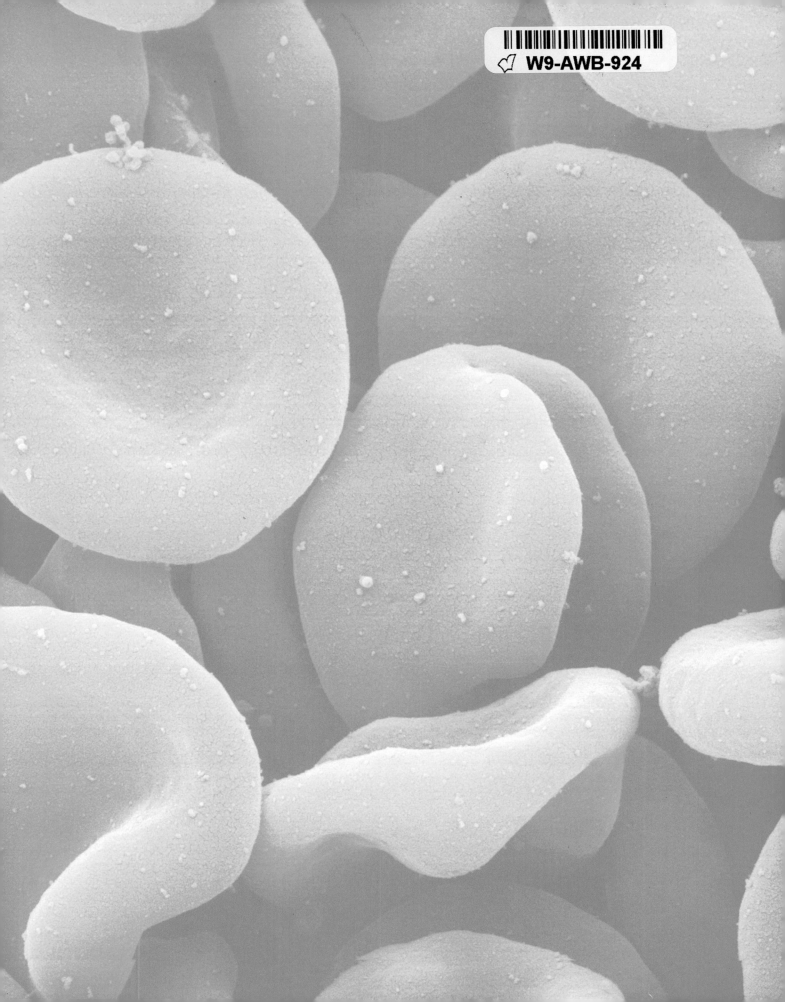

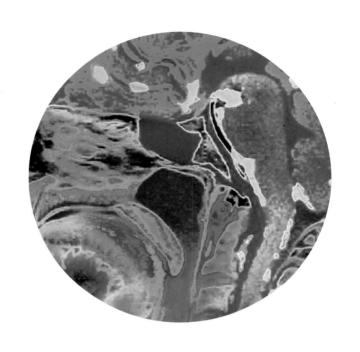

ENCYCLOPEDIA OF THE
HUMAN BODY

LONDON, NEW YORK, MUNICH,
MELBOURNE, and DELHI

Senior editors Selina Wood, Shaila Awan
Art editors Polly Appleton, Steven Laurie
Project editor Lucy Hurst
Managing art editor Clare Shedden
Managing editors Marie Greenwood, Andrew Macintyre
US editors Christine Heilman, Margaret Parrish
Digital artwork Robin Hunter
DTP design Siu Yin Ho
Production Kate Oliver
Picture research Sean Hunter
DK pictures Rose Horridge

for PAGE*One*:
Cairn House, Elgiva Lane,
Chesham, UK HP5 2JD

Creative director Bob Gordon
Managing editor Judith Hannam
Editors Naomi Mackay, Michael Spilling, Charlotte Stock
Art editor Robert Law
Designers Annie Hiew, Tim Stansfield
Special photography Andy Crawford
Digital artwork Anthony Duke, Mark Tattam, Peter Bull
Picture research John Farndon
With special thanks to Tania Fuller, Joe Gordon, Alex Jones,
Sophie Pateman, Adrian Phillips, and Henry Spilberg

Editorial consultant and author Richard Walker

Contributing authors David Burnie, Daniel Carter,
Phil Gates, Penny Preston, Frances Williams

First American Edition, 2002
02 03 04 05 10 9 8 7 6 5 4 3 2 1

Published in the United States by
DK Publishing, Inc.
375 Hudson Street
New York, New York 10014

Library of Congress Cataloging-in-Publication Data
Encyclopedia of the human body.
    p. cm.
Includes Index.
ISBN 0-7894-8672-5 (alk. paper)
  1. Human anatomy–Encyclopedias. 2. Human physiology–
Encyclopedias. 3. Body, Human–Encyclopedias. I. DK Publishing, Inc.
QM7.E53 2002
612'.003–dc21   2002073489

Color reproduction by Colourscan, Singapore
Printed and bound in Slovakia by Neografia

See our complete product line at
www.dk.com

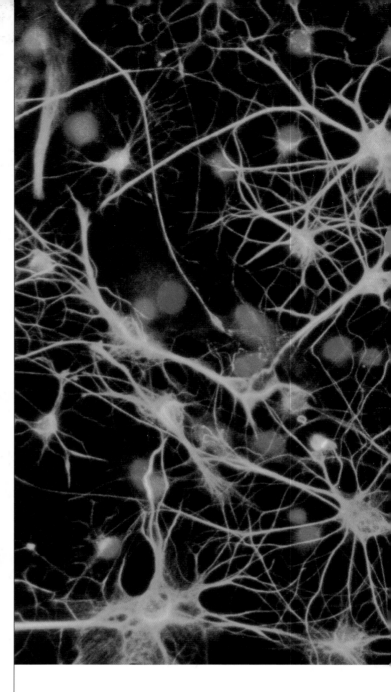

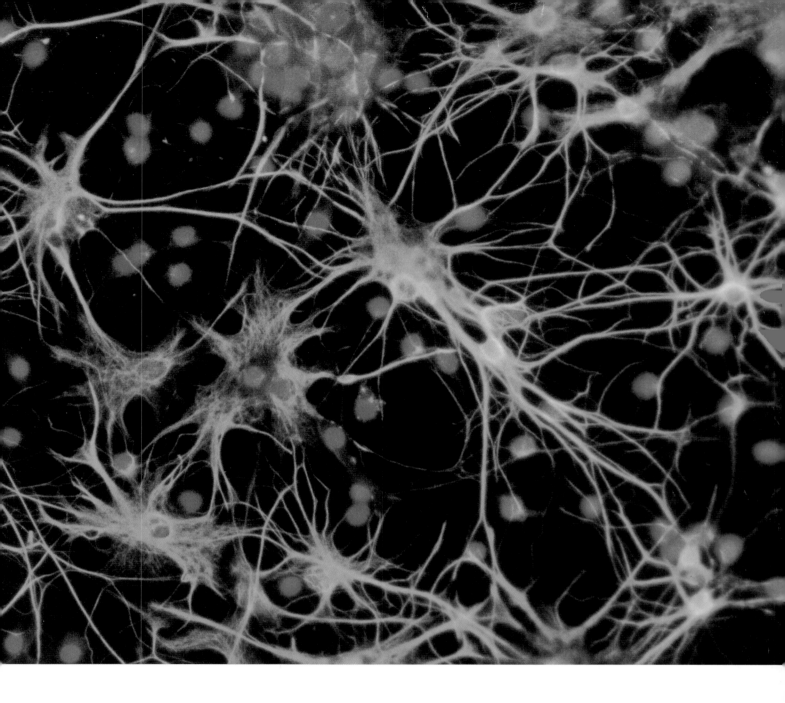

ENCYCLOPEDIA OF THE
HUMAN BODY

Richard Walker

DK Publishing

Contents

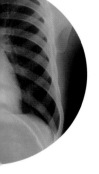

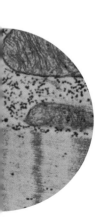

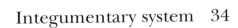

SUPPLY AND MAINTENANCE   126–209

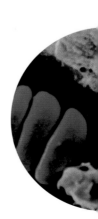

Contents

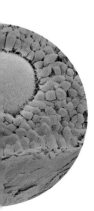

The following abbreviations have been
used for technical imaging techniques:

CT = Computed Tomography
LM = Light micrograph
NMR = Nuclear Magnetic Resonance Imaging
MRI = Magnetic Resonance Imaging
PET = Positron Emission Tomography
SEM = Scanning Electron Micrograph
TEM = Transmission Electron Micrograph

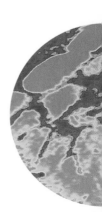

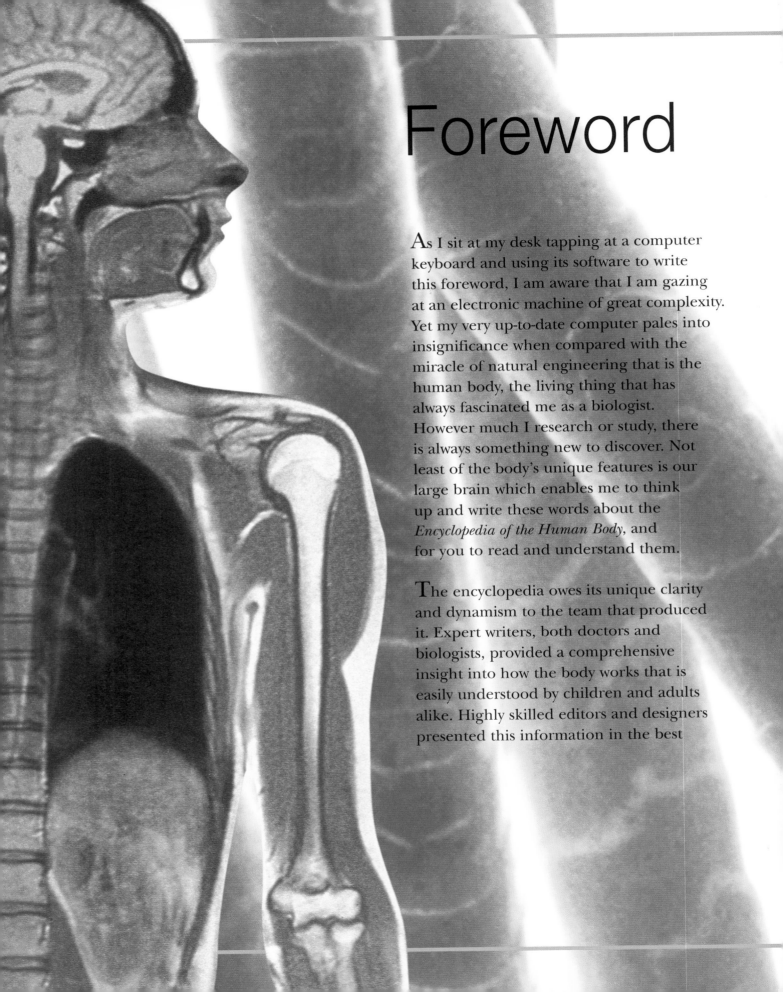

Foreword

As I sit at my desk tapping at a computer keyboard and using its software to write this foreword, I am aware that I am gazing at an electronic machine of great complexity. Yet my very up-to-date computer pales into insignificance when compared with the miracle of natural engineering that is the human body, the living thing that has always fascinated me as a biologist. However much I research or study, there is always something new to discover. Not least of the body's unique features is our large brain which enables me to think up and write these words about the *Encyclopedia of the Human Body*, and for you to read and understand them.

The encyclopedia owes its unique clarity and dynamism to the team that produced it. Expert writers, both doctors and biologists, provided a comprehensive insight into how the body works that is easily understood by children and adults alike. Highly skilled editors and designers presented this information in the best possible way, complementing the text with an incredible array of images that guide the reader on her or his journey through the body. These images include photographs, micrographs, scans, drawings, and diagrams that use color and detail to, for example, reveal the slimy lining of the intestines, expose the hordes of bacteria on the skin, explain why we do, or do not, have blue eyes, and describe how a baby is born from first contraction to first yell.

To make all this fascinating information accessible for the reader, we have organized the encyclopedia into seven sections. The first five deal with how the body is constructed, how it is supported and moved, how it is controlled, how it maintains itself, and how it reproduces and changes during life. Throughout these sections there are selected pages that focus on specific issues, such as "Understanding the mind" or "Art and anatomy", adding extra breadth to the topics covered in each section.

The final, seventh section contains a detailed timeline and glossary, but it is the sixth section that adds a whole new dimension to this encyclopedia. It explores how understanding of the human body and the development of medicine have gone hand in hand from the earliest times to the modern age. It explains how we know and understand so many of the things we take for granted today – such as how blood circulates around the body or why people get sick – that were a mystery to our ancestors and took all their intelligence and creativity to resolve.

One day, sometime in the future, a descendant of my desk computer may be smart enough to mimic the thoughts and actions of a human being, but, as you will see when you explore the body's remarkable structure and incredible workings in the *Encyclopedia of the Human Body*, it could never replace the real thing.

Richard Walker

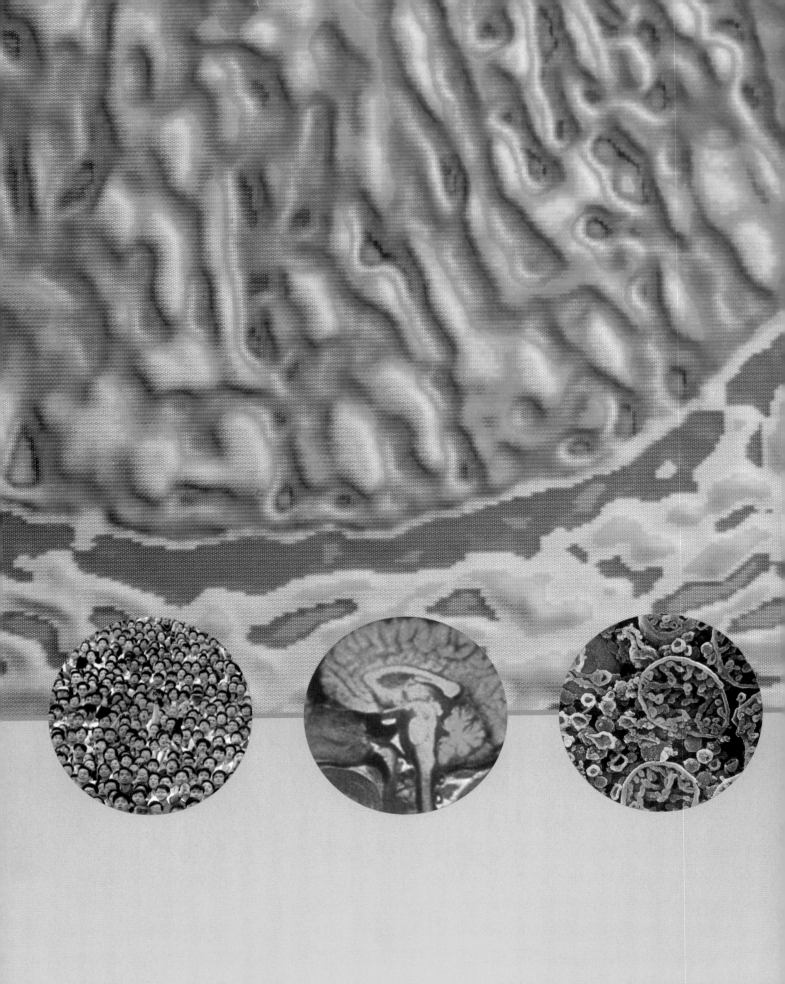

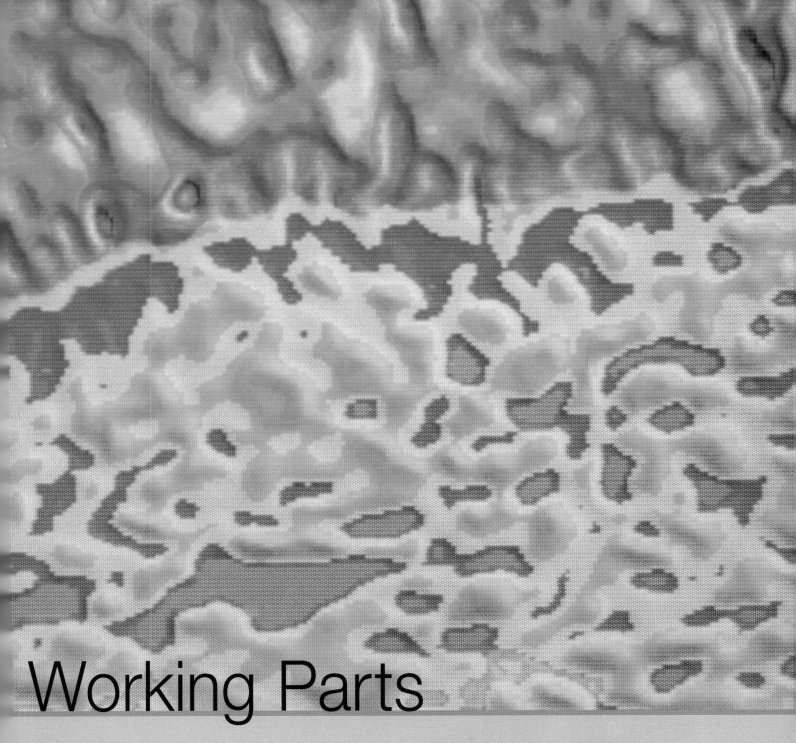

Working Parts

DESPITE THE INCREDIBLE VARIATION in body shapes and sizes, all humans share
the same working parts. At the microscopic level, the human body is built
from huge numbers of cells. Sharing the same basic structure, these tiny
chemical plants are grouped together to make the organs that pump blood,
digest food, take in air, and perform all other life-maintaining functions.
The structure and workings of the living body can be explored, without
cutting it open, using a range of different imaging techniques.

BEING HUMAN

Homo sapiens – Latin for "wise man" – is the name used by scientists to identify you, the reader, and the other six billion humans on planet Earth as a species (type) of animal. It may come as a surprise to some people to realize that humans are actually animals, and just one of the 1.5 million named species that make up the animal kingdom. At the same time, humans stand apart from other animals because their brain power is so superior, even when compared to their close relatives, the apes. Their unique intelligence, communication skills, curiosity, and ability to solve problems have enabled humans to colonize every continent, triumphing over environments and climates that have defeated other animal species, and to develop a complex understanding of themselves and the world around them.

SOCIAL ANIMALS
Humans are social animals that typically – although not always – live in family units led by a male and female partner, with one or more dependent children. Young humans usually remain with, and are nurtured by, their parents for about 18 years, until they are sufficiently mature and experienced to exist on their own. Several family units together form a larger social grouping or community, which can range in size from a village to a city. In modern industrial and agricultural societies, communities link together to form bigger units, the largest of which – nation states such as the United States or India – contain hundreds of millions of individuals.

Forward-facing eyes are characteristic of chimpanzees, humans, and all other primates

Chimpanzee
(*Pan troglodytes*)

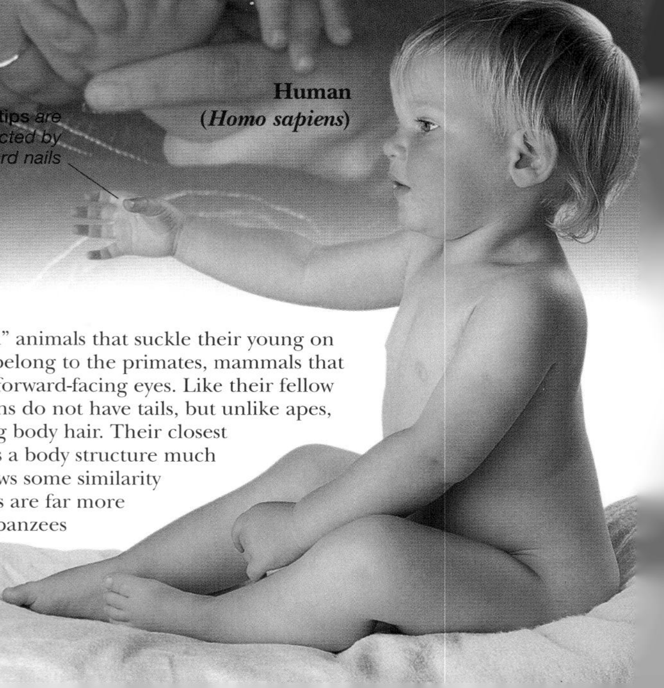

Fingertips are protected by hard nails

Human
(*Homo sapiens*)

CLOSEST RELATIVES
Humans are mammals – hairy, "warm-blooded" animals that suckle their young on milk. Along with apes and monkeys, humans belong to the primates, mammals that have five fingers and toes tipped by nails and forward-facing eyes. Like their fellow apes, such as chimpanzees and gorillas, humans do not have tails, but unlike apes, they walk upright and lack long body hair. Their closest relative, the chimpanzee, has a body structure much like that of humans, and shows some similarity in behavior. However, humans are far more intelligent and skillful than chimpanzees because their brain is much larger.

Inuits wear warm
clothing to survive
the harsh winters

PROTECTIVE CLOTHING

These two Inuit people from Nunavut are wearing thick boots, clothes, and hats to withstand the bitterly cold winters found in northern Canada. Humans are unique among animals in their making and wearing of clothes. This ability allowed humans to leave the confines of tropical Africa, where they first evolved, and move to cooler climates. While clothes have traditionally been made from animal and plant products, such as fur, wool, and cotton, today they are also made from synthetic materials such as nylon. Clothes do more than provide protection from the weather – they also send out messages about the wearer's status in society, their lifestyle, culture, and religious beliefs.

COMMUNICATION

The ability to communicate is essential for humans, as it is for all social animals, to ensure that they live together successfully. Like their ape relatives, humans use body language, gestures, and facial expressions to convey feelings and intentions to each other. But humans also have an additional, unique means of communication – language. By speaking and writing words they can share ideas, plans, decisions, memories, and wisdom. The existence of language means that information can be passed on from one generation to another, providing society with an ever-growing knowledge base.

HUMAN SPECIES FACT FILE

Class	Mammalia (mammals)	Body weight (average)	Males 165 lb (75 kg); females 115 lb (52 kg)
Order	Primates	Activity	Ground-living, diurnal (active during the day)
Species	Homo sapiens		
Distribution	Worldwide	Reproduction	Normally 1 young per litter
Habitat	Most land habitats, living in houses and other shelters	Maximum lifespan	90–100 years
Food	Animals, plants, and their products	Conservation status	Not endangered; population increasing worldwide

Keeping in touch by cellular phone

NATURAL VARIATION

IMAGINE STANDING IN a busy city watching the stream of humanity flowing past. One obvious thing an observer would notice is the sheer range of body variation. Everyone, unless they have an identical twin, has a unique combination of features – including their height, weight, shape, hair color and texture, skin tone, eye color, and the sound of their voice. However, these are but variations on a central theme that remains constant. Every human body is constructed to a fixed pattern and works in the same way, with minor differences between males and females. Externally, the basic design of a human is an upright body supported by two legs and feet, with two arms and hands that carry and hold, and a flattened face.

BODY REGIONS

Both female and male humans share the same body regions, although their overall shapes and reproductive organs differ. The main axis of the body is made up of the head and trunk. The head contains and protects the brain and sense organs, and is linked by the neck to the trunk, the center of the body. The thorax, or chest, forms the upper part of the trunk and contains the lungs and heart. The lower part, the abdomen, contains the digestive, reproductive, and urinary organs. Attached to the trunk are the limbs – the arms and legs.

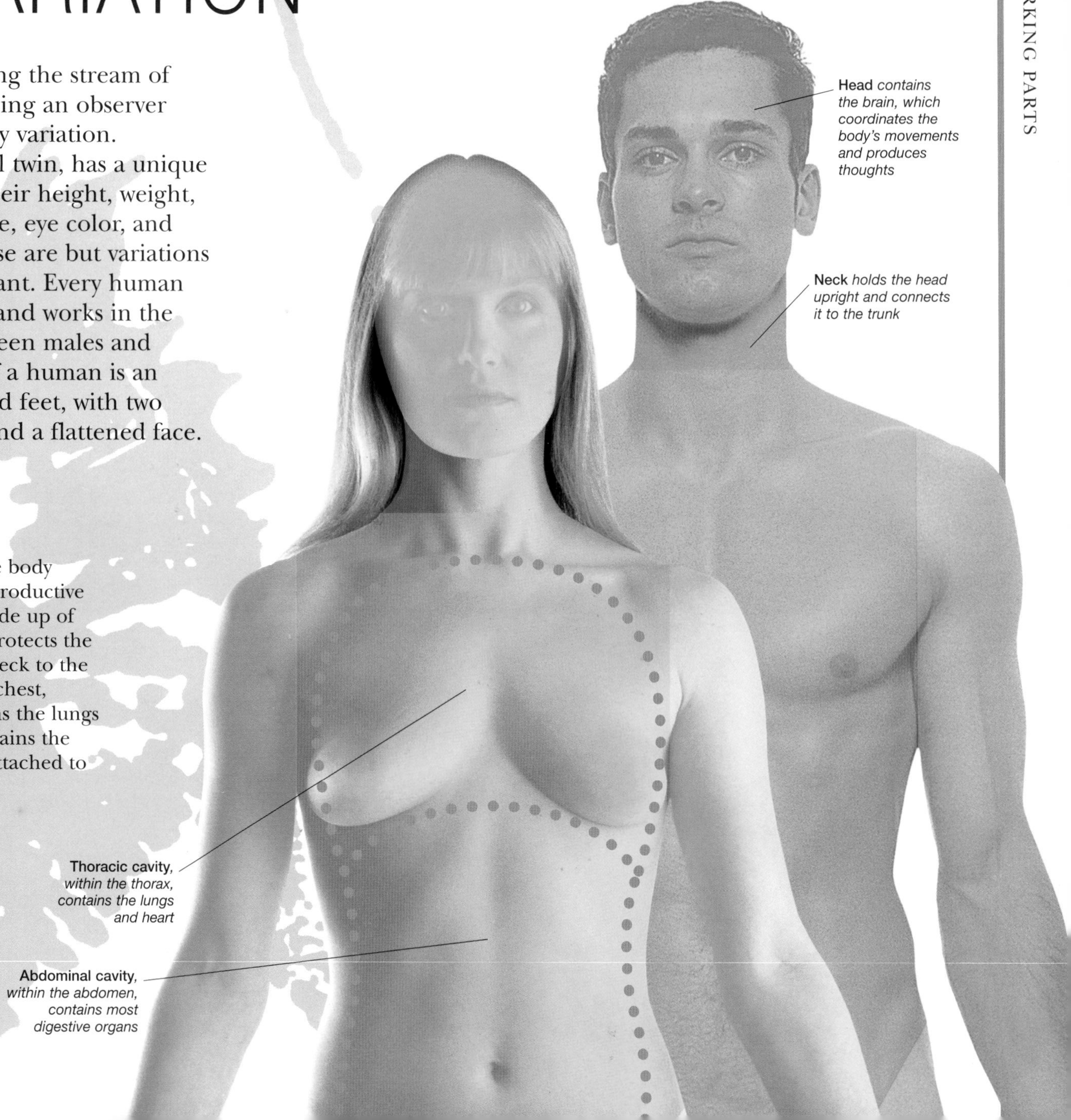

Head contains the brain, which coordinates the body's movements and produces thoughts

Neck holds the head upright and connects it to the trunk

Thoracic cavity, within the thorax, contains the lungs and heart

Abdominal cavity, within the abdomen, contains most digestive organs

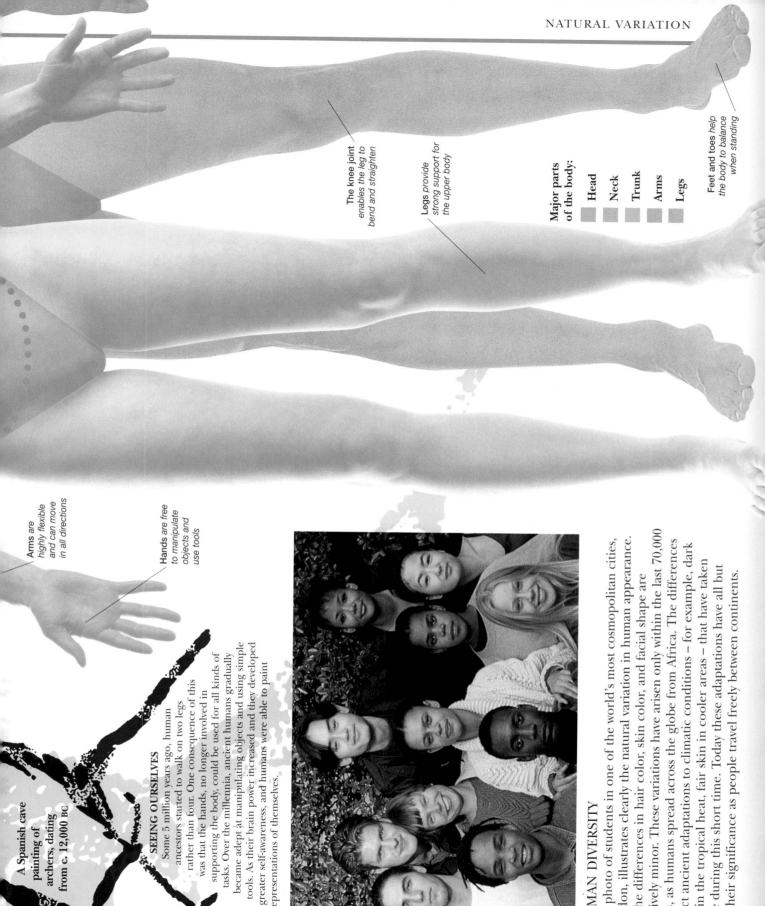

The knee joint *enables the leg to bend and straighten*

Legs *provide strong support for the upper body*

Major parts of the body:
- Head
- Neck
- Trunk
- Arms
- Legs

Feet and toes *help the body to balance when standing*

Arms are *highly flexible and can move in all directions*

Hands are *free to manipulate objects and use tools*

A Spanish cave painting of archers, dating from c. 12,000 BC

SEEING OURSELVES

Some 5 million years ago, human ancestors started to walk on two legs rather than four. One consequence of this was that the hands, no longer involved in supporting the body, could be used for all kinds of tasks. Over the millennia, ancient humans gradually became adept at manipulating objects and using simple tools. As their brain power increased and they developed greater self-awareness, and humans were able to paint representations of themselves.

HUMAN DIVERSITY

This photo of students in one of the world's most cosmopolitan cities, London, illustrates clearly the natural variation in human appearance. Yet the differences in hair color, skin color, and facial shape are relatively minor. These variations have arisen only within the last 70,000 years, as humans spread across the globe from Africa. The differences reflect ancient adaptations to climatic conditions – for example, dark skin in the tropical heat, fair skin in cooler areas – that have taken place during this short time. Today these adaptations have all but lost their significance as people travel freely between continents.

15

UNDER THE MICROSCOPE

THE END OF THE 16th century brought with it an invention that would open up a new world for scientists and doctors. In 1590, Dutch instrument maker Zacharias Janssen (1580–1638) made a magnifying device – later to be called the microscope – that, for the first time, made visible objects that were too small to be seen with the naked eye. Initially Janssen's invention made little impact, but in time it would be used to reveal the existence of cells and other previously unseen features of the living world. In the 20th century, the invention of the electron microscope took research into the microworld a step further.

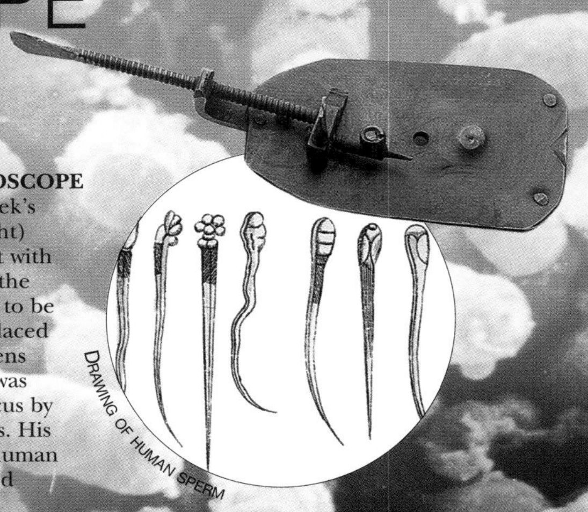

SIMPLE MICROSCOPE
Van Leeuwenhoek's microscope (right) was held upright with the eye close to the lens. The object to be examined was placed in front of the lens on a pin which was brought into focus by a series of screws. His drawing shows human sperm, discovered by him in 1677.

DRAWING OF HUMAN SPERM

THE DRAPER'S LENS
Following on from Janssen's invention, Dutch cloth merchant Anton van Leeuwenhoek (1632–1723) made a simple microscope by clamping a tiny convex lens between two brass plates. Although this device sounds primitive, it had a magnifying power of between 70 and 250 times. Van Leeuwenhoek's observations revealed the existence of single-celled organisms (now called protists), as well as some types of body cell. In 1683, he noted minute organisms in his own tooth scrapings, the first bacteria to be seen by the human eye.

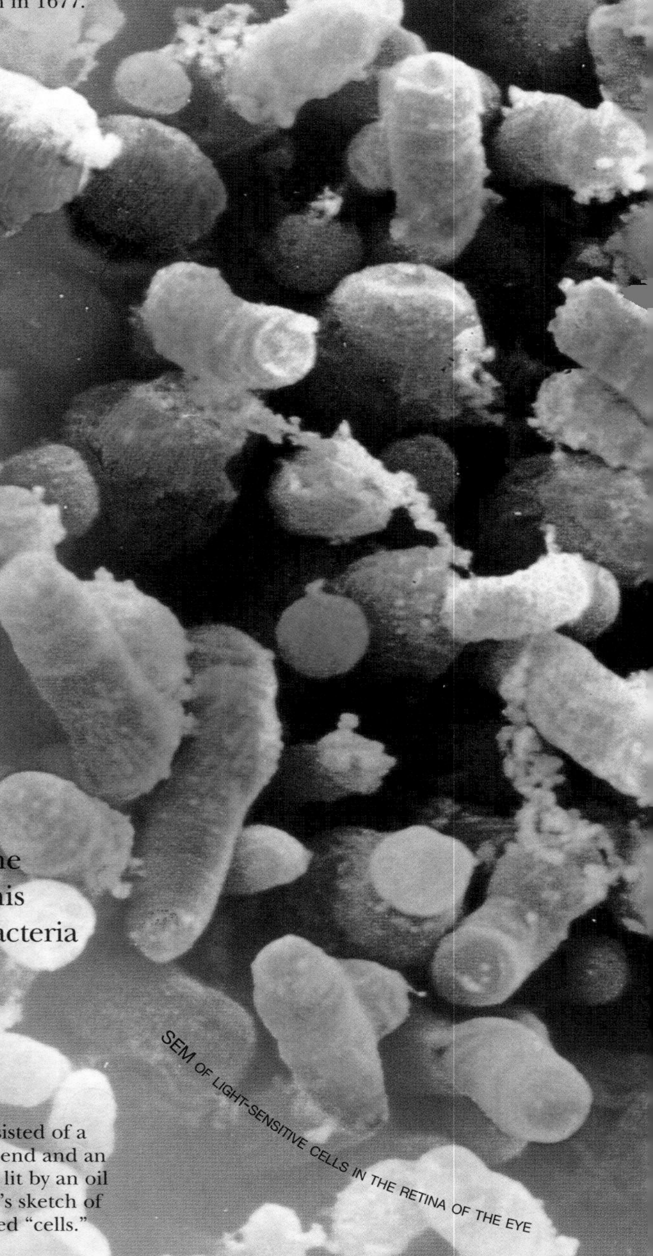

HOOKE'S DRAWING OF A CORK SECTION

B A

HOOKE'S VIEW
The microscope made by Robert Hooke (left) consisted of a pasteboard barrel, with an eyepiece lens at the top end and an objective lens at the bottom. Here, the specimen is lit by an oil lamp focused through a water-filled sphere. Hooke's sketch of a section through cork shows the chambers he called "cells."

SEM OF LIGHT-SENSITIVE CELLS IN THE RETINA OF THE EYE

COMPOUND MICROSCOPE

Despite van Leeuwenhoek's success, the future of microscopy lay in compound microscopes that used two or more lenses to produce their magnifying effects. British physicist Robert Hooke (1635–1703) made his own compound microscope and, in 1665, presented his observations in a book, illustrated with his own lavish drawings, called *Micrographia*. Among these observations was a section through cork, a dead plant material, showing tiny boxes that he called "cells." This term would later come into common use for a different purpose.

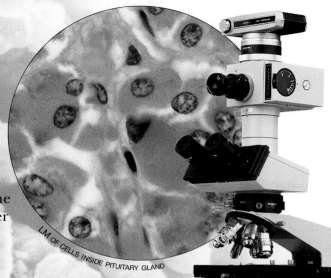

LM OF CELLS INSIDE PITUITARY GLAND

SEEING CELLS

Hooke's microscope and similar instruments of the time were hindered by poor-quality lenses. This defect prevented any great advances from being made in microscopy until 1830, when a solution was provided in the form of achromatic lenses, which removed blurring and color fringes. In the decades that followed, the improved compound microscope was used to discover, identify, and describe human cells and tissues.

THE MODERN VIEW
Used in science laboratories and hospitals worldwide, a modern compound microscope can provide a view of a section through the pituitary gland, as shown here. The otherwise transparent cells have been stained so the viewer can see their component parts.

GREATER MAGNIFICATION

Light, or optical, microscopes have always been restricted by an upper limit of magnification of about 2,000 times. German scientist Ernst Ruska (1906–88) devised an alternative microscope in 1930 that could magnify objects 200,000 times or more. Rather than using light for illumination, it sent a beam of electrons through the thinly sectioned object. This beam – focused not by glass lenses but by electromagnets – was projected onto a phosphor screen, producing a visual image of the object, called a transmission electron microscope. It revealed among other things the detailed internal structure of cells. The scanning electron microscope, invented in the 1960s, scans the object with an electron beam to produce a 3-D image.

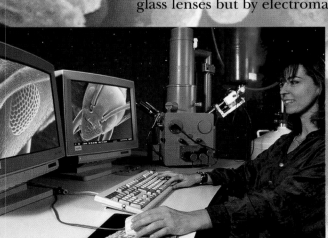

SCANNING ELECTRON MICROSCOPE
A scientist uses a scanning electron microscope to get a 3-D scanning electron micrograph (SEM) of an insect's head.

Cells

LIKE EVERY OTHER living thing on planet Earth, human beings are constructed from tiny, living units called cells. Individually, these cells are transparent, and so minute that they are only visible with a microscope. But the vast numbers of cells present in the body – about 100 trillion, or 100,000,000,000,000 – collectively form a recognizable human being. These cells are not all the same; just as within any society certain people play specific roles, so do different types of cell inside the body. This organization is dynamic, not static. Every day the body produces billions of new cells to replace those that have become diseased, damaged, or just worn out. In younger humans, these new cells also enable the body to grow.

Nucleus

Squamous (flat) epithelial cell

LM OF EPITHELIAL CELLS

EPITHELIAL CELLS
The light micrograph above shows epithelial cells from the lining of the cheek. These flat cells fit together like paving stones to protect the inside of the mouth. Other epithelial cells – which may be flat, cube-shaped, or column-shaped – line and protect the body's tubes and cavities, such as blood vessels and the intestines. They also cover the body, forming the epidermis, the upper layer of the skin.

CELL VARIETY
The trillions of cells that make up a person are all derived from a single fertilized egg cell. As this single cell divides repeatedly to make a human being, so groups of cells differentiate, or become specialized, each group taking on its own appearance and special role. By the time a person becomes an adult, they will have about 200 different types of cells, each adapted to a particular task. Four of these types – epithelial, bone, sperm, and blood cells – are described here as an example of how body cells differ, and how their appearance is related to their function.

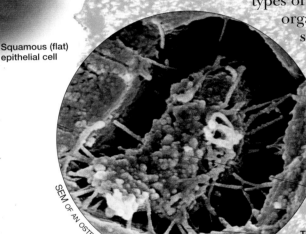

SEM OF AN OSTEOCYTE

Osteocyte *sits within its own cavity in bone*

Tiny "threads" *link osteocyte to other bone cells*

BONE CELLS
Osteocytes are bone cells that live isolated existences within their own tiny cavity, or lacuna, surrounded by the bony matrix that gives the body's bones their strength and hardness. Despite their isolation, these spider-like cells communicate with their neighbors through tiny "threads" that run along minute channels between lacunae. The role of these long-lived cells is day-to-day maintenance of the bony matrix.

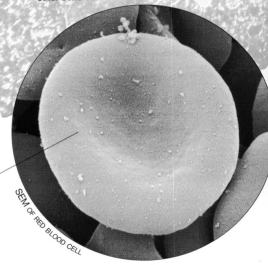

Red blood cell *has no nucleus*

SEM OF RED BLOOD CELL

Tail

Head

SEM OF SPERM

SPERMATOZOA
This scanning electron micrograph shows tadpole-shaped spermatozoa, or sperm, produced by a man's testes. The head of each sperm contains one part of the set of instructions needed to make a new human being; an ovum, or egg cell, produced by a woman, contains the other part. During sexual reproduction, the sperm's tail beats from side to side, pushing the streamlined cell toward an ovum. If the two fuse, a new human life is started.

RED BLOOD CELLS
As their name suggests, red blood cells, or erythrocytes, are found in the blood. Unlike other body cells, these dimpled, doughnut-shaped cells lack a nucleus. Instead they are packed with hemoglobin, a substance that both gives them their color and carries oxygen. During a four-month lifespan, each red blood cell makes millions of circuits, picking up oxygen in the lungs and delivering it elsewhere.

CELL DIVISION

Cells reproduce by cell division. In this micrograph, a cell's nucleus (red) has just divided in two, with the cytoplasm (blue) about to follow. Short-lived cells, such as skin cells, which are constantly worn away, are continually replaced by cell division. At the other extreme, nerve cells do not divide again once they have been formed. The majority of new body cells are produced by a type of cell division called mitosis. Sex cells – sperm and ova – are produced by a process of cell division called meiosis (see pp. 212–13).

Cytoplasm *of parent cell divides*

Nucleus of new cell

CELL THEORY

In 1838, German scientists Jakob Schlieden (1804–81) and Theodor Schwann (1810–82) put forward their cell theory, which states that all living things are made of cells. In 1858, German physician Rudolf Virchow (1821–1902) went one stage further by including newly discovered cell division. He stated that new cells can only be made from existing ones, discrediting the accepted idea that cells could arise spontaneously from non-living material.

Theodor Schwann

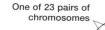
One of 23 pairs of chromosomes

Single body cell

New "daughter" cell *is identical to parent*

MITOSIS

This process produces two "daughter" cells that are identical to each other and to their "parent." The control center of a body cell is called the nucleus. It contains 46 thread-like chromosomes, which hold the genetic information needed to build and run a cell. Before mitosis, each chromosome copies itself. Then, during mitosis, these copies are pulled apart, each to their own new nucleus. The result, once the cytoplasm has divided, is two genetically identical "daughter" cells.

CANCER CELLS

Normally, cell division is strictly regulated. But if its genetic material is damaged beyond repair, a cell may start to divide uncontrollably and cause a disease called cancer. Once it is out of control, division of a cancer cell (right) produces an expanding clump of abnormal cells, called a tumor, that can affect normal body functions. Unless the tumor is treated and destroyed, its cancer cells can spread to produce tumors in other parts of the body, eventually causing death.

SEM OF A CANCER CELL

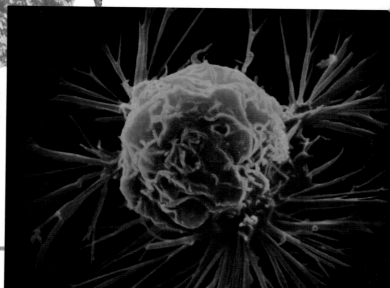

Cell structure

THE FACT THAT CELLS are small does not mean that they are simple. Regardless of their appearance and role, all cells share the same basic, highly organized internal structure. This structure was only revealed with the invention of the electron microscope in the 20th century. Before then, it was assumed that cells were made up of just three components: an outer cell membrane, central nucleus, and – between the two – the cytoplasm. The electron microscope revealed that, rather than being just a featureless jelly, the cytoplasm contained many different components. It is now known that these components work together rather like the different departments in a factory. Some manufacture the materials the cell needs, or recycle substances for reuse. Others generate the energy needed to power the cell's activities. All are controlled by instructions contained within the nucleus.

CYTOPLASM AND NUCLEUS
Lying between the cell membrane on the outside and the nucleus on the inside, cytoplasm consists of a clear, jellylike fluid – mainly made up of water – called cytosol. Here, organelles, such as mitochondria, float. In the cytoplasm, microfilaments and microtubules form the cell's support system. The nucleus is the cell's control center, containing the instructions that direct cell activities. The nucleus is surrounded by a nuclear membrane with pores (holes) that allow substances to move between nucleus and cytoplasm.

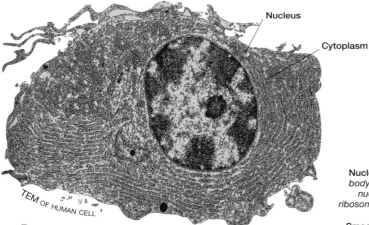

TEM OF HUMAN CELL

Nucleus

Cytoplasm

INSIDE A CELL
Just as each body part, or organ, has its own task, so do the tiny components, or organelles ("little organs"), inside a cell. Largest of these is the nucleus, the cell's control center. Organelles suspended in the cytoplasm include the endoplasmic reticulum and Golgi body, which manufacture, store, and transport substances, while the mitochondria release energy from glucose and other foods. These cytoplasmic organelles serve to organize the cell's interior into compartments, preventing the cell's many chemical reactions from interfering with each other. Many organelles are surrounded by a membrane, similar in structure to the cell membrane that controls the flow of substances into and out of the cell.

Microfilaments *support and shape the cell*

Nucleolus *is a body within the nucleus where ribosomes are made*

Smooth endoplasmic reticulum *is a system of membrane-enclosed channels where lipids are made*

Secretory vesicle *is a package of substances formed by the Golgi body. It opens at the cell's surface to release its contents*

Nuclear membrane *or envelope forms the boundary of the nucleus*

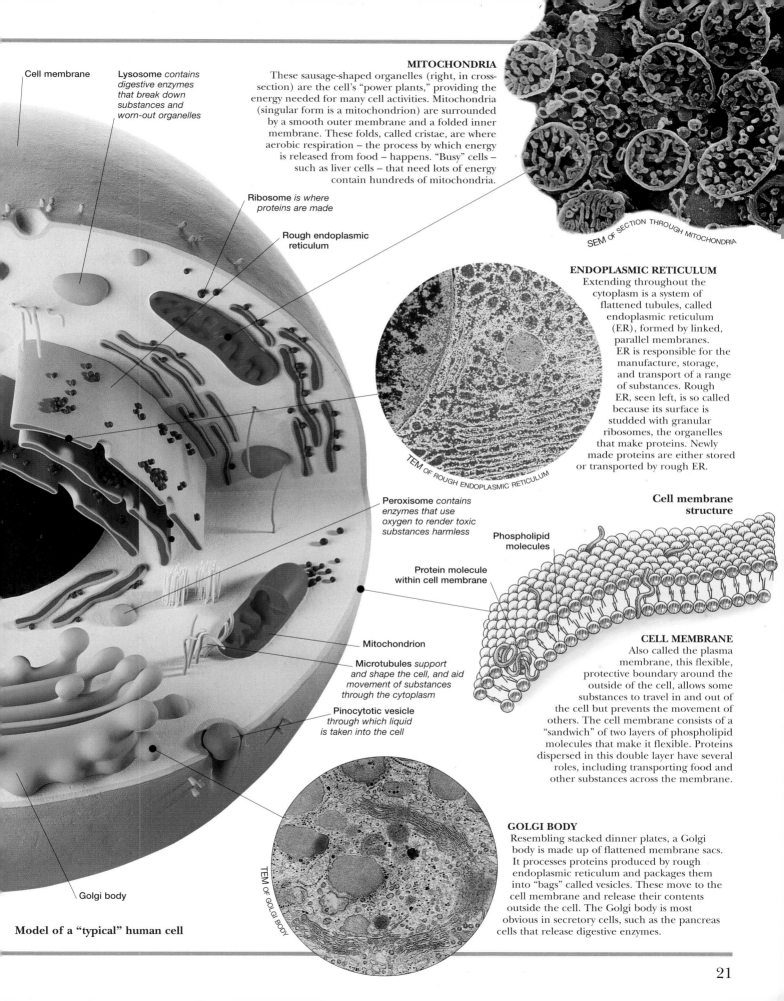

Cell membrane

Lysosome *contains digestive enzymes that break down substances and worn-out organelles*

Ribosome *is where proteins are made*

Rough endoplasmic reticulum

MITOCHONDRIA

These sausage-shaped organelles (right, in cross-section) are the cell's "power plants," providing the energy needed for many cell activities. Mitochondria (singular form is a mitochondrion) are surrounded by a smooth outer membrane and a folded inner membrane. These folds, called cristae, are where aerobic respiration – the process by which energy is released from food – happens. "Busy" cells – such as liver cells – that need lots of energy contain hundreds of mitochondria.

SEM OF SECTION THROUGH MITOCHONDRIA

ENDOPLASMIC RETICULUM

Extending throughout the cytoplasm is a system of flattened tubules, called endoplasmic reticulum (ER), formed by linked, parallel membranes. ER is responsible for the manufacture, storage, and transport of a range of substances. Rough ER, seen left, is so called because its surface is studded with granular ribosomes, the organelles that make proteins. Newly made proteins are either stored or transported by rough ER.

TEM OF ROUGH ENDOPLASMIC RETICULUM

Peroxisome *contains enzymes that use oxygen to render toxic substances harmless*

Cell membrane structure

Phospholipid molecules

Protein molecule within cell membrane

Mitochondrion

Microtubules *support and shape the cell, and aid movement of substances through the cytoplasm*

Pinocytotic vesicle *through which liquid is taken into the cell*

CELL MEMBRANE

Also called the plasma membrane, this flexible, protective boundary around the outside of the cell, allows some substances to travel in and out of the cell but prevents the movement of others. The cell membrane consists of a "sandwich" of two layers of phospholipid molecules that make it flexible. Proteins dispersed in this double layer have several roles, including transporting food and other substances across the membrane.

GOLGI BODY

Resembling stacked dinner plates, a Golgi body is made up of flattened membrane sacs. It processes proteins produced by rough endoplasmic reticulum and packages them into "bags" called vesicles. These move to the cell membrane and release their contents outside the cell. The Golgi body is most obvious in secretory cells, such as the pancreas cells that release digestive enzymes.

TEM OF GOLGI BODY

Golgi body

Model of a "typical" human cell

Cell chemistry

INSIDE A PERSON'S CELLS a multitude of chemical reactions is taking place, regardless of whether that person is asleep or awake. During each reaction, chemical compounds are modified to meet the needs of the cell. This mass of chemical activity is far from being chaotic. The organelles of the cell – such as mitochondria – organize chemical reactions into separate compartments so that they do not interfere with each other. Furthermore, reactions are greatly accelerated by special substances called enzymes, which also control how quickly cells consume raw materials and yield new products. Key to a cell's chemistry is the release of energy from food, by the process of cell respiration. Without energy, cells would have no driving force, and life simply could not exist.

THERMOGRAM OF WOMAN'S MOUTH AND TEETH

1 molecule
glucose

Glycolysis

ATP

2 molecules
pyruvic acid

CHEMICAL PROCESSES

Inside any cell, two basic processes – catabolism and anabolism – work side-by-side. In catabolism, energy-rich fuel molecules are broken down to release their energy to supply the cell's needs. In fact, only about 25 percent of this energy can be used by the cell; the rest is released as heat, which is used to maintain the body's temperature at 98.6°F (37°C). Anabolism takes simple building blocks to build up the more complex substances a cell needs, such as proteins and lipids. In order to work, anabolism uses the energy generated by catabolism. Together, anabolism and catabolism make up metabolism, the sum of all the chemical processes happening inside a cell.

ENZYMES

These proteins act as catalysts, speeding up the cell's chemical reactions by thousands or millions of times without being changed or used up. Without enzymes, these reactions would take place so slowly that life could not exist. Each enzyme is specific to a particular reaction. Molecules taking part in that reaction bind to the enzyme and react to form product molecules that are then released. Some enzymes work outside cells, including the digestive enzymes that speed up the breakdown of food during digestion.

Product
molecules
*move away
from enzyme*

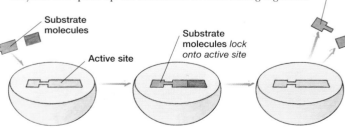

Substrate
molecules

Substrate
molecules *lock
onto active site*

Active site

1 *Molecules involved
in a reaction, called
substrates, fit into a
part of an enzyme
called the active site.*

2 *The enzyme holds
the substrates together.
The substrates react
and form product
molecules.*

3 *The products are
released. The enzyme is
unaffected by the reaction,
and is ready to attract
more molecules.*

RAW MATERIALS

Unless it has a constant stream of raw materials to supply its cells' needs, the body cannot survive. During digestion, the carbohydrates, lipids, proteins, and nucleic acids in food are broken down into simple molecules, taken into the blood, and carried to the body's cells. Once inside a cell these are assembled into new molecules by anabolism, or broken down by catabolism. Water is also vital because it provides the liquid medium inside cells in which chemical reactions take place.

AEROBIC RESPIRATION

Body cells get most of their energy from a type of cell respiration called aerobic respiration. Using oxygen, this breaks down fuel molecules such as glucose into carbon dioxide and water to release large amounts of energy. Aerobic respiration has two phases, each made up of several enzyme-catalyzed reactions. First, during glycolysis ("glucose splitting") in the cytoplasm, a glucose molecule is split into two molecules of pyruvic acid, with the release of a little energy. Then, inside mitochondria – the cell's "power plants" – a sequence of chemical reactions called the Krebs cycle (see p. 175) completely dismantles pyruvic acid molecules and, with the help of oxygen, releases all of their energy.

6 molecules oxygen

ATP

Krebs cycle

6 molecules carbon dioxide

6 molecules water

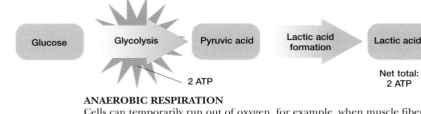

| Glucose | Glycolysis | Pyruvic acid | Lactic acid formation | Lactic acid |

2 ATP

Net total: 2 ATP

ANAEROBIC RESPIRATION

Cells can temporarily run out of oxygen, for example, when muscle fibers (cells) contract rapidly during vigorous exercise. This does not stop cells from releasing energy from glucose, however, even though they cannot use aerobic respiration. Instead, they use anaerobic ("without air") respiration. In the cytoplasm, glucose is broken down into pyruvic acid – as during glycolysis – which is then converted into lactic acid. This yields much less energy than aerobic respiration, but happens more rapidly. Once oxygen becomes available again, lactic acid is reconverted to pyruvic acid and broken down by the Krebs cycle.

Computer-generated model of ATP

ADENOSINE TRIPHOSPHATE (ATP)

Cells cannot use the energy stored inside glucose until it has been processed by cell respiration. This releases the stored energy in small bursts and uses it to make molecules of adenosine triphosphate (ATP), the cell's main energy store and carrier. When a chemical reaction requires energy, ATP is broken down to liberate its energy store and its components are recycled to pick up more energy from cell respiration. During aerobic respiration, each molecule of glucose yields 38 molecules – "energy packets" – of ATP. The yield from anaerobic is much lower – just 2 ATP.

CHEMICAL COMPONENTS

Molecular model of glycogen

Human cells – like those of all living things – contain chemical components that are unique to living systems. These are organic compounds, substances whose molecules are based on a "skeleton" of carbon atoms. The main types found in cells are carbohydrates, lipids, proteins, and nucleic acids.

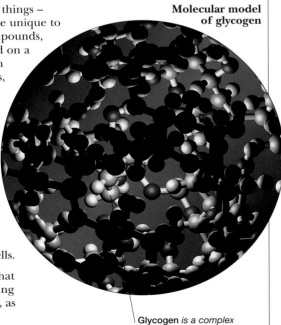

• Carbohydrates provide cells with energy. They include simple sugars, such as glucose, that deliver a source of energy, and complex polysaccharides, such as glycogen, that form fuel stores in the liver and muscle cells.

• Lipids (fats and oils) form the membrane around the cell and its organelles, and provide a long-term energy store in adipose (fat) tissue cells.

• Proteins are complex compounds that perform many different tasks, including forming part of cell membranes, and, as enzymes, controlling cell reactions.

• Nucleic acids such as DNA store the information (in coded form) needed to control cells. These codes tell cells how to make proteins.

Glycogen is a complex carbohydrate, or polysaccharide, which is made up of glucose subunits

THE DOUBLE HELIX

O N APRIL 2, 1953, the world of science changed forever. Two scientists – American James Watson (b. 1928) and Briton Francis Crick (b. 1916) – announced in the journal *Nature* that they had unraveled the structure of a molecule believed to hold the key to life itself. The molecule was DNA (deoxyribonucleic acid), which is found in the nucleus of every cell, and its structure they called the "double helix." This new understanding of DNA's structure enabled scientists to find out how it controls the activities of cells and of whole organisms, including humans.

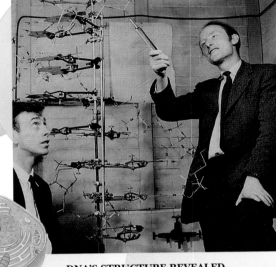

Cell

Chromosome *is made up of tightly coiled DNA*

DNA IN ACTION
Each of the 46 chromosomes in the nucleus of a human cell is made up of a long DNA molecule, sections of which form genes. The two strands of the DNA double helix are linked by bases that always join in a specific way.

"Unzipping" *DNA strands separate so that the bases contained in one strand can be copied*

Gene *is a section of DNA that carries the instructions for making a specific protein*

DNA'S STRUCTURE REVEALED
This photograph shows Watson (left) and Crick next to their model of DNA. Its completion was announced in the journal *Nature*: "We wish to suggest a structure for the salt of deoxyribose nucleic acid (DNA). This structure has novel features which are of considerable biological interest."

Guanine   **Thymine**

Adenine

mRNA nucleotide

Cytosine

DNA "backbone" *is made of linked phosphate and deoxyribose (sugar) molecules*

Transcription *is where free mRNA bases pair with corresponding bases on DNA to make an mRNA strand*

ROSALIND FRANKLIN
Born in 1920, British scientist Rosalind Franklin played a key role in the discovery of the structure of DNA. Her X-ray diffraction photographs provided Crick and Watson with vital evidence about DNA's spiral shape. Franklin died of cancer in 1958.

DISCOVERING DNA
Early in the 20th century it was realized that cells contain genes, a set of instructions for making and running an organism. Because genes are passed on from parents to offspring, they must be made of a molecule that can both replicate, or copy, itself and hold a store of information. In 1944, American bacteriologist Oswald Avery (1877–1955) showed that it was the nucleic acid DNA which was the carrier of genetic information.

It was known from work carried out during the 1930s that DNA is made up of units called nucleotides. Each nucleotide consists of a phosphate group, the sugar deoxyribose, and one of four nitrogenous bases called adenine, cytosine, guanine, and thymine. In 1953, using evidence from chemical analysis and X-ray diffraction – a method that bounces X-rays off atoms in a DNA of molecule to produce a photographic pattern that indicates its structure – Watson and Crick built their 3-D model of DNA, consisting of two parallel strands that spiral around each other.

UNDERSTANDING THE CODE

Watson and Crick's double helix resembles a twisted ladder. The uprights are made of a "backbone" of phosphate and deoxyribose, the "rungs" of paired bases, adenine with thymine, and cytosine with guanine. They soon realized that this arrangement also provided the means for replication – that the DNA double helix could "unzip," so that free nucleotides could bond to the exposed bases to produce two new DNA double helices. But how does DNA control cell activities?

Since the 1940s it had been known that genes control the production of proteins, many of which are enzymes, the biological catalysts that regulate chemical reactions inside cells. Each protein is made up of a specific sequence of amino acids,

COPYING THE MESSAGE
DNA has the unique ability to make an exact copy of itself. This TEM shows a DNA strand (shown right in yellow) that is "unzipping" to form two single "daughter" strands, each of which acts as a template to form a new double helix identical to the "parent."

DNA strand *has "unzipped" into two strands*

TEM OF REPLICATING DNA STRAND

MAKING PROTEINS

Protein synthesis happens in the cytoplasm of the cell, but DNA molecules are too large to move out of the nucleus. So how is the message conveyed from nucleus to cytoplasm? A section of DNA (a gene) "unzips," and one strand is copied (transcribed) by a smaller, single-stranded nucleic acid called messenger RNA (mRNA). This contains the same bases as DNA, except for uracil, which replaces thymine. The mRNA passes into the cytoplasm and attaches itself to a ribosome. Here, the mRNA is translated triplet by triplet so that amino acids are linked up in the correct sequence to make a specific protein.

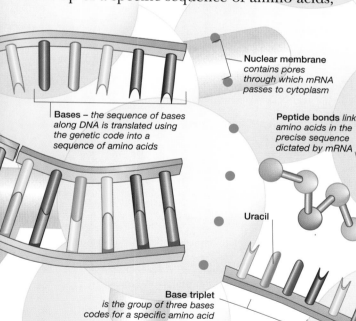

Nuclear membrane *contains pores through which mRNA passes to cytoplasm*

Bases – *the sequence of bases along DNA is translated using the genetic code into a sequence of amino acids*

Peptide bonds *link amino acids in the precise sequence dictated by mRNA*

Uracil

Free amino acids *in the cytoplasm are "assembled" to make a particular protein*

Base triplet *is the group of three bases codes for a specific amino acid*

mRNA

Ribosome *provides a site on which the mRNA message is translated into protein structure*

Newly assembled protein *detaches itself from the ribosome and folds up, its functional shape determined by the specific sequence of amino acids*

of which there are 20 different types. During the 1960s Marshall Nirenberg (b. 1927), an American biochemist, showed that within DNA an arrangement of three bases specifies one particular amino acid. This provides a genetic code in which base triplets form the "words" that instruct the cell to select the right amino acids to make a specific protein.

TRANSLATION
An organelle called a ribosome passes along the strand of mRNA using the genetic code to translate it into protein structure. Amino acids are lined up in the correct sequence, and then bond together to form a protein.

Tissues

If the body's trillions of cells all existed independently, it would be impossible to organize and operate a living human being. Instead, cells of the same or similar types are grouped together into tightknit communities in which they work together to carry out a specific task. These groups of similar cells form tissues – a word derived from the Latin for "woven" – just as cotton threads are interwoven to make cloth. The many different types of tissue fall into four basic categories – epithelial, connective, muscular, and nervous – that interface to make up the fabric of the body. If tissues are damaged, their cells divide to repair the damage. This process, called regeneration, happens more quickly in some tissues than others. Together, different types of tissue form organs such as the heart and kidneys, as described in more detail on pp. 28–29. The roles of the four basic types of tissue can be described very simply as follows: epithelial tissues cover; connective tissues support; muscle tissues move; and nervous tissues control.

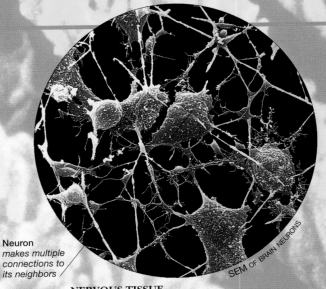

Neuron *makes multiple connections to its neighbors*

SEM OF BRAIN NEURONS

NERVOUS TISSUE

Restricted to the nervous system – the brain, spinal cord, and nerves – nervous tissue is responsible for controlling and coordinating most body processes, as well as providing humans with conscious thought and sensation. Two types of cells are found in nervous tissue. Neurons, or nerve cells, like the brain neurons shown in the scanning electron micrograph above, allow communication to take place by generating and carrying electrical signals at high speed. Glial cells, or neuroglia, support and nurture the neurons.

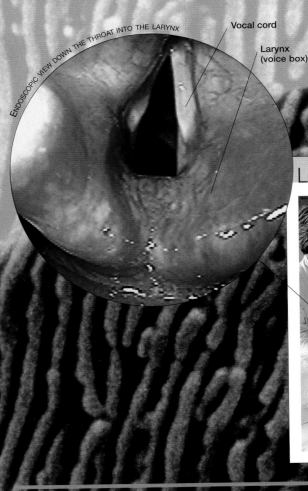

ENDOSCOPIC VIEW DOWN THE THROAT INTO THE LARYNX

Vocal cord

Larynx (voice box)

LOOKING INSIDE

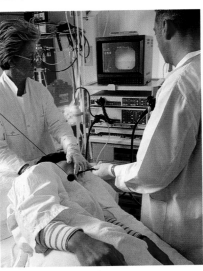

Doctors can look inside the body to examine tissues and organs by using a technique called endoscopy. Endoscopes are tubelike instruments that contain long optical fibers that transmit light. The endoscope can be inserted through a natural opening, such as the mouth, as shown here, or through a small incision made in the skin. Optical fibers carry light to illuminate the tissue being observed, while a miniature camera relays images to a screen for the doctor to see. The endoscope may also include tiny scissors or forceps to take a small sample of tissue for biopsy. Tissue is then looked at under the microscope for signs of disease.

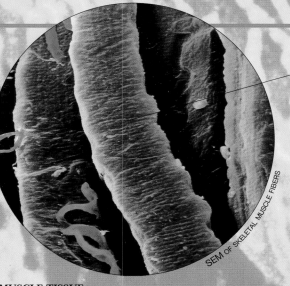

Muscle fiber

SEM OF SKELETAL MUSCLE FIBERS

Chondrocyte
*is a mature
cartilage cell*

CONNECTIVE TISSUES

Unlike other issues, connective tissues consist of cells
embedded in a matrix, or framework, secreted by the
cells. With major roles including binding and support,
protection and insulation, connective tissues are the
most abundant and diverse of all body tissues. They
hold the body together by supporting epithelial
tissues and packaging organs, and are also
found in tendons, ligaments, and the
dermis of the skin. Cartilage — left,
seen inside a joint — and bone
in the skeleton support and
protect the body's organs.
Adipose tissue, its cells
packed with fat, insulates
and cushions organs.
Blood, a connective tissue
with a liquid matrix,
transports materials
around the body.

Cartilage matrix *is
rich in collagen fibers*

LM OF SECTION THROUGH HYALINE CARTILAGE

MUSCLE TISSUE

The body's muscular tissues consist of cells, called fibers,
that can contract, or shorten. Skeletal muscle tissue,
seen in this micrograph, moves the body and maintains
its posture. Smooth muscle tissue, in the walls of hollow
organs, typically moves materials through the body.
Cardiac muscle tissue, found in the wall of the heart,
pumps blood around the body. Muscular tissues receive
a rich blood supply that brings the food and oxygen
needed to release energy for contraction.

EPITHELIAL TISSUE

Also called epithelium, epithelial tissue consists of a continuous
sheet of cells, which may be one cell or many layers thick. It
forms the outer layer of skin, and the inner linings of the
digestive system – including the folded lining of the
esophagus, shown here – and of the respiratory,
urinary, and reproductive systems, blood vessels
and the heart. By covering and lining,
epithelial tissues protect the body's surfaces,
form a barrier to microorganisms, and
provide an interface through which
all substances entering or leaving
the body must pass.

LM OF SECTION THROUGH NASAL MUCOUS MEMBRANE

SEM OF LINING OF ESOPHAGUS

MEMBRANES

Together, epithelial and connective tissues combine to
form the membranes that line hollow organs and body
cavities. This light micrograph (above) shows a section
through the membrane that lines the nasal cavity.
Epithelial tissue (blue-pink) secretes sticky mucus that traps
dust particles in the air. The connective tissue (green-gold)
is reinforced by tough collagen fibers and
stretchy elastin fibers, which underpin
and stabilize the epithelial
tissue above it.

Organs and systems

LOOKING AT THE pictures of living bodies on these pages, it is as if a door to each body's interior has been swung open to expose the brain, liver, and other organs. But however revealing these images may be, they provide no insight into how different organs work together to produce a living human. In fact, just as individual players in a soccer team collaborate to score goals, specific body organs operate as a team – called a system – to carry out a specific task. Digestive system organs, for example, interact to supply the body with food. In all, there are 12 systems, but they do not exist in isolation. Instead they work together to make a complete, walking, talking human being.

Larynx (voice box) *is the part of the respiratory system that produces sounds*

Kidney *removes wastes and excess water from the blood to form urine*

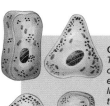

Cellular level
These are four types of cells found in the epithelial tissue that lines the stomach and together contribute to the digestive process.

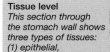

Tissue level
This section through the stomach wall shows three types of tissues:
(1) epithelial,
(2) connective,
(3) muscular.
Each is made up of specific types of cells.

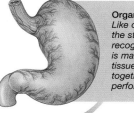

Organ level
Like other organs, the stomach has a recognizable shape and is made up of different tissues that work together so it can perform specific tasks.

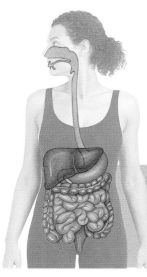

System level
The stomach, small intestine, and other digestive organs are linked together to form the digestive system, which is responsible for supplying the body with nutrients. Together, this and other systems make up the body.

Femur (thigh bone) *is the largest bone in the body, and it supports the body's weight*

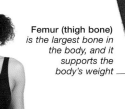

THE BODY HIERARCHY
The organization of the body can be seen as a sequence of levels, starting with the simplest – (the body's atoms and molecules) and progressing to the most complex (the body itself). Key molecules such as proteins and lipids – make up cells and their organelles. Similar cells that work together make up a tissue, while two or more tissues make up an organ. The stomach, for example, has a lining of epithelial tissue, layers of muscle tissue which contract to crush food during digestion, and connective tissue which holds the organ together. Linked organs work together to form a system, which interacts with the other systems to make up the body.

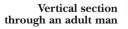

Vertical section through an adult man

WHAT IS AN ORGAN?

A glance into a mirror immediately reveals some organs. Eyes and skin are the most obvious, while inside an open mouth are the tongue, teeth, and tonsils. However, most organs are found inside the body, as these magnetic resonance imaging (MRI) scans show. Here the brain, lungs, kidneys, and liver can be seen in a vertical section, as can individual bones and muscles. Each organ is made of two or more tissues (a group of cells of the same type) and carries out one or more specific tasks that are essential for the body's survival.

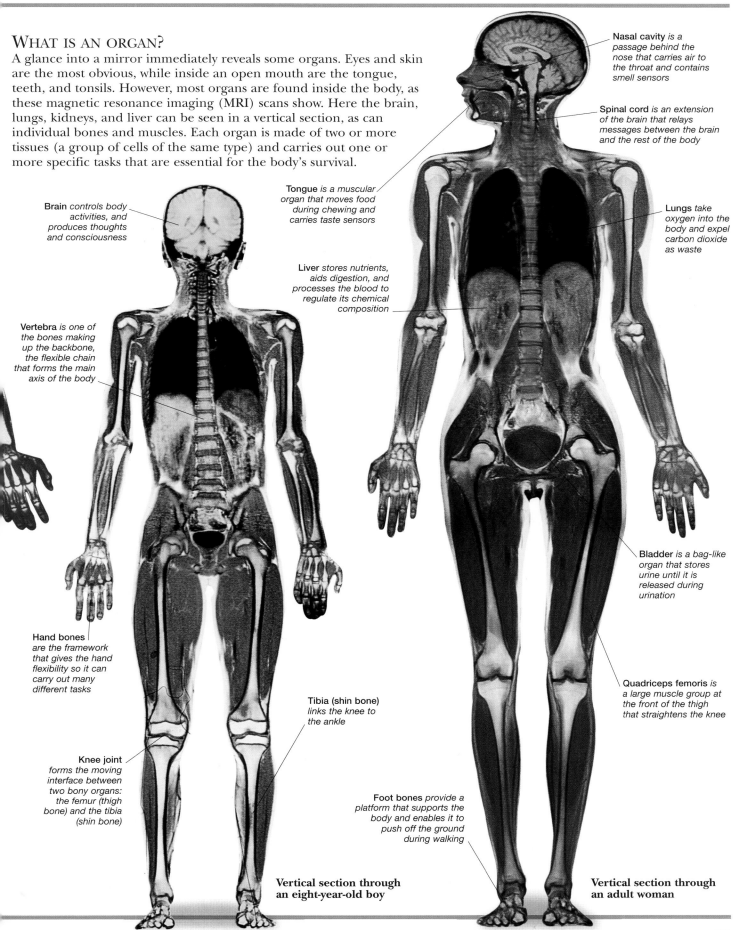

Nasal cavity *is a passage behind the nose that carries air to the throat and contains smell sensors*

Spinal cord *is an extension of the brain that relays messages between the brain and the rest of the body*

Tongue *is a muscular organ that moves food during chewing and carries taste sensors*

Brain *controls body activities, and produces thoughts and consciousness*

Lungs *take oxygen into the body and expel carbon dioxide as waste*

Liver *stores nutrients, aids digestion, and processes the blood to regulate its chemical composition*

Vertebra *is one of the bones making up the backbone, the flexible chain that forms the main axis of the body*

Hand bones *are the framework that gives the hand flexibility so it can carry out many different tasks*

Bladder *is a bag-like organ that stores urine until it is released during urination*

Knee joint *forms the moving interface between two bony organs: the femur (thigh bone) and the tibia (shin bone)*

Tibia (shin bone) *links the knee to the ankle*

Quadriceps femoris *is a large muscle group at the front of the thigh that straightens the knee*

Foot bones *provide a platform that supports the body and enables it to push off the ground during walking*

Vertical section through an eight-year-old boy

Vertical section through an adult woman

Imaging techniques

TODAY, DOCTORS AND researchers have access to many different methods of looking inside a living body. This allows them to explore tissues and organs to search for disease, or to find out how the body works. This has not always been the case. Until 40 years ago, X-rays – which do not clearly reveal softer body tissues – were the only means of seeing inside a living person without performing surgery. Since the 1970s, however, modern technology, especially advances in computers, has produced a variety of powerful imaging techniques, including CT and MRI scanning. Like X-rays, these techniques are noninvasive (do not require surgery), but they produce images – many examples of which are shown throughout this encyclopedia – that are considerably more detailed than anything obtained before.

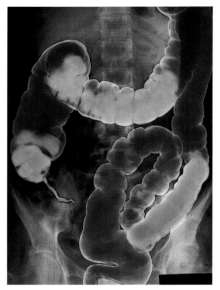

X-RAYS (RADIOGRAPHY)
With this technique, a high-energy form of radiation is passed through the body and projected onto a photographic film to produce an X-ray photograph, or radiograph. The film remains white where hard tissues, such as bone, have absorbed X-rays, but turns gray or black where X-rays have passed through soft tissues, such as muscle. In this contrast radiograph, barium sulfate – a substance that absorbs X-rays – has been introduced into the large intestine (made of soft tissues) so its outline (orange) can be clearly seen. The colors are false and were added afterward.

COMPUTED TOMOGRAPHY (CT)
Combining X-rays with a computer, CT scanning produces much more detailed images than ordinary X-ray photographs. As a person lies inside a scanner (below), it rotates around him, sending narrow beams of X-rays through his body and into a detector. A computer analyzes information from the detector to produce a "slice" through the organs in that part of the body. These slices can be built up to produce a 3-D image, like this one (right) of the skull and brain.

DIFFERENT METHODS

Imaging techniques vary in the way they work and in their applications. X-rays and CT scanning use high-energy radiation. Ordinary X-rays are typically used for looking at bones. Contrast X-rays use special substances to reveal hollow structures such as the intestines or blood vessels. CT scanning uses computers to produce detailed images, usually of the head or abdomen. PET and radionuclide scanning both use radioactive substances to reveal chemical activity in tissues rather than detailed structure. MRI scanning and ultrasound do not use radiation. MRI scans produce detailed images of any body tissue. Ultrasound can show both structure and movement, and is commonly used to observe the development of the fetus.

Patient undergoing CT scan

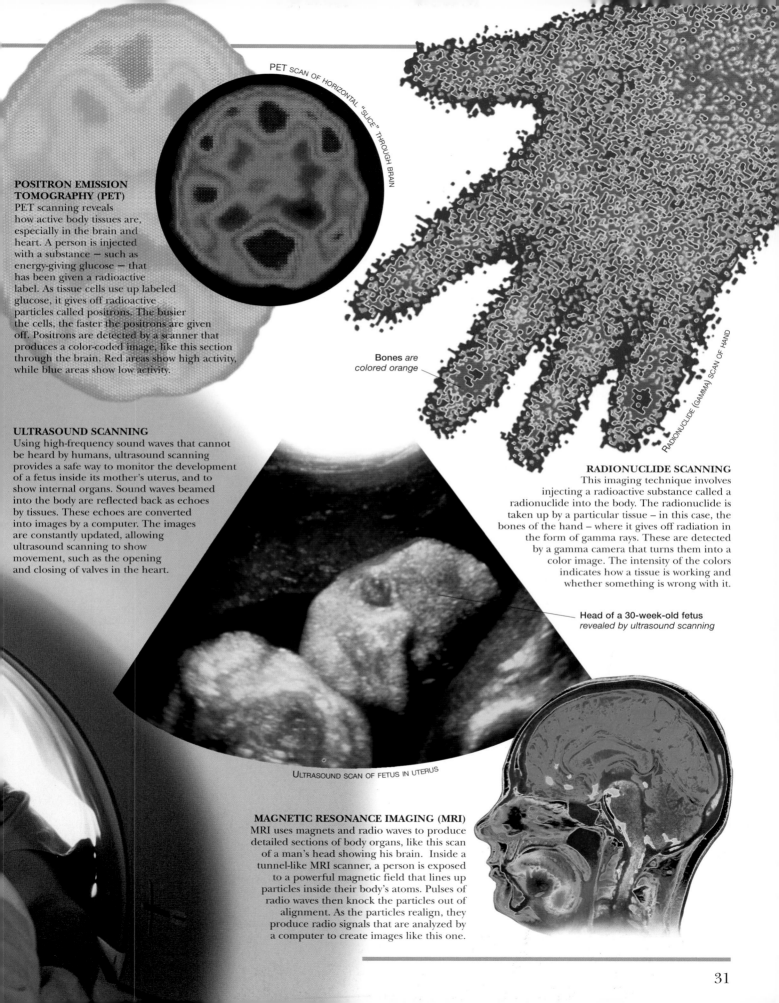

POSITRON EMISSION TOMOGRAPHY (PET)

PET scanning reveals how active body tissues are, especially in the brain and heart. A person is injected with a substance — such as energy-giving glucose — that has been given a radioactive label. As tissue cells use up labeled glucose, it gives off radioactive particles called positrons. The busier the cells, the faster the positrons are given off. Positrons are detected by a scanner that produces a color-coded image, like this section through the brain. Red areas show high activity, while blue areas show low activity.

Bones *are colored orange*

RADIONUCLIDE (GAMMA) SCAN OF HAND

ULTRASOUND SCANNING

Using high-frequency sound waves that cannot be heard by humans, ultrasound scanning provides a safe way to monitor the development of a fetus inside its mother's uterus, and to show internal organs. Sound waves beamed into the body are reflected back as echoes by tissues. These echoes are converted into images by a computer. The images are constantly updated, allowing ultrasound scanning to show movement, such as the opening and closing of valves in the heart.

RADIONUCLIDE SCANNING

This imaging technique involves injecting a radioactive substance called a radionuclide into the body. The radionuclide is taken up by a particular tissue – in this case, the bones of the hand – where it gives off radiation in the form of gamma rays. These are detected by a gamma camera that turns them into a color image. The intensity of the colors indicates how a tissue is working and whether something is wrong with it.

Head of a 30-week-old fetus *revealed by ultrasound scanning*

ULTRASOUND SCAN OF FETUS IN UTERUS

MAGNETIC RESONANCE IMAGING (MRI)

MRI uses magnets and radio waves to produce detailed sections of body organs, like this scan of a man's head showing his brain. Inside a tunnel-like MRI scanner, a person is exposed to a powerful magnetic field that lines up particles inside their body's atoms. Pulses of radio waves then knock the particles out of alignment. As the particles realign, they produce radio signals that are analyzed by a computer to create images like this one.

31

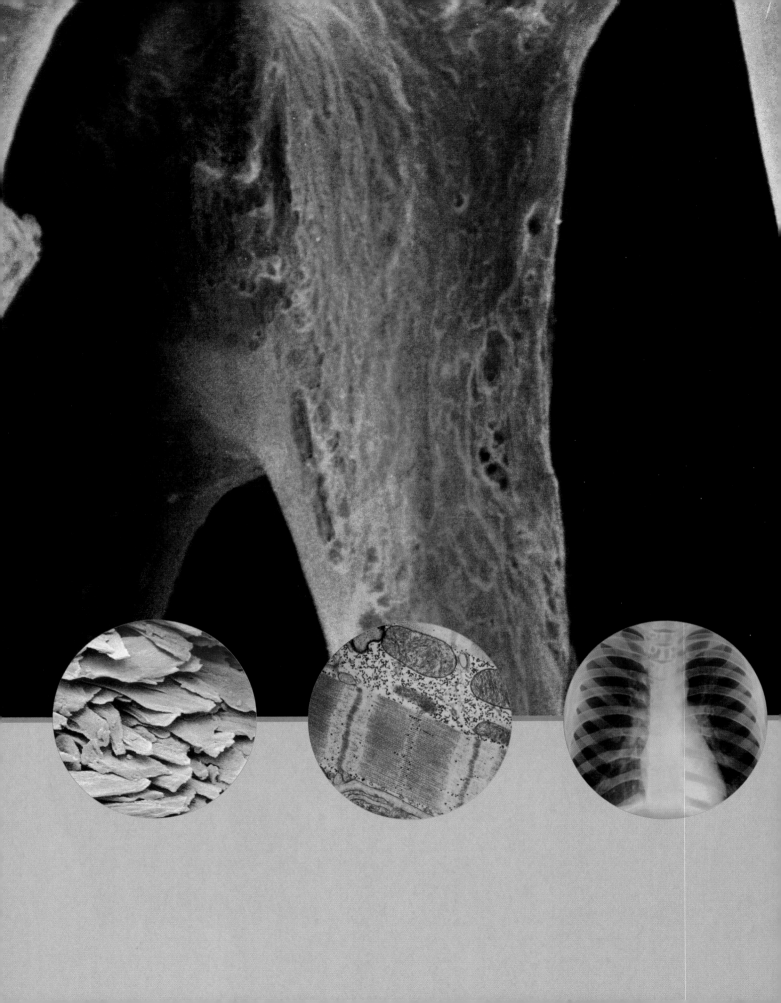

Moving Framework

THREE SYSTEMS COVER, move, shape, and support the body. Skin is
a living, stretchy overcoat that shields the delicate tissues inside the
body from the harsh conditions outside. Bones form the skeleton,
a structure strong enough to support the body's weight and prevent
its collapse, yet light and flexible enough to let the body move.
Muscles shape the body and, by pulling bones, produce a multitude
of movements, from raising an eyebrow to running a marathon.

INTEGUMENTARY system

Cornified layer *consists of flat, dead cells that are constantly worn away*

Clear layer *is most apparent in the thick skin that covers the soles and palms*

Granular layer *is where cells flatten and fill with tough keratin as they move toward the surface cells*

Basal layer *produces new cells to replace those lost from the surface*

Spiny layer *cells are linked by spinelike connections*

Dermal papillae *attach dermis to the epidermis*

SKIN, HAIR, AND NAILS make up the integumentary system. The skin, which covers the entire surface of the body and forms an essential barrier between the body and its surroundings, is the body's largest organ. In an average adult, it weighs about 11 lb (5 kg). It provides protection against injury, infection by microorganisms, and damage by harmful rays in sunlight. The skin is also a sense organ that can detect touch, warmth, cold, and pain. In addition, it helps to control body temperature and produces vitamin D, which is necessary for healthy bones. Hair and nails grow directly from the skin to provide additional covering and protection.

LIVING LAYERS
The skin has two layers. The upper layer, the epidermis, is made up of cell layers (left, shown separated) that become flatter and tougher toward the surface. The lower layer, the dermis, contains strong, flexible fibers, blood vessels, nerves, and sensory receptors. Lodged in the dermis are sebaceous glands and coiled sweat glands. Hairs grow from follicles that extend upward from the dermis through the epidermis. Beneath the dermis lies subcutaneous tissue, a fatty layer that insulates the body and stores energy.

Nerve *relays messages between skin receptors and the brain*

Arrector pili muscle *pulls hair upright to produce goose bumps*

Sebaceous gland *produces oily sebum which keeps skin and hair soft and flexible*

Subcutaneous fat *helps to insulate the body*

Touch receptor *detects light touch*

Sweat gland *releases sweat onto the skin's surface to cool the body*

Pressure receptor *detects pressure and vibrations*

Blood vessel *helps to regulate body temperature*

Hair follicle *is a cavity in the skin from which hair grows*

Section through the skin

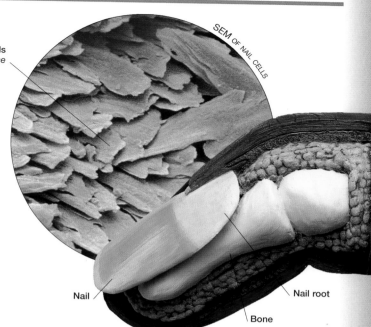

Flattened dead cells
from nail surface

SEM OF NAIL CELLS

Nail

Nail root

Bone

**Section through a finger
showing position of nail**

PROTECTIVE OVERCOAT

The epidermis provides a waterproof coating that protects the body from drying out or becoming waterlogged. Water is repelled from the skin's surface by the keratin that fills epidermal cells and by oily sebum produced by the sebaceous glands. As a person showers, skin keeps the water out. Meanwhile, receptors that are sensitive to heat or cold detect the temperature of the water, and receptors that are sensitive to touch detect the flow of water against the skin.

NAILS

The sensitive tips of the fingers and toes have hard plates called nails that provide protection and support. Each nail grows from a living root at its base, which is overlapped by a fold of skin, and consists mainly of flattened dead cells filled with the tough protein keratin. Nails grow faster in warm weather than cold, and fingernails grow three or four times faster than toenails.

INTEGUMENTARY SYSTEM FUNCTIONS

Protection	*Against the harmful effects of physical injury, chemicals, heat, sunlight, infection, and excessive water; also against water loss.*	Vitamin D synthesis	*Produces vitamin D in the presence of ultraviolet rays from the sun.*
		Excretion	*Eliminates small amounts of waste substances from the body in sweat.*
Temperature regulation	*Keeps body temperature stable by sweating and varying size of blood vessels in the skin; vessels narrow to conserve heat and widen to lose heat; hair limits heat loss from the head.*	Gripping	*Provides a surface with good grip for handling objects and to prevent slipping; nails make handling easier.*
Sensation	*Detects touch/pressure, pain, warmth, and cold.*	Absorption	*Can take small amounts of certain substances into the body from the surface.*

"NAKED" APES

Humans appear naked compared to great apes, our closest animal relatives. However, apes and humans have similar numbers of body hairs. While the ape's body is coated with long, coarse hair (terminal hair), the human body is mostly covered with short, fine hair (vellus). Humans have terminal hair on the scalp and in a few other areas only. A hairy coat helps keep the ape warm; humans rely mainly on clothing instead.

Light, downy vellus hair

Coarse terminal hair

Skin surface

Covering an area of up to 21.5 sq ft (2 sq m), the skin's surface is far from smooth. In fact, it is marked by numerous crisscrossing lines and by creases, grooves, ridges, and bumps. It is kept soft and supple by a thin coating of oil, called sebum. Scattered over the surface are the openings of millions of hair follicles and sweat ducts. Sweating is one of the ways in which the skin helps control body temperature. The surface of the skin is also home to a variety of bacteria, visible only under a microscope. Sometimes large numbers flourish, causing pimples or rashes.

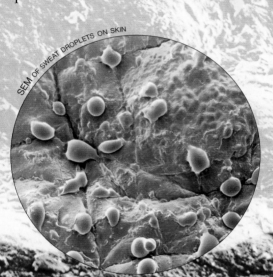

SEM OF SWEAT DROPLETS ON SKIN

Goose bumps

COOLING DOWN

If the body overheats, droplets of sweat ooze from sweat glands onto the skin's surface. Water in the sweat evaporates and draws heat away from the body, cooling it down. The sweat glands in the armpits produce a large amount of sweat, which many adults use antiperspirants to control. Cooling is also achieved by blood vessels in the skin, which widen to speed up heat loss from the body.

GOOSE BUMPS

When the body is cold, blood vessels in the skin narrow to conserve heat, and small bumps, called goose bumps, appear. Goose bumps are formed when a tiny muscle attached to the base of each hair shortens, pulling the hair upright and lifting the surrounding skin. In animals with thick coats, air becomes trapped between the upright hairs, creating a blanket that helps keep the body warm.

EPIDERMAL RIDGES

This close-up view shows the hundreds of tiny ridges on the surface of the skin on the palm of a hand. Sweat ducts open in rows along the crests of each ridge. The undersides of hands and feet are the only areas covered with these ridges, which are separated by fine parallel grooves and form curved patterns on the skin. They are also the only areas that have no hair or oil glands. A ridged, hairless surface provides good grip for handling objects and prevents slipping on surfaces, such as when walking or climbing.

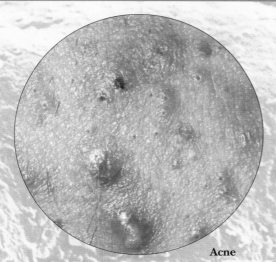

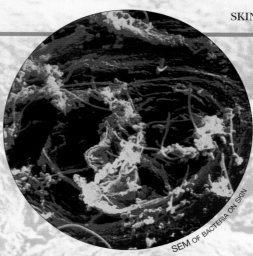

SEM OF BACTERIA ON SKIN

SKIN BACTERIA
This magnified view shows some of the millions of harmless bacteria that normally live on the skin. These bacteria help to keep the skin healthy by preventing harmful varieties from growing. The oil on the surface of the skin also helps eliminate harmful bacteria. Fungi are often present in deep folds in the skin, such as between the toes or in the groin.

Acne

PIMPLES AND ACNE
Bacteria or other microorganisms can infect the skin, resulting in pimples or acne. Skin problems are common during adolescence, when changes in hormone levels cause sebaceous glands to produce excess sebum that becomes trapped in hair follicles. Skin bacteria thrive in the sebum, causing inflammation of surrounding tissues, and often giving rise to acne, as shown above on the face of a teenage boy.

SEM OF SKIN ON THE PALM OF THE HAND

FINGERPRINTS AND CRIME DETECTION

The swirling epidermal ridges at the ends of the fingers and thumbs produce patterns that are unique to each individual. Well supplied with sweat glands, these ridges leave behind sweat patterns, better known as fingerprints, when they touch smooth surfaces. The unique nature of fingerprints makes them useful in crime detection. Investigators look for similarities between fingerprints found at a crime scene and those of suspects. During the 1880s, interest in the use of fingerprints grew, and the police in London, England, set up a fingerprint department in 1901 to help identify criminals. In 1902, a burglar named Jackson became the first criminal to be convicted on the basis of fingerprint evidence. In the United States, the first fingerprint file was established by J. Edgar Hoover, who became director of the FBI in 1924.

A fingerprint, with its unique pattern of whorls and arches

Skin features

TOGETHER, THE TWO layers of the skin – the epidermis and dermis – combine to give it depth. This can vary considerably – the skin is very thin and delicate in some areas, and much thicker and tougher in others. Regardless of its thickness, skin everywhere undergoes a continuous process of renewal. Dead, flattened cells are constantly worn away, to be replaced by new cells generated by the division of living cells in the lowest layer of the epidermis. Scattered within this multiplying layer are cells that produce melanin, the brown pigment that helps give skin its color.

TWO LAYERS

The SEM below shows the two skin layers: the epidermis above, and the thicker dermis beneath. The epidermis contains flat, overlapping cells that are filled with a tough protein called keratin and form a protective, waterproof covering. Below, the dermis contains collagen and elastin fibers that give the skin strength and flexibility, allowing it to stretch and return to its normal shape. The dermis is also supplied with nerves and blood vessels.

BRUISES
Bruising – which is usually caused by a blow or fall – occurs when blood leaks from damaged blood vessels. It can be very noticeable around the eye, because here the skin is not only very thin but also loosely anchored, so blood can easily collect, producing a black eye. Bruises usually look dark purple or blue at first, then turn brown, green, or yellow as they fade.

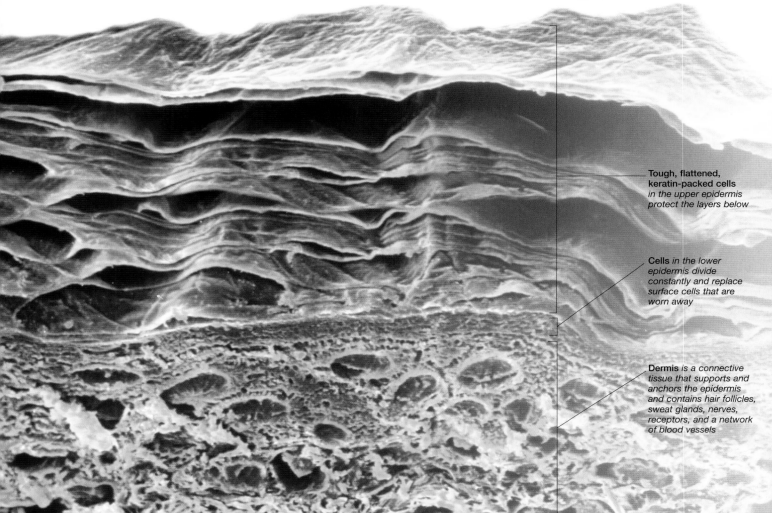

Tough, flattened, keratin-packed cells *in the upper epidermis protect the layers below*

Cells *in the lower epidermis divide constantly and replace surface cells that are worn away*

Dermis *is a connective tissue that supports and anchors the epidermis and contains hair follicles, sweat glands, nerves, receptors, and a network of blood vessels*

Sole of the foot: 0.16 in (4 mm)

Eyelid: 0.02 in (0.5 mm)

HOW THICK?

Skin varies in thickness over the surface of the body. It is very thin on the eyelids and lips, and very thick on the soles of the feet and palms of the hands. The epidermis of the skin tends to become thicker and harder if it experiences a lot of wear and tear. For example, people who often walk barefoot have tougher soles.

SUNTAN

Sunlight stimulates the skin to make more melanin – which is why skin darkens, or tans, in the sun. The extra melanin provides increased protection against harmful ultraviolet rays from the sun. Too much ultraviolet radiation can cause sunburn. It can also make the skin appear dry and wrinkled, and increases the risk of developing skin cancer in later life. Wearing a hat, and applying sunscreen regularly, helps reduce the sun's effects on the skin.

An Australian lifeguard with hat and sunscreen

SKIN FLAKES

Tens of thousands of dead, flattened cells are shed from the skin every minute. They constantly rub off or peel away from the skin surface, like flakes of old paint, to be replaced by new cells that push up from the lower epidermis toward the surface. These fallen flakes of dead skin, together with other particles and fibers, form household dust.

SEM OF SKIN FLAKES

MANY SHADES

Skin color ranges from nearly black through varying shades of brown to pale pink, and depends on how much melanin the skin contains. Melanin is a dark pigment made by cells called melanocytes in the lower epidermis. It serves to protect the skin against damage by ultraviolet rays. The amount each person has is determined by their ancestry. People with dark skin have a lot of melanin; people with fair skin have less.

Upper layers of epidermis

Epidermal cell

Pregnant female scabies mite *burrows into the epidermis*

ITCH MITES

The itch mite has been a human parasite for thousands of years. The tiny female mite burrows deep into the epidermis, where she lays her eggs, and a few weeks later an intensely itchy rash, called scabies, develops on the trunk and limbs. Passed on via close contact, such as holding hands with an infected person, the scabies mite can only be killed by special medicated lotions and creams.

Hair

ALMOST EVERY PART OF THE body – apart from the palms of the hands, soles of the feet, lips, and nipples – is covered by hair. Hairs are long filaments made up of dead cells that grow out of the skin. Short, fine vellus hair covers much of the body, while longer, thicker terminal hair is found in the eyebrows, eyelashes, nose hairs, and on the scalp. After puberty, terminal hair appears in the armpits and pubic regions of both sexes, as well as on the faces and chests of males. There are about 100,000 hairs on the scalp, of which about 100 are lost daily, to be replaced by new growth. Scalp hair serves to insulate the head and protect it from harmful sunlight radiation.

HEAD OF HAIR

Whether hair is straight, curly, or wavy depends on the shape of its shaft. In cross-section, shafts of straight hair are round, those of wavy hair are oval, and those of curly hair are flat. Hair color depends on how much of each of the three melanin variants – yellow, red, and brown-black – hair contains. The relative amounts of each determine whether hair is blond, red, brown, or black. In older people, a slowdown in melanin production produces gray hair.

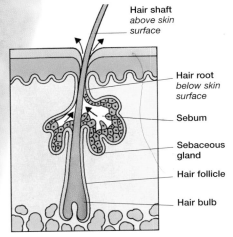

Hair follicle cross-section

Hair shaft *above skin surface*

Hair root *below skin surface*

Sebum

Sebaceous gland

Hair follicle

Hair bulb

Hair shaft

HAIR FOLLICLES

Hairs grow from tiny pits in the skin called follicles. Cells in the hair bulb at the bottom of the follicle divide to form the hair and push it upward. As cells move upward, they fill with keratin and die, which is why a haircut is painless. Oily sebum, released by sebaceous glands into hair follicles, keeps the hair shaft moist and flexible.

HAIR GROWTH

The terminal hairs on the scalp and, in the case of adult males, on the face, grow at a rate of about 0.4 in (10 mm) a month. Each hair has a growth phase lasting several years, then a resting phase, before it is pushed out by a new hair. People control the growth by cutting their hair, and many men also shave their beards. Here, beard hairs are regrowing after a shave.

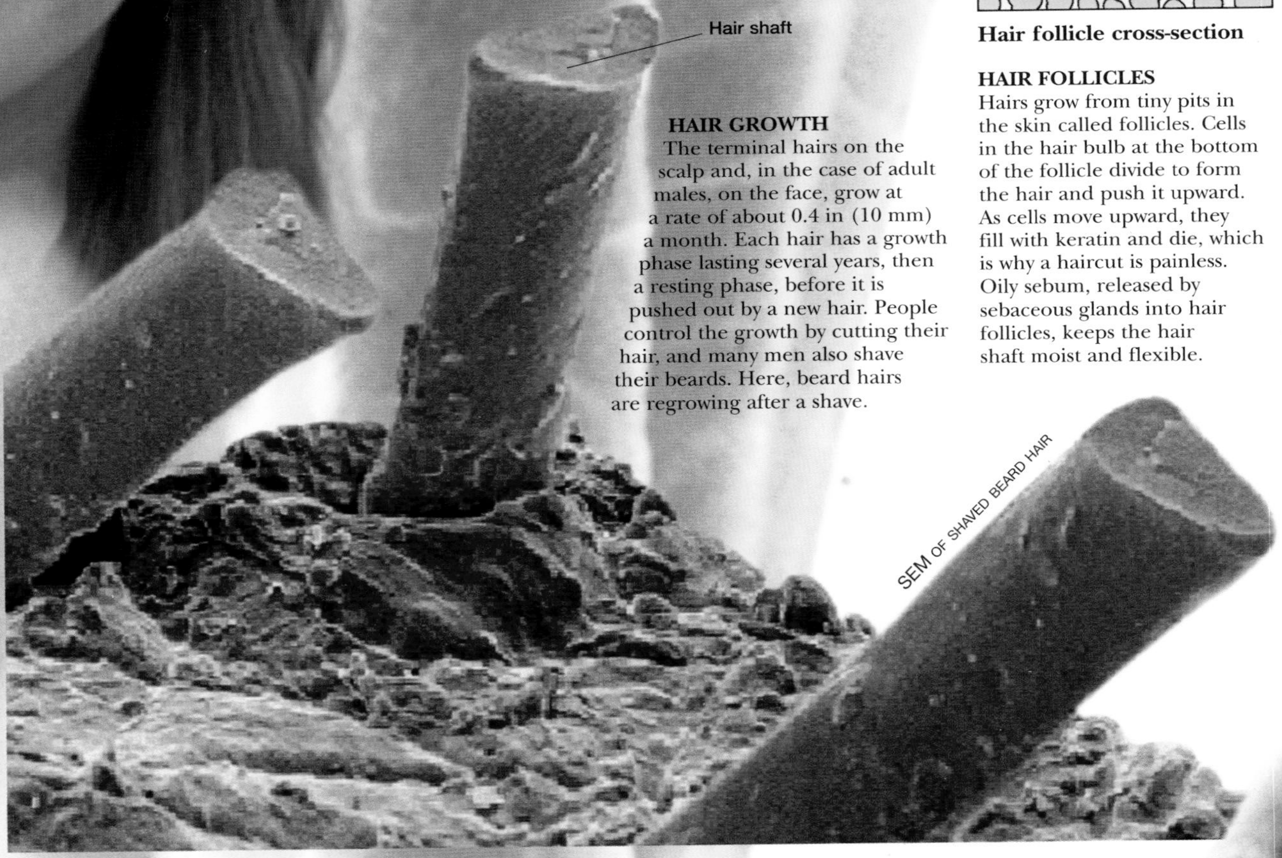

SEM OF SHAVED BEARD HAIR

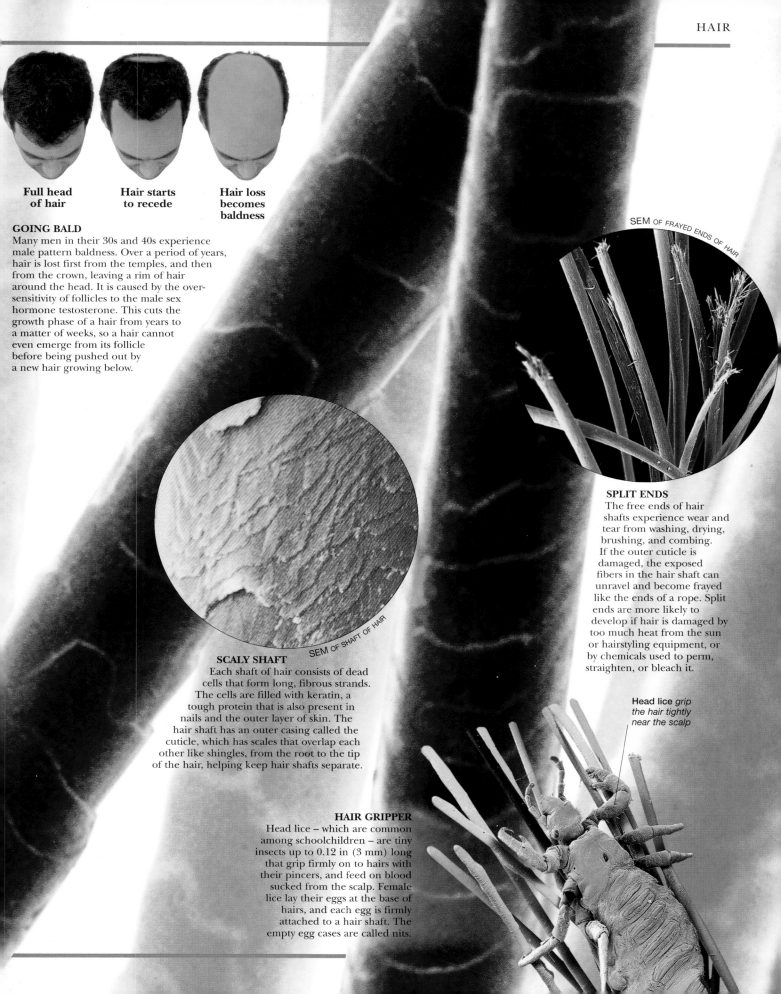

Full head of hair

Hair starts to recede

Hair loss becomes baldness

GOING BALD

Many men in their 30s and 40s experience male pattern baldness. Over a period of years, hair is lost first from the temples, and then from the crown, leaving a rim of hair around the head. It is caused by the over-sensitivity of follicles to the male sex hormone testosterone. This cuts the growth phase of a hair from years to a matter of weeks, so a hair cannot even emerge from its follicle before being pushed out by a new hair growing below.

SEM OF FRAYED ENDS OF HAIR

SPLIT ENDS

The free ends of hair shafts experience wear and tear from washing, drying, brushing, and combing. If the outer cuticle is damaged, the exposed fibers in the hair shaft can unravel and become frayed like the ends of a rope. Split ends are more likely to develop if hair is damaged by too much heat from the sun or hairstyling equipment, or by chemicals used to perm, straighten, or bleach it.

SCALY SHAFT

Each shaft of hair consists of dead cells that form long, fibrous strands. The cells are filled with keratin, a tough protein that is also present in nails and the outer layer of skin. The hair shaft has an outer casing called the cuticle, which has scales that overlap each other like shingles, from the root to the tip of the hair, helping keep hair shafts separate.

SEM OF SHAFT OF HAIR

Head lice grip the hair tightly near the scalp

HAIR GRIPPER

Head lice – which are common among schoolchildren – are tiny insects up to 0.12 in (3 mm) long that grip firmly on to hairs with their pincers, and feed on blood sucked from the scalp. Female lice lay their eggs at the base of hairs, and each egg is firmly attached to a hair shaft. The empty egg cases are called nits.

SKELETAL system

THE STRONG INNER framework of the body is formed by the skeletal system. Made up of separate bones that are linked together at joints, the skeletal system not only gives the body its shape, but also provides anchorage for the muscles that move it. It supports and protects vital organs, such as the brain, heart, and lungs. Although bones themselves are rigid, they are linked by joints that give the skeleton a great deal of flexibility. Before birth, the skeleton is made mostly of cartilage, and as a result is less rigid. As the body grows, cartilage is gradually replaced by bone, though some cartilage remains in the joints and also in the nose and ears.

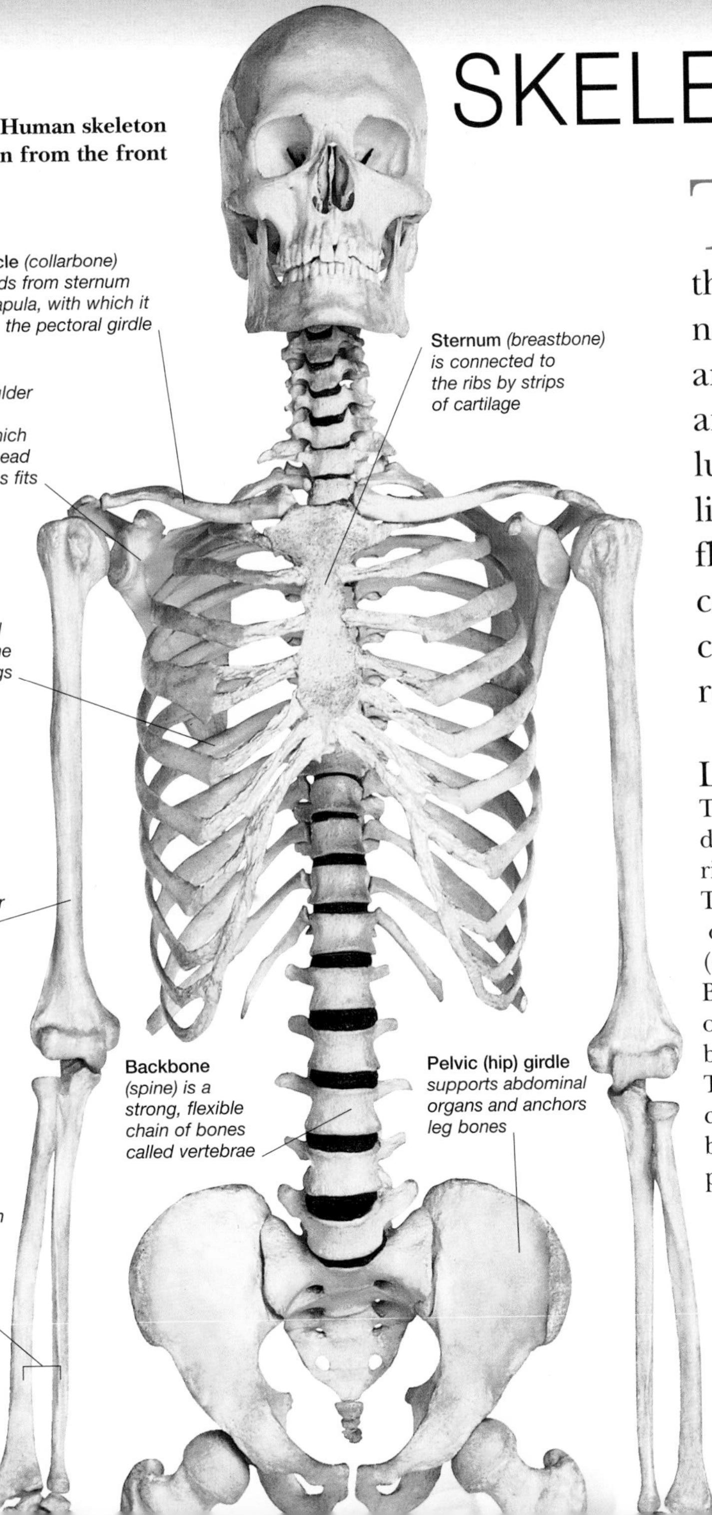

LIVING FRAMEWORK

The skeleton is made up of 206 separate bones, which differ in shape, size, and name. The skull, backbone, ribs, and sternum form the central part of the skeleton. The bones of the arms and legs hang symmetrically on either side, attached by the pectoral girdle (clavicle and scapula) and the pelvic girdle. Bones are not dry and lifeless, but are active organs containing living cells surrounded by protein fibers and mineral crystals. They act as mineral stores and are constantly exchanging calcium with blood. Inside some bones, marrow produces red and white blood cells.

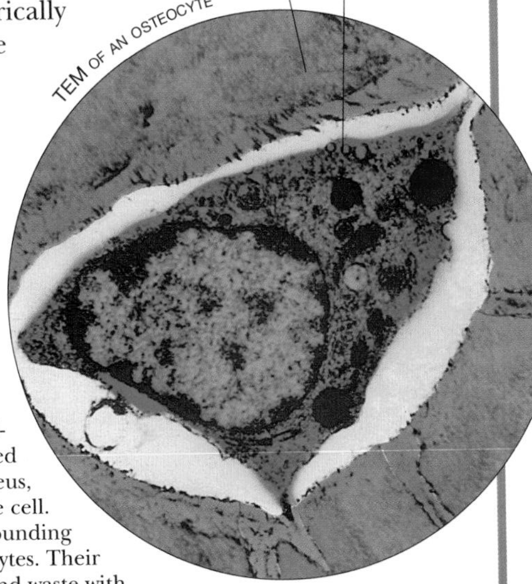

Osteocyte

Compact bone

TEM OF AN OSTEOCYTE

BONE CELL

This highly magnified image shows a mature bone cell called an osteocyte. It lies within a fluid-filled space called a lacuna, which is surrounded by compact bone. The cell has a large oval nucleus, which is visible in the lower part of the cell. Osteocytes send thin branches out into the surrounding bone to link with the branches of other osteocytes. Their role is to maintain bone, exchanging nutrients and waste with the blood. Other types of bone cell – called osteoblasts and osteoclasts – make bone and break it down, respectively.

Human skeleton seen from the front

Clavicle (collarbone) extends from sternum to scapula, with which it forms the pectoral girdle

Scapula (shoulder blade) has a hollow into which the rounded head of the humerus fits

Sternum (breastbone) is connected to the ribs by strips of cartilage

Ribs surround and protect the heart and lungs

Humerus (upper arm bone) is the longest bone in the arm and extends from shoulder to elbow

Backbone (spine) is a strong, flexible chain of bones called vertebrae

Pelvic (hip) girdle supports abdominal organs and anchors leg bones

Radius and ulna (forearm bones) run from the elbow to the wrist

RADIONUCLIDE (GAMMA) SCAN OF A HEALTHY SKELETON

18th-century engraving by Deuchar of Holbein's *Dance of Death*

SYMBOL OF DEATH
After death, once the flesh has rotted away, the bones are all that remain. Consequently, the skeleton has for centuries been used around the world as a symbol of death and disease. One example of this is the skull and crossbones, which was used on the flags of pirate ships to signal danger to others.

BONE SCAN
The image on the right is of a radionuclide (gamma) scan of the whole skeleton in a living person. Images such as these, which are produced in hospitals or clinics with special scanning equipment, can be very useful in medicine because they help doctors discover whether the bones are diseased. Doctors also use other tests, such as X-rays, magnetic resonance imaging (MRI), and ultrasound, to examine the skeletal system.

Tibia (shinbone) bears most of the weight in the lower leg; its sharp front edge forms the shin

SKELETAL SYSTEM FUNCTIONS

Support	Provides supportive framework for body tissues and organs; gives the body its shape.
Protection	Provides protection for internal organs: ribs protect heart and lungs; skull protects the brain; spine protects the spinal cord; pelvis protects the uterus and bladder.
Movement	Provides a strong yet light framework and anchorage for muscles; joints allow flexibility.
Blood cell production	Produces different types of blood cells in the red marrow of certain bones.
Mineral storage	Acts as a reservoir for minerals, particularly calcium and phosphorus.

Femur (thighbone) is the largest bone in the body. It has a rounded end that fits into the pelvic girdle; the other end has a wide, grooved surface that forms part of the knee

Metacarpal is one of 27 hand bones that form the most flexible part of the skeleton

RADIONUCLIDE (GAMMA) SCAN OF THE KNEE

FLEXIBLE SUPPORT
The image on the right shows a scan of the knees – the joints between each femur (thighbone) and tibia (shinbone). Joints are the parts of the skeleton where two or more bones meet. Held in place by strong bands of tissue called ligaments, they allow the bones to move and give the skeleton its flexibility. Each joint has its own range of movements, though most, like the knees, can move freely. In order to reduce friction, the ends of the bones at joints are covered with smooth cartilage.

Tarsal is one of 26 foot bones that support the body during walking and standing

BACKGROUND: SEM OF BONE MARROW

Skull

THE MOST COMPLEX PART of the skeleton, the skull shapes the head and face, protects the brain, and houses the special sense organs. It is made of 22 separate bones, 21 of which are locked together by immovable joints to form a structure of extraordinary strength. The only movable skull bone is the mandible, or lower jaw. Skull bones are divided into two sets. The cranial bones form the domed upper part, or cranium, which surrounds, supports, and protects the brain and the organs of hearing. The facial bones form the framework of the face and jaw, and provide attachment sites for the muscles that produce facial expressions. Together, both cranial and facial bones form the orbits, or eye sockets, and the nasal cavity.

Foramen magnum
in the occipital bone

LOWER OPENING
At the base of the skull is a large circular hole – the foramen magnum. The lowest part of the brain passes through this opening and continues downward as the spinal cord. Other smaller holes are for the passage of nerves and blood vessels.

X-ray of the skull, seen from the front, showing two pairs of sinuses

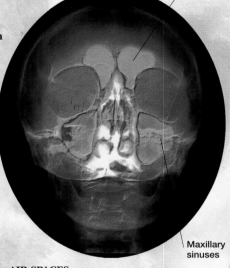

Frontal sinuses

Maxillary sinuses

AIR SPACES
Some of the bones surrounding the nasal cavity contain hollow, air-filled spaces called sinuses. The sinuses lighten the skull's weight, and act as an echo chamber, giving a slight "ring" to the voice. They are lined with a moist membrane and connect through small openings with the inside of the nasal cavity.

Occipital bone

Parietal bone

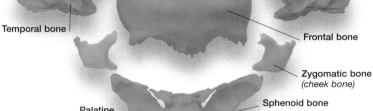

Temporal bone

Frontal bone

Zygomatic bone
(cheek bone)

Sphenoid bone

Palatine bone

Ethmoid bone

Maxilla
(upper jaw bone)

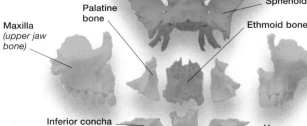

Inferior concha

Vomer

Bones of the skull

Cranial bones (8)

Facial bones (14)

Nasal bones

Mandible
(lower jaw)

COMPONENT PARTS
Eight bones form the cranium around the brain. The frontal bone is at the front, the two parietal bones form the sides and top, the occipital bone the back and (with the sphenoid) the base, the two temporal bones the side, and the ethmoid part of the nasal cavity. Each temporal bone has an opening to the inner parts of the ear, which are encased within. The remaining 14 facial bones form the skeleton of the face. The zygomatic bones are the cheek bones. The palatine bones, nasal bones, inferior conchae, vomer, and lacrimal bones (not shown here) surround the nasal cavity. The maxillae (upper jaw bones) and the mandible (lower jaw bone) contain sockets for the teeth.

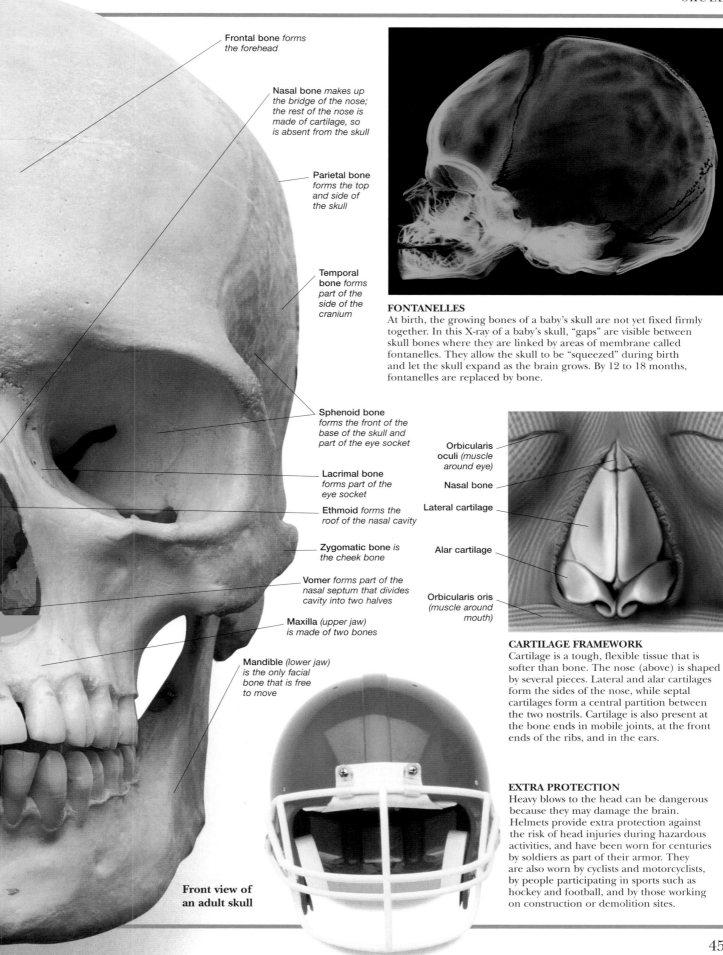

Frontal bone *forms the forehead*

Nasal bone *makes up the bridge of the nose; the rest of the nose is made of cartilage, so is absent from the skull*

Parietal bone *forms the top and side of the skull*

Temporal bone *forms part of the side of the cranium*

Sphenoid bone *forms the front of the base of the skull and part of the eye socket*

Lacrimal bone *forms part of the eye socket*

Ethmoid *forms the roof of the nasal cavity*

Zygomatic bone *is the cheek bone*

Vomer *forms part of the nasal septum that divides cavity into two halves*

Maxilla *(upper jaw) is made of two bones*

Mandible *(lower jaw) is the only facial bone that is free to move*

Front view of an adult skull

FONTANELLES

At birth, the growing bones of a baby's skull are not yet fixed firmly together. In this X-ray of a baby's skull, "gaps" are visible between skull bones where they are linked by areas of membrane called fontanelles. They allow the skull to be "squeezed" during birth and let the skull expand as the brain grows. By 12 to 18 months, fontanelles are replaced by bone.

Orbicularis oculi *(muscle around eye)*

Nasal bone

Lateral cartilage

Alar cartilage

Orbicularis oris *(muscle around mouth)*

CARTILAGE FRAMEWORK

Cartilage is a tough, flexible tissue that is softer than bone. The nose (above) is shaped by several pieces. Lateral and alar cartilages form the sides of the nose, while septal cartilages form a central partition between the two nostrils. Cartilage is also present at the bone ends in mobile joints, at the front ends of the ribs, and in the ears.

EXTRA PROTECTION

Heavy blows to the head can be dangerous because they may damage the brain. Helmets provide extra protection against the risk of head injuries during hazardous activities, and have been worn for centuries by soldiers as part of their armor. They are also worn by cyclists and motorcyclists, by people participating in sports such as hockey and football, and by those working on construction or demolition sites.

Backbone and ribs

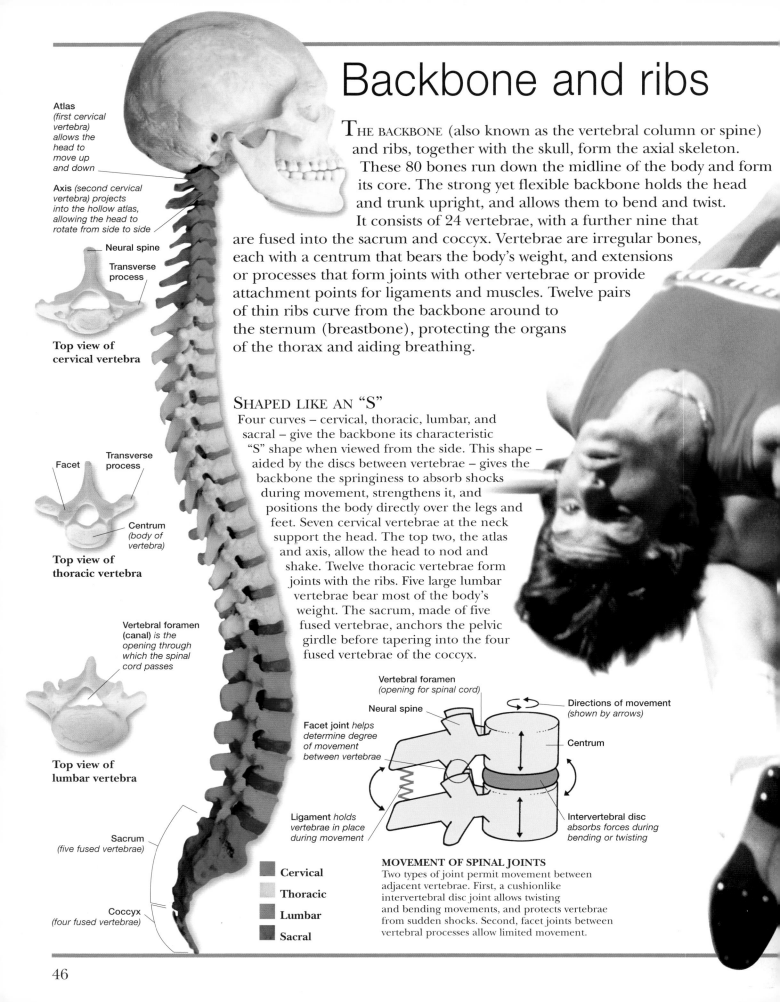

THE BACKBONE (also known as the vertebral column or spine) and ribs, together with the skull, form the axial skeleton. These 80 bones run down the midline of the body and form its core. The strong yet flexible backbone holds the head and trunk upright, and allows them to bend and twist. It consists of 24 vertebrae, with a further nine that are fused into the sacrum and coccyx. Vertebrae are irregular bones, each with a centrum that bears the body's weight, and extensions or processes that form joints with other vertebrae or provide attachment points for ligaments and muscles. Twelve pairs of thin ribs curve from the backbone around to the sternum (breastbone), protecting the organs of the thorax and aiding breathing.

SHAPED LIKE AN "S"

Four curves – cervical, thoracic, lumbar, and sacral – give the backbone its characteristic "S" shape when viewed from the side. This shape – aided by the discs between vertebrae – gives the backbone the springiness to absorb shocks during movement, strengthens it, and positions the body directly over the legs and feet. Seven cervical vertebrae at the neck support the head. The top two, the atlas and axis, allow the head to nod and shake. Twelve thoracic vertebrae form joints with the ribs. Five large lumbar vertebrae bear most of the body's weight. The sacrum, made of five fused vertebrae, anchors the pelvic girdle before tapering into the four fused vertebrae of the coccyx.

Atlas (first cervical vertebra) allows the head to move up and down

Axis (second cervical vertebra) projects into the hollow atlas, allowing the head to rotate from side to side

Neural spine

Transverse process

Top view of cervical vertebra

Facet

Transverse process

Centrum (body of vertebra)

Top view of thoracic vertebra

Vertebral foramen (canal) is the opening through which the spinal cord passes

Top view of lumbar vertebra

Sacrum (five fused vertebrae)

Coccyx (four fused vertebrae)

- Cervical
- Thoracic
- Lumbar
- Sacral

Vertebral foramen (opening for spinal cord)

Neural spine

Facet joint helps determine degree of movement between vertebrae

Ligament holds vertebrae in place during movement

Directions of movement (shown by arrows)

Centrum

Intervertebral disc absorbs forces during bending or twisting

MOVEMENT OF SPINAL JOINTS
Two types of joint permit movement between adjacent vertebrae. First, a cushionlike intervertebral disc joint allows twisting and bending movements, and protects vertebrae from sudden shocks. Second, facet joints between vertebral processes allow limited movement.

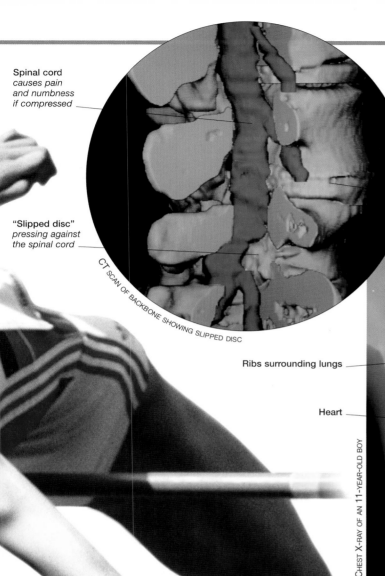

Spinal cord
*causes pain
and numbness
if compressed*

"Slipped disc"
*pressing against
the spinal cord*

CT SCAN OF BACKBONE SHOWING SLIPPED DISC

SLIPPED DISC

Each intervertebral disc between the vertebrae consists of a pad of fibrous cartilage with a jellylike center. Sometimes the fibrous coat breaks open, and part of the disc's core protrudes. If this happens, the core may put pressure on a spinal nerve or, as seen in this CT scan, the core (yellow) may press on the spinal cord itself (blue). This disc prolapse – known more commonly as a slipped disc – causes back pain, and may also cause weakness and pain in the arms and legs.

Intervertebral disc
in correct position

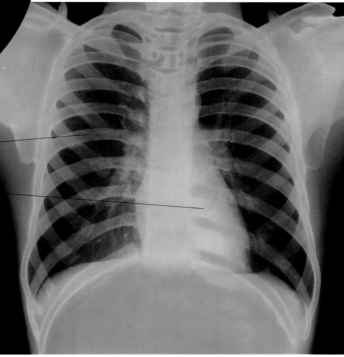

Ribs surrounding lungs

Heart

CHEST X-RAY OF AN 11-YEAR-OLD BOY

ORGAN PROTECTOR

This chest X-ray shows the cagelike structure formed by the ribs that protects the heart, lungs, and the organs of the upper abdomen. The 12 pairs of flat, curved ribs extend from the backbone, where the rear end of each rib forms a joint with one of the thoracic vertebrae, around the wall of the thorax to meet the sternum at the front. Flexible costal cartilage connects the upper ten ribs to the sternum. The up-and-down movements of the ribcage during breathing move air in and out of the lungs.

SPINE FLEXIBILITY

The joints between neighboring vertebrae, the bones that make up the chain running down the back, allow only limited movement. But added together, these small movements make the backbone as a whole very flexible. The backbone can bend forward and backward and from side to side, and permits rotation with the body twisting on its axis. The body can bend further forward (flexion) than it can backward (extension) because the shape of vertebrae limits backward movement. Of all the vertebrae, the cervical vertebrae allow the greatest flexibility, a feature that can be seen in human neck movements.

This highjumper demonstrates the flexibility of the spine

Limbs and girdles

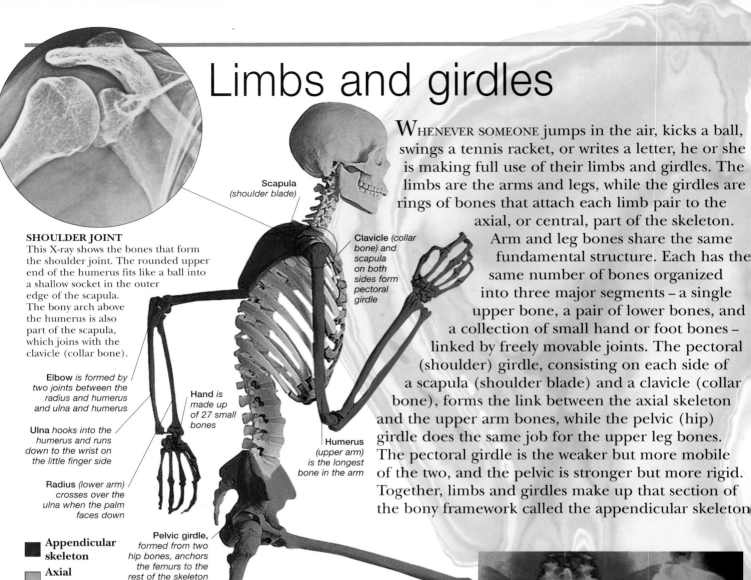

WHENEVER SOMEONE jumps in the air, kicks a ball, swings a tennis racket, or writes a letter, he or she is making full use of their limbs and girdles. The limbs are the arms and legs, while the girdles are rings of bones that attach each limb pair to the axial, or central, part of the skeleton. Arm and leg bones share the same fundamental structure. Each has the same number of bones organized into three major segments – a single upper bone, a pair of lower bones, and a collection of small hand or foot bones – linked by freely movable joints. The pectoral (shoulder) girdle, consisting on each side of a scapula (shoulder blade) and a clavicle (collar bone), forms the link between the axial skeleton and the upper arm bones, while the pelvic (hip) girdle does the same job for the upper leg bones. The pectoral girdle is the weaker but more mobile of the two, and the pelvic is stronger but more rigid. Together, limbs and girdles make up that section of the bony framework called the appendicular skeleton

SHOULDER JOINT
This X-ray shows the bones that form the shoulder joint. The rounded upper end of the humerus fits like a ball into a shallow socket in the outer edge of the scapula. The bony arch above the humerus is also part of the scapula, which joins with the clavicle (collar bone).

Scapula (shoulder blade)

Clavicle (collar bone) and scapula on both sides form pectoral girdle

Elbow is formed by two joints between the radius and humerus and ulna and humerus

Hand *is made up of 27 small bones*

Ulna hooks into the humerus and runs down to the wrist on the little finger side

Radius (lower arm) crosses over the ulna when the palm faces down

Humerus (upper arm) is the longest bone in the arm

■ **Appendicular skeleton**

▨ **Axial skeleton**

Pelvic girdle, formed from two hip bones, anchors the femurs to the rest of the skeleton

Femur (thigh bone) has a rounded top that fits into a hip bone, and a wide lower end that forms part of the knee

Tibia (shin bone) bears most of the weight in the lower leg, and has a sharp front, the shin

Fibula is the smaller of the lower leg bones; helps to swivel the foot

Knee joint is a hinge joint between the femur and tibia

APPENDICULAR SKELETON
The 126 bones of the appendicular skeleton (blue) "append," or hang on to, the axial skeleton. Thanks to the looseness of the pectoral girdle, arm bones have an incredible range of movement, which, coupled with the flexibility of the hand bones, makes them ideal for manipulating objects, a key skill for humans. Leg bones are thicker and firmly attached to the immobile pelvic girdle, reflecting their roles of moving and supporting the body's weight, but reducing their overall mobility compared with arm bones.

Foot is made up of 26 bones, and forms a flexible joint with the tibia and fibula at the ankle

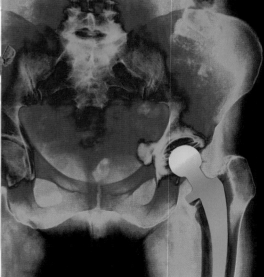

ARTIFICIAL JOINTS
This false-color X-ray shows an artificial left hip joint. Hips, knees, and sometimes other joints that have been damaged by arthritis or injury often need to be replaced in older people. During joint replacement surgery, the ends of the damaged bones are removed and replacement parts (yellow) made of metal or other synthetic materials are inserted instead.

Anatomy, the study of the structure of the human body, has been a subject of great interest since ancient times. In the past, it was made difficult because many cultures forbade the dissection, or cutting up, of dead bodies to look inside. For that reason, the easiest way to study anatomy was to look at the bones, the only part of the body to remain long after death. This illustration from 1363 shows a lesson in skeletal anatomy given by the French anatomist Guy de Chauliac.

Guy de Chauliac (right) giving an anatomy lesson

Head of femur (actual size)

Stapes (actual size)

LARGE AND SMALL

The largest bone in the body is the femur. In an average adult it is about 18 in (46 cm) long and has a tubelike shaft, making it longer and stronger than any other bone. At the upper end, its rounded head fits into a socket in the pelvis at the hip joint. The lower end has a wide, grooved surface that forms a junction with the tibia in the knee. The smallest bone in the body is the stapes – one of three tiny bones, called ossicles, situated inside the ear – which is shaped like a stirrup, and measures an average of 0.2 in (5 mm) in length.

Male pelvis

Hip bone *has a curved shape that supports the abdominal organs*

Pelvic inlet *is narrower in males*

Pubic symphysis *is the joint between hip bones at front of pelvic girdle*

Femur socket *is where the femur's rounded head fits into the pelvic girdle*

Sacrum — *part of the backbone — is attached by powerful ligaments to the pelvic girdle to form the pelvis*

PELVIC GIRDLE AND PELVIS

Two curved hip bones make up the pelvic girdle, the structure that forms the attachment point for the thigh bones and transmits weight downward from the upper body. The hip bones meet at the front of the girdle, while at the rear they are firmly attached to the sacrum. Together, the pelvic girdle and sacrum form the pelvis, a bowl-shaped structure that supports and protects digestive, reproductive, and urinary organs. The opening in the center of the pelvis – the pelvic inlet – is wider in females than in males, thus providing sufficient space for a baby's head to squeeze through during birth.

Female pelvis

Pelvic inlet *is wider in females*

Hands and feet

THE HINGED ATTACHMENTS at the lower ends of the limbs are called hands and feet. The hands are attached at the wrist joints, and the feet at the ankle joints. Although both hands and feet have five flexible digits, the hands are more versatile. They can perform an enormous range of movements. In particular, they can form a grip that allows them to hold and handle objects. The feet are mobile platforms for the body. They support its weight and also act as springboards to propel the body forward during walking, running, or jumping.

OPPOSABLE THUMB
The thumb is the most mobile digit. It can swing across the palm and turn towards the fingers, so that its tip touches the fingertips. This action is called opposition, and it enables the hand to form a grip. A precise grip between the thumb and forefinger, as shown in the above X-ray, is useful for handling small objects.

- Phalanges (14)
- Metacarpals (5)
- Carpals (8)

Little finger (fifth digit)

Ring finger (fourth digit)

Middle finger (third digit)

Index finger (second digit)

Thumb (first digit)

Threading a needle

Gripping a rope

PRECISION AND POWER
The hand can grip precisely with the thumb- and fingertips for delicate tasks such as holding a pen or threading a needle. It can also make a more secure and powerful grip by wrapping thumb and fingers around an object, as when pulling a rope.

HANDS
The hand contains 27 bones divided into three groups: carpals, metacarpals, and phalanges. Eight of the bones are carpals, or wrist bones. Connected to the carpals are five straight metacarpals, which form the palm. Each metacarpal is connected to a phalanx, or finger bone. The fingers each have three phalanges and the thumb has two. The hand has a total of 14 finger or thumb joints, called knuckles. These give the hand great flexibility and, when operated by the muscles of the hand and lower arm, enable the hand to perform a multitude of tasks.

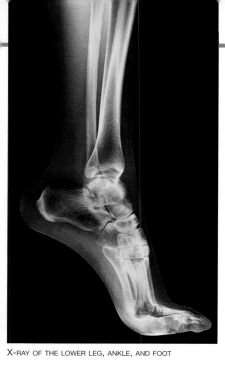

X-RAY OF THE LOWER LEG, ANKLE, AND FOOT

Big toe (first digit)

Second toe (second digit)

Third toe (third digit)

Fourth toe (fourth digit)

Little toe (fifth digit)

JUMP OFF
The feet provide support and stability to prevent the body from falling over while standing or moving on flat or uneven surfaces. The feet are also strong flexible levers that push the body off the ground during walking, climbing, running, and jumping. This X-ray shows the bones of the foot, ankle joint, and lower leg as the foot pushes the body up. The toes are the only part that remain in contact with the ground.

FEET
Each foot contains 26 bones arranged in three groups: tarsals, metatarsals, and phalanges. There are seven tarsals, or ankle bones. The largest of these is the calcaneus, or heel bone, which projects backward behind the ankle joint. The calcaneus is connected to the talus, which forms a joint with the bones of the lower leg. In front of the tarsals are five metatarsal bones, or sole bones, linked to the 14 phalanges, two of which are in the big toe and three in each other toe. The feet are less flexible than the hands because they are bound together by strong ligaments.

Talus *forms a joint with the tibia and fibula at the ankle*

FLEXIBLE ARCH
Footprints made by bare feet reveal that the soles are not flat and that only part of the foot touches the ground. Flexible curves, called arches, raise part of the foot off the ground. The arches are held up by ligaments and by tendons pulled by their associated muscles. Arches help spread out body weight and provide a springiness that absorbs shocks during running and walking. Feet with reduced arches are called flat feet.

Calcaneus *(heel bone)*

■ **Phalanges (14)**
■ **Metatarsals (5)**
■ **Tarsals (7)**

BONES IN EVOLUTION

MUCH OF OUR KNOWLEDGE of our ancestry comes from the study of the human skeleton. Bones and teeth are the only parts of the body that form fossils. This usually occurs when human remains become buried in mud and bone tissue is replaced by minerals. After death, bones become separated so it is extremely rare to find more than scattered fossilized bones and skull fragments. But painstaking searches in east Africa, followed by careful measurements and comparisons of bones, have allowed paleontologists to piece together the story of our evolution from our apelike ancestors.

PROCONSUL AFRICANUS
Skeletons of apelike *Proconsul africanus* (above), which lived about 20 million years ago, show long pelvic bones and arms typical of primates that walk using all four limbs. By 5 million years ago, hominids have strong leg bones and a broad pelvis suggesting that they walked on two legs.

ANCIENT FOOTPRINTS
This is the fossil footprint of *Australopithecus afarensis*, discovered in Laetoli, Tanzania, in 1972. The big toe (top right) hardly diverges from the rest of the foot, unlike that of primates such as chimpanzees, which walk on all fours and use this toe like a thumb. This fossil demonstrates conclusively that these early humans walked upright on two legs.

DOWN FROM THE TREES

Humans belong to a group of mammals called primates, and share a common ancestor with lemurs, monkeys, and apes. The hominids, a family of upright-walking humans to which we belong, arose some 6 million years ago, at a time when the climate in Africa became drier and grasslands began to replace forests. As our apelike ancestors spent more time foraging and hunting on the ground, a species that walked upright evolved. It seems likely that the ability to see approaching danger over tall grasses, the advantage of having hands free to manipulate objects, and the necessity to cool the body in a hot climate were all important factors in the transition from four legs to two.

EARLY FAMILY HISTORY

Fossil bones of apelike *Proconsul africanus*, which lived 20 million years ago, provide paleontologists with a point of reference for comparing more recent hominid fossils. *Proconsul* had the arched backbone, long pelvic bones, and long forelimbs that are typical of a primate that walks on all four limbs, with gripping hands and feet for climbing. The earliest hominids that walked upright were the Australopithecines (meaning "southern ape"). In 1974, American Donald Johanson (b. 1943) found the fossilized partial skeleton of *Australopithecus afarensis* in the Afar region of Ethiopia. "Lucy," as the specimen became

Clavicle
Large, projecting jaw
Humerus
Vertebra
Carpal
Femur (thighbone)
Knee joint
Tibia (upper piece)

AUSTRALOPITHECUS AFARENSIS
About 40 percent of the skeleton of "Lucy" has been found. She belonged to the species *Australopithecus afarensis*, the first primate known to have walked upright. Lucy was about 4 ft 9 in (143 cm) tall and is named after the Beatles' song "Lucy in the Sky with Diamonds," which was popular among the paleontologists who found her.

HOMO HABILIS

Fossil bones of *Homo habilis* (meaning "handy man") have been found among the stone tools that he used. This species was only about 4 ft 6 in (135 cm) tall and had a more rounded head, narrower jaw, and longer face than *Australopithecus*.

Homo habilis **used simple tools**

known, was 3 million years old. She had the curved, S-shaped spine and short pelvis that is typical of a primate that walks upright. Other key features of upright-walking primates include big toes aligned with all of the others, and feet with pronounced arches. In 1972, Mary Leakey (1913–96) found 3.5-million-year-old footprints in Laetoli, Tanzania, that had been left by feet just like this, preserved in hardened volcanic ash. These provide the earliest direct evidence of primates walking upright.

HUMANS APPEAR

Fossil bones of *Homo habilis*, the earliest member of our own genus, were found by Mary and Louis Leakey (1903–72) in 1960, in the Olduvai Gorge of Tanzania. This species lived about 2 million years ago and it had a small cranium, slightly protruding face, and long, thick leg bones. Fossil bones of *Homo erectus*, which evolved about 1.8 million years ago, have been found throughout Europe and

HOMO ERECTUS

Homo erectus was taller than *Homo habilis* and colonized Europe and Asia. Chinese fossils dating from 360,000 years ago have been found in caves among ash, charcoal, and charred bones – showing that this species had learned to use fire.

Asia, suggesting that this was the first species to travel out of Africa and colonize other continents. Fossil bones show that Neanderthals then evolved as a distinct species about 250,000 years ago, and modern humans evolved alongside them until Neanderthals became extinct, about 35,000 years ago.

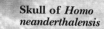

Eyebrow ridges *are very prominent in Neanderthals*

Skull of *Homo neanderthalensis*

HOMO NEANDERTHALENSIS

Studies of fossil hominid skulls show that skull size and brain volume have increased, teeth have become smaller, jaws less jutting, eyebrow ridges less prominent, and the chin more pronounced. Neanderthals had broad skulls and pronounced eyebrow ridges, but could easily pass unnoticed in the street today.

PALEONTOLOGIST AT WORK

Paleontologists rarely find more than fragments of skeletons. These are collected, photographed, carefully measured, and used to reconstruct the appearance of our earliest ancestors. Computer technology is often used to analyze and reconstruct skeletons.

Bone structure

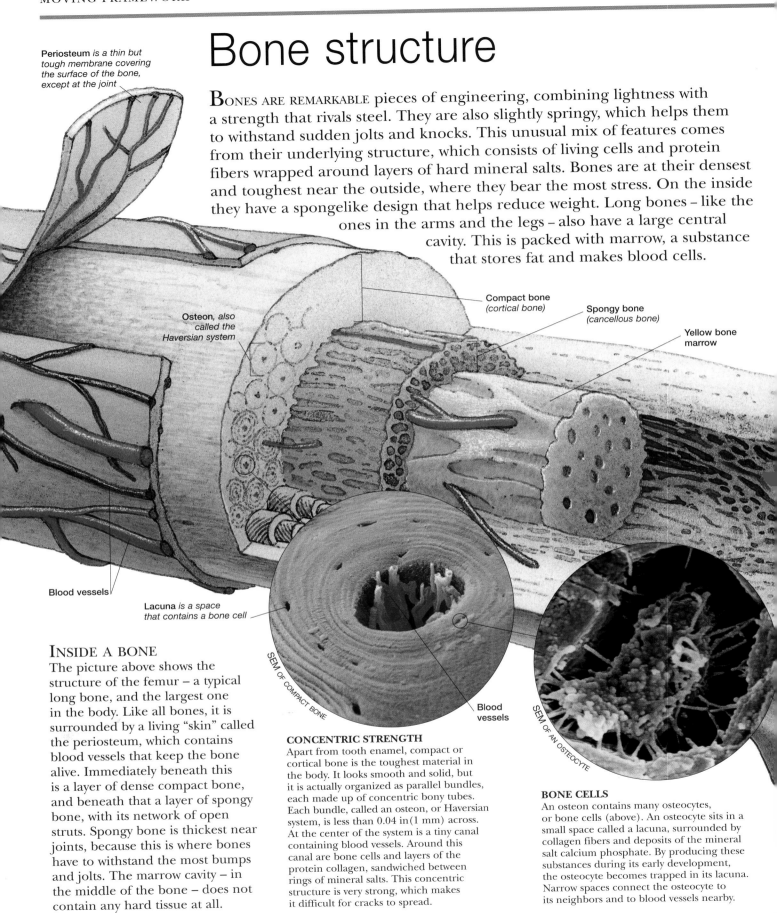

BONES ARE REMARKABLE pieces of engineering, combining lightness with a strength that rivals steel. They are also slightly springy, which helps them to withstand sudden jolts and knocks. This unusual mix of features comes from their underlying structure, which consists of living cells and protein fibers wrapped around layers of hard mineral salts. Bones are at their densest and toughest near the outside, where they bear the most stress. On the inside they have a spongelike design that helps reduce weight. Long bones – like the ones in the arms and the legs – also have a large central cavity. This is packed with marrow, a substance that stores fat and makes blood cells.

Periosteum *is a thin but tough membrane covering the surface of the bone, except at the joint*

Osteon, *also called the Haversian system*

Compact bone (cortical bone)

Spongy bone (cancellous bone)

Yellow bone marrow

Blood vessels

Lacuna *is a space that contains a bone cell*

SEM OF COMPACT BONE

Blood vessels

SEM OF AN OSTEOCYTE

INSIDE A BONE

The picture above shows the structure of the femur – a typical long bone, and the largest one in the body. Like all bones, it is surrounded by a living "skin" called the periosteum, which contains blood vessels that keep the bone alive. Immediately beneath this is a layer of dense compact bone, and beneath that a layer of spongy bone, with its network of open struts. Spongy bone is thickest near joints, because this is where bones have to withstand the most bumps and jolts. The marrow cavity – in the middle of the bone – does not contain any hard tissue at all.

CONCENTRIC STRENGTH

Apart from tooth enamel, compact or cortical bone is the toughest material in the body. It looks smooth and solid, but it is actually organized as parallel bundles, each made up of concentric bony tubes. Each bundle, called an osteon, or Haversian system, is less than 0.04 in (1 mm) across. At the center of the system is a tiny canal containing blood vessels. Around this canal are bone cells and layers of the protein collagen, sandwiched between rings of mineral salts. This concentric structure is very strong, which makes it difficult for cracks to spread.

BONE CELLS

An osteon contains many osteocytes, or bone cells (above). An osteocyte sits in a small space called a lacuna, surrounded by collagen fibers and deposits of the mineral salt calcium phosphate. By producing these substances during its early development, the osteocyte becomes trapped in its lacuna. Narrow spaces connect the osteocyte to its neighbors and to blood vessels nearby.

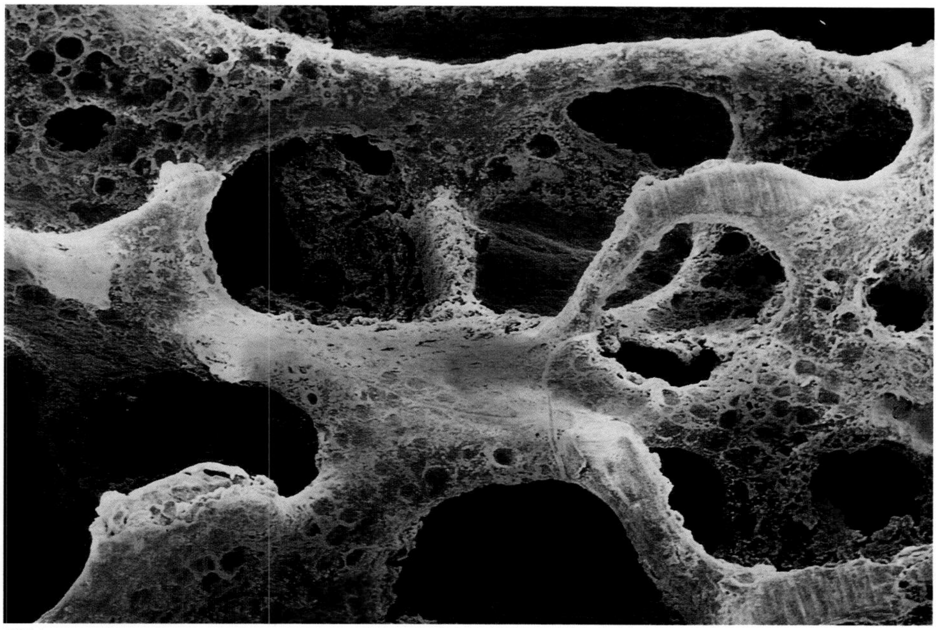

OSTEOPOROSIS

As people grow older, they can lose calcium and protein in their bones, causing the bones to become lighter and more likely to break. This condition, known as osteoporosis, affects both women and men, though women are particularly at risk, because of changes in their hormone levels following menopause (see p. 242). The photograph on the left shows spongy bone that has been weakened in this way. Compared with healthy spongy bone, shown below, its struts are full of spaces, or pores.

SEM OF SPONGY BONE AFFECTED BY OSTEOPOROSIS

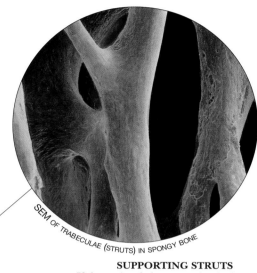

SEM OF TRABECULAE (STRUTS) IN SPONGY BONE

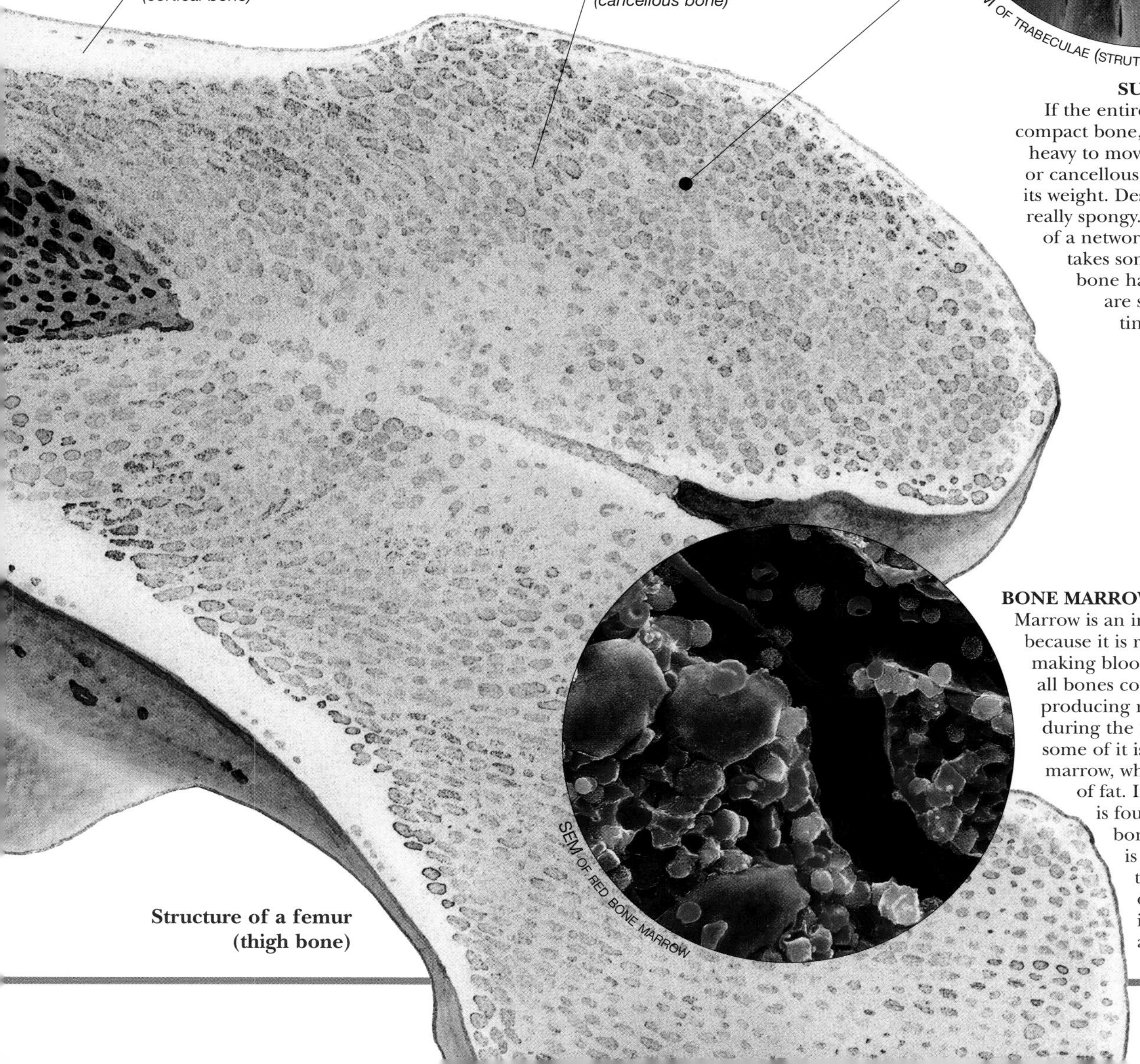

Compact bone
(cortical bone)

Spongy bone
(cancellous bone)

SUPPORTING STRUTS

If the entire skeleton consisted of compact bone, it would be much too heavy to move. Fortunately, spongy, or cancellous, bone helps to reduce its weight. Despite its name, it is not really spongy. Instead, it is made up of a network of rigid struts, which takes some of the load that the bone has to bear. These struts are separated by a maze of tiny spaces that are filled with bone marrow.

BONE MARROW

Marrow is an important tissue because it is responsible for making blood cells. At birth, all bones contain blood-cell-producing red marrow, but during the teenage years, some of it is replaced by yellow marrow, which consists mainly of fat. In adults, red marrow is found mainly in spongy bone. Yellow marrow is concentrated in the central cavity of long bones, where it acts mainly as a storage tissue.

SEM OF RED BONE MARROW

**Structure of a femur
(thigh bone)**

Growth and repair

Uₙₗₗₖₑ scₐffₒₗₐₙₙg or steel girders, bones change all the time.
They grow in step with the rest of the body, and can repair minor
fractures and some major breaks. Even when they have reached
adult size, they are constantly but invisibly renewed. How do they
do it? The answer lies in the cells that all bones contain. Some of
these cells, called osteoblasts, deposit protein and mineral salts,
forming new bone. At the same time, other cells, called osteoclasts,
do the reverse. By adjusting the balance between these two processes,
the body makes bones grow. It also ensures that bones keep strong, by
renewing or "remodeling" parts that get the most wear and tear.

Bone (dark areas) *replaces cartilage as the baby grows*

Joints *are one of the last areas to be ossified*

EARLY DEVELOPMENT

When the skeleton first forms, it consists
solely of cartilage. During a process called
ossification, osteoblast cells lay down
mineral salts in this framework, gradually
turning most of it into bone. This image
shows a fetus that is 14 weeks old. The
dark areas show that its bones are
partially ossified, but its joints still consist
of cartilage. Ossification continues after
birth and lasts throughout adult life.
For example, the flap of cartilage below
the breastbone, called the xiphoid process,
often ossifies at the age of 40 or older.

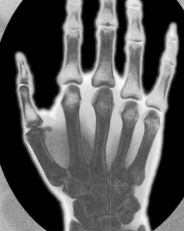

**A 14-week-old
fetus**

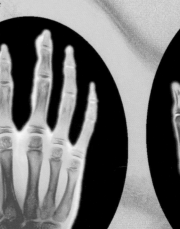

SEM OF OSTEOBLASTS

BUILDING BONES
This close-up view shows active
osteoblasts (bone-making cells) on
the surface of a bone. They lie just
underneath the bone's outer "skin"
or periosteum, and build up the
bone from the outside. As a bone
grows, they gradually become
embedded in the bone itself. Once
this has happened, they retire from
bone-making, and change into
mature bone cells, or osteocytes.

GROWING BONES
The X-rays below show how hand bones develop between
infancy and early adulthood. At first, the bones are only partially
ossified, and their ends consist of cartilage. But as the cartilage
grows, the ossified zone also expands, until finally the adult
bone is complete. When bones grow, most of the growth occurs
at their ends. Existing bone
tissue often has to be
broken down so
that the bone
can reach its
adult shape.

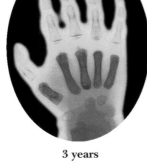

1 year

3 years

13 years

20 years

Compound fracture *leaves the broken end of the radius sticking through the skin and may need surgery*

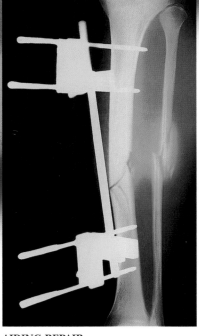

COLOURED X-RAY OF A PINNED FRACTURE OF THE TIBIA AND FIBULA BONES

Ulna *is one of the forearm bones (the other is the radius)*

X-RAY OF FRACTURE OF RADIUS AND ULNA

BONE FRACTURES

Although bones are tough, they sometimes break – particularly if they have been weakened by disease. The fractured ends may stay in place, but in a bad break they sometimes separate, as in the broken forearm shown here. If this happens, the fracture has to be realigned or "reduced" to produce a proper repair. In simple fractures, the broken ends remain beneath the skin, but in compound fractures they stick out and surgery may be required.

AIDING REPAIR

When a bone has been broken, the fractured ends need to stay together until the repair is complete. To ensure that this happens, the fracture is often immobilized in a plaster or plastic cast. With severe fractures, the bones are fixed with metal pins or screws (as above with this broken tibia), which keep them correctly aligned.

SETTING BONES

Until the modern health-care era, serious fractures could lead to permanent disabilities. One way to reduce this risk was to call in a bone-setter, who realigned broken bones so that they healed in the correct position. The art of bone-setting is thousands of years old, and arose in different cultures all over the world. Medieval bone-setters often doubled as blacksmiths, and, apart from a strong pair of hands, used little equipment. Later, more sophisticated techniques developed. The scene below, from the 1600s, shows a European bone-setter at work. Helped by an assistant tugging on a set of pulleys, the setter is about to reunite the ends of the patient's broken arm.

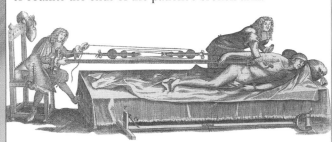

Engraving by E. A. Sohn in the scientific journal *Acta Eruditorum*

HOW BONES HEAL

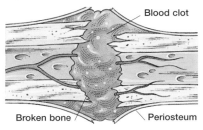

Blood clot

Broken bone — Periosteum

Blood clot formation
Within 6 hours of being fractured, a bone has already started the task of self-repair. A blood clot forms between the ends, sealing off any broken blood vessels within the bone. Cells in the periosteum start to divide, so that it can grow back around the site of the break.

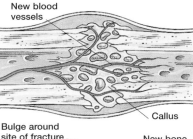

New blood vessels

Callus

Callus formation
After 3 weeks, the periosteum is complete, and the blood clot has been replaced by areas of fibrous tissue, forming a mass called a callus. Blood vessels grow through the callus, and osteoblasts start to lay down new bone tissue inside it, connecting the bone's broken ends.

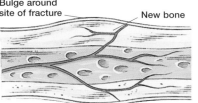

Bulge around site of fracture

New bone

New bone formation
By 3–4 months, the fracture is almost fully repaired. The callus has been replaced by new bone, with spongy bone on the interior and compact bone around the outside. Osteoclasts complete the operation by absorbing any remaining fragments of dead bone.

Joints

IF THE BONES IN THE SKELETON were solidly fixed together, nobody would be able to move. However, thanks to more than 400 separate joints, our skeletons are rigid but flexible at the same time. A joint is any part of the skeleton where two or more bones fit together. Some are big enough and strong enough to take all of the body's weight, while the smallest of them – between the tiny bones in the ear – are almost too small to see. As well as varying in size, joints also vary in the way they are built. Some hold bones together very firmly, so that they can hardly move at all. But in synovial joints, the most common type of joint, the bones slide over each other as smoothly as parts in a well-oiled machine.

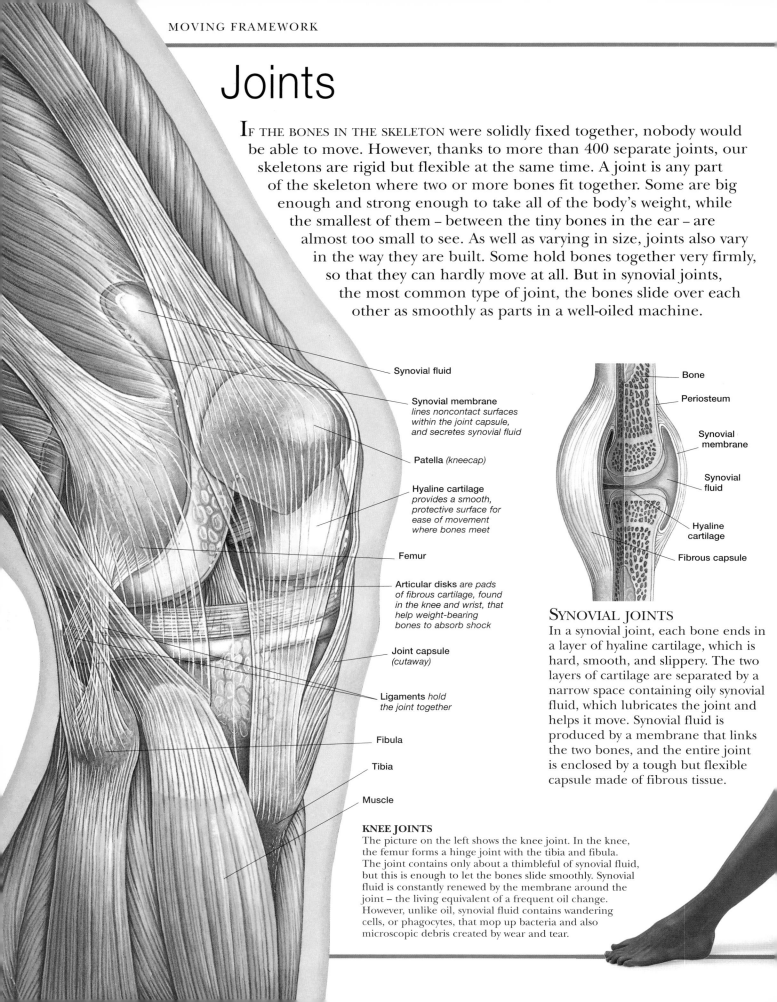

Synovial fluid

Synovial membrane *lines noncontact surfaces within the joint capsule, and secretes synovial fluid*

Patella *(kneecap)*

Hyaline cartilage *provides a smooth, protective surface for ease of movement where bones meet*

Femur

Articular disks *are pads of fibrous cartilage, found in the knee and wrist, that help weight-bearing bones to absorb shock*

Joint capsule *(cutaway)*

Ligaments *hold the joint together*

Fibula

Tibia

Muscle

Bone

Periosteum

Synovial membrane

Synovial fluid

Hyaline cartilage

Fibrous capsule

SYNOVIAL JOINTS
In a synovial joint, each bone ends in a layer of hyaline cartilage, which is hard, smooth, and slippery. The two layers of cartilage are separated by a narrow space containing oily synovial fluid, which lubricates the joint and helps it move. Synovial fluid is produced by a membrane that links the two bones, and the entire joint is enclosed by a tough but flexible capsule made of fibrous tissue.

KNEE JOINTS
The picture on the left shows the knee joint. In the knee, the femur forms a hinge joint with the tibia and fibula. The joint contains only about a thimbleful of synovial fluid, but this is enough to let the bones slide smoothly. Synovial fluid is constantly renewed by the membrane around the joint – the living equivalent of a frequent oil change. However, unlike oil, synovial fluid contains wandering cells, or phagocytes, that mop up bacteria and also microscopic debris created by wear and tear.

STRAPPED TOGETHER

Mobile joints are held together by straps of extra-tough tissue called ligaments. In some synovial joints, such as the hip and knee, there are ligaments inside the joint capsule, but the largest and strongest ones are on the outside. Ligaments connect the adjoining bones, and are made of densely packed fibers of collagen arranged in parallel rows. These fibers allow a joint to move, but because they are difficult to stretch, they stop the bones from being pulled apart. The hip joint has very strong ligaments, which is one reason why it rarely dislocates.

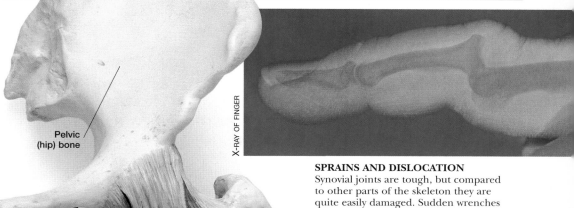

X-RAY OF FINGER

Pelvic (hip) bone

Ligament

Femur (thigh bone)

Hip joint showing ligaments

SPRAINS AND DISLOCATION

Synovial joints are tough, but compared to other parts of the skeleton they are quite easily damaged. Sudden wrenches sometimes result in a sprain – a painful injury involving damage to muscles and ligaments. But if the blow is really hard, it may force the two bones apart. This is known as a dislocation, and it is treated by carefully moving the bones back into position. The X-ray above shows a dislocated knuckle – one of the most common kinds of dislocation.

Fused joint

Sutures between skull bones

LOCKED TOGETHER

In the skull, most bones are locked together by joints called sutures. The wavy edges of skull bones fit tightly together like the pieces of a jigsaw puzzle. By adulthood, sutures are fully formed and cannot move, giving the skull its great strength.

LOOKING INSIDE JOINTS

Many things can go wrong with joints, particularly complicated ones such as the knee. During strenuous exercise, the knee's internal ligaments can be torn, and pieces of cartilage may break away, stopping it from moving altogether. To examine this kind of injury, doctors often use a special kind of endoscope (see p. 27) called an arthroscope. This slides into the joint capsule through a small incision, allowing the doctor to see the inside of the joint and carry out repairs.

(see p. 27)

ARTHROSCOPIC IMAGE OF KNEE CARTILAGE

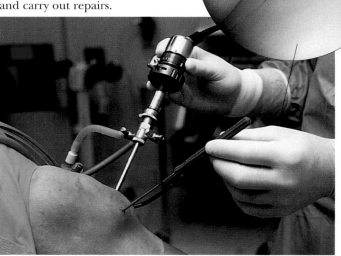

A surgeon using an arthroscope to see inside a knee joint

SEMI-MOVABLE JOINTS

In about a third of the body's joints, there is no synovial space, which means that the adjoining bones have much less freedom to move. In the backbone, for example, the joints between neighboring vertebrae are only slightly flexible, but because there are many of them, the whole backbone can bend.

Joints and movement

THE HUMAN BODY CAN CARRY OUT an incredible variety of movements, from threading a needle or typing on a keyboard to doing somersaults or leaping through the air. Each of these movements involves many different joints, acting together to produce a single action. The way individual joints move depends on their shape. Some joints, such as the knee, are hinged so that they move in just one dimension, or plane. Others, such as the shoulder, are much more flexible, and allow movement in many directions. Joints can also vary slightly from one person to another. People who are "double-jointed" – for example, in their fingers – have unusually flexible joints, although they have the same total number as everyone else.

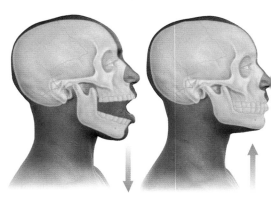

DEPRESSION AND ELEVATION
Used anatomically, depression means a downward movement, while elevation is an upward one. The lower jaw, or mandible, is depressed when the mouth is opened and elevated when it is closed.

TYPES OF JOINT

This skeleton shows six main types of synovial joints (see p. 58), with simplified diagrams showing how they work. Each joint allows a different set of movements between two neighboring bones. In most of these joints, the bones either hinge against each other, or they rotate. The exception is the plane joint, shown on the far right. Here, the bones glide past each other in the same plane.

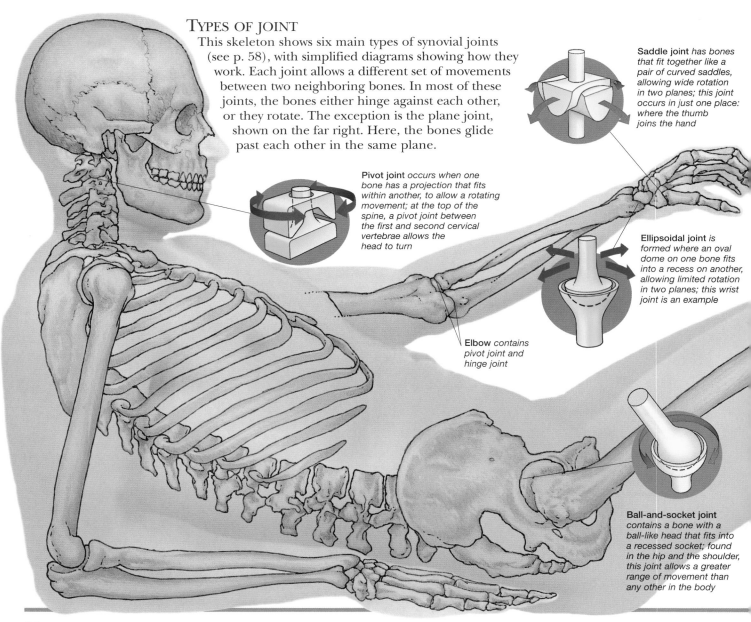

Saddle joint *has bones that fit together like a pair of curved saddles, allowing wide rotation in two planes; this joint occurs in just one place: where the thumb joins the hand*

Pivot joint *occurs when one bone has a projection that fits within another, to allow a rotating movement; at the top of the spine, a pivot joint between the first and second cervical vertebrae allows the head to turn*

Ellipsoidal joint *is formed where an oval dome on one bone fits into a recess on another, allowing limited rotation in two planes; this wrist joint is an example*

Elbow *contains pivot joint and hinge joint*

Ball-and-socket joint *contains a bone with a ball-like head that fits into a recessed socket; found in the hip and the shoulder, this joint allows a greater range of movement than any other in the body*

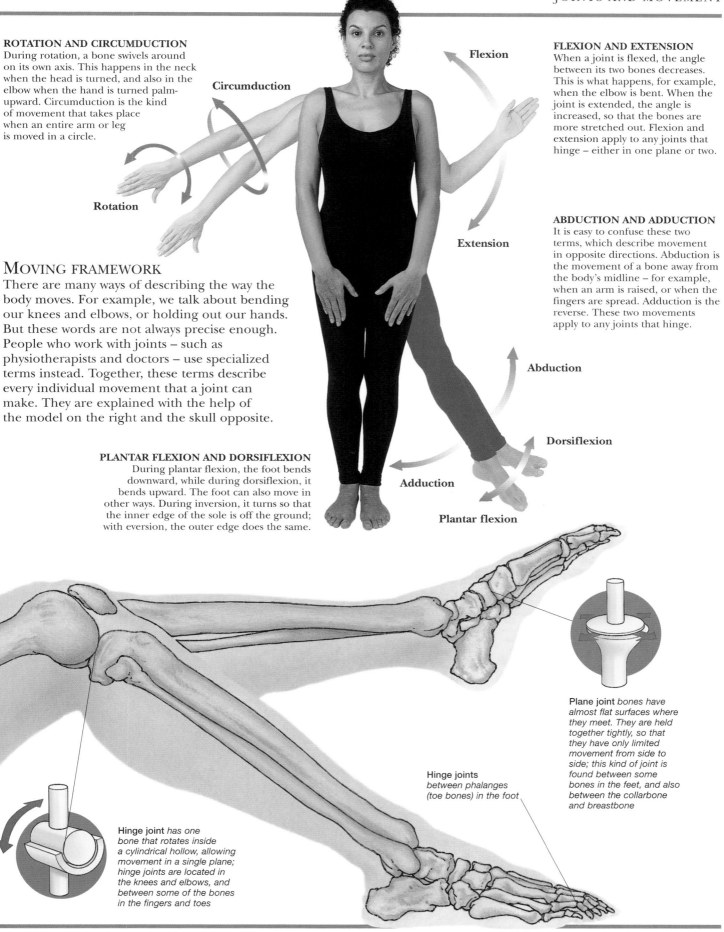

ROTATION AND CIRCUMDUCTION
During rotation, a bone swivels around on its own axis. This happens in the neck when the head is turned, and also in the elbow when the hand is turned palm-upward. Circumduction is the kind of movement that takes place when an entire arm or leg is moved in a circle.

Circumduction

Rotation

MOVING FRAMEWORK
There are many ways of describing the way the body moves. For example, we talk about bending our knees and elbows, or holding out our hands. But these words are not always precise enough. People who work with joints – such as physiotherapists and doctors – use specialized terms instead. Together, these terms describe every individual movement that a joint can make. They are explained with the help of the model on the right and the skull opposite.

Flexion

Extension

FLEXION AND EXTENSION
When a joint is flexed, the angle between its two bones decreases. This is what happens, for example, when the elbow is bent. When the joint is extended, the angle is increased, so that the bones are more stretched out. Flexion and extension apply to any joints that hinge – either in one plane or two.

ABDUCTION AND ADDUCTION
It is easy to confuse these two terms, which describe movement in opposite directions. Abduction is the movement of a bone away from the body's midline – for example, when an arm is raised, or when the fingers are spread. Adduction is the reverse. These two movements apply to any joints that hinge.

Abduction

Dorsiflexion

Adduction

Plantar flexion

PLANTAR FLEXION AND DORSIFLEXION
During plantar flexion, the foot bends downward, while during dorsiflexion, it bends upward. The foot can also move in other ways. During inversion, it turns so that the inner edge of the sole is off the ground; with eversion, the outer edge does the same.

Plane joint *bones have almost flat surfaces where they meet. They are held together tightly, so that they have only limited movement from side to side; this kind of joint is found between some bones in the feet, and also between the collarbone and breastbone*

Hinge joints *between phalanges (toe bones) in the foot*

Hinge joint *has one bone that rotates inside a cylindrical hollow, allowing movement in a single plane; hinge joints are located in the knees and elbows, and between some of the bones in the fingers and toes*

MUSCULAR system

ALL BODY MOVEMENTS – whether lifting a finger, running for a bus, or eating lunch – are produced by muscles. Many muscles are attached to bones, which they pull to move and support the skeleton. Others work automatically and invisibly within internal organs, often moving fluids or food through the body. Whatever their role, all muscle tissues share common features. Their cells, called fibers, possess the unique ability to use energy to contract, or get shorter, thereby producing a pulling force. Contraction of fibers is triggered by electrical nerve signals from the brain. Fibers are elastic enough to stretch yet still return to their original length.

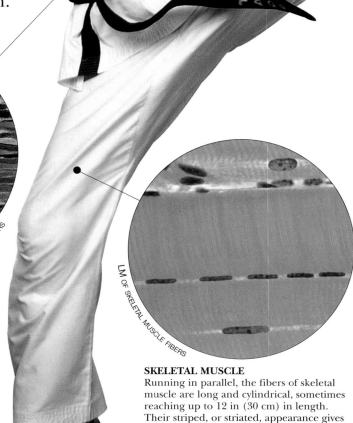

Skeletal muscles are used to produce these high kicks

SMOOTH MUSCLE

The fibers that make up smooth muscle are short, unstriped, and have tapering ends. They are packed closely together in muscle sheets in the walls of internal organs, such as the small intestine along which they push food. These sheets are often arranged in two layers – one circular and one longitudinal (lengthways) – with opposite effects. Smooth muscle is also called involuntary muscle because it cannot be controlled consciously – it is triggered by the autonomic nervous system (the part of the nervous system that automatically controls internal functions) and hormones (see p. 118).

LM OF SMOOTH MUSCLE FIBERS

LM OF SKELETAL MUSCLE FIBERS

MUSCLE TYPES

There are three distinct types of muscle tissue in the body: skeletal, cardiac, and smooth. Skeletal muscle tissue forms the muscles that move and support the skeleton. It contracts rapidly and powerfully but tires easily. Cardiac muscle tissue is found only in the wall of the heart. Here, for a lifetime, it contracts regularly, automatically, and without tiring to pump blood around the body. Smooth muscle tissue is found mainly in the walls of hollow organs, such as the bladder. It contracts slowly and rhythmically, performing actions such as pushing urine out of the bladder. The three types can be easily distinguished by the appearance of their fibers (cells).

SKELETAL MUSCLE
Running in parallel, the fibers of skeletal muscle are long and cylindrical, sometimes reaching up to 12 in (30 cm) in length. Their striped, or striated, appearance gives skeletal muscle its alternative name of striate muscle. It is also known as voluntary muscle because a conscious, or voluntary, decision is made by the nervous system to trigger contraction and move the body.

CARDIAC MUSCLE

The branched, striated fibers of cardiac muscle form an interconnected network in the heart wall. Cardiac muscle contracts automatically, with its own built-in rhythm, some 100,000 times each day. It cannot be controlled consciously. However, its rate of contraction is regulated by the autonomic nervous system, according to whether the body is active or at rest.

LM OF CARDIAC MUSCLE FIBERS

Skeletal muscle *is covered by a connective tissue sheath called the epimysium*

Tendon *makes a secure connection between the muscle and a bone*

Bone *is pulled by the tendon when a muscle contracts*

Periosteum *is the membrane that covers the bone's surface*

BONE CONNECTORS

Skeletal muscles are anchored to bones – and sometimes to each other – by strong cords or sheets called tendons that enable muscles to pull bones without tearing. Tendons have enormous tensile strength (pulling strength). They are packed with fibers of the tough protein collagen, which are arranged in parallel bundles. The connective tissue sheath that encloses the muscle extends to the tendon. The tendon then extends to the bone, where its fibers penetrate the periosteum (surface membrane) and embed themselves firmly in the bone's outer layer, completing the connection between muscle and bone.

HEAT GENERATORS

By making use of heat generated inside it, the body maintains a constant internal temperature of 98.6°F (37°C). About 85 percent of this heat is produced by muscle contraction. Of the energy converted by muscles, only 25 percent powers movement. The remaining 75 percent is "waste" energy, released as heat. This thermogram reveals how body heat is lost through the skin – lighter colors mark areas of greatest heat radiation.

MUSCULAR SYSTEM FUNCTIONS

Movement	Skeletal muscles produce a wide range of movements, including running, picking up objects, and changing facial expressions. Cardiac muscle in the heart pumps blood to all body tissues. Smooth muscle produces movement in internal organs, such as pushing food through the intestines.	Joint stability	When they contract, some skeletal muscles help stabilize highly mobile joints such as shoulders.
		Heat generation	Because they are not totally efficient, muscles generate heat as a by-product when they contract. Heat generation, or thermogenesis, is vitally important in maintaining normal body temperature. In cold conditions, the body uses involuntary contractions (shivering) to generate additional heat.
Posture maintenance	Certain skeletal muscles are kept in a partially contracted state to hold the body upright.		

Skeletal muscles

In any description of the muscular system, the skeletal muscles take center stage. Making up nearly half of the body's mass, skeletal muscles can perform a wide range of movements, from blinking an eyelid to wielding a sledgehammer. They are primarily attached to bones by tough, fibrous tendons. Typically, each muscle links two bones across a flexible joint so that muscle contraction, or shortening, either results in movement or assists in holding the body upright. A few muscles – such as those that produce facial expressions – work by tugging on the skin.

NAMING MUSCLES

Every skeletal muscle is given a Latin name according to one or more of its features, as described below. Some muscle names cover several features. The extensor carpi radialis longus, for example, extends (straightens) the wrist ("carpi"), lies close to the radius (lower arm) bone, and is longer than other wrist extensors.

MUSCLE FEATURES AND DESCRIPTIONS

Location Example: the frontalis runs over the frontal bone of the skull.

Relative size using terms such as maximus (largest), minimus (smallest), longus (long), and brevis (short). Example: the gluteus maximus is the biggest gluteal (buttock) muscle.

Shape Example: the two trapezius muscles form a trapezoid (four-sided) shape.

Action using terms such as flexor (bends a joint) and extensor (straightens a joint). Example: the flexor carpi ulnaris bends the hand at the wrist.

Origin and insertion Example: the sternocleidomastoid has origins (where bones do not move) on the breastbone – sternum – and collar bone – clavicle ("cleido") – and insertions (where bones do move) on the mastoid process of the skull's temporal bone.

Number of origins using terms such as biceps ("two heads"). Example: the biceps brachii (arm) has two origins on the scapula, or shoulder blade.

Frontalis *wrinkles the forehead*

Orbicularis oculi

Pectoralis major *pulls the arm forward, twists it, and pulls it toward the body*

Sternocleidomastoid *bends the head forward, and turns or tilts it to one side*

Biceps brachii *bends the arm at the elbow*

External oblique *twists the trunk and bends it sideways*

Rectus abdominis *bends the trunk forward and pulls in the abdomen*

Quadriceps femoris

Sartorius *rotates the thigh, and bends it at the hip*

Tibialis anterior *lifts the foot upward*

Adductor longus *pulls the leg inward toward the body's midline*

Quadriceps femoris

Extensor digitorum longus *lifts the foot and toes upward*

Front view of the body showing superficial (left) and deep (right) muscles

ORBICULARIS OCULI
Forming a ring around the eye, the orbicularis oculi (meaning "circular" and "of the eye") protects it from injury and intense light by causing blinking and squinting. The muscle is attached to the bony eye socket and to the eyelids. When the orbicularis oculi contracts, the ring gets smaller and the eyelids move to close the eye. A similar type of muscle, the orbicularis oris, surrounds the mouth and closes the lips.

QUADRICEPS FEMORIS
This powerful thigh muscle, which straightens the knee when running, climbing, and kicking, is actually not one muscle but four (quadriceps means "four heads"). Their upper ends are attached to the femur (thigh bone) or pelvic (hip) bone, while their lower ends are anchored to the tibia (shin bone) by a tendon that runs over the knee. When the muscles contract, the lower leg is pulled forward.

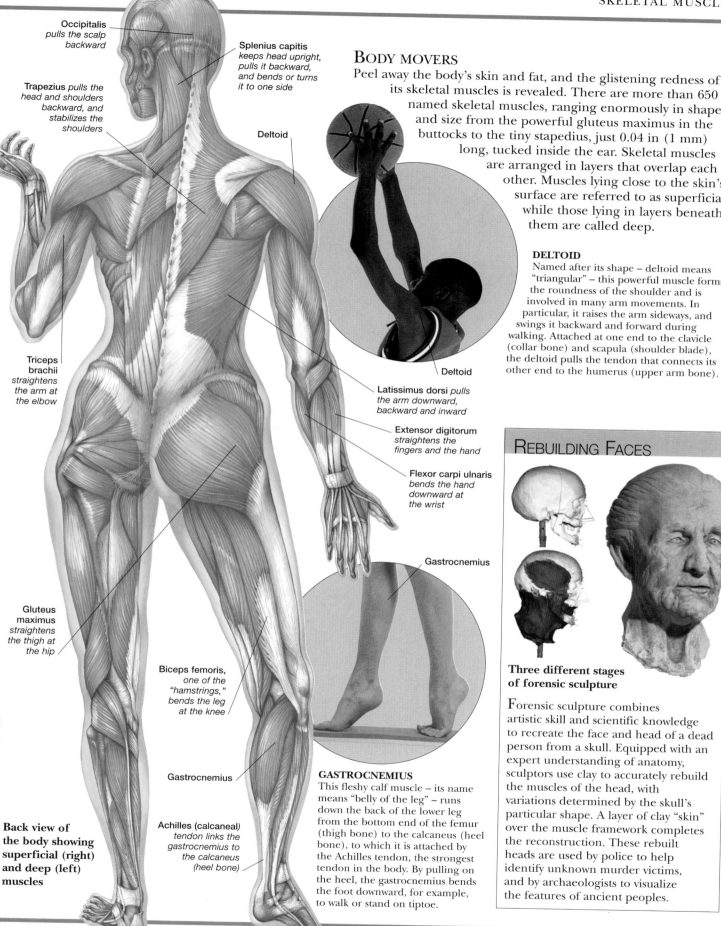

Occipitalis *pulls the scalp backward*

Splenius capitis *keeps head upright, pulls it backward, and bends or turns it to one side*

Trapezius *pulls the head and shoulders backward, and stabilizes the shoulders*

Deltoid

Triceps brachii *straightens the arm at the elbow*

Gluteus maximus *straightens the thigh at the hip*

Biceps femoris, *one of the "hamstrings," bends the leg at the knee*

Gastrocnemius

Achilles (calcaneal) *tendon links the gastrocnemius to the calcaneus (heel bone)*

Back view of the body showing superficial (right) and deep (left) muscles

Deltoid

Latissimus dorsi *pulls the arm downward, backward and inward*

Extensor digitorum *straightens the fingers and the hand*

Flexor carpi ulnaris *bends the hand downward at the wrist*

Gastrocnemius

BODY MOVERS

Peel away the body's skin and fat, and the glistening redness of its skeletal muscles is revealed. There are more than 650 named skeletal muscles, ranging enormously in shape and size from the powerful gluteus maximus in the buttocks to the tiny stapedius, just 0.04 in (1 mm) long, tucked inside the ear. Skeletal muscles are arranged in layers that overlap each other. Muscles lying close to the skin's surface are referred to as superficial, while those lying in layers beneath them are called deep.

DELTOID

Named after its shape – deltoid means "triangular" – this powerful muscle forms the roundness of the shoulder and is involved in many arm movements. In particular, it raises the arm sideways, and swings it backward and forward during walking. Attached at one end to the clavicle (collar bone) and scapula (shoulder blade), the deltoid pulls the tendon that connects its other end to the humerus (upper arm bone).

REBUILDING FACES

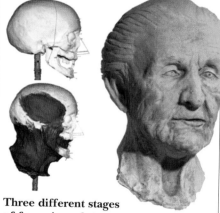

Three different stages of forensic sculpture

Forensic sculpture combines artistic skill and scientific knowledge to recreate the face and head of a dead person from a skull. Equipped with an expert understanding of anatomy, sculptors use clay to accurately rebuild the muscles of the head, with variations determined by the skull's particular shape. A layer of clay "skin" over the muscle framework completes the reconstruction. These rebuilt heads are used by police to help identify unknown murder victims, and by archaeologists to visualize the features of ancient peoples.

GASTROCNEMIUS

This fleshy calf muscle – its name means "belly of the leg" – runs down the back of the lower leg from the bottom end of the femur (thigh bone) to the calcaneus (heel bone), to which it is attached by the Achilles tendon, the strongest tendon in the body. By pulling on the heel, the gastrocnemius bends the foot downward, for example, to walk or stand on tiptoe.

How muscles contract

Muscle *is an organ that contracts to move, support, or stabilize part of the body*

UNDERSTANDING HOW muscle fibers are constructed is key to working out how muscles contract. Each long, cylindrical muscle fiber is filled with smaller fibers, called myofibrils, that are packed with a highly ordered array of protein filaments. The arrival of a nerve message from the brain causes these filaments to interact, making the muscle fiber – and muscle – shorten. The more signals that arrive, the more a muscle contracts, until it reaches about 70 percent of its resting length. The whole process involves the transformation of chemical energy stored in nutrients, such as glucose, into kinetic (movement) energy. In the absence of nervous stimulus, the muscle fiber relaxes.

Muscle fiber *is one of the long, thin cells that make up a muscle*

Fascicle *is one of the bundles of fibers that make up a muscle; it is surrounded by a connective tissue sheath, the perimysium*

Sarcomere *is a section of myofibril between Z lines*

Capillary *supplies muscle fibers with blood*

Myofibril *is one of the parallel, rod-like strands that pack the inside of a muscle fiber*

FROM FIBER TO FILAMENT

Hundreds of bundled muscle fibers run in parallel along the length of a muscle. Each fiber is packed with rodlike myofibrils that contain two types of protein filament – thick (myosin) and thin (actin). These filaments are arranged in repeating patterns called sarcomeres, that give muscle fibers their striped appearance. Extending from myosin filaments are small "heads" that, in resting muscle, extend toward acting filaments.

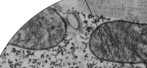

Mitochondrion

TEM OF SECTION THROUGH SKELETAL MUSCLE FIBER

Z line

Myofibril

ENERGY PROVIDERS

Energy-rich nutrients cannot be used directly for muscle contraction – they must first be converted into ATP (adenosine triphosphate). This substance stores energy, carries it to where it is needed, and releases it on demand. ATP is produced by aerobic respiration inside the mitochondria squeezed in between myofibrils. During respiration, glucose – delivered to muscle fibers by the blood or extracted from their glycogen store – is broken down using oxygen, releasing its energy to make ATP.

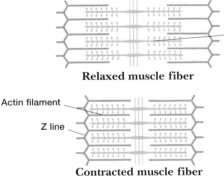

Sarcomere

Myosin filament

Relaxed muscle fiber

Actin filament

Z line

Contracted muscle fiber

SLIDING FILAMENTS

To make contractions happen, filaments in myofibrils slide over each other. In each sarcomere, myosin filaments are located centrally, while the actin filaments that surround and overlap them are attached to the Z line. When a muscle fiber is stimulated to contract, myosin heads bind to actin and, using energy supplied by ATP, repeatedly swivel toward the center of the sarcomere, repeatedly pulling actin filaments inward and making the sarcomere shorter until the stimulus stops.

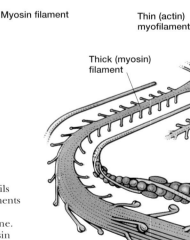

Thin (actin) myofilament

Thick (myosin) filament

Head of myosin molecule *is "charged" with ATP and interacts with actin during contraction*

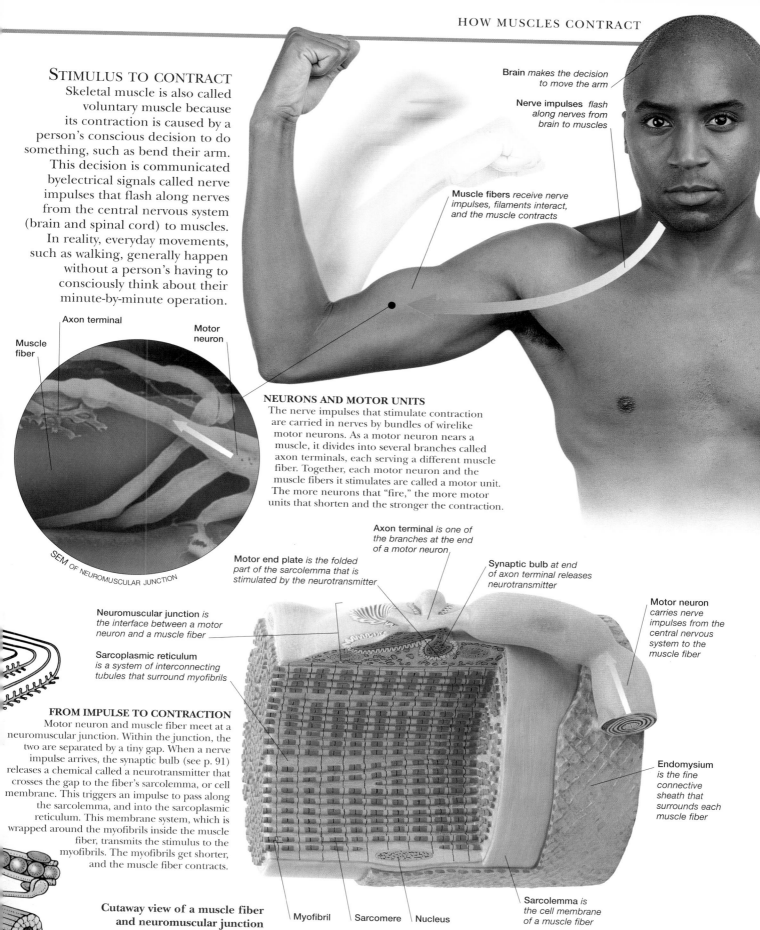

STIMULUS TO CONTRACT

Skeletal muscle is also called voluntary muscle because its contraction is caused by a person's conscious decision to do something, such as bend their arm. This decision is communicated byelectrical signals called nerve impulses that flash along nerves from the central nervous system (brain and spinal cord) to muscles. In reality, everyday movements, such as walking, generally happen without a person's having to consciously think about their minute-by-minute operation.

Brain *makes the decision to move the arm*

Nerve impulses *flash along nerves from brain to muscles*

Muscle fibers *receive nerve impulses, filaments interact, and the muscle contracts*

Axon terminal

Motor neuron

Muscle fiber

SEM OF NEUROMUSCULAR JUNCTION

NEURONS AND MOTOR UNITS

The nerve impulses that stimulate contraction are carried in nerves by bundles of wirelike motor neurons. As a motor neuron nears a muscle, it divides into several branches called axon terminals, each serving a different muscle fiber. Together, each motor neuron and the muscle fibers it stimulates are called a motor unit. The more neurons that "fire," the more motor units that shorten and the stronger the contraction.

Axon terminal *is one of the branches at the end of a motor neuron*

Motor end plate *is the folded part of the sarcolemma that is stimulated by the neurotransmitter*

Synaptic bulb *at end of axon terminal releases neurotransmitter*

Motor neuron *carries nerve impulses from the central nervous system to the muscle fiber*

Neuromuscular junction *is the interface between a motor neuron and a muscle fiber*

Sarcoplasmic reticulum *is a system of interconnecting tubules that surround myofibrils*

FROM IMPULSE TO CONTRACTION

Motor neuron and muscle fiber meet at a neuromuscular junction. Within the junction, the two are separated by a tiny gap. When a nerve impulse arrives, the synaptic bulb (see p. 91) releases a chemical called a neurotransmitter that crosses the gap to the fiber's sarcolemma, or cell membrane. This triggers an impulse to pass along the sarcolemma, and into the sarcoplasmic reticulum. This membrane system, which is wrapped around the myofibrils inside the muscle fiber, transmits the stimulus to the myofibrils. The myofibrils get shorter, and the muscle fiber contracts.

Endomysium *is the fine connective sheath that surrounds each muscle fiber*

Sarcolemma *is the cell membrane of a muscle fiber*

Cutaway view of a muscle fiber and neuromuscular junction

Myofibril   Sarcomere   Nucleus

ANATOMY AND ART

FOR THE PAST 500 YEARS, the science of anatomy – the study of the structure of the human body – and the art of anatomical illustration have developed hand in hand. Artists and doctors have combined efforts to produce visual representations of how muscles, bones, nerves, and other structures form the fabric of the body. The main purpose of such images has been to aid the teaching of anatomy to medical students by describing and explaining the confusing array of tissues and organs they come across inside bodies, both living and dead. Yet the sheer beauty of many of these illustrations and sculptures means that they have wider appeal.

SIMPLE IMAGES
This 15th-century image of the female body makes no pretense of accuracy. It was used to show wounds, diseases, and the influence of the zodiac on body parts.

EARLY BELIEFS

Until the Renaissance – the "rebirth" of arts and sciences between the 14th and 16th centuries – anatomical art was flat and schematic, owing less to reality and more to myth and astrology. Knowledge about the body was still firmly rooted in the ancient and often inaccurate teachings of the Greek physician Claudius Galen (c. AD 130–200). Only during the Renaissance, when dissection (cutting up) of bodies was finally allowed, did some people start to question Galen's legacy.

CLOSE OBSERVATION
Both scientist and artist, Leonardo da Vinci used his great skills as an observer, draftsman, and anatomist to produce over a thousand drawings of the human body, based on his own dissections.

LEONARDO DA VINCI

One of those dissectors was Italian artist and scientist Leonardo da Vinci (1452–1519). Cutting up bodies by candlelight, Leonardo meticulously recorded his observations in the form of detailed drawings that showed both depth and realism. But he never took advantage of the recent inventions of engraving and printing. His drawings remained unseen until his notebooks were rediscovered in the 19th century.

ANATOMICAL ACCURACY
Above is an accurate representation of the muscular system, taken from Vesalius's *De Humani Corporis Fabrica*, the first great book of anatomy to be published. In the style of the book, the figure is standing in a lifelike pose and is pictured against a landscape.

ANDREAS VESALIUS

The breakthrough in anatomical illustration came in 1543 with the publication of *De Humani Corporis Fabrica* (On the Structure of the Human Body) by Flemish0 doctor Andreas Vesalius (1514–64), who was based in

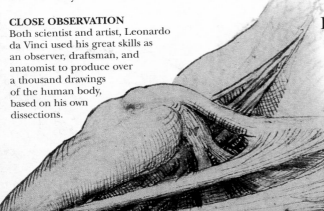

Superficial muscles, drawn by Leonardo da Vinci

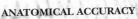

Padua, Italy. More than 300 illustrations by Jan Stefan van Kalkar, a favorite student of the Venetian artist Titian, used artistic form to show the detail of human anatomy exposed by Vesalius's careful and accurate dissections. By questioning and correcting Galen's works, Vesalius established the science of anatomy based on observation and realism, and initiated a new era in medicine.

THE SEARCH FOR REALISM

After Vesalius, artists sought to depict the dissected body realistically, as if it were still alive.

As well as sumptuous drawings, there was a fashion for wax models. These models gave medical students a three-dimensional view of the body but, unlike a dissected body, the wax sculpture did not rot and smell, and it could be colored to show clearly an individual muscle's nerves and blood vessels.

ANATOMY MANUALS

The 19th century brought with it printing and coloring techniques that could be used to mass-produce well-illustrated manuals of anatomy compiled by eminent anatomists and distinguished artists. Some, like the *Traité Complet de l'Anatomie d'Homme* (Complete Treatise of the Anatomy of Man) (1831–54) by Jean-Baptiste Bougéry (doctor) and Nicolas Jacob (artist), maintained the tradition of showing lifelike bodies.

MODELED IN WAX
This 19th-century wax model, made in Italy, shows in incredible detail and vibrant colors the muscles, bones, blood vessels, and nerves of the upper limb.

19th-century wax model made at the Specola Museum in Florence, Italy

MODERN METHODS

Some of today's anatomy manuals still use the beauty of artistic form to modify a raw dissection in order to reveal anatomy and function. But the medical illustrator now has other tools at his or her disposal. Computers can be used to create two- and three-dimensional images of the body, integrating input from drawings, photographs, or from imaging techniques such as CT and MRI scans (see pp. 30–1).

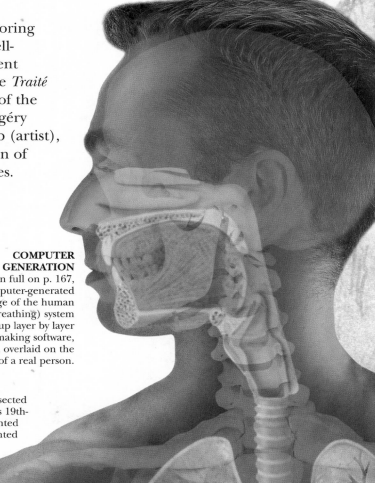

COMPUTER GENERATION
Shown in full on p. 167, this computer-generated image of the human respiratory (breathing) system was built up layer by layer using image-making software, and then overlaid on the photograph of a real person.

TEXTBOOK ILLUSTRATIONS
This detailed illustration of a dissected armpit from Bougéry and Jacob's 19th-century anatomical work was printed by lithography, a technique invented in 1798 that made it possible to produce inexpensive, well-illustrated medical textbooks.

Movement and posture

IF ITS MUSCLES WERE suddenly inactivated, the body would not only be immobilized but would also collapse. As well as moving the body, skeletal muscles hold it upright and maintain posture. To perform both roles, muscles pull the bones, to which they are attached by tendons, across a joint. When a muscle contracts, one of the bones to which it is attached – the insertion – moves, while the other attachment point – the origin – remains fixed. Since they can only pull and not push, muscles work in antagonistic pairs to produce opposing movements. Flexor muscles in the forearm, for example, bend fingers, while their antagonists, the extensor muscles, straighten them. Muscles that work together to produce the same movement are called synergists.

Triceps *contracts to straighten the arm*

Biceps *is fully contracted*

Brachioradialis *helps the biceps bend the arm by pulling the lower arm bones upward*

Biceps *contracts to bend the arm*

Triceps *relaxed and stretched*

Muscles that raise and lower the forearm

OPPOSING MUSCLES

When a muscle contracts, it shortens, pulling its insertion toward its origin. To produce movement in the opposite direction, there must be a separate antagonistic, or opposing, muscle. In the arm, for example, the biceps muscle pulls the forearm upward toward the shoulder to bend the arm. Its antagonist, the triceps, pulls the forearm downward to straighten the arm. The brachioradialis acts as a synergist to the biceps, helping it bend the arm.

MUSCLES, BONES, AND LEVERS

Muscles and bones interact to move the body using lever systems. A lever is a bar that moves on a fixed point, the fulcrum, when a force is applied to one part of it to move a weight on another. In the body, bones are levers, a joint is a fulcrum, and muscle contraction provides the force to move a body part (weight). Levers fall into three classes according to the relative positions of the force, weight, and fulcrum.

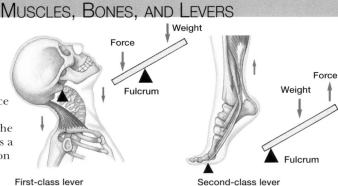

First-class lever
The fulcrum lies between force and weight, like a seesaw. Neck muscles pulling the back of the skull to tilt the head backward produce a similiar action.

Second-class lever
The weight lies between the force and the fulcrum, like a wheelbarrow (for example, raising of the heel and body weight by the calf muscles).

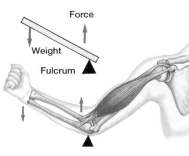

Third-class lever
In the most common type of lever in the body, the force is applied between fulcrum and weight, like tweezers (for example, bending the elbow).

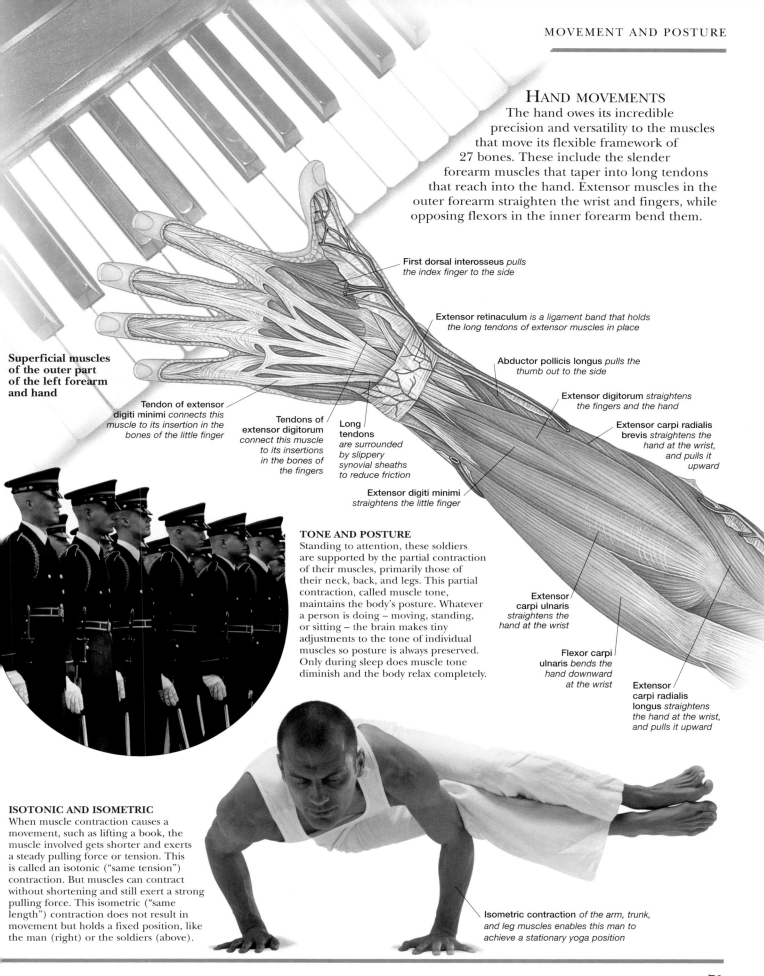

HAND MOVEMENTS

The hand owes its incredible precision and versatility to the muscles that move its flexible framework of 27 bones. These include the slender forearm muscles that taper into long tendons that reach into the hand. Extensor muscles in the outer forearm straighten the wrist and fingers, while opposing flexors in the inner forearm bend them.

First dorsal interosseus *pulls the index finger to the side*

Extensor retinaculum *is a ligament band that holds the long tendons of extensor muscles in place*

Abductor pollicis longus *pulls the thumb out to the side*

Extensor digitorum *straightens the fingers and the hand*

Extensor carpi radialis brevis *straightens the hand at the wrist, and pulls it upward*

Superficial muscles of the outer part of the left forearm and hand

Tendon of extensor digiti minimi *connects this muscle to its insertion in the bones of the little finger*

Tendons of extensor digitorum *connect this muscle to its insertions in the bones of the fingers*

Long tendons *are surrounded by slippery synovial sheaths to reduce friction*

Extensor digiti minimi *straightens the little finger*

Extensor carpi ulnaris *straightens the hand at the wrist*

Flexor carpi ulnaris *bends the hand downward at the wrist*

Extensor carpi radialis longus *straightens the hand at the wrist, and pulls it upward*

TONE AND POSTURE

Standing to attention, these soldiers are supported by the partial contraction of their muscles, primarily those of their neck, back, and legs. This partial contraction, called muscle tone, maintains the body's posture. Whatever a person is doing – moving, standing, or sitting – the brain makes tiny adjustments to the tone of individual muscles so posture is always preserved. Only during sleep does muscle tone diminish and the body relax completely.

ISOTONIC AND ISOMETRIC

When muscle contraction causes a movement, such as lifting a book, the muscle involved gets shorter and exerts a steady pulling force or tension. This is called an isotonic ("same tension") contraction. But muscles can contract without shortening and still exert a strong pulling force. This isometric ("same length") contraction does not result in movement but holds a fixed position, like the man (right) or the soldiers (above).

Isometric contraction *of the arm, trunk, and leg muscles enables this man to achieve a stationary yoga position*

Muscles and exercise

THE BODY IS capable of responding to all kinds of changes, both inside and outside itself. One of the most obvious responses is to increased activity or exercise. The heart, lungs, and muscles undergo changes – all carefully regulated by the brain – that ensure that muscle fibers obtain sufficient energy to contract more rapidly and more strongly. The ability of the body to react in this way depends on its fitness. A fit body is one that can carry out everyday activities, such as running for a bus or climbing stairs, without breathlessness or excessive tiredness. Fitness has three elements – stamina, strength, and flexibility – all of which can be increased by regular exercise. Some exercises focus on just one of these fitness elements, while others, such as swimming, improve all three.

Muscles *work harder during exercise and demand more energy*

Fibers *in the arm's muscles increase in size, which improves strength*

Weightlifting is an anaerobic exercise that increases strength

STRENGTH
The amount of force muscles exert when performing an action such as lifting or jumping, and their ability to hold the body upright without tiring, are determined by their strength. Exercises such as weightlifting improve strength by increasing the size of muscle fibers. These exercises are anaerobic. That is, they are intensive exercises that last for a very short time, and use energy released without the need for oxygen. They do not improve stamina.

STAMINA
Also called cardiovascular fitness or endurance, stamina reflects the ability of the heart and blood vessels to deliver oxygen and nutrients to the body's tissues, including muscles. Stamina is enhanced by aerobic exercises, such as running, brisk walking, or dancing, which use oxygen to release energy from "fuels" such as glucose. Performed for 20 minutes or more at least three times a week, and demanding enough to produce sweating and slight breathlessness, aerobic activities improve stamina by increasing the strength and efficiency of the heart.

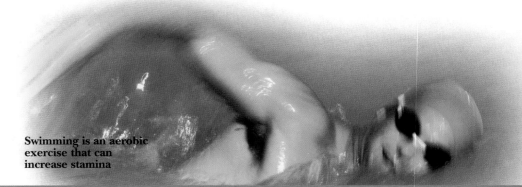

Swimming is an aerobic exercise that can increase stamina

ON THE MOVE

When exercise begins, several changes occur automatically to meet the demands for extra oxygen and nutrients needed by skeletal muscles that are working harder than normal. Blood flow to muscle fibers is dramatically increased during vigorous exercise from 2 to 25 pints (1 to 12 liters) per minute. This is achieved by widening blood vessels that serve muscle fibers, and by making the heart pump faster and more strongly so that blood flow rate increases from 10 to 42 pints (5 to 20 liters) per minute. At the same time, the volume of air taken in by the lungs goes from 0.2 up to 3.5 cu ft (6 to 100 liters) per minute by increasing the rate and depth of breathing.

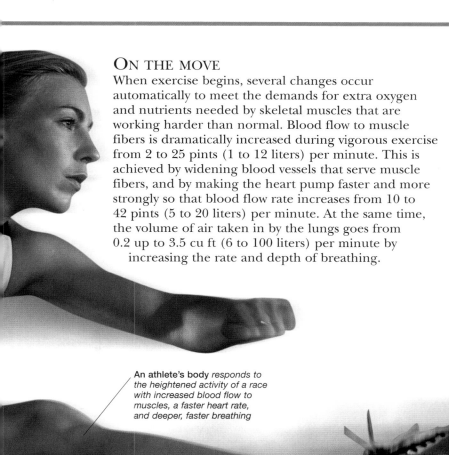

"Scorpion" yoga position

FLEXIBILITY

The body's flexibility is measured by the ability of its joints to move freely and without any discomfort. Activities that improve flexibility – including yoga and gymnastics – involve stretching and holding exercises, and ensure that muscles are supple and ligaments and tendons remain in good working order. Stretching the body just after exercise, while muscles are still "warmed up," also helps avoid muscle pain and stiffness.

An athlete's body *responds to the heightened activity of a race with increased blood flow to muscles, a faster heart rate, and deeper, faster breathing*

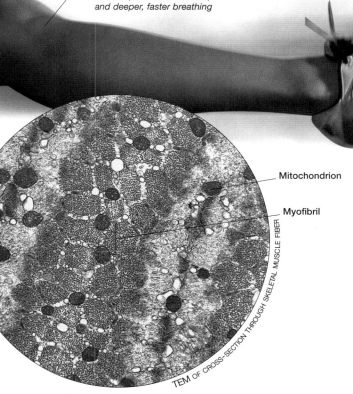

Mitochondrion

Myofibril

TEM OF CROSS-SECTION THROUGH SKELETAL MUSCLE FIBER

EXERCISE BENEFITS

Regular exercise combining elements that increase stamina, strength, and flexibility has numerous benefits. The heart pumps, and the lungs take in oxygen, more efficiently. Capillaries supplying muscle fibers with nutrients and oxygen increase in number. More mitochondria (organelles that release energy) and glycogen granules (energy stores) appear in muscle fibers, and there is more myoglobin (the substance that carries oxygen). Muscle fibers increase in size and work more efficiently, giving muscles greater strength and resistance to tiredness.

OXYGEN DEBT

An athlete pants after a race because his body needs to get extra oxygen to its cells – over and above their resting oxygen consumption – in order to "pay off" an "oxygen debt." This "debt" is generated during hard exercise by anaerobic respiration, when muscle fibers obtain energy without using oxygen. The waste product of this process – lactic acid – must be disposed of by aerobic respiration, a process that requires extra oxygen, before muscles can work normally again.

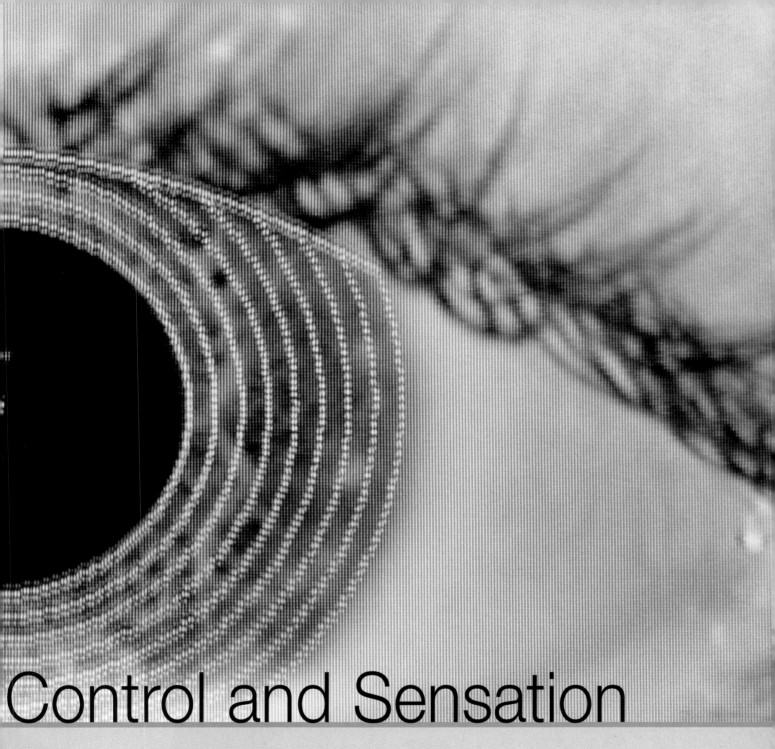

Control and Sensation

THE HUMAN BRAIN is a remarkable organ. It can simultaneously order leg muscles to run and the heart to beat faster. It gives humans their creativity, memory, intelligence, emotions, and personality. It turns messages received from sensors into the sensations that allow humans to see, hear, taste, smell, and touch. Together with its nerves and sensors, the brain forms the nervous system. A second, linked control system – the endocrine system – regulates growth, reproduction, and some other processes.

NERVOUS system

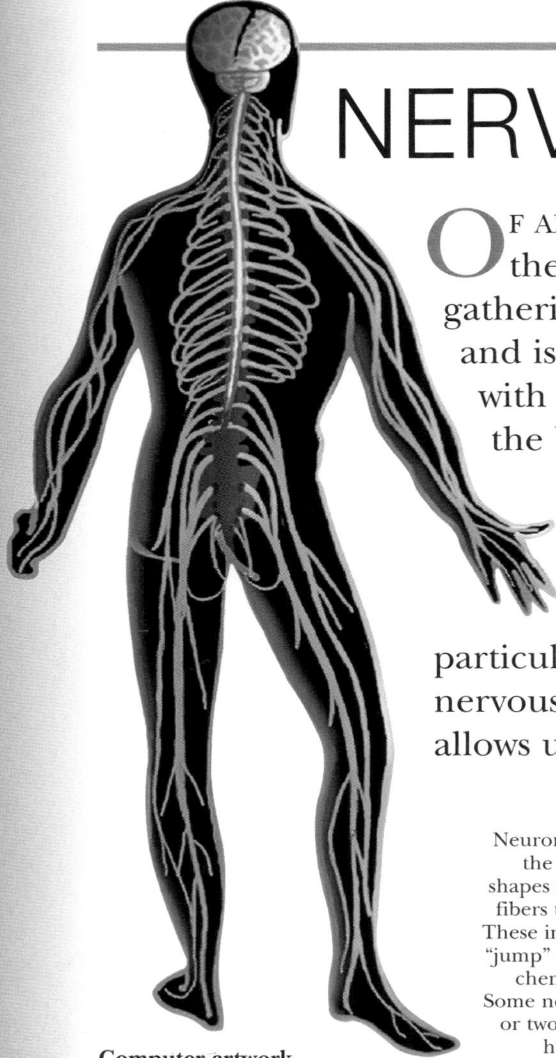

O F ALL THE HUMAN body's systems, the nervous system is the most complex. It is on duty every second of every day, gathering information about the body and its surroundings, and issuing instructions that make the body react. Together with the endocrine system (see p. 118), it controls everything the body does, and its speed and processing power mean that it can cope with an incredible range of tasks at the same time. It works through specialized cells called neurons, which carry signals in the form of tiny bursts of electricity. Some neurons carry signals to, or from, particular parts of the body, but most are packed into the nervous system's headquarters – the brain. This living computer allows us to think and to remember, and makes us who we are.

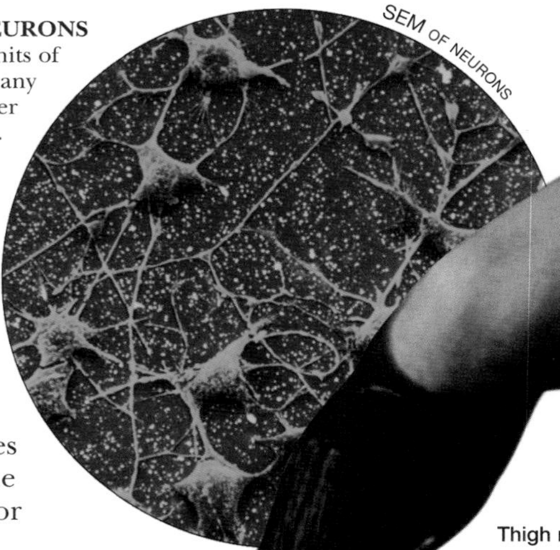

**Computer artwork
of the nervous system**

NEURONS
Neurons, or nerve cells, are the basic units of the nervous system. They come in many shapes and sizes, but they all have slender fibers that can carry electrical impulses. These impulses flash along the cell, and "jump" from one neuron to another at chemical junctions called synapses. Some neurons have synapses with one or two neurons, but others can have hundreds of these connections.

SEM OF NEURONS

COMMUNICATION NETWORK
The nervous system reaches almost every part of the body, from muscles and sense organs to the insides of teeth and bones. Nerves are the system's main communication cables, fanning out from the spinal cord and also from the brain. There are more than 80 major nerves, and each one may contain more than a million neurons. In the above diagram, the central nervous system, comprising the brain and spinal cord, is blue-white; the spine, shown around the spinal cord, is magenta, and the spinal nerves are orange.

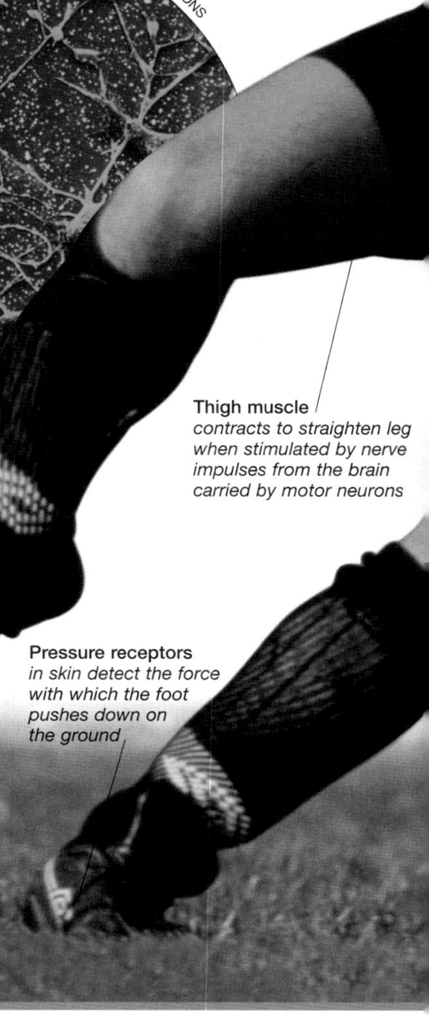

Thigh muscle *contracts to straighten leg when stimulated by nerve impulses from the brain carried by motor neurons*

Pressure receptors *in skin detect the force with which the foot pushes down on the ground*

NERVOUS SYSTEM FUNCTIONS

Sensory	*Senses changes (stimuli) inside and outside the body, in conjunction with receptors or sense organs. The changes include a wide range of physical factors, such as light, pressure, or the concentration of dissolved chemicals.*	Integrative	*Analyzes sensory information, and makes decisions on appropriate responses. Triggered or modified by information that is stored, and retrieved from memory.*
		Motor	*Triggers responses by muscles or glands. The nervous system can either stimulate muscles and glands into action, or inhibit them.*

Brain *analyzes incoming information from sensors, and sends out instructions to muscles to move the body and maintain its balance*

Optic nerve *from the eye sends a stream of signals to the brain, allowing it to track the ball*

Receptors *in the inner ear produce signals used to control balance*

Pressure receptors *in the hand tell the brain when the ball has been caught*

Motor neurons *of the autonomic nervous system stimulate the heart to beat faster to increase blood flow to the muscles*

Nerve impulses *carried by motor neurons make muscles straighten the arm to intercept the ball*

RAPID RESPONSE

On the playing field, split-second reactions are essential. The nervous system is ideally equipped for this; it can flash signals along neurons at up to 330 ft (100 m) per second. This gets sensory signals in record time to the brain or spinal cord, where they are processed. Motor signals are then flashed to selected muscles, making the body respond. With something as complicated as catching a ball, millions of signals race through the nervous system, ensuring that the body does the right thing at exactly the right time.

Stretch receptors *in the muscles detect muscle tone or tension and inform the brain so it can maintain balance*

HOW THE NERVOUS SYSTEM IS ORGANIZED

Central nervous system
The CNS coordinates the activities of the entire body. It receives and analyzes incoming information from sense organs and other receptors, and sends out instructions, based on past experience, to muscles and glands.

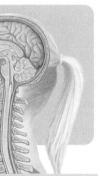

The nervous system is divided into two main parts: the central nervous system (CNS) and the peripheral nervous system (PNS). The CNS consists of the brain and spinal cord, and is the command center of the nervous system. The PNS consists of the nerves (bundles of neurons) that extend from the brain and spinal cord and relay messages between the CNS and the rest of the body.

Peripheral nervous system
The PNS has three divisions: one relaying information to the CNS, and two carrying instructions from the CNS.

Sensory division *gathers information from sensors to update the CNS about events occurring inside and outside the body.*

Somatic division *carries instructions to skeletal muscles to make them contract, enabling the body to respond under conscious control to outside events.*

Autonomic division *carries instructions to the body's internal organs to control their activities, thereby automatically regulating internal processes.*

Neurons

Found only in the nervous system, neurons are among the body's most specialized cells. They carry electrical signals, or impulses and pass them on through fibers called axons, which can be up to 1 yd (1 m) long. Neurons behave partly like wires and partly like batteries, because they charge themselves up. When something triggers a neuron to "fire," the charge reverses, creating a rapid burst of electricity that rushes along the cell. Some neurons are triggered by things that can be sensed. Others process this information, or carry signals that make the body react. Unlike most of the body's cells, neurons cannot divide once they are mature, and if they are badly damaged they cannot be replaced.

Axon terminals
The end of the axon divides to produce a collection of axon terminals that form synapses with other neurons, or with muscle or gland cells

Schwann cell *is a glial cell that wraps itself around an axon*

NEURON STRUCTURE

A typical neuron is divided into a part that receives signals, and a long axon, or fiber, that carries the signals from one place to another. In a motor neuron, shown here, the receiving end has a swelling, the cell body. Attached to this are short filaments called dendrites, which connect with neighboring neurons through chemical junctions called synapses. If one of these synapses is stimulated, an impulse flashes toward the cell body. It then travels along the neuron's axon, so that it can be passed on.

Axon, or nerve fiber, *conducts nervous impulses away from the cell body, so that they can be passed on to other neurons, or to muscles or glands*

Myelin sheath *insulates the axon and is formed in a Schwann cell*

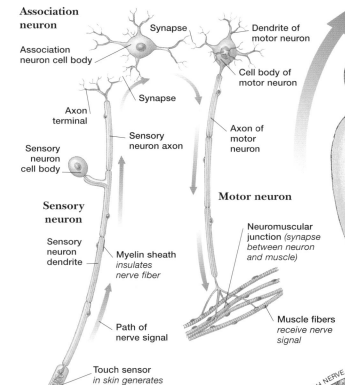

Association neuron

Synapse

Association neuron cell body

Synapse

Dendrite of motor neuron

Cell body of motor neuron

Axon terminal

Sensory neuron axon

Axon of motor neuron

Sensory neuron cell body

Sensory neuron

Sensory neuron dendrite

Myelin sheath *insulates nerve fiber*

Motor neuron

Neuromuscular junction *(synapse between neuron and muscle)*

Path of nerve signal

Muscle fibers *receive nerve signal*

Touch sensor *in skin generates the nerve signal*

TEM OF SECTION THROUGH NERVE FIBERS

Myelinated axon *surrounded by narrower nonmyelinated axons*

Nonmyelinated axon

Myelin sheath

TYPES OF NEURON

There are three main types of neuron. Sensory neurons are triggered by physical stimuli, such as light. The strength of the stimulus affects the rate at which the neuron fires. Association, or intermediate, neurons are triggered by sensory neurons. They process the information from sensory neurons and issue outgoing commands. These commands are passed on to motor neurons, which in turn make parts of the body respond.

MYELIN SHEATH

Bare axons do not carry impulses quickly, because their electrical charge leaks away. Many sensory and motor neurons are insulated by a fatty substance called myelin. Myelin is produced by Schwann cells, which wrap themselves around axons, forming layers like those in a jelly roll. The Schwann cells are separated by small gaps called nodes, and nerve impulses move by jumping from one node to the next.

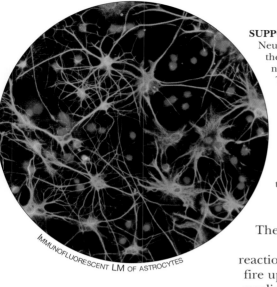

IMMUNOFLUORESCENT LM OF ASTROCYTES

SUPPORTING CELLS

Neurons make up only about one in ten of the nervous system's cells. The remaining nine-tenths are known as glial cells. They support the neurons and keep them alive. Glial cells called astrocytes, which are shown here, help to supply neurons with nutrients, while other glial cells mop up invading bacteria. Another type – Schwann cells – wrap themselves around neurons, providing protection and insulation. Unlike neurons, glial cells can replace themselves if they are damaged.

HIGH-SPEED IMPULSES

The nervous system works very quickly, as is illustrated by the split-second reactions of race car drivers. Neurons can fire up to 2,500 times per second and, in myelinated neurons, impulses sometimes travel at speeds of 218 mph (350 kmh). When a neuron is at rest, it uses energy to pump electrically charged particles, or ions, across its cell membrane. When the neuron is triggered by a synapse, the ions rush back across the cell membrane, and the charge is reversed. This reversal sweeps along the cell, and the result is a nerve impulse.

Direction of impulses

GOLGI'S STAIN

Because they are so slender, neurons are difficult to see – even when magnified several hundred times. Until the late 19th century, little was known about neurons. But in 1873, Italian histologist Camillo Golgi (1844–1926), who identified different neuron types, found that they could be stained black with silver nitrate, making their fine structure easier to see.

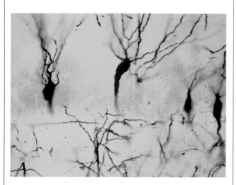

Section through the brain, showing neurons stained using Golgi's stain

Node of Ranvier *is a gap between adjacent Schwann cells that allows nervous impulses to leapfrog along the axon*

Nucleus

Cell body *contains most of the neuron's cytoplasm, as well as mitochondria and other organelles*

Branching dendrites *enable a single neuron to make contact with dozens, or even hundreds, of its neighbors*

Synapses

In the nervous system – just as in a computer – information is only useful if it can be communicated, or passed on. Neurons do this through microscopic junctions called synapses. At a synapse, a slender terminal fiber from a neuron reaches out to make contact with another cell. If a nerve impulse flashes along the fiber, it makes the synapse release a chemical called a neurotransmitter. In less than one-thousandth of a second, this chemical travels across a tiny gap between the two cells and triggers the second cell to respond. A single neuron can have several hundred of these minute connections, and the total number in the nervous system runs into many trillions. Together, they create a vast array of circuits that constantly interact with each other to control the body.

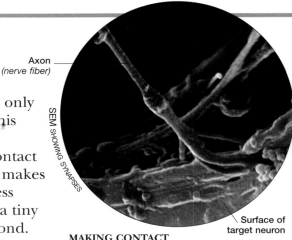

Axon
(nerve fiber)

SEM SHOWING SYNAPSES

Surface of
target neuron

MAKING CONTACT
In this electron microscope view of a nerve cell, an axon can be seen connecting one neuron to another. The axon (colored purple) divides into smaller fibers that end in small swellings, or synaptic bulbs. These produce neurotransmitters and release them when the axon fires. Most synapses are between neurons, though some synapses also connect neurons to other kinds of cells.

Myelinated axon,
or nerve fiber, is
surrounded by
Schwann cells

SYNAPSE CONNECTIONS

Nervous impulses travel throughout the body via synapses. Each synapse is like a one-way switch; it cannot work in reverse. Some neurons have just a handful of synapses, but association neurons in the brain – like the ones shown on the left – often form synapses with hundreds of neighboring cells. Synapses can change as time goes by. Extra synapses form in circuits that are used frequently, making it easier for nerve impulses to follow these particular paths. This explains why many things – such as playing a musical instrument or driving a car – get easier with practice.

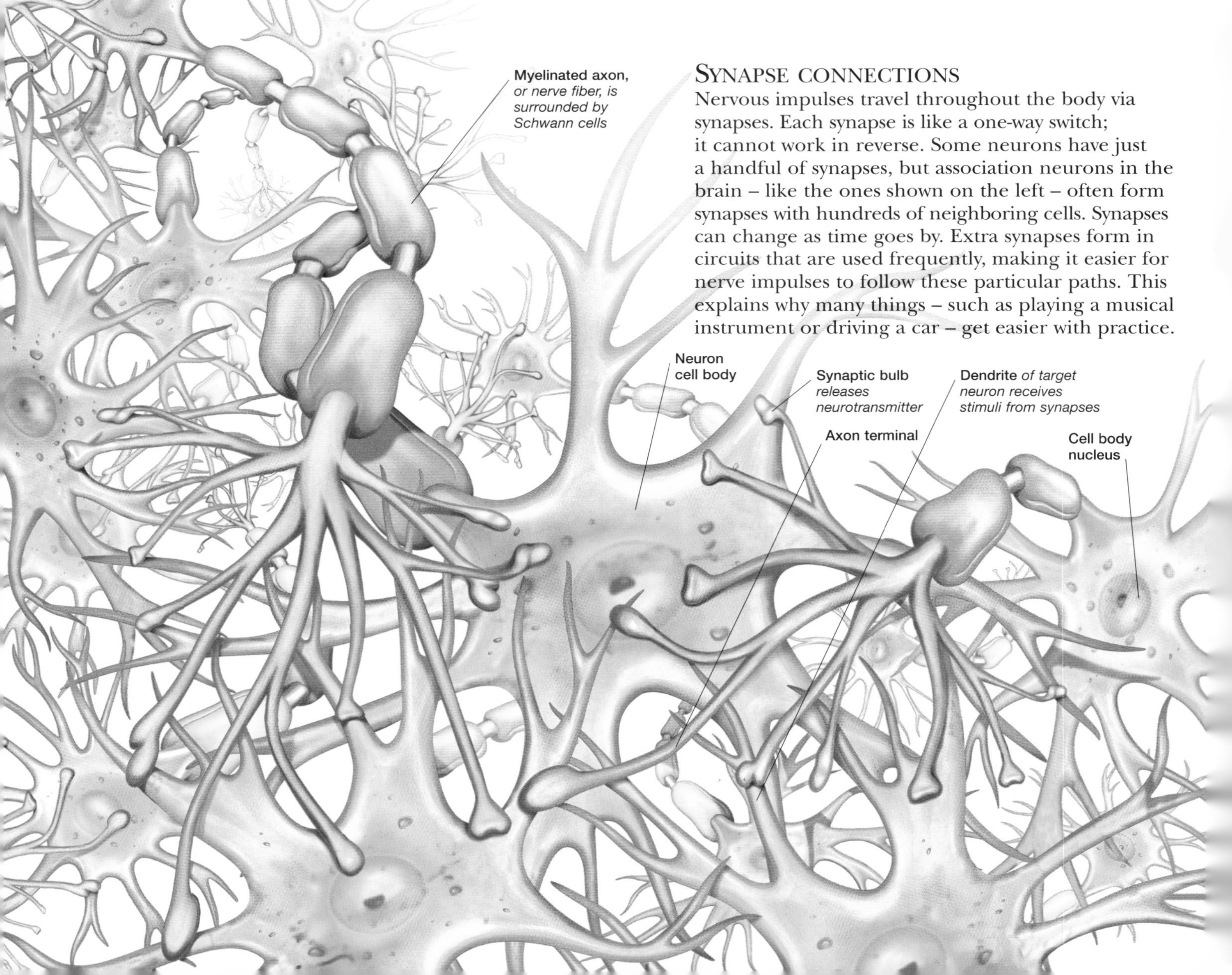

Neuron
cell body

Synaptic bulb
releases
neurotransmitter

Dendrite of target
neuron receives
stimuli from synapses

Axon terminal

Cell body
nucleus

DRUGS AND SYNAPSES

Many drugs work by interfering with the way that synapses work. For example, stimulants such as caffeine reduce the amount of neurotransmitter that is needed to make neurons fire. After several cups of coffee, the body's neurons are triggered more frequently than normal, producing a feeling of being more awake and alert. Depressants, including alcohol, have the opposite effect.

Coffee beans

NEUROTOXINS

Some of the most lethal substances in nature are ones that switch synapses permanently on or off. Known as neurotoxins, these include chemicals produced by some bacteria, and also secretions produced by black widow spiders and poison dart frogs. Neurotoxins that switch on synapses cause paralysis by making all the body's muscles contract at once. Those that switch off synapses stop muscles from contracting, which means that the victim cannot breathe. The fatal dose can be less than one-millionth of a gram.

Skin glands
release neurotoxins

Poison dart frog

CROSSING THE GAP

In the bulbous part of a synapse, neurotransmitters are stored in bubblelike packages called vesicles. When a nerve impulse arrives at the synapse, some of the vesicles migrate to the edge of the bulb and spill their neurotransmitter outside. The neurotransmitter crosses the gap to the target cell, where it activates special receptors. If the target cell is a neuron, the receptors trigger it to fire. The neurotransmitter is then broken down by enzymes.

Axon terminal

Synaptic bulb *lies close to the target neuron's cell body or dendrites*

Synaptic vesicles *store molecules of the neurotransmitter*

Dendrite *of target neuron*

Mitochondrion

Vesicle *discharges neurotransmitters into the synaptic cleft*

Cell membrane

Synaptic cleft or gap

Target cell membrane

Receptor sites *combine with the neurotransmitter on the target cell membrane, which then produces a nerve impulse in the target neuron*

Membrane channel *allows sodium ions (blue) in to trigger nerve impulse*

STAINS AND SYNAPSES

Spanish doctor and medical researcher Santiago Ramón y Cajal (1852–1934) studied the human nervous system using the staining techniques developed by Camillo Golgi (see p. 79). However, unlike Golgi, he believed that neurons met at synapses, without actually merging. He could not prove this with the microscopes of the time, but after the development of the electron microscope, his theory was shown to be correct. Golgi and Ramón y Cajal shared the Nobel Prize in 1906.

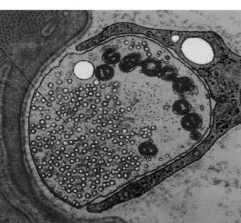

Vesicles *containing neurotransmitter chemicals*

Muscle fiber

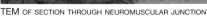

TEM OF SECTION THROUGH NEUROMUSCULAR JUNCTION

NEUROMUSCULAR JUNCTION

The cross-section above shows a special kind of synapse between neurons and skeletal muscle fibers that makes voluntary muscles contract. In the center is the synaptic bulb (blue), while the muscle cell that it triggers is to the left (red). The bulb is packed with vesicles of neurotransmitter waiting to be discharged. Smooth and cardiac muscles are triggered by synapses of a different kind, which pass electrical signals directly from one muscle cell to another.

Nerves

Regarded as the information highways of the nervous system, nerves can contain millions of individual neurons that fan out from the brain and spinal cord to reach every part of the body. Most carry two-way traffic, with sensory neurons flashing signals inward to the central nervous system, and motor neurons transmitting signals in the opposite direction. Nerves do not recover well from injury, and the majority are buried deep in the body, with only small branches reaching upward to make contact with the skin. The ulnar nerve, at the elbow, is one of the few that does sit close to the surface. If it is suddenly knocked against the humerus, or "funny bone," it sends a tingling sensation shooting down the arm.

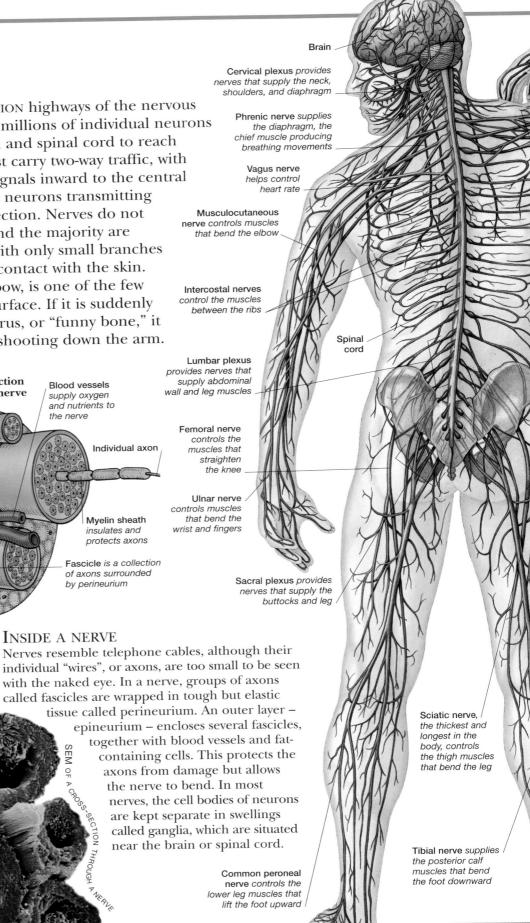

Brain

Cervical plexus *provides nerves that supply the neck, shoulders, and diaphragm*

Phrenic nerve *supplies the diaphragm, the chief muscle producing breathing movements*

Vagus nerve *helps control heart rate*

Musculocutaneous nerve *controls muscles that bend the elbow*

Intercostal nerves *control the muscles between the ribs*

Spinal cord

Lumbar plexus *provides nerves that supply abdominal wall and leg muscles*

Femoral nerve *controls the muscles that straighten the knee*

Ulnar nerve *controls muscles that bend the wrist and fingers*

Sacral plexus *provides nerves that supply the buttocks and leg*

Sciatic nerve, *the thickest and longest in the body, controls the thigh muscles that bend the leg*

Tibial nerve *supplies the posterior calf muscles that bend the foot downward*

Common peroneal nerve *controls the lower leg muscles that lift the foot upward*

Epineurium *surrounds the entire nerve*

Cross-section through nerve

Blood vessels *supply oxygen and nutrients to the nerve*

Individual axon

Myelin sheath *insulates and protects axons*

Fascicle *is a collection of axons surrounded by perineurium*

Fat-containing cells *act as a cushion against shocks*

Perineurium

Axons *(nerve fibers)*

Fascicle *surrounded by perineurium*

SEM OF A CROSS-SECTION THROUGH A NERVE

INSIDE A NERVE

Nerves resemble telephone cables, although their individual "wires", or axons, are too small to be seen with the naked eye. In a nerve, groups of axons called fascicles are wrapped in tough but elastic tissue called perineurium. An outer layer – epineurium – encloses several fascicles, together with blood vessels and fat-containing cells. This protects the axons from damage but allows the nerve to bend. In most nerves, the cell bodies of neurons are kept separate in swellings called ganglia, which are situated near the brain or spinal cord.

Radial nerve *controls muscles that straighten the elbow, wrist, and fingers*

Median nerve *controls muscles that bend the wrist and fingers*

Brachial plexus *provides the nerves that supply the arm and hand*

MICROSURGERY

If nerves, even small ones, are cut, it is possible to reconnect them using a delicate technique known as microsurgery. Surgeons use special binocular microscopes in the operating room. These devices enable the surgeons to see even the finest nerves – and blood vessels – in depth so that they can accurately rejoin the disconnected ends. Microsurgery allows severed fingers or limbs to be successfully reattached to the body with full feeling and control restored once the wound has healed.

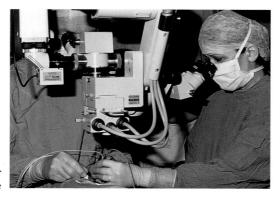

Surgeons using a binocular microscope as they operate

I Olfactory nerve *supplies the lining of the nose and relays signals from olfactory cells that are perceived as smells*

II Optic nerve *supplies the retina and relays signals from photoreceptors that are perceived as vision*

III Oculomotor nerve *controls movements of the eye and eyelid, and changes in shape of the pupil and lens*

IV Trochlear nerve, *in conjunction with the oculomotor and abducens nerves, controls movements of the eyeball*

VI Abducens nerve *controls movements of the eyeball*

V Trigeminal nerve *controls muscles involved in chewing and relays sensory information from the eye, teeth, and side of the face*

View of brain from underneath (front at top)

VII Facial nerve *controls muscles used in facial expressions, controls salivary and tear glands, and relays sensory information from the taste buds*

VIII Vestibulocochlear nerve *relays sensory signals from the inner ear that are perceived as sounds and allow balance*

XI Accessory nerve *controls muscles involved in swallowing and in moving the head*

IX Glossopharyngeal nerve *controls the salivary glands and relays sensory signals from the tongue and pharynx*

XII Hypoglossal nerve *controls the movement of the tongue*

MAJOR NERVES

Nerves are divided into two types, depending on where they connect with the central nervous system. The 12 pairs of cranial nerves (right) connect directly with the brain or brain stem and supply the head and neck. The 31 pairs of spinal nerves (left) connect with the spinal cord and supply the rest of the body. Nerves divide as they spread throughout the body, but some first converge in clusters called plexuses, which allow fine control of parts of the body such as the hand.

X Vagus nerve *controls muscles and glands in many internal organs, including the heart, lungs, and stomach*

CRANIAL NERVES

The 12 pairs of cranial nerves fan out from the underside of the brain. Other than the vagus nerve (X), cranial nerves control muscles in the head and neck region, or carry nerve impulses from sense organs, such as the eyes, to the brain. Cranial nerves are not only named but are also numbered I to XII, traditionally using Roman numerals. The main functions of each nerve are detailed above.

Spinal cord

TOGETHER WITH THE BRAIN, the spinal cord carries out the vital work of processing information and keeping the body coordinated. It starts at the base of the brain, and reaches most of the way down the spine, giving it an average length in adults of about 17 in (44 cm). Like the brain itself, it contains two kinds of nervous tissue – gray matter, which contains neuron cell bodies, and white matter, which contains axons that carry signals up or down the spine. The spinal cord has two main functions. It relays information between the spinal nerves and the brain, but it also controls many automatic reactions, or reflexes. When it triggers a reflex, it often works on its own, making the body react without waiting to consult the brain.

A PROTECTIVE TUNNEL

Although it is no thicker than a finger, the spinal cord is packed with millions of neurons, and it needs special protection to avoid being damaged. It gets this from the bony arches of the vertebrae, which form an open tunnel around it. The spinal cord is anchored at the top of the spine to the base of the brain, and to the vertebrae in between. This prevents it from being displaced by sudden jolts.

SPINAL CORD STRUCTURE

The spinal cord is surrounded by three layers of tissue, called meninges. The two innermost layers are separated by cerebrospinal fluid, which acts as a shock absorber. Inside this triple covering are the spinal cord's nerve cells, and a central canal. Between each pair of neighboring vertebrae, two spinal nerves emerge from the cord. Each nerve has two roots. One contains sensory neurons, which carry incoming signals toward the spinal cord. The other contains motor neurons, which carry outgoing signals that make the body respond.

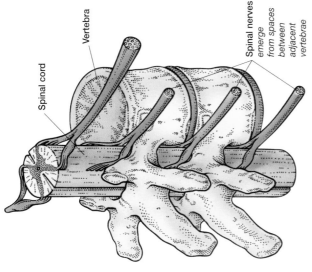

Vertebra

Spinal cord

Spinal nerves *emerge from spaces between adjacent vertebrae*

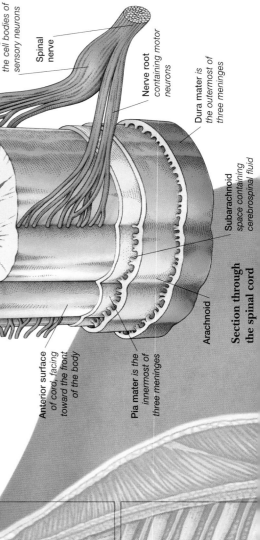

Nerve fiber tracts

Gray matter

White matter

Nerve root *containing sensory neurons*

Ganglion *is a swelling that contains the cell bodies of sensory neurons*

Spinal nerve

Nerve root *containing motor neurons*

Dura mater *is the outermost of three meninges*

Central canal *containing cerebrospinal fluid*

Anterior fissure

Cervical spinal nerves *(C1 to C8)*

Anterior surface *of cord, facing toward the front of the body*

Pia mater *is the innermost of three meninges*

Arachnoid

Subarachnoid *space containing cerebrospinal fluid*

Section through the spinal cord

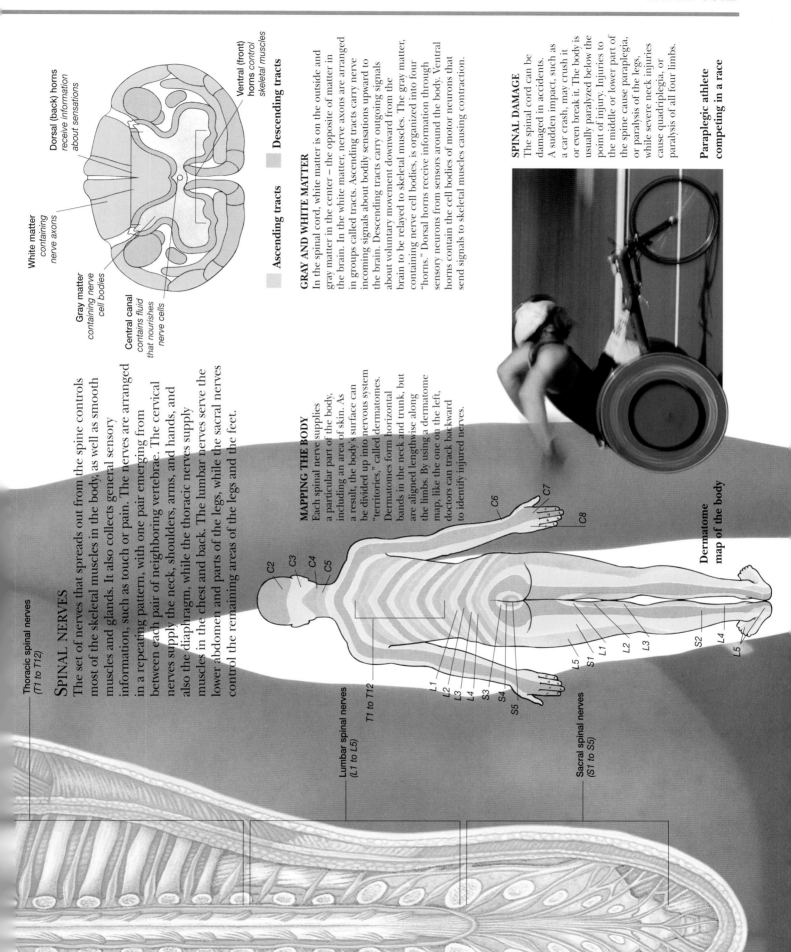

White matter
containing nerve axons

Dorsal (back) horns
receive information about sensations

Ventral (front) horns *control skeletal muscles*

Gray matter
containing nerve cell bodies

Central canal
contains fluid that nourishes nerve cells

■ Ascending tracts ■ Descending tracts

GRAY AND WHITE MATTER

In the spinal cord, white matter is on the outside and gray matter in the center – the opposite of matter in the brain. In the white matter, nerve axons are arranged in groups called tracts. Ascending tracts carry nerve incoming signals about bodily sensations upward to the brain. Descending tracts carry outgoing signals about voluntary movement downward from the brain to be relayed to skeletal muscles. The gray matter, containing nerve cell bodies, is organized into four "horns." Dorsal horns receive information through sensory neurons from sensors around the body. Ventral horns contain the cell bodies of motor neurons that send signals to skeletal muscles causing contraction.

SPINAL NERVES

The set of nerves that spreads out from the spine controls most of the skeletal muscles in the body, as well as smooth muscles and glands. It also collects general sensory information, such as touch or pain. The nerves are arranged in a repeating pattern, with one pair emerging from between each pair of neighboring vertebrae. The cervical nerves supply the neck, shoulders, arms, and hands, and also the diaphragm, while the thoracic nerves supply muscles in the chest and back. The lumbar nerves serve the lower abdomen and parts of the legs, while the sacral nerves control the remaining areas of the legs and the feet.

Thoracic spinal nerves
(T1 to T12)

MAPPING THE BODY

Each spinal nerve supplies a particular part of the body, including an area of skin. As a result, the body's surface can be divided up into nervous system "territories," called dermatomes. Dermatomes form horizontal bands in the neck and trunk, but are aligned lengthwise along the limbs. By using a dermatome map, like the one on the left, doctors can track backward to identify injured nerves.

Lumbar spinal nerves
(L1 to L5)

T1 to T12

C2
C3
C4
C5

C6
C7
C8

L1
L2
L3
L4
S3
S4
S5

L5
S1
L1
L2
L3

S2
L4
L5

Sacral spinal nerves
(S1 to S5)

Dermatome map of the body

SPINAL DAMAGE

The spinal cord can be damaged in accidents. A sudden impact, such as a car crash, may crush it or even break it. The body is usually paralyzed below the point of injury. Injuries to the middle or lower part of the spine cause paraplegia, or paralysis of the legs, while severe neck injuries cause quadriplegia, or paralysis of all four limbs.

Paraplegic athlete competing in a race

Reflexes

Brain *registers the painful stimulus, but after a reflex action has happened*

ALTHOUGH HUMANS are all individuals, there are times when we behave in exactly the same way. For example, we all pull our hands away if we accidentally touch something sharp or hot, and we blink if anything looks as though it is heading for our eyes. These responses are known as reflexes. They happen automatically, and are a key part of protecting the body from danger. Unlike more complicated kinds of behavior, reflexes are triggered by simple nervous pathways. A stimulus, such as pain, is picked up by a sensory nerve and then flashed to the spinal cord, or to the lower part of the brain. A motor signal travels back, making part of the body respond. As well as controlling emergency action, reflexes also manage many internal processes, such as movements involved in digesting food.

Spinal cord *carries sensory signal to the brain*

Association neuron *passes the signal to a motor neuron*

Motor neuron *carries signal to the biceps*

Biceps *contracts and pulls the arm away*

Pain receptor in fingertip

Sensory neuron *carries signal to spinal cord*

REFLEX ACTION

Fingers are packed with sensory receptors that respond to pain. Even before this girl is aware that she has been hurt, sensory signals arrive at her spinal cord. Within a few thousandths of a second, motor signals travel to the biceps, and to other muscles that flex the arm. The muscles respond by contracting, and they pull the girl's hand away. This automatic response is known as the withdrawal reflex, and it is shown by many other parts of the body, such as the legs and head. The withdrawal reflex normally works without involving the brain, but it can be modified, or even switched off entirely by conscious thought, such as when a person makes a decision not to flinch when something hurts.

REFLEX ARC

The withdrawal reflex, and reflexes like it, happen quickly because they typically involve just three sets of neurons. A sensory neuron carries a signal to the spinal cord, or to the lower part of the brain. An association neuron then passes the signal on to one or more motor neurons, which make muscles contract and the body react. This pathway is called a reflex arc.

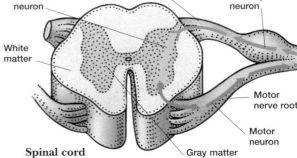

Association neuron

White matter

Spinal cord

Sensory nerve root

Sensory neuron

Spinal nerve

Motor nerve root

Motor neuron

Gray matter

TELLTALE TAP
In a healthy person, the stretch reflex maintains the body's posture by adjusting the tone, or tension, of skeletal muscles. It is activated by receptors deep inside muscles, and it makes muscles tighten if they stretch too far. Doctors test the stretch reflex by tapping a tendon just below the kneecap. The tapping stretches a muscle in the thigh, and the reflex makes the thigh muscle suddenly tighten, kicking the knee.

NEWBORN REFLEXES

Babies are born with many reflexes that help them to survive. For example, they instinctively suckle at their mother's breast, and they grasp anything that is put in the palm of their hands. If they are underwater, they hold their breath and make swimming movements – even if they have had no experience of water before. These newborn reflexes disappear with age. The grasping reflex is one of the briefest reflexes, fading away after about three months.

ANIMAL ELECTRICITY

Although nerves have been known about for centuries, how they work remained a mystery until recently. The first breakthrough was made by the Italian anatomist Luigi Galvani (1737–98), who found that frog legs would twitch when they were pinned on a metal frame. He thought that the twitching was caused by "animal electricity" – an idea that turned out to be partly right.

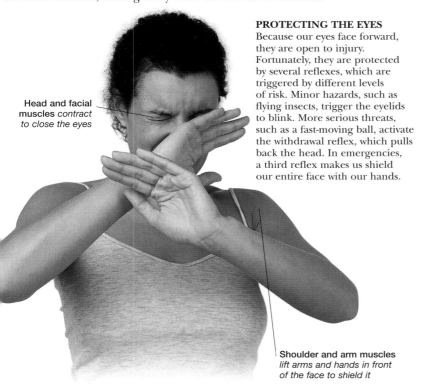

PROTECTING THE EYES
Because our eyes face forward, they are open to injury. Fortunately, they are protected by several reflexes, which are triggered by different levels of risk. Minor hazards, such as flying insects, trigger the eyelids to blink. More serious threats, such as a fast-moving ball, activate the withdrawal reflex, which pulls back the head. In emergencies, a third reflex makes us shield our entire face with our hands.

Head and facial
muscles *contract
to close the eyes*

Shoulder and arm muscles
*lift arms and hands in front
of the face to shield it*

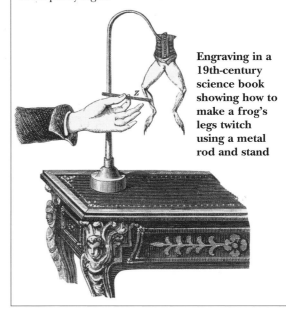

**Engraving in a
19th-century
science book
showing how to
make a frog's
legs twitch
using a metal
rod and stand**

The brain

As HEADQUARTERS of the nervous system, the brain is the control center of the body. Beneath its convoluted surface, more than 100 billion neurons sort and sift incoming information, and guide the body through an infinite variety of different movements. It is energy-demanding work, which explains why the brain uses up to one-fifth of the body's entire oxygen intake, even though it makes up only 2 percent of the body's total weight. Few other parts of the body are as delicate as the brain, but none is better protected. It floats in a shock-absorbing fluid and is surrounded by some of the toughest bones in the body. When the body's energy reserves are low, the brain gets first priority, ensuring that it can continue its vital work.

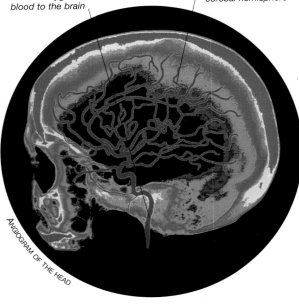

Internal carotid artery *delivers oxygen-rich blood to the brain*

Branches of the internal caroid artery *fan out through the cerebral hemisphere*

ANGIOGRAM OF THE HEAD

BLOOD SUPPLY
At any one time, up to one-fifth of the body's blood supply is on the move through the brain. Blood reaches the brain through an elaborate network of blood vessels, which is revealed by the angiogram above. The capillaries in the brain have a special structure that prevents potentially harmful substances from passing into the brain itself. This is known as the "blood-brain barrier."

EXTERNAL FEATURES
The cerebrum makes up 85 percent of the brain's weight. It overhangs the other main parts of the brain, the cerebellum and brain stem. It has a heavily folded surface with ridges called gyri (singular gyrus), and grooves called sulci (singular sulcus). Deep grooves are known as fissures. One of these fissures runs down the center of the cerebrum, dividing it into left and right hemispheres. Other sulci and fissures define the four main functional areas, or lobes, on each side of the cerebrum. Surface folding increases between infancy and adolescence, as the brain grows more complex and enlarges within the confines of the bony skull.

COMMUNICATION NETWORK
The brain's processing power comes from its association neurons – specialized nerve cells that form synapses with hundreds or even thousands of other nerve cells. Altogether, there are at least one trillion synapses in the brain, producing a vast web of pathways that signals can follow. This electron micrograph shows just a tiny fraction of the immense communication network.

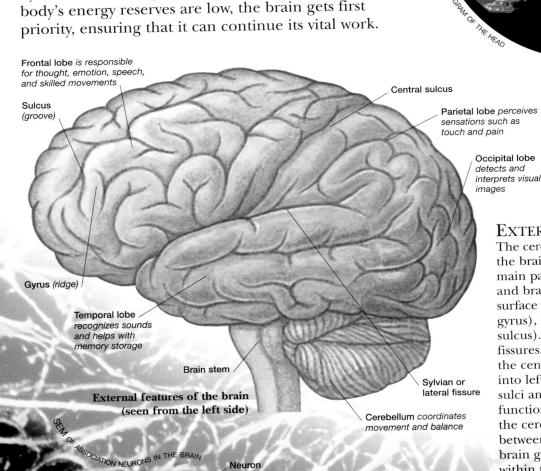

Frontal lobe *is responsible for thought, emotion, speech, and skilled movements*

Sulcus (groove)

Gyrus (ridge)

Temporal lobe *recognizes sounds and helps with memory storage*

Brain stem

External features of the brain (seen from the left side)

SEM OF ASSOCIATION NEURONS IN THE BRAIN

Neuron cell body

Axons and dendrites *that link neurons*

Central sulcus

Parietal lobe *perceives sensations such as touch and pain*

Occipital lobe *detects and interprets visual images*

Sylvian or lateral fissure

Cerebellum *coordinates movement and balance*

STROKE

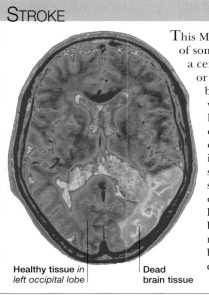

This MRI scan shows the brain of someone who has suffered a cerebrovascular accident, or stroke. This was caused by a ruptured blood vessel, which allowed blood to leak into the brain. The effect of a stroke depends on the part of the brain involved. Here, the stroke has cut off the supply of oxygen to part of the right occipital lobe, leading to partial blindness. Strokes are rare in young people, but become increasingly common with age.

Healthy tissue *in left occipital lobe*

Dead brain tissue

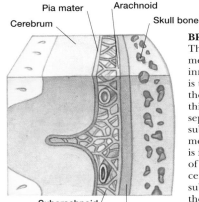

Pia mater

Arachnoid

Cerebrum

Skull bone

Subarachnoid space *filled with cerebrospinal fluid*

Dura mater

BRAIN PROTECTION
The brain is protected by three membranes, or meninges. The innermost of these membranes is the pia mater, which clings to the surface of the brain. Outside this is the arachnoid, which is separated from it by the weblike subarachnoid space. The outermost membrane, called the dura mater, is firmly attached to the inside of the skull. A watery liquid called cerebrospinal fluid, found in the subarachnoid space, surrounds the brain, flows through it, and cushions it against sudden jolts.

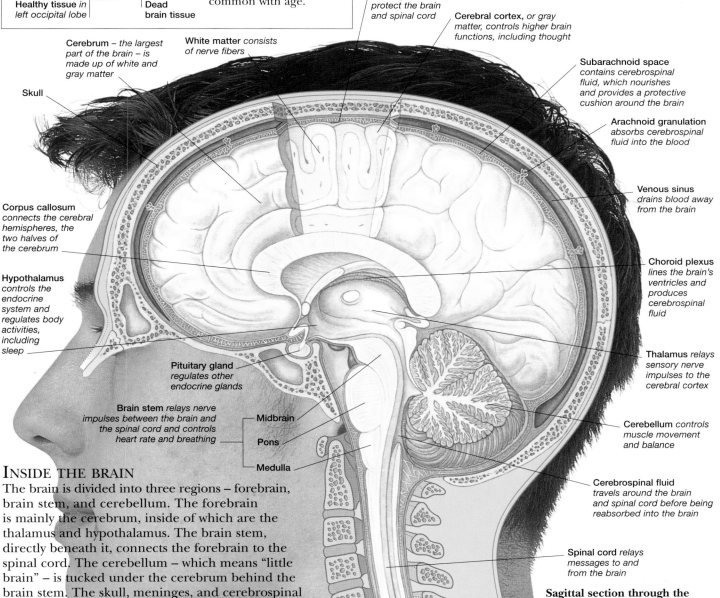

Meninges *protect the brain and spinal cord*

Cerebral cortex, *or gray matter, controls higher brain functions, including thought*

Cerebrum – *the largest part of the brain – is made up of white and gray matter*

White matter *consists of nerve fibers*

Subarachnoid space *contains cerebrospinal fluid, which nourishes and provides a protective cushion around the brain*

Skull

Arachnoid granulation *absorbs cerebrospinal fluid into the blood*

Corpus callosum *connects the cerebral hemispheres, the two halves of the cerebrum*

Venous sinus *drains blood away from the brain*

Choroid plexus *lines the brain's ventricles and produces cerebrospinal fluid*

Hypothalamus *controls the endocrine system and regulates body activities, including sleep*

Pituitary gland *regulates other endocrine glands*

Brain stem *relays nerve impulses between the brain and the spinal cord and controls heart rate and breathing*

Midbrain

Pons

Medulla

Thalamus *relays sensory nerve impulses to the cerebral cortex*

Cerebellum *controls muscle movement and balance*

Cerebrospinal fluid *travels around the brain and spinal cord before being reabsorbed into the brain*

Spinal cord *relays messages to and from the brain*

INSIDE THE BRAIN
The brain is divided into three regions – forebrain, brain stem, and cerebellum. The forebrain is mainly the cerebrum, inside of which are the thalamus and hypothalamus. The brain stem, directly beneath it, connects the forebrain to the spinal cord. The cerebellum – which means "little brain" – is tucked under the cerebrum behind the brain stem. The skull, meninges, and cerebrospinal fluid surround and protect the brain.

Sagittal section through the skull, brain, and spinal cord

MAPPING THE BRAIN

ANYONE READING a book that describes the human brain – as this encyclopedia does – is likely to come across a brain "map" (see p. 92). Just as a street map directs a person around a city and its sights, a brain map provides a guide not just to the brain's parts but also their roles, whether it be thinking thoughts, feeling pain, moving a hand, or distinguishing a cat from a caterpillar. The first proof that different regions of the brain have different functions came in the second half of the 19th century, when the pioneers of brain mapping started their investigations. Early clues came from an accident that occurred in the US.

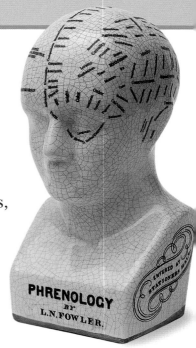

A mapped phrenology head

PHINEAS GAGE
A computerized reconstruction of Phineas Gage's skull, showing how the rod was driven upward through his cheek and eye, and out through the front of his brain.

CHANGED PERSONALITY
Phineas Gage was an American railroad construction worker. In 1848, as Gage used an iron tamping rod to push blasting powder into a hole, a spark set off an explosion that shot the rod up through Gage's left cheek and out through his forehead, taking with it part of the front of his brain. Remarkably, Gage recovered – but once friendly and reliable, he was now an antisocial drifter. Gage's misfortune did reveal, however, that although the front of the brain may not be vital for life, it does control personality. But the story of brain mapping began even earlier with the fanciful ideas of an Austrian doctor.

SPEECH AREA
French physician Pierre Paul Broca was a pioneer of brain mapping who discovered that a small area on the left side of the brain controls the production of speech. This region of the left cerebral cortex was named Broca's area in his honor.

READING THE BUMPS
Franz Josef Gall (1758–1828) claimed that the brain had separate parts that controlled 32 different aspects of personality, such as intelligence, humor, or aggression. Gall suggested that the stronger the characteristic, the bigger the brain part that controlled it, so the more it "pushed" on the skull to form a bump. By feeling, or "reading," a person's skull bumps, Gall believed he could analyse their personality. Given the name phrenology, Gall's nonsensical theory became very popular, and people flocked to have their bumps read.

LOST FOR WORDS
Phrenology met its match in the French doctor Pierre Paul Broca (1824–80). He was interested in which part of the brain controlled speech, and in 1861 examined a patient nicknamed "Tan," because that was the only sound he could utter. When Tan died, six days after the consultation, Broca found that part of his brain's left side was damaged, and concluded that this brain area was responsible for producing speech. Thirteen years later, Austrian doctor Karl Wernicke (1848–1905) was working with a patient who spoke fluently but talked gibberish. Wernicke later

discovered that he also had brain damage on the left side, but farther back. He concluded that this region – called Wernicke's area – dealt with choosing the right words to speak.

INVASIVE TECHNIQUES

Some researchers took a more direct approach. In 1870, when German army surgeon Eduard Hitzig (1838–1907) was treating wounded soldiers whose brains were exposed, he applied electrical currents to different parts of their brains and noted what happened. In the 1950s, Canadian brain surgeon Wilder Penfield (1891–1976) carried out similar, but more sophisticated, experiments. During surgery, when a patient's brain was exposed – but he or she was conscious – Penfield electrically stimulated different parts of the brain and carefully recorded which regions produced sensations, caused movements, or stored memories.

VICTIMS OF WAR
War inevitably produces head wounds, as sustained by these soldiers in World War I. Some wounded soldiers became subjects for researchers who were interested in using their exposed brains to find out which area controlled which action.

Soldiers wounded in the Somme Offensive, 1916

HAND CONTROL
These two MEG scans of the left side of brain show brain–hand control in real time. On the left, milliseconds (msecs) before the person moves their right index finger, neurons in the motor cortex "light up" as they send instructions to the finger-moving muscles. On the right, just 40 msecs later, the sensory cortex "lights up" as it receives a message from the muscles that the finger is moving.

SCANNING THE BRAIN

Today's brain mappers use noninvasive methods to investigate brain function. PET and MRI scans (see pp. 30–31) produce indirect images of activity in living brains by measuring oxygen uptake or blood flow in brain regions that are active. MEG (magnetoencephalography) scans measure brain activity directly and in real time – as it happens – by monitoring the electrical activity of brain cells themselves. What all these techniques have shown is that the brain is made up of interactive, not isolated, units.

BRAIN PROBE
Surgeons use a frame fixed to a patient's head to provide support and guidance for probes that will go into specific parts of the brain through holes drilled in the skull. These probes are used to remove diseased tissue, but have also been used to find out more about brain function.

Cerebral activities

Humans are not alone in having complex brains, but they are the only living things that have some idea about how their brains actually work. This ability – and countless others as well – comes about because our cerebral hemispheres are exceptionally well developed. Together, the two hemispheres give the human brain its amazing ability to process and store information, and they also initiate every deliberate movement that the body makes. These different tasks are carried out by gray matter which forms the surface of the brain (cerebral cortex) and "islands" deep inside it. Each region of gray matter carries out a particular function, and different regions work together to perform complex actions, such as reading and understanding this page. Together, they also generate consciousness – our sense of self-awareness.

Gray matter *is shown as yellow and blue areas*

Right hemisphere

White matter

MRI SCAN OF A VERTICAL SECTION THROUGH THE CEREBRUM

GRAY MATTER
This vertical slice through the brain shows gray matter spread over the surface or cortex of the cerebral hemispheres, with white matter beneath it. Gray matter consists of neuron cell bodies, while white matter consists of axons – the brain's equivalent of "wiring." These axons connect neurons with each other, and they also carry signals to and from other parts of the body.

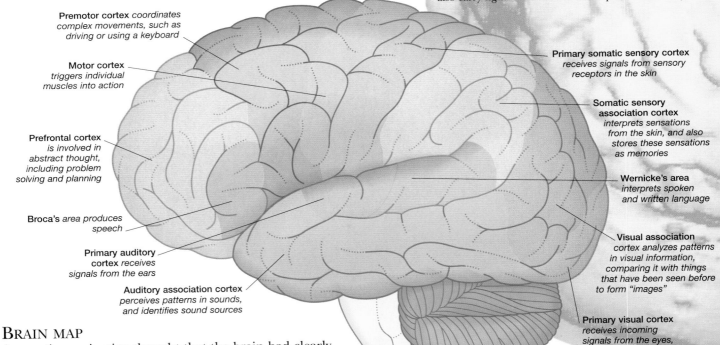

Premotor cortex *coordinates complex movements, such as driving or using a keyboard*

Motor cortex *triggers individual muscles into action*

Prefrontal cortex *is involved in abstract thought, including problem solving and planning*

Broca's *area produces speech*

Primary auditory cortex *receives signals from the ears*

Auditory association cortex *perceives patterns in sounds, and identifies sound sources*

Primary somatic sensory cortex *receives signals from sensory receptors in the skin*

Somatic sensory association cortex *interprets sensations from the skin, and also stores these sensations as memories*

Wernicke's area *interprets spoken and written language*

Visual association *cortex analyzes patterns in visual information, comparing it with things that have been seen before to form "images"*

Primary visual cortex *receives incoming signals from the eyes, and interprets shapes, colors, and movement*

Brain map of the left cerebral hemisphere

BRAIN MAP

At one time, scientists thought that the brain had clearly defined "departments" that dealt with every quirk of human behavior. Although this idea turned out to be wrong, the cerebral cortex does have distinct areas that carry out different tasks. Some parts of the cortex deal with information from the senses, while others trigger movement. A third type – called an association cortex – interprets and analyzes information, and is involved in learning, planning, and memory. More than three-quarters of the human cerebrum is devoted to association, compared with less than a quarter in many other mammals.

Left hemisphere

CT SCAN OF TOP OF BRAIN

LEFT AND RIGHT

The cerebrum is divided into left and right halves, or hemispheres, connected by a "bridge" of nerve fibers called the corpus callosum. The left hemisphere controls the body's right side, and the right hemisphere controls the left side. Usually the left hemisphere is dominant, which is why most people are right-handed. The left hemisphere is in charge of written and spoken language, numbers, and problem solving, among other things, while the right hemisphere deals with appreciation of art and music, and recognizing faces.

REACTION TIMES

In tennis and other fast-moving sports, rapid reactions are essential. For example, a tennis player may have less than half a second in which to judge the most appropriate movement to return a serve. This is not enough time to make a conscious decision about exactly how to move; the player's brain works subconsciously, triggering the right movements before the player becomes aware of having decided what to do.

Thalamus *relays incoming information to the cerebral cortex*

Motor neuron cell body

Motor cortex

Caudate nucleus

Putamen

Basal ganglia *plan, initiate, and monitor complex movement (links to other parts of the brain not shown)*

Globus pallidus

White matter *contains mainly nerve fibres*

Gray matter *contains neuron cell bodies and dendrites*

Cerebellum *coordinates body posture and muscular movements*

Spinal cord

Brain stem *relays messages between spinal cord and brain*

PRECISION MOVEMENT

Even a simple action, such as picking up a small object, involves several different parts of the brain. Movement is triggered by the motor cortex, which sends signals to muscles in the arm. Once it is underway, sensory signals travel back to the motor cortex, via the cerebellum and thalamus, where they modify the movement, making muscles contract by exactly the right amount. This kind of feedback control allows us to pick up delicate things without breaking them.

Skeletal muscles *receive instructions from the cortex and cerebellum and move the hand*

Sensory receptor *in muscle detects tension*

Voluntary movements *are continually corrected by messages from the cerebellum*

Signal sent from:

Motor cortex to muscle

Muscle's sensory receptor to cerebellum

Cerebellum via thalamus to cortex

Cerebellum via spinal cord to muscle

Memory and emotions

DESPITE THE HUGE SIZE of the human population, no two people behave in exactly the same way. One reason for this is that we learn from experience, and another is that emotions affect the way we respond. Memory and emotions both involve the limbic system, as well as other areas of the brain. Emotions are instant responses, but memory works in stages. Things that we experience pass first into the sensory memory, which holds them for a few seconds, and then into the short-term memory, which can store them for minutes or hours. Finally, they enter the long-term memory, which can store information for an entire lifetime. To prevent the brain being overwhelmed by data, only about 1 percent of what we experience actually reaches this final stage.

Limbic system (blue) shown within the cerebral hemispheres

Cingulate gyrus *is the part of the limbic cortex that modifies behavior and emotions*

Thalamus

Fornix *is pathway of nerve fibers links different parts of the limbic system together*

Cerebrum

Olfactory bulb

Amygdala

Hippocampus

Parahippocampal gyrus *is the part of the limbic cortex that modifies emotions such as rage and fright*

Playing the violin depends on learned skills stored in procedural memory

THE LIMBIC SYSTEM

Without the limbic system, life would be more hazardous, and also much less interesting. This part of the brain guards us against everyday hazards, and also controls sexual instincts, pleasure, and pain. The limbic system is deep within the brain, and it consists of a curve of structures that stretch around the brain stem. Among them are the hippocampus, which plays a part in establishing memories, and the amygdala, which triggers an inbuilt fear of danger, such as falling or being attacked. The olfactory bulbs are also part of the limbic system, which is why smells can trigger memories and emotions.

Sensory memory
Retains input from, say, sights or sounds for a few seconds.

Short-term memory
Receives sensory input, and may retain and interpret it.

Consolidation
Transfer from short-term to long-term memory by the hippocampus.

Long-term memory
Provides both memory storage and retrieval, and has three basic forms.

MEMORY

Sensory memory makes a person aware of their surroundings from moment to moment. This input is briefly stored in short-term memory, where thoughts, words, and emotions are analysed. Most short-term memories are quickly lost, but "significant" ones are shunted to the hippocampus. Here, they are replayed repeatedly, over weeks or years, to the cerebral cortex. Each repetition etches the event, experience, or skill ever deeper until it is lodged in long-term memory.

Information forgotten
Most information is stored only briefly, then lost.

Procedural memory
Involves skills learned through practice, such as riding a bicycle.

Semantic memory
Deals with words, language, facts, and their meanings.

Episodic memory
Records specific events and experiences, such as a holiday.

Inner surface of right cerebral hemisphere

CT SCAN OF SECTION THROUGH BRAIN

Hypothalamus

HYPOTHALAMUS

Positioned near the base of the brain, the hypothalamus plays a key part in emotional responses, such as anger or fear. It does this by controlling the autonomic nervous system, and also by releasing hormones into the nearby pituitary gland. Linked to the limbic system (and sometimes described as part of it), the hypothalamus also acts as the body's thermostat, its energy and water manager, and its clock.

Laughter reflects a state of happiness

EMOTIONS

Anger, amusement, sadness, and disappointment are all examples of emotions. These deep-seated feelings – produced by the interaction of the limbic system and the cerebral cortex – help to make us human, and seem to have no direct equivalent in the animal world. Although emotions are mental states, they often express themselves through body language. Crying and laughter are two common examples.

PHOBIAS

Fear is a vital part of everyday life, because it keeps us on guard against potentially dangerous situations. It usually matches the potential threat, which means that we are most fearful of things that can do us the most harm. But some people develop an irrational fear of things that are largely harmless – a condition known as a phobia. Phobias can be triggered by all kinds of objects and situations, from spiders and mice to open spaces and air travel. In severe cases, medical treatment is needed to help sufferers lead a normal life.

Arachnophobia is the fear of spiders

Arms are used to help balance the body

Brain remembers "errors" such as falling over, so they can be improved on next time

Child is ready to progress from standing on two feet to walking

LEARNING

Humans are born with some instincts, but most of our behavior – and all of our knowledge – is learned. In infants, learning takes place by trial and error, which is how a baby discovers how to walk. But as the brain develops, insight and imagination become increasingly important. Learning creates electrical pathways between neurons in the brain. Repetition reinforces these pathways, making information "stick" in the memory.

Consciousness and sleep

EVERY DAY, THE BRAIN switches between two quite different states – being awake and fully conscious, and being asleep. When the brain is awake, it is aware of its surroundings and is able to think in a purposeful way, so that it can meet the demands of daily life. During sleep, its activity is reduced, and its thought patterns are largely disconnected from the outside world. Sleep allows the body to rest, but just as importantly, it gives the brain time to sort and store the information it has accumulated during the day. Consciousness and sleep are both triggered and maintained by neurotransmitters. These chemicals are made and released by the reticular activating system – a regulator located in the brain stem at the base of the brain.

Alpha waves *occur when someone is awake but resting, or in light sleep*

Beta waves *occur when someone is awake and mentally alert*

EEG OF BRAIN WAVE PATTERNS

Delta waves *occur during deep sleep*

BRAIN WAVES

The invention of the electroencephalograph in the 1920s revealed the existence of brain waves – patterns of electrical activity created by the combined output of millions of neurons. Alpha waves are produced when the brain is awake but relaxed, while beta waves occur during times of intense activity. Widely spaced delta waves occur during deep sleep, when the brain is at its least active. The reading produced by the instrument is caused an electroencephalogram (EEG).

Cell bodies of neurons *in RAS produce the neurotransmitter acetylcholine*

Acetylcholine *travels along axons that reach all parts of the cerebral cortex – the folded outer layer of the brain*

Radiating signals

Visual impulses *from the eye stimulate the RAS*

RAS *in the brain stem*

Auditory impulses *from the ear stimulate the RAS*

Nerve impulses *traveling up the spinal cord stimulate the RAS*

Section of the brain showing the reticular activating system (RAS) and its nerve fiber pathways

STAYING ALERT

When a person is awake, their brain deals with a torrent of sensory information from inside and outside the body. To do this, its association neurons have to work with maximum efficiency. This level of activity is triggered by neurons in the reticular activating system (RAS). These reach throughout the cerebral cortex – the "thinking" part of the brain – where they release acetylcholine, a neurotransmitter that aids alertness and concentration. The brain also uses many neurotransmitters. One of them, called serotonin, triggers sleep and affects mood. Another, called dopamine, helps regulate movements. People suffering from Parkinson's disease have low levels of dopamine, causing weakness and muscle tremors.

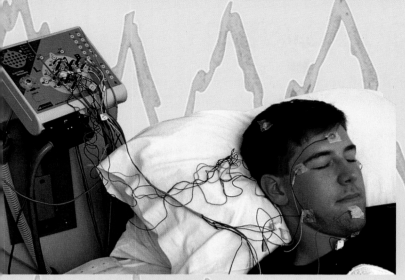

A circadian, or daily, rhythm experiment is conducted on a sleeping patient

SLEEPING

The amount of sleep that people need varies greatly from one person to another. Most adults sleep between seven and eight hours a day even though their bodies need less than half this time, while infants and young children need much more. Scientists do not know exactly why the brain needs sleep, but the most likely explanation is that freedom from external distractions allows it to carry out internal "housekeeping," which makes memory storage more efficient. During sleep, the brain is still partly alert, and an unexpected sound or movement will quickly rouse it.

SLEEP PATTERNS

During a typical night, two kinds of sleep follow each other in succession. In the first type, called NREM (nonrapid eye movement sleep) the sleeper often moves about, but their brain activity drops to a low level. By contrast, in REM (rapid eye movement sleep) the body becomes immobile, but the eyes dart around. Most dreams occur during REM sleep.

DREAMS

Almost everyone dreams – although they may forget their dreams before they wake up – but exactly why we dream is still unknown. One possibility is that dreams are simply the results of nerve cells firing at random; another is that dreams play some part in the brain's memory storage, with old experiences being retrieved, and new ones filed away. Repeated dreams may reveal hidden anxieties, and some psychiatrists believe that they can be used as a window into the human subconscious – an idea proposed by the founder of psychoanalysis, Austrian doctor Sigmund Freud (1856–1939).

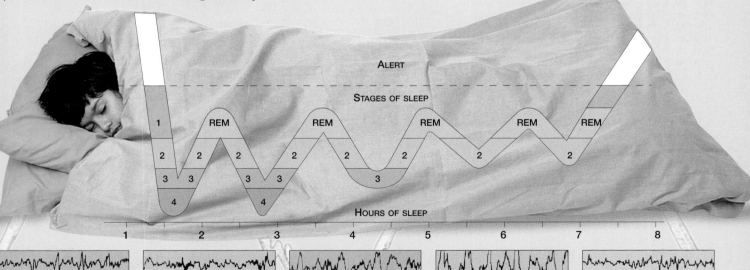

ALERT

STAGES OF SLEEP

| 1 | REM | REM | REM | REM | REM |

HOURS OF SLEEP

1   2   3   4   5   6   7   8

NREM SLEEP: STAGE 1
EEG shows alpha waves. The body is relaxed but the person wakes immediately if disturbed.

NREM SLEEP: STAGE 2
The EEG pattern becomes more irregular. It becomes more difficult to wake the sleeper.

NREM SLEEP: STAGE 3
Delta waves appear in the EEG. Vital signs – breathing, heart rate, and body temperature – decrease.

NREM SLEEP: STAGE 4
In deep sleep, delta waves dominate the EEG. Vital signs are at their lowest. Arousal is difficult.

REM SLEEP
Alpha waves appear. Vital signs increase, while skeletal muscles are inhibited. Dreaming occurs.

Autonomic nervous system

Every day, the nervous system issues streams of instructions that enable the body to deal with the outside world. These are handled by the somatic branch, which is chiefly concerned with body movements. But the nervous system also helps with the body's internal "housekeeping" through its autonomic branch, which works without any conscious control. The autonomic nervous system (ANS) acts mainly on smooth and cardiac muscle – the kinds found in internal organs and the heart, respectively. It has two separate divisions, the sympathetic and parasympathetic, which often have opposite effects. By triggering one or the other in response to changing internal or external conditions, the brain can adjust all kinds of physical factors, from the size of the eyes' pupils, to the speed of digestion. By so doing, the ANS helps maintain homeostasis – stable conditions inside the body.

SYMPATHETIC GANGLION CHAIN
After leaving the spinal cord, nerves of the sympathetic division connect with a chain of ganglia. They then travel onward through the body, sometimes connecting with more ganglia on the way. Ganglia are like junction boxes. They allow nerve signals to be passed on from one neuron to several, so that they reach a wide variety of organs.

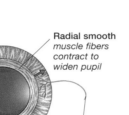

Iris

Circular smooth *muscle fibers contract to narrow pupil*

Pupil

Radial smooth *muscle fibers contract to widen pupil*

Parasympathetic *nerve fiber*

Sympathetic *nerve fiber*

CHANGING PUPIL SIZE
Pupil size is constantly adjusted by the iris under the control of the autonomic nervous system to change the amount of light entering the eyes. Pupil narrowing occurs when the iris's concentrically arranged smooth muscle fibers are stimulated by parasympathetic nerve fibers. Pupil widening occurs when radial smooth muscle fibers – arranged like the spokes of a wheel – are stimulated by sympathetic nerve fibers. This is one of the many autonomic reflexes of which people are usually unaware.

THE SYMPATHETIC DIVISION

This division of the ANS activates a wide range of organs and tissues. It also steps up processes that help the body to cope with stress. For example, it triggers the release of glucose into the blood, and increases the blood's oxygen level by speeding up the heart rate and widening the airways in the lungs. The nerves of this division all emerge from the central section of the spinal cord. Unlike motor nerves that drive skeletal muscles, they have two consecutive sets of neurons. One set runs from the spinal cord to swellings called ganglia, and another set carries signals from these ganglia to their final destination.

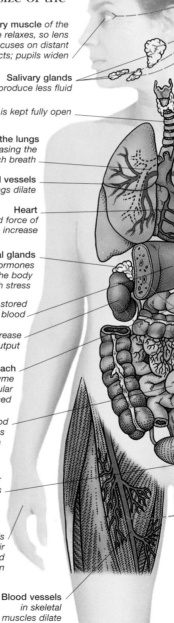

Ciliary muscle *of the eye relaxes, so lens focuses on distant objects; pupils widen*

Salivary glands *produce less fluid*

Trachea *is kept fully open*

Airways in the lungs *dilate, increasing the volume of each breath*

Blood vessels *in the lungs dilate*

Heart *rate and force of contraction increase*

Adrenal glands *produce hormones that prepare the body to deal with stress*

Liver *releases stored glucose into the blood*

Kidneys *decrease urine output*

Stomach *decreases enzyme production, and muscular movements are reduced*

Movement *of food through the intestines slows down*

Bladder *sphincter muscle constricts*

Skin: *blood vessels constrict, hair stands on end, and sweat pores open*

Blood vessels *in skeletal muscles dilate*

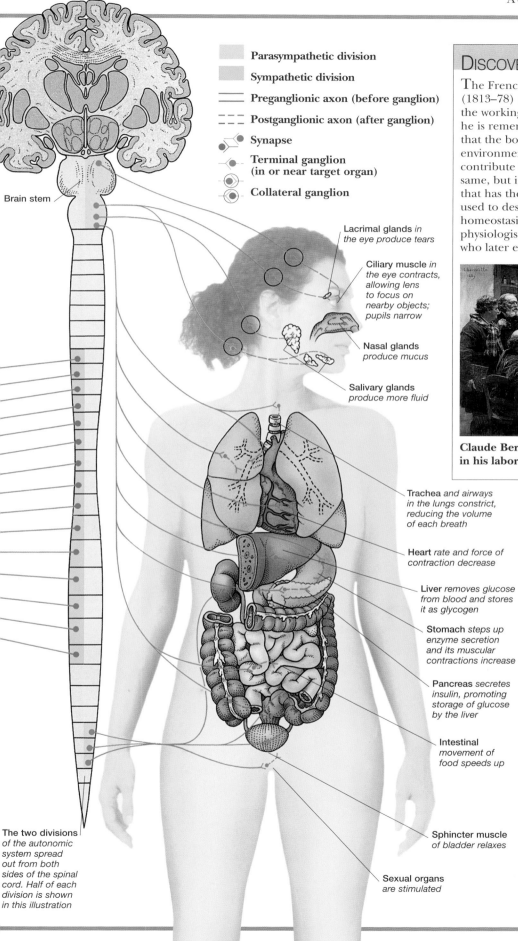

Parasympathetic division

Sympathetic division

Preganglionic axon (before ganglion)

Postganglionic axon (after ganglion)

Synapse

Terminal ganglion
(in or near target organ)

Collateral ganglion

Brain stem

Lacrimal glands *in the eye produce tears*

Ciliary muscle *in the eye contracts, allowing lens to focus on nearby objects; pupils narrow*

Nasal glands *produce mucus*

Salivary glands *produce more fluid*

Trachea *and airways in the lungs constrict, reducing the volume of each breath*

Heart *rate and force of contraction decrease*

Liver *removes glucose from blood and stores it as glycogen*

Stomach *steps up enzyme secretion and its muscular contractions increase*

Pancreas *secretes insulin, promoting storage of glucose by the liver*

Intestinal *movement of food speeds up*

Sphincter muscle *of bladder relaxes*

Sexual organs *are stimulated*

The two divisions *of the autonomic system spread out from both sides of the spinal cord. Half of each division is shown in this illustration*

DISCOVERING HOMEOSTASIS

The French physiologist Claude Bernard (1813–78) made several discoveries about the workings of the human body. However, he is remembered particularly for the idea that the body's cells need a constant internal environment to survive. All body systems contribute to keeping internal conditions the same, but it is the autonomic nervous system that has the most important role. The word used to describe maintaining a stable state – homeostasis – was coined by the American physiologist Walter Cannon (1871–1945), who later expanded the concept.

Claude Bernard performing an experiment in his laboratory at the College de France

THE PARASYMPATHETIC DIVISION

This division of the ANS comes into play when the body needs to conserve its resources, rather than getting them ready for use. It gives priority to digestion, because this supplies the body with raw materials and energy, and it ensures that glucose is stored away in the liver for future use. The parasympathetic division is also involved in the regulation of sexual response – which is reduced when the body is under stress. The nerves of this division originate from the brain stem and base of the spine. Like the sympathetic division, they have two consecutive sets of neurons. In the parasympathetic division, however, the ganglia – called terminal ganglia – are near or inside the target organs.

Communication

HUMANS ARE INTENSELY social beings, and communication plays a central role in the way we live. We communicate not only to show how we feel, but also to pass on information. Today, people often communicate via machines, but the most natural way of expressing ourselves still involves face-to-face contact. When people meet, they communicate in various ways. Facial expressions and body language convey a multitude of signals about a person's mood, but they relate only to the present time. Spoken language is far more powerful. It conveys an unlimited range of ideas, not only about what is actually happening, but also about the past and future. Together with our intelligence, it is one of the features that makes humans unique.

Smiling
This infectious expression is produced mainly by the risorius muscles. A really broad smile also involves the zygomaticus major, which stretches the mouth and lifts its corners up. These muscles – and more – are also used in laughing.

Frontalis *raises the eyebrow and wrinkles the forehead*

Levator labii superioris *raises the upper lip and makes it curl*

Corrugator supercilii *(under orbicularis oculi) pulls the eyebrow down and wrinkles it*

Orbicularis oculi *closes the eye*

Levator anguli oris *turns corner of mouth upward*

Orbicularis oris *purses the lips and shapes them when speaking*

Mentalis *protrudes the lower lip and wrinkles the chin*

Zygomaticos major *pulls the corner of the mouth outward and upward when smiling*

Risorius *pulls the corner of the mouth outward when smiling*

Depressor anguli oris *pulls the corner of the mouth downward*

Depressor labii inferioris *pulls the lower lip downward*

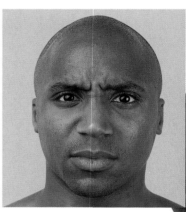

Frowning
Frowning involves the two corrugator supercilii muscles, which contract to pull the eyebrows down, making them wrinkle. Frowning conveys many emotions, from suspicion to deep thought. It also helps to shade the eyes from bright sunshine.

FACIAL EXPRESSIONS

Compared to most other animals, humans have extremely expressive faces. These expressions are produced by a set of more than 30 muscles, which pull small areas of facial skin when they contract. Most of these muscles work as pairs, but with a little practice, some – such as the ones that raise the eyebrows – can be used individually as well. Some facial expressions mean different things in different parts of the world, but many, such as smiling and crying, can be understood by anybody anywhere.

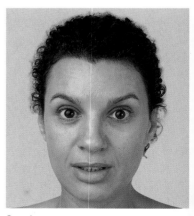

Surprise
When someone shows surprise, the frontalis muscle contracts, raising the eyebrows and making the forehead wrinkle. People use a variant of this expression, called the "eyebrow flash," to acknowledge people they know without stopping to talk.

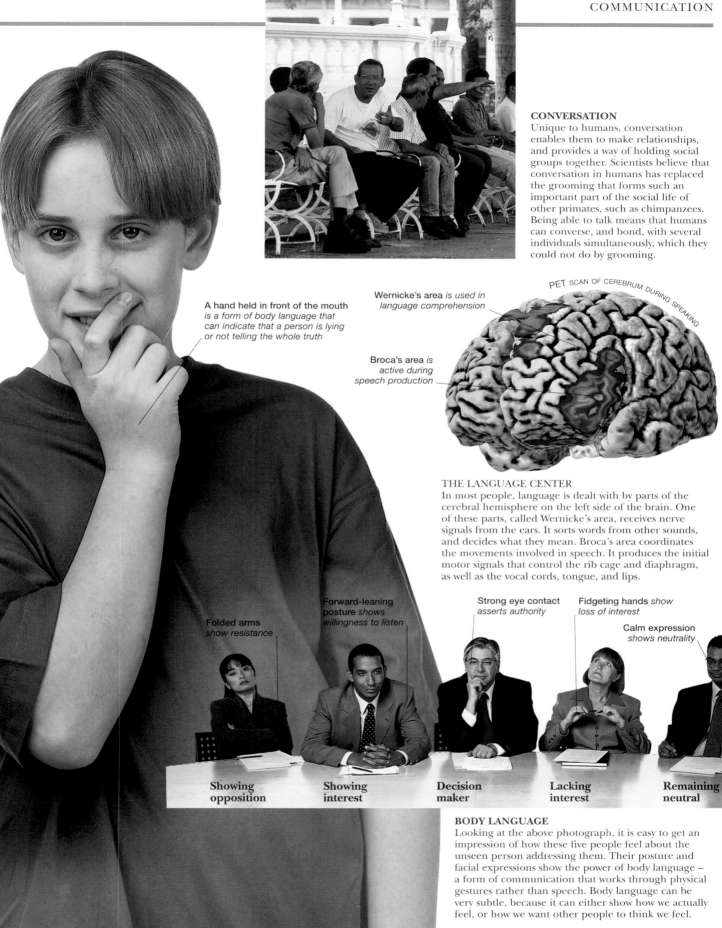

CONVERSATION

Unique to humans, conversation enables them to make relationships, and provides a way of holding social groups together. Scientists believe that conversation in humans has replaced the grooming that forms such an important part of the social life of other primates, such as chimpanzees. Being able to talk means that humans can converse, and bond, with several individuals simultaneously, which they could not do by grooming.

A hand held in front of the mouth is a form of body language that can indicate that a person is lying or not telling the whole truth

PET SCAN OF CEREBRUM DURING SPEAKING

Wernicke's area *is used in language comprehension*

Broca's area *is active during speech production*

THE LANGUAGE CENTER

In most people, language is dealt with by parts of the cerebral hemisphere on the left side of the brain. One of these parts, called Wernicke's area, receives nerve signals from the ears. It sorts words from other sounds, and decides what they mean. Broca's area coordinates the movements involved in speech. It produces the initial motor signals that control the rib cage and diaphragm, as well as the vocal cords, tongue, and lips.

Folded arms *show resistance*

Forward-leaning posture *shows willingness to listen*

Strong eye contact *asserts authority*

Fidgeting hands *show loss of interest*

Calm expression *shows neutrality*

| **Showing opposition** | **Showing interest** | **Decision maker** | **Lacking interest** | **Remaining neutral** |

BODY LANGUAGE

Looking at the above photograph, it is easy to get an impression of how these five people feel about the unseen person addressing them. Their posture and facial expressions show the power of body language – a form of communication that works through physical gestures rather than speech. Body language can be very subtle, because it can either show how we actually feel, or how we want other people to think we feel.

UNDERSTANDING THE MIND

FOR THOUSANDS of years, philosophers and scientists have tried to explain the mind, the intangible "thing" that gives a person his or her unique thoughts, feelings, behavior, and sense of being. Until the 18th century, it was believed that the mind and brain were separate entities, but today it is widely accepted that the mind is a product of brain activity. One way of exploring the mind is through the study of mental illness. In the past, sheer ignorance made people react to mental illness in others with fear and hostility. But in the 19th century, a more scientific approach was taken to understanding the mind's problems.

RELEASING SPIRITS
This skull from around 2000 BC shows clearly the holes made by trepanning. This ancient practice of drilling, or cutting, holes in the skull was believed to "cure" mental illnesses, or milder conditions such as migraines, by releasing "evil spirits" from the head.

EVIL SPIRITS
What makes disorders of the mind different from other diseases is that they affect how a person behaves. Ancient peoples believed mental illness was the result of someone being "possessed" by evil spirits. Treatment, if any, came in the

PINEL THE REFORMER
The reformer Philippe Pinel (center left, with cane) is celebrated in heroic style as he orders the removal of chains from mental patients at the Bicêtre Asylum, Paris, in 1795.

form of magical amulets or charms, or, more drastically, by drilling holes into the head so those spirits could escape.

VIEWS OF MENTAL ILLNESS
In the Middle Ages, the Church saw mental illness as a sign of the devil at work, a belief that led to the persecution of people as witches. Doctors, however, viewed it as an imbalance in the four humors, the fluids that were believed to make up the body.

Most mentally-ill people were treated as less than human, with many languishing locked up in madhouses. But by the end of the 18th century, reformers were suggesting a more humane approach. French doctor Philippe Pinel controversially insisted that his patients be released from their chains and allowed to receive medical attention. The work of Pinel helped establish the field of psychiatry, the branch of medicine that deals with mental illness.

SCIENCE IN MIND

In the 19th century, large mental hospitals were established that enabled doctors to observe patients and catalog a wide range of disorders. The work of Broca and Wernicke (see pp. 90–1) proved that abnormal brain structure could alter behavior, indicating that the mind really was part of the brain. In Paris, physician Jean-Martin Charcot (1825–93) drew together all that had been learned about mental illness and the brain to create a scientific approach to understanding the mind.

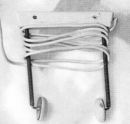

SHOCK TREATMENT
An electroconvulsive therapy (ECT) machine from 1950 is attached to a headset complete with paired electrodes. These padded electrodes were placed on the side of the head in order to deliver an electrical pulse – or shock – to the brain.

PRESSURE ON THE BRAIN
This MRI scan of a vertical section through the brain (orange) shows an abnormal growth, or tumor (blue), in the right hemisphere. Tumors like these may cause changes in behavior and sensation, but can, in some cases, be removed by surgery.

PROBING THE UNCONSCIOUS

In 1885, an Austrian doctor called Sigmund Freud visited Charcot in Paris. On returning to Vienna, Freud evolved a method by which some patients could discuss their problems by free association – talking openly about their feelings and emotions to a person, called the analyst. Freud believed that problems were caused by subconscious fears, worries, and conflicts, often developed in childhood. His technique, called psychoanalysis, raises problems to a conscious level – by talking about them – so that the patient, with the help of the analyst, can deal with them.

THE MODERN APPROACH

But by the middle of the 20th century, there were still few treatments for mental illnesses, because there was little idea of their causes. Electroconvulsive therapy (ECT), for example, was used to treat severe depression, but its mode of action was unknown. But since then there have been considerable advances. Drugs have been developed that treat specific mental illnesses. Research has shown that in many cases these drugs work because they correct imbalances of neurotransmitters (see pp. 80–1) in the brain. Modern scanning techniques, such as MRI and PET scans, enable doctors and researchers to look for abnormal brain structures and to watch brain activity in action. Psychotherapy allows people to talk through and address their problems.

FOUNDER OF ANALYSIS
Austrian doctor Sigmund Freud (1856–1939), seen here at his desk, developed the earliest form of psychotherapy – psychoanalysis – to treat mental health problems. Freud left Austria when the Nazis took over in 1938 and moved to London.

PSYCHOTHERAPY
A person with a mental or emotional problem seeks help from a psychotherapist. The person is encouraged to talk about their symptoms and problems, while the therapist is trained to listen to and evaluate what has been said, and help the person to understand themselves more.

Touch

OF ALL THE SENSES, touch is the most direct because it tells us about the state of our own bodies. It allows us to perceive an amazing range of physical sensations, from the pain of a sudden blow to the movement of individual hairs when they are ruffled by the breeze. It is also responsible for registering heat and cold, and for some of the sensory signals that tell us about our posture – in other words, how our bodies are arranged. Unlike the special senses – such as hearing and vision – touch is a general sense, meaning that it works through receptors that are scattered all over the body. There are several kinds of receptors, and each one responds to a different type of stimulus, contributing to the sense of touch as a whole.

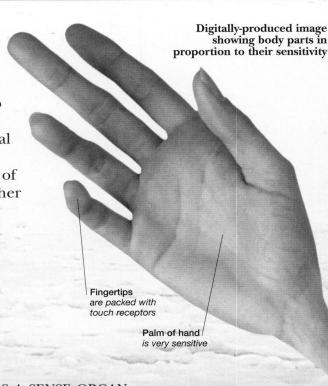

Digitally-produced image showing body parts in proportion to their sensitivity

Fingertips *are packed with touch receptors*

Palm of hand *is very sensitive*

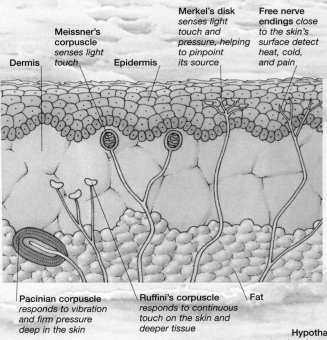

Meissner's corpuscle *senses light touch*

Dermis

Epidermis

Merkel's disk *senses light touch and pressure, helping to pinpoint its source*

Free nerve endings *close to the skin's surface detect heat, cold, and pain*

Pacinian corpuscle *responds to vibration and firm pressure deep in the skin*

Ruffini's corpuscle *responds to continuous touch on the skin and deeper tissue*

Fat

SKIN AS A SENSE ORGAN

The skin contains more sensory receptors than any other organ in the body. Most of them are mechanoreceptors that trigger nerve impulses when they are physically pulled or pressed. The structure and position of these receptors affect what they detect. Merkel's disks, for example, are small and close to the surface of the skin – the ideal combination for detecting light touch and pinpointing its exact source. Pacinian corpuscles, on the other hand, are larger and deeper, and respond to firmer pressure and to being stretched. The skin also contains free nerve endings that detect the movement of hairs, physical contact, and pain, as well as heat and cold.

TEMPERATURE DETECTORS

To keep its own temperature steady, the body needs to monitor temperature changes around it. It does this with the help of nerve endings in the skin. These respond to cold or heat, and they send signals to the body's temperature control center in the hypothalamus located in the brain (see p. 122). Skin temperature sensors are best at detecting rapid changes – such as a plunge into icy water taken by the man in the picture on the right. Once the change has taken place, the sensors soon adapt to it.

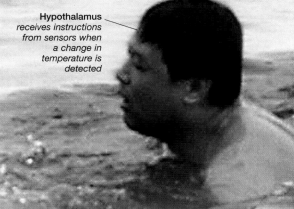

Hypothalamus *receives instructions from sensors when a change in temperature is detected*

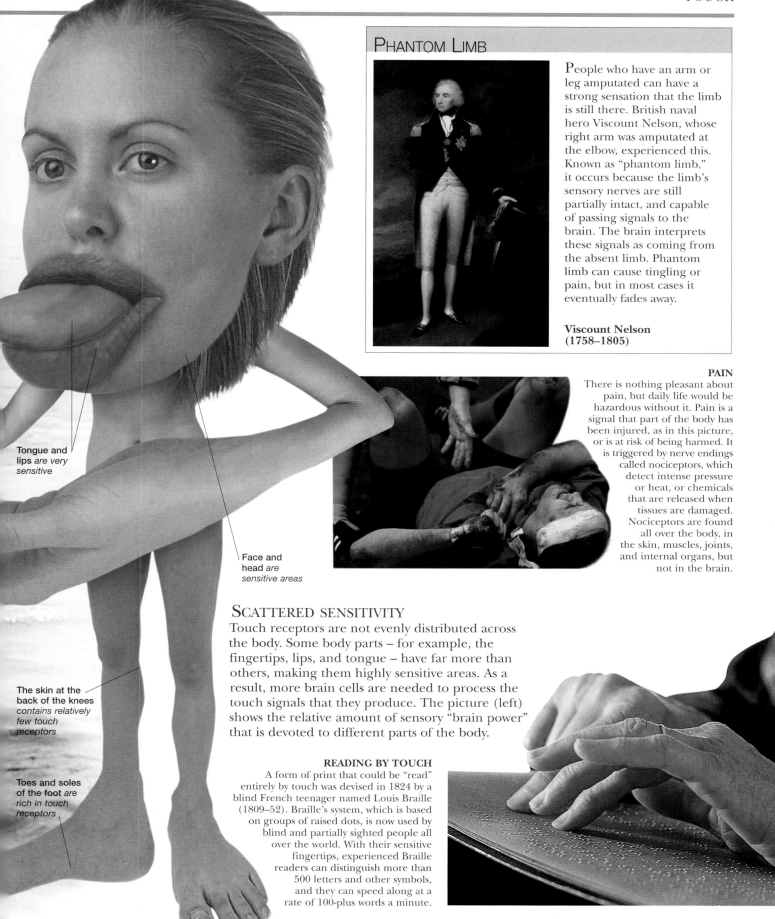

PHANTOM LIMB

People who have an arm or leg amputated can have a strong sensation that the limb is still there. British naval hero Viscount Nelson, whose right arm was amputated at the elbow, experienced this. Known as "phantom limb," it occurs because the limb's sensory nerves are still partially intact, and capable of passing signals to the brain. The brain interprets these signals as coming from the absent limb. Phantom limb can cause tingling or pain, but in most cases it eventually fades away.

Viscount Nelson (1758–1805)

Tongue and lips *are very sensitive*

Face and head *are sensitive areas*

The skin at the back of the knees *contains relatively few touch receptors*

Toes and soles of the foot *are rich in touch receptors*

PAIN
There is nothing pleasant about pain, but daily life would be hazardous without it. Pain is a signal that part of the body has been injured, as in this picture, or is at risk of being harmed. It is triggered by nerve endings called nociceptors, which detect intense pressure or heat, or chemicals that are released when tissues are damaged. Nociceptors are found all over the body, in the skin, muscles, joints, and internal organs, but not in the brain.

SCATTERED SENSITIVITY
Touch receptors are not evenly distributed across the body. Some body parts – for example, the fingertips, lips, and tongue – have far more than others, making them highly sensitive areas. As a result, more brain cells are needed to process the touch signals that they produce. The picture (left) shows the relative amount of sensory "brain power" that is devoted to different parts of the body.

READING BY TOUCH
A form of print that could be "read" entirely by touch was devised in 1824 by a blind French teenager named Louis Braille (1809–52). Braille's system, which is based on groups of raised dots, is now used by blind and partially sighted people all over the world. With their sensitive fingertips, experienced Braille readers can distinguish more than 500 letters and other symbols, and they can speed along at a rate of 100-plus words a minute.

Smell and taste

Compared with the other special senses, taste and smell are close partners and work in similar ways. Both are chemical senses: taste detects substances that are dissolved in saliva, while smell detects those present in the air. To do this, they use chemoreceptors, which are specialized cells that respond to specific molecules. Together, these two senses allow us to identify things that are good to eat or drink, but they also warn us about things that might be dangerous. The ability to taste and smell varies a great deal from person to person. This explains why some people make good wine tasters or perfumiers, while others have trouble perceiving some flavors or odors at all.

CHEMICAL DETECTORS

Taste receptors are found on the tongue, while smell receptors are located in the roof of the nasal cavity. Both are triggered by contact with chemicals, but their sensitivity is quite different. Taste receptors can detect only four overall tastes – sweet, salty, sour, and bitter – but smell receptors can distinguish between more than 10,000 different odors. Smell receptors are also much better at detecting faint chemical traces. They can pick up some particularly smelly substances in concentrations of just a few parts per billion, which is why a skunk's scent can be smelled some distance away.

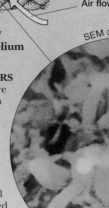

Olfactory bulb
carries nerve impulses to brain from smell receptors

Olfactory epithelium
contains smell sensors

Odor molecules
breathed in with air through nostrils

Taste sensors
located on surface of tongue

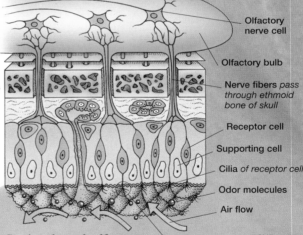

Olfactory nerve cell

Olfactory bulb

Nerve fibers *pass through ethmoid bone of skull*

Receptor cell

Supporting cell

Cilia *of receptor cell*

Odor molecules

Air flow

Section through olfactory bulb and olfactory epithelium

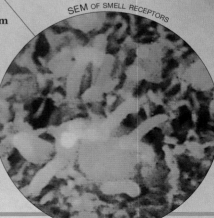

SEM OF SMELL RECEPTORS

SMELL RECEPTORS
Located deep inside the nasal cavity are smell receptors, or olfactory cells, in a thumbnail-sized patch of tissue called the olfactory epithelium. One end of each receptor connects with the olfactory bulb, which is an extension of the brain. The other ends in a cluster of cilia, which look like microscopic hairs. These hairs project into the mucous film lining the nasal cavity, where they respond to dissolved molecules from the incoming air.

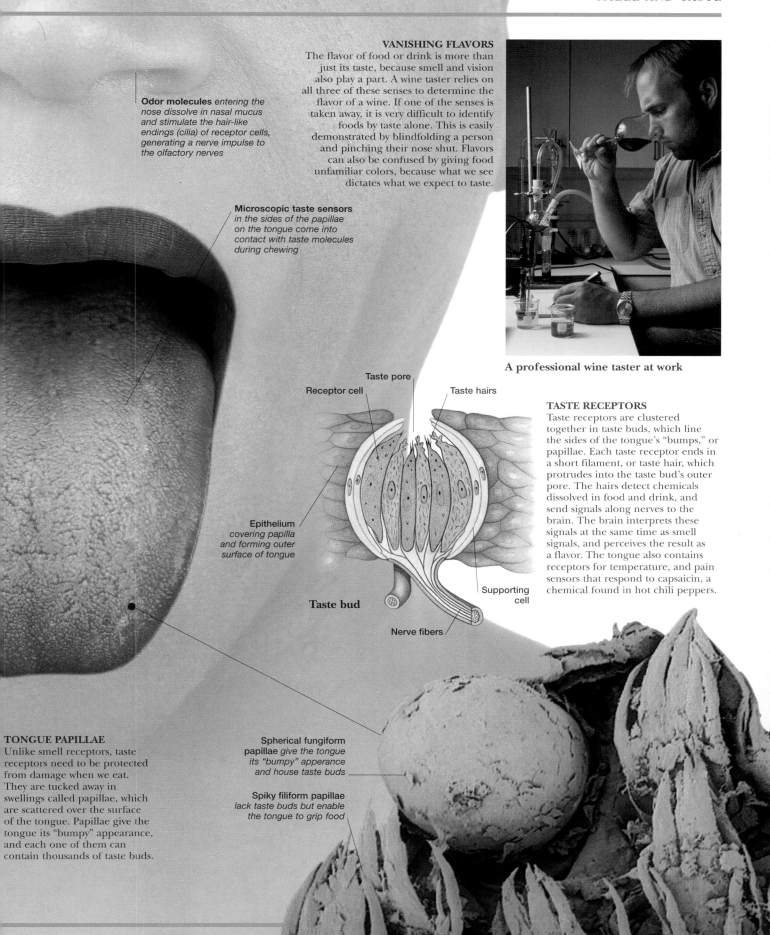

Odor molecules *entering the nose dissolve in nasal mucus and stimulate the hair-like endings (cilia) of receptor cells, generating a nerve impulse to the olfactory nerves*

VANISHING FLAVORS
The flavor of food or drink is more than just its taste, because smell and vision also play a part. A wine taster relies on all three of these senses to determine the flavor of a wine. If one of the senses is taken away, it is very difficult to identify foods by taste alone. This is easily demonstrated by blindfolding a person and pinching their nose shut. Flavors can also be confused by giving food unfamiliar colors, because what we see dictates what we expect to taste.

A professional wine taster at work

Microscopic taste sensors *in the sides of the papillae on the tongue come into contact with taste molecules during chewing*

Taste pore

Receptor cell

Taste hairs

TASTE RECEPTORS
Taste receptors are clustered together in taste buds, which line the sides of the tongue's "bumps," or papillae. Each taste receptor ends in a short filament, or taste hair, which protrudes into the taste bud's outer pore. The hairs detect chemicals dissolved in food and drink, and send signals along nerves to the brain. The brain interprets these signals at the same time as smell signals, and perceives the result as a flavor. The tongue also contains receptors for temperature, and pain sensors that respond to capsaicin, a chemical found in hot chili peppers.

Epithelium *covering papilla and forming outer surface of tongue*

Supporting cell

Taste bud

Nerve fibers

TONGUE PAPILLAE
Unlike smell receptors, taste receptors need to be protected from damage when we eat. They are tucked away in swellings called papillae, which are scattered over the surface of the tongue. Papillae give the tongue its "bumpy" appearance, and each one of them can contain thousands of taste buds.

Spherical fungiform **papillae** *give the tongue its "bumpy" apperance and house taste buds*

Spiky filiform **papillae** *lack taste buds but enable the tongue to grip food*

Hearing

WHENEVER ANYTHING MOVES or vibrates, it creates waves of pressure that travel through the air. Hearing is the sense that detects these waves and turns them into the sensation of sound. It is one of the most versatile of the human senses, because it alerts us to things that are nearby or far away, and it often allows us to pinpoint their direction, even if they cannot be seen. It also enables us to communicate, through music as well as the spoken word. Sound waves are gathered by the outer ear, but sound detection takes place deep within the skull. Here, the waves are channeled into one of the body's most sophisticated sense organs – the organ of Corti in the inner ear.

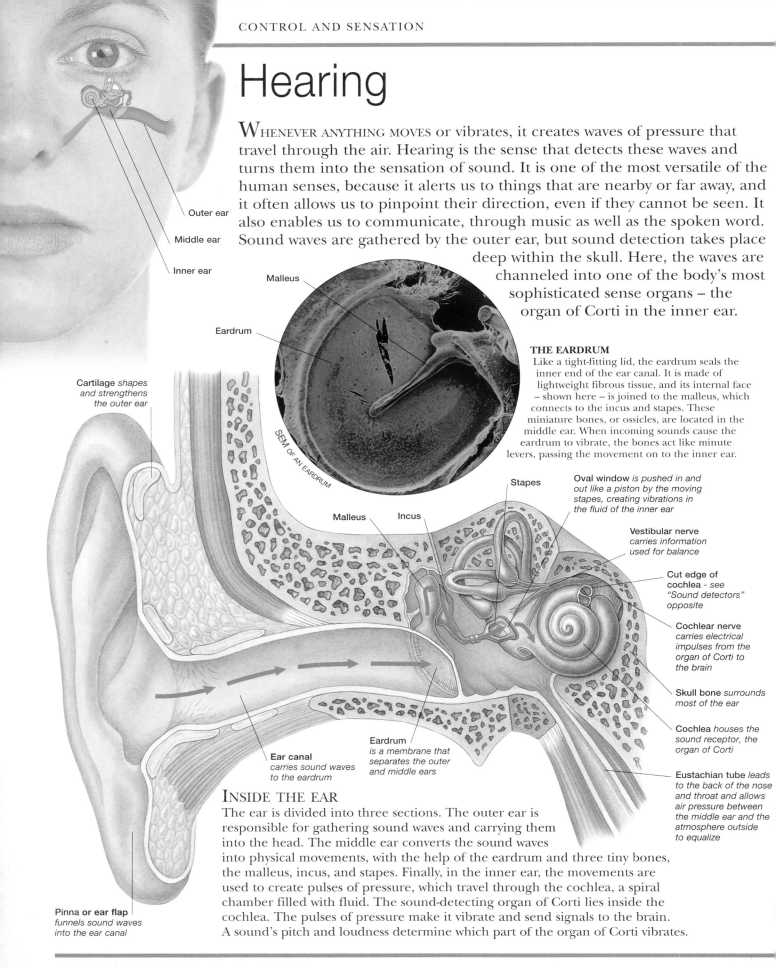

Outer ear

Middle ear

Inner ear

Malleus

Eardrum

SEM OF AN EARDRUM

THE EARDRUM
Like a tight-fitting lid, the eardrum seals the inner end of the ear canal. It is made of lightweight fibrous tissue, and its internal face – shown here – is joined to the malleus, which connects to the incus and stapes. These miniature bones, or ossicles, are located in the middle ear. When incoming sounds cause the eardrum to vibrate, the bones act like minute levers, passing the movement on to the inner ear.

Cartilage *shapes and strengthens the outer ear*

Stapes

Malleus

Incus

Oval window *is pushed in and out like a piston by the moving stapes, creating vibrations in the fluid of the inner ear*

Vestibular nerve *carries information used for balance*

Cut edge of cochlea - *see "Sound detectors" opposite*

Cochlear nerve *carries electrical impulses from the organ of Corti to the brain*

Skull bone *surrounds most of the ear*

Cochlea *houses the sound receptor, the organ of Corti*

Eustachian tube *leads to the back of the nose and throat and allows air pressure between the middle ear and the atmosphere outside to equalize*

Ear canal *carries sound waves to the eardrum*

Eardrum *is a membrane that separates the outer and middle ears*

Pinna or ear flap *funnels sound waves into the ear canal*

INSIDE THE EAR

The ear is divided into three sections. The outer ear is responsible for gathering sound waves and carrying them into the head. The middle ear converts the sound waves into physical movements, with the help of the eardrum and three tiny bones, the malleus, incus, and stapes. Finally, in the inner ear, the movements are used to create pulses of pressure, which travel through the cochlea, a spiral chamber filled with fluid. The sound-detecting organ of Corti lies inside the cochlea. The pulses of pressure make it vibrate and send signals to the brain. A sound's pitch and loudness determine which part of the organ of Corti vibrates.

SOUND DETECTORS

This enlarged view of the cutaway cochlea (below) shows three parallel ducts separated by two membranes. The organ of Corti consists of hair cells – supported by the basilar membrane – the "hairs" of which are embedded in the rooflike tectorial membrane. Incoming sounds create pressure pulses in the cochlear fluid that make the basilar membrane move up and down. This squashes the "hairs" against the tectorial membrane, making the hair cells generate nerve impulses which are relayed to the brain and interpreted as sounds.

Vestibular duct

Vestibular membrane

Cochlear duct

Organ of Corti

Basilar membrane
supports the hair cells

Tympanic duct

Tectorial membrane

Cochlear nerve

TACKLING HEARING LOSS

Deafness is a common effect of aging, but it can strike younger people too. Sometimes it is caused by problems with the sound-conducting parts of the ear, but it can also be caused by disorders that affect hair cells or nerves. This kind of deafness can be treated by a cochlear implant – an electronic device (above) that turns sounds directly into electrical signals that are sent to the brain.

HEARING RANGE

A sound's pitch depends on its frequency, which is how fast it makes the air vibrate. Frequency is measured in cycles per second, or hertz (Hz), or in kilohertz(kHz), where 1 kHz = 1,000 Hz. Few people can hear sounds that have frequencies below 20Hz, but the upper limit depends on age. Children's ears are good at hearing high frequencies, but as people grow older, their upper limit gradually declines. As the chart below shows, many animals are able to hear sounds that are so high pitched that we cannot detect them at all.

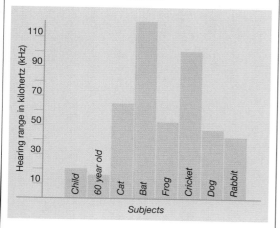

SEM OF HAIR CELLS

"Hairs" of hair cells
arranged in a "V" shape

HAIR CELLS

This SEM shows the three rows of outer hair cells (red) that, with a single row of inner hair cells, form the organ of Corti. Nerve fibers leaving the bases of these hair cells join together to form the cochlear nerve. The V-shaped tuft of "hairs" sprouting from each hair cell is enmeshed in the tectorial membrane. Nerve fibers leaving the bases of these hair cells join together to form the cochlear nerve.

SOUNDS DANGEROUS

The human ear can differentiate between more than a billion-fold difference in volume, from the whine of a mosquito, which measures about 10 decibels, to the roar of a passenger jet, which measures 130 decibels or more. It has built-in safeguards against very loud sounds, including the body's smallest muscle, called the stapedius, which prevents the ear ossicles from being shaken too much. However, persistent exposure to loud noise can damage hearing unless ear protection is worn.

Minor using drill wears ear protectors

Hearing range in kilohertz (kHz)

110
90
70
50
30
10

Child
60 year old
Cat
Bat
Frog
Cricket
Dog
Rabbit

Subjects

Balance

OFTEN UNNOTICED until it lets people down, balance not only keeps us upright, but also informs us whether or not we are on the move. With practice, it enables people to carry out some remarkable feats of coordination, from surfing and snowboarding to walking tightropes high above the ground. Compared to some senses, balance is easily disturbed. Its main input comes from sensors deep in the inner ear. This information, however, is only part of staying balanced, because the brain draws on information from vision and touch as well. Vertigo – the dizzy feeling tha can happen when the body is moving quickly, or sometimes even when it is perfectly still – is one of the most common symptoms of disturbed balance.

Utricle and saccule

Semi-circular canals

Cochlea

Fluid-filled duct

Semi-circular canals

Ampulla

Vestibular nerve

Macula of saccule

Cupula

Utricle

Macula of utricle

Hair cells

Gelatinous mass

Nerve fibers

Sacule

INNER EAR ORGANS

The inner ear contains two sets of fluid-filled organs that produce the sense of balance. The first consists of two chambers – the utricle and saccule – which contain hair cells that detect both acceleration and the downward pull of gravity. The second consists of three semicircular canals, arranged at right angles to each other. Their hair cells detect rotation of the head in any direction. Together, the organs of balance make up the vestibular system.

DETECTING POSITION AND MOVEMENT

The brain is constantly updated on the body's position and movement by balance organs located in the inner ear. They send nerve signals to the brain along the vestibular nerve. The two types of balance organs have distinct roles. The utricle and saccule detect the position of the head when not moving. They also detect linear (straight-line) acceleration, such as when an elavator moves or a car speeds up. The archlike semicircular canals pick up rotational movement, such as when a dancer performs a pirouette or when the head is thrown in all directions during a rough boat ride.

POSITION

Information about position is supplied by the utricle and saccule, the two chambers in the inner ear. These contain the macula, a gelatinous membrane consisting of sensitive hair cells projecting into a layer of jelly containing mineral crystals. If the head tilts, the weight of the crystals makes the jelly slide, and this triggers the hair cells to send signals to the brain. Other movements have a similar effect.

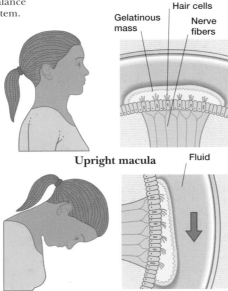

Upright macula

Fluid

Displaced macula

MOVEMENT

The three semicircular canals work together to detect rotation of the head. Each one contains a chamber, called an ampulla, which is almost filled by the cupula – a jellylike cap that sits over a set of hair cells. If the head turns, the cupula bends as fluid flows past it, stimulating the hair cells. Because the semicircular canals are in three different planes, they can detect rotation in any direction.

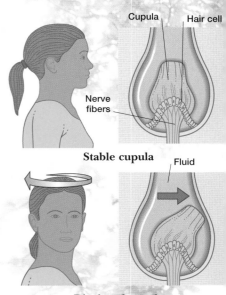

Cupula

Hair cell

Nerve fibers

Stable cupula

Fluid

Displaced cupula

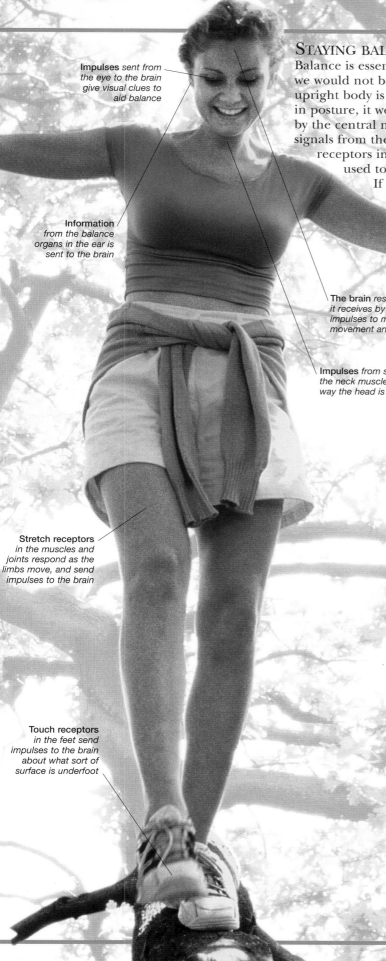

Impulses *sent from the eye to the brain give visual clues to aid balance*

Information *from the balance organs in the ear is sent to the brain*

Stretch receptors *in the muscles and joints respond as the limbs move, and send impulses to the brain*

Touch receptors *in the feet send impulses to the brain about what sort of surface is underfoot*

STAYING BALANCED

Balance is essential for activities such as climbing, and without it we would not be able to stand upright at all. This is because an upright body is naturally unstable – without constant adjustments in posture, it would soon fall down. These adjustments are made by the central nervous system, which receives a constant stream of signals from the organs of the inner ear, as well as from stretch receptors in muscles, and from the eyes. These signals are used to regulate the tension, or tone, of skeletal muscles. If the body starts to tip even slightly, groups of muscles tighten up to bring it back into line.

The brain *responds to the information it receives by sending out motor impulses to muscles to control movement and thus help balance*

Impulses *from stretch receptors in the neck muscles indicate which way the head is turned*

MOTION SICKNESS
Sudden movements often make people dizzy, but motion sickness is a longer-lasting and much more unpleasant experience. It usually happens when the brain receives conflicting information from the organs of balance and from the eyes. For example, inside a ship on a stormy sea, there are few visual clues that the ship is moving up and down. However, the organs of balance detect these movements, and send signals to the brain. The result is seasickness—a condition that some people still suffer from even after years afloat. Cars and planes can also cause motion sickness, but even watching movement at the movies may be enough to trigger it.

The eye

Vision is the foremost of the special senses, and the one that dominates our impressions of the outside world. We use it every moment we are awake, and we dream with visual images when we sleep. Visual expressions crop up almost every time we speak, and when we think of ourselves or other people, it is almost always in a visual way. The organ responsible for triggering this imagery – the eye – is one of the most complex in the body. Set in a protective socket inside the skull, it is always on the move and is quick to adapt to changing light conditions. It automatically focuses on anything that comes into view, collecting light and converting it into a stream of billions of nervous impulses. Once they have arrived in the brain, these signals have to be analyzed – an awesomely complex process that makes sense of what we see.

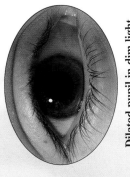

Dilated pupil in dim light

Contracted pupil in bright light

PUPIL SIZE
Human eyes have to cope with a huge range of light intensity. In bright conditions, muscles in the iris contract, narrowing the pupil and cutting down the amount of light entering the eye. If it is dim, the reverse happens. This reflex action takes about a one-fifth of a second. Pupils also narrow when the eyes look at something very close, because this increases the eye's depth of field.

Tears move down and across the eye, carrying debris with them

The tear gland is under the outer edge of the eyebrow and produces tears

Tear ducts empty tears onto the surface of the eye

Pupil is the hole that lets light into the eye

Eyebrows direct sweat away from the eye and help keep out some light

Eyelashes stop too much light from entering the eye, as well as protecting it from foreign particles

Eyelids protect the eye from bright light and foreign objects; when we blink, they wipe the eyes and keep them clear of dust

Iris color is determined by the amount of melanin present – brown eyes have the most melanin and blue eyes the least

EYE PROTECTION
Only about one-sixth of each eyeball – the iris and pupil – can be seen from the outside. The rest lies inside the eye socket, or orbit, where it is cushioned by pads of fat. Most features surrounding the eye have a protective function – the eyebrows, eyelashes, and eyelids all help shield the eye from excessive light and dust. The front of the eye is kept moist by tears, which wash away specks of dust and help prevent infection. Tears are washed across the eye by blinking – a reflex action that also helps to protect the eye if anything heads its way.

Tears drain away through two tear openings in the corner of the eye

Nasolacrimal duct drains tears into the nasal cavity

Opening into nasal cavity

Nostril

SEM OF THE INNER SURFACE OF THE IRIS

Ciliary processes form part of the ciliary body whose muscles alter the shape of the lens during focusing

Iris surface folds mark the position of circular and radial muscle fibers that contract to alter pupil size

Suspensory fibers run from the ciliary processes to the lens (not shown, to the left of the SEM)

INSIDE VIEW

This SEM shows an inside view of the eyeball, looking forward from behind the iris (purple). Visible here are the inner surface of the iris and the ciliary processes (red) that lie behind the iris and surround its base. These folded processes are the point of attachment of the suspensory fibers (yellow and green) that hold the lens in place. They also secrete the fluid that fills the front section of the eyeball.

KEEPING ON THE MOVE

Eyes move smoothly when they follow a moving object, but they jump rapidly when they are looking at different parts of a scene, words on a page, or a face. These abrupt jumps – represented in the photograph on the left by green lines – are called saccades. Eyes also make much smaller movements called tremors. Tremors are essential to vision. If they are stopped – for example, by an anesthetic – signals from the eye fade away.

IRIS IDENTIFICATION

People often share the same eye color, but the precise pattern of pigment in their irises is as personal as a fingerprint. Security systems have been developed to recognize iris patterns, so that people can come and go without keys or special codes. Some people believe that a wide range of disorders can be diagnosed by examining the iris, but this procedure – called iridology – is not recognized by most doctors.

Computer image of an iris being scanned

Ciliary body controls the thickness of the lens so it focuses correctly

Suspensory ligament fibers attach the lens to the ciliary body

Lens changes shape to focus light from both near and far objects

Lateral rectus pulls the eyeball so that it looks out toward the side

Inferior oblique makes the eye look upward and outward

Inferior rectus makes the eye look downward and inward

Fat cells cushion eyeball inside bony eye socket

Superior oblique swivels the eye so that it looks downward and outward

Superior rectus makes the eyeball look upward

Medial rectus pulls the eyeball in, so that it looks toward the nose

Optic nerve

Side view of right eye

EYE MOVEMENT

The eyeball is moved by six small, strap-shaped muscles. Five of them are anchored to the back of the eye socket, although one of them – called the superior oblique – initially runs forward, before doubling back through a "pulley" made of cartilage. The sixth, called the inferior oblique muscle, is anchored to the point nearest the nose. Compared to other voluntary muscles, all six can make extremely precise movements, allowing the eye to track objects on the move.

Eye structure

ALTHOUGH IT IS one of the most familiar parts of the body, most of the eye is hidden away. In an adult, it measures about 1 in (2.5 cm) across, and contains about 125 million photoreceptors, or light-sensing cells. These are spread out in an ultrathin screen called the retina, and light is focused onto them by a lens. Unlike a camera lens, the eye's lens is flexible, and it focuses by changing shape. These changes, which are controlled by a ring of muscle fibers, take place automatically, within a split second of anything coming into view. If the eye is in good working order, the result is a sharp image on the retina – exactly what the photoreceptors need to send precise information to the brain.

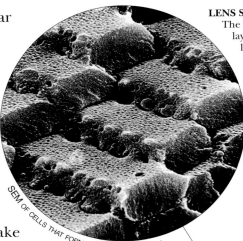

SEM OF CELLS THAT FORM THE LENS OF THE EYE

LENS STRUCTURE
The lens is layered like an onion, with each layer consisting of six-sided fibers, or cells, locked together like puzzle pieces. Lens fibers contain proteins called crystallins that give them their transparency, essential for letting light through, and elasticity, needed for focusing on both near and far objects. Since blood vessels would interfere with transparency, the lens has none.

Conjuctiva *is a moist layer over the cornea*

Iris *is the colored part of the eye that adjusts the amount of light entering the eye by changing the pupil's diameter*

Pupil

Aqueous humor is *a clear fluid between the lens and the cornea that keeps the cornea curved outward*

Vertical cross-section through the eye

Object
reflects light in all directions

Light ray

Cornea *partly focuses light rays*

Lens – *made of layers of crystal-clear proteins, it changes shape to focus incoming light*

Ciliary muscles *form a ring of muscle that focuses light by changing the shape of the lens*

OPHTHALMOSCOPE

As a mathematician and physicist, Hermann von Helmholtz (1821–94) made several important discoveries, including the fact that energy cannot be created or destroyed. He also made notable breakthroughs in physiology – the study of how the body works. On a practical level, one of his most important inventions was the ophthalmoscope, an instrument that shines light into the eye, allowing doctors and opticians to directly examine the retina. Disorders of the retina are often warning signs of problems elsewhere in the body.

INSIDE THE EYE
The eyeball is divided into two unequal cavities, on either side of the lens. The rear cavity, which makes up most of the eye, is filled with a transparent, jellylike substance called the vitreous humor ("humor" is an old word for a body fluid). The front cavity is filled with the aqueous humor, which is more watery. Both the humors are under slight pressure, and they keep the eye in shape. The front chamber is covered by a clear, domed layer called the cornea, while the rest of the eye is jacketed by the sclera, which is slippery and white. The retina lies in the rear half of the eye, and is directly connected to the optic nerve.

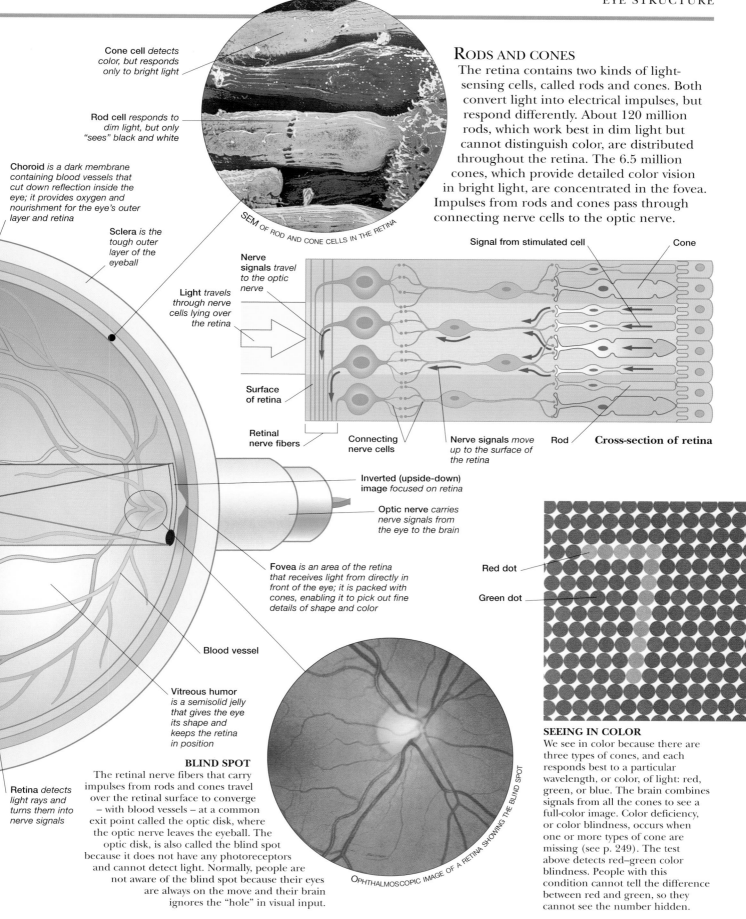

Cone cell *detects color, but responds only to bright light*

Rod cell *responds to dim light, but only "sees" black and white*

Choroid *is a dark membrane containing blood vessels that cut down reflection inside the eye; it provides oxygen and nourishment for the eye's outer layer and retina*

Sclera *is the tough outer layer of the eyeball*

SEM OF ROD AND CONE CELLS IN THE RETINA

RODS AND CONES

The retina contains two kinds of light-sensing cells, called rods and cones. Both convert light into electrical impulses, but respond differently. About 120 million rods, which work best in dim light but cannot distinguish color, are distributed throughout the retina. The 6.5 million cones, which provide detailed color vision in bright light, are concentrated in the fovea. Impulses from rods and cones pass through connecting nerve cells to the optic nerve.

Signal from stimulated cell

Cone

Nerve signals *travel to the optic nerve*

Light *travels through nerve cells lying over the retina*

Surface of retina

Retinal nerve fibers

Connecting nerve cells

Nerve signals *move up to the surface of the retina*

Rod

Cross-section of retina

Inverted (upside-down) image *focused on retina*

Optic nerve *carries nerve signals from the eye to the brain*

Fovea *is an area of the retina that receives light from directly in front of the eye; it is packed with cones, enabling it to pick out fine details of shape and color*

Blood vessel

Vitreous humor *is a semisolid jelly that gives the eye its shape and keeps the retina in position*

Retina *detects light rays and turns them into nerve signals*

BLIND SPOT

The retinal nerve fibers that carry impulses from rods and cones travel over the retinal surface to converge – with blood vessels – at a common exit point called the optic disk, where the optic nerve leaves the eyeball. The optic disk, is also called the blind spot because it does not have any photoreceptors and cannot detect light. Normally, people are not aware of the blind spot because their eyes are always on the move and their brain ignores the "hole" in visual input.

OPHTHALMOSCOPIC IMAGE OF A RETINA SHOWING THE BLIND SPOT

Red dot

Green dot

SEEING IN COLOR

We see in color because there are three types of cones, and each responds best to a particular wavelength, or color, of light: red, green, or blue. The brain combines signals from all the cones to see a full-color image. Color deficiency, or color blindness, occurs when one or more types of cone are missing (see p. 249). The test above detects red–green color blindness. People with this condition cannot tell the difference between red and green, so they cannot see the number hidden.

How we see

IN ANCIENT TIMES, eyes were thought to give
out light, making things visible. Today, we
have a far better idea of how eyes really work,
and why they sometimes fail to give perfect
results. Collecting light is only the first step.
To see, we have to interpret a barrage of visual
information, a task that is carried out by the
brain, which compares what it sees now with
what it saw a moment ago, and also with what
it expects to be there. The result is a mental
"map" that seems like the real outside world.
Thanks to this map, we can tell how far away
things are and whether or not they are on the
move. Most important of all, we can recognize
what – or who – we see.

WHAT'S THAT?
The brain is very good at identifying what it sees, even if
signals from the eyes are unclear. For example, the animal
in the picture above is easy to recognize, though the detail
is extremely poor. This kind of processing is carried out by
the brain's visual association cortex. If this area is damaged,
the person may have difficulty recognizing everyday objects.

VISUAL PATHWAYS

Because their eyes face forward, humans have
binocular vision, which means that they see the same
view from two slightly different angles. As a result,
the brain's initial processing center – the primary
visual cortex – receives two slightly different sets of
visual information. In the visual pathway from the
eyes to the brain, there is a crossover called the optic
chiasma, which directs signals from the same side of
both eyes to one side of the brain. By comparing
the differences between these signals, the brain can
judge distance or depth, and see objects in three
dimensions. The primary visual cortex can identify
outlines and movement, but several other areas of
the brain are involved in recognizing specific objects.

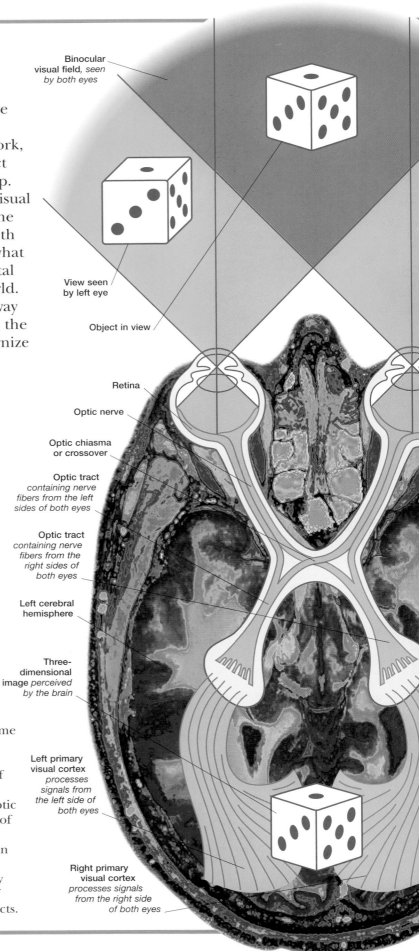

Binocular
visual field, *seen
by both eyes*

View seen
by left eye

Object in view

Retina

Optic nerve

Optic chiasma
or crossover

Optic tract
*containing nerve
fibers from the left
sides of both eyes*

Optic tract
*containing nerve
fibers from the
right sides of
both eyes*

Left cerebral
hemisphere

Three-
dimensional
image *perceived
by the brain*

Left primary
visual cortex
*processes
signals from
the left side of
both eyes*

Right primary
visual cortex
*processes signals
from the right side
of both eyes*

IN FOCUS

Two parts of the eye – the cornea and the lens – focus light on the retina, so that the brain produces a clear, not blurred, view of the outside world. The cornea does most of the work, but it cannot change shape, so fine adjustments are carried out by the lens. With faraway objects, the ring of ciliary muscle relaxes, allowing ligaments to pull on the lens, making it slimmer and flatter. With nearby objects, the ciliary muscle contracts, the ligaments stop pulling, and the elastic lens returns to its natural shape, which is rounder. These changes – called accommodation – are under the control of the brain.

View seen by right eye

Diagram of visual pathway

CT SCAN OF HORIZONTAL SECTION THROUGH BRAIN

Right cerebral hemisphere

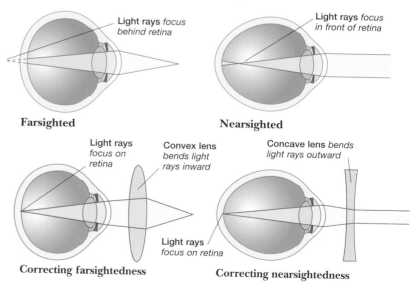

Fibers of suspensory ligament are less taut and allow lens to become more rounded

Ring of ciliary muscle around lens contracts

Divergent light rays from nearby object

Image of nearby object in sharp focus on retina

Cornea

Round lens refracts (bends) light rays more

Accommodation – nearby objects

Pupil

Thin lens refracts (bends) light rays less

Inverted (upside-down) image on retina is turned the right way up by the brain

Distant object

Cornea

Parallel light rays from distant object

Retina

Ring of relaxed ciliary muscle is stretched by pressure of fluid inside eye

Fibers of suspensory ligament pull on lens to make it thinner

Accommodation – distant objects

TRICKING THE BRAIN

The brain uses a variety of clues to decide what it is seeing. But sometimes these clues are confusing, tricking the brain into drawing the wrong conclusions. Take, for example, this tribar, an impossible three-dimensional shape that could never exist in real life. It confuses the brain's mechanism for determining depth, so it can never be seen as a complete object. Other optical illusions trick the brain into seeing dots or lines where none actually exist.

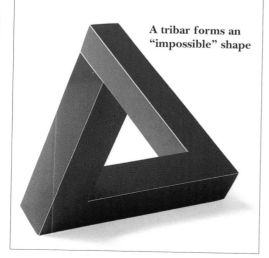

A tribar forms an "impossible" shape

EYE PROBLEMS
Visual disorders, or eye problems, are very common. The most common – affecting people of all ages – are farsightedness and nearsightedness, both involving errors of focusing, and both of which can be corrected by the use of glasses or contact lenses. Another disorder, called presbyopia, affects many people over the age of 40 who lose the ability to focus on near objects as their lenses becomes less elastic.

Light rays focus behind retina

Light rays focus in front of retina

Farsighted

Nearsighted

Light rays focus on retina

Convex lens bends light rays inward

Concave lens bends light rays outward

Light rays focus on retina

Correcting farsightedness

Correcting nearsightedness

In farsightedness, or hypermetropia, the eyeball is too short; light rays are therefore not bent enough, so they reach the retina before they have been focused. This is corrected by wearing glasses or contact lenses that make the light rays converge.

In nearsightedness, or myopia, the eyeball is too long; light rays are therefore bent too much, so the image on the retina is blurred. This is corrected by wearing glasses or contact lenses that make the light rays diverge.

ENDOCRINE system

THE TWO CONTROL systems of the human body work in very different ways. While the nervous system uses electrical signals to make cells respond, the endocrine system uses chemical messengers, called hormones, that are released into the blood. Hormones often take a longer time than nerves to react, and they can have important and long-lasting effects. They regulate the speed of thousands of chemical processes, and they are also responsible for the physical changes that occur during puberty. Hormones are produced by endocrine glands, which empty directly into the bloodstream. Many of these glands influence each other, and some are also triggered by nerves. The result is an intricate web of controls – one that keeps the whole body in a stable state.

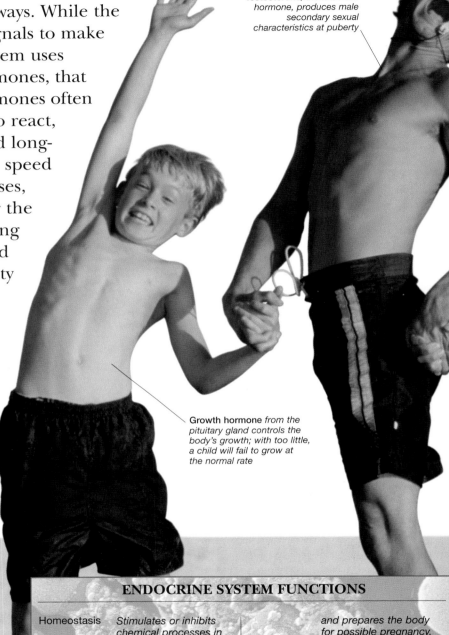

Testosterone, the male sex hormone, produces male secondary sexual characteristics at puberty

Growth hormone *from the pituitary gland controls the body's growth; with too little, a child will fail to grow at the normal rate*

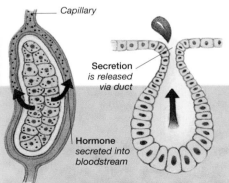

Capillary

Secretion is released via duct

Hormone secreted into bloodstream

Endocrine gland   **Exocrine gland**

HORMONE-SECRETING GLANDS

Endocrine glands produce their secretions in tiny amounts, releasing the hormones directly into capillaries, so that they can be carried away by the bloodstream. Endocrine glands are found in two types of organs. Some of these organs are devoted exclusively to making hormones, while others – such as the stomach and kidneys – carry out different functions as well. In contrast, exocrine glands such as salivary or sweat glands, release their secretions through a duct into body cavities or onto the skin.

ENDOCRINE SYSTEM FUNCTIONS

Homeostasis	Stimulates or inhibits chemical processes in cells to keep body in a stable state. These adjustments can affect just one type of target cells, or a wide range across the body.		and prepares the body for possible pregnancy. After fertilization, it maintains the uterus lining, prepares the mammary glands for milk production, and initiates birth.
Reproduction	Initiates and maintains production of sex cells. In women, it also initiates and controls the release of eggs cells,	Development	Initiates and governs physical changes that lead to sexual maturity and bring the body to adult size.

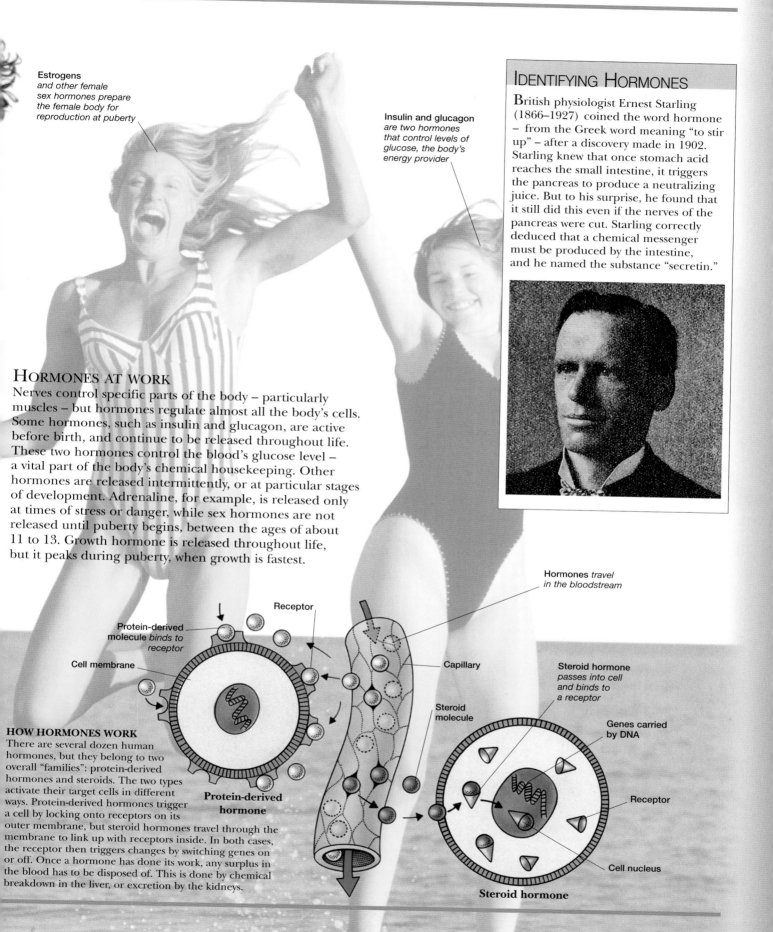

Estrogens *and other female sex hormones prepare the female body for reproduction at puberty*

Insulin and glucagon *are two hormones that control levels of glucose, the body's energy provider*

HORMONES AT WORK

Nerves control specific parts of the body – particularly muscles – but hormones regulate almost all the body's cells. Some hormones, such as insulin and glucagon, are active before birth, and continue to be released throughout life. These two hormones control the blood's glucose level – a vital part of the body's chemical housekeeping. Other hormones are released intermittently, or at particular stages of development. Adrenaline, for example, is released only at times of stress or danger, while sex hormones are not released until puberty begins, between the ages of about 11 to 13. Growth hormone is released throughout life, but it peaks during puberty, when growth is fastest.

Hormones *travel in the bloodstream*

Receptor

Protein-derived molecule *binds to receptor*

Cell membrane

Capillary

Steroid hormone *passes into cell and binds to a receptor*

Steroid molecule

Genes carried by DNA

Protein-derived hormone

Receptor

Cell nucleus

HOW HORMONES WORK

There are several dozen human hormones, but they belong to two overall "families": protein-derived hormones and steroids. The two types activate their target cells in different ways. Protein-derived hormones trigger a cell by locking onto receptors on its outer membrane, but steroid hormones travel through the membrane to link up with receptors inside. In both cases, the receptor then triggers changes by switching genes on or off. Once a hormone has done its work, any surplus in the blood has to be disposed of. This is done by chemical breakdown in the liver, or excretion by the kidneys.

Steroid hormone

Endocrine glands

Unlike the nervous system, the endocrine system consists of separate "outposts" scattered across the body. Three major endocrine glands – including the pituitary – are in the head, while the rest are in the neck and trunk. Together with some more diffuse regions of endocrine tissue, these glands produce all the hormones that keep the body under control. Each hormone has a specific list of target tissues, and in many cases these include other endocrine glands. This means that one hormone can stimulate the production of another, or counteract its effects. This kind of interaction is called feedback, and it lies behind almost all the subtle changes in hormone levels that keep the body on an even keel.

Hormone producers

Endocrine glands can be organs in their own right, or they can form part of organs that also carry out other tasks. The pituitary gland acts as the system's overall coordinator, and is directly linked to the hypothalamus, a hormone-producing region of the brain. Several glands, including the thyroid and pancreas, adjust the body's rate of energy use, while the adrenals produce an unusually fast-acting hormone that is released in moments of sudden stress. Sex hormones are released by the ovaries and the testes, but only once puberty has been reached. Endocrine tissue is also found in some other organs, such as the kidneys and the heart.

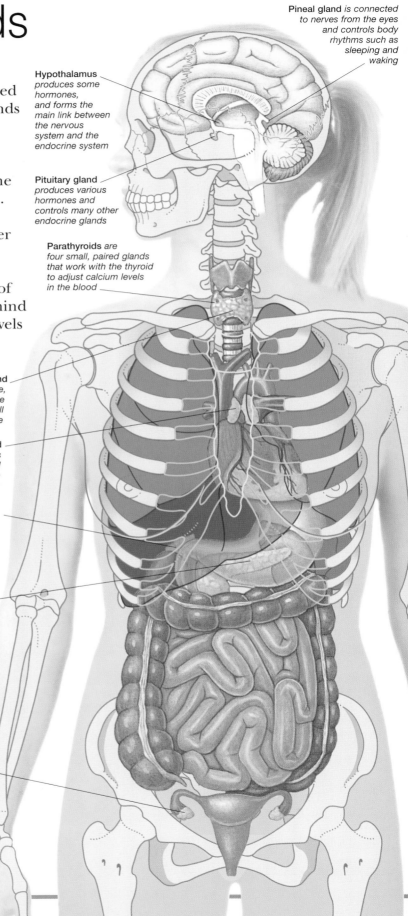

Pineal gland *is connected to nerves from the eyes and controls body rhythms such as sleeping and waking*

Hypothalamus *produces some hormones, and forms the main link between the nervous system and the endocrine system*

Pituitary gland *produces various hormones and controls many other endocrine glands*

Parathyroids *are four small, paired glands that work with the thyroid to adjust calcium levels in the blood*

Thyroid gland *produces thyroxine, which increases the body's overall metabolic rate*

Thymus gland *produces hormones needed for normal development of the immune system*

Adrenal glands *are paired glands that produce adrenaline, the hormone that prepares the body for action in emergencies*

Pancreas *releases insulin and glucagon – two opposing hormones that control the level of glucose in the blood*

Ovaries *are paired organs in women that form part of the reproductive system and endocrine system; their endocrine tissue releases female sex hormones*

Testes *are paired organs in men that form part of the reproductive system and endocrine system; their endocrine tissue releases male sex hormones*

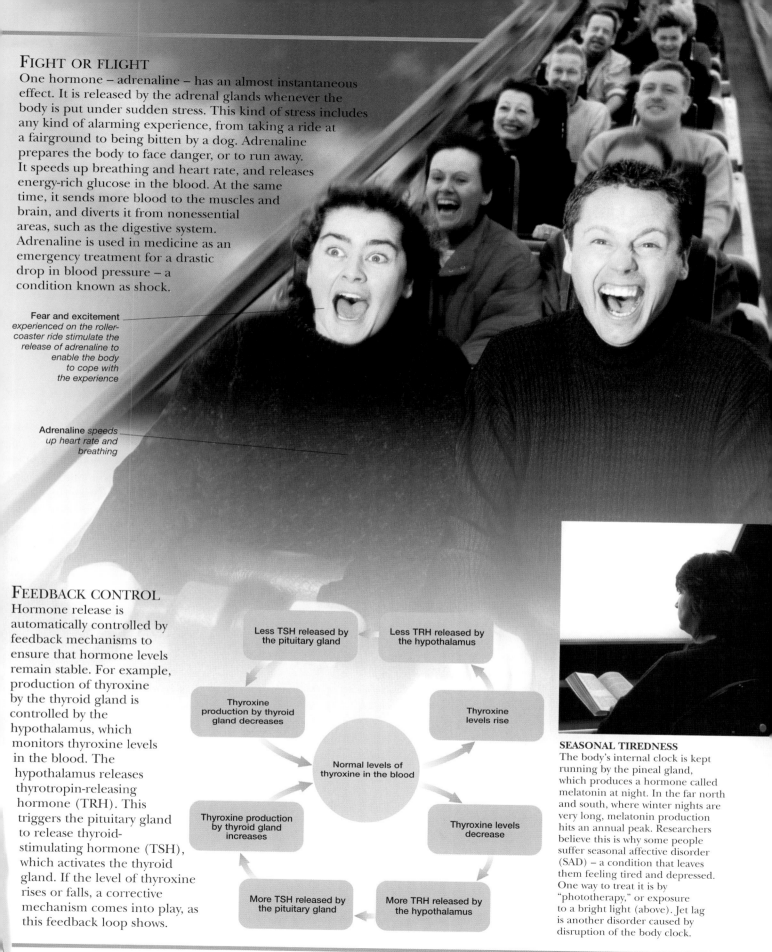

FIGHT OR FLIGHT

One hormone – adrenaline – has an almost instantaneous effect. It is released by the adrenal glands whenever the body is put under sudden stress. This kind of stress includes any kind of alarming experience, from taking a ride at a fairground to being bitten by a dog. Adrenaline prepares the body to face danger, or to run away. It speeds up breathing and heart rate, and releases energy-rich glucose in the blood. At the same time, it sends more blood to the muscles and brain, and diverts it from nonessential areas, such as the digestive system. Adrenaline is used in medicine as an emergency treatment for a drastic drop in blood pressure – a condition known as shock.

Fear and excitement experienced on the roller-coaster ride stimulate the release of adrenaline to enable the body to cope with the experience

Adrenaline speeds up heart rate and breathing

FEEDBACK CONTROL

Hormone release is automatically controlled by feedback mechanisms to ensure that hormone levels remain stable. For example, production of thyroxine by the thyroid gland is controlled by the hypothalamus, which monitors thyroxine levels in the blood. The hypothalamus releases thyrotropin-releasing hormone (TRH). This triggers the pituitary gland to release thyroid-stimulating hormone (TSH), which activates the thyroid gland. If the level of thyroxine rises or falls, a corrective mechanism comes into play, as this feedback loop shows.

Less TSH released by the pituitary gland

Less TRH released by the hypothalamus

Thyroxine production by thyroid gland decreases

Thyroxine levels rise

Normal levels of thyroxine in the blood

Thyroxine production by thyroid gland increases

Thyroxine levels decrease

More TSH released by the pituitary gland

More TRH released by the hypothalamus

SEASONAL TIREDNESS

The body's internal clock is kept running by the pineal gland, which produces a hormone called melatonin at night. In the far north and south, where winter nights are very long, melatonin production hits an annual peak. Researchers believe this is why some people suffer seasonal affective disorder (SAD) – a condition that leaves them feeling tired and depressed. One way to treat it is by "phototherapy," or exposure to a bright light (above). Jet lag is another disorder caused by disruption of the body clock.

Pituitary gland

TUCKED AWAY underneath the brain, the pituitary gland is the control center of the endocrine system. Although not much bigger than a raisin, it releases a total of nine different hormones, many of which trigger other endocrine glands to secrete hormones of their own. A unique feature of this gland is that it is directly connected to the hypothalamus – a part of the brain that monitors the temperature and chemistry of the blood. The hypothalamus makes hormones that affect the pituitary and is involved in many of the feedback mechanisms that keep hormone levels under control. Together, the hypothalamus and the pituitary gland form the chief link between the nervous and endocrine systems, ensuring that they work as a team.

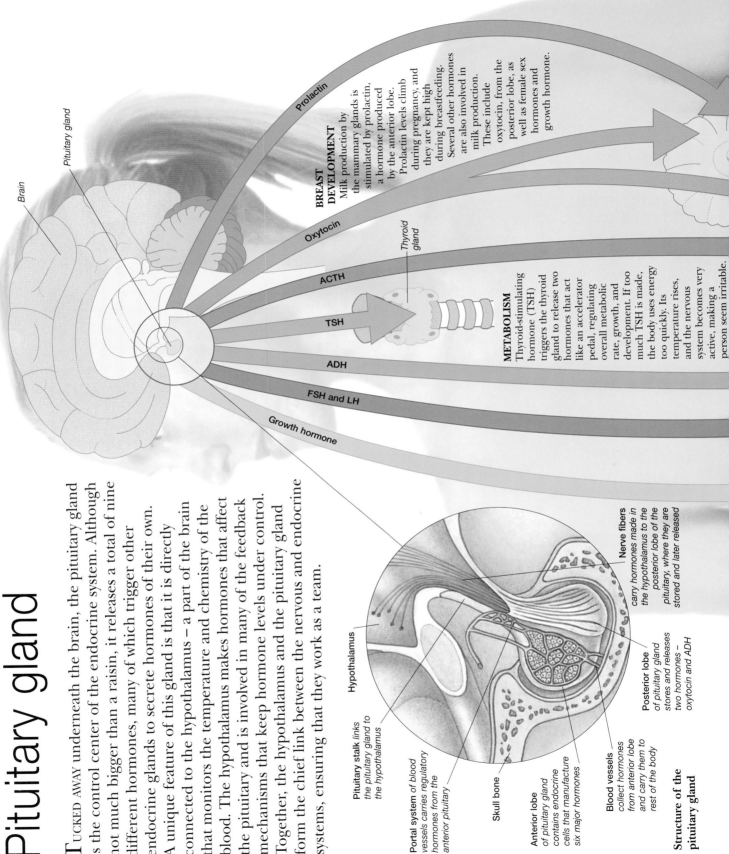

Brain

Pituitary gland

Prolactin

Oxytocin

ACTH

TSH

ADH

FSH and LH

Growth hormone

Thyroid gland

BREAST DEVELOPMENT
Milk production by the mammary glands is stimulated by prolactin, a hormone produced by the anterior lobe. Prolactin levels climb during pregnancy, and they are kept high during breastfeeding. Several other hormones are also involved in milk production. These include oxytocin, from the posterior lobe, as well as female sex hormones and growth hormone.

METABOLISM
Thyroid-stimulating hormone (TSH) triggers the thyroid gland to release two hormones that act like an accelerator pedal, regulating overall metabolic rate, growth, and development. If too much TSH is made, the body uses energy too quickly. Its temperature rises, and the nervous system becomes very active, making a person seem irritable.

Structure of the pituitary gland

Hypothalamus

Pituitary stalk links the pituitary gland to the hypothalamus

Portal system of blood vessels carries regulatory hormones from the anterior pituitary

Skull bone

Anterior lobe of pituitary gland contains endocrine cells that manufacture six major hormones

Blood vessels collect hormones from anterior lobe and carry them to rest of the body

Posterior lobe of pituitary gland stores and releases two hormones – oxytocin and ADH

Nerve fibers carry hormones made in the hypothalamus to the posterior lobe of the pituitary, where they are stored and later released

INSIDE THE PITUITARY

The pituitary has two lobes attached to the same slender stalk. The front or anterior lobe is the larger of the two, and contains endocrine cells. It produces most of the hormones that the pituitary releases into the blood. The posterior lobe is made up mainly of nervous tissue, and does not make hormones itself. But its nerve fibers originate in the hypothalamus and carry hormones to the pituitary. The hormones are stored there and later released. This process is called neurosecretion. The nerves release their hormones when they are stimulated by other nerves in the brain.

STEROID PRODUCTION

Adrenocorticotropic hormone (ACTH) stimulates the outer part, or cortex, of the adrenal glands to produce and release steroid hormones, including aldosterone and cortisol. These hormones help to control the level of water and salts in the blood, and they play an important part in regulating metabolism. They also help the body react to stress – for example, when it is recovering from a severe injury.

URINE PRODUCTION

Antidiuretic hormone (ADH) is made in the hypothalamus, and then transported to the posterior lobe by nerve fibers. When it is released from the pituitary, it acts on the nephrons of the kidney, reducing the rate of urine production. It also cuts down perspiration, and makes blood vessels constrict. These changes help to maintain the body's water balance. ADH release is triggered by the hypothalamus when it detects a drop in the blood's water content.

Adrenal gland

Kidney

Uterus

Ovary

BIRTH AND MILK PRODUCTION

Oxytocin plays a key role in birth, and is also involved in the production of breast milk. During birth, it stimulates the contractions of the uterus. The contractions stimulate the release of yet more oxytocin, and through this positive feedback mechanism the contractions become more and more powerful. Oxytocin is also released when a baby starts sucking at its mother's breast. This triggers a reflex that ejects milk through the nipple.

REPRODUCTION

The male and female reproductive systems respond to the same pituitary hormones, although in different ways. In women, follicle-stimulating hormone (FSH) triggers the development of egg cells, or ova. Luteinizing hormone (LH) causes their release, and stimulates the production of estrogen, or female sex hormone (see p. 220). In men (left), FSH stimulates sperm production. LH stimulates cells in the testes to produce the male sex hormone testosterone (see p. 217).

Penis

Testis

Male reproductive organs

GROWTH AND REPAIR

Growth hormone, or somatotropin, makes nearly all the body's cells multiply and grow. It is important not only for normal growth, but also for tissue repair. During early life, growth hormone stimulates ossification, or the conversion of cartilage into bone. It is also involved in bone remodeling – the process that renews bone tissue, so that it can cope with everyday wear and tear.

PITUITARY DISORDERS

In the early 1900s, the American neurosurgeon Harvey Cushing (1869–1939) began to study the pituitary gland, partly by noting what happened when it malfunctions. He discovered that an under- or overactive pituitary can cause disorders in metabolism and growth, and he gave his name to one of them, known as Cushing's syndrome. Caused by too much adrenocorticotropic hormone, this condition can produce wasted limbs and brittle bones. Cushing described the pituitary as the "conductor of the endocrine orchestra," but it has since become clear that the hypothalamus is actually the conductor-in-chief.

THE SEARCH FOR INSULIN

DIABETES MELLITUS IS A DISEASE that prevents sufferers from breaking down glucose in their cells. The glucose level in their blood rises rapidly and their body tries to remove it by increasing urine production, leading to uncontrollable thirst. Glucose is the major source of energy for the body, but diabetes prevents cells from using it, so body fat is broken down instead and the body wastes away. Diabetes was always fatal until Canadian physiologists Frederick Banting and Charles Best discovered an effective treatment in 1922 – one of the greatest achievements in modern medicine.

THOMAS WILLIS
English physician Thomas Willis (1621–75) showed that sugar was excreted in diabetics' urine, and rediscovered the ancient Chinese test of the sweet taste of urine indicating diabetes. "Taste thy patient's urine," he advised fellow doctors. "If it be sweet like honey, he will waste away, grow weak, fall into a sleep and die."

ISLETS OF LANGERHANS
The hormone insulin is produced in the pancreas, in distinctive groups of cells called islets of Langerhans. They are named after Paul Langerhans, who first described them in 1869, although it was left to others to discover their function.

EARLY DESCRIPTIONS OF THE SYMPTOMS

Symptoms of diabetes, including frequent urination, thirst, and weakness, were recognized by the ancient Egyptians, who left a description in the Ebers papyrus, dating from 1500 BC. Later, in the 2nd century AD, Aretaeus of Cappadocia referred to the way in which patients "never stop making water and the flow is incessant, like the opening of aqueducts." Aretaeus named the disease "diabetes," which comes from the Greek word meaning "siphon" and refers to a constant flow of water. By the 6th century, Indian physicians had recognized that sufferers have sweet urine, but the presence of sugar in their urine was not confirmed in Western medicine until the 17th century, when Thomas Willis showed that sugar crystals remain when urine is evaporated.

THE ROLE OF THE PANCREAS

The first conclusive proof that the pancreas played the central role in diabetes came in 1889, when German doctors Joseph von Mering (1849–1907) and Oskar Minkowski (1858–1931) showed that dogs developed diabetes if their pancreas was removed.

Exocrine *part of pancreas produces digestive enymes*

LM OF SECTION THROUGH THE PANCREAS

Islet of Langerhans *produces insulin*

BANTING AND BEST

Frederick Banting (1899–1978), far right, and Charles Best (1891–1941) isolated insulin. They injected it into Marjorie, a dying diabetic dog whose pancreas had been removed. She recovered. Banting won a Nobel Prize for his work but Best's achievement was overlooked, although Banting shared the prize money with him.

1922. The crucial test with a human patient came in 1923, when they treated Leonard Thompson, a 14-year-old diabetic who was close to death. The effect was miraculous. His blood sugar level fell, one day later he was on his feet, and he soon returned home to lead a normal life with the aid of insulin injections. The Eli Lilly pharmaceutical company immediately began large-scale production of insulin, extracted from pig pancreas. This method has now been superseded by the use of laboratory-produced human insulin. Diabetes is still an incurable disease, but diabetics, once condemned to a short and painful existence, can now live a full and active life.

INSULIN PEN

Some diabetics control their blood glucose by injecting insulin into their blood. The insulin pen gives a measured dose, according to the patient's varying blood glucose levels.

Twenty years earlier, a German scientist, Paul Langerhans (1847–88), had described unique groups of cells within the pancreas, later named islets of Langerhans. British scientist Edward Sharpey-Schafer (1850–1935) showed that a substance regulating glucose metabolism in the body was produced by these islets and called it "insuline" (later shortened to insulin), from the Latin *insula*, meaning island. English physiologist Ernest Starling (1866–1927) coined the name "hormone" in 1905 to describe substances secreted by endocrine glands, like the pancreas, that control metabolism. So now the race was on to isolate the pancreatic hormone, insulin.

ISOLATION OF INSULIN

Attempts to treat diabetics by feeding them pancreas failed, so extracting the hormone and injecting it into their blood was the only option. After many unsuccessful attempts, Frederick Banting and Charles Best succeeded in isolating insulin in

Insulin is a small protein made up of two amino acid chains

Six insulin molecules shown in green and purple are bound together here

COMPUTER-GENERATED IMAGE OF INSULIN MOLECULE

ROLE OF INSULIN

Insulin molecules bind to the outer membrane of cells, triggering chemical processes inside that break down glucose molecules, so removing the sugar from the blood and generating energy. Insulin also inhibits breakdown of glycogen to glucose by the liver.

MAKING INSULIN

Initially, insulin was laboriously extracted from pig pancreas, obtained from slaughterhouses. In some patients, the immune system reacts against pig insulin. This can be avoided by using human insulin, made in the laboratory using *E. coli* bacteria that have human insulin genes inserted into them.

Insulin production sites are stained orange

TEM OF GENETICALLY ALTERED E. COLI BACTERIA

Escherichia coli bacteria are genetically engineered to produce insulin

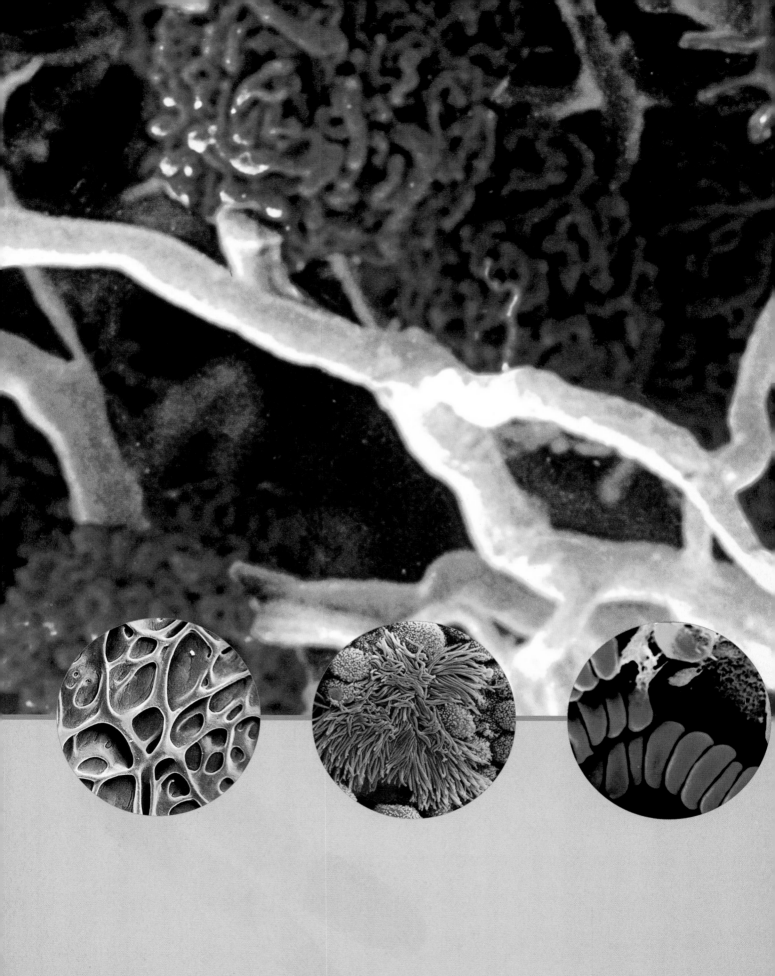

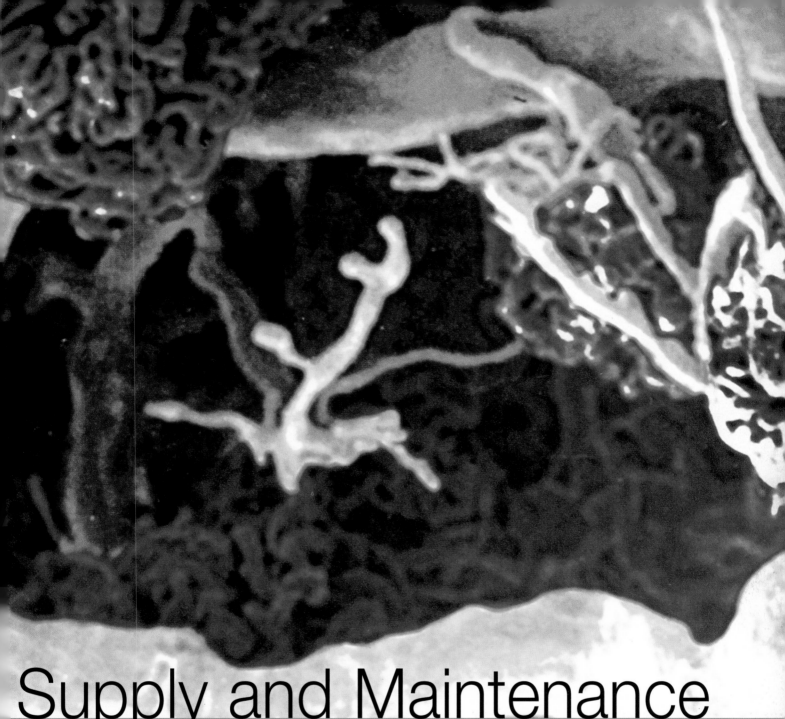

Supply and Maintenance

TO WORK AT THEIR BEST, the body's trillions of cells must be kept in a stable environment, regardless of conditions outside the body. This stability is provided by the systems that supply and maintain body tissues. Together they ensure that all cells have sufficient food and oxygen to meet their energy requirements, have their wastes removed, are protected from disease-causing pathogens, are kept at a constant, warm temperature of 98.6°F (37°C), and are bathed by a nurturing fluid, the composition of which fluctuates little.

CARDIOVASCULAR system

THROUGHOUT EVERY SECOND of every day of life, as the body's cells perform their incredible variety of functions, they are dependent on the continuous delivery of oxygen and nutrients, and the removal of wastes. These are carried by blood, a tissue made up of cells suspended in fluid that is transported by the cardiovascular, or circulatory, system. Consisting of a muscular pump (the heart) and an intricate network of tubes called blood vessels, the cardiovascular system ensures that blood reaches every part of the body. The amount of blood supplied to the various tissues can be adjusted whenever necessary to meet the body's continually changing needs. In addition to being responsible for transportation, the cardiovascular system plays a key role in defending the body against infection through the white blood cells that it carries. It also helps maintain a stable environment within the body.

TRANSPORTATION NETWORK

The intricate network of blood vessels extends to just about every part of the body. These vessels range in size from the thickness of a thumb to a fraction of a hair's width, visible only under the microscope. So extensive is the network, in fact, that if a person's blood vessels were laid end to end they would stretch out over 62,500 miles (100,000 km). In this "body map" (right), only the major blood vessels are shown, along with the heart, which pumps blood along them. Arteries – vessels carrying blood away from the heart – generally transport oxygen-rich blood (red) to the tissues, while veins – vessels carrying blood to the heart – usually carry oxygen-poor blood (blue). Connecting arteries and veins – but not visible here – is a massive system of microscopically narrow capillaries.

RECEIVING BLOOD
A blood transfusion can be given to restore blood volume. This can be lifesaving if blood loss is severe. Blood is grouped according to the presence of certain proteins on the surface of red blood cells. The blood to be transfused and the recipient's blood must be "typed" to ensure they are compatible.

Pulmonary arteries
carry oxygen-poor blood from the right side of the heart to the lungs

Oxygen-poor blood (blue)

Pulmonary veins
carry oxygen-rich blood from the lungs to the left side of the heart

The heart *(shown here cut open) is a muscular pump that propels blood around the circulatory system*

Inferior vena cava *is the main vein carrying blood from the abdomen and legs to the heart*

Aorta *is the main artery through which blood leaves the heart*

White blood cell

BLOOD

This liquid tissue keeps the body's cells working normally by ensuring that they are nurtured and kept warm in constant surroundings. Its red color is produced by the red blood cells that float in plasma, the liquid part of blood. These cells carry oxygen to where it is needed, while plasma delivers essential nutrients to cells and removes their unwanted wastes. Also present are white blood cells that destroy invading germs before they can cause any harm.

Femoral vein
drains blood from the muscles and other tissues of the thigh

Femoral artery
supplies the muscles of the thigh

Oxygen-rich blood *(red)*

Ulnar artery supplies
the forearm and hand

Muscular layer makes
arteriole wider or narrower to control blood flow to tissues

Red blood cells traveling
through the central lumen of arteriole

Outer layer
protects the arteriole

Red blood cell

LIVING TUBES

The different types of blood vessel vary in structure and size. Arteries have elastic, muscular walls that enable them to carry blood away from the heart at very high pressures. Capillaries have thin walls that allow oxygen and other substances to pass through easily. Veins have relatively thin walls, since they carry blood at low pressures, and valves to prevent backflow of blood away from the heart.

SEM OF CROSS-SECTION THROUGH AN ARTERIOLE (SMALL ARTERY)

CARDIOVASCULAR SYSTEM FUNCTIONS

Distribution	*Delivers oxygen from the lungs, and nutrients – such as glucose – from the digestive system, to all body cells. Removes waste products from all body cells to elimination sites from the body, such as carbon dioxide to the lungs or urea to the kidneys. Transports hormones ("chemical messengers") from endocrine glands to their target tissues.*
Protection	*Defends the body against infection by foreign microorganisms such as bacteria. Prevents blood loss by initiating the formation of clots.*
Regulation	*Distributes heat to keep body temperature at 98.6°F (37°C). Maintains normal pH (balance of acidity and alkalinity) in the tissues. Keeps the right amount of fluid in the circulatory system.*

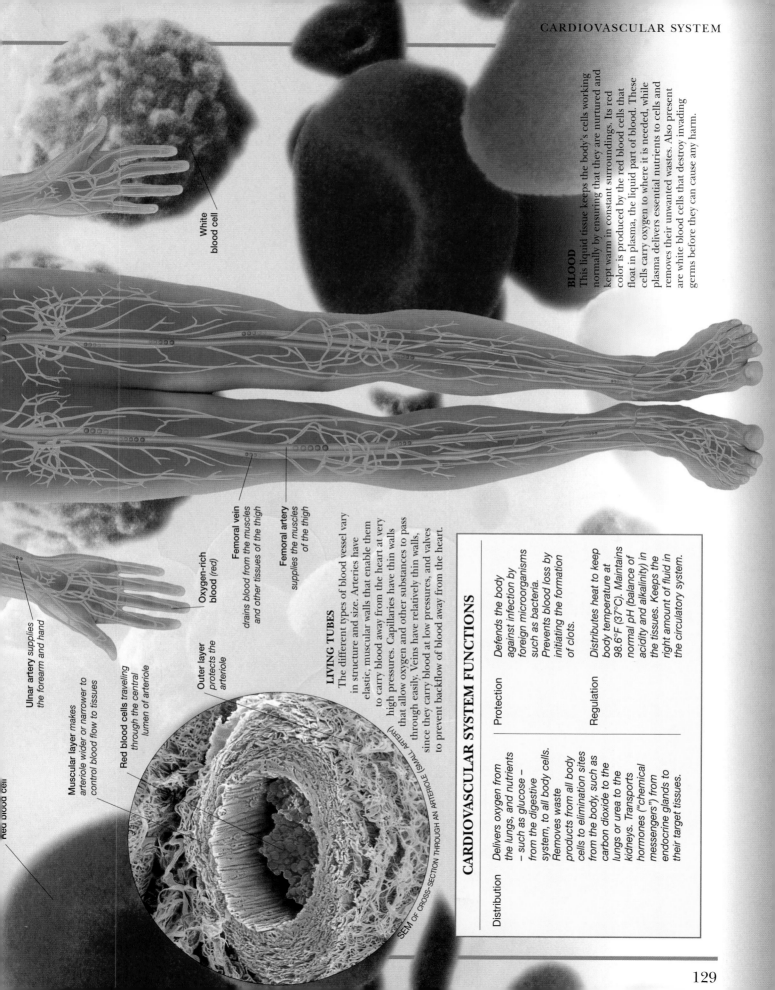

Blood

COURSING CONTINUOUSLY through the network of blood vessels, blood supplies the needs of each of the body's trillions of cells, ensuring that they are kept in safe, constant surroundings. It fulfills this demanding role in three ways. First, it acts as the body's delivery and collection service, carrying food, oxygen, hormones, and other essentials to cells, and removing wastes. Second, it distributes heat around the body, keeping cells at a steady 98.6°F (37°C). Third, it helps defend the body against infection. Blood itself is not a simple liquid but consists of different types of cells floating in fluid plasma. Each component – whether cellular or liquid – has a particular role within the body.

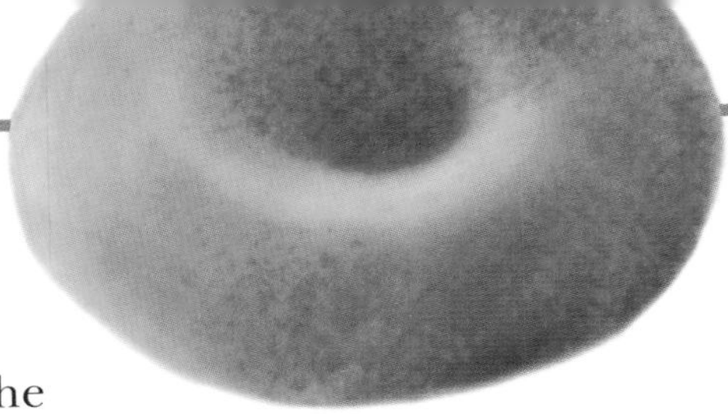

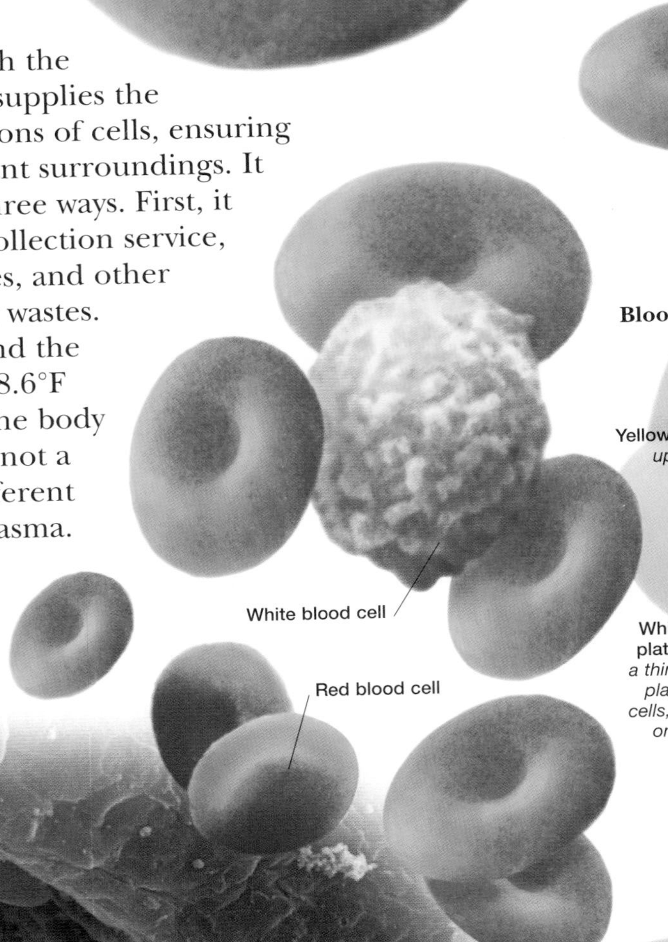

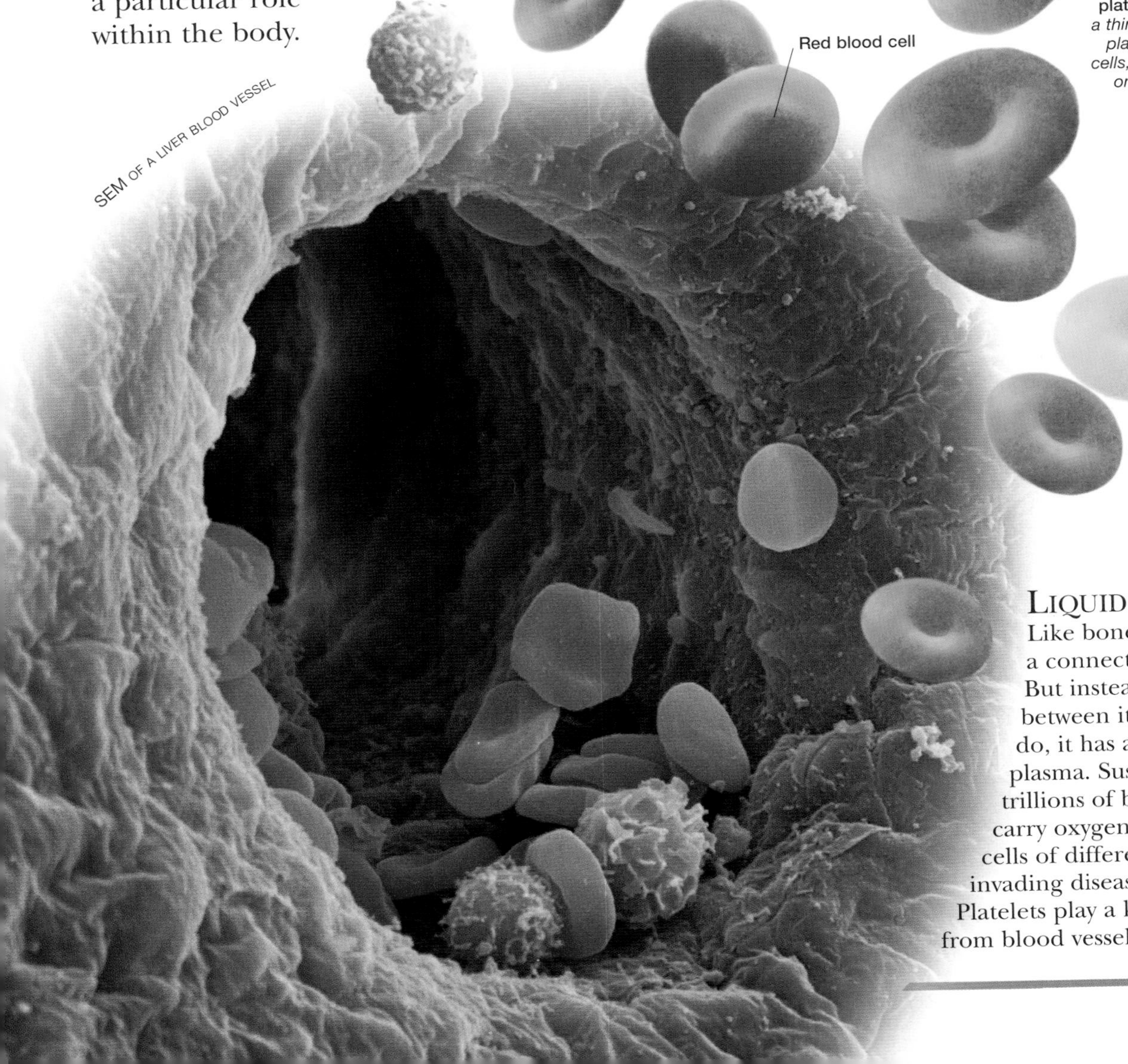

SEM OF A LIVER BLOOD VESSEL

White blood cell

Red blood cell

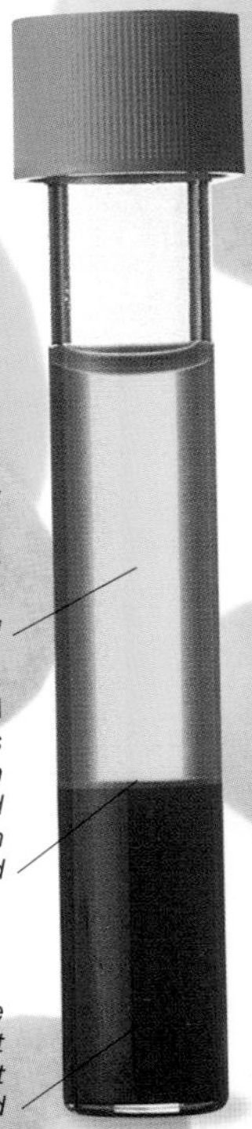

Blood components

Yellowish plasma *makes up about 55 percent of blood, and consists mostly of water, in which many different substances are dissolved*

White blood cells and platelets, *seen here as a thin pale line between plasma and red blood cells, make up less than one percent of blood*

Red cells *make up about 44 percent of blood*

BLOOD COMPOSITION

This blood sample has been spun at high speed in a centrifuge to separate its main components. Plasma makes up about 55 percent of the total volume, while red and white blood cells make up 45 percent. Blood cells and platelets are incredibly tiny. In a single drop of blood, there are approximately 250 million red blood cells, 16 million platelets, and 375,000 white blood cells.

LIQUID TISSUE

Like bone and cartilage, blood is a connective tissue (see pp. 26–7). But instead of having a solid matrix between its cells as the other tissues do, it has a liquid matrix called plasma. Suspended in plasma are trillions of blood cells. Red blood cells carry oxygen to the tissues. White blood cells of different types detect and destroy invading disease-causing microorganisms. Platelets play a key role in stopping leaks from blood vessels by making blood clot.

PLASMA

This straw-colored liquid consists of about 90 percent water, with the remaining 10 percent made up of some 100 solutes (dissolved substances) that are either carried by the blood or help maintain its stable composition. Key solutes are listed (far right) with a description of their function or delivery destination.

Transfusion bag containing plasma

SUBSTANCES DISSOLVED IN PLASMA	FUNCTION
Proteins	Plasma proteins have various functions:
• albumin	Maintains water balance between blood and tissues, and helps regulate blood volume
• alpha and beta globulins	Helps transport some lipids, vitamins, and hormones
• gamma globulins	Antibodies that help defend the body against pathogens
• clotting proteins, including fibrinogen	Play an essential role in blood clotting
• others	Metabolic enzymes and antibacterial proteins
Nutrients: e.g. glucose, amino acids, and fatty acids	Products of digestion carried from the small intestine to be used by cells, stored, or broken down
Carbon dioxide	Waste product of cell respiration carried to lungs for disposal
Nitrogenous wastes	Products of protein breakdown, including urea carried from liver to kidneys and other points of excretion
Hormones	Chemical messengers carried from endocrine glands to target tissues
Electrolytes (ions)	Including sodium and potassium ions, which help maintain normal blood concentration

HOW MUCH?

Blood makes up about 8 percent of body weight. This amounts to 8–10 pints (4–5 liters) in women and 10–12 pints (5–6 liters) in men. Blood volume is regulated by the kidneys (see pp. 206–7), which increase or decrease the amount of fluid they filter from blood and pass out of the body as urine.

Blood cells *are made in the parts of the skeleton shaded red*

The average person has 10 pints (5 liters) of blood

Ten of these 1-pint (500-ml) bottles *contain the same amount of blood as an average person*

Red blood cells

White blood cell

Platelet

SEM OF BONE MARROW

Sinusoid channel *carries blood cells*

MAKING BLOOD CELLS

Red blood cells, platelets, and some white blood cells are made by the red bone marrow found in the flat bones of the axial skeleton – cranium, collar bones, shoulder blades, breast bone, ribs, vertebrae, hip bones – and the top of each humerus (upper arm bone) and femur (thigh bone). All cell types arise from the same basic stem cells, called hemocytoblasts ("blood cell sprouts"), but each type of cell follows a different development pathway.

Red blood cells

THE AVERAGE ADULT HAS around 25 trillion red blood cells in their blood at any one time. Also known as erythrocytes, these tiny cells make up 99 percent of the cells in the blood and perform the vital function of carrying oxygen to all the tissues of the body. They are produced at a rate of over 2 million per second in the red marrow of certain bones. Their unique structure means they are able to squeeze through the tiniest blood vessels and can pick up oxygen in the lungs and unload it in the tissues. In addition to transporting oxygen, they also carry some of the carbon dioxide produced as a waste product by the cells of the body.

Oxygen-poor blood

Oxygen-rich blood

LARGE SURFACES
As this cutaway view shows, a red blood cell resembles a flattened, dimpled disk, a shape that gives the cell a large surface area in relation to its volume. It means that no oxygen-carrying hemoglobin molecule is ever far from the cell membrane, which explains why red blood cells are very efficient at both picking up and depositing oxygen.

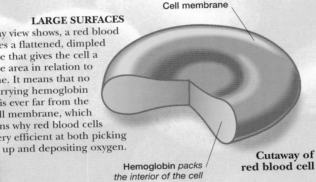

Cell membrane

Hemoglobin packs the interior of the cell

Cutaway of red blood cell

CHANGING COLOR
The redness of blood alters as it travels around the body because hemoglobin changes its color as it picks up or deposits oxygen. After hemoglobin picks up oxygen in the lungs, oxygen-rich blood traveling along the arteries to the tissues is bright red. After hemoglobin unloads oxygen in the tissues, the oxygen-poor blood returning along veins to the heart is now a dull, dark red. This gives thin-walled veins just under the skin's surface a blue appearance.

OXYGEN CARRIERS
Red blood cells have a number of special features, including their dimpled shape and flexibility. They are also the only cells in the body that do not have a nucleus. Instead, they are packed with hemoglobin, a protein that is responsible for their red color, and for the redness of the blood itself. Hemoglobin molecules pick up oxygen in the lungs and release it in the tissues. The formation and destruction of red blood cells takes place continuously. They begin their life as immature stem cells in the bone marrow, becoming fully developed and capable of transporting oxygen over a period of about five days. Each red blood cell lasts for about 120 days.

SEM OF RED BLOOD CELLS

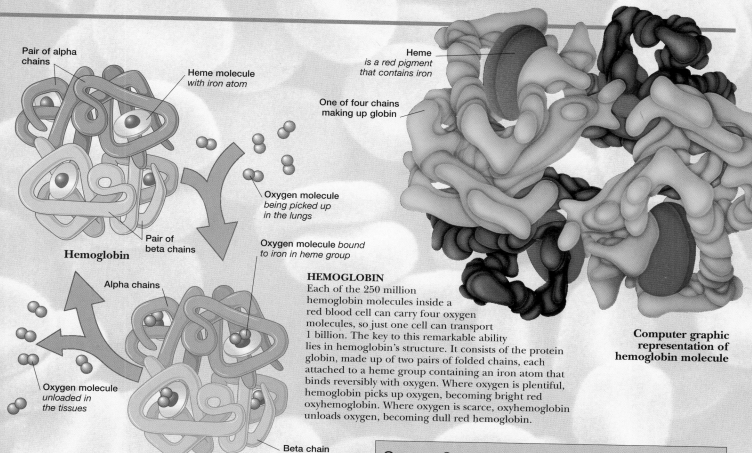

Pair of alpha chains

Heme molecule with iron atom

Hemoglobin

Pair of beta chains

Oxygen molecule *being picked up in the lungs*

Oxygen molecule *bound to iron in heme group*

Alpha chains

Oxygen molecule *unloaded in the tissues*

Beta chain

Oxyhemoglobin

Heme *is a red pigment that contains iron*

One of four chains making up globin

Computer graphic representation of hemoglobin molecule

HEMOGLOBIN

Each of the 250 million hemoglobin molecules inside a red blood cell can carry four oxygen molecules, so just one cell can transport 1 billion. The key to this remarkable ability lies in hemoglobin's structure. It consists of the protein globin, made up of two pairs of folded chains, each attached to a heme group containing an iron atom that binds reversibly with oxygen. Where oxygen is plentiful, hemoglobin picks up oxygen, becoming bright red oxyhemoglobin. Where oxygen is scarce, oxyhemoglobin unloads oxygen, becoming dull red hemoglobin.

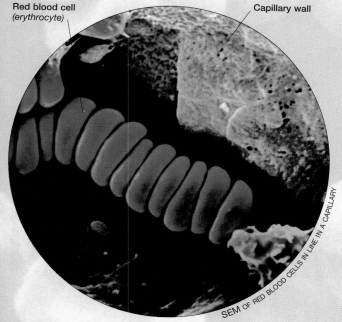

Red blood cell *(erythrocyte)*

Capillary wall

SEM OF RED BLOOD CELLS IN LINE IN A CAPILLARY

LINING UP

The cell membrane of red blood cells contains a protein called spectrin that makes them very flexible. This, together with their minute size, enables them to pass through tiny capillaries. Often they must pass along blood vessels in single file, since many of the smallest capillaries are just wider than one blood cell.

SICKLE CELL ANEMIA

Sickle cell anemia is an inherited disorder. Caused by a defect of the gene responsible for producing hemoglobin, it results in an abnormality of the red blood cell structure. While a normal red blood cell maintains its shape in oxygen-poor areas of the body, these cells become sickle-shaped, lose their flexibility, and obstruct narrow blood vessels, blocking the blood supply and causing pain. People with sickle cell anemia have inherited two copies of the abnormal gene, one from each parent. The ability of their blood to carry oxygen is reduced. Sickle cell trait is a milder form that often does not cause symptoms; it is the result of one abnormal and one normal gene. For reasons that are unknown, sickle cell trait seems to give some protection against the infectious disease malaria.

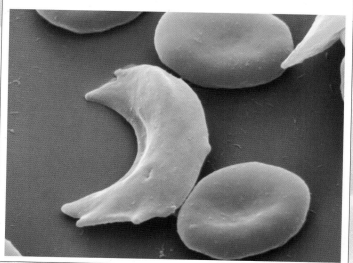

White blood cells

As BLOOD COURSES around the body, it carries with it a mobile defense force that is ready at all times to destroy invading pathogens before they can cause disease. Manning this force are the white blood cells, or leukocytes. White blood cells are outnumbered by oxygen-carrying red blood cells by about 700 to 1, but they are larger and have a nucleus, which their red partners lack. They can also change shape and slip out through capillary walls into the tissues in order to hunt down their prey. That prey is not limited to foreign invaders such as disease-causing bacteria, viruses, protists, or fungi. White blood cells also tackle enemies from within, such as the rogue cells that cause cancer.

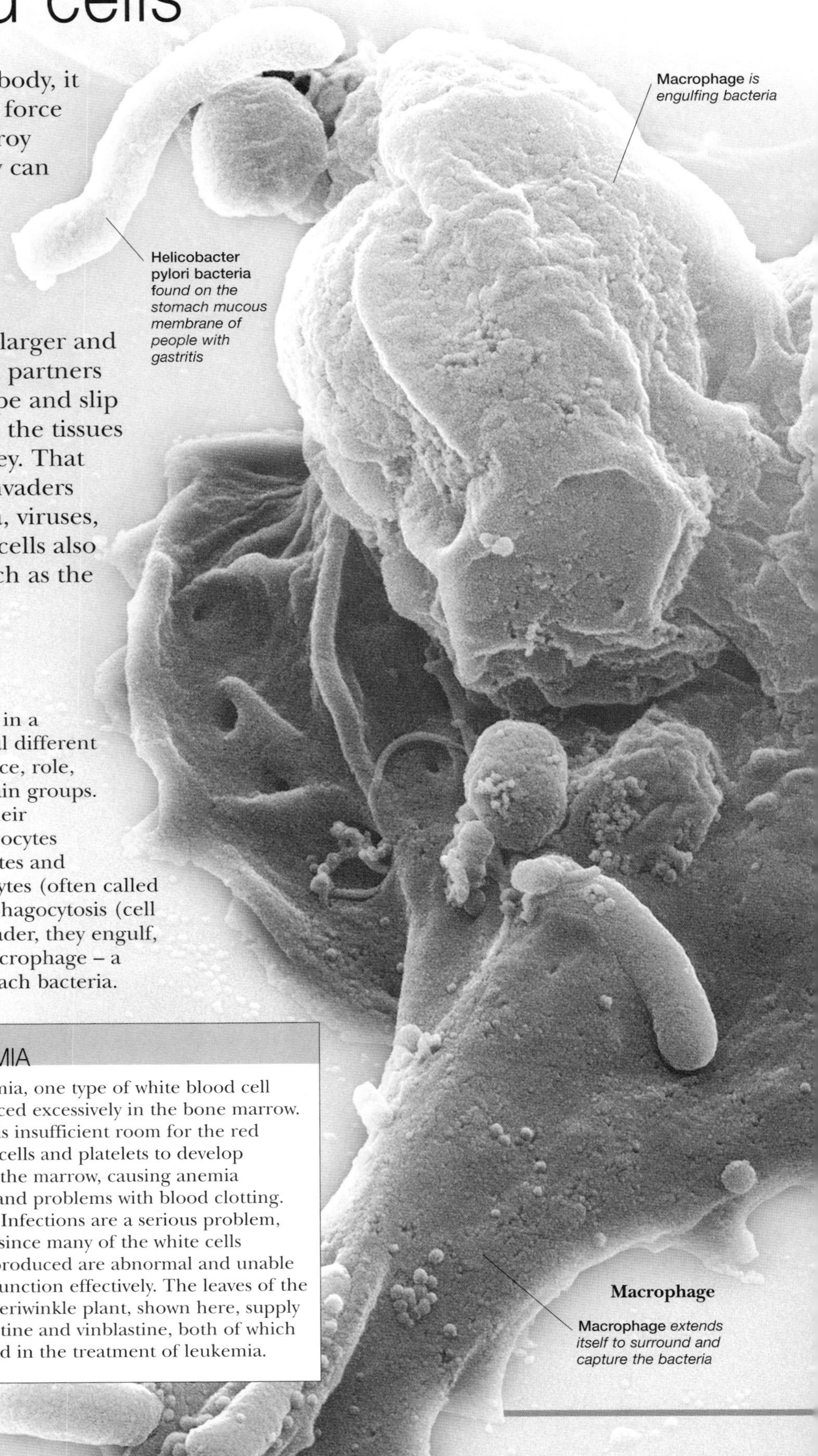

Macrophage is engulfing bacteria

Helicobacter pylori bacteria found on the stomach mucous membrane of people with gastritis

BODY DEFENDERS

Among the 375,000 white blood cells in a single drop of blood, there are several different types – each with their own appearance, role, and life span – which fall into two main groups. Granulocytes are so called because their cytoplasm contains granules. Agranulocytes (without granules) include lymphocytes and monocytes. Granulocytes and monocytes (often called phagocytes) destroy their quarry by phagocytosis (cell eating). Having tracked down an invader, they engulf, then digest it. Here, a marauding macrophage – a monocyte – is doing just that to stomach bacteria.

LEUKEMIA

In leukemia, one type of white blood cell is produced excessively in the bone marrow. There is insufficient room for the red blood cells and platelets to develop in the marrow, causing anemia and problems with blood clotting. Infections are a serious problem, since many of the white cells produced are abnormal and unable to function effectively. The leaves of the rosy periwinkle plant, shown here, supply vincristine and vinblastine, both of which are used in the treatment of leukemia.

Macrophage

Macrophage extends itself to surround and capture the bacteria

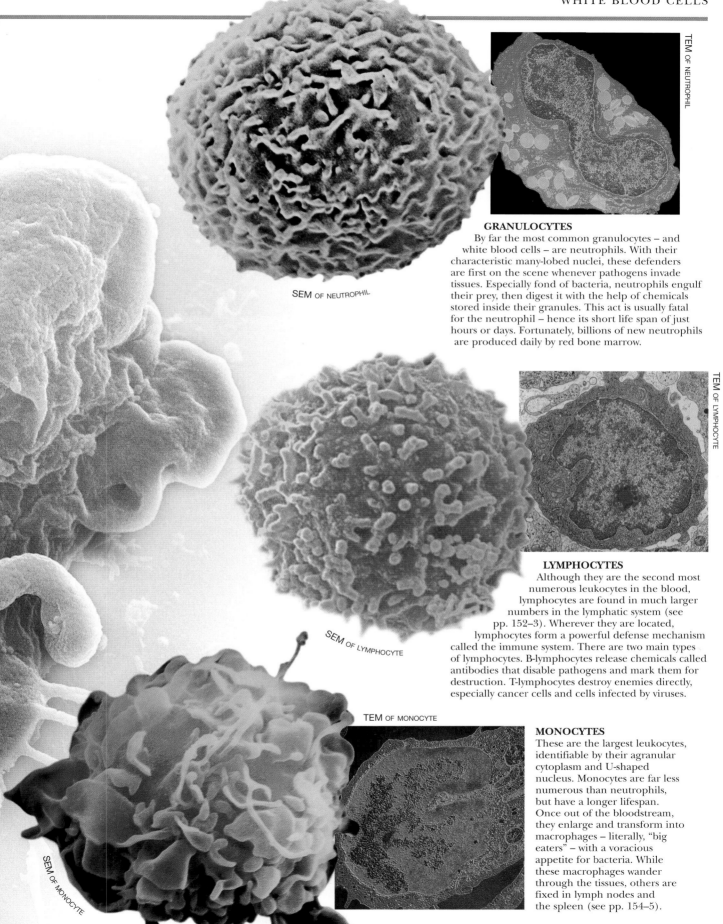

TEM OF NEUTROPHIL

SEM OF NEUTROPHIL

GRANULOCYTES

By far the most common granulocytes – and white blood cells – are neutrophils. With their characteristic many-lobed nuclei, these defenders are first on the scene whenever pathogens invade tissues. Especially fond of bacteria, neutrophils engulf their prey, then digest it with the help of chemicals stored inside their granules. This act is usually fatal for the neutrophil – hence its short life span of just hours or days. Fortunately, billions of new neutrophils are produced daily by red bone marrow.

TEM OF LYMPHOCYTE

SEM OF LYMPHOCYTE

LYMPHOCYTES

Although they are the second most numerous leukocytes in the blood, lymphocytes are found in much larger numbers in the lymphatic system (see pp. 152–3). Wherever they are located, lymphocytes form a powerful defense mechanism called the immune system. There are two main types of lymphocytes. B-lymphocytes release chemicals called antibodies that disable pathogens and mark them for destruction. T-lymphocytes destroy enemies directly, especially cancer cells and cells infected by viruses.

TEM OF MONOCYTE

SEM OF MONOCYTE

MONOCYTES

These are the largest leukocytes, identifiable by their agranular cytoplasm and U-shaped nucleus. Monocytes are far less numerous than neutrophils, but have a longer lifespan. Once out of the bloodstream, they enlarge and transform into macrophages – literally, "big eaters" – with a voracious appetite for bacteria. While these macrophages wander through the tissues, others are fixed in lymph nodes and the spleen (see pp. 154–5).

Platelets and clotting

IF A WATER PIPE develops a hole, water will leak out until the supply is turned off. But if a blood vessel is similarly damaged, the hole is rapidly sealed by the circulatory system's self-repair mechanism. This mechanism, called hemostasis ("blood halting"), springs into action whenever a blood vessel breaks. Hemostasis involves three phases that happen in a rapid sequence. First, chemicals released by the damaged vessel make the vessel constrict (narrow) so that the flow of blood is immediately slowed down. Next, tiny platelets carried by the blood congregate around the damaged site and form a temporary plug to stop the leak. Finally, blood coagulates (clots) to form a more permanent seal where new tissue will grow to repair the hole in the blood vessel.

MEDICINAL LEECHES
When blood-sucking leeches like these bite through human skin, chemicals in their saliva stop blood from clotting and increase blood flow. Until the 19th century, doctors regularly used leeches to bleed their patients as a "cure" for all kinds of disorders. Today, leeches are still used in special cases, such as when severed body parts are reattached to the body, because they get blood flowing and drain any excess.

PLATELETS
Unlike blood cells, platelets are not complete cells, but are tiny cell fragments, round or oval in shape, each about one-third the size of a red blood cell. The 1,500 billion platelets circulating in the blood play a vital role in stopping bleeding, by first plugging the leak and then triggering the events that lead to the formation of a clot (see opposite). Under normal conditions, the lining of a blood vessel, or endothelium, is smooth, allowing blood to flow easily over it. But if the vessel is cut and its endothelium disrupted, blood platelets at the scene undergo a remarkable transformation. They swell, form spiky processes, and stick as if glued to the damaged site. These sticky, activated platelets release chemicals that attract more platelets. Within a few minutes, the mass of platelets forms a temporary plug to stop blood loss. Now the clotting process can begin.

Platelets *are normally round or oval*

Projections *enable activated platelets to contact each other*

SEM OF PLATELETS

SEM OF ACTIVATED PLATELETS

WOUND HEALING

Damage to blood vessels can happen deep inside the body or, as in this case, near the surface of the skin. Wherever the wound is, the body responds in the same way, except that a hard scab does not form inside the body. As soon as an injury occurs, platelets stick together to form a temporary plug in the wound. Once this plug is formed, the next stage of healing – coagulation – is triggered. A chain of events is set off that results in the formation of a clot, a more permanent structure than the plug, that remains in place until the damage has been repaired by cell division.

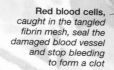

Red blood cells, *caught in the tangled fibrin mesh, seal the damaged blood vessel and stop bleeding to form a clot*

Threads of fibrin *form a mesh, like a fishing net, trapping red blood cells to form a clot*

SEM OF A BLOOD CLOT

CLOT FORMATION

Within minutes of an injury, a gel-like clot begins to form at the wound site as a result of coagulation of the blood. Platelets trigger the activation of chemicals called clotting factors that normally circulate in the blood in inactive form unless mobilized. Activation happens as a "cascade" sequence, with one factor activating the next, until, finally, the soluble blood protein fibrinogen is converted into insoluble fibrin, which forms a mesh of tough threads that traps blood cells to make a clot.

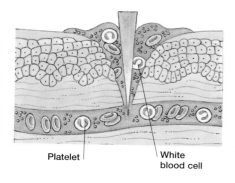

INJURY
A pin has punctured a small blood vessel just below the skin's surface. As blood oozes out, the damage to the blood vessel causes platelets to change and become "sticky." White blood cells track down any invading microorganisms.

Platelet | White blood cell

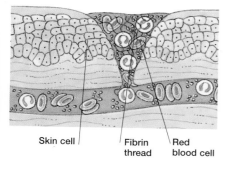

CLOT FORMATION
The "sticky" platelets clump together in the wound, forming a plug that stops blood from leaking out. They also release chemicals that turn the soluble blood protein fibrinogen into fibrin threads. These trap blood cells and more platelets to make a clot.

Skin cell | Fibrin thread | Red blood cell

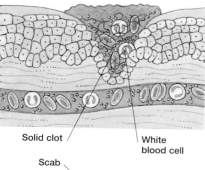

OLDER CLOT
In time, the clot becomes firmer and tightens, pulling the edges of the damaged blood vessel closer together so that blood loss is reduced even more. Cells in the skin and blood vessel wall divide, providing new cells to repair the damage.

Solid clot | White blood cell

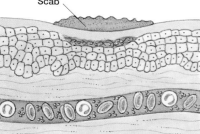

Scab

SCAB
On the skin's surface, the clot dries to form a hard scab. Beneath the scab, the clot shrinks as cell division continues to repair the skin and blood vessel. As wound repair reaches completion, the scab loosens and falls off, leaving fully healed tissue below.

HEMOPHILIA

Affecting only males, hemophilia prevents blood from clotting properly, so excessive bleeding occurs. It is caused by an abnormal gene, located on the X chromosome, one of the sex chromosomes (see pp. 248–49). This stops production of one of the clotting factors described above, so that the clotting process is halted before a clot forms. Girls who inherit an abnormal gene are unaffected, but they can pass on the disease, because they have two X chromosomes, one of which contains a normal gene. The son of a female carrier has a 1 in 2 chance of inheriting hemophilia. Boys with a defective gene get the disease because they have only one X chromosome. The most famous occurrence of the condition was in the British royal family in the 19th century. Queen Victoria was a carrier, as were two of her daughters, but only one of her sons was affected.

Prince Albert | Queen Victoria

■ **Carrier of hemophilia**　　■ **Sufferer of hemophilia**　　■ **Normal male or female**

BLOOD TRANSFUSIONS

BRITISH PHYSICIAN William Harvey announced in 1628 that theheart is responsible for pumping blood around the body in arteries and veins, overthrowing the long-held belief that the body makes and consumes large amounts of blood daily. This discovery led to a new way of treating patients whose lives were threatened by blood loss or illness, by transfusing, or transferring, blood into their veins from a healthy donor. Early attempts at blood transfusions usually failed and were sometimes fatal. Routine, safe transfusions finally became possible in the early years of the 20th century, when scientists recognized that blood carries a complex defense system for destroying invading cells – including transfused blood cells.

FIFTY-FIFTY SUCCESS RATE
Early person-to-person transfusions involved joining arteries and veins surgically, an awkward and painful method. Some surgeons used syringe to inject blood, but failure rates by b methods were high. Only 114 of the 243 patients transfused before 1873 fully recovered from the ordeal.

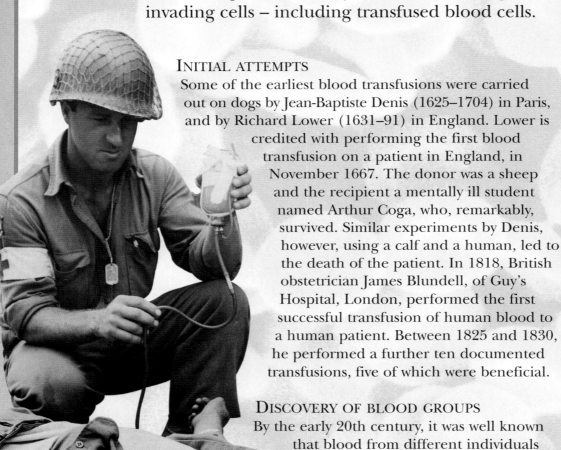

INITIAL ATTEMPTS

Some of the earliest blood transfusions were carried out on dogs by Jean-Baptiste Denis (1625–1704) in Paris, and by Richard Lower (1631–91) in England. Lower is credited with performing the first blood transfusion on a patient in England, in November 1667. The donor was a sheep and the recipient a mentally ill student named Arthur Coga, who, remarkably, survived. Similar experiments by Denis, however, using a calf and a human, led to the death of the patient. In 1818, British obstetrician James Blundell, of Guy's Hospital, London, performed the first successful transfusion of human blood to a human patient. Between 1825 and 1830, he performed a further ten documented transfusions, five of which were beneficial.

DISCOVERY OF BLOOD GROUPS

By the early 20th century, it was well known that blood from different individuals often thickened (coagulated) when it was mixed, blocking

KARL LANDSTEINER
Austrian-born American scientist Karl Landsteiner discovered the ABO blood group system in the early 1900s, the M, N, and P systems in 1927, and the rhesus system in 1940. Landsteiner was awarded the Nobel Prize in 1930.

TRANSFUSIONS IN THE FIELD
Landsteiner's discovery of blood groups had an impact on the survival of wounded soldiers. From World War 1 onward, improved methods for storing blood made it possible to stockpile blood and transfuse casualties on the battlefield.

BLOOD GROUP COMPATIBILITY

Blood is always typed before transfusion to make sure a person receives blood that matches their own ABO and Rh blood groups to avoid adverse reactions. In an emergency, however, group O blood can be given to anyone, while someone who is group AB can receive blood from any donor. This chart shows compatible donors and recipients.

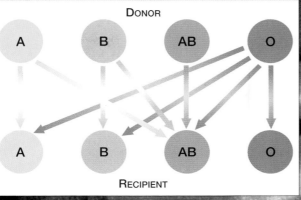

DONOR

A   B   AB   O

A   B   AB   O

RECIPIENT

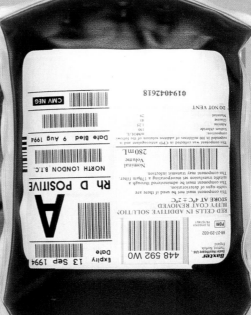

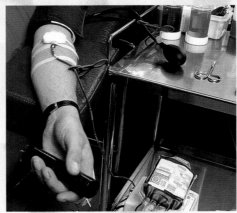

BLOOD BANK
Blood is tested for diseases and checked for its blood group. Chemicals are added to increase its shelf life, and it is stored at low temperature in hospitals until it is needed. It can be stored either as blood, or as one of its components, such as plasma.

blood vessels. The explanation for this was provided by Karl Landsteiner (1868–1943), who in 1901 discovered that within the human population there were different blood groups. Which of the four blood groups a person belonged to – A, B, AB, or O – depended on the presence or absence of two molecular markers called antigens – identified as A and B – carried on the surface of their red blood cells. Group A has the A antigen, group B the B antigen, group AB both antigens, and group O neither antigen. Also present in blood plasma are antibodies that act against antigens not present on a person's own red blood cells. Group A blood contains anti-B antibodies, group B blood contains anti-A antibodies, group O blood contains both antibodies, and group AB blood contains neither. This explains why, for example, if a group A person is given group B blood, their anti-B antibodies "recognize" the B antigens on the foreign red blood cells, make them stick together, and block blood vessels.

In 1940, Landsteiner recognized the rhesus antigen (Rh), first identified in rhesus monkeys. About 85 percent of people are rhesus positive (Rh+) because they carry the antigen, while the remainder lack the antigen and are therefore rhesus negative (Rh-).

SAFE TRANSFUSIONS

Once an individual's blood group could be identified by simple tests, safe blood transfusions became routine. But obtaining enough blood for emergency use is still a problem. Blood can be stored at low temperature in blood banks, but only for limited periods, so an important long-term goal is to develop artificial blood that can be given to a member of any blood group.

GIVING BLOOD
Healthy individuals can donate 1 pint (500 ml) of blood every 16 weeks. They can also donate parts of their blood, such as red cells, white cells, plasma, or platelets, more frequently. To give blood, the donor lies down and has a needle inserted into a vein near the elbow. Blood flows down a plastic tube and into a storage bag.

Heart

ONCE THOUGHT TO BE the source of feelings of love and emotion, the heart is actually the powerhouse of the circulatory system. Rhythmic contractions of this muscular pump push blood along the blood vessels to all parts of the body, even its far extremities, and back to the heart again. The beating heart ensures that every cell of the body has an uninterrupted supply of food, oxygen, and other essentials. So powerful is the heart that it can pump the body's entire blood volume of 10 pints (5 liters) around the body about once every minute. On average it beats, or pumps, 70 times a minute when the body is at rest, yet can increase this rate if the body is more active. Over a lifetime of 70 years, the heart beats some 2.5 billion times without tiring or stopping for a rest, thanks to the cardiac muscle in its walls.

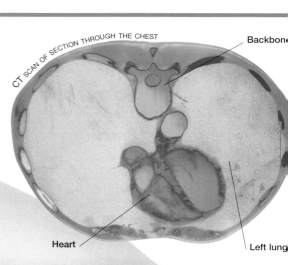

CT SCAN OF SECTION THROUGH THE CHEST

Backbone

Heart

Left lung

HEART AND LUNGS

This CT scan "slices" through the chest to show clearly how the heart is surrounded by right and left lungs. Being this close is important. It cuts to a minimum the distance blood has to travel from the heart to pick up oxygen in the lungs.

TWO SIDES

Divided into the left and right sides, the heart is two pumps in one. On each side, blood enters the atrium, then passes into the ventricle to be pumped on its onward journey. On the right side, oxygen-poor blood (blue) enters the right atrium, flows into the right ventricle, and is pumped to the lungs. On the left side, oxygen-rich blood (red) enters the left atrium, flows into the left ventricle, and is pumped to the rest of the body.

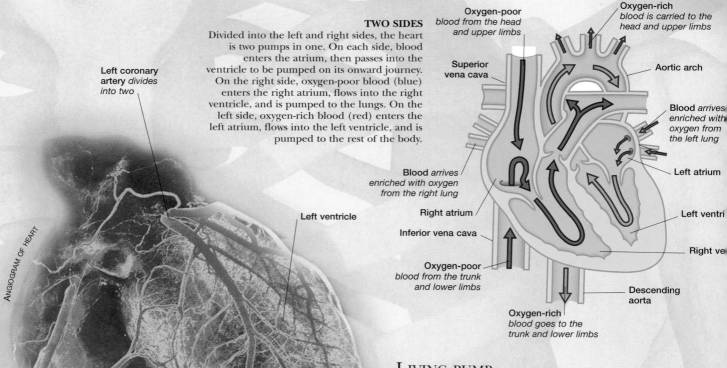

Left coronary artery *divides into two*

Left ventricle

Right ventricle

Right coronary artery

Network of blood vessels *supplies heart muscle with oxygen and food*

Heart *is tilted toward the left side of the body*

ANGIOGRAM OF HEART

Oxygen-poor *blood from the head and upper limbs*

Superior vena cava

Blood *arrives enriched with oxygen from the right lung*

Right atrium

Inferior vena cava

Oxygen-poor *blood from the trunk and lower limbs*

Oxygen-rich *blood goes to the trunk and lower limbs*

Oxygen-rich *blood is carried to the head and upper limbs*

Aortic arch

Blood *arrives enriched with oxygen from the left lung*

Left atrium

Left ventri[cle]

Right ve[ntricle]

Descending aorta

LIVING PUMP

As this angiogram of the heart shows, the heart is the size of a clenched fist and lies in the middle of the thorax (chest) with its apex (tip) pointing downward and to the left. The angiogram also reveals the coronary blood vessels on the surface of the heart. Because the heart is a pump made out of living tissue, it too requires a supply of blood. However, the blood that gushes through it every second cannot meet the demands of the heart muscle for food and oxygen. To overcome this problem, coronary arteries arise from the aorta as it leaves the heart, and branch to carry oxygen-rich blood to the cardiac muscle in the heart wall (see also pp. 144–5).

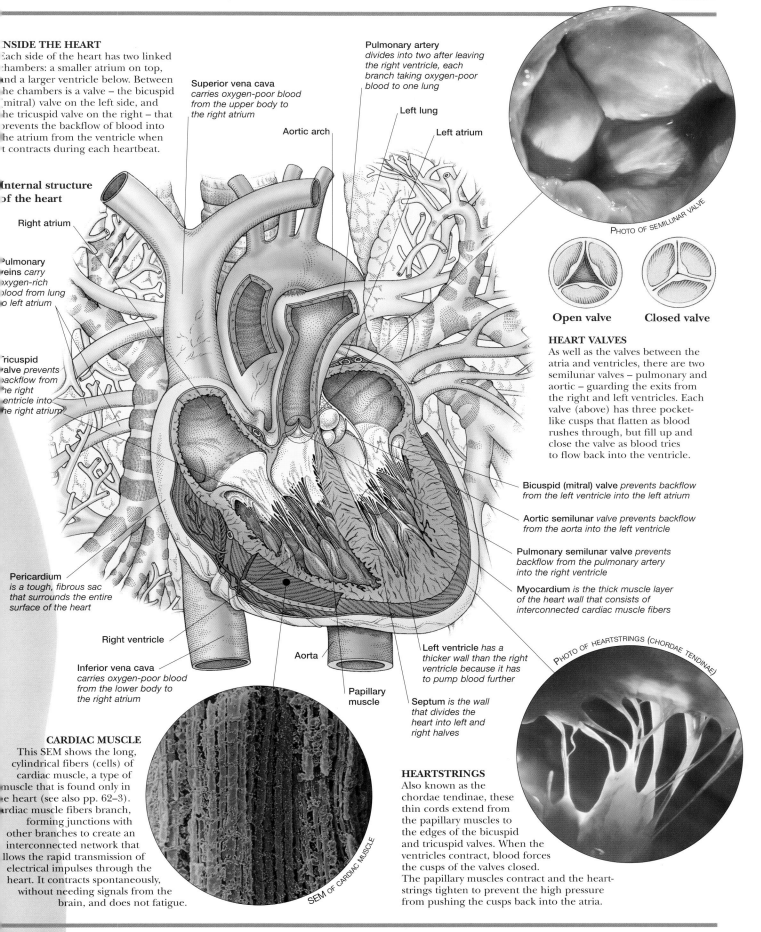

INSIDE THE HEART

Each side of the heart has two linked chambers: a smaller atrium on top, and a larger ventricle below. Between the chambers is a valve – the bicuspid (mitral) valve on the left side, and the tricuspid valve on the right – that prevents the backflow of blood into the atrium from the ventricle when it contracts during each heartbeat.

Internal structure of the heart

Right atrium

Pulmonary veins *carry oxygen-rich blood from lung to left atrium*

Tricuspid valve *prevents backflow from the right ventricle into the right atrium*

Pericardium *is a tough, fibrous sac that surrounds the entire surface of the heart*

Right ventricle

Inferior vena cava *carries oxygen-poor blood from the lower body to the right atrium*

Superior vena cava *carries oxygen-poor blood from the upper body to the right atrium*

Aortic arch

Pulmonary artery *divides into two after leaving the right ventricle, each branch taking oxygen-poor blood to one lung*

Left lung

Left atrium

Aorta

Papillary muscle

PHOTO OF SEMILUNAR VALVE

Open valve   **Closed valve**

HEART VALVES

As well as the valves between the atria and ventricles, there are two semilunar valves – pulmonary and aortic – guarding the exits from the right and left ventricles. Each valve (above) has three pocket-like cusps that flatten as blood rushes through, but fill up and close the valve as blood tries to flow back into the ventricle.

Bicuspid (mitral) valve *prevents backflow from the left ventricle into the left atrium*

Aortic semilunar *valve prevents backflow from the aorta into the left ventricle*

Pulmonary semilunar valve *prevents backflow from the pulmonary artery into the right ventricle*

Myocardium *is the thick muscle layer of the heart wall that consists of interconnected cardiac muscle fibers*

Left ventricle *has a thicker wall than the right ventricle because it has to pump blood further*

Septum *is the wall that divides the heart into left and right halves*

PHOTO OF HEARTSTRINGS (CHORDAE TENDINAE)

CARDIAC MUSCLE

This SEM shows the long, cylindrical fibers (cells) of cardiac muscle, a type of muscle that is found only in the heart (see also pp. 62–3). Cardiac muscle fibers branch, forming junctions with other branches to create an interconnected network that allows the rapid transmission of electrical impulses through the heart. It contracts spontaneously, without needing signals from the brain, and does not fatigue.

SEM OF CARDIAC MUSCLE

HEARTSTRINGS

Also known as the chordae tendinae, these thin cords extend from the papillary muscles to the edges of the bicuspid and tricuspid valves. When the ventricles contract, blood forces the cusps of the valves closed. The papillary muscles contract and the heart-strings tighten to prevent the high pressure from pushing the cusps back into the atria.

Heartbeats

MOST PEOPLE HAVE experienced the feeling of a pounding heart, especially after running fast and then stopping suddenly. Every rhythmic pulsation represents one heartbeat, but not just one event. Each beat is made up of three stages called the heartbeat cycle. The entire cycle is masterminded by a patch of modified cardiac muscle called the sinoatrial (SA) node that acts as a pacemaker, sending out regular electrical impulses to stimulate contraction of the heart's chambers. Heart contraction happens spontaneously, but outside control in the form of the autonomic nervous system (ANS) is needed to alter the rate and strength of heartbeats in order to meet the ever-changing needs of the body.

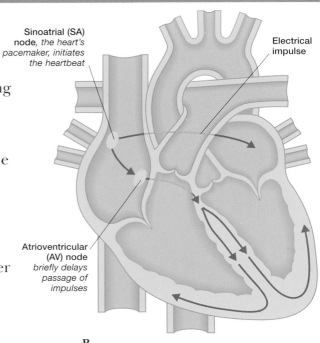

Sinoatrial (SA) node, the heart's pacemaker, initiates the heartbeat

Electrical impulse

Atrioventricular (AV) node briefly delays passage of impulses

HEARTBEAT CYCLE

The three diagrams below show the stages of a heartbeat cycle. During diastole (relaxation), the heart relaxes, the atria fill with blood, and the pulmonary and aortic semilunar valves close to prevent backflow. During atrial systole (contraction), the atria contract to push blood into their respective ventricles. During ventricular systole, as the two ventricles contract together to pump blood out of the heart, blood pressure forces the semilunar valves open and the bicuspid and tricuspid valves shut. The three stages correspond to different sections of an ECG recording, an example of which extends across these pages and is explained (right).

ELECTRICAL PATHWAYS

Electrical impulses spread through the atria from the SA node, then are briefly delayed at the atrioventricular (AV) node, giving the atria time to contract before impulses spread through the ventricles and trigger their contraction. This electrical activity, recorded as an electrocardiogram (ECG), below, shows characteristic peaks. The P wave occurs as impulses travel over the atria, the QRS peak as impulses pass through the ventricles, and the T wave as the ventricles relax.

R

P

T

Q

S

ECG recording

Stage 1

Stage 2

Stage 3

Aorta

Contracted right atrium

Right atrium fills with oxygen-poor blood from the body

Oxygen-rich blood from lungs fills left atrium

Semilunar valves closed

Oxygen-poor blood from lower body

Contracted left atrium

Semilunar valves open

Semilunar valves closed

Tricuspid and bicuspid valves open

Full right ventricle

Full left ventricle

Tricuspid and bicuspid valves closed

Oxygen-rich blood flows to upper and lower body

Oxygen-poor blood flows to the lungs

Pulmonary artery

Contracted ventricles

Stage 1. Diastole
The heart muscle is relaxed, allowing oxygen-rich blood from the lungs and oxygen-poor blood from the body to enter the left and right atria, respectively.

Stage 2. Atrial systole
The atria contract to squeeze their remaining blood into the ventricles. The tricuspid and bicuspid valves open to allow this, but the semilunar valves remain closed.

Stage 3. Ventricular systole
Contraction of the ventricles sends blood to the lungs and around the body. The semilunar valves are pushed open by the surge of blood, while the tricuspid and bicuspid valves are closed.

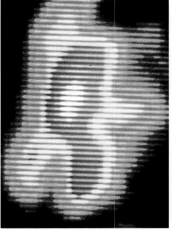

Left ventricle contracted **Left ventricle relaxed**

LISTENING TO HEARTBEATS

The effective working of the valves can be assessed by listening to the sounds they make as they close. Early physicians listened to the heartbeat by placing an ear to the chest, but a one-ear stethoscope, invented by French doctor René Laënnec (1781–1826) in 1816, made the sounds much clearer and easier to hear. About 40 years later, the principles of this instrument were used to develop the two-ear, or binaural, stethoscope, which is still used today. In addition to assessing the heart, a stethoscope can be used to listen to breathing sounds made by the lungs and to sounds generated by the intestines.

Laënnec-type stethoscope, c. 1820

HEART SOUNDS

The gamma camera scans (above) provide one way for doctors to follow the heartbeat cycle in action. Another is to use a stethoscope to listen for the sounds produced when the heart's valves close. Each heartbeat produces two sounds: a longer, louder "lub" sound when bicuspid and tricuspid valves close, and a shorter, sharper "dub" sound when the semilunar valves close. Unusual heart sounds can indicate that a valve is leaking.

CONTROLLING HEART RATE

Heart rate is controlled by the sympathetic and parasympathetic sections of the ANS (see pp. 98–9), whose nerve fibers terminate in the heart's pacemaking SA node. Under orders from the cardioregulatory center in the brain stem, which monitors conditions inside the body, sympathetic signals speed up heart rate during exercise or stress, while parasympathetic signals slow heart rate when the body is at rest to about 70 beats per minute.

Sympathetic *speeds up heart rate during exercise*

Parasympathetic *slows heart rate after exercise*

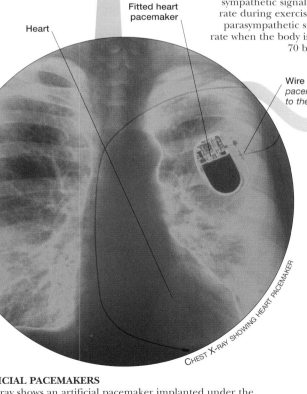

Fitted heart pacemaker

Heart

Wire *connects pacemaker to the heart*

CHEST X-RAY SHOWING HEART PACEMAKER

ARTIFICIAL PACEMAKERS

This X-ray shows an artificial pacemaker implanted under the skin of a person whose SA node has stopped working normally, or whose heart does not conduct electrical impulses properly. Powered by a long-life battery, the pacemaker sends electrical impulses along a wire to stimulate the heart to beat. Some send out impulses at a fixed rate, some switch on if the heart misses a beat, and some vary their rate to match body activity levels.

Exercise can increase heart rate significantly

HEART PROBLEMS

UNSEEN INSIDE THE CHEST, the heart is taken for granted – until something goes wrong. A common cause of heart problems is a narrowing or blocking of the coronary arteries, which provide heart muscle with oxygen – a condition known as coronary artery disease. Its main symptom is chest pain, noticed during stress or exercise, when extra demands are put on the heart. The chances of developing this problem are increased by smoking, high blood pressure, a high-fat diet, obesity, and inactivity. But before looking at the consequences and treatment of this disease, consider a drastic measure that can deal with a badly damaged heart.

FIRST HEART TRANSPLANTS
In 1967, Christiaan Barnard led a team of 20 surgeons to perform the first human heart transplant.

HEART TRANSPLANTS

First performed in 1967 in South Africa by Professor Christiaan Barnard (1922–2001), a heart transplant involves the replacement of a diseased heart with a healthy one. Before the damaged heart is removed, the recipient's major blood vessels are connected to a bypass machine that pumps oxygen-rich blood to the brain and other organs. Once in place, the healthy heart is connected to the recipient's vessels and the bypass machine is switched off. Rejection of the new heart by the recipient's immune system is a major risk, and the patient must take preventive medication.

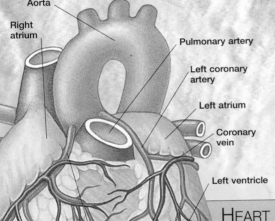

Aorta
Right atrium
Pulmonary artery
Left coronary artery
Left atrium
Coronary vein
Left ventricle
Right ventricle
Right coronary artery

Front view of heart

CORONARY VESSELS

Both main coronary arteries originate from the aorta. The right coronary artery branches to deliver blood mainly to the right side of the heart; the left artery and its branches supply both ventricles and the left atrium, as well as the septum, the muscular wall that divides the heart. The smallest arterial branches connect to the smallest veins by capillaries. Coronary veins return oxygen-poor blood to the coronary sinus, a large vein at the back of the heart that empties into the right atrium.

HEART ATTACKS

Narrowing of coronary arteries can occur as a result of atheroma, a common condition in which fatty substances are deposited on the lining of arterial walls, causing scarring. If a narrowed artery becomes blocked by a blood clot, the blood supply to an area of the heart is cut off, causing permanent damage to this area. This occurrence is known as a heart attack or myocardial infarction.

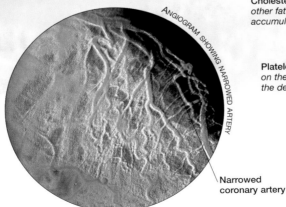

ANGIOGRAM SHOWING NARROWED ARTERY

Narrowed coronary artery

Cholesterol *and other fatty substances accumulate*

EARLY ATHEROSCLEROSIS
The first signs of atherosclerosis, the narrowing of arteries, are the gradual accumulation of fatty substances in the artery wall.

Platelets *collect on the surface of the deposits*

ADVANCED STAGES
The yellow deposits, called atheroma, cause the muscle layer to thicken. They restrict blood flow and narrow the artery.

HEALTHY HEART

The well-being of the heart can be assessed by performing a walking electrocardiogram (ECG), which records the electrical activity within the heart during a period of exercise on a treadmill. The speed of walking is gradually increased – and the treadmill may also be inclined – so that the stress on the heart slowly rises. Some conditions, such as coronary artery disease, may be diagnosed if particular changes are seen on the trace.

PHOTO OF DEFLATED ANGIOPLASTY BALLOON

WIDENING VESSELS

When coronary heart disease has been diagnosed, a doctor may perform balloon angioplasty to prevent a heart attack. A catheter (tube) carrying a deflated "balloon" is fed through an artery in the leg and into the affected coronary artery. The balloon is inflated to enlarge the coronary artery and improve blood flow. Once this is achieved, the balloon is deflated and withdrawn from the body.

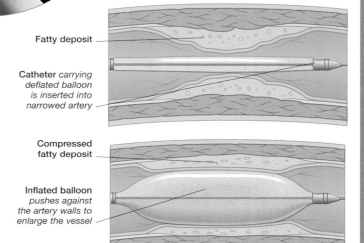

Fatty deposit

Catheter *carrying deflated balloon is inserted into narrowed artery*

Compressed fatty deposit

Inflated balloon *pushes against the artery walls to enlarge the vessel*

Balloon angioplasty

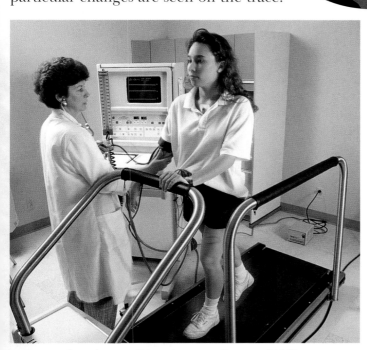

Patient undergoing a walking electrocardiogram (ECG)

EMERGENCY DEFIBRILLATION

Coronary heart disease may result in a heart attack which can cause fibrillation. This occurs when cardiac muscle fibers contract individually and chaotically rather than together, as happens ordinarily. As a consequence, the ventricles cannot pump blood, a condition known as cardiac arrest. To counteract this problem, emergency defibrillation, or cardioversion ("turning the heart"), can be performed by giving the heart a brief electric shock through two metal plates applied to the chest (right). The shock may restore normal synchronized contractions.

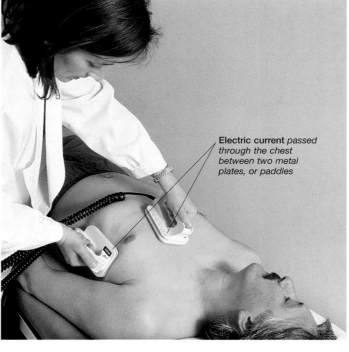

Electric current *passed through the chest between two metal plates, or paddles*

Blood circulation

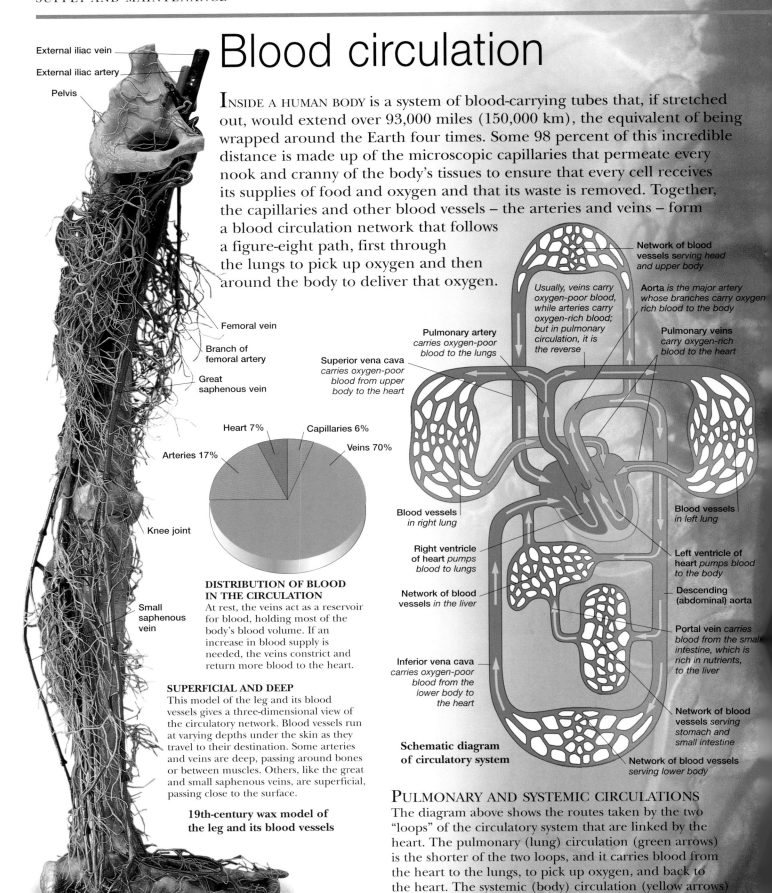

INSIDE A HUMAN BODY is a system of blood-carrying tubes that, if stretched out, would extend over 93,000 miles (150,000 km), the equivalent of being wrapped around the Earth four times. Some 98 percent of this incredible distance is made up of the microscopic capillaries that permeate every nook and cranny of the body's tissues to ensure that every cell receives its supplies of food and oxygen and that its waste is removed. Together, the capillaries and other blood vessels – the arteries and veins – form a blood circulation network that follows a figure-eight path, first through the lungs to pick up oxygen and then around the body to deliver that oxygen.

External iliac vein

External iliac artery

Pelvis

Femoral vein

Branch of femoral artery

Great saphenous vein

Knee joint

Small saphenous vein

Bones of the foot

Heart 7%

Capillaries 6%

Veins 70%

Arteries 17%

DISTRIBUTION OF BLOOD IN THE CIRCULATION
At rest, the veins act as a reservoir for blood, holding most of the body's blood volume. If an increase in blood supply is needed, the veins constrict and return more blood to the heart.

SUPERFICIAL AND DEEP
This model of the leg and its blood vessels gives a three-dimensional view of the circulatory network. Blood vessels run at varying depths under the skin as they travel to their destination. Some arteries and veins are deep, passing around bones or between muscles. Others, like the great and small saphenous veins, are superficial, passing close to the surface.

19th-century wax model of the leg and its blood vessels

Network of blood vessels serving head and upper body

Usually, veins carry oxygen-poor blood, while arteries carry oxygen-rich blood; but in pulmonary circulation, it is the reverse

Aorta is the major artery whose branches carry oxygen rich blood to the body

Pulmonary artery carries oxygen-poor blood to the lungs

Pulmonary veins carry oxygen-rich blood to the heart

Superior vena cava carries oxygen-poor blood from upper body to the heart

Blood vessels in right lung

Blood vessels in left lung

Right ventricle of heart pumps blood to lungs

Left ventricle of heart pumps blood to the body

Network of blood vessels in the liver

Descending (abdominal) aorta

Portal vein carries blood from the small intestine, which is rich in nutrients, to the liver

Inferior vena cava carries oxygen-poor blood from the lower body to the heart

Schematic diagram of circulatory system

Network of blood vessels serving stomach and small intestine

Network of blood vessels serving lower body

PULMONARY AND SYSTEMIC CIRCULATIONS
The diagram above shows the routes taken by the two "loops" of the circulatory system that are linked by the heart. The pulmonary (lung) circulation (green arrows) is the shorter of the two loops, and it carries blood from the heart to the lungs, to pick up oxygen, and back to the heart. The systemic (body) circulation (yellow arrows) carries blood to all body tissues and back to the heart.

Major arteries and veins

Internal jugular vein *drains the brain*

Common carotid artery *supplies the head and brain*

Pulmonary artery *carries blood from the heart to the lungs*

Subclavian artery *supplies the arm and thorax*

Pulmonary vein *carries blood from the lungs to the heart*

Superior vena cava *drains blood from the upper body*

Brachial vein *drains the arm*

Aortic arch *is first portion of the aorta, which curves behind the heart*

Hepatic vein *drains the liver*

Heart

Hepatic artery *supplies the liver*

Brachial artery *supplies the upper arm*

Renal vein *drains the kidney*

Renal artery *supplies the kidney*

Superior mesenteric artery *supplies the intestines*

Inferior vena cava *drains blood from the lower body*

Descending (abdominal) aorta *supplies the abdomen and legs*

Common iliac artery *supplies the pelvis and legs*

Common iliac vein *drains the pelvis and legs*

Femoral artery *supplies the thigh and knee*

Femoral vein *drains the thigh*

Great saphenous vein *drains the foot and leg*

Splenic artery

Renal artery

Small saphenous vein *drains the foot and leg muscles*

Backbone

Arterior tibial artery *supplies lower leg and foot*

Descending (abdominal) aorta

Common iliac artery

ABDOMINAL ARTERIES
This angiogram of the arteries in the abdomen shows the descending (abdominal) section of the aorta, which delivers blood from the heart to the abdomen and legs. Arteries arising from it include the splenic artery, which supplies the pancreas, stomach, and spleen, and the renal arteries, which supply the kidneys. Lower down, the aorta splits into the two common iliac arteries, which supply the legs.

ARTERIES
Some 1 in (2.5 cm) wide, the aorta emerges from the top of the left side of the heart, curves around and behind it, and descends to the lower abdomen, where it splits into the two arteries that serve the legs. The aorta has many branches that supply the body's organs with oxygen-rich blood.

VEINS
Blood that has passed through the tissues and is depleted of oxygen and food is directed into the many veins that empty into the body's main veins – the inferior vena cava from the lower body, and the superior vena cava from the upper body. These large veins finally empty into the right side of the heart.

Blood vessels

BLOOD IS TRANSPORTED around the body in three main types of blood vessels – arteries, veins, and capillaries. Arteries carry oxygen-rich blood from the heart to the tissues. Their walls have a wide middle layer of muscle fibers and elastic tissue that enables them to expand and recoil as blood surges through them at high-pressure when the heart contracts. Veins have thinner walls, with valves to prevent backflow as they carry blood under low pressure back to the heart. Capillaries are the smallest, and most numerous, blood vessels. Within walls just one cell thick, they carry blood through the tissues, linking the smallest branches of arteries (arterioles) and veins (venules).

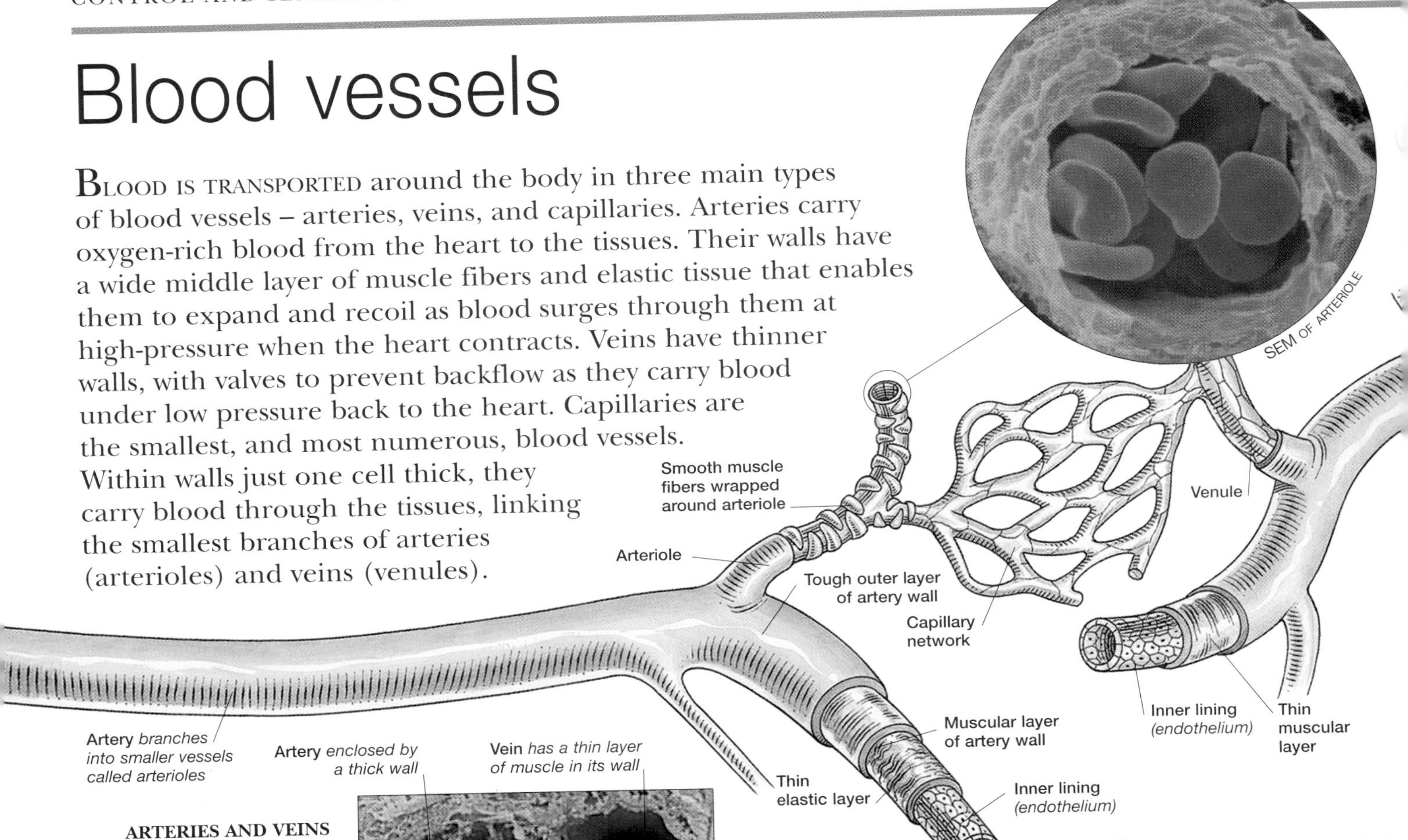

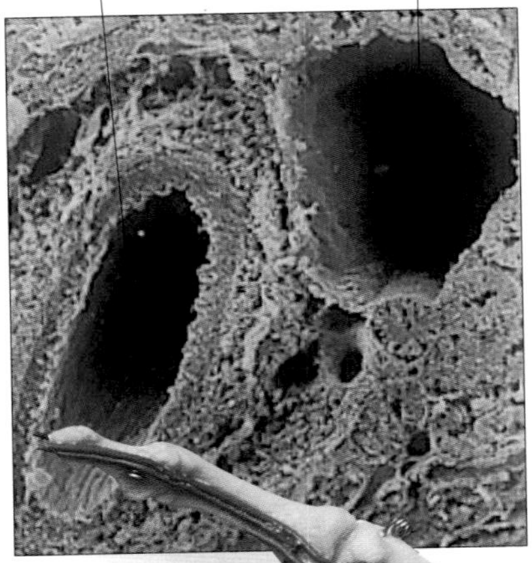

SEM OF ARTERIOLE

Smooth muscle fibers wrapped around arteriole

Venule

Arteriole

Tough outer layer of artery wall

Capillary network

Inner lining (endothelium)

Thin muscular layer

Muscular layer of artery wall

Artery branches into smaller vessels called arterioles

Artery enclosed by a thick wall

Vein has a thin layer of muscle in its wall

Thin elastic layer

Inner lining (endothelium)

ARTERIES AND VEINS

This SEM shows a section cut through a piece of tissue, through which an artery and a vein run in parallel. It clearly reveals the difference between arteries and veins. Although they both have about the same diameter, the artery has a narrower lumen (space in the middle through which blood flows) because it has a thicker, more muscular wall, while the vein has a wider lumen but a thinner, less muscular wall.

NETWORK OF VESSELS

The diagram above shows how oxygen-rich blood is carried into the tissues by arteries, which divide to form arterioles less than 0.001 in (0.3 mm) in diameter. The smallest arterioles are wrapped in smooth muscle fibers, which contract or relax to control blood flow. Arterioles divide to form capillaries that pass close to, and serve, tissue cells. The capillaries then unite to form tiny vein branches called venules, which merge to form the larger veins that return oxygen-poor blood to the heart. The model below shows the major blood arteries and veins of the arm, although the capillaries that link them are too small to be visible.

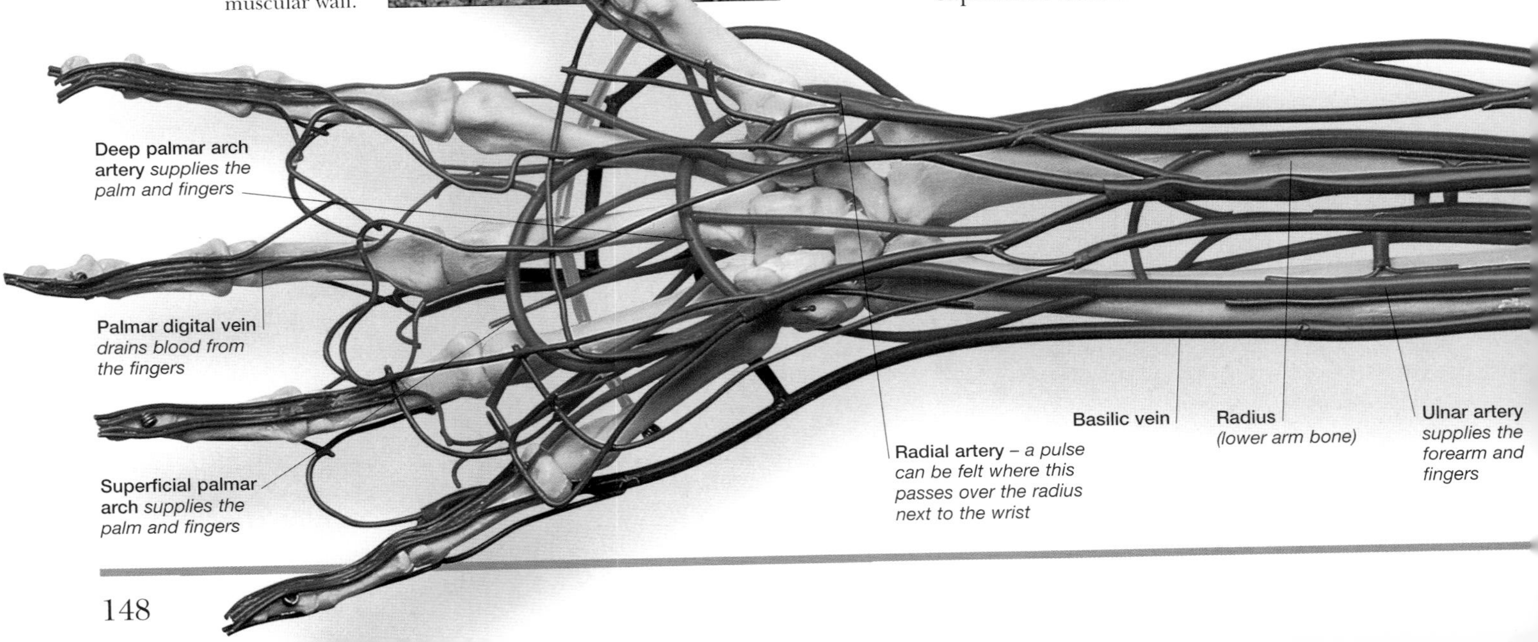

Deep palmar arch artery supplies the palm and fingers

Palmar digital vein drains blood from the fingers

Superficial palmar arch supplies the palm and fingers

Radial artery – a pulse can be felt where this passes over the radius next to the wrist

Basilic vein

Radius (lower arm bone)

Ulnar artery supplies the forearm and fingers

Valve *prevents blood from flowing backward*

Nucleus *of endothelial cell that forms the capillary wall*

Vein *branches into smaller tubes called venules*

Red blood cell *inside a capillary*

TEM OF SECTION THROUGH A BLOOD CAPILLARY

TISSUE DELIVERY

This section through a capillary shows how narrow it is – just wider, in fact, than a red blood cell passing through it. It reveals, too, how thin its wall is – only one cell thick. The wall is also quite "leaky," allowing fluid carrying food and oxygen to pass out of the blood and into the tissue fluid that surrounds the cells, and return in the opposite direction carrying the cells' wastes.

VENOUS RETURN

Blood pressure in the veins is much lower than that in arteries. Despite this lack of "push," various mechanisms make sure that there is adequate venous return – the return of blood along veins back to the heart. Many deep veins lie within muscles, and when the muscles contract, they squeeze blood back toward the heart. Similarly, low pressure in the thorax (chest) produced during breathing in (see pp. 172–3) also draws blood to the heart.

Direction of blood flow

Vein surrounded by muscle

Relaxed muscle

One-way valve

Direction of increased blood flow

Contracted muscle

Squeezed vein

RELAXED MUSCLE
When a person is standing still, the leg muscles surrounding a deep vein are relaxed and blood flow in the vein is sluggish, although one-way valves prevent backflow.

CONTRACTED MUSCLE
During movement, leg muscles surrounding the vein contract providing a muscular pump that squeezes the vein and pushes blood upward toward the heart.

Air inhaled

Chest cavity *at low pressure*

Blood *drawn toward heart*

Diaphragm

RESPIRATORY PUMP
During inhalation, pressure inside the thoracic cavity decreases. Pressure is higher in the rest of the body, so blood is pushed toward the heart.

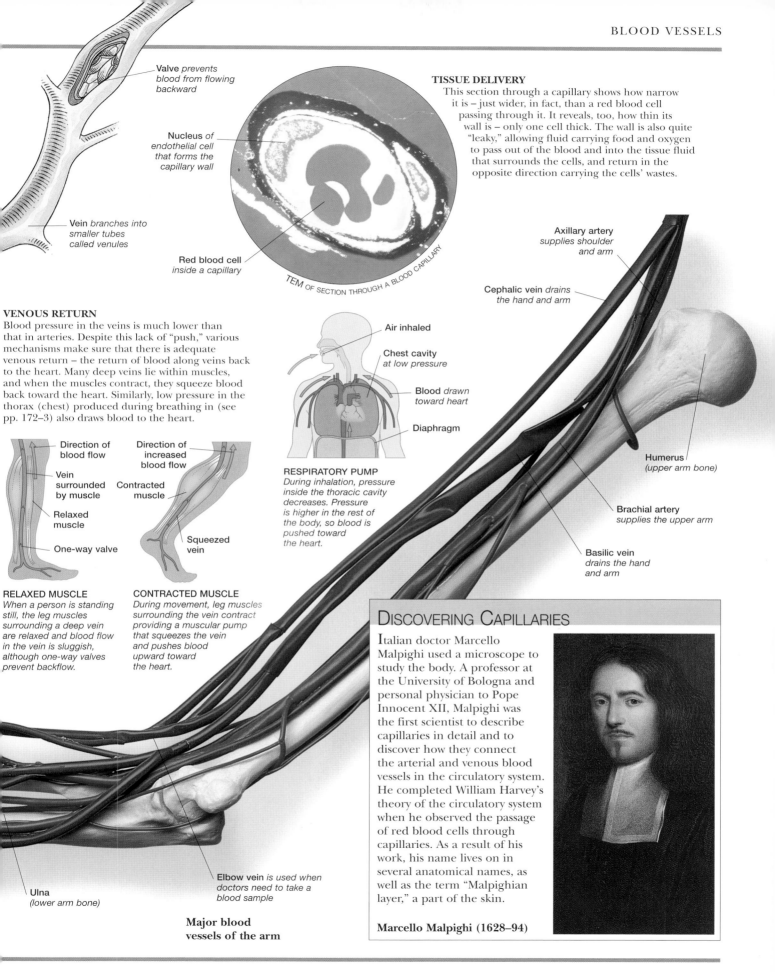

Axillary artery *supplies shoulder and arm*

Cephalic vein *drains the hand and arm*

Humerus *(upper arm bone)*

Brachial artery *supplies the upper arm*

Basilic vein *drains the hand and arm*

Ulna *(lower arm bone)*

Elbow vein *is used when doctors need to take a blood sample*

Major blood vessels of the arm

DISCOVERING CAPILLARIES

Italian doctor Marcello Malpighi used a microscope to study the body. A professor at the University of Bologna and personal physician to Pope Innocent XII, Malpighi was the first scientist to describe capillaries in detail and to discover how they connect the arterial and venous blood vessels in the circulatory system. He completed William Harvey's theory of the circulatory system when he observed the passage of red blood cells through capillaries. As a result of his work, his name lives on in several anatomical names, as well as the term "Malpighian layer," a part of the skin.

Marcello Malpighi (1628–94)

Pressure and flow

EACH TIME THE HEART'S ventricles contract, they squeeze out blood, which exerts pressure on artery walls. This pressure provides the force that pushes blood around the circulatory system. It changes with each heartbeat, rising as the ventricles contract and falling as they relax. In addition to this constant fluctuation, blood pressure increases during exercise as the heart contracts faster and expels a greater volume of blood. Exercise also alters the pattern of blood flow, as blood vessels supplying muscles widen to allow them to receive extra oxygen and nutrients. In a healthy person, blood pressure is kept within strict limits by the brain and hormones. If blood pressure remains too high over long periods, it can cause health problems.

A pulse can be felt by pressing an artery – like the radial artery in the wrist – where it runs over a bone

PULSE
After each heartbeat, a pressure wave – or pulse – passes along an artery as its walls bulge and then recoil to withstand the surge of blood. By pressing on an artery, the number of pulses – or heartbeats – per minute can be counted.

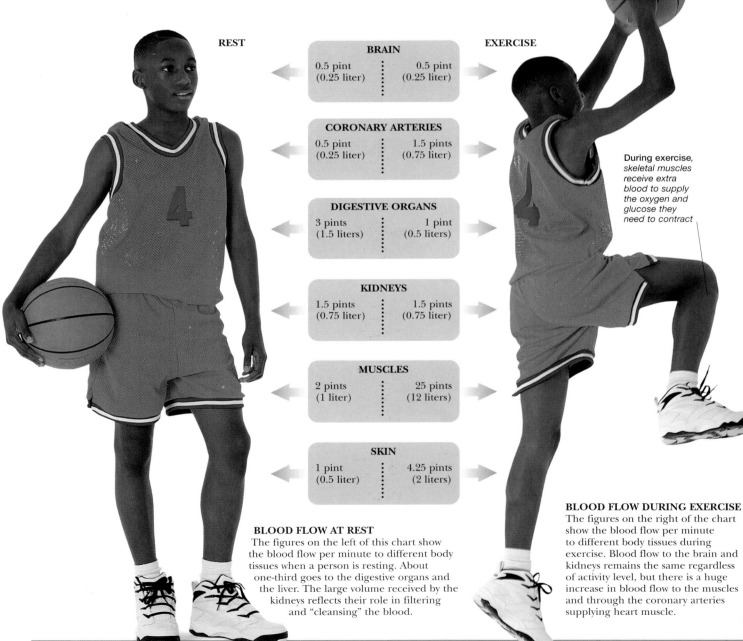

REST   EXERCISE

BRAIN
0.5 pint (0.25 liter)   0.5 pint (0.25 liter)

CORONARY ARTERIES
0.5 pint (0.25 liter)   1.5 pints (0.75 liter)

DIGESTIVE ORGANS
3 pints (1.5 liters)   1 pint (0.5 liters)

KIDNEYS
1.5 pints (0.75 liter)   1.5 pints (0.75 liter)

MUSCLES
2 pints (1 liter)   25 pints (12 liters)

SKIN
1 pint (0.5 liter)   4.25 pints (2 liters)

During exercise, skeletal muscles receive extra blood to supply the oxygen and glucose they need to contract

BLOOD FLOW AT REST
The figures on the left of this chart show the blood flow per minute to different body tissues when a person is resting. About one-third goes to the digestive organs and the liver. The large volume received by the kidneys reflects their role in filtering and "cleansing" the blood.

BLOOD FLOW DURING EXERCISE
The figures on the right of the chart show the blood flow per minute to different body tissues during exercise. Blood flow to the brain and kidneys remains the same regardless of activity level, but there is a huge increase in blood flow to the muscles and through the coronary arteries supplying heart muscle.

MEASURING BLOOD PRESSURE

Blood pressure is measured using a sphygmomanometer (literally a "pulse pressure measurer") that consists of an inflatable cuff linked to a pressure gauge, and a stethoscope. In fact, two pressures, not one, are measured (see below) – systolic and then diastolic. The cuff is wrapped around the upper arm and inflated to squeeze the arm until blood flow along the brachial artery (see p. 149) stops. Placing the end of the stethoscope on the skin over the brachial artery, the doctor now deflates the cuff until a pulse can just be heard. The reading on the gauge shows the higher, systolic pressure, which is sufficient to push blood along the narrowed artery. The cuff is deflated further until the pulse sound just disappears, indicating that blood is flowing freely along the artery. The gauge now shows the lower, diastolic pressure.

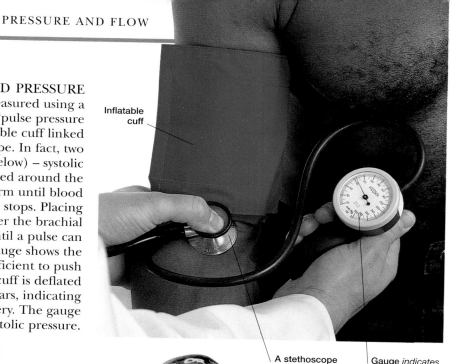

Inflatable cuff

A stethoscope is used by a doctor to listen to blood flow

Gauge indicates pressure

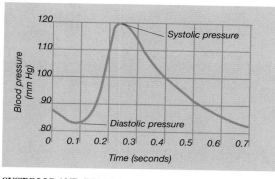

SYSTOLIC AND DIASTOLIC
During each heartbeat cycle (see pp. 142–3), the heart contracts (systole), causing a peak in arterial blood pressure called systolic pressure (see graph, above), then relaxes (diastole), causing a fall to the minimum, diastolic pressure. Pressure, measured in millimeters of mercury (mm Hg), varies according to age, sex, and health, but in a healthy young adult should be about 120/80 (120 mm Hg systolic and 80 mm Hg diastolic).

FROSTBITE
At temperatures below 32°F (0°C), the small arteries supplying the skin and underlying tissues narrow, restricting the supply of blood. If the cold conditions persist, ice forms in the tissues, causing damage. The fingers, toes, and nose are particularly susceptible to this condition, known as frostbite. The damage may be permanent, requiring amputation of the affected tissue in very severe cases.

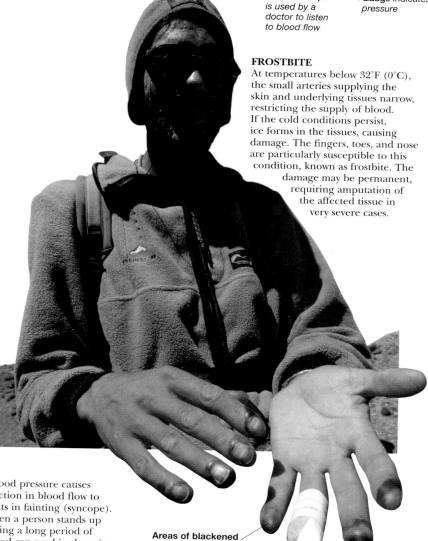

FAINTING
A sudden fall in blood pressure causes a momentary reduction in blood flow to the brain and results in fainting (syncope). This may occur when a person stands up suddenly, or following a long period of standing, when blood can pool in the veins of the legs. Lying down and elevating the legs will help restore normal blood pressure.

Areas of blackened skin indicate tissue death caused by prolonged frostbite

LYMPHATIC AND IMMUNE systems

T HE BODY HAS a second transportation system, which consists of a network of lymphatic vessels and lymphoid organs. Called the lymphatic system, it has two major functions. First, it ensures that blood volume stays the same. Each day, some 51 pints (24 liters) of fluid leave the blood as it passes through the tissues. Most returns to capillaries, but some 6–8 pints (3–4 liters) remains. This surplus, now called lymph, drains into lymphatic vessels and is emptied back into the bloodstream. Second, it plays a major part in body defense. It contains cells, also found in the blood, called lymphocytes and macrophages, which form the immune system, the body's most powerful defense against disease (see pp. 160–1).

LYMPHATIC SYSTEM

There is a one-way flow of lymph along the network of lymphatic vessels. Tiny, dead-end lymph capillaries pick up lymph in the tissues, and then merge to form larger lymphatic vessels. These eventually drain into two ducts that empty lymph into the subclavian veins, thereby restoring the blood's "lost" fluid. Contracting skeletal muscles surrounding lymphatic vessels help push lymph along them, while valves, like those in veins, prevent backflow. Associated lymphoid organs include the lymph nodes, tonsils, thymus gland, and spleen.

Skin forms a barrier against invading pathogens

Cluster of lymph nodes in armpit

Tonsils trap and destroy eaten or inhaled organisms

Left subclavian vein

Right lymphatic duct receives lymph from the upper right side of the body and empties it into right subclavian vein

Thymus gland processes lymphocytes

Thoracic duct empties into left subclavian vein

Spleen is the largest lymphoid organ and lies next to the stomach

Peyer's patch is a cluster of lymphatic tissue found in the lower part of the small intestine

LYMPHATIC AND IMMUNE SYSTEMS FUNCTIONS

Draining tissue fluid — Lymph vessels form a one-way transportation system that drains excess fluid from the tissues and empties it into the blood in order to restore and maintain blood volume.

Transporting dietary fats — Tiny lymph vessels called lacteals collect tiny globules of digested fat from inside the villi of the small intestine, transport them in lymph, and empty them into the blood.

Protection against disease — The immune system consists of cells contained in the lymphatic and cardiovascular systems that protect the body from pathogens and cancer cells.

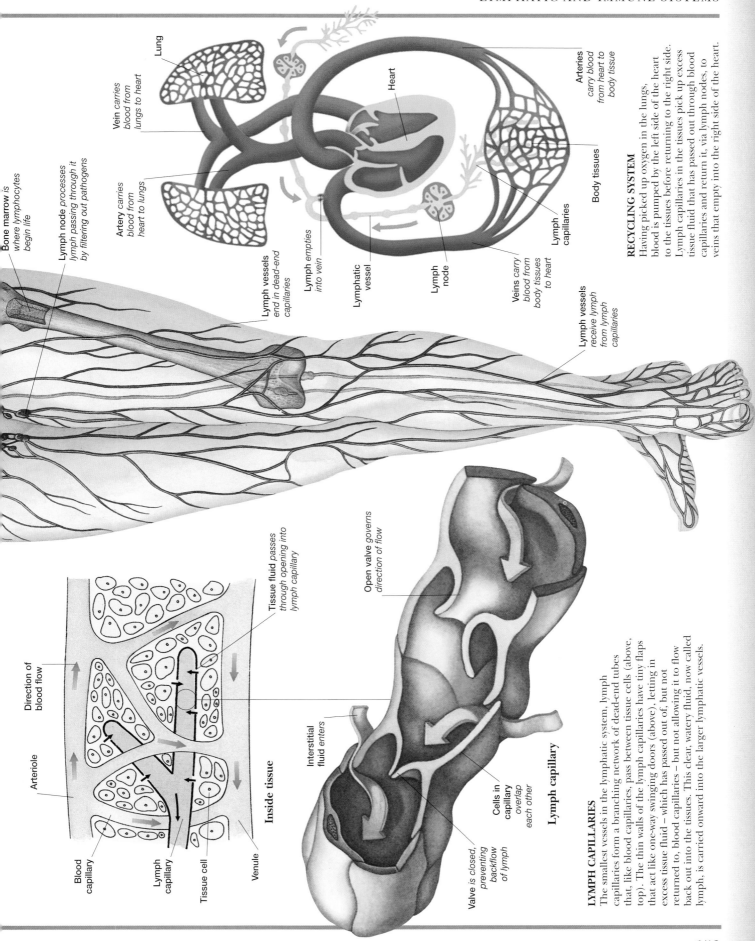

Lung

Vein carries
blood from
lungs to heart

Heart

Arteries
*carry blood
from heart to
body tissue*

Bone marrow *is
where lymphocytes
begin life*

Lymph node *processes
lymph passing through it
by filtering out pathogens*

Artery carries
blood from
heart to lungs

Lymph empties
into vein

Lymphatic
vessel

Lymph
node

Veins carry
*blood from
body tissues
to heart*

Lymph
capillaries

Body tissues

Lymph vessels
*end in dead-end
capillaries*

Lymph vessels
*receive lymph
from lymph
capillaries*

RECYCLING SYSTEM

Having picked up oxygen in the lungs, blood is pumped by the left side of the heart to the tissues before returning to the right side. Lymph capillaries in the tissues pick up excess tissue fluid that has passed out through blood capillaries and return it, via lymph nodes, to veins that empty into the right side of the heart.

Tissue fluid *passes
through opening into
lymph capillary*

Open valve *governs
direction of flow*

Direction of
blood flow

Interstitial
fluid enters

Arteriole

Cells in
capillary
*overlap
each other*

Inside tissue

Lymph capillary

Blood
capillary

Lymph
capillary

Tissue cell

Venule

Valve *is closed,
preventing
backflow
of lymph*

LYMPH CAPILLARIES

The smallest vessels in the lymphatic system, lymph capillaries form a branching network of dead-end tubes that, like blood capillaries, pass between tissue cells (above, top). The thin walls of the lymph capillaries have tiny flaps that act like one-way swinging doors (above), letting in excess tissue fluid – which has passed out of, but not returned to, blood capillaries – but not allowing it to flow back out into the tissues. This clear, watery fluid, now called lymph, is carried onward into the larger lymphatic vessels.

Lymphoid organs

THE LYMPHOID, or lymphatic organs, which include the lymph nodes, spleen, and tonsils, are the parts of the lymphatic system that fight disease. They have a similar structure, and are filled with fibers that support macrophages and lymphocytes. Macrophages ingest and destroy pathogens and cancer cells, while lymphocytes play a key role in the immune system (see pp. 160–1), either by attacking pathogens directly, or by disabling them with antibodies. The most numerous lymphoid organs are the lymph nodes, which are scattered throughout the body and filter pathogens out of the lymph passing through them. The spleen removes pathogens from the blood, while the tonsils intercept those passing toward the throat. The thymus gland plays a vital role during childhood in the development of the immune system.

LYMPH NODES

These small, bean-shaped swellings, each 0.04–1 in (1–25 mm) across, occur along lymph vessels like beads on a string. Lymph nodes filter lymph as it passes through them. Surrounded by a tough capsule, the spaces, or sinuses, inside the lymph node are filled with a network of fibers that support macrophages and lymphocytes. These fibers slow the flow of lymph passing through, while macrophages engulf and destroy bacteria, cancer cells, and debris, and lymphocytes launch their immune defenses. During infections, lymph nodes may swell up and become tender, a condition known as "swollen glands."

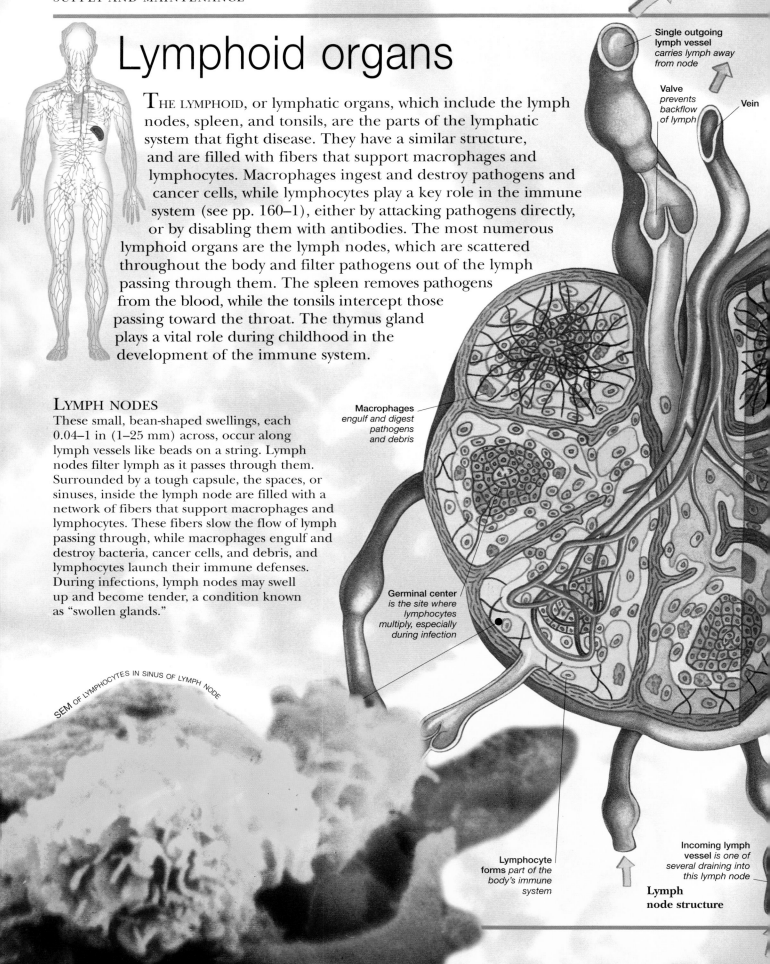

Single outgoing lymph vessel *carries lymph away from node*

Valve *prevents backflow of lymph*

Vein

Macrophages *engulf and digest pathogens and debris*

Germinal center *is the site where lymphocytes multiply, especially during infection*

SEM OF LYMPHOCYTES IN SINUS OF LYMPH NODE

Lymphocyte forms *part of the body's immune system*

Incoming lymph vessel *is one of several draining into this lymph node*

Lymph node structure

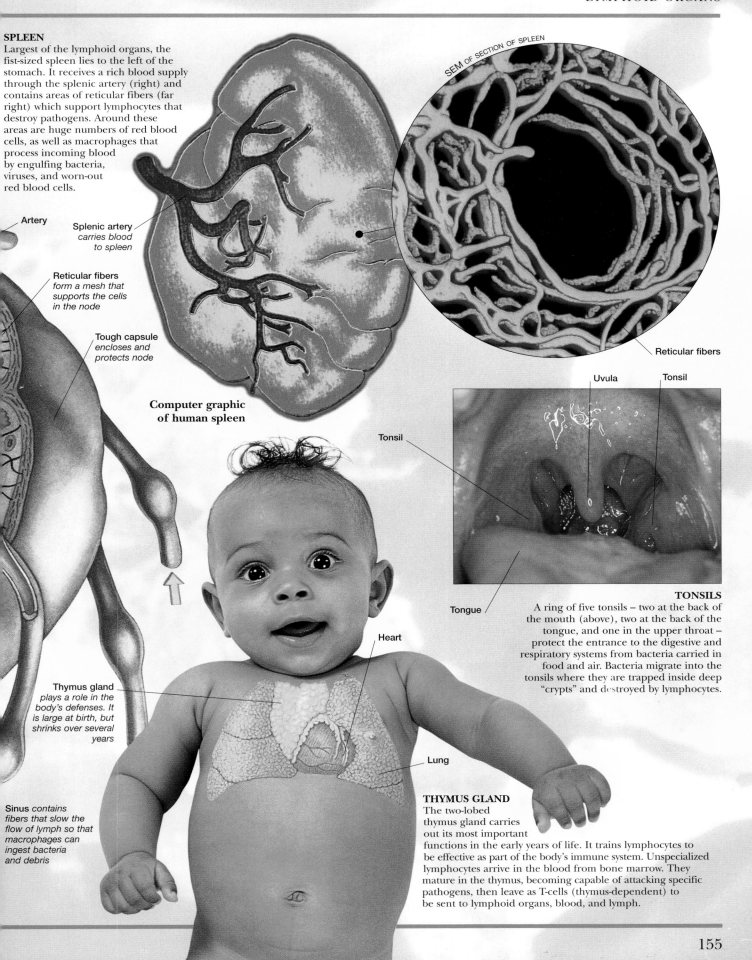

SPLEEN
Largest of the lymphoid organs, the fist-sized spleen lies to the left of the stomach. It receives a rich blood supply through the splenic artery (right) and contains areas of reticular fibers (far right) which support lymphocytes that destroy pathogens. Around these areas are huge numbers of red blood cells, as well as macrophages that process incoming blood by engulfing bacteria, viruses, and worn-out red blood cells.

Artery

Splenic artery
*carries blood
to spleen*

Reticular fibers
*form a mesh that
supports the cells
in the node*

Tough capsule
*encloses and
protects node*

**Computer graphic
of human spleen**

SEM OF SECTION OF SPLEEN

Reticular fibers

Uvula   Tonsil

Tonsil

Tongue

TONSILS
A ring of five tonsils – two at the back of the mouth (above), two at the back of the tongue, and one in the upper throat – protect the entrance to the digestive and respiratory systems from bacteria carried in food and air. Bacteria migrate into the tonsils where they are trapped inside deep "crypts" and destroyed by lymphocytes.

Heart

Thymus gland
*plays a role in the
body's defenses. It
is large at birth, but
shrinks over several
years*

Lung

Sinus *contains
fibers that slow the
flow of lymph so that
macrophages can
ingest bacteria
and debris*

THYMUS GLAND
The two-lobed thymus gland carries out its most important functions in the early years of life. It trains lymphocytes to be effective as part of the body's immune system. Unspecialized lymphocytes arrive in the blood from bone marrow. They mature in the thymus, becoming capable of attacking specific pathogens, then leave as T-cells (thymus-dependent) to be sent to lymphoid organs, blood, and lymph.

Diseases

FROM TIME TO TIME, the body fails to work properly because one or more of the mechanisms that maintain homeostasis – constant, stable conditions inside the body – goes wrong. Any such breakdown is called a disease. Some diseases are short-lived and easily overcome by the body's natural defense systems, while others are more serious and require outside intervention in the form of drugs. Humans are affected by two types of disease – infectious and noninfectious. Infectious diseases are caused by parasitic organisms called pathogens that break through the body's defenses and grow and multiply in its tissues. Most pathogens are microorganisms. Noninfectious diseases are those not caused by pathogens, and include cancer, nervous system disorders, and autoimmune conditions (see p. 165).

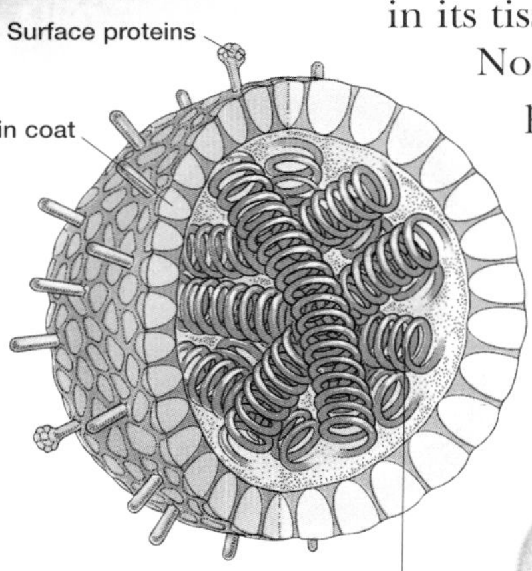

VIRUSES

Chemical packages rather than living things, viruses are about one-hundredth the size of bacteria and consist of genetic material, either DNA or RNA, surrounded by a protein coat. Once inside the body, a virus invades a cell and hijacks its metabolism to make copies of itself that break out and infect other cells. Viral diseases include colds and polio.

Surface proteins

Protein coat

Cross-section of a virus

Nucleic acid (DNA or RNA)

SEM OF ATHLETE'S FOOT FUNGUS

Spores *released by the fungus spread infection*

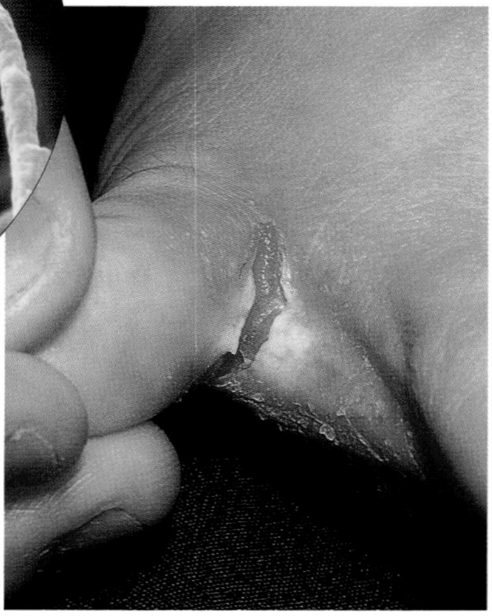

FUNGI

Many fungi are helpful to humans, such as mushrooms or moulds used to produce antibiotics, that feed on dead material. But some fungi are parasitic on humans, including the fungus whose filaments (above) feed on skin and cause athlete's foot (right), and the yeast that causes candidiasis (thrush).

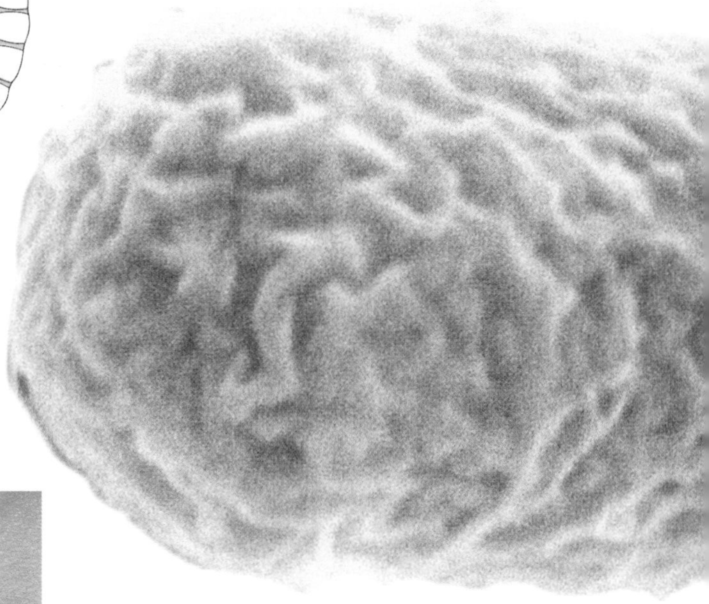

BACTERIA

The smallest living organisms, bacteria, are found by the trillion living harmlessly in the soil, air, and in water, as well as in or on the human body. But some bacteria – known more commonly as germs – are pathogenic and cause diseases such as cholera, diphtheria, whooping cough, tuberculosis (TB), and typhoid. Pathogenic bacteria thrive at body temperature and reproduce by splitting in two about once every 20 minutes. They damage the body by releasing poisons called toxins.

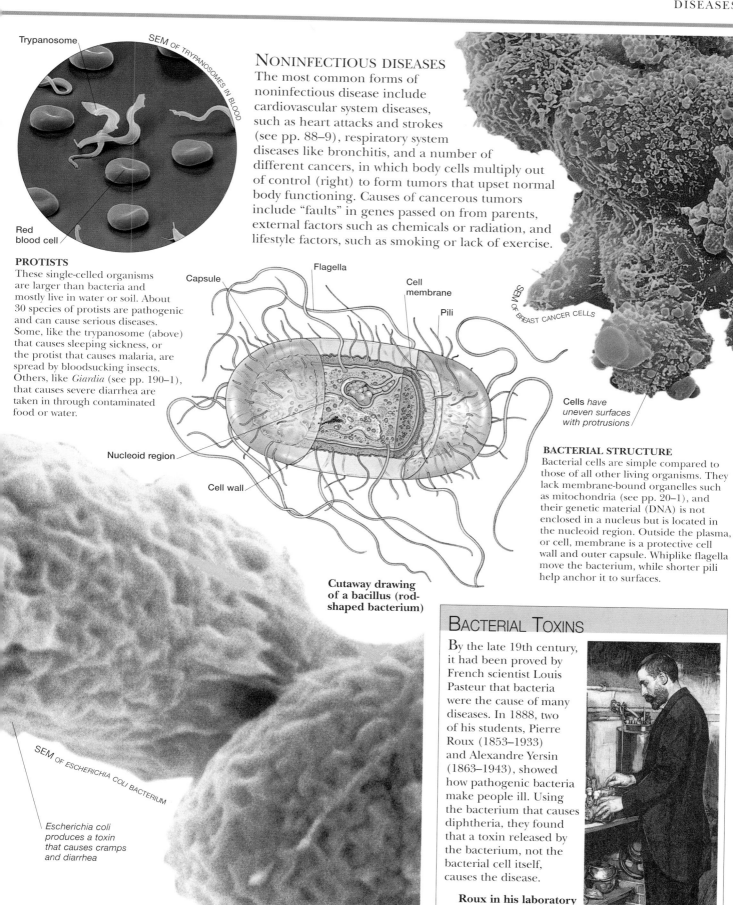

Trypanosome

SEM OF TRYPANOSOMES IN BLOOD

Red
blood cell

NONINFECTIOUS DISEASES

The most common forms of
noninfectious disease include
cardiovascular system diseases,
such as heart attacks and strokes
(see pp. 88–9), respiratory system
diseases like bronchitis, and a number of
different cancers, in which body cells multiply out
of control (right) to form tumors that upset normal
body functioning. Causes of cancerous tumors
include "faults" in genes passed on from parents,
external factors such as chemicals or radiation, and
lifestyle factors, such as smoking or lack of exercise.

SEM OF BREAST CANCER CELLS

PROTISTS

These single-celled organisms
are larger than bacteria and
mostly live in water or soil. About
30 species of protists are pathogenic
and can cause serious diseases.
Some, like the trypanosome (above)
that causes sleeping sickness, or
the protist that causes malaria, are
spread by bloodsucking insects.
Others, like *Giardia* (see pp. 190–1),
that causes severe diarrhea are
taken in through contaminated
food or water.

Capsule

Flagella

Cell
membrane

Pili

Nucleoid region

Cell wall

**Cutaway drawing
of a bacillus (rod-
shaped bacterium)**

Cells *have
uneven surfaces
with protrusions*

BACTERIAL STRUCTURE

Bacterial cells are simple compared to
those of all other living organisms. They
lack membrane-bound organelles such
as mitochondria (see pp. 20–1), and
their genetic material (DNA) is not
enclosed in a nucleus but is located in the
nucleoid region. Outside the plasma,
or cell, membrane is a protective cell
wall and outer capsule. Whiplike flagella
move the bacterium, while shorter pili
help anchor it to surfaces.

SEM OF ESCHERICHIA COLI BACTERIUM

*Escherichia coli
produces a toxin
that causes cramps
and diarrhea*

BACTERIAL TOXINS

By the late 19th century,
it had been proved by
French scientist Louis
Pasteur that bacteria
were the cause of many
diseases. In 1888, two
of his students, Pierre
Roux (1853–1933)
and Alexandre Yersin
(1863–1943), showed
how pathogenic bacteria
make people ill. Using
the bacterium that causes
diphtheria, they found
that a toxin released by
the bacterium, not the
bacterial cell itself,
causes the disease.

Roux in his laboratory

Nonspecific defenses

THROUGHOUT LIFE, the body is exposed to an array of infectious pathogens that would, if left unchecked, invade, exploit, and ultimately destroy it. Fortunately, the body has a highly sophisticated defense system, which consists of two main parts: the nonspecific defenses described here, and the immune system (see pp. 160–1). Nonspecific defenses are built into the body at birth, and respond in the same way to all invading pathogens. First, skin and other outer defenses present a physical barrier. Then, if pathogens breach this, a system of defensive cells and antimicrobial chemicals in blood and tissue fluids springs into action.

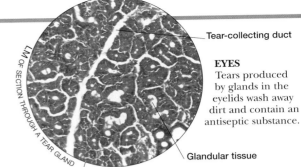

Tear-collecting duct

EYES
Tears produced by glands in the eyelids wash away dirt and contain an antiseptic substance.

LM OF SECTION THROUGH A TEAR GLAND

Glandular tissue

Enzyme-secreting cells

Mucus-secreting cells

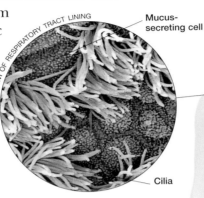

SEM OF RESPIRATORY TRACT LINING

Mucus-secreting cell

Cilia

RESPIRATORY TRACT
Mucus is produced in the lining of the respiratory tract. It traps pathogens and is carried to the throat by cilia.

LM OF SECTION THROUGH SALIVARY GLAND

MOUTH
Watery saliva, produced by glands around the mouth, washes the mouth out, and contains bacteria-killing lysozyme.

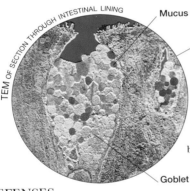

TEM OF SECTION THROUGH INTESTINAL LINING

Mucus

Goblet cell

INTESTINES
The lining of the intestines is protected from harmful organisms and chemicals by mucus produced by goblet cells.

Opening of gastric gland

Stomach lining

SEM OF GASTRIC GLAND

STOMACH
Glands in the stomach lining produce hydrochloric acid, which kills most invading organisms.

OUTER DEFENSES
This diagram shows the main parts of the body's outer defenses. The tightly knit cells of the skin, and those of the mucous membrane lining the respiratory, digestive, urinary, and reproductive systems, stop pathogens from entering the tissues. Tears contain a bacteria-killing substance called lysozyme, as do saliva and sweat. Mucus lining the respiratory system traps pathogens, and then passes them to the throat for swallowing. Stomach acid destroys most swallowed bacteria. On the skin, and in the digestive and female reproductive system, colonies of harmless bacteria prevent harmful bacteria from establishing themselves.

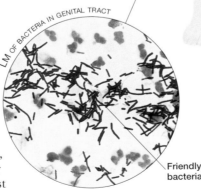

LM OF BACTERIA IN GENITAL TRACT

Friendly bacteria

GENITAL AND URINARY TRACTS
The expulsion of urine in the urinary tract and the presence of friendly bacteria in the genital tract prevent harmful organisms from multiplying in these areas.

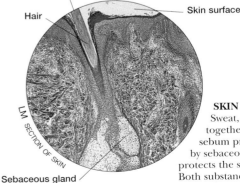

Hair

Skin surface

LM SECTION OF SKIN

Sebaceous gland

SKIN
Sweat, together with sebum produced by sebaceous glands, protects the skin. Both substances have antiseptic properties.

Interferon binds *to cells to protect them against viruses*

POLARIZED LM OF INTERFERON CRYSTALS

ANTIMICROBIAL SUBSTANCES

Two sets of blood proteins – interferon and the complement system – form a key part of the defense force. Interferon is released by body cells already infected with viruses. It stimulates neighboring cells to protect themselves against viral infection. The complement system's 20-plus proteins aid the inflammation process (see below). The proteins attach themselves to bacteria, either to make them more "tasty" for phagocytes to eat or to destroy them by making the cell membranes burst open.

Macrophage *tracks down pathogen*

FEVER

The body may respond to infection by bacteria or viruses by raising its temperature above the normal 98.6°F (37°C) in order to stop the invaders from multiplying. This strategy, called fever or pyrexia, is often accompanied by sweating, shivering, and a feeling of thirst. It is triggered by white blood cells that release chemicals called pyrogens, which reset the body's "thermostat" in the brain's hypothalamus so that body temperature rises above normal.

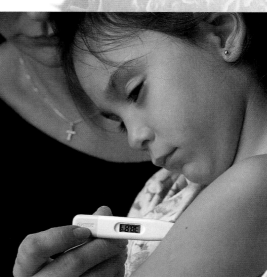

Extension of macrophage *engulfs protist prior to digestion*

Parasitic protist *that causes the tropical disease leishmaniasis*

SEM OF MACROPHAGE ENGULFING PROTIST

CELL EATERS

Phagocytes are white blood cells that engulf and destroy invading organisms. There are two types: neutrophils and macrophages. Neutrophils circulate in the blood before being transferred to the tissues, where they seek out organisms. Macrophages also start in the bloodstream, where they are known as monocytes, before moving to the tissues where they become macrophages. Some macrophages stay in one place; others travel around looking for invading organisms. All phagocytes flow around organisms, wrapping them within a membrane that fuses with granules called lysosomes. These granules contain strong chemicals that digest the organisms, producing harmless substances that pass out through the cells' membrane.

Chemicals *that attract white blood cells*

Pathogen

Injured skin

White blood cells *engulf bacteria*

Inflamed tissue

Blood vessel *widens*

Damage

Response

INFLAMMATORY RESPONSE

This is the familiar warm, reddish, tender swelling that appears after an injury. At the site of the damage, tissue cells release histamine and other chemicals. They make the blood vessels wider, so that extra blood arrives, and more leaky, so that fluid passes into the tissues, aiding repair and making the area red, swollen, and warm. These chemicals also attract phagocytes that destroy pathogens.

Immune system

Antigen of bacterium

Macrophage

Bacterium *enters the body and is surrounded by a macrophage*

Non-matching B-cells

Engulfed bacterium

Antigen of bacterium

Matching B-cell *multiplies to produce plasma cells and memory B-cells – plasma cells create antibodies to destroy bacteria, while memory B-cells are stored for future use*

Memory B-cell *rapidly produces plasma cells when it encounters the same bacteria the second time around*

Inactivated bacterium

Plasma cell

Antibodies released by the plasma cells lock on to bacterial antigens and inactivate the bacterium; the antibodies also attract phagocytes to the area to help destroy the bacteria

Antigen of bacterium

Phagocyte destroys bacterium

THE MOST POWERFUL PART of the body's defenses, the immune system consists of billions of white blood cells, called lymphocytes, found in the circulatory and lymphatic systems and in other tissues. While nonspecific defenses provide unchanging protection against all pathogens, the immune system attacks specific pathogens and remembers them so that if they should attack again, it can respond with lightning speed. This gives a person long-term protection, or immunity, against diseases. The immune system is triggered by foreign antigens, or cell markers, that distinguish pathogens and cancer cells from the body's own cells. This system has two linked parts. The humoral part works by releasing antibodies to disable pathogens, while the cellular part directly attacks and destroys invaders.

COMPUTER MODEL OF AN ANTIBODY

ANTIBODIES

Also called immunoglobulins, these proteins are made by B-lymphocytes and are found in blood, lymph, and other tissue fluids. Most of each Y-shaped antibody molecule is identical in all antibodies, but parts of the "arms" of the Y are unique to each particular type of antibody. It is this unique, variable region that binds the antibody to a specific antigen carried by its target pathogen, just as a key fits into a lock. Disabled by antibodies, the pathogen is now marked for destruction.

HUMORAL IMMUNITY

This part of the immune system uses antibodies to attack invaders – particularly bacteria and some viruses – and involves lymphocytes called B-cells, which are found in the lymphoid organs of the lymphatic system (see pp. 154–55). A pathogen entering the body is engulfed by a pathogen-destroying cell called a macrophage. This presents the antigens carried by the pathogen to a matching B-cell that is primed to recognize that specific antigen. The B-cell then divides rapidly to produce plasma cells that flood blood, lymph, and tissue fluid with antibodies, and memory B-cells that remember the pathogen and will respond rapidly to it if it returns. The antibodies bind to the pathogens and mark them for destruction by phagocytes or chemicals.

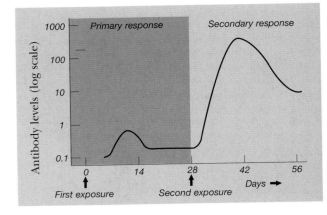

IMMUNE RESPONSE
When a pathogen invades the body for the first time, its antigens stimulate the immune system to produce antibodies. This primary response takes several days (see above). If, subsequently, a second invasion takes place, the immune system leaps into action, releasing high levels of antibodies that target the specific pathogen. A person is now immune to the disease caused by that pathogen, and should never suffer from it again.

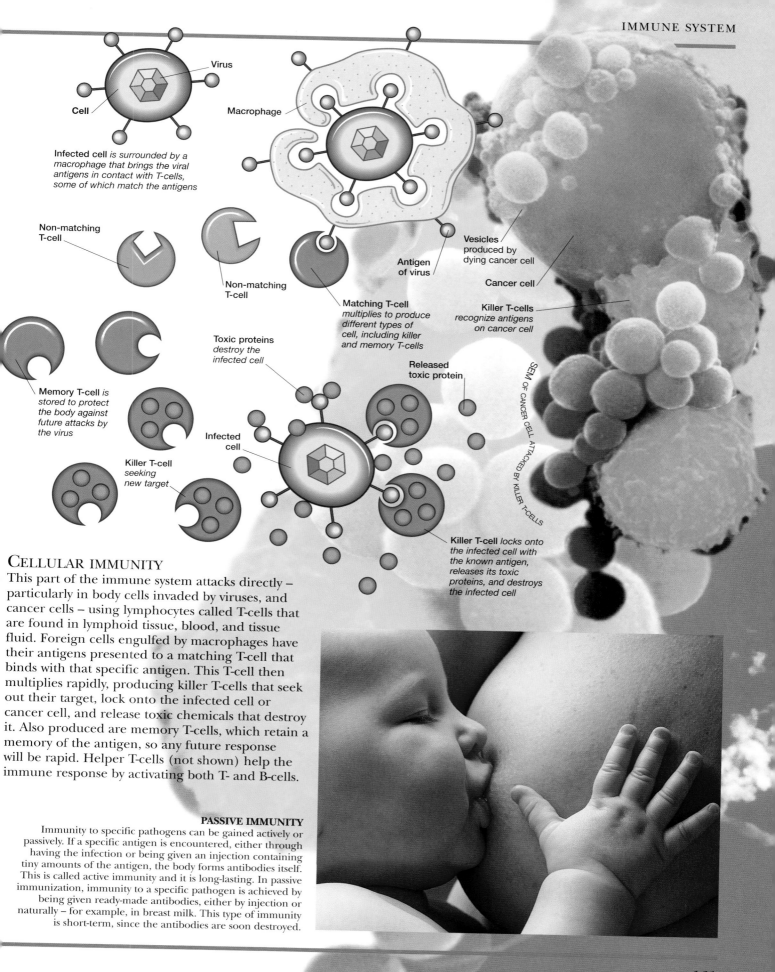

Infected cell *is surrounded by a macrophage that brings the viral antigens in contact with T-cells, some of which match the antigens*

Virus

Cell

Macrophage

Non-matching T-cell

Non-matching T-cell

Vesicles produced by dying cancer cell

Cancer cell

Antigen of virus

Matching T-cell *multiplies to produce different types of cell, including killer and memory T-cells*

Killer T-cells *recognize antigens on cancer cell*

Toxic proteins *destroy the infected cell*

Released toxic protein

Memory T-cell *is stored to protect the body against future attacks by the virus*

Infected cell

Killer T-cell *seeking new target*

Killer T-cell *locks onto the infected cell with the known antigen, releases its toxic proteins, and destroys the infected cell*

SEM OF CANCER CELL ATTACKED BY KILLER T-CELLS

CELLULAR IMMUNITY

This part of the immune system attacks directly – particularly in body cells invaded by viruses, and cancer cells – using lymphocytes called T-cells that are found in lymphoid tissue, blood, and tissue fluid. Foreign cells engulfed by macrophages have their antigens presented to a matching T-cell that binds with that specific antigen. This T-cell then multiplies rapidly, producing killer T-cells that seek out their target, lock onto the infected cell or cancer cell, and release toxic chemicals that destroy it. Also produced are memory T-cells, which retain a memory of the antigen, so any future response will be rapid. Helper T-cells (not shown) help the immune response by activating both T- and B-cells.

PASSIVE IMMUNITY

Immunity to specific pathogens can be gained actively or passively. If a specific antigen is encountered, either through having the infection or being given an injection containing tiny amounts of the antigen, the body forms antibodies itself. This is called active immunity and it is long-lasting. In passive immunization, immunity to a specific pathogen is achieved by being given ready-made antibodies, either by injection or naturally – for example, in breast milk. This type of immunity is short-term, since the antibodies are soon destroyed.

VACCINATION FOR ALL

THROUGHOUT HISTORY, people have lived in fear of infectious diseases such as smallpox, which killed 40 percent of those infected and left gruesome scars on the faces of survivors. By the 17th century, smallpox had become the most serious infectious disease in the West. The turning point in the fight against it came with the discovery of vaccination, when exposure to harmless cowpox was found to protect people from catching its deadlier relative. The technique, pioneered by English doctor Edward Jenner in the late 18th century, has saved millions of lives, but it was preceded by another, albeit more risky, method of prevention.

TURKISH TECHNIQUE
Lady Mary Wortley Montagu noticed that Turkish women carried pus from a mild form of smallpox in walnut shells, and used it to inoculate children to protect them from the dangerous form of the disease. She encouraged people in England to use the technique, called variolation.

Ivory blade

Tortoiseshell handle

Vaccination lancet

VARIOLATION

In 1717, a technique called variolation – which originated in 10th-century China – came to the notice of Lady Mary Wortley Montagu (1689–1762), wife of the British Ambassador to Turkey. Turkish children were inoculated by scratching their skin and applying pus taken from the blisters of people with mild smallpox. Lady Mary, who had her own children treated in this way, introduced variolation when she returned to England in 1721. But there was an element of chance in the procedure, with some patients developing full-blown smallpox.

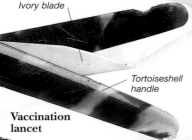

Large, pus-filled sore

Drawing from Jenner's book showing cowpox

LIFE-SAVER
Within three years of Edward Jenner's discovery, more than 100,000 people had been vaccinated against smallpox. His technique became the most important life-saving discovery of the 18th century, and was the forerunner of today's mass immunization programs against infectious diseases.

Sculpture showing Jenner vaccinating James Phipps

VACCINATION
Jenner used a lancet (above, left) to scratch James Phipp's arm, then inoculated him with pus taken from a blister on a milkmaid's hand. Phipps became immune to smallpox – a disease that, in Jenner's day, killed 3,000 people a year in London alone.

JENNER'S BREAKTROUGH

It was Edward Jenner (1749–1823) who developed a more reliable method of preventing smallpox. He noticed that milkmaids contracted a similar but mild infection called cowpox from their cows but never caught smallpox, even when in close contact with smallpox victims. Reasoning that cowpox infection could protect against smallpox, Jenner carried out a bold experiment. On May 14, 1796, he took pus from a cowpox blister and introduced it into the arm of eight-year-old James Phipps. Six weeks later, when he deliberately inoculated Phipps with smallpox, the boy did not develop the disease. Jenner's treatment, called vaccination, quickly caught on, even though how it worked would not be understood until the 20th century. Jenner's work inspired the great French bacteriologist Louis Pasteur, who nearly 100 years later produced a vaccine to protect against rabies.

Louis Pasteur produced a rabies vaccine

THE END OF SMALLPOX

Even in the mid-1960s, smallpox still infected 10 million and killed 2 million people worldwide every year. But a concerted vaccination program by the World Health Organization (WHO) finally eliminated the disease in 1977. This was the first time in history that a disease had been eradicated by human intervention. It now only exists in laboratories in Russia and the United States.

PROTECTING CHILDREN

Although smallpox has been defeated, many other infectious diseases still kill millions. Vaccinating, or immunizing, children remains the single most important preventative treatment. Vaccines – medications that prime the immune system to fight infection – have been developed to protect against many life-threatening diseases. In several countries, health authorities implement an immunization schedule for children that starts at two months and continues until the teenage years.

EARLY PROTECTION
Babies are very vulnerable to infection, so immunization provides vital protection.

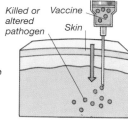

FIGHTING RABIES
In 1885, Louis Pasteur (1822–95) tested a vaccine, made from rabbit spinal cord on Joseph Meister, a nine-year-old who had been bitten by rabid dogs. Meister recovered from rabies, a horrific and fatal disease, and public acclaim for Pasteur's achievement led to the foundation of the Pasteur Institute in 1888.

HOW IMMUNIZATION WORKS

Immunization, or vaccination, prepares the body to fight a specific infection. In active immunization, shown here, a vaccine is injected into a person to stimulate their immune system to produce antibodies (see pp. 160–61) that will destroy the "real" pathogen if it invades the body.

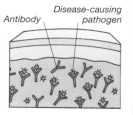

1. To immunize them against a specific disease, a person is injected with a vaccine containing a killed or altered version of the pathogen that causes that disease.

2. Within days, the immune system produces antibodies against the disease, as well as long-lived memory cells that "remember" the pathogen's identity for future reference.

3. Should the "real" pathogen enter the body at a later date, the immune system launches an immediate response, producing large numbers of antibodies that immobilize the invader.

Immune system disorders

THE IMMUNE SYSTEM of the human body can be disrupted. Allergies, such as hay fever, are common and result from an excessive immune reaction to what would normally be regarded as a harmless substance. Extreme allergies can cause anaphylaxis, a rare but life-threatening condition. Sometimes the immune system can react inappropriately, rather than excessively, by forming antibodies against its own cells. This is known as autoimmunity. Even though they are appropriate, immune responses to transplanted tissue and organs are unwanted, so drugs are taken long-term to try to prevent the immune system from rejecting the new transplants. Immunodeficiency (weakening of the immune system) may develop for a number of reasons, including diseases of the bone marrow, kidney failure, and the human immunodeficiency virus (HIV).

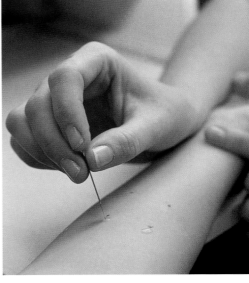

TESTING FOR ALLERGIES
Skin-prick tests are often performed on individuals with allergies to try to identify the allergens responsible. Small drops of allergen solutions are placed on the skin, which is then pricked with a needle. If the test is positive, a red lump will form at the site of the allergen, usually within half an hour.

ALLERGIES

When the immune system reacts excessively to specific antigens, allergies are said to be present. Various substances, known as allergens, can provoke such a response. Common allergens include the dust mite and pollen. Allergens may cause a reaction when they are breathed in or eaten, or when they come in contact with the skin. When the body encounters an allergen for the first time, it becomes "sensitized." On subsequent encounters the immune system mounts an excessive response. Allergies may cause a variety of conditions. Hay fever, one of the most common, is a reaction to pollen and produces watery eyes, a runny nose, and sneezing.

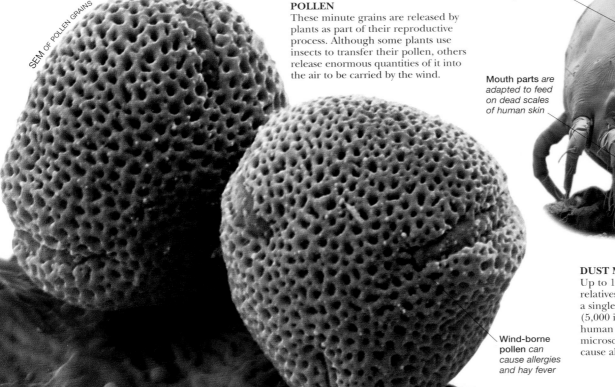

SEM OF POLLEN GRAINS

POLLEN
These minute grains are released by plants as part of their reproductive process. Although some plants use insects to transfer their pollen, others release enormous quantities of it into the air to be carried by the wind.

Wind-borne pollen *can cause allergies and hay fever*

Carcasses and droppings *of dust mites can cause allergic reactions*

Mouth parts *are adapted to feed on dead scales of human skin*

DUST MITES
Up to 140,000 of these tiny relatives of spiders can live in a single ounce of house dust (5,000 in a gram). They feed on human skin flakes and release microscopic droppings that can cause allergies when breathed in.

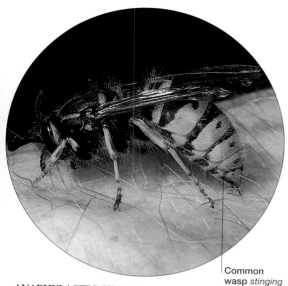

Common wasp *stinging a human*

ANAPHYLACTIC SHOCK

Some people have excessive and potentially life-threatening allergic responses to specific allergens, such as wasp stings and peanuts. The response is so strong that contact with the allergen results in a major fall in blood pressure. Symptoms of a severe allergic response (anaphylactic shock) may include difficulty in breathing, a skin rash, and loss of consciousness. The condition, which requires urgent treatment, is fortunately rare.

REJECTED TISSUES

The first attempts at transplanting human tissue from one person to another were made early in the 20th century. They were unsuccessful because the body "rejected" the transplanted tissue. In the late 1940s, British immunologist Peter Medawar (1915–87) showed that the immune system regards the cells of the transplanted tissue as foreign – as it would pathogenic bacteria – and destroys it. His work helped to make organ transplantation – in which drugs are given to suppress the immune system – possible. In 1960, Medawar was awarded the Nobel Prize for Medicine.

Whitened area *shows pigment loss*

Vitiligo causes the skin to lose its pigment

AUTOIMMUNITY

If the body does not recognize its own cells, it will regard them as foreign and produce an immune response, which attacks and damages them. Known as autoimmunity, this forms the basis for a number of conditions affecting various parts of the body. An example is rheumatoid arthritis, in which antibodies are produced against the lining of joints, causing pain and swelling. Another autoimmune disorder is vitiligo, in which antibodies cause patches of skin to lose their color. It is still not known why autoimmunity develops, but genetic factors are thought to play a part in many of these diseases.

HIV AND AIDS

There are several reasons why the immune system can fail to work properly: one of them is the human immunodeficiency virus (HIV). This virus infects T-helper cells. These are lymphocytes (see pp. 160–1) that play a key role in enabling the immune system to target and destroy pathogens and cancer cells. If the number of T-helper cells drops significantly, serious infections and certain types of cancer can develop due to major weakening of the immune system. This is called acquired immunodeficiency syndrome (AIDS). Drugs have now been developed that can limit the progress of the virus.

HIV particle

Infected T-cells *typically have a lumpy appearance*

SEM OF T-CELL INFECTED WITH HIV

RESPIRATORY system

WHILE THE BODY can do without food or water for a short time, it cannot survive without a continuous supply of oxygen. Its trillions of cells relentlessly consume oxygen in order to release from sugars energy to power their activities. This process – called cell, or internal, respiration – also produces waste carbon dioxide. The body's oxygen supply is provided by the respiratory system, which draws air into the body, transfers its oxygen to the bloodstream, then pushes air out, expelling unwanted carbon dioxide.

Air passes through the nasal cavity, being warmed, moistened, and cleaned as it does so

Hairs in nostrils filter out large particles

SEM OF CILIA INSIDE NASAL CAVITY

ENDOSCOPIC VIEW OF TRACHEA

SEM OF LINING OF TRACHEA

NASAL CAVITY

The entrance to the respiratory system is through the nasal cavity, the hollow space behind the nose. Air contains dust and dirt particles that could damage the lungs if they got that far. Fortunately, the nose and nasal cavity provide a filtration service. Hairs guarding the nostrils remove larger particles as air is inhaled (breathed in). Then dust is trapped by sticky mucus, secreted by the nasal cavity lining, which is then moved by cilia to the back of the throat for swallowing. Inhaled air is moistened and warmed as it passes through the nasal cavity.

LUNGS AND AIRWAYS

The respiratory system consists of the lungs and the airways – nose, pharynx (throat), larynx (voice box), trachea (windpipe), and bronchi – that carry air between the lungs and the outside atmosphere. Inhaled air travels along the nose, pharynx, larynx, and trachea before entering one of two branches – the bronchi. Inside the lungs, bronchi divide into smaller and smaller branches that finally end in pouchlike alveoli where oxygen and carbon dioxide are exchanged. Exhaled air returns in the opposite direction.

TRACHEA

The trachea (windpipe) is the flexible tube through which air travels from the larynx toward the lungs. At its lower end, it divides into two main bronchi, one for each lung. The trachea is held open by C-shaped rings of cartilage embedded in its walls. The lining of the trachea continues the work of the nasal cavity in removing dust and dirt from air.

Right lung

Cilia projecting from cells lining the trachea move rhythmically to waft dust-laden mucus up to the throat so it can be swallowed or spat out

RESPIRATORY SYSTEM FUNCTIONS

Ventilation	*Muscle contractions alter the volume of the chest, drawing air along the respiratory tract and into and out of the lungs.*
External respiration	*Within the lungs, oxygen diffuses from the air into the bloodstream, and carbon dioxide diffuses in the opposite direction.*
Internal respiration	*Throughout the body, oxygen diffuses out of the blood into cells, where it is used in the chemical processes that release energy. Carbon dioxide diffuses in the opposite direction.*

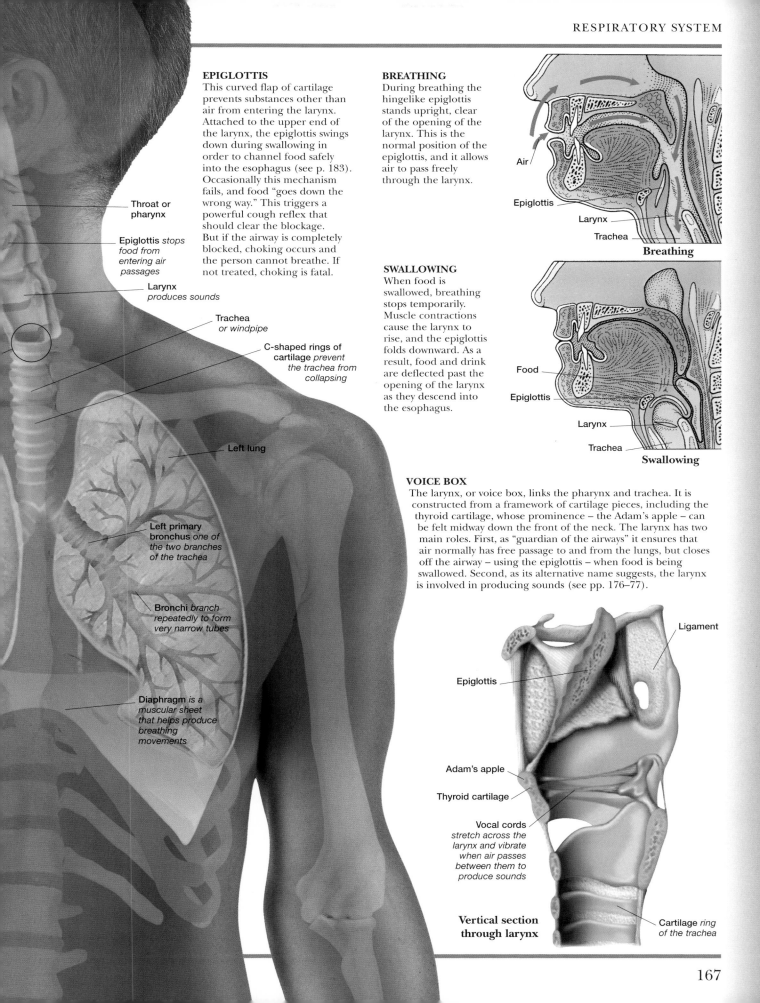

EPIGLOTTIS

This curved flap of cartilage prevents substances other than air from entering the larynx. Attached to the upper end of the larynx, the epiglottis swings down during swallowing in order to channel food safely into the esophagus (see p. 183). Occasionally this mechanism fails, and food "goes down the wrong way." This triggers a powerful cough reflex that should clear the blockage. But if the airway is completely blocked, choking occurs and the person cannot breathe. If not treated, choking is fatal.

BREATHING

During breathing the hingelike epiglottis stands upright, clear of the opening of the larynx. This is the normal position of the epiglottis, and it allows air to pass freely through the larynx.

Air

Epiglottis

Larynx

Trachea

Breathing

SWALLOWING

When food is swallowed, breathing stops temporarily. Muscle contractions cause the larynx to rise, and the epiglottis folds downward. As a result, food and drink are deflected past the opening of the larynx as they descend into the esophagus.

Food

Epiglottis

Larynx

Trachea

Swallowing

VOICE BOX

The larynx, or voice box, links the pharynx and trachea. It is constructed from a framework of cartilage pieces, including the thyroid cartilage, whose prominence – the Adam's apple – can be felt midway down the front of the neck. The larynx has two main roles. First, as "guardian of the airways" it ensures that air normally has free passage to and from the lungs, but closes off the airway – using the epiglottis – when food is being swallowed. Second, as its alternative name suggests, the larynx is involved in producing sounds (see pp. 176–77).

Throat or pharynx

Epiglottis *stops food from entering air passages*

Larynx *produces sounds*

Trachea *or windpipe*

C-shaped rings of cartilage *prevent the trachea from collapsing*

Left lung

Left primary bronchus *one of the two branches of the trachea*

Bronchi *branch repeatedly to form very narrow tubes*

Diaphragm *is a muscular sheet that helps produce breathing movements*

Ligament

Epiglottis

Adam's apple

Thyroid cartilage

Vocal cords *stretch across the larynx and vibrate when air passes between them to produce sounds*

Vertical section through larynx

Cartilage *ring of the trachea*

Lungs

THESE TWO ORGANS SURROUND the heart, occupying most of the space inside the thorax. While the rest of the respiratory system is concerned with getting air into and out of the body, the lungs concentrate on getting oxygen into, and carbon dioxide out of, the bloodstream. To do this, they interact closely with the circulatory system, whose mass of blood vessels gives the lungs their pinky-red color. The lungs have a spongy feel as a result of their internal structure – a system of air-filled, progressively branching tubes terminating in microscopic "air bags" through which oxygen enters the blood and waste carbon dioxide leaves it.

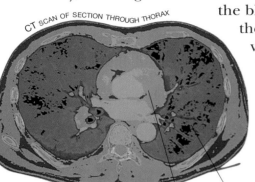

CT SCAN OF SECTION THROUGH THORAX

Heart   Lung

The right lung is separated into three lobes, the left lung into two

LUNG STRUCTURE

The lungs are light, spongy structures that are approximately conical in shape. The uppermost part of each lung extends above the clavicle (collarbone) into the neck, and their bases rest on the diaphragm. Each lung is divided into separate portions called lobes: the right lung consists of three lobes, whereas the left lung, which is slightly smaller in order to make space for the heart, consists of two. Surrounding the lungs are two membranes called pleura, between which lies a thin layer of pleural fluid which ensures that the lungs expand and shrink smoothly with each breath. The rib cage protects the lungs, and its muscles assist in breathing.

BRONCHIAL TREE

This resin cast (right) shows the system of airways that carries air into the lungs. The trachea divides into two primary, or main, bronchi, each supplying one lung. These split into secondary bronchi, which then subdivide into narrower, tertiary bronchi. Bronchi further divide into terminal bronchioles. This structure is called the bronchial tree as it resembles an upside-down tree with the trachea as "trunk," bronchi as "branches," and bronchioles as "twigs."

Trachea   Primary (or main) bronchus

Respiratory bronchiole   Bronchiole

ALVEOLAR SACS

As terminal bronchioles penetrate more deeply into the lungs, they divide into microscopic respiratory bronchioles. These lead into alveolar sacs resembling bunches of grapes. Each "grape," or alveolus, shares with other alveoli an opening into a duct connecting it to the respiratory bronchiole. Alveoli are the site of gas exchange.

Alveoli *surrounded by blood capillaries*

Tertiary bronchus *branches from the secondary bronchus, which subdivides repeatedly to form terminal bronchioles*

Secondary bronchus *– there are three secondary bronchi in the right lung, each supplying one lobe of the lung*

Right primary bronchus

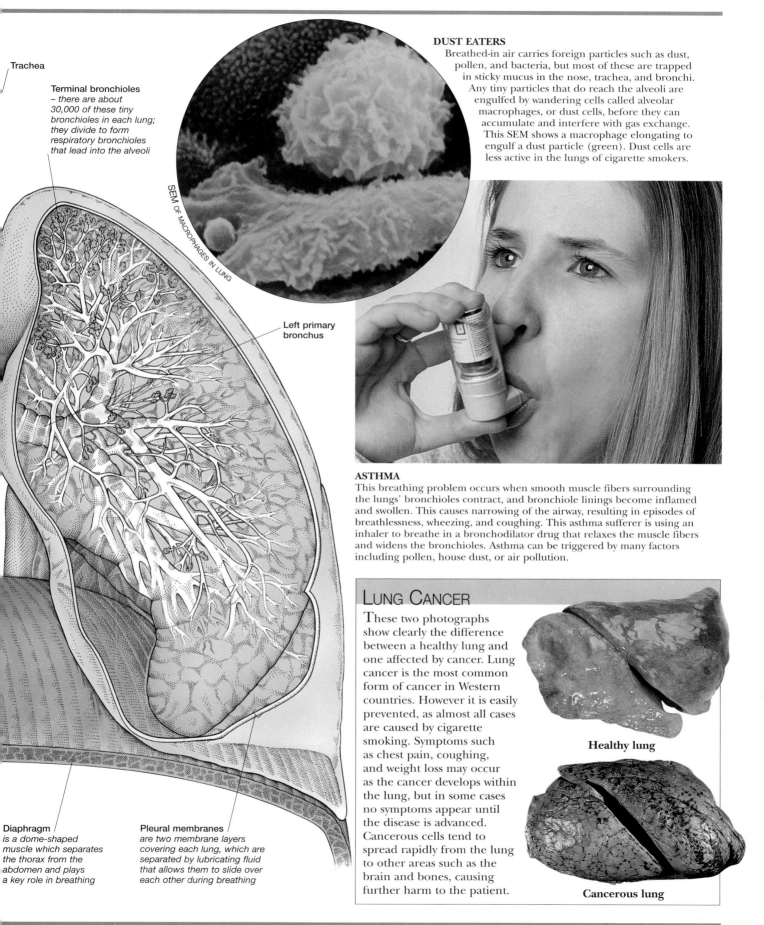

Trachea

Terminal bronchioles
– there are about
30,000 of these tiny
bronchioles in each lung;
they divide to form
respiratory bronchioles
that lead into the alveoli

SEM OF MACROPHAGES IN LUNG

Left primary
bronchus

Diaphragm
is a dome-shaped
muscle which separates
the thorax from the
abdomen and plays
a key role in breathing

Pleural membranes
are two membrane layers
covering each lung, which are
separated by lubricating fluid
that allows them to slide over
each other during breathing

DUST EATERS
Breathed-in air carries foreign particles such as dust, pollen, and bacteria, but most of these are trapped in sticky mucus in the nose, trachea, and bronchi. Any tiny particles that do reach the alveoli are engulfed by wandering cells called alveolar macrophages, or dust cells, before they can accumulate and interfere with gas exchange. This SEM shows a macrophage elongating to engulf a dust particle (green). Dust cells are less active in the lungs of cigarette smokers.

ASTHMA
This breathing problem occurs when smooth muscle fibers surrounding the lungs' bronchioles contract, and bronchiole linings become inflamed and swollen. This causes narrowing of the airway, resulting in episodes of breathlessness, wheezing, and coughing. This asthma sufferer is using an inhaler to breathe in a bronchodilator drug that relaxes the muscle fibers and widens the bronchioles. Asthma can be triggered by many factors including pollen, house dust, or air pollution.

LUNG CANCER
These two photographs show clearly the difference between a healthy lung and one affected by cancer. Lung cancer is the most common form of cancer in Western countries. However it is easily prevented, as almost all cases are caused by cigarette smoking. Symptoms such as chest pain, coughing, and weight loss may occur as the cancer develops within the lung, but in some cases no symptoms appear until the disease is advanced. Cancerous cells tend to spread rapidly from the lung to other areas such as the brain and bones, causing further harm to the patient.

Healthy lung

Cancerous lung

Gas exchange

EVERY MINUTE, LARGE AMOUNTS OF life-giving oxygen is taken into the bloodstream, while potentially poisonous carbon dioxide is expelled. This happens through a mechanism called gas exchange, which occurs in the lungs' tiny saclike alveoli. Two features of alveoli make gas exchange fast and efficient. Firstly, the wall of an alveolus is just one cell thick, as is the wall of the blood capillaries that surround it. Where the two meet, they form a respiratory membrane just 0.00002 in (0.0005 mm) wide, across which oxygen can move rapidly into, and carbon dioxide out of, the blood. The two lungs contain some 300 million alveoli that collectively provide a surface area for gas exchange of 750 sq ft (70 sq m) – 35 times the surface area of the skin – squeezed into a space inside the chest that is no bigger than a shopping bag.

Before diffusion **After diffusion**

DIFFUSION
The natural tendency of molecules to move randomly from an area of high concentration to one of low until evenly spread out is called diffusion. Some molecules (above, red) can diffuse through cell membranes (green). This is exactly what happens to oxygen during gas exchange in the alveoli, except that breathing brings more oxygen into the alveoli, while blood capillaries carry it away, never allowing it to be evenly distributed.

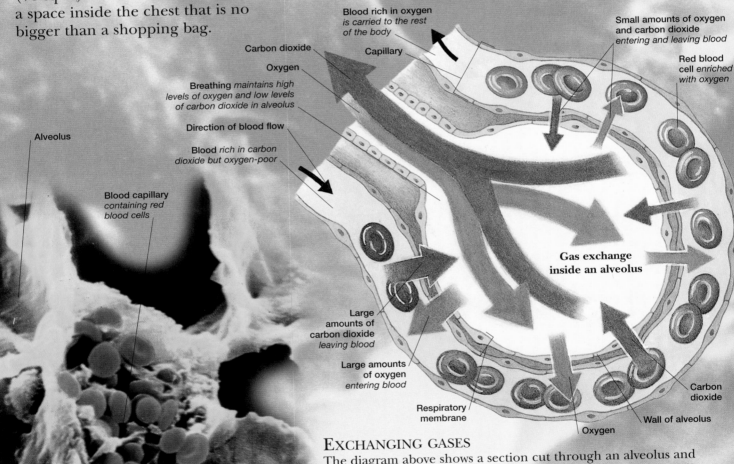

Blood rich in oxygen *is carried to the rest of the body*

Carbon dioxide

Oxygen

Capillary

Breathing *maintains high levels of oxygen and low levels of carbon dioxide in alveolus*

Direction of blood flow

Blood *rich in carbon dioxide but oxygen-poor*

Alveolus

Blood capillary *containing red blood cells*

Small amounts of oxygen and carbon dioxide *entering and leaving blood*

Red blood cell *enriched with oxygen*

Gas exchange inside an alveolus

Large amounts of carbon dioxide *leaving blood*

Large amounts of oxygen *entering blood*

Respiratory membrane

Oxygen

Carbon dioxide

Wall of alveolus

SEM OF LUNG SECTION

EXCHANGING GASES
The diagram above shows a section cut through an alveolus and the blood capillary that surrounds it. Oxygen in inhaled air diffuses across the thin respiratory membrane, and passes into red blood cells. Inhalation replenishes oxygen supplies in the alveolus, while blood flow removes oxygen-enriched blood. This creates a diffusion "gradient" across the respiratory membrane – high levels of oxygen in the alveolus, low levels in the blood – that ensures a constant flow of oxygen into the bloodstream. The same applies to carbon dioxide, but in the opposite direction. Carbon dioxide diffuses from newly arrived blood into the alveolus, where levels of carbon dioxide are low because it is continually exhaled.

BLOOD SUPPLY

This angiogram of a lung shows a pulmonary artery and its branches. The left and right pulmonary arteries carry the dark red, oxygen-poor blood that is pumped by the heart into the two lungs. Then, they follow the bronchi and bronchioles, branching repeatedly into smaller and smaller vessels until they form the dense networks of capillaries that surround and cling to the alveoli. As they leave the alveoli, these capillaries merge to form progressively larger and larger veins that empty their bright red, oxygen-rich blood into the two pulmonary veins that return blood from each lung to the heart for distribution around the body.

THE BENDS

As a diver descends underwater, the pressure on their body rises steadily because of the increasing weight of water pushing down on them. Under these conditions, nitrogen in inhaled air dissolves in the blood. If a diver then ascends to the surface too rapidly, the nitrogen comes out of solution in the blood and forms bubbles, like those that appear in a bottle of soda when the cap is unscrewed. The result is decompression sickness, or the "bends," as nitrogen bubbles cause excruciating pains in joints or muscles, or affect brain function, sometimes with fatal results.

SUPPLYING CELLS

The final stage of the respiratory process involves the delivery of oxygen to, and the removal of carbon dioxide from, the body's trillions of cells. During gas exchange in the tissues, oxygen diffuses from blood carried by capillaries into the surrounding cells, while carbon dioxide diffuses from tissue cells into the blood.

Respiratory bronchiole

Air space inside alveolus

Wall of alveolus

Capillary

Oxygen diffuses *from the alveolus and binds with hemoglobin in red blood cells*

Carbon dioxide diffuses *from blood plasma into the alveolus*

Gas exchange in the lungs

Oxygen-poor blood *returns from the tissues to the lungs via the heart*

Oxygen-rich blood *travels from the lungs to the tissues via the heart*

Fluid *between cells*

Tissue cell

Red blood cell

Blood plasma

Capillary

Carbon dioxide *diffuses from tissue cells into a capillary and dissolves in plasma, the liquid part of blood*

Oxygen *is unloaded from red blood cells and diffuses from the capillary into tissue cells*

Gas exchange in the tissues

Breathing

THE AIR INSIDE THE LUNGS is constantly renewed by breathing, or ventilation, which pumps fresh air in and stale air out. Lacking muscles of their own, the lungs themselves do not play an active part in the process. Instead, these spongy, elastic organs are forced passively to expand, to suck in air, or shrink, to push out air, as the volume of the thoracic cavity, in which they are encased, increases or decreases. These volume changes, which make breathing happen, are produced by the diaphragm and the intercostal muscles. The whole sequence of events is controlled by the brain stem, which can alter the rate and depth of breathing according to the body's needs.

GAS	% IN INHALED AIR	% IN EXHALED AIR
Oxygen	20.8	15.6
Carbon dioxide	0.04	4.0
Water vapor	0.56	1.8
Nitrogen	78.6	78.6
Total	100.0	100.0

CHANGE IN COMPOSITION
The nonstop process of gas exchange taking place inside the lungs' millions of alveoli removes oxygen from the air and adds carbon dioxide to it. As a result, exhaled air contains less oxygen, but more carbon dioxide, than inhaled air. It also contains more water vapor because it is moistened as it travels along the airways.

INHALATION AND EXHALATION

Breathing in, or inhalation, and breathing out, or exhalation, involve the diaphragm and the intercostal muscles. During inhalation, the diaphragm contracts and flattens, while the intercostal muscles contract, raising the ribs upward and outward. These two actions increase the volume of the thoracic (chest) cavity. This makes the elastic lungs enlarge, and reduces the pressure inside them so that air is sucked in from outside. During exhalation, the diaphragm relaxes and is pushed upward, while the intercostal muscles relax so that the ribs move downward and inward. These two actions decrease the volume inside the thoracic cavity, squeezing the passive lungs and increasing the pressure inside them so that air is pushed to the outside.

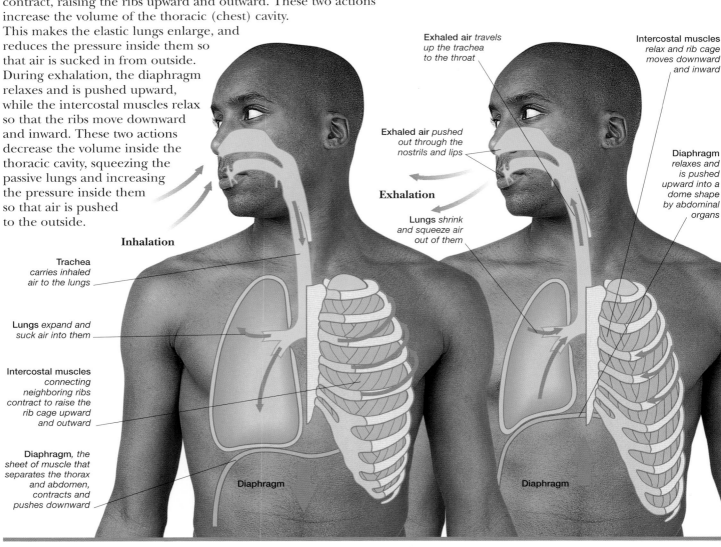

Inhalation

Trachea *carries inhaled air to the lungs*

Lungs *expand and suck air into them*

Intercostal muscles *connecting neighboring ribs contract to raise the rib cage upward and outward*

Diaphragm, *the sheet of muscle that separates the thorax and abdomen, contracts and pushes downward*

Diaphragm

Exhaled air *travels up the trachea to the throat*

Exhaled air *pushed out through the nostrils and lips*

Exhalation

Lungs *shrink and squeeze air out of them*

Intercostal muscles *relax and rib cage moves downward and inward*

Diaphragm *relaxes and is pushed upward into a dome shape by abdominal organs*

Diaphragm

Respiratory volumes for a young adult male, measured using a spirometer

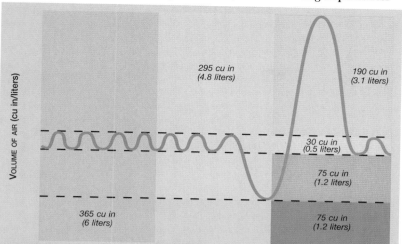

VOLUME OF AIR (cu in/liters)

295 cu in
(4.8 liters)

190 cu in
(3.1 liters)

30 cu in
(0.5 liters)

75 cu in
(1.2 liters)

365 cu in
(6 liters)

75 cu in
(1.2 liters)

RESPIRATORY VOLUME

Tidal volume (TV) is the amount of air breathed in and out at rest.
Inspiratory reserve volume (IRV) is air forcibly inhaled beyond
TV. Expiratory reserve volume (ERV) is air that can be forcibly
exhaled beyond TV. Residual volume (RV) is air that remains in
the lungs and prevents their collapse. Vital capacity (VC) is the
total amount of air that can be breathed in and out (TV +
IRV + ERV). Total lung capacity equals VC + RV.

- Total lung capacity
- Vital lung capacity
- Inspiratory reserve volume
- Resting tidal volume
- Expiratory reserve volume
- Residual volume

Spirometer
*measures the
volume of air
inhaled and
exhaled through
a mouthpiece
attached to
the patient*

CONTROLLING BREATHING

Breathing is controlled by the
respiratory center in the brain
stem. It receives input from
sensors that monitor carbon
dioxide and oxygen levels in
blood, and from stretch
receptors in muscles.
It sends nerve signals to the
diaphragm and intercostal
muscles, setting the rate and
depth of breathing. At rest,
the breathing rate is between
12 to 15 times per minute.
During exercise, this rate can
more than double, as the
respiratory center increases
breathing rate and
depth to get more
oxygen to hard-
working muscles.

Respiratory center,
*located in the brain
stem, controls the
breathing process*

Diaphragm and
intercostal muscles
*are stimulated
by messages from
the respiratory center*

Stretch receptors *in
muscles detect how
active they are and
send signals to the
respiratory center*

ARTIFICIAL RESPIRATION

If a person suddenly stops breathing through
illness or injury, the brain begins to die within
minutes because its oxygen supply is being cut
off. In such an emergency, artificial respiration
may save the person's life. The technique
involves ensuring that the airway is not
blocked, and then delivering the "kiss of life"
in order to blow air into the lungs. This
maintains the supply of oxygen to the lungs,
and may cause breathing to restart.

OTHER BREATHING MOVEMENTS

In sneezing, which clears the upper airways, air from
the lungs builds up behind the closed vocal cords,
which then open to release a 100 mph (160 kmh)
surge of air through the nasal passages. Coughing
is similar, but air exits out through the mouth.
In hiccups, the diaphragm suddenly contracts,
air rushes into the lungs, and the vocal cords noisily
snap shut. Yawning takes a deep breath into the
lungs to "flush out" accumulated carbon dioxide.

SCHLIEREN PHOTOGRAPH OF PERSON SNEEZING

Air turbulence
*caused by
a sneeze*

THE VITAL FLAME

THE FIRST SIGN of death occurs when breathing stops. What happens next, as the lifeless corpse grows cold? The ancient Greeks thought that a vital flame within the body, which heated the blood, went out. They were, in a sense, correct. Burning is a key element of life, but the burning involved is much slower than combustion in a flame. It occurs in the form of cell respiration – the chemical breakdown of glucose within the body's cells, fueled by oxygen drawn into the lungs and transported in the blood. Heat released by respiration warms the body. When breathing stops, the supply of oxygen for respiration is cut off, and the body dies and cools.

GALEN'S PNEUMA
The writings of the Roman physician Galen (above) influenced medicine for more than a thousand years. Galen proposed that a vital spirit in air, the pneuma, entered the lungs and passed to the heart, where it mixed with and "vitalized" the blood.

INNER WARMTH

When ancient Greek philosophers such as Aristotle (above, 384–322 BC) claimed that breathed-out air was warm because it had been heated by a fire burning in the heart, they were making a logical, but incorrect, deduction. They believed that this vital (or "life-giving") flame provided the warmth that was essential for life, and was fueled by food taken into the body. The air brought in by breathing served to control and cool the flame. If the flame went out, of course, the body lost its warmth and went cold.

VITALIZING THE BLOOD

The Romans inherited many ideas from the Greeks, including that of a vital spirit, called pneuma, contained in the air. The influential Greek-born physician Claudius Galen (AD 130–200) proposed that pneuma passed down the airways into the lungs, and then to the left ventricle of the heart. He also suggested that blood was manufactured, enriched with food in the liver, and then carried away in a tidal movement by the veins to the organs, where it was consumed. Blood entering the right ventricle followed two courses. Some went to the lungs to get rid of waste. The rest moved through "pores" into the left ventricle, where it was "vitalized" by being mixed with pneuma, and then carried the "life force" to all parts of the body through the arteries. For Galen, therefore, veins and arteries formed separate, sealed-off systems. No further progress in understanding the respiratory system would be made until the true nature of the circulatory system was discovered in 1628, when English doctor William Harvey (see pp. 268–9) showed that the heart pumped blood around the body through the arteries and veins.

BOYLE'S PUMP
Physicist Robert Boyle used a vacuum pump to suck air from containers with birds or small mammals inside. They died. When he repeated the experiment with a burning candle, the flame went out. From these outcomes, it was clear to Boyle that animals need "fresh" air to stay alive, just as candles need it to keep burning.

DISCOVERING OXYGEN

During Harvey's lifetime, there was considerable interest in why both an animal and a flame need air to survive. This question was explored by English physicist Robert Boyle (1627–91). The invention of the vacuum pump, which sucked air out of sealed containers, allowed Boyle to show that animals could not survive without air, nor would a candle burn. English doctor John Mayow (1640–79) showed that if a mouse, or a lighted candle, was placed in a confined space, only part of the air was used up before the animal died, or the candle went out, a part that he called nitroaerial spirit. It was left to French chemist Antoine Lavoisier (1743–94) to identify this as oxygen. Lavoisier showed that the human body consumes oxygen during cell respiration and exhales carbon dioxide, just as a burning candle consumes oxygen and generates carbon dioxide. He thought cell respiration occurred only in the lungs, but Italian physiologist Lazzaro Spallanzani (1729–99) proved that cell respiration occurs in every tissue of the body.

RELEASING ENERGY

By 1856, it was known that muscles respire, taking in oxygen, giving out heat, and generating energy for their contraction. It was not until the 1930s, however, that German-born British biochemist Hans Krebs (1900–81) described the complex chemical reactions of aerobic respiration (called the Krebs cycle) that use oxygen – produced by the world's plant life – to break down glucose derived from food. These reactions, which occur inside cell

ANTOINE LAVOISIER
Seen here experimenting in his laboratory, Antoine Lavoisier gave the name "oxygen" to the part of air that supports life. Lavoisier lost his own life prematurely when he was guillotined by French revolutionaries in 1794.

organelles called mitochondria, release energy to power cell activities. They are also the source of the heat thought by Aristotle to be generated by the vital flame.

Cell respiration *takes place on these inner fields*

TEM OF A MITOCHONDRION

Oxygen *is released by leaves as a product of photosynthesis*

Leaves *absorb carbon dioxide from the air*

OXYGEN PRODUCERS
Plants generate oxygen, which is essential for life. They take in water through their roots and absorb carbon dioxide from air into their leaves. From these, in a reaction called photosynthesis, they manufacture sugars used for growth and release oxygen as a waste product.

MITOCHONDRIA
These sausage-shaped organelles are found inside body cells. Oxygen, taken in through the lungs and carried to cells by the blood, is used inside mitochondria to help release energy from glucose during cell respiration (see pp. 22–3). The waste product of this process, carbon dioxide, is delivered to the lungs, breathed out, and then used by plants for photosynthesis.

Making sounds

FROM THE MOMENT of birth, humans make sounds. At first these sounds are inarticulate noises, but as children grow, they learn to articulate, producing distinctive words and phrases. This ability to communicate with a voice – whether by speaking, singing, shouting, or whispering – is unique to humans. Sounds originate in the larynx, or voice box, which links the base of the pharynx (throat) to the trachea. Air expelled from the lungs makes vocal cords in the larynx vibrate and produce sounds, which are amplified by the pharynx, and shaped into recognizable words by the tongue and lips. The whole process is controlled by several parts of the brain, notably Broca's area, found on the left side of the brain.

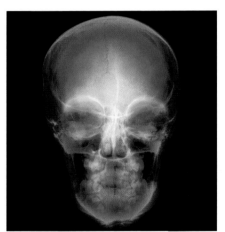

COLORED X-RAY OF HUMAN SKULL

IMPROVING QUALITY
Sounds produced by the larynx are improved by other parts of the respiratory system. In particular, the pharynx, nasal cavities, mouth, and sinuses (hollow chambers in the bones of the skull, seen as black triangles below the eye sockets in this X-ray) act as resonators. They help to amplify the voice and give it a distinctive quality, in a manner similar to the soundbox of a guitar.

VOCAL CORDS

These membrane folds extend horizontally from the front to the back of the larynx. Muscles attached to the vocal cords alter both their length and the size of the opening between them. To make sounds, the vocal cords are drawn together, and air is expelled from the lungs. As the air pushes between the vocal cords, they vibrate, creating sounds. Tightly stretched vocal cords vibrate rapidly to produce high-pitched sounds, while looser cords produce low-pitched sounds. Men have lower-pitched voices than women because their vocal cords are longer and thicker and vibrate more slowly. Loudness depends on the force with which air passes between the cords – the greater the force, the louder the sound.

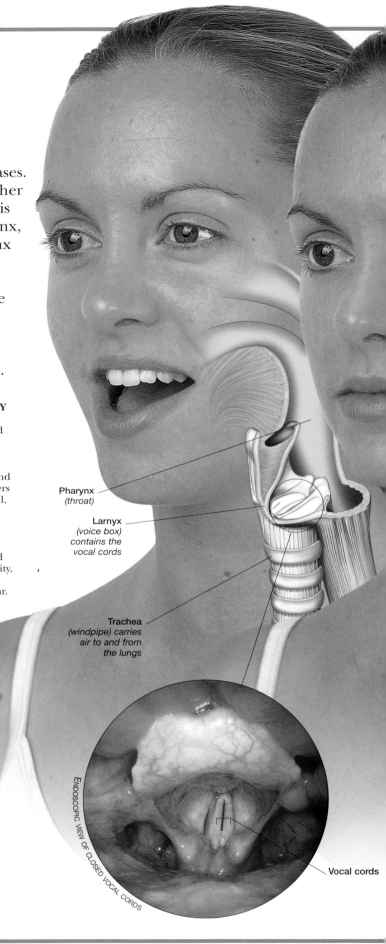

Pharynx
(throat)

Larnyx
(voice box)
contains the
vocal cords

Trachea
(windpipe) carries
air to and from
the lungs

ENDOSCOPIC VIEW OF CLOSED VOCAL CORDS

Vocal cords

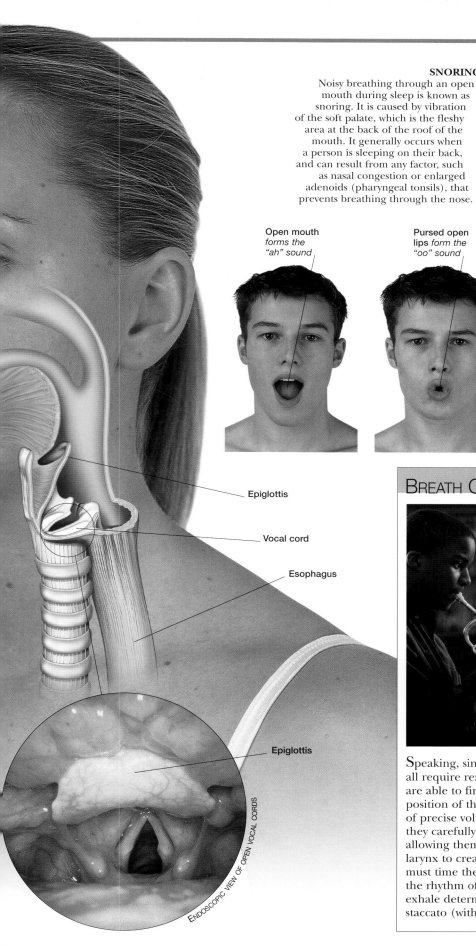

SNORING

Noisy breathing through an open mouth during sleep is known as snoring. It is caused by vibration of the soft palate, which is the fleshy area at the back of the roof of the mouth. It generally occurs when a person is sleeping on their back, and can result from any factor, such as nasal congestion or enlarged adenoids (pharyngeal tonsils), that prevents breathing through the nose.

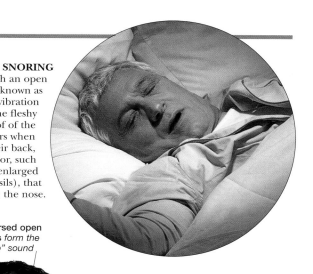

Open mouth *forms the "ah" sound*

Pursed open lips *form the "oo" sound*

SHAPING SPEECH

In a process called articulation, muscles controlling the tongue, cheeks, and lips shape the basic sounds arriving from the throat into recognizable vowels and consonants in order to form the subtle and varied sounds of speech. For example, separation of the lips so that air suddenly escapes from between them produces the sound "p."

Epiglottis

Vocal cord

Esophagus

Epiglottis

ENDOSCOPIC VIEW OF OPEN VOCAL CORDS

BREATH CONTROL

Speaking, singing, and the playing of wind instruments all require remarkable breathing control. Singers are able to finely coordinate the shape, tension, and position of their vocal cords in order to produce sounds of precise volume, pitch, and quality. In addition, they carefully control the pattern of their breathing, allowing them to regulate the flow of air through the larynx to create the desired sounds. Similarly, musicians must time their breathing so that it does not interrupt the rhythm of the music, and the way in which they exhale determines whether the sound is prolonged or staccato (with each note detached), soft or powerful.

DIGESTIVE system

URING THEIR lifetime, the average person eats their way through at least 20 tons of food. The job of the digestive system is to turn this mountain of nourishment into substances that the body can use, both for energy and for growth and repair. It works like an assembly line in reverse, turning complex nutrients into simpler ones that the body can then absorb. Food contains three major kinds of nutrients – carbohydrates, fats, and proteins – and the digestive system deals with each kind in a different way. Once these and other nutrients have been extracted, the digestive system gets rid of any undigested waste.

ESSENTIALS AND ACCESSORIES

The core of the digestive system is a long tube called the alimentary canal, or gastrointestinal tract. It runs from the mouth to the anus, and is divided into distinct regions – the esophagus and stomach, and the small and large intestines – that carry out different tasks. Attached to the tube are a number of accessory organs that help in the process of digestion. They include the teeth, tongue, and salivary glands, as well as the liver, gallbladder, and pancreas. Cells lining the alimentary canal experience a lot of wear and tear, and they often have a working life of just three or four days.

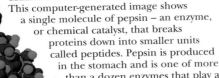

CHEMICAL AND MECHANICAL
This computer-generated image shows a single molecule of pepsin – an enzyme, or chemical catalyst, that breaks proteins down into smaller units called peptides. Pepsin is produced in the stomach and is one of more than a dozen enzymes that play a part in digestion. The mechanical side of digestion includes chewing and also muscular "churning" by the stomach and intestines. This helps enzymes get at the substances that they break down.

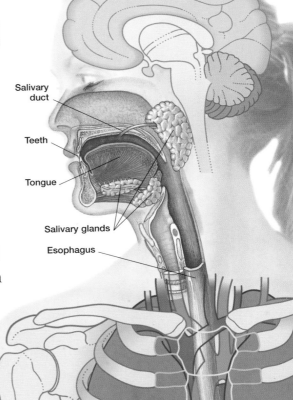

Salivary duct

Teeth

Tongue

Salivary glands

Esophagus

Liver

Stomach

Gallbladder

Pancreas

Small intestine

Large intestine

Rectum

Anus

FOOD ON THE MOVE

The alimentary canal operates by muscle power and works at a range of different speeds. Food is only briefly in the mouth and esophagus, but once it reaches the stomach, it can stay there several hours. From here, food moves into the small intestine, where it is nudged through the lengthy twists and turns at about 0.5 in (1 cm) per minute. Once in the large intestine, it slows down again, particularly if the body is short of water. The times shown below are for a typical meal.

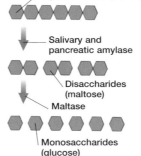

`00:00:10`

Food enters the stomach about ten seconds after it has been swallowed

`03:00:00`

If food contains only a small amount of fat, it leaves the stomach within three hours. Fatty or protein-rich food can stay in the stomach for twice as long as this

`06:00:00`

Semidigested food, *called chyme, reaches the halfway point of the small intestine about three hours after it left the stomach. By now, many of its nutrients have been absorbed*

Small intestine

`08:00:00`

Ileocecal sphincter
(beginning of large intestine)

About eight hours after being swallowed, watery, indigestible waste completes its journey to the end of the small intestine

Large intestine
has a 1-in (2-cm) layer of bacteria

By the time it reaches the midpoint of the large intestine, a large proportion of the waste's water has been removed and reabsorbed

`20:00:00`

During the 12 to 36 hours in the large intestine, liquid waste is transformed into semi-solid feces

`32:00:00`

Feces *reach the rectum, the end of the large intestine, between 20 and 44 hours after swallowing*

DIGESTING FOOD

Although food is full of nutrients, most of them are complex molecules that the body cannot absorb. These have to be broken down into smaller and simpler chemicals that can travel through the lining of the small intestine and into the body itself. These simple substances are formed by enzymes. Enzymes work like chemical scissors, cutting up the large molecules at specific points.

Polysaccharides (starch)

Salivary and pancreatic amylase

Disaccharides (maltose)

Maltase

Monosaccharides (glucose)

Carbohydrate digestion
Complex carbohydrates, such as starch, are broken down by enzymes in saliva and in the small intestine. An enzyme called amylase splits long starch molecules to produce maltose. Maltase then splits maltose molecules to produce glucose. Through this process, long carbohydrate molecules, or polysaccharides, are turned into monosaccharides, or simple sugars.

Protein digestion
The first step in protein digestion takes place in the stomach, where pepsin breaks down protein molecules into smaller units called peptides. In the small intestine, an enzyme called trypsin continues this work, while other enzymes, called peptidases, cut up the peptide molecules to produce individual amino acids.

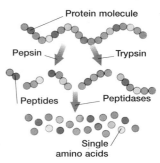

Protein molecule

Pepsin

Trypsin

Peptides

Peptidases

Single amino acids

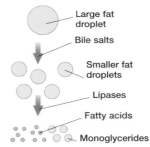

Large fat droplet

Bile salts

Smaller fat droplets

Lipases

Fatty acids

Monoglycerides

Fat digestion
Fats do not normally dissolve in water, but bile salts turn them into an emulsion of droplets. They are then digested by an enzyme called lipase, which produces fatty acids and monoglycerides. These travel to the sides of the small intestine in microscopic globules, called micelles.

DIGESTIVE SYSTEM FUNCTIONS

Ingestion	*Takes food and drink into the body through the mouth.*
Propulsion	*Moves food and indigestible waste through the alimentary canal by waves of muscle contraction (peristalsis).*
Mechanical digestion	*Physically breaks down food by chewing, and by muscular movements of the alimentary canal.*
Chemical digestion	*By using enzymes, breaks down complex nutrient molecules into simpler substances that the body can absorb.*
Absorption	*Moves digested nutrients from the alimentary canal to the bloodstream or the lymphatic system so that they can be distributed to the body's cells.*
Egestion	*During defecation, disposes of indigestible waste and waste products produced by the body.*

Teeth

Located at the entrance of the digestive system, teeth are the hardest objects in the body. They can withstand tremendous pressure when they bite – thanks not only to their extra-tough crowns, but also to their shock-absorbing roots. Teeth cut, crush, and chew the food that we eat, making it easier to both swallow and digest. Humans have two sets of teeth, and in each, different teeth carry out different work. But teeth all share one important characteristic: once they have appeared, or "erupted," above the gums, their hard outer enamel cannot be repaired or replaced. Enamel can be damaged by acids from food, and if it is breached, the inner part of teeth can decay. But with regular cleaning and a healthy diet, adult teeth can last for life.

TYPES OF TEETH

When someone opens their mouth wide, the differences between individual teeth become easy to see. The incisors, at the front, are the only teeth that have a flat cross-section, with a single cutting edge. They take large chunks out of food and slice it up. The canines, to each side of them, have a single point for gripping and tearing. Behind them are the premolars and molars, which are used for chewing food, grinding it down into a paste. These teeth have two or four cusps, or raised edges, and because they are near the back of the jaw, they have an exceptionally powerful bite.

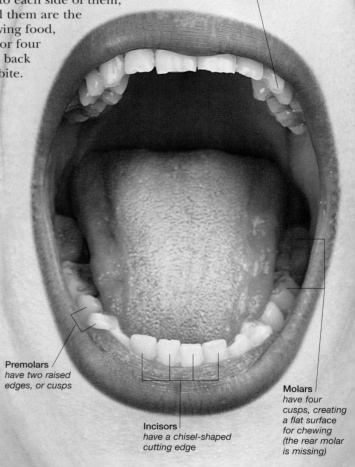

Canines end in a single rounded point

Premolars have two raised edges, or cusps

Incisors have a chisel-shaped cutting edge

Molars have four cusps, creating a flat surface for chewing (the rear molar is missing)

TWO SETS

Baby teeth, also known as deciduous teeth, have small crowns and relatively shallow roots. They begin to appear at the age of about six months, and are complete by about 32 months. From the age of about six years onward, they are shed and replaced by adult or permanent teeth, which are larger, with longer roots. Most people have 20 baby teeth and 32 adult teeth. Baby teeth appear in a set order, starting with the central incisors and ending with the second molars. Adult teeth start appearing at the front of the jaw, and work backward as the jaw grows. However, in some people, the third molars, or wisdom teeth, remain embedded in the jaws.

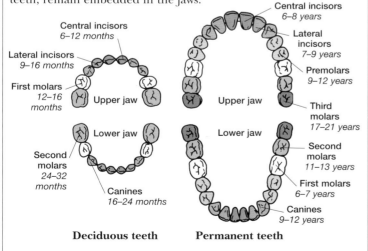

Central incisors
6–12 months

Lateral incisors
9–16 months

First molars
12–16 months

Upper jaw

Lower jaw

Second molars
24–32 months

Canines
16–24 months

Deciduous teeth

Central incisors
6–8 years

Lateral incisors
7–9 years

Premolars
9–12 years

Upper jaw

Third molars
17–21 years

Lower jaw

Second molars
11–13 years

First molars
6–7 years

Canines
9–12 years

Permanent teeth

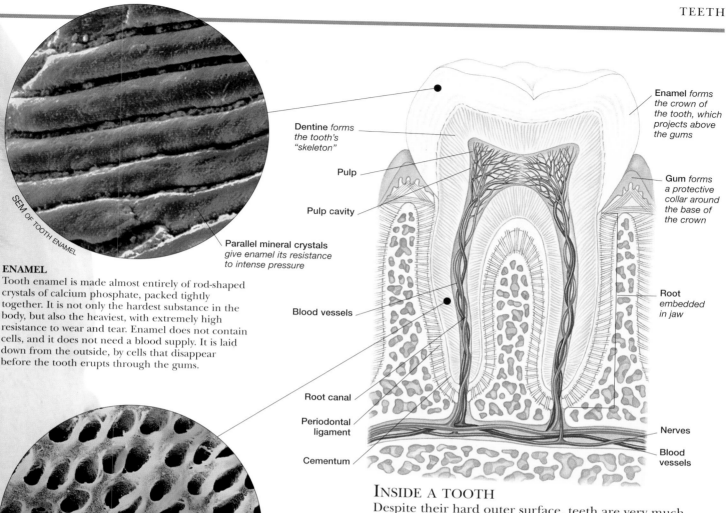

Enamel *forms the crown of the tooth, which projects above the gums*

Dentine *forms the tooth's "skeleton"*

Pulp

Pulp cavity

Parallel mineral crystals *give enamel its resistance to intense pressure*

Gum *forms a protective collar around the base of the crown*

Blood vessels

Root *embedded in jaw*

Root canal

Periodontal ligament

Cementum

Nerves

Blood vessels

SEM OF TOOTH ENAMEL

ENAMEL

Tooth enamel is made almost entirely of rod-shaped crystals of calcium phosphate, packed tightly together. It is not only the hardest substance in the body, but also the heaviest, with extremely high resistance to wear and tear. Enamel does not contain cells, and it does not need a blood supply. It is laid down from the outside, by cells that disappear before the tooth erupts through the gums.

SEM OF DENTINE

Struts *in dentine contain a higher proportion of minerals than in bone, making it harder*

DENTINE

Compared to enamel, dentine has a more open structure, but it is still heavier and harder than most types of bone. When a tooth bites, it acts like crumple-resistant scaffolding, transmitting the force of the bite between the crown and the jaw. Unlike enamel, dentine is produced by cells in the pulp cavity, and it needs a blood supply to stay alive.

INSIDE A TOOTH

Despite their hard outer surface, teeth are very much alive. Their inner framework is made of a substance called dentine, which resembles bone. Dentine supports the tooth's enamel crown, and it also forms the roots that anchor the tooth in the jaw. The roots are held in place by a chemical cement that glues them to a ligament lining the socket. At the center of the tooth is a natural cavity, which is full of living tissue, called pulp. This contains blood vessels and nerves, which reach the cavity through hollow root canals. The nerves enable teeth to sense changes in temperature – and unfortunately, to sense pain.

PROBLEMS WITH PLAQUE

Magnified about 100 times, this photograph shows a layer of plaque on the surface of a tooth. Plaque is a mixture of bacteria and food that builds up on teeth that are not properly brushed. Bacteria in plaque release acids as they feed, and these can eat through tooth enamel, creating holes that lead to the pulp cavity inside. If this is left untreated, the result is dental cavities, or tooth decay – an infection that destroys pulp cells and dentine. Plaque can be hard to remove, because many bacteria produce a sticky "glue" that fastens them in place.

Bacteria *release acids when they break down the sugars in fragments of food*

Chewing and swallowing

COMPARED WITH SOME ANIMALS, people are slow eaters. The human digestive system is not designed to cope with food in large chunks, so instead, it has to be chewed. Chewing grinds food down into a more manageable form, so that it can be swallowed. Chewing and swallowing happen almost without our noticing, but they both involve complicated movements and rapid reflexes. The tongue maneuvers food into position between the teeth, while making sure that it does not get bitten itself. The teeth close with exactly the right amount of force, but they immediately stop if they touch something unexpectedly hard. Once the food has been reduced to a pulp, the tongue pushes it to the back of the throat. This triggers swallowing, which sends another mouthful on its way to the stomach.

LM OF A SECTION THROUGH A SALIVARY GLAND

Parotid salivary gland *located in front of the ear*

Salivary duct *carries saliva into the mouth*

Teeth *break up food*

Tongue *maneuvers food during chewing*

ENDOSCOPIC VIEW OF ESOPHAGUS

Sublingual salivary gland *is found under the tongue*

Submandibular salivary gland *is found deep in the floor of the mouth*

Esophagus *conveys food to the stomach*

Entrance to the stomach

INSIDE THE MOUTH

The mouth is the reception center of the digestive system, and the place where food gets its initial processing before being passed on. As soon as it arrives, food is given a rapid check by taste buds in the tongue, to make sure that it does not contain anything that might be dangerous. At the same time, the food is bathed in saliva from the three pairs of salivary glands, which moistens it so that it is easier to swallow. Saliva contains the enzyme amylase, and this starts to digest any starch that the food contains. As chewing begins, the lips and cheeks work with the tongue to help guide the food between the teeth.

INSIDE THE ESOPHAGUS

The lining of the esophagus is coated with mucus, which helps food to slide through on its way to the stomach. Cells lining the esophagus have tiny folds called microplicae, and these trap mucus, keeping the inner surface slippery. Unlike the trachea, or windpipe, the esophagus is not reinforced by cartilage because it does not need to be open at all times. When it is not in use, its upper reaches – in the throat – are usually pressed flat.

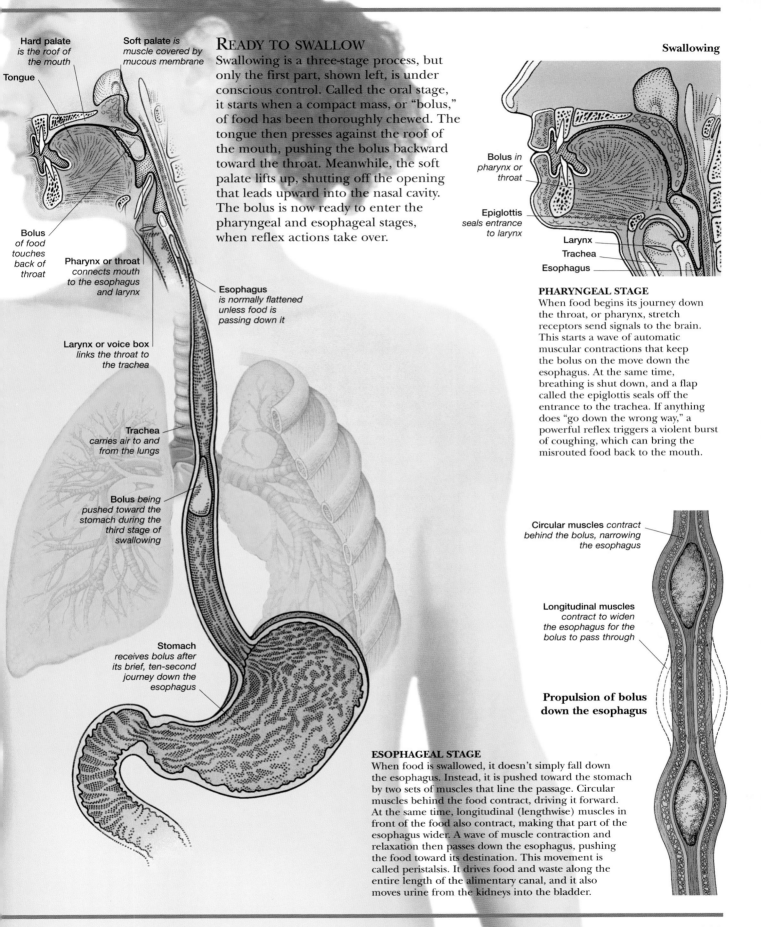

Hard palate *is the roof of the mouth*

Soft palate *is muscle covered by mucous membrane*

Tongue

Bolus *of food touches back of throat*

Pharynx or throat *connects mouth to the esophagus and larynx*

Larynx or voice box *links the throat to the trachea*

Trachea *carries air to and from the lungs*

Bolus *being pushed toward the stomach during the third stage of swallowing*

Stomach *receives bolus after its brief, ten-second journey down the esophagus*

Esophagus *is normally flattened unless food is passing down it*

READY TO SWALLOW

Swallowing is a three-stage process, but only the first part, shown left, is under conscious control. Called the oral stage, it starts when a compact mass, or "bolus," of food has been thoroughly chewed. The tongue then presses against the roof of the mouth, pushing the bolus backward toward the throat. Meanwhile, the soft palate lifts up, shutting off the opening that leads upward into the nasal cavity. The bolus is now ready to enter the pharyngeal and esophageal stages, when reflex actions take over.

Swallowing

Bolus *in pharynx or throat*

Epiglottis *seals entrance to larynx*

Larynx

Trachea

Esophagus

PHARYNGEAL STAGE

When food begins its journey down the throat, or pharynx, stretch receptors send signals to the brain. This starts a wave of automatic muscular contractions that keep the bolus on the move down the esophagus. At the same time, breathing is shut down, and a flap called the epiglottis seals off the entrance to the trachea. If anything does "go down the wrong way," a powerful reflex triggers a violent burst of coughing, which can bring the misrouted food back to the mouth.

Circular muscles *contract behind the bolus, narrowing the esophagus*

Longitudinal muscles *contract to widen the esophagus for the bolus to pass through*

Propulsion of bolus down the esophagus

ESOPHAGEAL STAGE

When food is swallowed, it doesn't simply fall down the esophagus. Instead, it is pushed toward the stomach by two sets of muscles that line the passage. Circular muscles behind the food contract, driving it forward. At the same time, longitudinal (lengthwise) muscles in front of the food also contract, making that part of the esophagus wider. A wave of muscle contraction and relaxation then passes down the esophagus, pushing the food toward its destination. This movement is called peristalsis. It drives food and waste along the entire length of the alimentary canal, and it also moves urine from the kidneys into the bladder.

Stomach

Of all the body's internal organs, the stomach is probably the best known but most misunderstood. This J-shaped bag is tucked beneath the ribs, and although it can stretch to fill with food, it does not absorb any of the nutrients that food contains. Instead, the stomach has two main functions: it gets digestion under way, storing any semidigested food, and then releases it at a slow and steady rate. In the stomach, highly acidic gastric juice allows enzymes to break down proteins, while powerful waves of muscle contraction churn the food to mix it up. After several hours of this kind of treatment, the runny result – called chyme – is ready to move on.

INSIDE THE STOMACH

The stomach is the widest and most elastic part of the alimentary canal. When it is empty, it can be smaller than a fist, but its volume can increase by more than 20 times after a meal, because the rugae (deep folds) of its inner surface become smoother as it fills. Unlike the rest of the alimentary canal, the stomach's lining has three layers of smooth muscle, arranged at angles to each other. By contracting in turn, these muscles churn up the food. At the base of the stomach, a ring of muscle called the pyloric sphincter acts like a valve, controlling the release of semi-digested food.

Esophagus

Lower esophageal sphincter *closes the junction between the esophagus and stomach to keep the stomach contents in place*

Longitudinal muscle *runs the length of the stomach*

Outer covering of stomach

Circular muscle *wraps around the stomach*

Rugae *are deep folds formed when the stomach is empty, reducing its volume to a minimum, and stretch as it fills*

Duodenum

Gastric pit *in the stomach wall leads to a gastric gland*

Pyloric sphincter *opens to allow semi-digested food to leave the stomach at a measured rate*

SEM OF STOMACH INNER LINING

GASTRIC GLANDS

Cells in the stomach's millions of gastric glands produce the components of gastric juice – mucus, hydrochloric acid, and pepsinogen, a substance that is converted into protein-digesting pepsin as it flows into the stomach. The stomach does not digest itself because its lining is covered with protective mucus, and because pepsin becomes active only when it has been "primed" by acid.

Oblique muscle *runs diagonally*

FILLING AND EMPTYING

By the time food reaches the stomach, the stomach is ready to receive it because it has been primed by the autonomic nervous system (see pp. 98–99). During its stay here – which can last for up to four hours – nerves and hormones work together to keep the digestive process working smoothly. These two control systems ensure that the stomach secretes enough gastric juice, and also trigger muscular movements (peristalsis) in the stomach wall. When digestion has progressed far enough, the pyloric sphincter relaxes, and the stomach's contents flow into the small intestine.

Pyloric sphincter *partially relaxes to allow food to pass through*

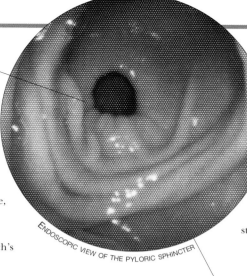

ENDOSCOPIC VIEW OF THE PYLORIC SPHINCTER

AUTOMATIC VALVE

Seen through an endoscope, the pyloric sphincter guards the entrance to the duodenum – the first part of the small intestine. When this ring of muscle is tightly contracted, nothing can leave the stomach, but as digestion proceeds, it begins to relax. This relaxation is controlled by a feedback mechanism, which ensures that semi-digested food leaves the stomach at the right rate.

Stomach muscles *push food through pyloric sphincter*

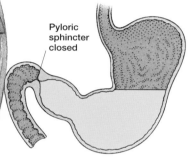

Pyloric sphincter closed

Filling
As it fills, the stomach releases gastric juice, which is mixed with food by waves of muscular contraction, or peristalsis.

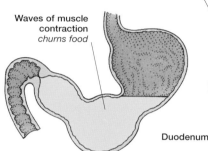

Waves of muscle contraction *churns food*

Digestion
Vigorous peristalsis churns food as gastric juice digests it into creamy liquid chyme.

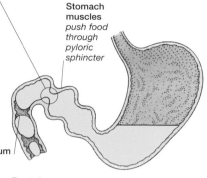

Duodenum

Emptying
If chyme is liquid enough, the pyloric sphincter relaxes and opens slightly to let small quantities of food pass into the duodenum.

Stomach wall *contains millions of microscopic glands that secrete gastric juice*

ACID ATTACK

When food enters the stomach, it is mixed with a digestive fluid called gastric juice. This juice contains hydrochloric acid, and it is strong enough to dissolve small pieces of bone. These acidic conditions are needed for protein digestion, which is carried out by an enzyme called pepsin.

Long flagella *enable the bacterium to move through mucus on the stomach's lining*

STOMACH BUG

Stomach acid kills most bacteria, but one kind, called *Helicobacter pylori*, manages to thrive in these hazardous conditions. In recent years, this bacterium has been closely studied, and there is mounting evidence that it is linked to two different forms of stomach disease, one of which is stomach cancer. The other disease is gastritis – an inflammation that often leads to ulcers. How the bacterium spreads is not known.

STOMACH STUDY

In 1822, American surgeon William Beaumont treated Alexis St. Martin, who had been shot during a hunting trip. Beaumont saved the man's life, but his patient was left with a permanent opening from his stomach to the outside. For the next decade, Beaumont monitored St. Martin's stomach, and the fluid that it produced. Although gruesome, the research produced a great deal of useful information, and the patient lived to the ripe age of 82.

Beaumont (1785–1853) examining St. Martin's stomach

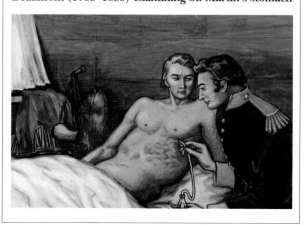

Small intestine

DESPITE ITS MODEST-SOUNDING NAME, the small intestine is the most important part of the entire digestive system. Measuring up to 20 ft (6 m) in length, this intricately folded tube is the site where food is fully broken down, and where its nutrients are absorbed. By the time food has been gently squeezed through all its twists and turns, nearly all its useful ingredients have been removed, leaving just watery waste. The small intestine is only about 1 in (2.5 cm) across, but its inner lining has a huge surface area, thanks to microscopic projections called villi. With the help of the pancreas and the liver, the intestine breaks down food into simple substances, and the villi absorb these into the body itself.

ENDOSCOPIC VIEW OF THE SMALL INTESTINE

HOW THE SMALL INTESTINE WORKS

The small intestine is divided into three regions that work in different ways. Starting "upstream," the first part is the duodenum – a 12-in (30-cm) section that receives digestive fluids from the pancreas and the liver. This is where stomach acid is neutralized, and where digestion of food begins in earnest. The second section, called the jejunum, is about 6.5 ft (2 m) long and secretes large amounts of digestive enzymes. The third and longest section, called the ileum, works mainly at absorbing nutrients, rather than breaking food down. All three sections push food along by peristalsis, but they also contract into short segments, ensuring that the food is mixed up.

Duodenum is the first section of the small intestine, in which chyme is mixed with bile and pancreatic juice

Jejunum, the middle section of the small intestine, secretes digestive enzymes

Circular ridges increase the surface area of the small intestine

Villi are 0.04 in (1 mm) long projections that absorb nutrients

Ileum, the final and longest section of the small intestine, has a rich supply of blood and lymph

VILLI

The small intestine has circular internal ridges, but the greatest boost to its surface area comes from tightly packed villi (singular villus) – fingerlike projections that protrude inward from the intestine's lining. Villi contain capillaries, and also lacteals, which are minute branches of the lymphatic system. Together, these collect the nutrients that the villus absorbs from food, so that they can be carried around the body. Most of the cells that line the villi have even smaller projections, called microvilli. These form "brush borders," which are like chemical countertops. Enzymes are fastened to the brush borders, and they carry out the last stages of digestion before food is absorbed.

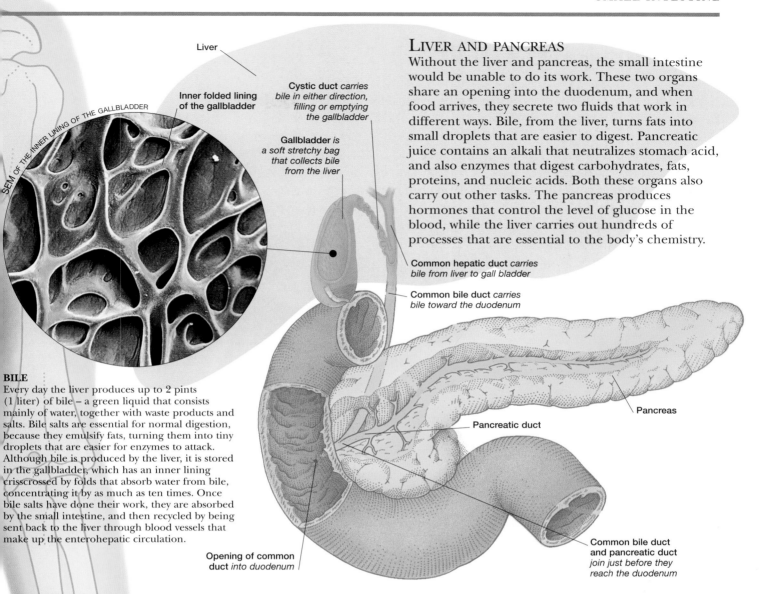

Liver

Inner folded lining
of the gallbladder

SEM OF THE INNER LINING OF THE GALLBLADDER

Cystic duct *carries
bile in either direction,
filling or emptying
the gallbladder*

Gallbladder *is
a soft stretchy bag
that collects bile
from the liver*

LIVER AND PANCREAS

Without the liver and pancreas, the small intestine would be unable to do its work. These two organs share an opening into the duodenum, and when food arrives, they secrete two fluids that work in different ways. Bile, from the liver, turns fats into small droplets that are easier to digest. Pancreatic juice contains an alkali that neutralizes stomach acid, and also enzymes that digest carbohydrates, fats, proteins, and nucleic acids. Both these organs also carry out other tasks. The pancreas produces hormones that control the level of glucose in the blood, while the liver carries out hundreds of processes that are essential to the body's chemistry.

Common hepatic duct *carries
bile from liver to gall bladder*

Common bile duct *carries
bile toward the duodenum*

BILE

Every day the liver produces up to 2 pints (1 liter) of bile – a green liquid that consists mainly of water, together with waste products and salts. Bile salts are essential for normal digestion, because they emulsify fats, turning them into tiny droplets that are easier for enzymes to attack. Although bile is produced by the liver, it is stored in the gallbladder, which has an inner lining crisscrossed by folds that absorb water from bile, concentrating it by as much as ten times. Once bile salts have done their work, they are absorbed by the small intestine, and then recycled by being sent back to the liver through blood vessels that make up the enterohepatic circulation.

Pancreas

Pancreatic duct

Opening of common
duct *into duodenum*

Common bile duct
and pancreatic duct
*join just before they
reach the duodenum*

ENZYMES IN ACTION

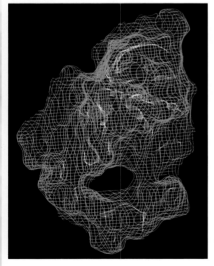

Enzymes are proteins that speed up chemical reactions in the body. If they did not exist, it would take several decades to digest even a single meal. There are two main groups of digestive enzymes: those made by the pancreas and released in pancreatic juice, and those on the "brush borders" of the small intestine. Each enzyme acts on one particular type of nutrient, turning it into smaller and simpler products. Enzyme molecules are not used up when they do their work. This means that they can do the same job thousands or even millions of times in succession.

**Computer-generated image
of the enzyme amylase**

ENZYME	ACTS ON	PRODUCT
PANCREATIC		
Amylase	Starch	Maltose
Trypsin	Proteins	Peptides
Chymotrypsin	Proteins	Peptides
Carboxypeptidase	Proteins	
Lipase	Fats and oils	Fatty acids and monoglycerides
Nuclease	Nucleic acids	Pentoses and bases
BRUSH BORDER		
Peptidases	Peptides	Amino acids
Maltase	Maltose	Glucose
Sucrase	Sucrose	Glucose and fructose
Lactase	Lactose	Glucose and galactose
Nuclease	Nucleic acids	Pentoses and bases

Large intestine

THE LARGE INTESTINE IS the final stretch of the alimentary canal. It is more than twice as wide as the small intestine, but only about one-fourth as long. Instead of twisting and turning, it follows a more straightforward path, with just a handful of sharp bends. The large intestine does not produce any enzymes, and it does not play a direct part in digestion. Instead, its chief function is to reabsorb water to help the body's fluid balance, and to make waste easier to expel. The large intestine also has another role: it absorbs vitamins that are made by bacteria. Huge numbers of microbes thrive in its warm and moist interior, and they break down substances that have escaped digestion, before eventually being expelled themselves.

INSIDE THE COLON
Endoscopes are often used to examine the colon for signs of disease. This view shows the inside of a healthy colon, with a corridor of pockets, called haustra, separated by narrower parts of the intestine wall. The intestine looks triangular in cross-section because it has three taeniae, (bands of muscle) running almost all the way along it.

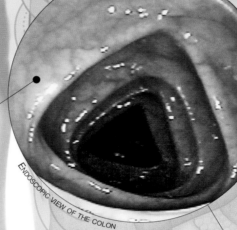

ENDOSCOPIC VIEW OF THE COLON

Glands *produce mucus to lubricate passage of feces*

Descending colon *travels down the left side of the abdominal cavity*

Tenia omentalis *is one of three parallel bands of muscle that run along the colon*

Transverse colon *travels across the abdominal cavity, below the liver and spleen*

SEM OF COLON WALL

ABSORPTIVE LINING
Magnified about 400 times, the lining of the large intestine (above) looks much smoother than other parts of the alimentary canal. Unlike the small intestine, it does not have villi, but it does have small glands, which can clearly be seen in the picture (blue). These contain cells that produce mucus. Water-absorbing cells are spread all over the large intestine's lining, and in the sides of its glands.

Ascending colon *travels up the right side of the adominal cavity*

COLON

The large intestine begins at the ileocecal sphincter, or valve, and it ends at the rectum and anus. The section between these points is called the colon and measures about 5 ft (1.5 m) in length. The colon follows a path shaped like the edge of a shield, traveling up, across, and then down the lower part of the abdominal cavity. Unlike the small intestine, the colon has muscle bands (teniae), which gather it up into a series of pockets (haustra) that help to compact waste before passing it on. The rectum collects waste once most of its water has been removed, and holds the waste ready for disposal.

Appendix

Small intestine

Anus

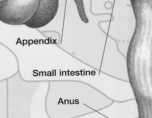

Sigmoid colon *leads down to the rectum*

Rectum

FLUID IN, FLUID OUT

Water entering the alimentary canal

Saliva	2 pints (1 liter)
Water in beverages	5 pints (2.3 liters)
Bile	2 pints (1 liter)
Pancreatic juice	4.25 pints (1.9 liters)
Gastric juice	4.25 pints (1.9 liters)
Intestinal juice	2 pints (1 liter)
TOTAL	19.5 pints (9.3 liters)

Water reabsorbed by the alimentary canal

Small intestine	17.5 pints (8.3 liters)
Large intestine	1.8 pints (0.9 liters)
TOTAL	18.3 pints (9.2 liters)
Water lost in feces	0.2 pints (0.1 liters)

This diagram shows how much water moves in and out of the alimentary canal during a typical day. About 19.5 pints (9.3 liters) of water are needed to move food and nutrients, and to create the right conditions for enzymes to work. However, the digestive system reabsorbs and recycles almost all of this water, so that the body does not become dehydrated. Reabsorption is a vital part of the body's water balance: if it breaks down, as happens in dysentery and other diseases that produce severe diarrhea, people can become seriously ill.

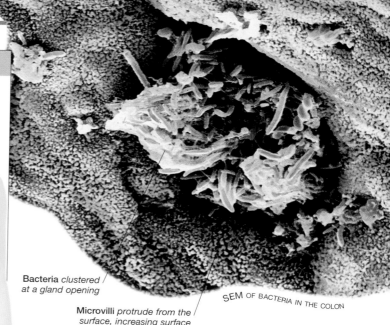

Bacteria *clustered at a gland opening*

Microvilli *protrude from the surface, increasing surface area for water absorption*

SEM OF BACTERIA IN THE COLON

INTESTINAL BACTERIA

There are more bacteria in the large intestine than in the rest of the body put together – so many, in fact, that they are estimated to form a layer 1 in (2 cm) thick. Their function is to break down organic matter in waste, and to produce gas. Bacteria also make a range of useful chemicals, such as vitamin K, which the body absorbs and uses. Bacteria make up nearly 50 percent of waste by the time its gets expelled.

DEFECATION

After spending about five to ten hours in the large intestine, compacted waste, known as feces, is ready for disposal. Feces contain a variable amount of water, together with undigested fiber, dead gut cells, and living and dead bacteria. They also contain digested bile pigments, which give them their color. Feces are pushed into the rectum by peristalsis, and are expelled through the anus during defecation – an essential final stage in the digestive process. Preparations for defecation are made by automatic reflexes, but it begins when the outer sphincter of the anus relaxes, a movement that is initiated by voluntary control.

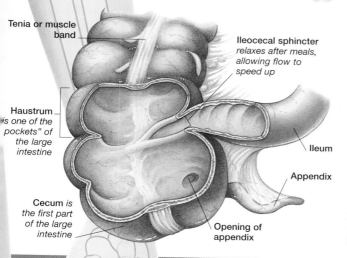

Tenia or muscle band

Haustrum *is one of the "pockets" of the large intestine*

Cecum *is the first part of the large intestine*

Ileocecal sphincter *relaxes after meals, allowing flow to speed up*

Ileum

Appendix

Opening of appendix

SPHINCTER AND APPENDIX

The ileocecal sphincter is a muscular ring that controls the flow of digested waste into the large intestine. It joins the side of the intestine, just above a pocket called the cecum. Attached to the cecum is the appendix. Long ago in human evolution, this narrow, dead-end tube played a part in the digestion of plant food, but in modern humans it has no useful function. Inflammation of the appendix, known as appendicitis, is potentially dangerous and is often treated by surgery.

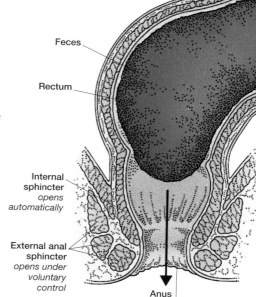

Feces

Rectum

Internal sphincter *opens automatically*

External anal sphincter *opens under voluntary control*

Anus

Nutrition

NUTRIENTS PROVIDE US with all the substances we need to keep our bodies working normally. Macronutrients, which include carbohydrates, fats, and proteins, make up most of what we eat. They supply energy, as well as building materials that the body uses for growth and maintenance. Micronutrients, which include vitamins and minerals (see pp. 194–95), are usually present in much smaller amounts, but without them, the body's chemistry cannot work. In nature, some animals manage to get all their nutrients from just one kind of food, but humans are not like this. We need to eat a mixture of different foods to get the nutrients we need in the right amounts. This mixture is known as a balanced diet, and it is one of the most important factors in staying healthy.

Fats, oils, and sugar-rich foods contain essential lipids, but only small quantities are needed because lipids are present in other foods; sugary foods are tempting, but in a well-balanced diet, most carbohydrate should come from starchy foods.

WATER AND FIBER
Two other essential nutrients are water and fiber. Water makes up over 50 percent of body weight and is constantly being lost. Fiber adds bulk to food and improves the efficiency of the muscles in the intestinal wall.

NUTRIENTS IN FOOD

For most of human history, nothing was known about the chemistry of food. Today, food labels usually indicate the exact contents of a food. The richest sources of carbohydrates are sugar, cereals, and potatoes, and anything made from them, such as pasta and bread. Protein is found in all kinds of meat, as well as in some plant-based food, such as nuts and beans. Lipids are found in vegetable oils and animal fats, and also in foods that contain butter or milk. Plant-based food is often rich in two other ingredients essential for a healthy diet – water and dietary fiber.

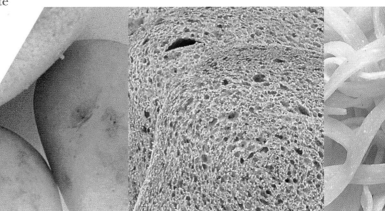

Cereals and potatoes contain plenty of starch, a complex polysaccharide. During digestion, starch is converted into glucose – the body's main source of energy. Many of these foods also contain vitamins and minerals, such as iron.

FOOD PYRAMID

We eat many different things, so it can be difficult to decide whether or not a diet is well balanced. This food pyramid helps to solve the problem. It organizes food into categories, according to the main nutrients that they contain, and it also shows how much of each category the body needs. Foods rich in carbohydrates make up the base of the pyramid, because they are needed in large amounts. Fruit and vegetables come next, as sources of vitamins, minerals, and dietary fiber (roughage). Protein-rich food is close to the top, while fats, oils, and sugar-rich foods are at the peak. They contain useful nutrients, but are best eaten in small amounts.

Meat, fish, eggs, and nuts *all supply protein, which is digested to produce amino acids; some animal proteins can supply all the amino acids that the body needs.*

A healthy stir-fry

FAST FOOD
In today's busy world, fast food (left) can make a convenient and often tasty alternative to something that has to be prepared and cooked. But unlike meals made using a mixture of fresh ingredients (above), fast food does not add up to a balanced diet. One reason for this is that it often contains extremely high levels of sugars and fats, but very low levels of minerals and vitamins and the dietary fiber needed to keep the digestive system working smoothly.

Dairy products *such as milk, butter, cheese, and yogurt contain variable amounts of protein and animal fat. They are good sources of calcium, while their fat content ranges from about 70 percent in butter, to zero in some kinds of yogurt.*

A fast food meal of a burger and chips

Vegetables *are a prime source of vitamins and minerals and contain lots of dietary fiber; this indigestible plant matter adds bulk to food and digested waste, helping it to move easily through the alimentary canal.*

Fruit *contains water and dietary fiber, and is often a good source of vitamins. Its sweetness comes from simple carbohydrates or sugars, which are useful as a rapid energy boost.*

FOOD POISONING

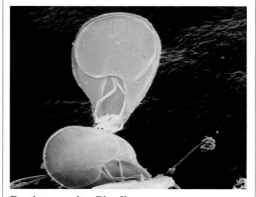

Protist parasite *Giardia*

Even with careful hygiene, food and beverages can be contaminated with microorganisms, some of which can produce acute food poisoning or long-running illnesses. The protist parasite *Giardia* causes fairly minor symptoms, but some bacteria, such as *Salmonella*, cause severe diarrhea and vomiting, leaving a person feeling weak and dehydrated. The best way to treat these symptoms is to drink plenty of water, to make up for the fluid that the body has lost.

THE SEARCH FOR VITAMINS

By THE END OF the 19th century, any uncertainty about the cause of diseases had all but disappeared. Accepted by doctors and scientists alike, Louis Pasteur's germ theory maintained that diseases were caused by bacteria and other microorganisms. But in the early 1900s, a few innovative scientists proved that some diseases were the result not of germs but instead a lack, or deficiency, of "factors" – later called vitamins – found in tiny amounts in food. The realization that there was a link between diet and disease sparked off a search to identify these "factors" and their deficiency diseases. That poor diet could cause disease had, however, been suspected much earlier.

TREATING SCURVY
On board ship, Scottish naval surgeon James Lind examines sailors he has treated for scurvy to determine which of his remedies has worked best. Lind conducted the first-ever serious clinical trial of possible cures for disease, using carefully controlled experiments.

SCURVY AT SEA

In the 18th century, sailors on long sea voyages survived for many months on an unvarying diet of preserved food. Many succumbed to scurvy, a disease that resulted in loose teeth, bleeding gums, bruising, and even death. All remedies failed until Scottish naval surgeon James Lind (1716–94) took an interest in the matter. Lind selected 12 crewmen with scurvy, divided them into pairs, and gave each pair different foods for two weeks. The two sailors fed citrus fruits – oranges and lemons – recovered rapidly. Lind published his results in 1753, but it was not until 1795 that the British Admiralty put them into practice, and it would be another 100 years before any link between diet and disease was made.

BEATING BERIBERI
For people whose diet consists mainly of rice, the type of rice consumed could make a big difference to their health. Polished (white) rice has been stripped of the outer husk retained in whole (brown) rice. This husk contains the vitamin B_1, which is necessary to prevent the disease beriberi.

White rice

Brown rice

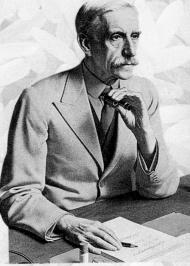

HOPPY'S FACTORS
Known as "Hoppy" by his colleagues at England's Cambridge University, biochemist Frederick Gowland Hopkins was a pioneer of nutrition research. He found that tiny amounts of "accessory food factors" – later called vitamins – were necessary for the body to function normally.

FOOD FACTORS

In 1900, Dutch physician Christiaan Eijkmann (1858–1930) was despatched to Indonesia to investigate the cause of beriberi, a disease that causes numbness and muscle weakness. Eijkmann discovered that if chickens were fed on polished (white) rice with the outer husk removed they developed a disease very similar to beriberi. Remarkably, if fed on whole (brown) rice, they rapidly recovered. Eijkmann concluded that the husk

MALFORMED BONES
A girl with rickets, caused by a lack of vitamin D, pictured with her brother in Budapest, Hungary, around 1920. She shows the characteristic bowing of the legs caused by her upper body weight pushing downward on weakened leg bones.

contained an "essential food factor." Eijkmann's work was paralleled by that started in 1906 by Frederick Gowland Hopkins (1861–1947). By feeding rats carefully controlled diets, Hopkins showed that to stay healthy they – and presumably humans too – needed tiny amounts of what he termed "accessory food factors."

NAMING VITAMINS

"Food factors" were given a new name – "vitamins" – in 1912 by Polish-American chemist Casimir Funk (1884–1967). Funk's idea that diseases such as beriberi and scurvy are caused by the lack of a particular vitamin set in motion a new era of

scientific research. In 1914, Joseph Goldberger (1874–1929) of the US Public Health Service demonstrated that pellagra – a disease that causes dermatitis, diarrhea, and dementia – was not spread by insects but was the result of poor diet, and could be reversed by a vitamin (niacin) found in protein-rich foods. British physician Edward Mellanby (1884–1955) showed in 1918 that a substance in cod liver oil – later identified by American scientist E.V. McCollum (1879–1967) as vitamin D – could prevent rickets, a deficiency disease characterized by weakened bones.

VITAMIN SUPPLEMENTS

By the end of the 1930s, scientists had identified vitamins A, C (the scurvy-preventing vitamin in citrus fruits), D, E, and the B vitamins, including B_1, B_2, and B_{12}. This wealth of knowledge about vitamins means that deficiency diseases have been all but eliminated in the developed world.

SUPPLEMENTS
A wide range of vitamin supplements like these are available from pharmacies. How effective vitamin supplements are is the subject of considerable debate. Many nutritionists believe that, for most people, a mixed diet containing fresh produce provides all the vitamins they need.

EXTRA VITAMINS
During World War II, food was rationed in Britain, but the government took measures to protect young children from vitamin deficiencies. Here, mothers in wartime London receive free vitamin supplements in the form of orange juice (vitamin C) and cod liver oil (vitamins A and D) for their children.

Vitamins and minerals

ESSENTIAL TO ANY BALANCED DIET are the micronutrients – minerals and vitamins – needed for growth, vitality, and general well-being. All minerals, and most vitamins, can only be obtained from food, and are not made by the body. Minerals, such as calcium, are chemical elements. Seven are required in relatively large amounts, while others – trace minerals – including iron, are needed only in minute amounts. Vitamins are organic (carbon-containing) substances. Without them the body cannot utilize macronutrients – carbohydrates, proteins, and fats – to supply energy or for building and growth. Vitamins are classified according to whether they dissolve in fats (A, D, E, K) or in water (B complex, C). The lists below reveal their major sources, functions, and the symptoms of a deficiency (shortage).

MICRONUTRIENTS
A diet that contains a wide variety of foods, including plenty of fresh fruit and vegetables, will provide all the micronutrients needed by humans. Avocado, for example, is a fruit that is rich in the mineral potassium and the vitamin folic acid. It also contains the minerals calcium, iron, magnesium, phosphorus, sodium, zinc, copper, and manganese, as well as the vitamins A, B_1, B_2, B_6, niacin, pantothenic acid, and vitamin C.

WATER-SOLUBLE VITAMINS

VITAMIN	SOURCE	ROLE IN BODY	DEFICIENCY SYMPTOMS
B_1 (THIAMINE)	Whole grains, peas, beans, nuts, yeast, egg white, fish, liver, milk	Needed by enzymes that break down sugars, and for normal nerve and muscle function	Beriberi (a disease causing nerve inflammation and muscle weakness)
B_2 (RIBOFLAVIN)	Milk, cheese, liver, meat, egg white, leafy green vegetables, whole grains, peas, and beans	Needed by enzymes involved in carbohydrate and protein metabolism	Cracked skin, defective vision, cataracts, ulceration of the cornea
NIACIN (B_3, NICOTINAMIDE)	Meat, fish, wholegrain cereals, liver, peanuts, yeast, leafy green vegetables, potatoes	Plays part in breakdown of carbohydrates and fats during cell respiration	Pellagra (a disease causing skin disorders, diarrhea, and dementia)
B_6 (PYRIDOXINE)	Meat, poultry, fish, liver, wholegrain cereals, egg yolks, potatoes, spinach	Needed by enzymes involved in amino acid and fatty acid metabolism	In children, anemia, convulsions; in adults, sores around the eyes and nose
B_{12} (CYANOCOBALAMIN)	Animal foods – meat, liver, kidney, poultry, fish, milk, eggs, oysters – and yeast	Needed by enzymes involved in synthesis of DNA and proteins; promotes red blood cell formation	Pernicious anemia – a disease causing paleness, weight loss, and impaired nervous system function
PANTOTHENIC ACID	Meat, liver, egg yolks, wholegrain cereals, peas, beans, yeast	Needed by enzymes involved in cell respiration, fatty acid metabolism; also involved in synthesis of steroid hormones	Disorders of the digestive and nervous systems
BIOTIN	Liver, egg yolks, wholegrain cereals, yeast, peas, beans, nuts	Involved in carbohydrate, fat, and amino acid metabolism	Skin disorders, muscle pain, tiredness, depression, nausea
FOLIC ACID (FOLATE, FOLACIN)	Leafy green vegetables, liver, whole grains, eggs, yeast	Needed by enzymes involved in amino acid and DNA synthesis; involved in red blood cell formation	Digestive system disorders, anemia
C (ASCORBIC ACID)	Citrus fruits, green peppers, tomatoes, other fruits, broccoli, fresh potatoes	Promotes collagen formation and growth of teeth, bones, and blood vessels; aids normal wound healing	Poor bone growth and wound healing; in severe cases, scurvy (bleeding gums, anemia, weight loss, internal bleeding)

FAT-SOLUBLE VITAMINS

VITAMIN	SOURCE	ROLE IN BODY	DEFICIENCY SYMPTOMS
A (RETINOL)	Dark green leafy vegetables, yellow-orange vegetables and fruit, egg yolks, oily fish, milk, liver	Needed for production of pigments in the eye, bones, and teeth, and for healthy skin and linings of organs	Night blindness, clouding of the cornea, dry skin and hair, lowered resistance to infection
D (CHOLECALCIFEROL)	Primary source is action of sunlight on the skin; also oily fish, egg yolks, dairy products	Aids absorption of calcium from intestines; helps bone and tooth formation	Rickets (disease where bones do not develop properly)
E (TOCOPHEROLS)	Vegetable oils, leafy green vegetables, wholegrain cereals, egg yolks, liver	Formation of red blood cells; protects cell membranes from damage	Damaged red blood cells
K (PHYLLOQUINONE)	Made by bacteria in large intestine; also pork liver, cauliflower, cabbage	Needed to make substances involved in blood clotting	Easy bruising and bleeding

KEY MINERALS

MINERAL	SOURCE	ROLE IN BODY	DEFICIENCY SYMPTOMS
CALCIUM (Ca)	Milk, dairy products, shellfish, fish, leafy green vegetables, egg yolks, nuts, and seeds	Helps build healthy bones and teeth; involved in muscle contraction, nerve impulse conduction, and blood clotting	Stunted growth and rickets (see vitamin D) in children; osteoporosis in adults
CHLORINE (Cl)	Many foods, table salt	Helps maintain balance of water and ions in blood and tissue fluid; needed to form acid in stomach juices	Muscle cramps, mental apathy
MAGNESIUM (Mg)	Wholegrain cereals, leafy green vegetables, milk, dairy products, meat, nuts	Helps build bones; involved in muscle contraction, nerve impulse conduction; needed for activity of many enzymes	Stunted growth, behavioral problems, tremors
PHOSPHORUS (P)	Eggs, fish, meat, milk and dairy products, nuts, peas, beans, wholegrain cereals	Component of bones and teeth; key part of ATP (energy storage and transfer) and DNA (genetic material)	Weak and poorly formed bones
POTASSIUM (K)	Dried fruits, bananas, nuts, beans, wholegrain cereals, green leafy vegetables, meat, milk, dairy products, fish	Helps maintain balance of water and ions in blood and tissue fluid; involved in muscle contraction, nerve impulse conduction, and regular heart rhythm	Muscle weakness, paralysis, heart failure
SODIUM (Na)	Most foods (except fruits); table salt	Helps maintain balance of water and ions in blood and tissue fluid; involved in muscle contraction and nerve impulse conduction	Nausea, muscle cramps, convulsions, mental apathy
SULFUR (S)	Foods rich in protein: meat, eggs, milk, nuts, seeds	Essential part of many proteins	Impaired protein synthesis
TRACE MINERALS			
COPPER (Cu)	Liver, meat, shellfish, mushrooms, beans, peas, wholegrain cereals	Needed for production of the hemoglobin in red blood cells and melanin in skin	Anemia
FLUORINE (F)	Fish, shellfish, fluoridated tap water	Needed for strong teeth and bones	Tooth decay (caries)
IODINE (I)	Fish, shellfish, iodized table salt	Needed to make thyroid hormones	Goiter, reduced metabolic rate
IRON (Fe)	Liver, red meat, shellfish, nuts, egg yolks, leafy green vegetables, wholegrain cereals	Essential for making the hemoglobin in red blood cells	Anemia
MANGANESE (Mn)	Vegetables, fruit, nuts, wholegrain cereals	Assists action of many enzymes	Poor growth
SELENIUM (Se)	Fish, shellfish, meat, wholegrain cereals, dairy products	Antioxidant (prevents damage to cells and tissues by oxidation)	Not known
ZINC (Zn)	Fish, shellfish, meat, wholegrain cereals, beans, nuts, eggs	Constituent of several enzymes; necessary for normal growth, wound healing, sperm production	Retarded growth, learning impairment, loss of taste and smell

Metabolism

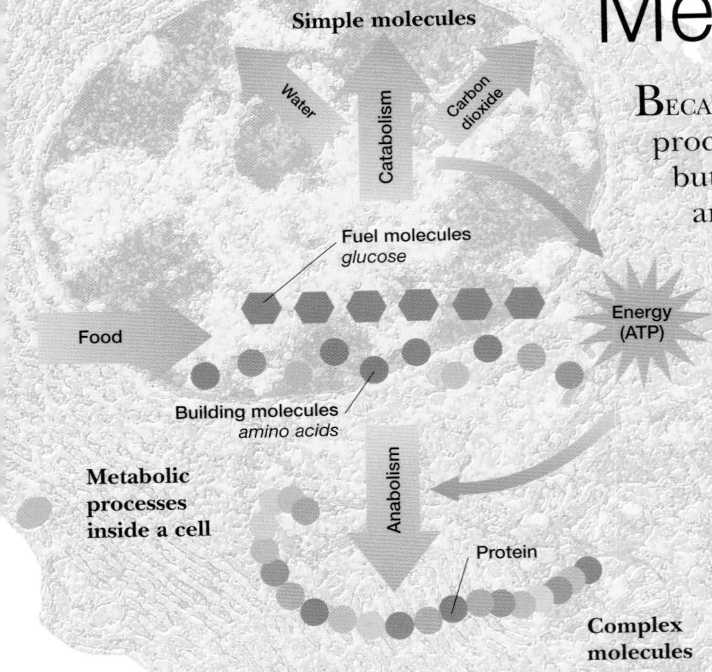

B ECAUSE THE BODY IS MADE OF CELLS, it depends on chemical processes to stay alive. Exactly how many is still uncertain, but the known total already runs into many thousands, and more are being discovered all the time. Together, they make up the body's metabolism – the sum of all the chemical reactions that it carries out. Metabolism has two sides, which are closely interlinked. On the one hand, catabolic processes break down substances and release energy from them. On the other, anabolic ones take in energy, and use it to build substances and make the body work. During this energy interchange, some energy escapes, chiefly in the form of heat. The body's metabolic rate shows how fast it produces heat, and therefore how quickly it is "burning" its fuel.

Simple molecules
Water
Catabolism
Carbon dioxide

Fuel molecules
glucose

Food

Energy (ATP)

Building molecules
amino acids

Metabolic processes inside a cell

Anabolism

Protein

Complex molecules

CATABOLISM AND ANABOLISM

The diagram above shows the effect of metabolism inside a cell. In catabolism, shown in the upper half of the cell, energy-rich substances from food are oxidized in a process called cellular respiration. This releases energy that is used to drive anabolic processes (shown in the lower half of the cell). Anabolic processes make complex molecules – such as proteins – from simpler raw materials. In cells, energy is transferred between catabolic and anabolic reactions by a substance called adenosine triphosphate (ATP). This acts like a shuttle service, picking up energy when it is released, and delivering it where it is needed.

FOOD AND METABOLISM

During digestion, the complex carbohydrates, fats, and proteins in food are broken down into, respectively, glucose, fatty acids and glycerol, and amino acids. These simple nutrients are the raw materials of metabolism. This diagram reveals what happens to these nutrients after they have been processed by the liver (see pp. 198–99) and are then carried by the bloodstream to be used by body cells or stored until required.

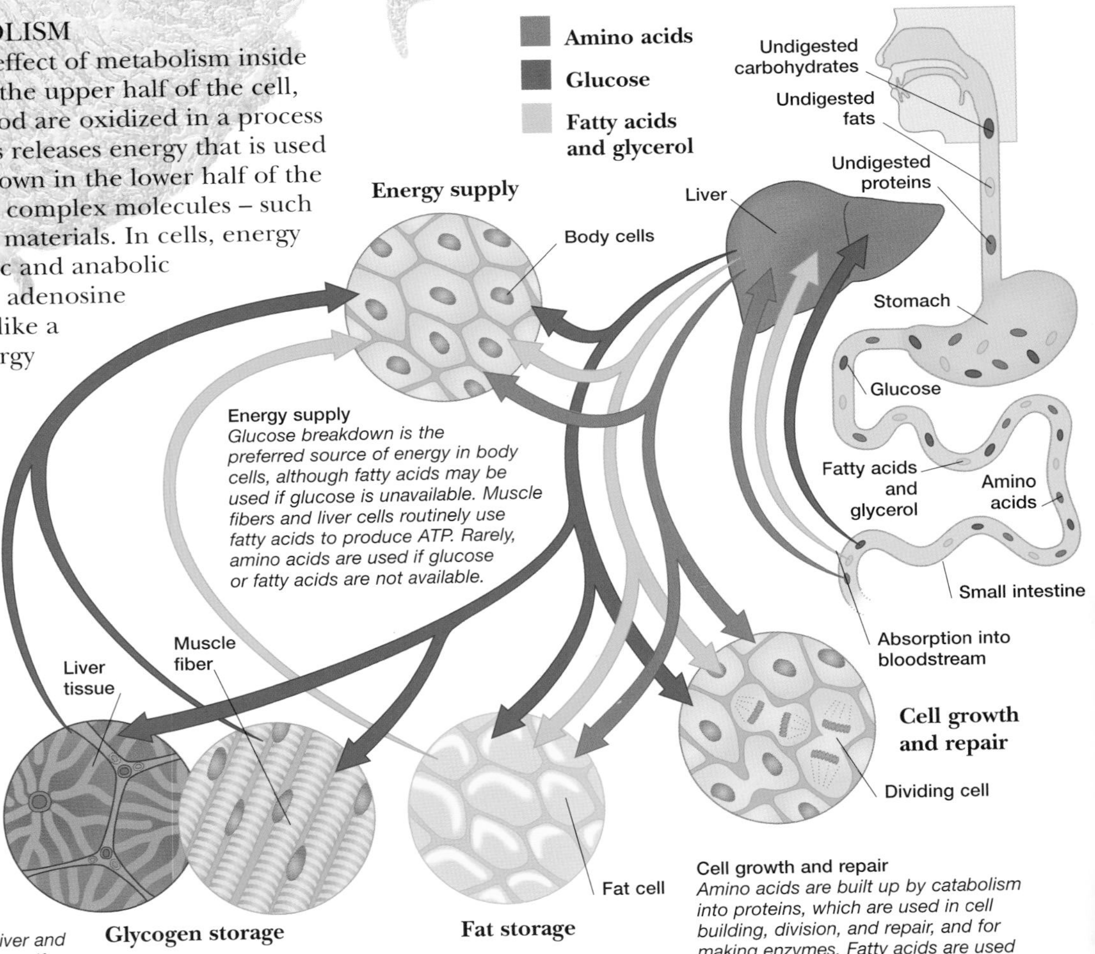

Amino acids
Glucose
Fatty acids and glycerol

Undigested carbohydrates
Undigested fats
Undigested proteins

Energy supply

Liver
Body cells
Stomach

Glucose

Energy supply
Glucose breakdown is the preferred source of energy in body cells, although fatty acids may be used if glucose is unavailable. Muscle fibers and liver cells routinely use fatty acids to produce ATP. Rarely, amino acids are used if glucose or fatty acids are not available.

Fatty acids and glycerol
Amino acids

Small intestine

Absorption into bloodstream

Muscle fiber
Liver tissue

Cell growth and repair

Dividing cell

Fat cell

Glycogen storage

Fat storage

Nutrient storage
Excess glucose is stored as glycogen in liver and muscle cells, and converted back to glucose if blood glucose levels drop. Excess fatty acids are stored as fat in adipose (fat) cells, as is glucose if glycogen stores are full. Excess amino acids cannot be stored, but can be converted to fat.

Cell growth and repair
Amino acids are built up by catabolism into proteins, which are used in cell building, division, and repair, and for making enzymes. Fatty acids are used to make cell membranes and the myelin sheaths around nerve axons, and, with glucose, provide the energy for cell growth and repair.

SANTORIO'S BALANCE

The Italian physician Santorio (or Sanctorius) (1561–1636) devised a simple but ingenious way of investigating metabolism. He devised a balance (right) that he could sit in, and used it to measure changes in his weight after eating, sleeping, and exercise. Santorio found that the body loses weight when it is at rest, through something he called "insensible perspiration." This weight loss is a sign of catabolism – the breakdown of substances to release energy.

TAKING A TEMPERATURE

If the body is fighting an infection, its temperature often rises by 2–3.5°F (1–2°C). As a result, taking a temperature is a useful way of checking someone's health. Temperatures used to be taken with mercury thermometers, which took a minute or more to produce a reading. Now, digital thermometers give an almost instant result. A slight rise in temperature can be beneficial, because it helps to check the growth of bacteria and viruses.

Digital temperature reading *is taken in the ear*

TEMPERATURE CONTROL

Whatever the conditions outside, the body's internal temperature remains steady, at almost exactly 98.6°F (37°C). To stay at this temperature, the body has to produce heat at the same rate that it loses it. This balancing act is controlled by the hypothalamus. If the blood's temperature falls, the hypothalamus triggers actions that produce more heat, and ones that make it harder for heat to escape. If the blood's temperature rises, it cuts down heat production, and makes it easier for the body to lose some of its warmth.

In cold weather, people wrap up warmly

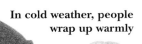

The hypothalamus initiates heat loss

Body temperature increases during exercise or when in a hot climate, etc

Normal body temperature 98.6°F (37°C)

Body temperature decreases when in a cold climate, etc

The hypothalamus initiates heat gain

Heat loss
- *Blood vessels in the skin dilate (widen), increasing heat loss to the outside from blood flowing through them, and making the skin flushed*
- *Sweat glands release more sweat on to the skin's surface from where it evaporates to cool the skin*

Body temperature decreases and heat loss mechanism shuts off

Body temperature increases and heat gain mechanism shuts off

Heat gain
- *Blood vessels in the skin constrict (narrow), diverting blood away from the skin so less heat is lost to the outside*
- *Shivering (involuntary contraction of skeletal muscles) generates extra heat*
- *Erection of hairs slightly reduces heat loss from the head*

Dilated blood vessels   Hair   Sweat droplet

Sweat gland

Sections through skin

Constricted blood vessels

Erect hair

Contracted arrector pili muscle

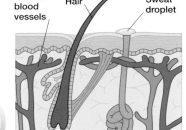

HYPOTHERMIA AND HEATSTROKE

When it is cold, people keep warm by wearing several layers and having hot drinks (as in the picture, left); when it is hot, they tend to discard their clothes. In extremely hot or cold conditions, the body's temperature-control mechanisms can sometimes break down. If someone suffers heatstroke, their temperature can reach 106°F (41°C) or more. In the opposite condition – called hypothermia – it drops below 95°F (35°C). Both conditions can be dangerous. However, hypothermia is sometimes used during surgery, particularly in heart operations. By slowing the body's metabolism, hypothermia reduces its need for oxygen during an operation.

Prolonged exposure to hot sun can cause heatstroke

Liver

Liver

Weighing about 3 lb (1.4 kg) in adults, the liver is the largest internal organ in the body. One of its jobs is to make bile (used in digestion), but its real work starts once nutrients from food have been absorbed into the blood. Its task is to process these nutrients, so that substances in the blood stay at the correct levels, keeping the body in a stable state. This mammoth operation involves more than 500 different chemical processes, which are carried out by cells called hepatocytes. Packed into columns called lobules, they are bathed by blood transported from the digestive system by the portal vein. The lobules absorb and release substances as the blood flows past. The liver also contains phagocytes (see pp. 134–5), white blood cells that remove bacteria, together with blood cells whose useful life has ended.

PROCESSING PLANT

The liver fits into the top of the abdominal cavity. It is lopsided, with a large right lobe and a smaller left lobe, and it partially covers the stomach. The two lobes are divided by a thick ligament, and the entire liver is covered by a sheet of tough connective tissue. The liver is unusual because it receives blood from two separate sources – the heart and the alimentary canal. It also has a remarkable ability to regenerate after injuries, growing back even if two-thirds of its cells have been lost.

Hepatic veins *empty blood into the inferior vena cava, which carries it to the heart*

Inferior vena cava

Right lobe *of the liver*

Common heptic duct *carries bile to the gall bladder*

Gall bladder *stores bile produced by the liver*

Cystic duct *carries bile in either direction, filling or emptying gall bladder*

Common bile duct *carries bile to the duodenum*

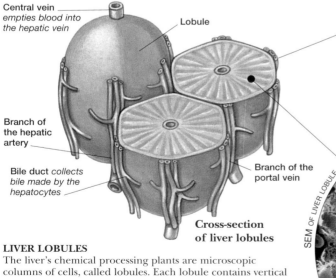

Central vein *empties blood into the hepatic vein*

Lobule

Branch of the hepatic artery

Bile duct *collects bile made by the hepatocytes*

Branch of the portal vein

Cross-section of liver lobules

SEM OF LIVER LOBULE

Red blood cells *in a sinusoid*

LIVER LOBULES

The liver's chemical processing plants are microscopic columns of cells, called lobules. Each lobule contains vertical sheets of hepatocytes, just one cell thick, which are separated by spaces called sinusoids. Blood pumps through the sinusoids from the outside of each lobule. The hepatocytes process the blood; they remove some substances for storage, break down others, and release those that the body needs. In the sinusoids, phagocytes called Kupffer cells destroy old blood cells and bacteria. Processed blood leaves the lobule via a central vein.

HEPATOCYTES

This SEM of the inside of a sesame seed–sized lobule shows the hard-working hepatocytes, or liver cells (brown), that perform the liver's many functions. The hepatocytes surround sinusoids (blue), the leaky capillaries that provide a delivery and removal service. Between the sheets of hepatocytes are tiny canals called bile canaliculi (yellow). These carry bile secreted by hepatocytes into the bile ducts.

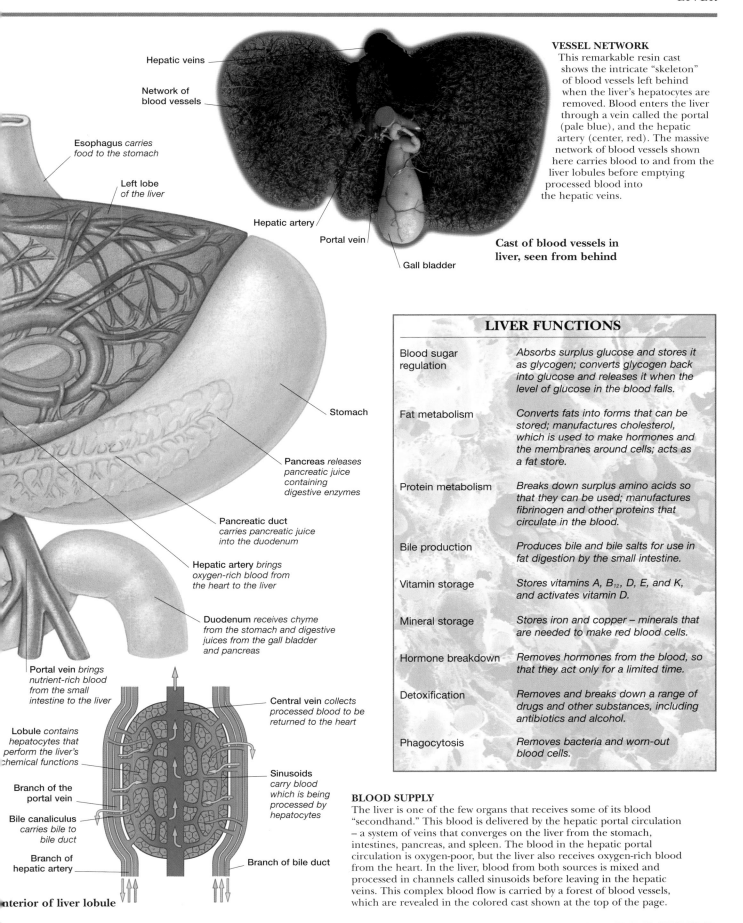

Hepatic veins

Network of
blood vessels

Esophagus *carries
food to the stomach*

Left lobe
of the liver

Hepatic artery

Portal vein

Gall bladder

VESSEL NETWORK

This remarkable resin cast
shows the intricate "skeleton"
of blood vessels left behind
when the liver's hepatocytes are
removed. Blood enters the liver
through a vein called the portal
(pale blue), and the hepatic
artery (center, red). The massive
network of blood vessels shown
here carries blood to and from the
liver lobules before emptying
processed blood into
the hepatic veins.

**Cast of blood vessels in
liver, seen from behind**

Stomach

Pancreas *releases
pancreatic juice
containing
digestive enzymes*

Pancreatic duct
*carries pancreatic juice
into the duodenum*

Hepatic artery *brings
oxygen-rich blood from
the heart to the liver*

Duodenum *receives chyme
from the stomach and digestive
juices from the gall bladder
and pancreas*

Portal vein *brings
nutrient-rich blood
from the small
intestine to the liver*

Lobule *contains
hepatocytes that
perform the liver's
chemical functions*

Branch of the
portal vein

Bile canaliculus
*carries bile to
bile duct*

Branch of
hepatic artery

Central vein *collects
processed blood to be
returned to the heart*

Sinusoids
*carry blood
which is being
processed by
hepatocytes*

Branch of bile duct

Interior of liver lobule

LIVER FUNCTIONS

Blood sugar regulation	*Absorbs surplus glucose and stores it as glycogen; converts glycogen back into glucose and releases it when the level of glucose in the blood falls.*
Fat metabolism	*Converts fats into forms that can be stored; manufactures cholesterol, which is used to make hormones and the membranes around cells; acts as a fat store.*
Protein metabolism	*Breaks down surplus amino acids so that they can be used; manufactures fibrinogen and other proteins that circulate in the blood.*
Bile production	*Produces bile and bile salts for use in fat digestion by the small intestine.*
Vitamin storage	*Stores vitamins A, B_{12}, D, E, and K, and activates vitamin D.*
Mineral storage	*Stores iron and copper – minerals that are needed to make red blood cells.*
Hormone breakdown	*Removes hormones from the blood, so that they act only for a limited time.*
Detoxification	*Removes and breaks down a range of drugs and other substances, including antibiotics and alcohol.*
Phagocytosis	*Removes bacteria and worn-out blood cells.*

BLOOD SUPPLY

The liver is one of the few organs that receives some of its blood
"secondhand." This blood is delivered by the hepatic portal circulation
– a system of veins that converges on the liver from the stomach,
intestines, pancreas, and spleen. The blood in the hepatic portal
circulation is oxygen-poor, but the liver also receives oxygen-rich blood
from the heart. In the liver, blood from both sources is mixed and
processed in channels called sinusoids before leaving in the hepatic
veins. This complex blood flow is carried by a forest of blood vessels,
which are revealed in the colored cast shown at the top of the page.

Energy balance

Humans share one feature with machines: we need energy to make our bodies work. Energy cannot be touched or even seen, but without it, nerves cannot transmit signals, muscles cannot contract, and cells cannot divide and grow. We use energy when we are completely at rest, but our energy expenditure soars by 10 times or more when we are really on the move. The body obtains all its energy from food, and it manages its resources as carefully as someone running a bank account. Its "cash" consists of glucose in the blood – a supply of chemical energy that is instantly available to the body's cells. Its "savings" consist mainly of glycogen and fat, which take longer to be brought out of store. Hunger is a sign that the body's energy reserves are running low, and that more food needs to be taken on board.

Hypothalamus
detects a fall in the blood's glucose level

USING ENERGY

Most of the body's energy is produced by oxidizing or "burning" glucose, its chief fuel. Once this energy has been released, it is used to drive chemical reactions that keep cells alive, and it is also converted into kinetic (movement) energy, and heat energy. The body normally matches the energy that it takes in with the energy that it uses, so an Olympic sprinter needs more food than someone who has a less active way of life. But whatever a person's lifestyle, a healthy diet – combined with exercise – helps the body to keep its energy budget balanced.

FEELING HUNGRY

There is more to feeling hungry than having an empty stomach. Hunger is actually controlled by the hypothalamus – a region of the brain that monitors the concentration of glucose in the blood. An adult's bloodstream usually contains just 0.2 oz (5 g) of glucose, but the level is kept steady by the liver, which releases more glucose as existing stocks are used. However, if the glucose level starts to fall, the hypothalamus soon reacts, triggering the feeling of hunger. After eating, glucose from food then brings it back to the correct level. The hypothalamus also creates the feeling of fullness – an important sensation, because the digestive system cannot cope with too much food at one time.

Eating brings the blood's glucose level back to normal

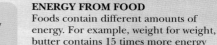

Pizza
1,115 kJ (266 kcal)/ 3.5 oz (100 g). Pizzas are energy-rich because of their high fat content, but also provide some other nutrients.

Banana
339 kJ (81 kcal)/ 3.5 oz (100 g). Bananas supply slowly released energy, are very low in fat, and provide certain vitamins and minerals.

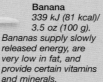

ENERGY FROM FOOD
Foods contain different amounts of energy. For example, weight for weight, butter contains 15 times more energy than an apple. Traditionally, food energy is measured in calories (kcal), but most dieticians and food manufacturers now use the kilojoule (kJ) (1 kcal = 4.187 kJ). These four foods illustrate differences in energy content and show how, eaten in excess, some high-energy foods can unbalance the diet.

Salmon
837 kJ (200 kcal)/ 3.5 oz (100 g). Oily fish, like salmon, are rich in unsaturated fatty acids – "good" for the heart – proteins and certain vitamins.

Chips
2,172 kJ (519 kcal)/ 3.5 oz (100 g). Chips are very energy-rich because of their high fat content; they also contain a lot of salt.

A 125 lb (55 kg) cyclist traveling at 13 mph (21 kph1) uses 2,220 kJ (534 kcal) during a one-hour ride

OUT OF BALANCE
The body uses fat as its long-term energy store, and as an "insurance policy" against hungry times. If a person takes in more food energy than they use, these fat stores slowly increase, and the person puts on weight. Reducing food intake and increasing activity levels will cause the body to dip into its fat reserves, and the weight begins to fall. Obesity is often caused by bad eating habits. However, weight loss can be a sign of disease, as well as of a shortage of food.

Obesity is a problem that affects not only adults, but also children who lead inactive lives

ENERGY REQUIREMENTS

A person's daily energy requirements depend not only on whether they are male or female, but also on how old they are, and how active – or inactive – they are. Sex and age influence a person's basal metabolic rate (BMR), which is the rate at which the body releases energy when it is at rest. During adolescence, the body's energy need climbs steeply – not just because this is an active time of life, but also because the body is rapidly growing. Pregnant women, and mothers who breastfeed their babies, also have a high energy requirement, because they are literally "eating for two."

AVERAGE DAILY ENERGY REQUIREMENTS

Infant 9–12 months 891 kcal (3,730 kJ)
Child 5 years 1,627 kcal (6,810 kJ)
Child 8 years 1,853 kcal (7,760 kJ)
Child 11 years 2,029 kcal (8,495 kJ)
Girl 15 years 2,207 kcal (9,240 kJ)
Boy 15 years 2,875 kcal (12,035 kJ)
Woman (inactive) 1,917 kcal (8,025 kJ)
Woman (active) 2,150 kcal (9,000 kJ)
Woman (breastfeeding) 2,687 kcal (11,250 kJ)
Man (inactive) 2,515 kcal (10,530 kJ)
Man (active) 3,000 kcal (12,560 kJ)

kcal PER DAY   0   500   1,000   1,500   2,000   2,500   3,000

URINARY system

Several times each day, a person stops what they are doing in order to urinate. The urine they release is produced by the urinary system, a system that plays a key part in homeostasis – keeping conditions stable inside the body. At the core of the system are the two kidneys. Second by second, they process blood, removing two main components from it – unwanted wastes that must be excreted (eliminated) from the body before they build up and poison it, and water and salts that are surplus to requirements. The resulting watery waste – called urine – can then be expelled from the body.

EXCRETION

This is the elimination of chemical wastes from the body. Most of these wastes are unwanted products formed by metabolism in the body's cells, but some are substances taken in, but no longer required, by the body. The kidneys, for example, excrete urea, a nitrogenous (nitrogen-containing) waste produced in the liver. Other excretory processes include the loss of carbon dioxide from the lungs and sweat from the skin.

WASTE DISPOSAL SYSTEM

The major organs of the urinary system are the kidneys and the bladder. The kidneys filter the blood and produce urine, and the bladder stores urine until it can be expelled. The kidneys lie on either side of the back of the upper abdomen, whereas the bladder is found inside the pelvis. Urine is transported from the kidneys to the bladder along two tubes called the ureters, one from each kidney. A third tube called the urethra carries urine from the bladder so that it can leave the body during urination: in males the urethra runs along the length of the penis, and in females it comes to an end just in front of the opening of the vagina.

WATER CONTENT

Water is essential for the reactions that take place within cells, and it is the major component of the fluid that bathes the tissues of the body. Maintenance of constant water levels in the body is therefore essential, and this is one of the key functions of the kidneys. Factors such as age, sex, and fat content produce differences in the amount of water in different people's bodies, but the kidneys ensure that the water content of any one person remains constant.

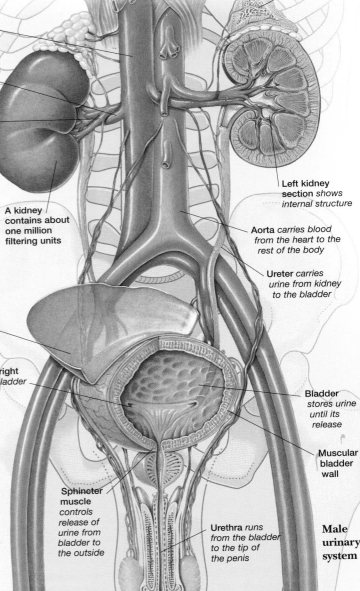

Inferior vena cava *returns blood from lower body to heart*

Renal vein *removes blood from kidney*

Renal artery *supplies the kidney with blood*

A kidney contains about one million filtering units

Adrenal gland

Left kidney section *shows internal structure*

Aorta *carries blood from the heart to the rest of the body*

Ureter *carries urine from kidney to the bladder*

Peritoneum *lines the abdomen and covers the surface of the bladder*

Opening of right ureter *into bladder*

Bladder *stores urine until its release*

Muscular bladder wall

Sphincter muscle *controls release of urine from bladder to the outside*

Urethra *runs from the bladder to the tip of the penis*

Male urinary system

WATER CONTENT % chart

- Infant: 73%
- Young man: 60%
- Young woman: 50%
- Older person: 45%

WATER CONTENT % (y-axis: 0–100)

AGE/SEX

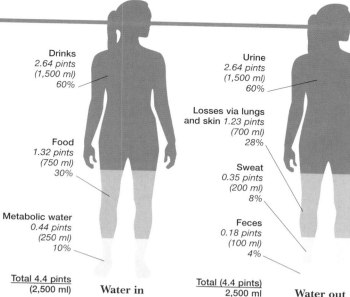

Drinks
*2.64 pints
(1,500 ml)
60%*

Food
*1.32 pints
(750 ml)
30%*

Metabolic water
*0.44 pints
(250 ml)
10%*

Total 4.4 pints
(2,500 ml)
Water in

Urine
*2.64 pints
(1,500 ml)
60%*

Losses via lungs
and skin *1.23 pints
(700 ml)
28%*

Sweat
*0.35 pints
(200 ml)
8%*

Feces
*0.18 pints
(100 ml)
4%*

Total (4.4 pints)
2,500 ml
Water out

WATER BALANCE

The body matches the amount of water that leaves it to the amount that enters it, so that the total amount of water in the body remains constant. Water is obtained from food, drink, and the chemical reactions that take place within the body. Loss of water occurs not just in the urine, but also in sweat and feces, and in evaporation from the lungs and skin. The more water that enters the body, and the less that is lost in forms such as sweat, the more the kidneys must dispose of in the urine.

Drinking is a response to a signal issued by the thirst center in the brain

INTRAVENOUS INFUSION

Commonly known as an IV drip, an intravenous ("into a vein") infusion is used to introduce fluid directly into the bloodstream of patients who cannot maintain water balance. They may be unable to drink, or have lost large amounts of body fluid through vomiting, diarrhea, or blood loss. The intravenous fluid passes downwards from a plastic container (above) into a vein in the arm.

CONTROLLING THIRST

Inside the brain's hypothalamus is a thirst center which monitors the concentration of plasma – the liquid part of blood – passing through it. Plasma concentration increases as the body loses water. This leaves the mouth feeling dry because less saliva is produced, and the thirst center generates a feeling of thirst. Having a drink soon quenches thirst, as plasma concentration returns to normal.

FUNCTIONS OF THE URINARY SYSTEM

Excretion	*Removal of waste products and foreign chemicals from the blood.*	Osmoregulation	*Removal of excess salt and water ensures balance of concentration of body fluid.*
Regulation of the blood pH	*Hydrogen ions are removed from the blood and bicarbonate ions are added to control blood pH (acid-base balance).*	Regulation of blood volume and composition	*The various functions of the kidneys combine to maintain the correct volume and composition of the blood.*
Regulation of blood pressure composition	*Kidneys secrete renin which increases the amount of salt and water in the blood, and leads to constriction of blood vessels.*	Other homeostatic roles	*The kidneys release erythropoietin, a hormone that stimulates red blood cell production; and help synthesize the active form of vitamin D.*

Kidneys

ATTACHED HIGH ENOUGH at the back of the abdominal cavity to be protected by the lowest ribs, the kidneys are perfectly adapted to their role of "cleansing" the blood and helping to keep its composition constant. The outer part of each kidney contains about one million tightly packed, coiled, tubular filtration units called nephrons. Each nephron receives a share of the copious supply of blood that is delivered every second by the renal artery and removed by the renal vein. Having filtered fluid from the blood, the nephron then processes the fluid to produce waste urine – as described in more detail on pp. 206–7. A continuous stream of urine trickles from the nephrons into the center of the kidney, from where it is directed to the bladder.

KIDNEY STRUCTURE

About 5 in (12 cm) long and 1 in (3 cm) thick, each kidney is surrounded by a thin renal capsule. Internally, as this section (right) shows, the kidney is clearly divided into three zones: cortex, medulla, and pelvis. The outer cortex, and the medulla it surrounds, are the site of urine production. Fluid is filtered out of the blood in the cortex, while in the medulla, substances needed by the body are reabsorbed back from that fluid into the blood. The remaining urine is collected by ducts that open at the tips of the medulla's cone-shaped pyramids into the pelvis. This flattened, funnel-shaped tube channels urine into the ureter, which carries it to the bladder.

Angiogram of a human kidney

BLOOD SUPPLY
As this angiogram shows, the kidneys receive an abundant blood supply. So important are the kidneys in processing blood that they receive one quarter of the heart's output, which amounts to some 125 pints (72 liters) per hour. Every hour about 12 pints (7 liters) of fluid are filtered from blood into the nephrons, but most of this is returned to the blood, with only about 1 percent leaving the body as urine.

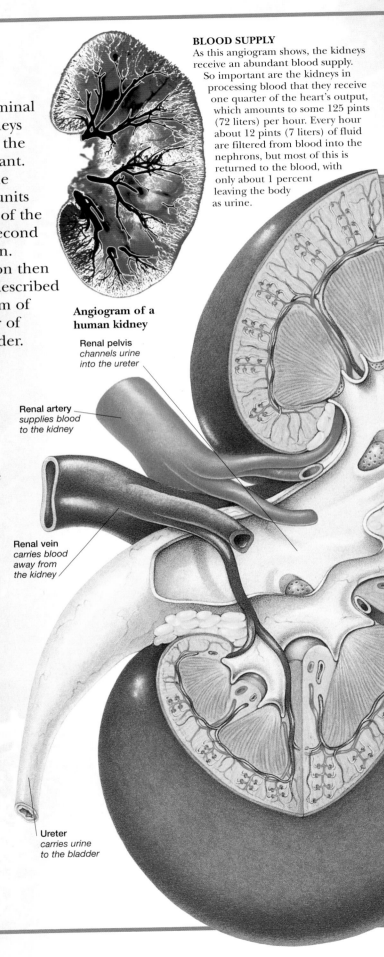

Renal pelvis
channels urine into the ureter

Renal artery
supplies blood to the kidney

Renal vein
carries blood away from the kidney

Ureter
carries urine to the bladder

KIDNEY TRANSPLANTS
For people suffering from serious kidney disease, kidney transplantation is a life-saving treatment. The operation replaces a patient's defective kidney with a healthy one received from a donor. As with most forms of transplantation, drugs are required to prevent the patient's immune system (see pp. 160–61) from rejecting the donor organ. Kidney transplantation is one of the most frequently performed types of transplantation.

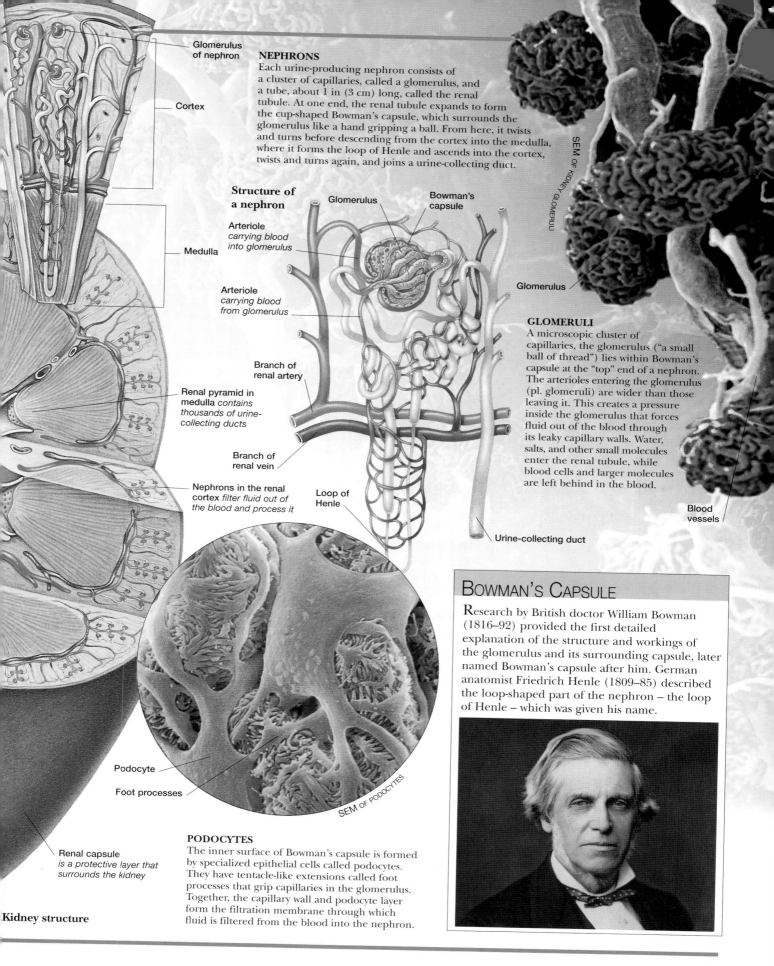

Glomerulus of nephron

Cortex

Medulla

Renal pyramid in medulla *contains thousands of urine-collecting ducts*

Nephrons in the renal cortex *filter fluid out of the blood and process it*

Renal capsule *is a protective layer that surrounds the kidney*

Kidney structure

NEPHRONS

Each urine-producing nephron consists of a cluster of capillaries, called a glomerulus, and a tube, about 1 in (3 cm) long, called the renal tubule. At one end, the renal tubule expands to form the cup-shaped Bowman's capsule, which surrounds the glomerulus like a hand gripping a ball. From here, it twists and turns before descending from the cortex into the medulla, where it forms the loop of Henle and ascends into the cortex, twists and turns again, and joins a urine-collecting duct.

Structure of a nephron

Glomerulus

Bowman's capsule

Arteriole *carrying blood into glomerulus*

Arteriole *carrying blood from glomerulus*

Branch of renal artery

Branch of renal vein

Loop of Henle

Urine-collecting duct

SEM OF KIDNEY GLOMERULI

Glomerulus

GLOMERULI

A microscopic cluster of capillaries, the glomerulus ("a small ball of thread") lies within Bowman's capsule at the "top" end of a nephron. The arterioles entering the glomerulus (pl. glomeruli) are wider than those leaving it. This creates a pressure inside the glomerulus that forces fluid out of the blood through its leaky capillary walls. Water, salts, and other small molecules enter the renal tubule, while blood cells and larger molecules are left behind in the blood.

Blood vessels

Podocyte

Foot processes

SEM OF PODOCYTES

PODOCYTES

The inner surface of Bowman's capsule is formed by specialized epithelial cells called podocytes. They have tentacle-like extensions called foot processes that grip capillaries in the glomerulus. Together, the capillary wall and podocyte layer form the filtration membrane through which fluid is filtered from the blood into the nephron.

BOWMAN'S CAPSULE

Research by British doctor William Bowman (1816–92) provided the first detailed explanation of the structure and workings of the glomerulus and its surrounding capsule, later named Bowman's capsule after him. German anatomist Friedrich Henle (1809–85) described the loop-shaped part of the nephron – the loop of Henle – which was given his name.

Kidney functions

Bowman's capsule

Glomerulus

Proximal convoluted tubule

Distal convoluted tubule

Urine

Artery

Vein

Collecting duct

Ascending part of the loop of Henle

Descending part of the loop of Henle

Loop of Henle

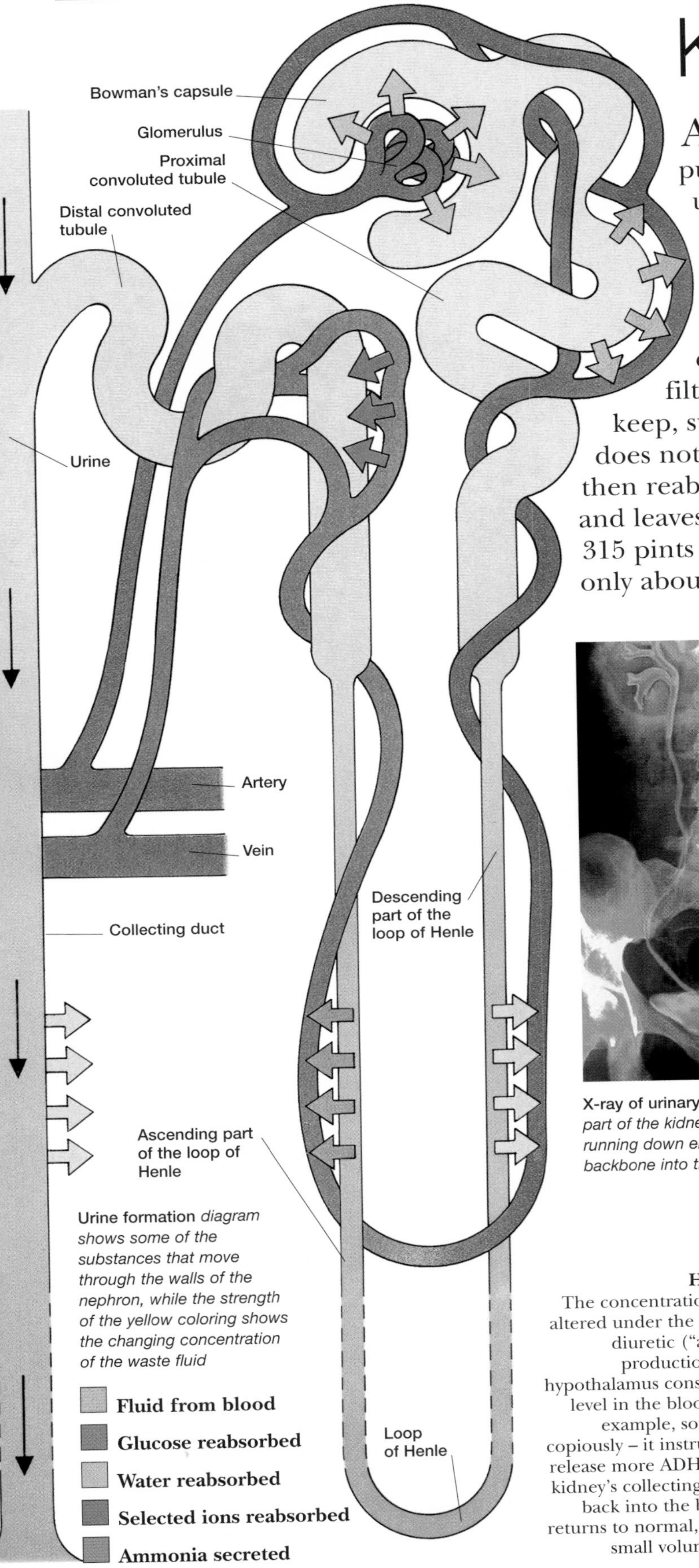

Urine formation diagram shows some of the substances that move through the walls of the nephron, while the strength of the yellow coloring shows the changing concentration of the waste fluid

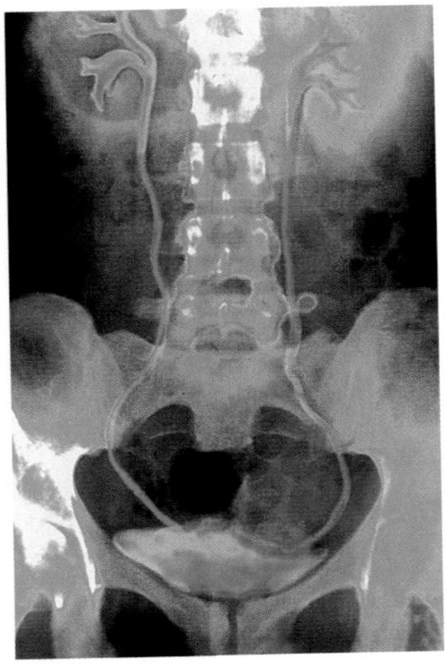

Fluid from blood

Glucose reabsorbed

Water reabsorbed

Selected ions reabsorbed

Ammonia secreted

ALTHOUGH THEY DO HAVE other roles, the primary purpose of the kidneys is to form urine by removing unwanted wastes and surplus water from the blood. Urine production happens in the million or so nephrons found inside each kidney. A crude filtrate is produced by filtering blood through the leaky walls of a nephron's glomerulus, leaving cells and protons behind in its capillaries. This filtrate contains both substances the body wants to keep, such as glucose and most of the water, and those it does not, such as urea. With great efficiency, the nephron then reabsorbs the wanted substances back into the blood, and leaves the unwanted ones behind to form urine. Of the 315 pints (180 liters) that is filtered into the nephrons daily, only about 2.5 pints (1.5 liters) leaves the body as urine.

PRODUCING URINE

The diagram (left) shows the process of urine formation in the nephron. As the filtrate (fluid filtered from blood) passes through the twisted proximal (near) tubule, all the nutrients – such as glucose and amino acids – and most of the water and salts, are reabsorbed back into the blood. As the filtrate passes further along the nephron, it is further processed, so that by the time it reaches the common collecting duct, it has lost all the substances useful to the body, retaining only wastes and surplus water to become urine. This is further concentrated as it passes down the collecting duct to empty into the inner pelvis of the kidney.

X-ray of urinary system *shows part of the kidneys and the ureters running down either side of the backbone into the bladder below*

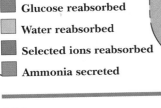

Kidney produces urine in quantities regulated by ADH

HORMONAL CONTROL

The concentration and volume of urine is altered under the control of ADH, the anti-diuretic ("against diuresis," or urine production) hormone. The brain's hypothalamus constantly monitors the water level in the blood. If this falls – when, for example, someone has been sweating copiously – it instructs the pituitary gland to release more ADH. This, in turn, makes the kidney's collecting ducts absorb more water back into the blood so its concentration returns to normal, and the kidneys release a small volume of concentrated urine.

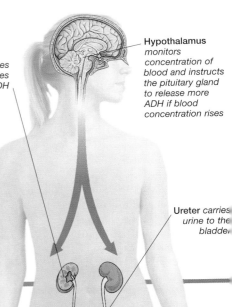

Hypothalamus monitors concentration of blood and instructs the pituitary gland to release more ADH if blood concentration rises

Ureter carries urine to the bladder

KIDNEY DIALYSIS

The kidneys are sometimes so damaged by disease that they are unable to filter the blood adequately by themselves. When this happens, a procedure called dialysis can be used, in which the function of the kidneys is carried out artificially. In one form of dialysis, a machine pumps the patient's blood around a circuit and through a filter containing membranes. Harmful substances such as urea migrate out of the blood, across these membranes, and into a solution called dialysate. People with kidney failure need to undergo dialysis on a regular basis, often several times a week.

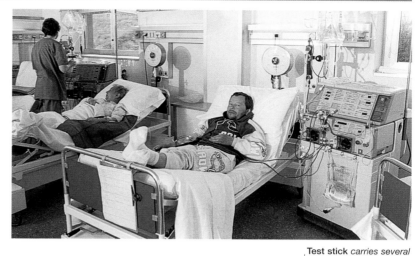

URINE COMPOSITION
About 95 percent of urine consists of water containing dissolved substances that are not needed by the body. Predominant among these is the nitrogenous waste urea, generated in the liver from excess amino acids. Other dissolved substances include potassium, sodium, chloride, phosphate, and sulfate ions, and uric acid and creatinine. Urine composition varies according to conditions in the body. For example, it will contain less water if the body is dehydrated. The presence of certain substances, such as glucose, can indicate disease.

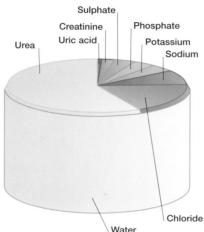

Sulphate · Creatinine · Uric acid · Urea · Phosphate · Potassium · Sodium · Chloride · Water

URINE TESTING
Doctors use urine testing to look for abnormal levels of substances in urine that help to diagnose certain disorders. Testing uses a dipstick that has several colored squares of chemically impregnated paper, each of which detects a different substance. The dipstick is dipped into a patient's urine sample, and any color changes are matched against a color chart to find the amounts of substances in the urine.

Test stick *carries several pads, each of which tests for a different chemical*

Color chart *is used to find a color match with the result on the test stick*

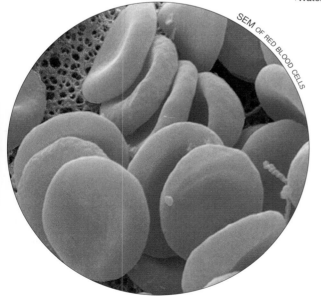

SEM OF RED BLOOD CELLS

OTHER ROLES
The kidneys have several other roles in addition to making urine. They release the hormone erythropoietin, which stimulates red marrow inside bones to produce more red blood cells, should numbers in the blood decline. The kidneys activate vitamin D, made by the action of sunlight on the skin. Activated vitamin D stimulates absorption of calcium into the blood from the small intestine. The enzyme renin, released by the kidneys, forms part of a system that regulates blood pressure.

DISCOVERING KIDNEY FUNCTIONS

Carl Ludwig was born in Witzenhausen, in Germany, in 1816. After studying medicine, he became a researcher in the fields of anatomy and physiology, and had become an associate professor by the age of 30. In 1844, Ludwig put forward a theory which stated that the walls of kidney tubules act as filters for the production of urine, and that concentration of urine occurs when water is drawn out of the tubules, across these walls and into the bloodstream. This thinking contributed to our modern understanding of the physiology of the kidneys.

Carl Ludwig (1816–95)

Bladder and urination

WHILE THE TWO KIDNEYS actually process blood to produce urine, it is the other parts of the urinary system that channel, and control the flow of, urine to the outside of the body. Urine is produced in a continuous trickle by the kidneys at a rate of about 0.002 pints (1 ml) per minute. If it were to be released directly from the body as it was produced, the constant dribble of urine would make normal life impossible, unless everyone wore diapers. Instead, urine travels along the ureters, narrow tubes that carry it to the urinary bladder. This stretchy, muscular storage bag gradually fills with urine until a sufficient amount has accumulated to be released – when a person wants to – in one short gush to the outside along an exit tube called the urethra.

URINARY BLADDER

Responsible for both urine storage and release, this elastic, muscular bag is located within the protective bony walls of the pelvic girdle. It receives urine through the two ureters, which open at the lower rear of the bladder. When empty, the bladder can be as small as a plum, but as it fills it can swell to the size of a large grapefruit. So distensible is the bladder that, although it can hold 0.3–0.5 pints (200–300 ml) before a person feels the need to urinate, it can fill to double that volume before urination becomes essential. At its base, the bladder opens into the urethra, the tube that carries urine to the outside.

URETER

Urine is carried from kidney to bladder by a ureter, a hollow tube that is 10–12 in (25–30 cm) long. The ureter starts out as a continuation of the hollow pelvis of the kidney, then travels vertically downward to enter the lower part of the back wall of the bladder. Ureters are more than just passive tubes. Smooth muscles in the ureter's wall contract rhythmically, creating waves of contraction, called peristalsis, that push urine towards the bladder.

LM OF SECTION THROUGH A URETER

Lumen
(inner channel)
through which
urine travels

Muscular layer
of ureter wall

Inner surface *folded
when muscle layer
is relaxed*

Folded inner
lining of bladder

SEM OF BLADDER EPITHELIUM

BLADDER WALL

The highly stretchy bladder wall contains layers of smooth muscles. When the bladder is empty, the smooth muscles remain relaxed, and the inner epithelial lining (left) forms folds called rugae. As the bladder swells with urine, the wall muscles stretch, causing the rugae to smooth out and disappear. Receptors in the bladder wall detect the extent of stretching in the wall muscles. These receptors relay that information to the central nervous system (CNS), which initiates the emptying of the bladder.

Urine | Bladder | Contracted internal sphincter

Filling bladder (female)

Vagina
Pelvic floor muscle *contracted around urethra*

Bladder wall *contracts*
Relaxed internal sphincter

Urethra
Pelvic floor muscle *relaxed*

Emptying bladder (female)

Urine *passes out through urethral opening*

URINATION

As these diagrams show, an internal sphincter – a ring of smooth muscle – at the junction of the bladder and urethra contracts to hold urine inside the filling bladder. A lower, external sphincter is provided by pelvic floor muscles contracting around the urethra. As the bladder fills, stretch receptors in its wall send nerve impulses to the spinal cord. In a reflex action, this returns signals telling the internal sphincter to relax and the bladder wall muscles to contract. At the same time, messages sent to the brain make a person feel the need to urinate. At a time of her choosing, she voluntarily relaxes the external sphincter, and bladder wall contractions push urine out.

BABY DIAPERS

Until they reach about two years of age, children are unable to control the pelvic floor muscle – a skeletal (voluntary) muscle – that forms the external sphincter. As a result, as soon as the bladder has filled enough to trigger the spinal reflex, the internal sphincter opens, and the bladder contracts and empties through the external sphincter, which is already open. For that reason, babies and toddlers wear absorbent diapers until they have learned to control bladder emptying.

UROSCOPY

In medieval times, doctors had few methods available to them for diagnosing diseases. Of those few, uroscopy, or "urine gazing," was the most common. There were up to 30 features of the patient's urine a doctor might note, including its color, smell, cloudiness, and even its taste. These features were believed to provide information about the patient's health, thus enabling the doctor to prescribe a suitable course of treatment. In reality, uroscopy was of doubtful value, although it persisted until the 19th century. It was replaced then by urinology, the chemical analysis of urine for purposes of diagnosis, a practice that still continues today (see p. 207).

15th-century print of a doctor examining urine

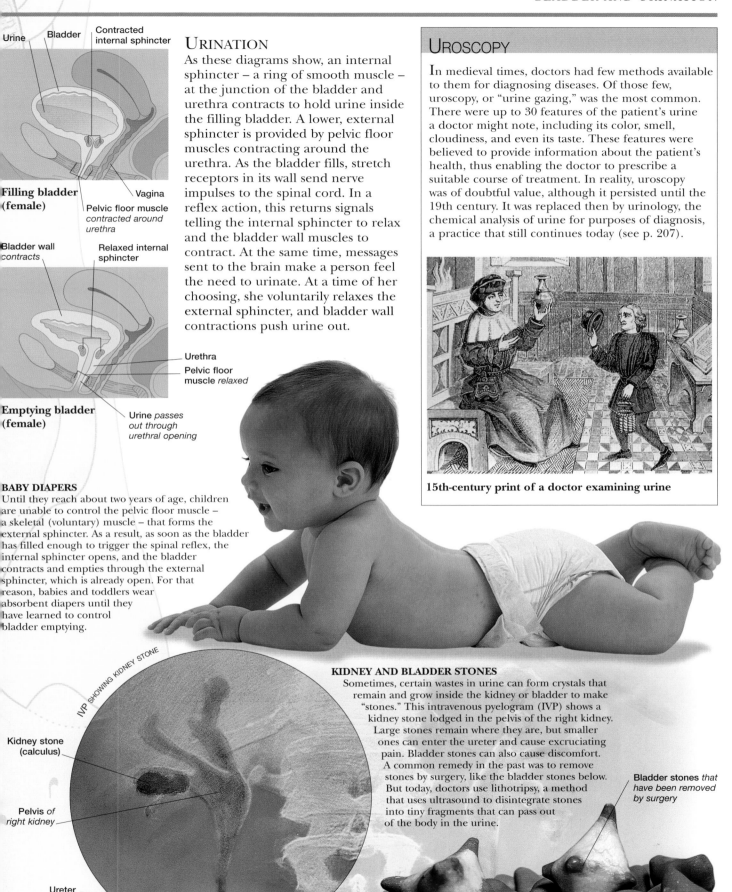

IVP SHOWING KIDNEY STONE

Kidney stone (calculus)

Pelvis *of right kidney*

Ureter

KIDNEY AND BLADDER STONES

Sometimes, certain wastes in urine can form crystals that remain and grow inside the kidney or bladder to make "stones." This intravenous pyelogram (IVP) shows a kidney stone lodged in the pelvis of the right kidney. Large stones remain where they are, but smaller ones can enter the ureter and cause excruciating pain. Bladder stones can also cause discomfort. A common remedy in the past was to remove stones by surgery, like the bladder stones below. But today, doctors use lithotripsy, a method that uses ultrasound to disintegrate stones into tiny fragments that can pass out of the body in the urine.

Bladder stones *that have been removed by surgery*

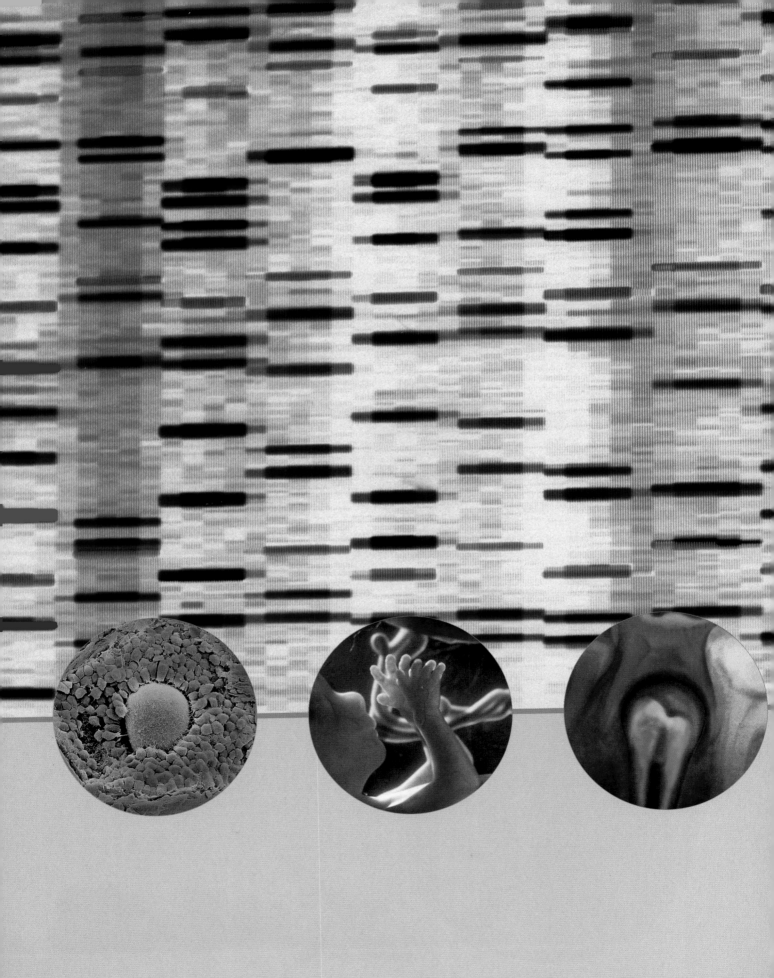

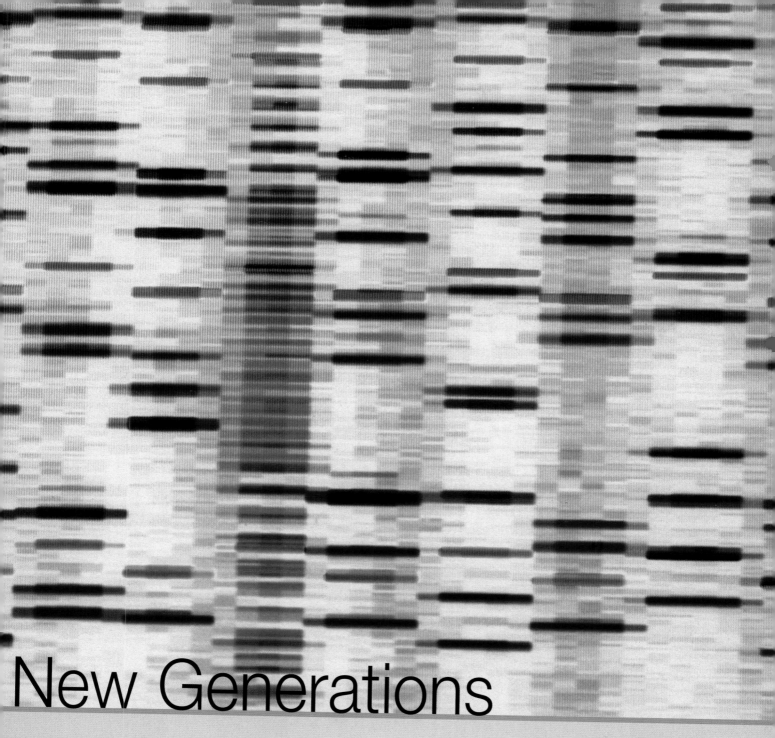

New Generations

EVERY PERSON ON EARTH follows the same life history, which starts with their birth and ends with their death. During that life, many men and women reproduce, producing and nurturing a new generation of children who will eventually succeed them. Each child resembles their parents, but is not identical to either of them. These similarities and differences are controlled by thousands of chemical instructions, called genes, found inside every body cell. The identity and structure of these genes are currently under investigation.

REPRODUCTIVE systems

REPRODUCTION IS A complex process in which genetic material from two parents is brought together to form a new human being. This material is contained within special sex cells – sperm, which are produced by males, and ova (or eggs), produced by females. For reproduction to occur, a sperm and an ovum must join to form a single cell containing a full set of genetic material, half each from the father and mother. The reproductive process continues over nine months of pregnancy, when this single cell develops into a fully formed baby, culminating in childbirth.

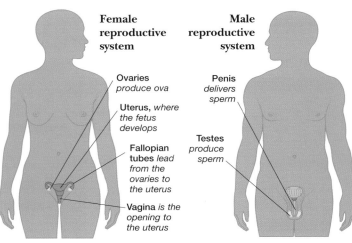

Female reproductive system

Ovaries *produce ova*

Uterus, *where the fetus develops*

Fallopian tubes *lead from the ovaries to the uterus*

Vagina *is the opening to the uterus*

Male reproductive system

Penis *delivers sperm*

Testes *produce sperm*

REPRODUCTIVE SYSTEMS

Males and females each have specialized reproductive organs. In the male these are the testes and the penis, while the female organs are the ovaries, the fallopian tubes, the uterus, and the vagina. The reproductive systems of both sexes produce sex cells and enable these cells to meet so that fertilization can occur. The female system has a further function not found in the male – it provides an environment in which conception and fetal development occur, and from which the baby emerges during birth.

Daughter *has received half her genetic material from each parent*

NEW GENERATIONS

All living organisms have a limited lifespan, and so new generations must be produced to replace those that die. Some species produce new generations rapidly, but humans reproduce relatively infrequently. This is because humans live longer than many other animals, and put a great deal of time and care into nurturing their offspring while they are in the uterus and as they develop following birth. Having a family is not only a biological urge – it also creates strong social bonds of support and love.

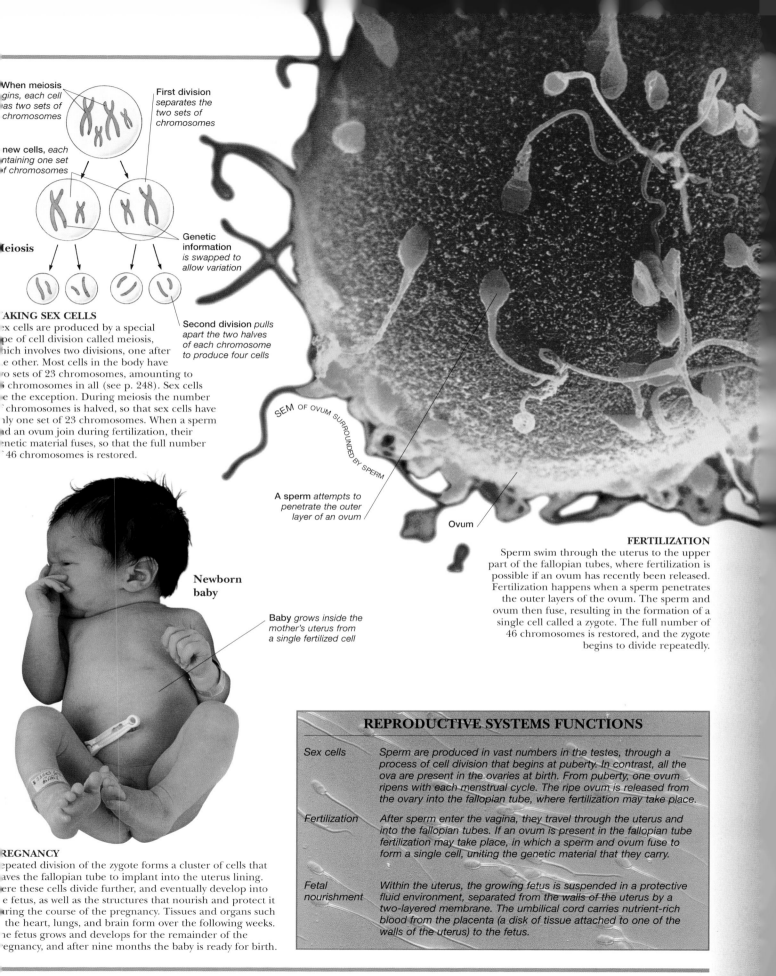

When meiosis begins, each cell has two sets of chromosomes

First division *separates the two sets of chromosomes*

new cells, *each containing one set of chromosomes*

Genetic information *is swapped to allow variation*

Meiosis

Second division *pulls apart the two halves of each chromosome to produce four cells*

MAKING SEX CELLS

Sex cells are produced by a special type of cell division called meiosis, which involves two divisions, one after the other. Most cells in the body have two sets of 23 chromosomes, amounting to 46 chromosomes in all (see p. 248). Sex cells are the exception. During meiosis the number of chromosomes is halved, so that sex cells have only one set of 23 chromosomes. When a sperm and an ovum join during fertilization, their genetic material fuses, so that the full number of 46 chromosomes is restored.

SEM OF OVUM SURROUNDED BY SPERM

A sperm *attempts to penetrate the outer layer of an ovum*

Ovum

Newborn baby

Baby *grows inside the mother's uterus from a single fertilized cell*

FERTILIZATION

Sperm swim through the uterus to the upper part of the fallopian tubes, where fertilization is possible if an ovum has recently been released. Fertilization happens when a sperm penetrates the outer layers of the ovum. The sperm and ovum then fuse, resulting in the formation of a single cell called a zygote. The full number of 46 chromosomes is restored, and the zygote begins to divide repeatedly.

PREGNANCY

Repeated division of the zygote forms a cluster of cells that leaves the fallopian tube to implant into the uterus lining. Here these cells divide further, and eventually develop into the fetus, as well as the structures that nourish and protect it during the course of the pregnancy. Tissues and organs such as the heart, lungs, and brain form over the following weeks. The fetus grows and develops for the remainder of the pregnancy, and after nine months the baby is ready for birth.

REPRODUCTIVE SYSTEMS FUNCTIONS

Sex cells	Sperm are produced in vast numbers in the testes, through a process of cell division that begins at puberty. In contrast, all the ova are present in the ovaries at birth. From puberty, one ovum ripens with each menstrual cycle. The ripe ovum is released from the ovary into the fallopian tube, where fertilization may take place.
Fertilization	After sperm enter the vagina, they travel through the uterus and into the fallopian tubes. If an ovum is present in the fallopian tube fertilization may take place, in which a sperm and ovum fuse to form a single cell, uniting the genetic material that they carry.
Fetal nourishment	Within the uterus, the growing fetus is suspended in a protective fluid environment, separated from the walls of the uterus by a two-layered membrane. The umbilical cord carries nutrient-rich blood from the placenta (a disk of tissue attached to one of the walls of the uterus) to the fetus.

Male reproductive system

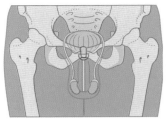

Male reproductive system

THE ORGANS OF A MAN'S reproductive system enable him to make sperm and fertilize ova (eggs) produced by a woman. The outer, visible parts of the male reproductive system are the penis and a pouch called the scrotum. Inside the scrotum is a pair of oval glands called testes, which are the main reproductive organs of the male. The testes produce millions of minute sex cells, called sperm, and also make male sex hormones. The sperm are carried from the testes through a series of internal tubes. They are released from the body in a fluid called semen, which is formed from liquids secreted by the seminal vesicles and the prostate gland.

REPRODUCTIVE ORGANS

The testes, where sperm is made, hang outside the body, inside the scrotum and below the penis. A complicated tube system delivers sperm from the testes to the penis. Small tubes lead from each testis into the long, tightly coiled epididymis, located behind the testis. Each epididymis leads into another tube, called the vas deferens, which joins with a small tube from one of the seminal vesicles to form the ejaculatory duct. The two ejaculatory ducts then join the urethra as it passes through the prostate gland. The urethra is the channel that passes from the bladder to the tip of the penis, through which sperm are released.

PENIS

The penis contains three columns of spongy tissue. During sexual arousal, the spongy columns fill with blood to make the penis erect, ready for sexual intercourse. Sperm are ejaculated through the urethra, a tube that passes through the middle of the penis to its tip. Urine from the bladder also passes out of the body through the urethra. The tip of the penis is covered by the foreskin, which is often removed during an operation called circumcision.

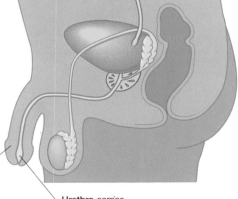

Penis *becomes erect when blood fills the spongy tissue inside*

Urethra *carries sperm and urine out of the body*

Vas deferens *is a tube that carries sperm from a testis to an ejaculatory duct*

Penis *delivers sperm into the female's vagina during sexual intercourse*

Urethra *is a tube that carries sperm and urine to the outside of the body*

Corpora cavernosa *are two parallel cylinders of tissue that fill with blood to make the penis erect*

Corpus spongiosum *is spongy tissue that surrounds the urethra and fills with blood to make the penis erect*

Foreskin *covers and protects the head of the penis*

Glans penis *is the head of the penis*

Testes *produce sperm and sex hormones*

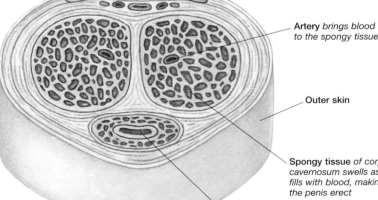

Artery *brings blood to the spongy tissue*

Outer skin

Spongy tissue *of corpus cavernosum swells as it fills with blood, making the penis erect*

Urethra *travels through the center of the spongy tissue of the corpus spongiosum*

Cross-section of penis showing internal structure

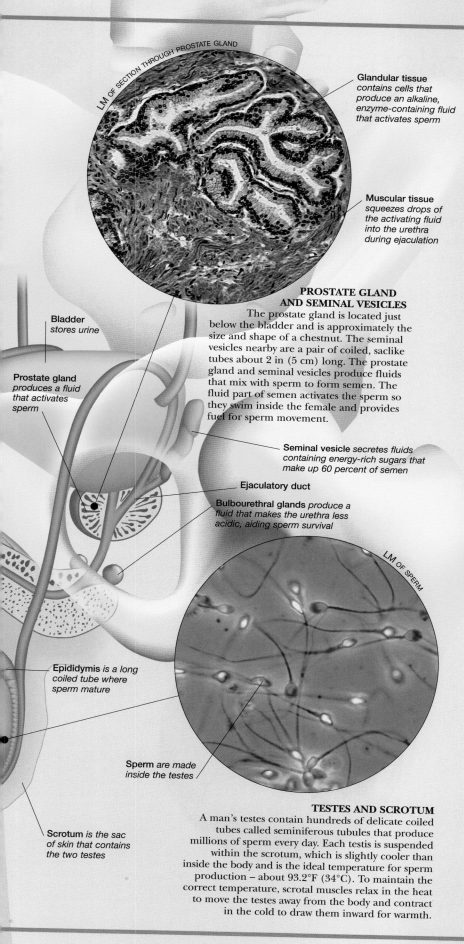

LM OF SECTION THROUGH PROSTATE GLAND

Glandular tissue *contains cells that produce an alkaline, enzyme-containing fluid that activates sperm*

Muscular tissue *squeezes drops of the activating fluid into the urethra during ejaculation*

Bladder *stores urine*

Prostate gland *produces a fluid that activates sperm*

PROSTATE GLAND AND SEMINAL VESICLES

The prostate gland is located just below the bladder and is approximately the size and shape of a chestnut. The seminal vesicles nearby are a pair of coiled, saclike tubes about 2 in (5 cm) long. The prostate gland and seminal vesicles produce fluids that mix with sperm to form semen. The fluid part of semen activates the sperm so they swim inside the female and provides fuel for sperm movement.

Seminal vesicle *secretes fluids containing energy-rich sugars that make up 60 percent of semen*

Ejaculatory duct

Bulbourethral glands *produce a fluid that makes the urethra less acidic, aiding sperm survival*

LM OF SPERM

Epididymis *is a long coiled tube where sperm mature*

Sperm *are made inside the testes*

TESTES AND SCROTUM

A man's testes contain hundreds of delicate coiled tubes called seminiferous tubules that produce millions of sperm every day. Each testis is suspended within the scrotum, which is slightly cooler than inside the body and is the ideal temperature for sperm production – about 93.2°F (34°C). To maintain the correct temperature, scrotal muscles relax in the heat to move the testes away from the body and contract in the cold to draw them inward for warmth.

Scrotum *is the sac of skin that contains the two testes*

BEING MALE
This man and his son are both readily identifiable as being male. Their maleness was determined during the first weeks of development inside the uterus. At this stage, the genetic material of the tiny embryo may or may not stimulate the growth of testes. If testes do grow, they release male sex hormones that stimulate the development of a complete male reproductive system. Years later, at the onset of puberty, the same hormones cause the testes to start producing sperm and make a boy grow into a man.

TINY BODIES

Sperm were discovered in 1677 by a Dutch microscopist, Antoni van Leeuwenhoek (1632–1723). During the next century, scientists called animalculists believed that a complete preformed miniature human – sometimes called a homunculus – was enclosed within a sperm. Another group, called ovists, believed that preformed offspring were contained inside the ova, or eggs, of females. It was later recognized that babies are not preformed but develop gradually after a sperm has fertilized an ovum.

An illustration of a homunculus, based on a drawing by N. Hartsoeker (1656–1725) made in 1694

Sperm production

THE ROLE OF SPERM IS TO fertilize female ova (eggs) in order to produce new human beings. Each sperm has a flattened oval head containing the cell's nucleus, a midpiece, and a long whiplike tail that enables it to swim. After puberty, sperm are continuously produced inside the two testes, a process controlled by hormones from the pituitary gland and testes. Once the sperm have formed, they mature in the epididymis. Muscular contractions then force the sperm, which are mixed in a fluid called semen, to move up the vas deferens and the urethra and out of the man's penis during ejaculation. Each milliliter (0.03 oz) of semen contains 50–150 million sperm.

Each testis *produces sperm and hormones*

Seminiferous tubules *are tightly coiled tubes where sperm grow from spermatogonia*

The scrotum *consists of a pouch of loose skin and an inner muscular layer that supports the testes*

Sperm mature *inside a coiled duct (here shown in cross-section)*

Epididymis *is a highly coiled duct where sperm are stored and mature*

Vas deferens *holds sperm that have matured and moved out of the epididymis*

Efferent ducts *connect the seminiferous tubules to the epididymis*

Cross-section of the scrotum

LM OF A SECTION THROUGH THE EPIDYMIS

EPIDIDYMIS

The epididymis lies behind the testis. It is here that sperm become mature and start moving. Sperm move to the epididymis from the seminiferous tubules via several efferent ducts. It takes about 20 days for the sperm to become fully mature, before they are pushed into a tube called the vas deferens. They are propelled along this tube during ejaculation.

MAKING SPERM

Sperm are made in the testes by a process called spermatogenesis. This happens in tiny coiled tubes, the seminiferous tubules, which, if unraveled, would be 1,644 ft (500 m) long. Sperm develop from cells called spermatogonia, which are present in the testes at birth. From puberty onward, spermatogonia start to divide into sperm. As each sperm develops, its number of chromosomes is halved from 46 to 23 so that a union with an ovum will restore the correct number. Up to about 250 million sperm may form per day – nearly 3,000 per second – and any that are not released are broken down and absorbed by the body. The testes also contain interstitial cells which make the hormone testosterone.

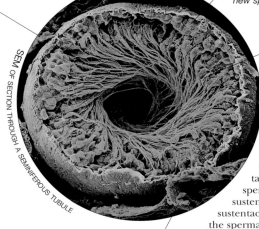

SEM OF SECTION THROUGH A SEMINIFEROUS TUBULE

Interstitial (Leydig) cells *around the tubules release testosterone*

Sustentacular (Sertoli) cells *nurture the new sperm*

Growing sperm cells *are released into the center and head toward the epididymis*

SEMINIFEROUS TUBULES

Each testis contains about 300 compartments, each containing 1–4 tightly coiled seminiferous tubules where spermatogenesis takes place. Inside these tubes, spermatogonia and other cells, called sustentacular cells, line the walls. The sustentacular cells support and nurture the spermatogonia as they develop through several stages into mature sperm. As they do so, they swirl away from the sustentacular cells into the central cavity of the tubules before heading toward the epididymis.

SPERMATOZOA

Sperm, or spermatozoa, measure about 0.002 in (0.05 mm) in length and are very well adapted to their function of transporting a genetic load. The head contains a flattened nucleus, inside which is genetic material in the form of 23 DNA-packed chromosomes. This material determines the sex of the future offspring and other characteristics. The cylindrical midpiece contains organelles called mitochondria (see p. 21). These release the energy needed by the sperm to swim inside the female's reproductive system. The long tail whips from side to side to push the streamlined, tadpolelike cell toward its destination.

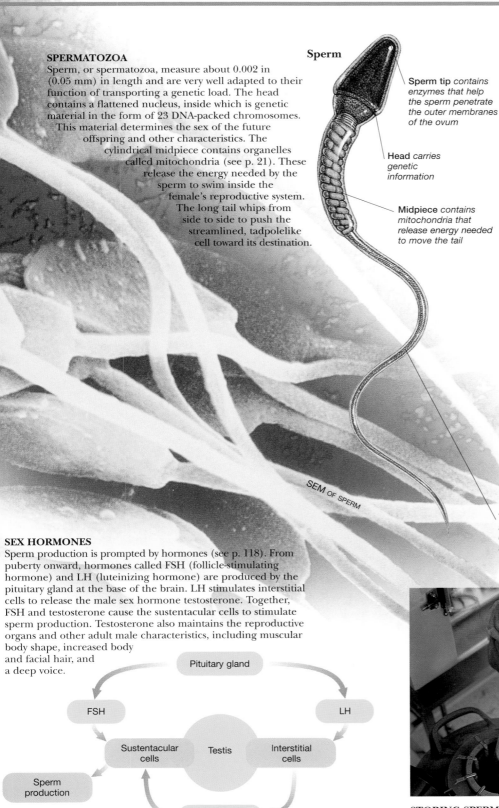

Sperm

Sperm tip *contains enzymes that help the sperm penetrate the outer membranes of the ovum*

Head *carries genetic information*

Midpiece *contains mitochondria that release energy needed to move the tail*

SEM OF SPERM

Tail *beats from side to side, enabling the sperm to swim*

DISCOVERING SPERM

Rudolf Albrecht von Kolliker (1817–1905), above, was a Swiss–German biologist and anatomist who became one of the first scientists to recognize that spermatozoa were cells. He described the site of sperm formation in the testes. His work followed that of a previous scientist, Lazzaro Spallanzani (1729–99), an Italian. Spallanzani attacked the belief known as "spontaneous generation" – that living organisms appeared from nonliving material. He showed that sperm were necessary for fertilization.

SEX HORMONES

Sperm production is prompted by hormones (see p. 118). From puberty onward, hormones called FSH (follicle-stimulating hormone) and LH (luteinizing hormone) are produced by the pituitary gland at the base of the brain. LH stimulates interstitial cells to release the male sex hormone testosterone. Together, FSH and testosterone cause the sustentacular cells to stimulate sperm production. Testosterone also maintains the reproductive organs and other adult male characteristics, including muscular body shape, increased body and facial hair, and a deep voice.

Pituitary gland

FSH

LH

Sustentacular cells

Testis

Interstitial cells

Sperm production

Testosterone

Maintains male reproductive structures and secondary sexual characteristics

STORING SPERM

Sperm can be frozen and stored in plastic tubes in liquid nitrogen at –321°F (–196°C) for long periods. In special clinics, sperm are stored for the treatment of couples who are unable to have children. After thawing, sperm become mobile again and are capable of fertilizing ova. A man's sperm may also be stored if he needs to have medical treatment that could damage his testes. This provides a backup supply of sperm in case he wants to be a father.

Female reproductive system

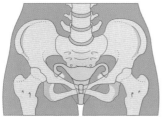

Female reproductive system

T̶HE ORGANS OF A WOMAN'S REPRODUCTIVE system produce female sex cells called ova (eggs), and enable her to become pregnant and give birth. The organs are all located inside the pelvis except for the outer visible part, called the vulva. The most important organs are a pair of almond-shaped glands called ovaries. These produce ova and make sex hormones. Each month, a single ovum is released from an ovary. If the ovum is fertilized by a sperm from a male, the female may become pregnant. During pregnancy, the fertilized ovum develops into a baby inside the uterus, or womb. The baby is born through the vagina, which is a tube of flexible muscle. After birth, the baby can be fed milk from the mother's breasts.

Pelvic girdle *protects the reproductive organs and other parts of the lower abdomen*

R̶EPRODUCTIVE ORGA̶
The main female reproducti̶ organs are the ovaries, which̶ contain thousands of immatu̶ female sex cells called ova. The other organs include both̶ internal and external parts. Externally, the vulva contains fo̶ of skin (the labia, or labium as singular) which surround and protect the entrance to the vagin̶ and the clitoris. Internally, the vagina leads into the uterus, which̶ is hollow and has muscular walls. The uterus connects to a pair of narrow tubes, called the fallopian tubes, one on each side. The outer̶ end of each tube has a funnel-shaped opening that lies very close to an ovary, ready to "catch" an ovum when it is released.

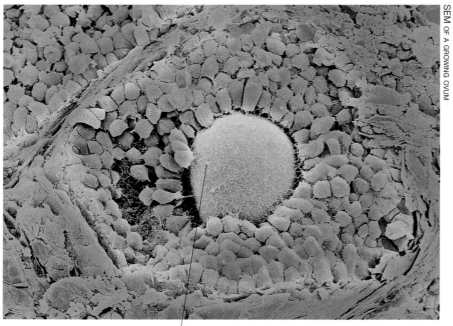

SEM OF A GROWING OVUM

Ovum matures inside a follicle

OVARIES AND OVA

At birth, each ovary, which is about 1.2 in (3 cm) long, contains thousands of immature ova. Each ovum (above, center) is enclosed within a "bag" called a follicle (pink), which also contains nurturing tissue called granulosa cells (blue). After puberty, several ovarian follicles start to mature each month and become fluid-filled bubbles on the ovary's surface. Only one of these follicles matures fully and its ovum bursts out during ovulation. The ovaries usually alternate, each one releasing an ovum every other month until the woman is about 50.

DISCOVERING OVA?

The Dutch biologist Regnier de Graaf (1641–73) made a detailed study of the human reproductive system and published a famous book describing the female reproductive organs. De Graaf discovered what he thought was the human ovum in the ovary. In fact, what he had found was a maturing follicle, not the actual smaller ovum inside. Maturing follicles are still sometimes called Graafian follicles in his memory.

Regnier de Graaf

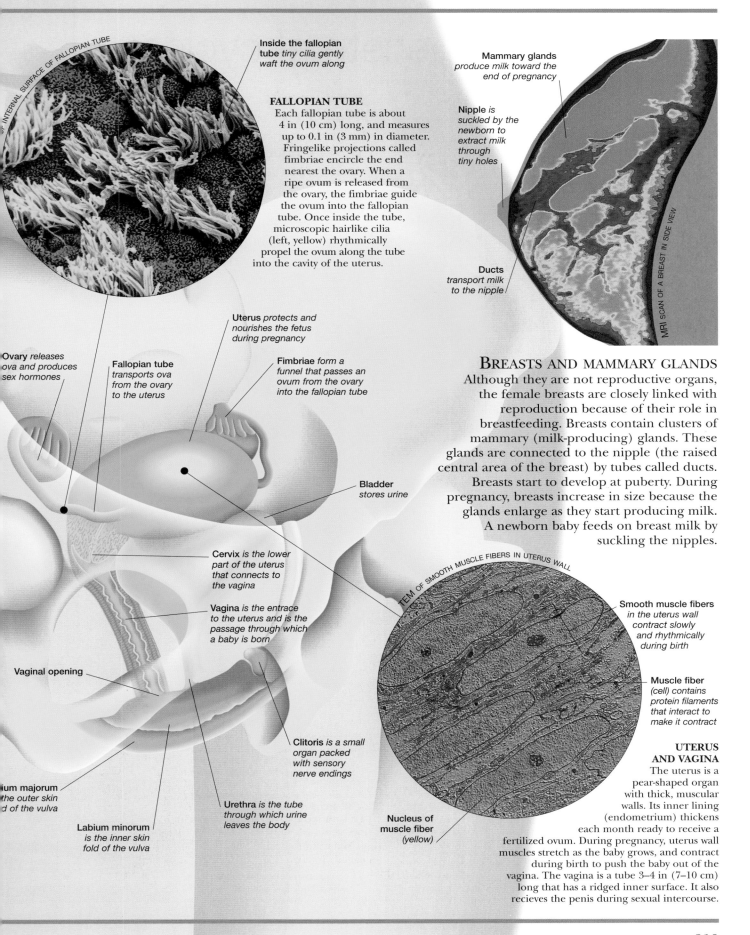

OF INTERNAL SURFACE OF FALLOPIAN TUBE

Inside the fallopian tube *tiny cilia gently waft the ovum along*

FALLOPIAN TUBE
Each fallopian tube is about 4 in (10 cm) long, and measures up to 0.1 in (3 mm) in diameter. Fringelike projections called fimbriae encircle the end nearest the ovary. When a ripe ovum is released from the ovary, the fimbriae guide the ovum into the fallopian tube. Once inside the tube, microscopic hairlike cilia (left, yellow) rhythmically propel the ovum along the tube into the cavity of the uterus.

Mammary glands *produce milk toward the end of pregnancy*

Nipple *is suckled by the newborn to extract milk through tiny holes*

Ducts *transport milk to the nipple*

MRI SCAN OF A BREAST IN SIDE VIEW

Uterus *protects and nourishes the fetus during pregnancy*

Ovary *releases ova and produces sex hormones*

Fallopian tube *transports ova from the ovary to the uterus*

Fimbriae *form a funnel that passes an ovum from the ovary into the fallopian tube*

Bladder *stores urine*

BREASTS AND MAMMARY GLANDS
Although they are not reproductive organs, the female breasts are closely linked with reproduction because of their role in breastfeeding. Breasts contain clusters of mammary (milk-producing) glands. These glands are connected to the nipple (the raised central area of the breast) by tubes called ducts. Breasts start to develop at puberty. During pregnancy, breasts increase in size because the glands enlarge as they start producing milk. A newborn baby feeds on breast milk by suckling the nipples.

TEM OF SMOOTH MUSCLE FIBERS IN UTERUS WALL

Cervix *is the lower part of the uterus that connects to the vagina*

Vagina *is the entrace to the uterus and is the passage through which a baby is born*

Vaginal opening

Clitoris *is a small organ packed with sensory nerve endings*

Urethra *is the tube through which urine leaves the body*

Nucleus of muscle fiber *(yellow)*

ium majorum the outer skin d of the vulva

Labium minorum *is the inner skin fold of the vulva*

Smooth muscle fibers *in the uterus wall contract slowly and rhythmically during birth*

Muscle fiber *(cell) contains protein filaments that interact to make it contract*

UTERUS AND VAGINA
The uterus is a pear-shaped organ with thick, muscular walls. Its inner lining (endometrium) thickens each month ready to receive a fertilized ovum. During pregnancy, uterus wall muscles stretch as the baby grows, and contract during birth to push the baby out of the vagina. The vagina is a tube 3–4 in (7–10 cm) long that has a ridged inner surface. It also recieves the penis during sexual intercourse.

Ovarian and menstrual cycles

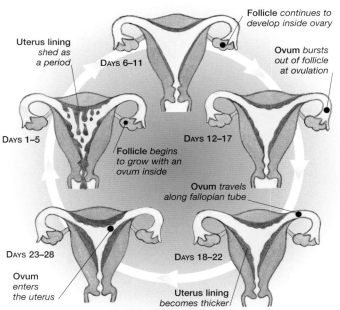

Follicle *continues to develop inside ovary*

Uterus lining *shed as a period*

DAYS 6–11

Ovum *bursts out of follicle at ovulation*

DAYS 1–5

DAYS 12–17

Follicle *begins to grow with an ovum inside*

Ovum *travels along fallopian tube*

DAYS 23–28

DAYS 18–22

Ovum *enters the uterus*

Uterus lining *becomes thicker*

EACH MONTH, A WOMAN'S REPRODUCTIVE SYSTEM goes through a set sequence of changes – a cycle – that prepares her body for the possibility of pregnancy. This reproductive cycle has two interlinked parts – the ovarian cycle and the menstrual cycle. During the ovarian cycle, an ovum (egg) ripens inside one of the ovaries and is then released. During the menstrual cycle, the lining of the uterus (the endometrium) thickens in readiness to receive the ovum if it is fertilized. If fertilization does not happen, the endometrium breaks down and is shed through the vagina during menstruation (a period). The monthly changes in the ovaries and the uterus are controlled by hormones from the brain and the ovaries.

REPRODUCTIVE CYCLES

The menstrual and ovarian cycles usually begin when a girl is between 11 and 14 years of age and stop when a woman reaches the menopause (at about 50). The cycles repeat every 28 days on average, but this varies between women and can be different each month. From puberty until the menopause, the endometrium is repeatedly shed during a period and then thickens again, while a follicle in the ovary matures and releases its ovum into the fallopian tube. If it reaches the uterus unfertilized, the ovum is shed with the endometrium, marking the end of one cycle and the beginning of the next.

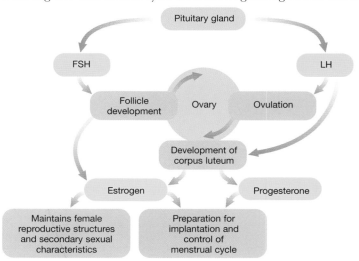

Pituitary gland

FSH

LH

Follicle development

Ovary

Ovulation

Development of corpus luteum

Estrogen

Progesterone

Maintains female reproductive structures and secondary sexual characteristics

Preparation for implantation and control of menstrual cycle

SEX HORMONES

Four hormones control the female reproductive system: FSH (follicle-stimulating hormone) and LH (luteinizing hormone) from the pituitary gland; and the sex hormones estrogen and progesterone from the ovaries. After puberty, FSH and LH stimulate follicle maturation and ovulation. Ripening follicles release estrogen, which makes the endometrium thicken and maintains the female sexual organs. After ovulation, progesterone is released; this also has a controlling role in the menstrual cycle.

OVARIAN CYCLE

At the start of each ovarian cycle, several follicles – each containing an ovum – begin to enlarge and fill up with fluid. One follicle becomes fully mature and bursts, releasing its ovum from the surface of the ovary during ovulation. The empty follicle forms the corpus luteum, a mass of cells that release hormones.

MENSTRUAL CYCLE

At the start of each cycle, the endometrium is shed during menstruation. The bleeding lasts an average of five days, and contains the unfertilized ovum as well as cells from the uterine lining. Hormones are then released that cause the endometrium to increase in size to a thickness of 0.25 in (6 mm) before being shed again.

HORMONE LEVELS

Hormone levels fluctuate over the month because of the interaction between them. Initially, FSH causes an ovum to mature, and its follicle releases estrogen. Increasing estrogen inhibits FSH, but stimulates LH, which surges, stimulating the ripe follicle to burst and release its ovum. The newly formed corpus luteum then releases progesterone, which further stimulates endometrial thickening and some estrogen. Both hormones suppress FSH and LH. Without fertilization, the corpus luteum breaks down, progesterone and estrogen levels fall, and the cycle begins again.

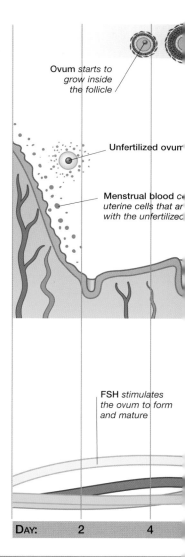

Ovum *starts to grow inside the follicle*

Unfertilized ovum

Menstrual blood c[...] *uterine cells that ar[...] with the unfertilized*

FSH *stimulates the ovum to form and mature*

DAY: 2   4

OVULATION

About halfway through the ovarian (and menstrual) cycle, ovulation occurs. One follicle outgrows the others and matures, producing a blisterlike swelling just under the surface of the ovary. The follicle eventually bursts, and the ovum is released from the ovary. It is then moved along the fallopian tube, where it may be fertilized, and into the uterus.

SEM OF AN OVUM AT OVULATION

Ovum *(pink) bursts from the ovary's surface*

Uterus lining *has folds and a spongy surface after ovulation*

SEM OF ENDOMETRIUM

SPONGY SURFACE

Both before and after ovulation, hormones from the ovaries cause the endometrium to thicken and its blood supply to increase. As the tissue gets thicker and starts to look spongy, it is ready to receive a fertilized ovum if one embeds itself into the tissue. Glands in the surface (darker areas) secrete nutrients, such as lipids and sugars, to nourish the fertilized ovum.

Ruptured follicle *forms the corpus luteum, which secretes progesterone and estrogen*

Corpus luteum *degenerates if the ovum is unfertilized*

Fluid-filled cavity

Ovulation *occurs when the follicle bursts and the ovum is released*

Unfertilized ovum *is shed to begin the next menstrual cycle*

Follicle cells *surround the developing ovum*

Mature ovum *bulges from the ovary surface and produces more estrogen*

Thickened lining *with increased blood supply, caused by an increase in progesterone*

Blood vessels *lengthen as more estrogen is produced*

Estrogen, *which is produced by the growing follicle, peaks just before ovulation*

LH *surges to trigger ovulation at about day 14*

Progesterone *is produced by the corpus luteum and makes the endometrium thicken*

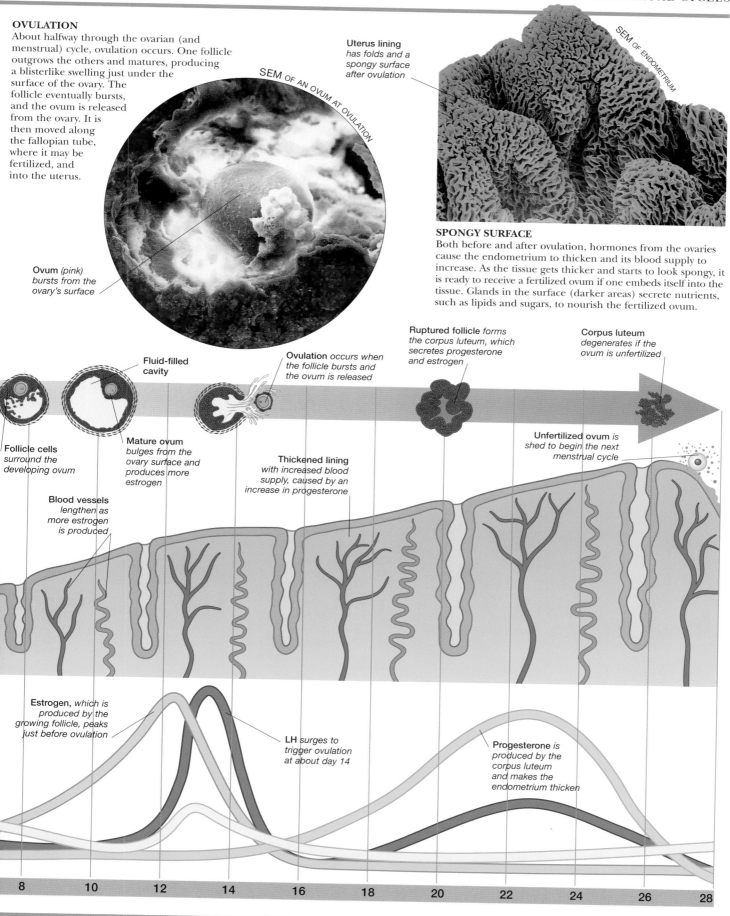

8   10   12   14   16   18   20   22   24   26   28

Conception

THE CREATION OF EACH NEW HUMAN LIFE starts with fertilization. This is the union of an ovum (egg) from a female with a sperm from a male. The male and female cells are brought together when the millions of sperm in the semen swim through the cervix into the uterus and toward the ovum in the fallopian tube, although only a few actually reach the ovum. Fertilization usually takes place inside a fallopian tube, but it can only occur if a sperm meets the ovum in the first 24 hours after the ovum's release from the ovary. Once a sperm penetrates the ovum, its nucleus fuses with that of the ovum and a single new cell (zygote) is produced that contains genetic material from both parents. The new cell divides repeatedly to form a ball-shaped cluster of cells, which travels along the fallopian tube into the uterus. About a week after fertilization, the tiny ball of cells burrows, or implants, into the lining of the uterus. The start of pregnancy, which begins with fertilization and implantation, is called conception.

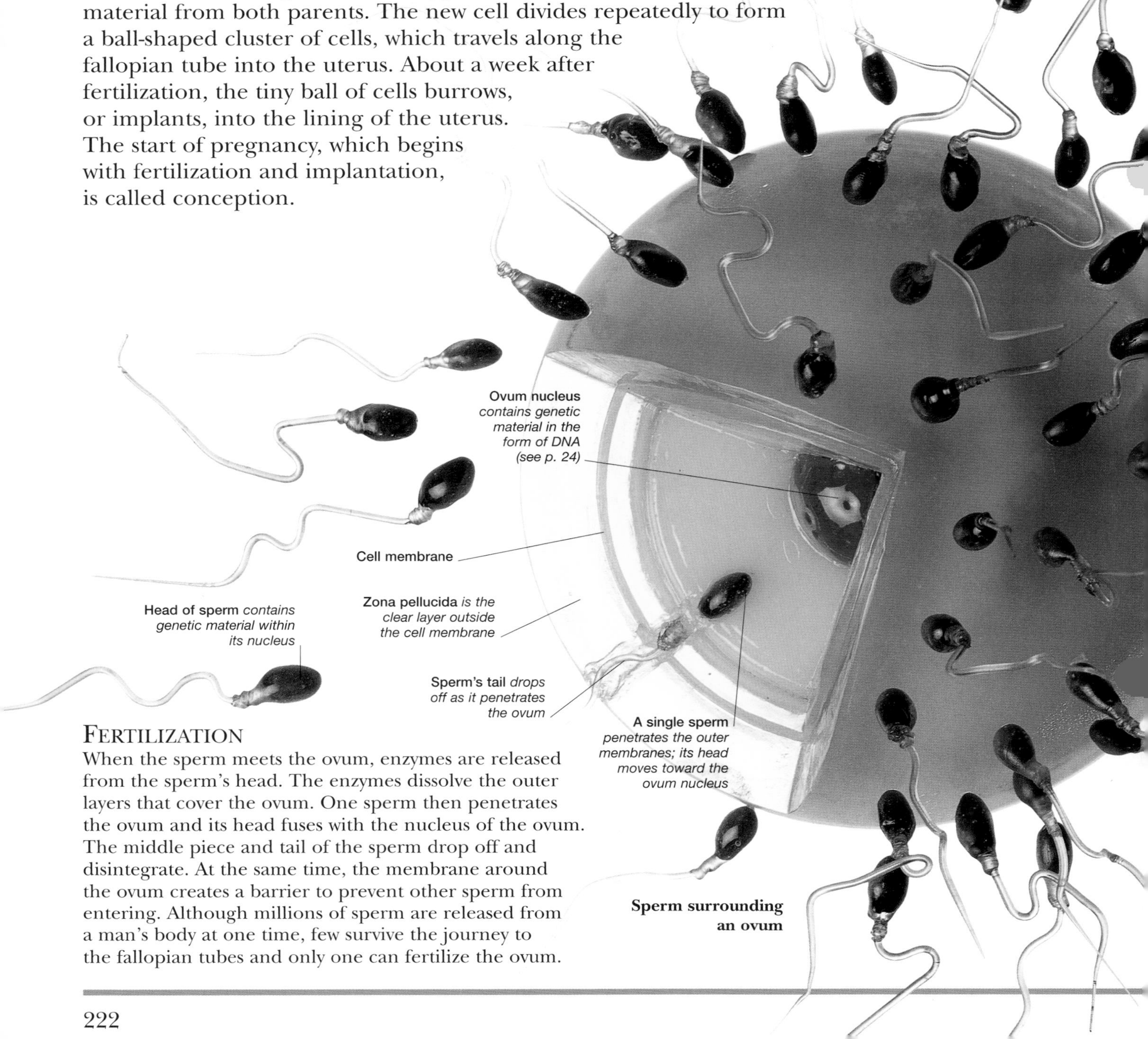

Ovum nucleus *contains genetic material in the form of DNA (see p. 24)*

Cell membrane

Zona pellucida *is the clear layer outside the cell membrane*

Head of sperm *contains genetic material within its nucleus*

Sperm's tail *drops off as it penetrates the ovum*

A single sperm *penetrates the outer membranes; its head moves toward the ovum nucleus*

Sperm surrounding an ovum

FERTILIZATION

When the sperm meets the ovum, enzymes are released from the sperm's head. The enzymes dissolve the outer layers that cover the ovum. One sperm then penetrates the ovum and its head fuses with the nucleus of the ovum. The middle piece and tail of the sperm drop off and disintegrate. At the same time, the membrane around the ovum creates a barrier to prevent other sperm from entering. Although millions of sperm are released from a man's body at one time, few survive the journey to the fallopian tubes and only one can fertilize the ovum.

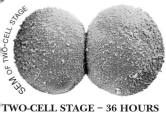

SEM OF TWO-CELL STAGE

TWO-CELL STAGE – 36 HOURS
It takes about 36 hours for the fertilized cell to divide into two (above) as it continues along the fallopian tube. Cell division by mitosis (see p. 19) creates two identical new cells, each with an exact copy of all the genetic information contained in the original cell. At this stage, the zygote measures about 0.004 in (0.1 mm) across.

Fertilization *occurs as a sperm penetrates the ovum, creating a zygote*

Two-cell stage *occurs as the zygote begins to divide and grow*

Fallopian tube

Four-cell stage

Ovulation *is when an egg bursts from the ovary and moves along the fallopian tube*

Ovary

SEM OF FOUR-CELL STAGE

FOUR-CELL STAGE – 48 HOURS
As the zygote travels farther along the fallopian tube, it continues to divide. Here, after about 48 hours, the cells divide again to become a four-cell ball. As its journey continues, the cells divide every 12 hours or so.

EARLY DAYS
After fertilization, the zygote divides into two, then again into four, and so on. Muscular contractions combine with beating cilia to gently waft the growing ball of cells along the fallopian tube. After about three days, the dividing cells have formed a berrylike cluster called a morula, which reaches the end of the fallopian tube and enters the uterus. About a week after fertilization, the morula develops into a fluid-filled ball of cells called a blastocyst and implants into the uterus lining, beginning pregnancy.

16-cell stage *is a cluster of dividing cells called a morula*

Uterus

Implantation *occurs when the blastocyst reaches the uterus and embeds itself into the lining*

Journey of the fertilized ovum

SEM OF SIXTEEN-CELL STAGE

SIXTEEN-CELL STAGE – 72 HOURS
Three days after fertilization, the cells create a sixteen-cell, solid, berrylike ball called a morula (left). This stage gets its name from the Latin word for "mulberry." The morula eventually finishes its journey down the fallopian tube and enters the uterus. It then changes into a hollow ball of cells called a blastocyst.

SEM OF IMPLANTED EMBRYO

IMPLANTATION – SIX DAYS
Six days after fertilization, the blastocyst (orange) implants itself into the lining of the uterus (pink), marking the end of conception. Its inner cells become the embryo, while the outer cells help form the placenta. The placenta connects the growing embryo to its mother and nourishes it. After day 10, the embryo is completely embedded and continues its growth.

FERTILITY

MODERN MEDICINE HAS DEVELOPED ways to control human fertility (the ability to produce children) – both to prevent it and aid it. The fact that women can produce large numbers of children over 30 or 40 fertile years, and the need to give each child a long period of parental care, has led to the search for methods of contraception to control the number of births and the length of time between them. Conversely, some people have difficulty conceiving children due to problems in their reproductive systems. Modern fertility treatments have made it possible for many childless couples to have a family by joining ova and sperm in a laboratory.

DR. MARIE STOPES
Dr. Marie Stopes campaigned for the right for women to use birth control, publishing two best-selling books on the subject. In 1921, she opened the first British family planning clinic.

BIRTH CONTROL PILL
There are two main types of birth control pill, the combined pill and the progestogen-only pill. The hormones in them usually prevent a woman from ovulating. This means that no ova are released, so they cannot be fertilized by sperm.

BARRIER METHODS

The earliest attempts at contraception centered on the use of physical barriers that stopped sperm from reaching the ovum; for example, condoms that cover the penis. Their widespread availability today, as both a contraceptive and a barrier to sexually transmitted diseases, was first pioneered by Margaret Sanger (1879–1966) in the US and Marie Stopes (1880–1958) in Britain. They both overcame strong social and religious opposition to make contraception freely available so that women could choose when they would become pregnant.

IUD AND BIRTH CONTROL PILLS

More sophisticated methods of contraception, based on treatments that interfere with the processes of ovum production and fertilization,

became available in the second half of the 20th century. Small interuterine devices (IUDs), implanted inside the uterus, work by preventing fertilized ova from implanting. More recent interuterine systems (IUS) contain the hormone progestogen, which stops sperm from entering the uterus.

The use of hormones to regulate ovulation was pioneered by several scientists whose studies explained how hormones controlled human fertility. They developed artificial hormones that stop ova from maturing, and these formed the basis of orally

Fallopian tube
*is blocked by
a clip during
sterilization*

FEMALE STERILIZATION
This method of contraception is permanent and involves surgery. Two small incisions are made into the abdomen. The fallopian tubes are then sealed with clips or cut and tied, so that sperm cannot travel through the tubes to fertilize ova. Males can be sterilized by cutting the vas deferens.

administered birth control pills. Their widespread introduction in the 1960s meant that women had more control over family planning and fertility.

INFERTILITY TREATMENTS

Until late last century, the inability to conceive, either through failure of ovulation, blockage of the female reproductive tract, or defective sperm production in men, meant that many couples could not have their own children. Then an understanding of how hormones control ovulation allowed doctors to use fertility drugs to trigger ovulation. Ova could then be collected, fertilized outside the

TEST-TUBE BABY
The first baby to be born as a result of successful IVF was Louise Brown (pictured right, with her father). She was born on 12 August, 1978, in Great Britain. IVF was pioneered by Dr. Patrick Steptoe (1913–88).

body, and reimplanted into the womb. This technique, called in vitro fertilization (IVF), led to the birth of "test-tube" babies. Male infertility caused by sperm with low mobility can now be overcome by intracytoplasmic sperm injection (ICSI), a technique that uses microscopic needles to inject sperm into an ovum in a laboratory. The fertilized ovum is then reimplanted into the uterus.

Fertilization *occurs during IVF treatment when sperm are mixed with an ovum*

LM OF AN OVUM DURING FERTILIZATION

INTRACYTOPLASMIC SPERM INJECTION
In a lab, a technician (below) takes a sperm cell and injects it directly into the ovum before it is implanted back into the female.

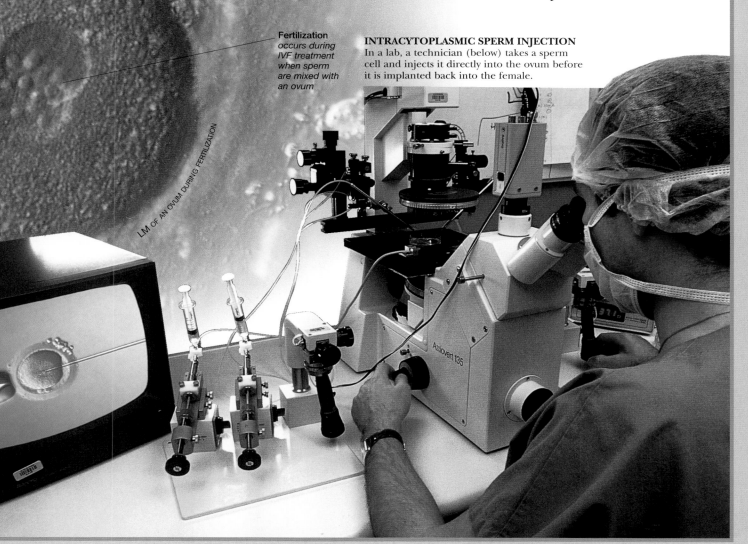

Early pregnancy

DURING THE FIRST TWELVE WEEKS of pregnancy (the first trimester), the fertilized ovum develops from a single cell into a complex structure in which the internal organs, face, and limbs have all completed their basic development. At first, the developing baby is called an embryo and bears little resemblance to a human – at four weeks its face has not yet formed, and it has a taillike extension in place of legs. However, its heart has already started beating, and other internal organs have begun to form. Once eight weeks have passed, the baby is referred to as a fetus, and by the end of the first trimester it has limbs, a face that is recognizably human, and internal organs that are well developed. Meanwhile, the placenta has become well established in the wall of the uterus, and the mother has begun to experience many of the effects of pregnancy.

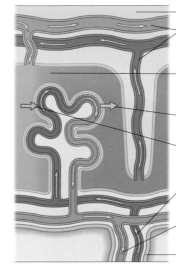

- Uterus wall
- Maternal blood vessels *supply fresh blood and take away wastes*
- Intervillous space *filled with pools of the mother's blood*
- Wastes *pass through thin villus walls into the placenta*
- Nutrients *pass through thin villus walls into blood vessels*
- Umbilical artery *carries wastes away from the fetus*
- Umbilical vein *carries nutrients to the fetus*
- Umbilical cord

PLACENTA BLOOD EXCHANGE
Inside the placenta, blood from the fetus is distributed into a complex network of small vessels (villi) that protrude into chambers called intervillous spaces, through which maternal blood flows freely. These vessels and the tissue that surrounds them are thin, so nutrients and waste products have only a short distance to cross between fetal and maternal blood. Unfortunately, potentially harmful substances, such as drugs and viruses, are also able to cross with little difficulty.

PREGNANCY IN THE FIRST TRIMESTER
Complex changes take place within a woman's body as it works hard to adjust to pregnancy and provide for the developing embryo and placenta. The metabolic rate (see p. 22) increases by 10–25 percent, and the pulse and breathing rate rise as more oxygen and other nutrients are sent to the fetus and more carbon dioxide is exhaled. The fluid content of the body increases, as does the mother's weight. Even though the pregnancy is not yet far advanced, the mother's body begins to prepare for the birth – the walls of the uterus become more muscular, and the breasts begin to swell and form new milk-producing ducts.

Breasts *become tender and swell, and the area around the nipples darkens*

Internal organs *such as the lungs, heart, and kidneys work harder*

Abdomen *begins to swell slightly as the fetus grows*

Uterus *protects the growing fetus, while the placenta and umbilical cord nourish it*

Hormones *cause menstruation to stop. An increase in hormones can also cause nausea (morning sickness)*

Placenta *provides an interface between mother and fetus. About 1.1 pints (600 ml) of maternal blood passes through the placenta every minute*

Umbilical cord *takes blood to and from the fetus. Its flexibility allows the baby to move around freely*

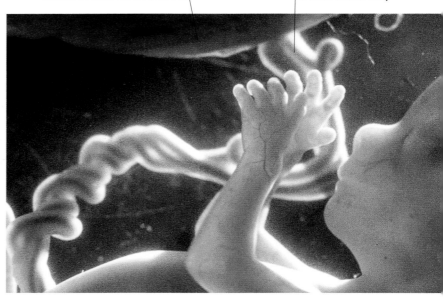

PLACENTA AND UMBILICAL CORD
The growing fetus has no direct contact with the maternal circulatory system. Instead, it is nourished by the placenta, a disk of tissue located on the internal surface of the uterus. The fetus and placenta are connected by the umbilical cord. In the placenta, blood from the fetus flows through an elaborate network of vessels that are bathed in the mother's blood. This allows oxygen and other nutrients to pass from the mother's blood into that of the fetus, while waste products travel in the opposite direction. Nutrient-rich, refreshed blood then returns to the fetus along the umbilical cord, which is about 24 in (60 cm) long.

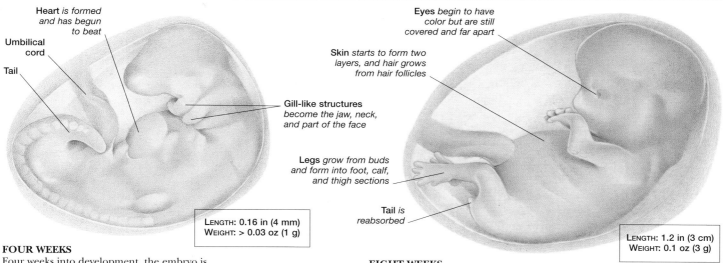

Heart *is formed and has begun to beat*

Umbilical cord

Tail

Gill-like structures *become the jaw, neck, and part of the face*

Eyes *begin to have color but are still covered and far apart*

Skin *starts to form two layers, and hair grows from hair follicles*

Legs *grow from buds and form into foot, calf, and thigh sections*

Tail *is reabsorbed*

| LENGTH: 0.16 in (4 mm) |
| WEIGHT: > 0.03 oz (1 g) |

| LENGTH: 1.2 in (3 cm) |
| WEIGHT: 0.1 oz (3 g) |

FOUR WEEKS

Four weeks into development, the embryo is roughly the size of a pea. It resembles a tadpole more than a human, and has a taillike protrusion instead of legs. Within the embryo, many changes have taken place. Cells have become specialized, so the heart is forming and has been beating for about a week, and the beginnings of a spinal cord are present. Many other vital organs, such as the brain, liver, and intestine, have begun to develop.

EIGHT WEEKS

The developing baby is now about the size of a strawberry and is called a fetus. Most organs are already established, and the head has grown to accommodate the rapidly developing brain, the basic structure of which is in place. The main features of the face are formed, and the tail-like protrusion is gone. The arms and legs have grown from buds, and the fingers and toes – initially paddlelike limbs – are now separated from one another as individual digits. The heart is pumping blood around new blood vessels as the fetus moves around inside the uterus.

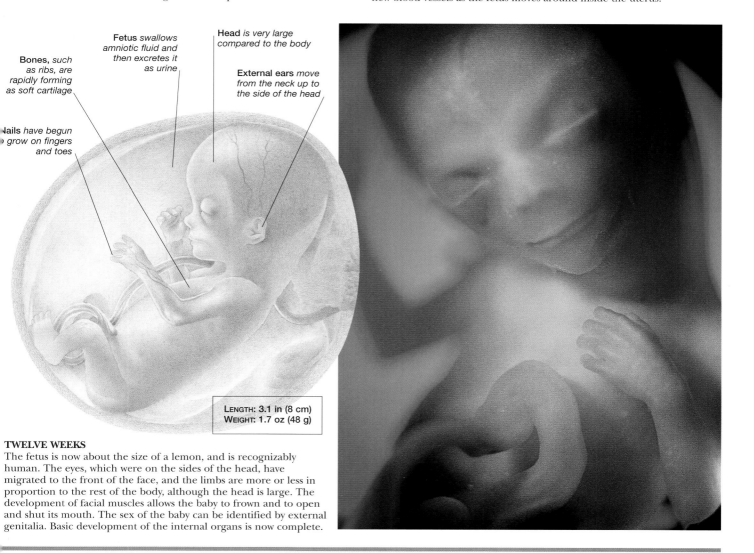

Bones, *such as ribs, are rapidly forming as soft cartilage*

Fetus *swallows amniotic fluid and then excretes it as urine*

Head *is very large compared to the body*

Nails *have begun to grow on fingers and toes*

External ears *move from the neck up to the side of the head*

| LENGTH: 3.1 in (8 cm) |
| WEIGHT: 1.7 oz (48 g) |

TWELVE WEEKS

The fetus is now about the size of a lemon, and is recognizably human. The eyes, which were on the sides of the head, have migrated to the front of the face, and the limbs are more or less in proportion to the rest of the body, although the head is large. The development of facial muscles allows the baby to frown and to open and shut its mouth. The sex of the baby can be identified by external genitalia. Basic development of the internal organs is now complete.

Growing fetus

BY THE END OF THE FIRST TRIMESTER of pregnancy, the major organs of the fetus are in place. The second and third trimesters (weeks 13–28 and 29–birth) primarily involve fetal growth and final maturation. At first, the fetus grows rapidly in size but gains little weight, but later he or she becomes heavier and plumper as fat accumulates beneath the skin. Growth of the fetus causes the uterus to expand, so that the mother's abdomen swells noticeably. She may also experience effects such as breathlessness and frequency of urination as the uterus begins to press on nearby organs such as the diaphragm and bladder. Toward the end of pregnancy the fetus undergoes final preparations for life outside the uterus and usually turns head down, ready to pass through the birth canal headfirst.

Fetus *is thin but has grown in length, and muscles and bones are maturing*

Skin *sensitive t touch, so th fetus moves the mother abdomen is presse*

LENGTH: 8.7 in (22 cm)
WEIGHT: 1 lb 12 oz (800 g)

PREGNANCY IN THE SECOND TRIMESTER

During the second trimester, the mother's abdomen begins to swell noticeably as the uterus expands beyond the boundaries of the pelvis in order to accommodate the growing fetus. A pigmented streak called the *linea nigra* may appear down the center of the abdomen, and other pigmented areas such as the nipples may darken. Changes in the digestive system can cause heartburn and reduced frequency of bowel movements, and the gums may become spongy. In order to supply extra blood to the uterus and kidneys, the heart works twice as hard as normal.

24-WEEK FETUS
Fetal development in the second trimester is mainly a matter of growth. After six months the baby's length has increased rapidly, so the head is more in proportion, but the fetus is only about a quarter of its final weight. Brain and nerve cells and an immune system are maturing, and the ears begin to hear sounds inside and outside the uterus. By the end of the second trimester, the hands, fingers, and face are fully developed.

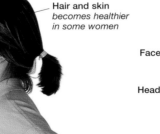

Hair and skin *becomes healthier in some women*

Uterus *enlarges, making the abdomen swell and sometimes causing stretch marks*

Fetal *movements are first felt by the mother as a "fluttering" sensation between weeks 16 and 22*

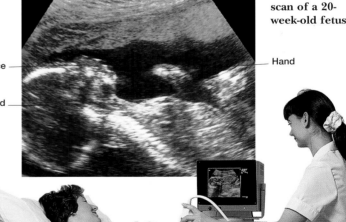

Ultrasound scan of a 20-week-old fetus

Face

Hand

Head

Transducer *sends and receives high-frequency sound waves*

Back pain *may be caused by the increased weight of the fetus*

ULTRASOUND SCAN
A low-risk test called an ultrasound scan is used to view the fetus and assess its health inside the uterus. Ultrasound can also help identify the sex of the baby. High-frequency sound waves are beamed into the abdomen through a handheld instrument called a transducer, which is placed on the skin. Waves are reflected back from the contents of the abdomen into the transducer, creating an image of the uterus and fetus on a television screen

EXERCISING IN PREGNANCY

Regular, suitable exercise during pregnancy has several benefits – it helps the mother's body adapt to the pregnancy and prepare for labor, and it enables her to recover more quickly following childbirth. Exercise also helps with relaxation, and can promote improved sleep. Swimming can be particularly enjoyable and beneficial. Muscles are toned and stamina improves, while the water supports the mother's increased weight, making injuries very unlikely.

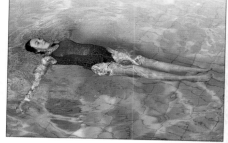

PREGNANCY IN THE THIRD TRIMESTER

The growing fetus causes the uterus to fill the abdomen, so that it displaces the digestive tract and presses against the diaphragm. This, combined with the oxygen demands of the fetus, causes the mother to breathe more rapidly and deeply. Meanwhile, pressure of the uterus on the bladder often leads to an increased frequency of urination. Aches and pains occur due to stretching of ligaments, especially in the hips and pelvis.

Breasts *may secrete colostrum, a yellowish fluid that provides nourishment for the baby after birth*

Squashed intestine

Fetus *has undergone a growth spurt and takes up much of the abdomen*

Mucus plug *protects the fetus from infection*

Amniotic sac *is now filled with about 1.8 pints (1 litre) of fluid*

FULL-TERM BABY

The weight of the fetus increases rapidly during the last trimester of pregnancy. Fat is deposited beneath the skin in order to provide the baby with energy and insulation after birth, and as a result the fetus becomes more rounded. The lungs become well-developed and produce a substance called a surfactant, which will play a vital role in breathing. In many ways the fetus behaves as it will after birth – it has periods of sleep and wakefulness, responds to music and voices, and is startled by loud noises.

Eyes *are blue but may change color after birth*

LENGTH: 14.2 in (36 cm)
WEIGHT: 6–8 lb (3–4 kg)

Mother's backbone

Fetus *usually turns head down to fit into the pelvis during engagement*

READY FOR BIRTH

By the end of the pregnancy the fetus is quite plump – it only just fits into the uterus by curling up. If the fetus is not already positioned head down in the uterus, it usually turns now so that it can pass through the birth canal headfirst. Once it has turned, the fetus may descend slightly so that its head settles into the lowest part of the uterus (a process called engagement), although in many cases this does not happen until the start of labor.

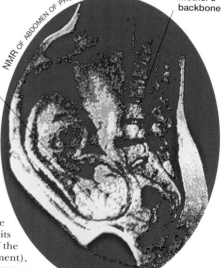

NMR OF ABDOMEN OF PREGNANT WOMAN

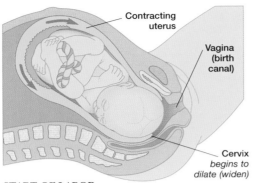

START OF LABOR
Labor begins with contractions of the uterus that become painful and frequent. Often, the amniotic sac lining the uterus breaks at this stage, and the fluid surrounding the fetus pours out through the vagina. The cervix begins to widen so that the fetus can pass through it. Widening of the cervix is brought about by the softening of its tissues, and by pressure from the head of the fetus as it is pushed downward with each contraction.

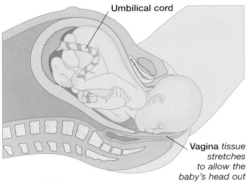

STAGE TWO
During the second stage of labor, which begins once the cervix has widened fully, the baby is born. At first, the fetus faces the mother's side, but as it gradually descends its head rotates so that its face is toward the mother's back. The mother usually now develops an irresistible desire to push with each contraction, adding to the forces that propel the fetus along the birth canal.

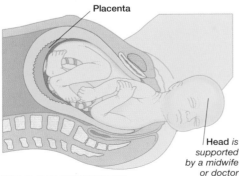

HEAD AND SHOULDERS
As soon as the head of the fetus has emerged from the vagina it rotates back into line with the rest of the body, allowing the shoulders to be delivered with the next contraction. Normally, the shoulder nearest the mother's belly appears first, soon followed by the other. Once the shoulders have been delivered, the rest of the body can pass through the birth canal quickly, with little difficulty.

Birth

BIRTH OCCURS WHEN THE FETUS LEAVES the uterus to enter the outside world. This usually happens about 38 weeks after fertilization. In most cases birth begins when the mother goes into labor, which is the process by which powerful contractions of the muscular walls of her uterus gradually expel the fetus through the vagina. There are three distinct stages of labor: the first of these prepares the birth canal for the baby to pass through it; the second involves the birth of the baby; and the third consists of the delivery of the placenta. The length of time that these stages take varies, and is influenced by the number of previous pregnancies the mother has had. As soon as the baby is born it takes its first breaths and begins to adjust to its new environment, allowing it to survive outside its mother's body.

NEWBORN BABY
Sudden contact with the world outside the uterus normally stimulates the baby to take its first breath, moments after it leaves the birth canal and is lying between its mother's legs. The baby's circulatory system begins to adjust so that blood circulates through the lungs rather than the placenta. Much of the nutritious blood in the placenta flows back along the umbilical cord into the baby's body so that it is not wasted when the cord is cut. As soon as the cord has been cut, the baby can be given to the mother to suckle. On average, a baby is 20 in (51 cm) long and weighs 7 lb 11 oz (3.5 kg) at birth. The baby's skull bones are not completely fused, so its head might be temporarily misshapen by the journey down the birth canal.

FORCEPS SECRET
18th-century forceps Obstetric forceps consist of two interlocking tongs that are inserted into the vagina during difficult deliveries to help the baby's head move through the birth canal. They were developed in the 17th century by an English family, the Chamberlens, and represented a significant breakthrough, as previous means of assisting in difficult deliveries generally resulted in the death of the baby. However, the Chamberlens kept their invention secret, and it was not until the 18th century that the forceps became more widely used. Numerous versions have evolved since, although many forceps in use today are based on early designs.

FINAL STAGE

The final stage of labor begins as soon as the baby has been born, and lasts until the placenta is delivered. Mild contractions continue after the birth of the baby, and the placenta gently peels away from the inner surface of the uterus and follows the umbilical cord out through the vagina. Blood vessels in the wall of the uterus that previously supplied the placenta clamp shut, preventing excessive bleeding. The placenta, or afterbirth, is usually delivered about 5–30 minutes after the birth of the baby, and consists of a disc of spongy, blood-rich tissue about 8 in (20 cm) in diameter.

Cut umbilical cord

Placenta *peels away from the uterus lining*

APGAR SCORE

At birth, and during the following minutes, the baby's well-being can be assessed using a tool called the Apgar score, developed by an American doctor, Virginia Apgar, in which vital signs are evaluated. A low Apgar score indicates that the baby is unwell.

SIGN	SCORE: 0	SCORE: 1	SCORE: 2
Activity	Limp	Some bending of limbs	Active movements
Pulse	None	Below 100 bpm	Over 100 bpm
Grimace	None	Grimace or whimpering	Cry, sneeze, or cough
Appearance	Pale, blue	Blue extremities	Pink
Respiration	None	Slow or irregular breaths, weak cry	Regular breaths, strong cry

Vernix *is a greasy substance that covers and protects the baby's skin until it is born*

Umbilical cord *is clamped and cut once blood has flowed back to the baby*

BREASTFEEDING

During pregnancy, hormones activate the milk-producing glands of the breasts, so that food is available for the newborn. At first, the breasts produce colostrum, a yellowish fluid that is rich in antibodies, that protect the baby from infection. During the second day after birth, colostrum is replaced by ordinary breast milk, which contains lactose (a type of sugar), protein, and fat. Usually, a mother produces about 1.8 pt (1 liter) of milk a day for as long as she wishes to breastfeed.

SAVING MOTHERS

THE BIRTH OF A BABY SHOULD be a time of happiness for parents. Yet although the process is natural, it is never risk-free, and a few mothers die during or following childbirth. The number of fatalities today is tiny when compared with earlier centuries. In the 18th and 19th centuries, for example, many women died within a week or two of giving birth from a disease called puerperal (childbed) fever, particularly in hospitals. In Europe and the United States, a handful of doctors realized how puerperal fever might be spread. But their findings were ignored, and it took decades before measures were taken to save mothers.

IGNAZ SEMMELWEIS
Deaths of women from puerperal fever in Vienna General Hospital were greatly reduced by the work of Ignaz Semmelweis.

WASHING HANDS
To many 19th-century doctors, the idea that washing their hands would stop the spread of disease seemed ridiculous. Today, hand-washing is a vital part of stopping infection from passing from doctor or midwife to patient.

THE MENACE OF INFECTION

By the end of the 18th century there had been great advances in the understanding of pregnancy and childbirth, with the training of specialist doctors, called obstetricians, and the opening of maternity hospitals. Although these hospitals provided bed rest for poorer expectant mothers, they also had appalling death rates. Within days of giving birth, many mothers died of puerperal

EARLY MATERNITY WARD
This illustration, taken from the book *Microcosm of London*, published in 1808, shows the scene inside a women's ward in the Middlesex Hospital, London, England. The view was probably idealized by the artist, since conditions were certainly more crowded and dirty than shown here.

fever, an infection
that spreads through
the vagina and uterus.
Why so many deaths
occurred in these
hospitals was unknown.

In 1846, Hungarian obstetrician
Ignaz Semmelweis (1818–65) started
work in Vienna General Hospital.
He was shocked to discover that many
more women died from puerperal fever
in Maternity Ward 1 than in Ward 2.
The difference between the wards was
that in Ward 1, women were attended
by doctors who also carried out autopsies
(dissections of dead patients), while in
Ward 2, women were attended by midwives who
did not. Semmelweis deduced that the doctors,
who rarely washed their hands, were transferring
infection from corpses to live patients.
He ordered medical staff to wash their
hands carefully before attending to
their patients and, as a result, the
death rate in Ward 1 dropped to the
same level as Ward 2. But when he
reported his findings, Semmelweis was
ridiculed by fellow doctors. He had
dared to question the accepted
medical view that infections were
spread not by human contact but
by a mysterious miasma, or "bad air."

HARMFUL BACTERIA
This is *Streptococcus pyogenes*, the
bacterium that causes most cases of puerperal
fever. Streptococcal bacteria are spherical and are
linked together in a chain. Infection may take place
during or after birth when a woman is examined by
someone whose fingers are contaminated with *S. pyogenes*.

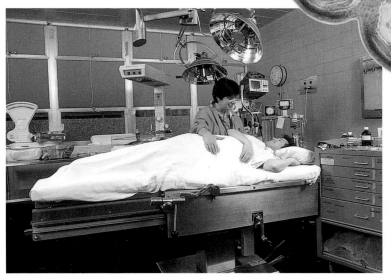

MODERN DELIVERY ROOM
In the photo above, an expectant mother is being attended by a nurse in
the delivery room of a modern hospital. She will give birth here safe in
the knowledge that conditions are clean and hygienic, and that medical
care is at hand should there be any complications during the birth.

IDENTIFYING THE CAUSE

Semmelweis was not alone in his views.
In the Untited States, the physician
and writer Oliver Wendell Holmes
(1809–94) presented a paper in
1843 entitled *On the Contagiousness
of Puerperal Fever* at the Boston
Society of Medical Improvement.
Like Semmelweis, he suggested that
infection was spread to women by
unhygienic medical practices.
Holmes was also ridiculed, but he
persisted in his campaign to stop
the unnecessary deaths of new
mothers. Both Semmelweis and
Holmes were finally vindicated by
Louis Pasteur (1822–95), the great French scientist
who, in 1879, proved that puerperal fever was caused
by the *Streptococcus* bacterium, thus destroying the
miasma theory forever.

MODERN PRACTICES

As a result of Pasteur's findings, and those of
physicians such as Joseph Lister (see p. 270), there
was a gradual acceptance of the need for clean
conditions in hospital wards. Modern maternity
wards provide a safe and sterile environment for
childbirth, and obstetricians and midwives are
educated to a high standard. If bacterial infection
does occur, it can be treated using antibiotics.

LIFE STORY

Throughout life, each individual undergoes a continuous process of mental and physical development. A newborn is highly dependent on others, but it rapidly grows into an infant and acquires movement skills and an understanding of the world. These skills provide a base for childhood development – the body matures and becomes agile, and intellectual abilities are gained. During puberty, the individual undergoes physical and psychological changes to move into adulthood. As an adult, the body matures and the person goes through various life experiences. Gradually, signs of aging appear as the individual enters old age.

Fertility begins to decline after the mid-twenties for both women and men

Male physique may still be maturing

NEWBORN BABY

From birth, a baby begins to adapt to life outside the uterus. Basic instincts, such as the ability to cry when hungry and to suck from the nipple, enable the baby to survive early life. Otherwise, it is entirely dependent on others to provide food, warmth, and comfort. Very soon after birth, interaction with parents takes place through crying, eye contact, and facial expressions.

TWENTIES

By the age of twenty, the transition into adulthood is largely complete, although further development of the male muscles may still occur. As an adult, the individual has achieved a large degree of independence, although this is accompanied by responsibilities such as the need to earn a living. Often, this is a time during which important relationship, parenthood, and career decisions are made.

Infant begins to control his muscles as he stands and walks

TEN YEAR OLD

After a decade of life, physical development is continuing, although at a slower pace than in early childhood. Complex movements such as walking and running have been mastered, and the shape of the body is more mature. The child is capable of complex thought and is rapidly acquiring new skills and knowledge. He or she is able to speak fluently, and enjoys interaction with others.

ONE YEAR OLD

By the end of the first year of life, the infant has grown in height and weight. He or she is also able to control his or her muscles so that it can manipulate objects and stand and walk with assistance. A basic understanding of language has been achieved, and a powerful emotional bond has been established between the infant and his or her parents, creating the basis for future social development.

Child has grown taller and become coordinated and sociable

Adolescent's body matures and begins to take on an adult form

TEENAGERS

Physical development speeds up as the individual undergoes the transition from childhood to adulthood. During puberty, hormones trigger the maturation of sexual organs, and features such as male facial hair and female breasts appear. Complex emotional development takes place as the individual becomes more sophisticated and evolves into an adult.

THIRTIES AND FORTIES

By the age of forty, signs of aging such as gray hair are more prominent, and organs such as the kidneys have passed their peak performance. Some may sense a decline in physical capacity, but those who are active remain in better shape than sedentary people of a younger age. Lifestyles vary enormously, but for some people this will be a time devoted to parenthood and work, during which one's knowledge and experience are consolidated.

Neuron

Neural network

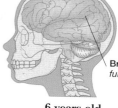

Birth

Seams (fontanelles) in the cranium *allow the skull to grow as the brain expands*

Number of connections *between neurons increases*

Neural network

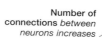

The activity of internal organs *such as the kidneys, heart, and lungs may start to decline slightly*

Brain *is almost full-size*

6 years old

Neural network

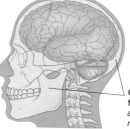

Cranium and facial bones *are now fully mature*

18 years old

BRAIN AND SKULL DEVELOPMENT

When a baby is born, it has all the billions of neurons (nerve cells) that its brain needs. These neurons make contact with each other to form a communication, or neural, network. Initially there are few connections, but as a child learns and experiences more, the number of connections rapidly increases. This causes the brain to expand. By age 18, the network is fully developed, but continues to be modified throughout life.

Effects of age *may be prominent but many people remain active*

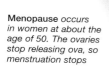

Menopause *occurs in women at about the age of 50. The ovaries stop releasing ova, so menstruation stops*

FIFTIES TO SEVENTIES

In an older adult, signs of aging are more apparent – wrinkling of the skin and graying of the hair have progressed. By now women have stopped having periods. Further changes, such as gradual conversion of muscle into fat, have also taken place, and the body as a whole is less resilient. However, most people are still able to participate in vigorous activity, particularly if they were active when younger.

EIGHTIES AND OVER

For those who remain healthy and are financially secure, this can be a fulfilling time of life. The responsibilities of employment and parenthood are over, and one has a wealth of memories and experience to look back on. The physical effects of aging are now pronounced. Sadly, for some, this results in disability and illness, but many people remain healthy and active well into their old age.

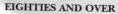

Infancy

INFANCY IS DEFINED AS THE 12 months after birth, and is a time of great transition and fast growth. A newborn baby has a number of reflexes (see p. 86) that help in activities such as feeding, but is otherwise helpless and relies completely on others to fulfill its needs. Most of the infant's functions, such as posture and movement, are poorly developed. During the first weeks and months, the baby learns to control his or her muscles, sleep patterns become more regular, and the infant participates more actively in routines such as feeding. Meanwhile, vital interaction between the infant and his or her parents provides a foundation for future emotional development. By the end of infancy, a child is eating solid foods, crawling, can stand and walk with assistance, and has formed a solid emotional bond with his or her parents.

Grasp reflex *is strong in a newborn baby's hands and feet*

REFLEXES
Newborn babies are equipped with a number of reflexes that help them to survive in the first few weeks, but which fade within a few months. For example, a baby can suck and swallow as soon as it is born, and automatically turns his or her head when the cheek is touched, helping the baby to find the nipple during feeding. A baby will also have a strong grasp reflex (above) for the first three months. Other reflexes, such as a rapid recoil in response to pain, remain for life.

MOVEMENT
At birth, a baby has poor muscle control – the body and arms are stiff, and the neck is floppy, so that the head needs support. Gradually, movements become smoother and more controlled, so that by six months the infant moves purposefully and is beginning to support the weight of its own body. After about a year, he or she can crawl, sit up, stand, and walk when held by the hand.

BONDING
A secure early relationship between an infant and his or her parents is crucial because it helps a child to be confident and balanced in the future. Soon after birth, an infant uses eye contact, facial expression, and crying to interact with others, and his or her parents reciprocate with nurturing and comforting behavior. This relationship becomes more sophisticated and within a few months a solid and profound emotional bond has formed, and the infant becomes upset when separated from his or her parents.

Eye contact *between mother and baby helps to form a strong emotional bond*

Muscles develop *to support the infant's weight, while increased co-ordination allows movement*

INFANCY MILESTONES
Infants pass through a predictable pattern of development, although each progresses differently. The following are general guidelines only:

1 MONTH	6 MONTHS	9 MONTHS	12 MONTHS
• Watches mother's face • Smiles at about 5 or 6 weeks • Hands are normally closed but grasp finger • Startled by loud noises • Lifts head 45°	• Sits up unsupported and can roll over • Turns head to look around • Digests semisolid food • Can see a full range of colors and shades • Can distinguish voices from other sounds • Grasps between thumb and index finger • Can pick up a small object • Turns to the sound of a familiar voice • First lower baby teeth appear • Plays with own feet	• Pokes at objects with index finger • Babbles • Shouts to attract attention • Crawls • Walks holding onto furniture • Stands without help • First upper baby teeth appear • Eats with fingers	• Walks with one or two hands held • Understands simple commands • Holds arms and legs out to be dressed • Learns single words • Can drink from a cup

MANIPULATION

A newborn infant has little ability to manipulate things, but will spontaneously grasp objects, such as a parent's finger, that are placed in his or her palm (left). This reflex fades as more complex movements of the hands develop over the ensuing months. By six months, an infant can pick up objects by pinching them between the fingers and thumb. At one year of age (below), this action has become more refined. The infant can now grasp objects delicately, and can also drop and throw them. Other skills of fine movement, such as the ability to point, have also been acquired by the end of infancy.

Hands *develop to complete complex movements such as picking up and throwing a ball*

FEEDING

At first, feeding is based on reflex responses – the infant cries for food, spontaneously turns its head toward the nipple or bottle, and then automatically begins to suck from it. During infancy, the frequency of feeding declines, and the infant becomes more active in the process. It begins to grasp the breast or bottle, and by the end of infancy is able to use a spoon. Meanwhile, teeth emerge from the gums, the infant can hold, chew, and swallow pieces of food, and the gradual transition to a solid diet can take place.

A baby *should always be put on his or her back to sleep*

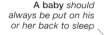

SLEEPING

A newborn baby sleeps for about 20 hours a day, but wakes every couple of hours for feeding, with little variation between day and night. During the following weeks the infant begins to have longer periods of wakefulness in the day and sleeps longer at night, and after about two months it is able go through much of the night without waking. Later in infancy, sleep becomes increasingly regular and less is needed – by six months sleep primarily occurs during the hours of darkness, and has decreased to about 15 hours a day.

Childhood

CHILDHOOD SPANS THE YEARS from infancy to adolescence. During early childhood, the achievements of infancy provide a foundation for further learning and development. The child begins to walk and run, and gradually becomes more skilled and graceful in his or her movement. The secure emotional bond between the child and his or her parents allows and encourages an interaction with others, and learning takes place through active engagement with the world. During the ensuing years, intellectual skills such as reading are acquired, and abstract thinking and complex social behavior evolve. Rapid physical change also takes place – the child grows steadily, the body shape becomes more mature, and baby teeth emerge, which are later replaced with permanent teeth. By the time adolescence approaches, the child has become a sophisticated being, and has undergone remarkable personal, intellectual, and physical development.

MOVEMENT

Basic movement skills that were acquired during infancy develop further during early childhood. Walking and running are achieved by the age of two, by which time a child is also adept at manipulating objects. With each passing year, new skills are acquired, such as jumping, walking on tiptoe, and riding a tricycle. As the child develops, these skills are refined, so that by the age of 10, movement is smooth and coordinated, and complex tasks such as juggling can be carried out with practice.

Girls and boys *interact well together for the first 10 years*

Reading *usually begins by the age of six*

LEARNING

Early childhood is largely concerned with physical exploration – for example, learning about colors and shapes. With time, concepts such as size, direction, and time are grasped. As new knowledge is gained, it is incorporated into the child's understanding of the world. Specific skills such as reading and counting are acquired. Analytical thinking develops, so that by about the age of 12 the child is capable of complex reasoning.

Play *is an important part of development and learning*

SOCIAL BEHAVIOR

The secure emotional bonds a young child shares with his or her parents encourage interaction with others. By the age of three or four he or she enjoys playing with other children, and is upset when others are hurt. Play becomes more imaginative and complex, and an independence from adults develops. Older children begin to work well in groups and enjoy team-based activities. Personal development continues so that by adolescence, children are well developed socially and capable of complex thought.

Speech and vocabulary *becomes complex as childhood progresses*

SPEECH

Speech develops at varying rates in young children. Gradually actual words replace the "babble" of infancy. From about the age of two the child begins to combine groups of words to convey more complex ideas, and by four he or she is usually able to engage in simple conversation. During the remaining years of childhood, speech rapidly increases in complexity as vocabulary and grammatical understanding develop.

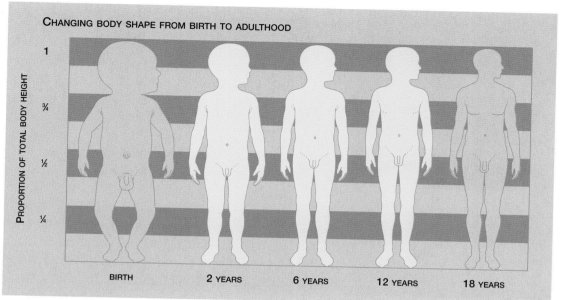

CHANGING BODY SHAPE FROM BIRTH TO ADULTHOOD

PROPORTION OF TOTAL BODY HEIGHT

1
¾
½
¼

BIRTH 2 YEARS 6 YEARS 12 YEARS 18 YEARS

BODY PROPORTIONS

Children grow rapidly during the first two years of life. Growth then continues at a reduced rate for the remainder of childhood – usually about 2.75 in (7 cm) in height and 6 lb (2.7 kg) in weight each year. Different parts of the body grow at varying rates. In a young child the head accounts for a large part of the total height of the body, but it becomes less prominent as the limbs and trunk grow longer. Over time, the proportions of the body gradually begin to resemble those of an adult.

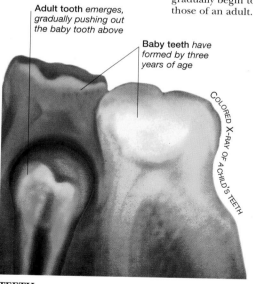

Adult tooth *emerges, gradually pushing out the baby tooth above*

Baby teeth *have formed by three years of age*

COLORED X-RAY OF A CHILD'S TEETH

COLORED X-RAY OF A CHILD'S SKULL

FACE SHAPE

At birth and throughout infancy, copious reserves of fat beneath the skin give the face a rounded appearance. This persists well into childhood, so that during the first years of life the finer features of the face have yet to become apparent. At about the age of five, this begins to change – the fat reserves of babyhood ebb away, and the face becomes leaner and the features more distinct. Family resemblances that may previously have been vague often become more pronounced at this time. Facial bones become larger and stronger as childhood passes, also changing the face shape.

TEETH

By the end of infancy, a child usually has two front teeth in the upper jaw and two in the lower. More teeth emerge during the following months, so that the full set of 20 baby teeth (deciduous teeth) is in place by about the age of three. Teething can be painful, so while a tooth is emerging the child may be irritable and tearful. At about the age of six, permanent teeth begin to emerge, and as they do so, each dislodges the overlying baby tooth, which falls out. Permanent teeth have usually replaced all the baby teeth by adolescence (see pp. 180–1).

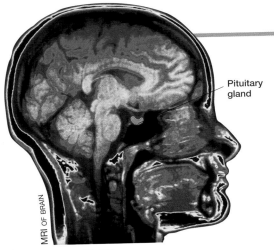

SWITCHING ON
Puberty is triggered by the hypothalamus (see p. 95) which sends hormones to the pituitary gland, located at the base of the brain. The pituitary gland then releases hormones of its own that stimulate the ovaries and testes to mature. As these organs become active, they too secrete hormones. These cause changes such as female breast growth and the deepening male voice.

Pituitary gland

MRI OF BRAIN

Adolescence

ADOLESCENCE IS A TIME OF transition from childhood to adulthood, and involves both physical and psychological changes. Through a process called puberty, the sexual organs become functional. As a result, sex cells (sperm in males and ova in females) become available so that the individual is capable of reproduction. Other physical characteristics, such as facial hair in males and breasts in females, also appear, and a growth spurt takes place so that adult height is achieved. Meanwhile, vital personal development takes place. As childhood ends, the individual becomes more self-aware and sophisticated, and independence and an adult identity are forged through a process that can be emotionally turbulent. By the end of the late teens, the individual has progressed both physically and personally, and is ready for adult life.

PUBERTY FOR BOYS

In boys, puberty usually begins between the ages of 12 and 14, although this varies greatly. The first sign of puberty is enlargement of the testes as they prepare to produce sperm. The penis then begins to grow, and reaches its full adult size after about two years. Pubic, facial, armpit, and chest hair grows. Structures of the larynx (voice box) increase in size, making the voice deeper. As sexual development progresses, the growth rate accelerates, the shoulders broaden, and muscles develop.

FACIAL HAIR
An increase in the hormone testosterone causes facial hair to grow as boys progress through puberty. This photo (left) shows facial hairs that have been shaved, and are now growing back. The first hairs are fluffy, but later become thicker and stronger.

SEM OF BEARD STUBBLE

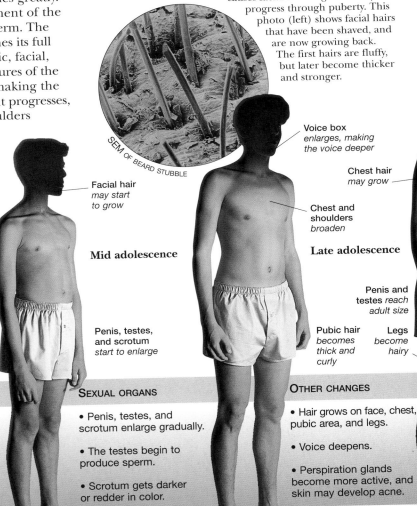

Pimples *may appear*

Underarm hair *begins to grow*

Early adolescence

Sweat glands *may perspire more*

Pubic hair *may grow*

Facial hair *may start to grow*

Mid adolescence

Penis, testes, and scrotum *start to enlarge*

Voice box *enlarges, making the voice deeper*

Chest and shoulders *broaden*

Late adolescence

Chest hair *may grow*

Penis and testes *reach adult size*

Pubic hair *becomes thick and curly*

Legs *become hairy*

BODY PROPORTION

• By the end of adolescence, adult height is reached.

• Shoulders and chest broaden as muscles develop.

SEXUAL ORGANS

• Penis, testes, and scrotum enlarge gradually.

• The testes begin to produce sperm.

• Scrotum gets darker or redder in color.

OTHER CHANGES

• Hair grows on face, chest, pubic area, and legs.

• Voice deepens.

• Perspiration glands become more active, and skin may develop acne.

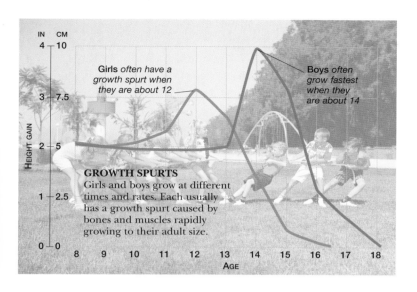

Girls *often have a growth spurt when they are about 12*

Boys *often grow fastest when they are about 14*

HEIGHT GAIN

IN CM
4 — 10
3 — 7.5
2 — 5
1 — 2.5
0 — 0

8 9 10 11 12 13 14 15 16 17 18
AGE

GROWTH SPURTS
Girls and boys grow at different times and rates. Each usually has a growth spurt caused by bones and muscles rapidly growing to their adult size.

PUBERTY FOR GIRLS

Girls usually begin puberty between the ages of 10 and 12, and the first period (when ova start to be released) occurs about two years later. Puberty in girls is heralded by enlargement of the ovaries, but as this is hard to see, the first sign is usually breast growth. By the time of the first period, pubic and armpit hair are well developed. At first, periods may be irregular, but they gradually become predictable. Meanwhile, rapid growth, a change in the distribution of body fat, and widening of the pelvis take place.

ACNE
During puberty, hormones affecting both boys and girls cause glands in the skin to secrete more oil than previously. If the duct leading from the gland to the skin's surface becomes blocked with dead cells or hardened oil, pimples form. The surrounding skin can become infected, making it sore and red.

CHANGING FEELINGS
During adolescence, individuals become more sophisticated and independent. Complex choices about issues such as sexual identity, relationships, and the future are faced. Childhood is abandoned, and the individual faces the daunting search for an adult identity. This can be a challenging, stressful time, and as a result, adolescents may experience feelings of anxiety, depression, and poor self-esteem. However, adolescents are generally less confrontational than is commonly perceived.

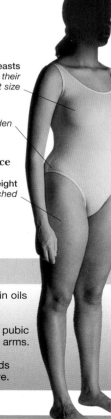

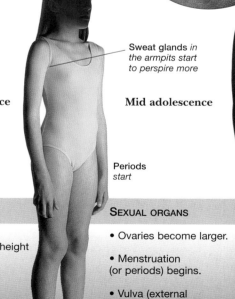

Pimples *may appear*

Underarm hair *may start to grow*

Early adolescence

Nipples *start to enlarge*

Pubic hair *may start to grow*

Sweat glands *in the armpits start to perspire more*

Mid adolescence

Periods *start*

Breasts *become rounder*

Late adolescence

Breasts *reach their full adult size*

Hips *widen*

Adult height *is reached*

Pubic hair *becomes thick and curly*

BODY PROPORTION

• By the end of adolescence, adult height is reached.

• Breasts develop.

• Hips widen and the waist becomes curvy.

SEXUAL ORGANS

• Ovaries become larger.

• Menstruation (or periods) begins.

• Vulva (external genitals) enlarges and becomes fleshy.

OTHER CHANGES

• An increase in skin oils can cause acne.

• Hair grows in the pubic area and under the arms.

• Perspiration glands become more active.

Adulthood and aging

AN INDIVIDUAL'S PERSONALITY AND lifestyle evolve as he or she progresses through adulthood. The way in which this takes place is unique to everyone, and is influenced by factors such as personal preference, opportunities and circumstances, and social and cultural expectations. In fact, the lifestyles of two adults of similar age often differ just as much as those of two people from separate generations. As an individual's life progresses, physical changes also take place. The dramatic development of childhood and adolescence is replaced by a subtler, more gradual transition, and in due course signs of aging begin to appear in the bones, skin, senses, and other organs. Despite these changes, modern medicine allows many elderly people to have an enjoyable and healthy old age.

ADULTHOOD

The nature of adulthood varies enormously depending on personality, decisions made, circumstances, and social context. However, commonly this is a time of independence and responsibility. Adulthood allows personal freedom but this is often accompanied by duties – adults are generally held accountable for their actions, and are expected to support themselves and their families financially. Meanwhile, choices must be made about careers, relationships, and parenthood, all of which involve taking on responsibilities.

COLORED X-RAY OF A LOWER SPINE WITH OSTEOPOROSIS

Osteoporosis has caused this vertebra to collapse

MENOPAUSE

Menopause is when a woman stops having periods, usually between the ages of about 45 and 54. Menopause represents the end of a woman's reproductive potential, and this can have emotional and psychological impacts. Also, as the ovaries cease to work, levels of the hormone estrogen decline. This may cause symptoms such as hot flashes, loss of sexual desire, and wrinkling of the skin, and also increases the risk of disorders such as stroke and osteoporosis. Women may therefore choose to use hormone replacement therapy, in which artificial estrogen is taken in pills (right) or through patches (top right).

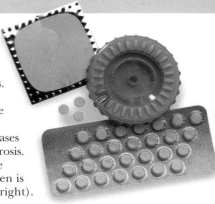

BONE DEGENERATION
This X-ray shows the spine of a 65-year-old woman who has developed a bone condition called osteoporosis. This disease causes the outer layer of bones to become thinner, while the inner layer becomes more porous, with fewer blood cells and less calcium. Bones are therefore more brittle and likely to be damaged. Here, a vertebra has become compressed and wedge-shaped, distorting the spine. Osteoporosis is common in older women, particularly after menopause.

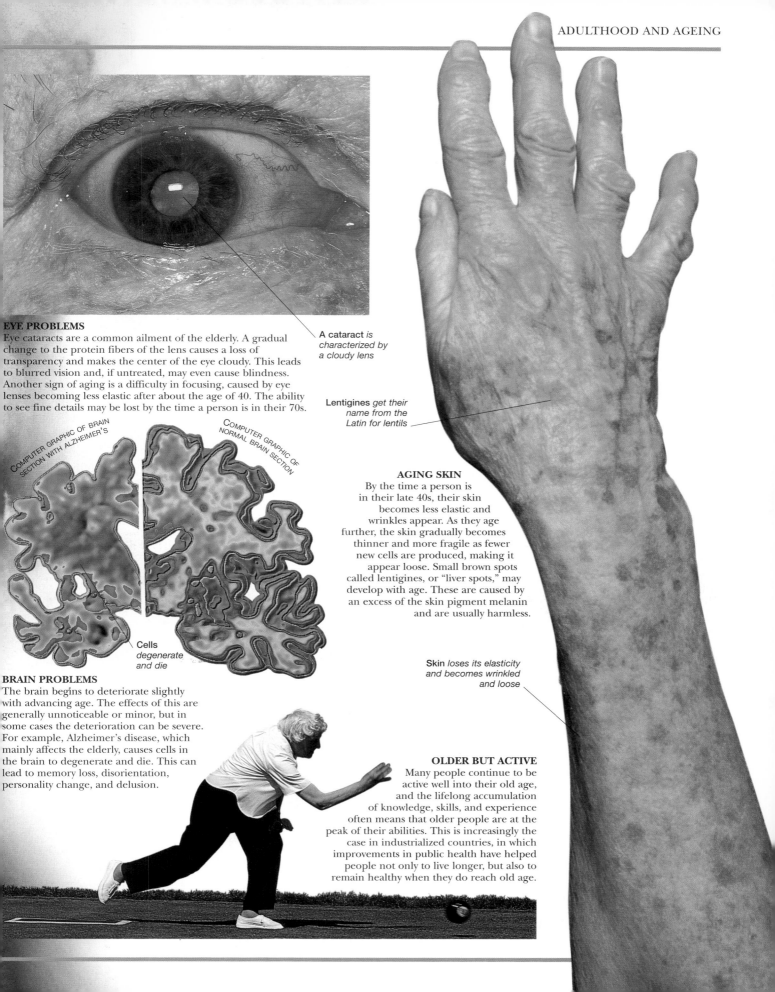

EYE PROBLEMS
Eye cataracts are a common ailment of the elderly. A gradual change to the protein fibers of the lens causes a loss of transparency and makes the center of the eye cloudy. This leads to blurred vision and, if untreated, may even cause blindness. Another sign of aging is a difficulty in focusing, caused by eye lenses becoming less elastic after about the age of 40. The ability to see fine details may be lost by the time a person is in their 70s.

A cataract is characterized by a cloudy lens

Lentigines get their name from the Latin for lentils

COMPUTER GRAPHIC OF BRAIN SECTION WITH ALZHEIMER'S

COMPUTER GRAPHIC OF NORMAL BRAIN SECTION

Cells degenerate and die

AGING SKIN
By the time a person is in their late 40s, their skin becomes less elastic and wrinkles appear. As they age further, the skin gradually becomes thinner and more fragile as fewer new cells are produced, making it appear loose. Small brown spots called lentigines, or "liver spots," may develop with age. These are caused by an excess of the skin pigment melanin and are usually harmless.

BRAIN PROBLEMS
The brain begins to deteriorate slightly with advancing age. The effects of this are generally unnoticeable or minor, but in some cases the deterioration can be severe. For example, Alzheimer's disease, which mainly affects the elderly, causes cells in the brain to degenerate and die. This can lead to memory loss, disorientation, personality change, and delusion.

Skin loses its elasticity and becomes wrinkled and loose

OLDER BUT ACTIVE
Many people continue to be active well into their old age, and the lifelong accumulation of knowledge, skills, and experience often means that older people are at the peak of their abilities. This is increasingly the case in industrialized countries, in which improvements in public health have helped people not only to live longer, but also to remain healthy when they do reach old age.

HUMAN INHERITANCE

IT IS OFTEN EASY TO recognize members of a family because of the remarkable similarity between them. Just as striking, though, are the differences. Why individuals inherit some features but not others has been studied over the past century by scientists. The key to inheritance lies inside body cells, where chromosomes store the information needed to construct and run each cell in units called genes. Since cells make up the body, they also determine its appearance. When humans reproduce, the chromosomes in their sperm and ova are passed on to the next generation.

FAMILY TREE

This photo shows four generations from the same family. Each individual developed from a zygote, or fertilized ovum, produced when their father's sperm fertilized their mother's ovum. Both ovum and sperm have the same number of chromosomes, but some of the genes (genetic instructions) that they carry differ. Passing on a new combination of genes to an offspring means that, while one generation resembles the previous one, a daughter is not identical to her mother (or father). Everyone, therefore, apart from identical twins, has a unique combination of genes in their chromosomes.

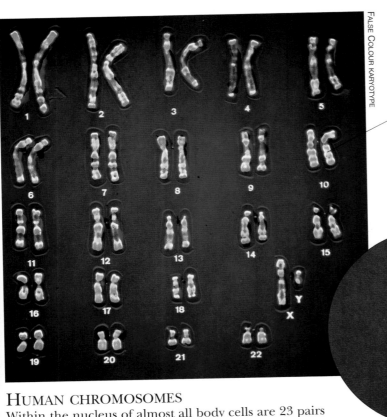

FALSE COLOUR KARYOTYPE

Each chromosome pair *contains many genes, with instructions for particular characteristics*

X chromosomes *of a female match each other*

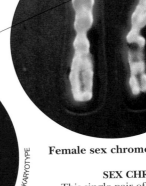

CLOSE-UP OF FALSE COLOR KARYOTYPE

CLOSE-UP OF FALSE COLOR KARYOTYPE

Female sex chromosome

SEX CHROMOSOMES

This single pair of chromosomes is responsible for determining a person's sex. Not surprisingly, they differ between females and males. A female's body cells each contain a matching pair of sex chromosomes called X chromosomes. A male's sex chromosomes do not match. His body cells each contain one X chromosome paired with a Y chromosome.

Male sex chromosome

X and Y chromosomes of a male are of different length

HUMAN CHROMOSOMES

Within the nucleus of almost all body cells are 23 pairs of threadlike chromosomes. Normally, chromosomes are difficult to see under the microscope because they are long, thin, and tangled. But they can be seen when a cell is about to divide because they get shorter and thicker. A photograph of the chromosomes is cut up to produce a karyotype like this one. Pairs of matching chromosomes are arranged in order of size from 1 (largest) to 22 (smallest). These 22 pairs of chromosomes, called autosomes, control most body characteristics. The remaining pair are the sex chromosomes.

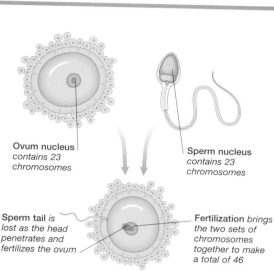

Ovum nucleus *contains 23 chromosomes*

Sperm nucleus *contains 23 chromosomes*

Sperm tail *is lost as the head penetrates and fertilizes the ovum*

Fertilization *brings the two sets of chromosomes together to make a total of 46*

HAPLOID TO DIPLOID

Most body cells are diploid ("double") because they have two sets of chromosomes. But sex cells – sperm and ova – are different. Produced by a special kind of cell division called meiosis (see p. 213), sperm and ova contain just one set of chromosomes and are referred to as haploid ("single"). After fertilization, when a sperm and an ovum combine, the resulting fertilized ovum, or zygote, has a full complement of 46 chromosomes. Two haploid cells have joined to form a diploid one.

CLONING

The process of cloning produces new individuals, called clones, that are genetically identical to their "parent" and does not involve sexual reproduction. In 1997, scientists in Scotland produced Dolly the sheep, the first mammal to be cloned from a cell taken from an adult. The cell's nucleus was injected into an ovum from another sheep that had had its nucleus removed. This "ovum" was then implanted into a sheep's uterus, where it developed into Dolly. Could this happen in humans? Cloning a human has never been achieved, and most countries have made it illegal to even try.

Dolly the sheep

Tongue rolling *is a characteristic controlled by a person's genes, which means some people can do it while others cannot*

GENETIC VARIATION

Around 99.8 percent of the genetic information contained within chromosomes is identical in all people. It ensures that bodies are constructed and work in the same way. The remaining 0.2 percent is variable and produces differences between individuals. Some features show discontinuous variation – for example, people can either roll their tongue or not; there is no in-between stage. Other characteristics show continuous variation – for example, people's height covers a wide range from short to tall.

Chromosomes and genes

EVERY BODY CELL CONTAINS a blueprint for life. Within its nucleus are 23 pairs of chromosomes, each constructed from deoxyribonucleic acid (DNA). Sections of DNA, called genes, contain the coded instructions needed for a cell to build proteins. These proteins control the growth and development of the organs which give the body its individual shape and form. A cell's 23 pairs of chromosomes contain an instruction set of some 30,000–50,000 pairs of genes. One member of the gene pair is inherited from the mother and one is inherited from the father. Each may control the same or alternative versions of a body characteristic, such as eye color. A person's features are not produced by a "blending" of all their genes. Instead, some genes are expressed while others remain inactive, giving each person a unique appearance.

FLUORESCENT MICROGRAPH OF CHROMOSOMES

Gene position
marked on a
chromosome

GENES

DNA is divided up into sections called genes. Genes provide the means by which characteristics are passed from parents to children. Body cells contain homologous (matching) pairs of chromosomes. Each pair contains matching pairs of genes carried at identical locations on each chromosome. Within each gene pair, one gene may be an identical copy of its partner, or they may occur in slightly different versions called alleles.

CHROMOSOME STRUCTURE

The nucleus of every body cell – apart from red blood cells, which lack a nucleus – contains a store of chromosomes. These are normally long and threadlike, but as a cell is about to divide they become (as shown here) much shorter, and duplicate to form identical strands, or chromatids, linked by a centromere. Each chromosome is made up of a molecule of DNA, tightly packed into a supercoil – a coil within a coil. When a cell divides, its 46 chromosomes split into equal halves so that each daughter cell receives an identical package of DNA instructions.

Cell nucleus
contains a full set
of chromosomes

One half of the
chromosome has
doubled because a
cell is about to divide

Centromere joins the duplicated
half of the chromosome to the
original half until the cell divides

Backbone is made from
sugar and phosphate

DNA coils up tightly to
form a chromosome

A gene is a
section of DNA

Bases protrude from the
backbone and meet in
the middle of the ladder

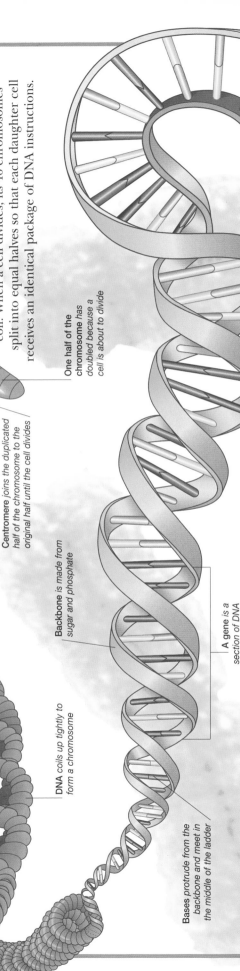

DNA

This giant molecule consists of two linked strands that spiral around each other like a twisted ladder to form what is known as a double helix. Each strand has a "backbone" made up of linked sugar and phosphate molecules. Linking the two strands are four types of nucleotide bases – adenine, cytosine, guanine, and thymine – that bond to form the "rungs" of the "ladder." The specific sequence of bases in sections of DNA form the "words" of the cell's "instruction manual" (see also pp. 24–5).

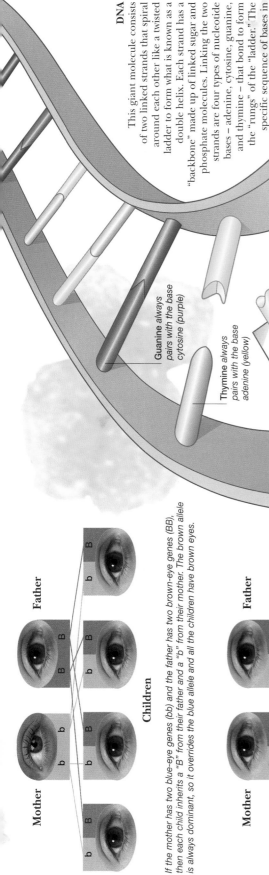

Guanine always pairs with the base cytosine (purple)

Thymine always pairs with the base adenine (yellow)

Free bases attach themselves to the unzipping DNA to make a new strand

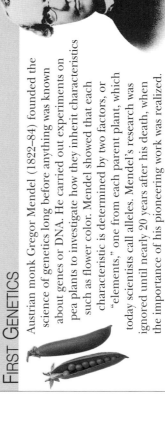

First Genetics

Austrian monk Gregor Mendel (1822–84) founded the science of genetics long before anything was known about genes or DNA. He carried out experiments on pea plants to investigate how they inherit characteristics such as flower color. Mendel showed that each characteristic is determined by two factors, or "elements," one from each parent plant, which today scientists call alleles. Mendel's research was ignored until nearly 20 years after his death, when the importance of his pioneering work was realized.

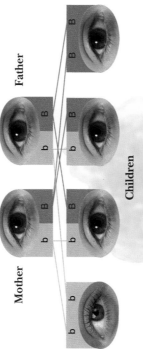

Father

Children

If the mother has two blue-eye genes (bb) and the father has two brown-eye genes (BB), then each child inherits a "B" from their father and a "b" from their mother. The brown allele is always dominant, so it overrides the blue allele and all the children have brown eyes.

Mother

Father

Children

If each parent has one brown-eye gene (B) and one blue-eye gene (b), then there is a one-in-four chance of their child being blue-eyed. This happens when the recessive gene (b) is inherited from both parents, so the blue is not suppressed.

Mother

b	**Gene for blue eyes**	B	**Gene for brown eyes**

DOMINANT AND RECESSIVE

Every person shares some characteristics with their parents, but has others that are different. The explanation for this lies in the nature of alleles, or gene pairs. A cell may contain an identical pair of alleles for a characteristic, or a different pair. If two different alleles are present, only one – the dominant allele – has any effect, because it suppresses the other – the recessive allele. A simple diagram, here showing the inheritance of eye color, shows how alleles interact. A dominant allele is represented by a capital letter (here, B for brown eyes), while a recessive allele is represented by a lower case letter (here, b for blue eyes).

Chance and heredity

MANY ASPECTS OF HUMAN INHERITANCE depend on random, chance events. Whether a human is destined to be female or male is determined by the fifty–fifty chance at fertilization that a mother's ovum is fertilized by a sperm carrying an X sex chromosome or a Y sex chromosome. While most pregnancies result in a single offspring, the random event of two ova being released and fertilized at the same time, or of one fertilized ovum splitting into two, will from time to time produce twins. Random mutations, or changes, can affect single genes or whole chromosomes. Mutated genes may sometimes cause disorders that can be passed on to the next generation. Extra chromosomes, picked up by chance during meiosis, may be carried by ova or sperm at fertilization, resulting in conditions such as Down's syndrome.

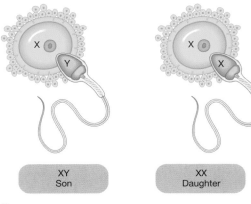

XY
Son

XX
Daughter

SEX DETERMINATION

A person's sex is determined at fertilization by the identity of the sex chromosome carried by the fertilizing sperm. A sperm may carry either an X chromosome or a Y chromosome, whereas an ovum always contains an X chromosome. If a Y-carrying sperm fertilizes an ovum, the resulting child will be a boy because a few weeks after fertilization, a gene on the Y chromosome initiates development of the embryo's testes. Fertilization by an X-carrying sperm produces a girl because the Y chromosome and its gene are not present. The X chromosome carries many genes that control other body characteristics, but the smaller Y chromosome carries far fewer genes.

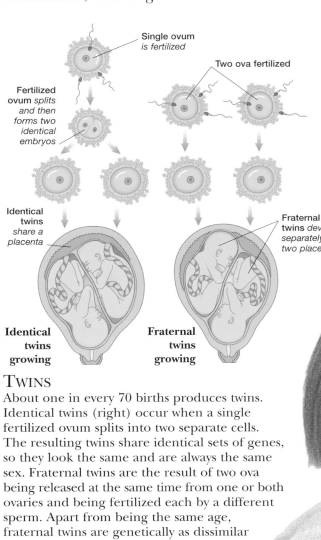

Single ovum *is fertilized*

Two ova fertilized

Fertilized ovum *splits and then forms two identical embryos*

Identical twins *share a placenta*

Fraternal twins *develop separately with two placentas*

Identical twins growing

Fraternal twins growing

TWINS

About one in every 70 births produces twins. Identical twins (right) occur when a single fertilized ovum splits into two separate cells. The resulting twins share identical sets of genes, so they look the same and are always the same sex. Fraternal twins are the result of two ova being released at the same time from one or both ovaries and being fertilized each by a different sperm. Apart from being the same age, fraternal twins are genetically as dissimilar as any other brothers and sisters, and may be the same sex or different sexes.

GENES AND DISEASE

In addition to carrying genes that control normal body structure and function, chromosomes may also carry genes that cause diseases, which may be passed on from parents to children. Scientists map genes to identify which ones may, in a mutated form, cause disease. This map shows the location of some of these genes on an X chromosome. Each gene is present twice, with one on each of the chromosome's linked strands, or chromatids.

Test for color blindness

Cleft palate *is caused by a gene mutation in this area*

Color-blind *people often have trouble distinguishing between red and green, so this type of pattern is used as a test*

Hemophilia *(see p. 137) occurs when a gene located here is mutated*

Color blindness *(see p. 115) is caused by a mutation to a gene here*

Inheriting color blindness

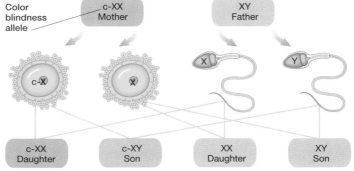

Color blindness allele

c-XX Mother

XY Father

c-X

X

X

Y

c-XX Daughter

c-XY Son

XX Daughter

XY Son

Key

Carrier female

Normal sight

Color blind

SEX-LINKED INHERITANCE

Some inherited disorders, for example color blindness, are determined by sex. If the color blindness allele ("c," above), which is recessive, appears on one of a woman's X chromosomes, it will usually be "masked" by a dominant allele on the other. She may pass the gene to her children but will have normal vision herself. But if a man has the recessive allele on his single X chromosome, there is no opposing allele on his smaller Y chromosome, so he will be color blind. Therefore, a carrier mother has a 25 percent chance of having a color-blind son and a 25 percent chance of having a carrier daughter.

Down's syndrome *is caused by the presence of a third copy of chromosome 21*

Chromosome 21 in a Down's syndrome child

EXTRA CHROMOSOMES

Children with Down's syndrome have flattened facial features, folds of skin that cover the inner corners of their eyes, and learning difficulties. Down's syndrome, also called trisomy 21, is the result of inheriting an extra number 21 chromosome from the mother or, more rarely, the father. Down's syndrome children are affectionate and friendly and, despite their disabilities, are usually able to lead fulfilling lives.

HUMAN GENOME PROJECT

H AILED AS THE FIRST GREAT SCIENTIFIC achievement of the 21st century, the Human Genome Project has unlocked the store of genetic instructions needed to build a human body – the genome – which are held inside every body cell. On 26 June, 2000, at the White House in Washington, D.C., two competing teams of scientists announced jointly that they had prepared the first draft of the human genome, having deciphered some 90 percent of its coded blueprint for life. But this is just the beginning. It should, in time, be possible to identify all human genes, as well as the genetic causes of human disease. The Project also raises ethical issues about the ownership and use of genetic information.

Enzyme *cuts DNA between cytosine and guanine and nowhere else*

CUTTING UP DNA
A DNA molecule is cut at a specific point using "precision scissors" in the form of restriction enzymes. Each type of restriction enzyme recognizes a specific base sequence in DNA and cuts the giant molecule at that point and nowhere else.

AN AMBITIOUS PROJECT
The Human Genome Project had its origins in 1985, when several scientists suggested it might be possible to identify the coded messages, or genes, contained within DNA (see pp. 24–5 and pp. 246–7). Just one body cell contains 6.6 ft (2 m) of tightly coiled DNA, which contains several billion substances called bases whose precise sequence makes up the coded instructions for life. There are four bases in all – adenine (A), cytosine (C), guanine (G), and thymine (T). Within each gene, groups of three bases contain the letters

in genetic code – say, GGT or ACT – that dictate the specific order in which amino acid building blocks are fitted together to make the proteins that control cell activities. Finding out the precise sequence of these bases became the daunting task of a multi-billion-dollar project, that lasted 15 years and involved 16 research institutes in 6 countries.

SEQUENCING THE GENOME
Scientists split chromosomes into fragments using special enzymes that cut DNA at specific points. These were loaded on to a special gel, across which an electric charge was applied. This process, called electrophoresis, separated fragments by size, producing patterns that, when analysed by a computer, revealed the base sequence of chromosome fragments. By 2000, the fragments had been pieced together like a jigsaw puzzle to produce the draft.

CHROMOSOMES AND GENOMES
A genome is contained within each of the two sets of 23 chromosomes (pink) found inside a body cell. The two genomes inside a person's cells – one inherited from each parent – differ very slightly, giving that person their individual characteristics.

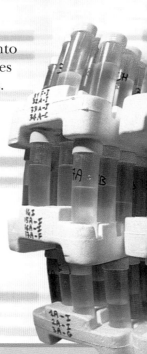

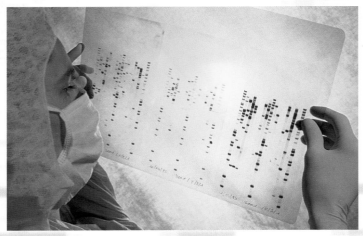

GENETIC FINGERPRINT
A technician examines the banding pattern, or genetic fingerprint, produced when DNA is cut up into fragments and separated by electrophoresis, a key process in sequencing. A computer analyzes the banding pattern and turns it into a sequence of bases.

FIRST RESULTS AND NEXT STEPS

The draft contained some fascinating revelations about the human genome. It showed that the varying but precise sequence of bases along the genome consists of about 3,200 million "letters." That is enough to fill a pile of standard paperback-sized books 197 ft (60 m) high. Incredibly, about 97 percent of DNA is "junk," with just 3 percent making up the genes that contain coded instructions to make a protein. Rather than 100,000 genes, as previously thought, there are probably between 30,000 and 50,000.

The next steps in the Human Genome Project

involve identifying all those genes, discovering which protein each gene produces, and what these proteins do. However, the first benefits – and problems – of the Human Genome Project are already evident.

BENEFITS AND CHALLENGES

It should soon be possible to identify the base sequence of defective genes that cause inherited diseases, such as cystic fibrosis, and understand how they actually work. This in turn will lead to the use of gene therapy – inserting "normal" genes into people to overrule defective versions – or the design of specific drugs that can "switch off" or modify defective genes. For the first time, too, people will know their own, individual genome. This could be screened for genetic problems that may develop, or be passed on to children, so that people can take preventative measures.

The disadvantage of having this information about a person's genome is that it could also be used by insurance companies to increase life insurance premiums for people

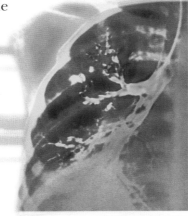

CYSTIC FIBROSIS
This inherited disease may one day become curable thanks to knowledge gained from the Human Genome Project. Its symptoms include the secretion of thick mucus (seen in this chest X-ray as green) that blocks airways in the respiratory system.

more likely to die younger. Also, employers might discriminate against potential employees who could develop health problems or have a shorter working life. Furthermore, drug companies might claim ownership of genes through patenting, which would give them all the profits from the development of new treatments. Hundreds of new cures might become available, but only for a small, wealthy section of humanity. These are but a few of the ethical challenges of the Human Genome Project to be faced and resolved in the years to come.

GENE BANK
These refrigerated tubes together contain a complete human genome. Inside each tube is one particular region of DNA. Gene banks like this one are found in laboratories taking part in the Human Genome Project.

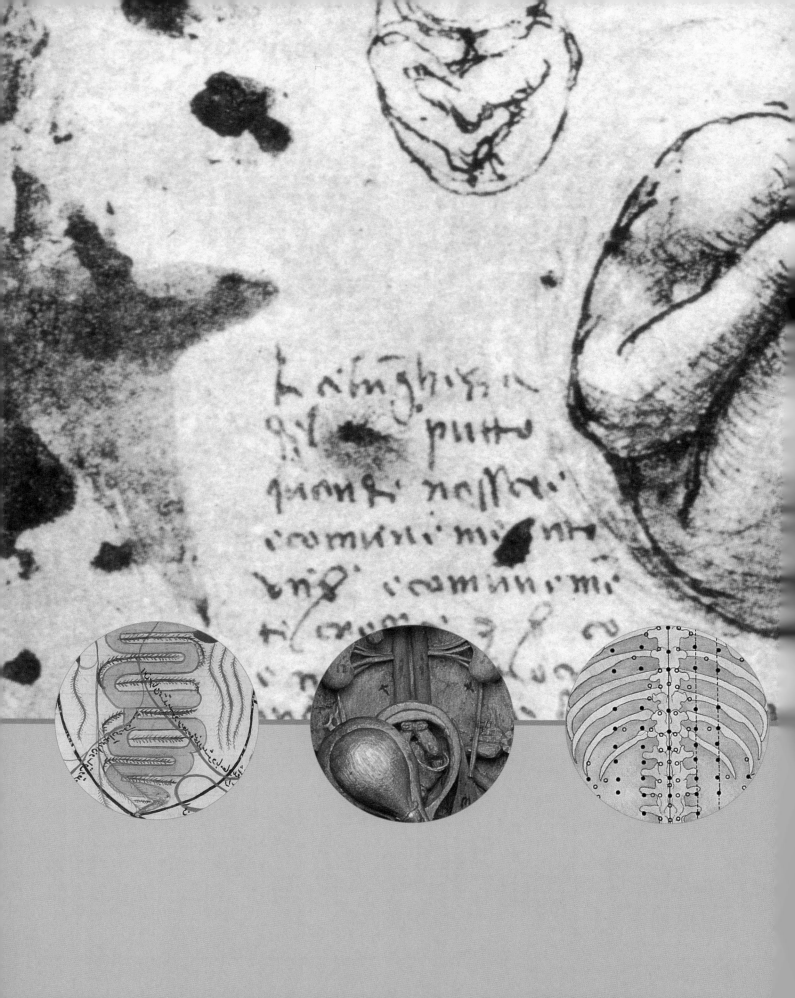

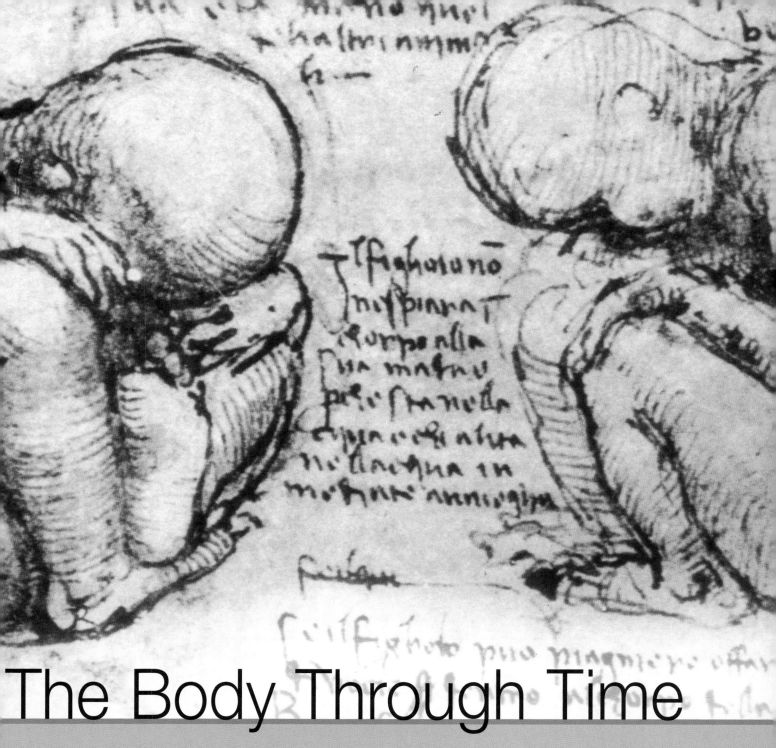

The Body Through Time

THEIR POWERFUL INTELLIGENCE, and ability to analyze, communicate, and record, make human beings unique in the living world. Driven by a natural curiosity, humans have used these skills to study themselves in order to understand both how the body works and why it goes wrong. Over the millennia, human biology and medicine have evolved together across many cultures. The resulting accumulation of knowledge enables 21st-century humans to stay healthier and live longer than their ancient relatives.

Early humans

Scientific measurements of skulls show that larger brain size evolved quickly in ancient human relatives, while walking on two legs instead of four left their hands free to use stone tools. Increasing intelligence and skill in tool use made early humans formidable hunter-gatherers. They may even have learned by trial and error to use herbs to treat illnesses, in the same way as some apes are thought to do today. Combined use of intelligence and hands also allowed them to produce early works of art, revealing an awareness of themselves and their surroundings, which is a characteristic that distinguishes humans from apes.

Proconsul
20 million years ago

ANCIENT RELATIVES
This chart shows the evolutionary sequence from an apelike ancestor, *Proconsul*, that walked on all fours, to ancient hominid (humanlike) relatives and modern humans. The sequence is not a straight line, but a "tree" with dead ends that do not necessarily indicate ancestry.

30,000 years ago

40,000 years ago

100,000 years ago

HUMAN EVOLUTION
Homo ergaster ("handy man") was one of our earliest hominid ancestors and evolved about 1.75 million years ago. *Homo ergaster* was probably a very close relative of *Homo erectus*, the first human species to migrate out of Africa. By hunting and killing animals, it is likely that early humans would have learned about the heart and other organs.

Australopithecus
("southern ape")
5–2 million
years ago

Homo erectus
("upright man")
1.7 million–250,000
years ago

Homo neanderthalensis
(Neanderthal man)
250,000–35,000
years ago

Homo sapiens
(modern man)
100,000 years ago

Traces of our ancestors

Humans belong to the genus *Homo*, and evolved from an apelike ancestor, *Proconsul*. All early humans would have been hunter-gatherers, living on a diet of plants and animals. Neanderthals, an ancient relative of modern *Homo sapiens*, appeared about 250,000 years ago. Archaeological evidence supports the argument that they looked after their sick and probably knew how to set broken bones: the remains of a Neanderthal man found in a cave in Shanidar, Iraq, show crushing injuries that did not directly cause his death. This is deduced from the fact that the bones show signs of healing. Neanderthals also buried their dead. In one Shanidar burial, pollen from seven different flowers was found. Six of these plants have medicinal properties. Was this a coincidence or were these ancient relatives using medicinal plants?

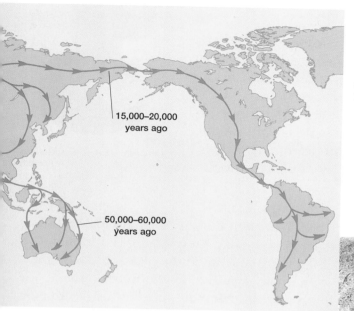

OUT OF AFRICA
The distribution of genes in modern humans shows that *Homo sapiens* evolved in East Africa. They migrated out of Africa about 100,000 years ago. They then traveled across Asia, Europe, Australia, and into North America, eventually reaching South America.

15,000–20,000 years ago

50,000–60,000 years ago

Area of healed bone

EVIL SPIRITS
This preserved skull shows three trepanned holes for allowing evil spirits to escape – a previous hole has healed, which suggests that the person survived the practice. Cave paintings showing men dressed as animals may represent shamans driving away the demons.

MODERN HUMANS
Our ancient ancestors would have used sounds and facial expressions to communicate desires and emotions, just as humans do today. Although they would have had some understanding of the use of plants, they did not know how the body worked and would have explained illnesses in terms of evil spirits. Cave paintings left by *Homo sapiens* are difficult to interpret. But it is likely that the cave painting above right shows a shaman (healing priest) dancing or chanting to drive away evil and illness. Shamans are still found today, practicing their blend of priest's and doctor's duties. There is also evidence to suggest that by 5000 BC, *Homo sapiens* carried out trepanning, or making holes in the skull, to release the evil spirits believed to have caused the illness.

NATURAL REMEDIES
By watching apes, we can find clues to the ways in which early medicine might have begun. Chimpanzees deliberately pick and chew leaves of certain plants, then spit them out. Have they learned that some plants can cure sickness? This might be the way in which our human ancestors learned to use plants as medicines. Unlike apes, humans developed sophisticated language skills, allowing them to pass on this knowledge to their young.

INSTINCTS
Gorillas in West Africa eat several types of plant that are known to help joint pains and other conditions.

The ancient world

MODERN MEDICAL TECHNIQUES have been used to analyze mummified bodies from ancient tombs. The results show that the people of ancient civilizations suffered from illnesses that are still prevalent today, such as gallstones and appendicitis. In the ancient world, sick people believed that they were being punished by their gods for wrongdoing. Although they turned to physicians for treatment, they often put their faith in the hands of priests, who used magic and called upon the gods to take pity and deliver a cure.

IMHOTEP
One of the first great physicians in Egypt was Imhotep (c. 2686–2613 BC), who was elevated to the status of a god

ASSYRIAN STONE TABLET
This stone tablet from the library of Ashurbanipal (668–627 BC), the last great Assyrian ruler, contains advice on remedies for stomach disorders.

MESOPOTAMIAN MEDICINE

Physicians practiced in Mesopotamia – the land between the Tigris and Euphrates rivers, and home to the Sumerian, Assyrian, and Babylonian civilizations. A Sumerian stone tablet dating from 2150 BC shows how physicians provided first aid by washing and binding wounds, and applied poultices made from prunes, pine, and lizard dung. In Assyria, priests were also physicians. They learned their skills from thousands of inscribed stone tablets, such as the one above. Professional physicians existed by the reign of King Hammurabi of Babylon, who ruled from 1792-1750 BC. He established a set of laws called the Code, which stated that surgeons were responsible for their errors. There were rewards for surgeons who cured noblemen and severe punishments, such as cutting off hands, for surgeons whose operations killed patients of high status. But if a slave died, the surgeon only had to replace the slave. Religion also played an important part in Babylonian medicine. This took the form of ritual incantations and appealing to the heavens for help in curing diseases.

EGYPTIAN MEDICINE

Physicians in ancient Egypt were undoubtedly the best doctors of the day. Even kings of Babylonia and of the Hittites wrote to the pharaohs, asking for Egyptian physicians to be sent to treat them. The Ebers papyrus, the oldest medical text, contains remedies that included hippopotamus dung and onions. But such ingredients were only used when all else failed. Surgeons, who were also priests, carried out a limited amount of internal surgery, while providing spiritual comfort to the sufferer.

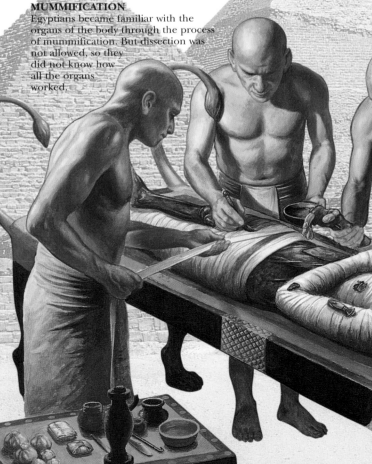

MUMMIFICATION
Egyptians became familiar with the organs of the body through the process of mummification. But dissection was not allowed, so they did not know how all the organs worked.

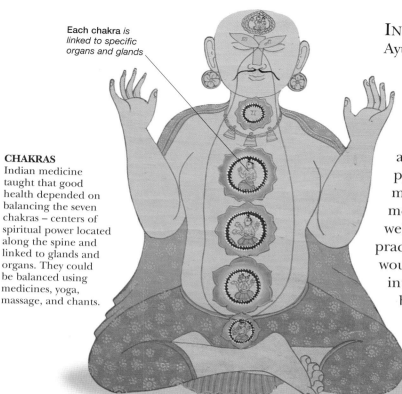

Each chakra *is linked to specific organs and glands*

CHAKRAS
Indian medicine taught that good health depended on balancing the seven chakras – centers of spiritual power located along the spine and linked to glands and organs. They could be balanced using medicines, yoga, massage, and chants.

INDIAN MEDICINE
Ayurveda, which means "knowledge of life," is a system of medicine that was used in ancient India and is still in use today. It treats illnesses by correcting imbalances in the body's three humors – wind (*vaya*), bile (*pitta*), and phlegm (*kapha*). It is likely that the ancient Greek theory of the four humors (see pp. 258–9) orginated in India with Ayervedic medicine. Physicians used chants along with medicine and operations. Surgery was particularly well-developed in ancient India, where practitioners used fine steel needles to sew up wounds, with biting black ants as sutures to close internal wounds. Susruta, who lived some time between 100 BC and AD 100, carried out cosmetic surgery, repairing amputated noses by using skin grafted from the forehead. Trainee surgeons often practiced their skills on meat and leather bags filled with slime before working on real patients.

CHINESE MEDICINE
Harmony and balance were also key elements of Chinese medicine, which by 400 BC had become separated from religion. According to Chinese medical philosophy, harmony between two opposing forces, yin and yang, is essential for good health. The great reference book of Chinese medicine, the *Nei Ching*, was compiled between 479 and 300 BC, based on the wisdom of Emperor Huang Ti (2629–2598 BC). Many of the techniques it describes have survived in traditional medicine in China to the present day. It includes details of using acupuncture to balance yin and yang by controlling the flow of energy (chi) in the body.

PULSE TAKING
Taking the pulse gave Chinese physicians information on how well the chi energy of the body was balanced. Six pulses were counted on each wrist, and described in poetic phrases before treatment was prescribed.

YIN AND YANG
The two fundamental forces in Chinese philosophy – including medicine – are yin and yang. Yin is dark, cool, moist, passive, negative, and female, while yang is light, dry, active, warm, positive, and male. It is believed that illness is caused by an imbalance of these forces.

Ancient Greece and Rome

THE GREEKS WERE INFLUENCED CONSIDERABLY by the Egyptians, and even identified their god of medicine, Asklepios, with the Egyptian god of medicine, Imhotep. Greek medicine was based on a combination of supernatural and natural beliefs. The Greeks prayed to Asklepios for a cure and went to the temples to be healed. However, Hippocrates believed that a disease was not sent or cured by the gods, but had a natural cause and cure. Roman medicine had many similarities, but with emphasis on the importance of preventing disease by providing clean water and sewers in crowded cities. The Romans also adopted the ideas of Greek-born Claudius Galen.

CLAUDIUS GALEN
The influence of the writings of Claudius Galen (c. AD 130–200) lasted until the Renaissance. Many of his teachings contained mistaken ideas about human anatomy.

THE BASIS OF GREEK MEDICINE

Greek medicine taught that illnesses were caused by a lack of balance between four body fluids called humors. These were blood, phlegm, yellow bile, and black bile. The physician Hippocrates (c.460–377 BC) founded a school of medicine on the island of Cos, where pupils learned to diagnose and treat diseases by rebalancing humors. His Hippocratic Oath, which committed doctors to maintaining confidentiality in their consultations with patients and acting only in the patient's best interests, is still followed by doctors today.

THE FOUR HUMORS
The Greeks developed the idea that health was controlled by the balance of four bodily humors. Excess blood was removed by bleeding, while other humors were altered by prescribing herbs or a change in diet.

GREEK PHYSICIANS

Patients visiting a Greek physician would be closely questioned about their symptoms, diet, and lifestyle, and were provided with a prognosis, advising them on the likely progress of their illness. Dissection of human bodies was not allowed in Greece, but was practiced in the city of Alexandria, founded by the Greeks in Egypt. There Herophilus (c. 300 BC), a skilled anatomist, learned to identify arteries and nerves and investigated the structure of the brain.

GREEK DOCTORS
Greek doctors followed the teachings of Hippocrates, who separated magic from medicine. They diagnosed symptoms using methods that included feeling for palpitations and listening to sounds from the patient's chest.

Rome's debt to Greek medicine

When Rome was founded, its people placed great reliance on gods for healing, and when plague struck in 293 BC they called in help from the Greek god Asklepios. They adopted him as their own god and welcomed Greek physicians. Doctors enjoyed privileged status in Rome, free from military service and taxes, so there were many practitioners. There were also women doctors, who worked as midwives and specialists in female disorders.

ASKLEPIOS
Asklepios remains patron saint of physicians. His staff, with its sacred snake, is seen in logos of modern medical organizations such as the World Health Organization.

ROMAN SURGERY
The army of Julius Caesar (c. 100–44 BC) included battlefield surgeons who set up dressing stations. Injured soldiers were sent back to field hospitals (*valetudinaria*), the forerunners of today's hospitals. Roman surgeons were skilled in operations ranging from removal of splinters to amputation of limbs.

Development of Roman medicine

The Roman army was responsible for many of the important developments in medicine. Military campaigns had taught Roman doctors about the nature of wounds and surgery, and they also used gladiators' wounds as "windows into the body." Cornelius Celsus (c. 20 BC–AD 45) compiled an encyclopedia, *De Medicina*, that described in Latin everything there was to know about medicine. It provided advice on clamping veins so casualties would not bleed to death, and included details of delicate operations, such as eye surgery and the removal of bone splinters from head wounds.

Galen and his legacy

Claudius Galen was the most influential physician in Rome. Prevented from dissecting humans, he studied anatomy by dissecting pigs and other animals. Although he made some significant discoveries, such as nerve function, many of his ideas were wrong, such as his reliance on bloodletting. But because they were backed by the Christian church, Galen's ideas would dominate medicine for the next 1,500 years.

Arabic medicine

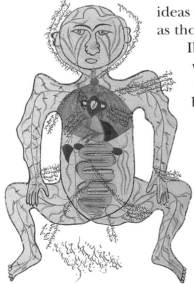

WHEN BARBARIANS DESTROYED THE ROMAN EMPIRE and medicine fell into decline, sick people in Western Europe once again placed their faith in religion and magic. The teachings of Galen and the ancient Greeks survived only because they had been carried eastward to Persia, where Arab scholars translated them into their own languages. As the new religion of Islam spread explosively through the Middle East and North Africa and into Europe, medicine flourished, based on the Greek-Roman model. Hospitals and medical schools were established in cities, where new treatments and more advanced methods of surgery were available. In the 12th century, ancient medical knowledge, saved and enhanced by the Arabs, traveled back to Europe through Spain and Italy.

Scalpel

RHAZES
Although Rhazes (above) was a follower of Galen, he recommended that his teaching should not be followed slavishly, and advocated the use of reason and science in medicine.

MEDICAL ADVANCES

Physicians added new knowledge to the teachings of the Greeks and Romans. Rhazes (c. 850–932) was the first to describe measles and smallpox as separate diseases, and reasoned that fever was part of the body's defense against illness. Avicenna of Persia (980–1037), also known as Ibn Sina, produced his *Canon of Medicine*, which superseded Galen's work and remained influential in medical teaching until the 17th century. Some Arabic ideas were very advanced, such as those of the Syrian physician Ibn an-Nafis (d. 1288 AD), who argued that blood circulated around the body – a theory that would not be proven until the work of William Harvey, 400 years later.

REMEDIES
Medicinal preparations were dispensed by physicians as well as pharmacists. Physicians trained at a *madrasah* (place of lessons), which was attached to a mosque or hospital.

ANATOMICAL DRAWINGS
Anatomical drawings followed the teachings of Galen, and perpetuated his errors. A more accurate understanding of the human body was not possible, since dissection was forbidden under Islamic law.

Scissors

Camphor

Pestle

Surgical knife

Mortar

HERBAL TRADITIONS

During the 9th century, the first private pharmacies opened in Baghdad. Pharmacy came to be viewed as a separate profession from medicine, which was practiced by skilled specialists who had to pass exams and be licensed. The use of herbs played a major role in this development. Arab pharmacists helped to introduce a number of new drugs, such as camphor, senna, and nutmeg. They were the first to develop sweet-tasting syrups for medicine, and used pleasant flavorings, such as rose water and orange blossom water, as a way of disguising the medicine. Eventually, extracting and preparing the medicine became a fine art.

TOOLS OF THE TRADE
Surgeons used finely crafted tools for carrying out operations, while a mortar and pestle was often used for crushing substances. These would then be incorporated into other preparations, such as ointments, pills, and confections.

Cautery irons *were heated like branding irons, and then placed on the affected area to seal the wound*

ARAB SURGEONS
Although surgery did not progress much, surgeons carried out complex operations, and put much faith in cauterizing. They learned their trade from illustrated manuals of surgery, such as *Al-tasrif,* compiled by Abulcasis of Córdoba.

SURGERY

There were three types of surgery carried out by Arab surgeons: vascular, general, and orthopedic (ophthalmic surgery was seen as a separate specialty). Abulcasis (936–1013) was the most famous surgeon in Arabic medicine. His book includes descriptions of various operations, such as correction of spinal deformities, removal of eye cataracts, and even tracheotomy. Today, surgeons still carry out several procedures introduced by Abulcasis.

The Middle Ages

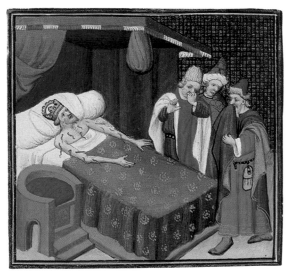

MEDIEVAL TREATMENTS
Bleeding patients to balance their humors and remove poisons remained as important in medieval medicine as it had been in Roman times. Blood was usually drained by applying leeches or cutting open veins from the part of the body closest to the source of illness.

IN THE MIDDLE AGES, between the 5th and 15th centuries, sick people throughout Western Europe accepted illnesses as God's punishment for their sins and believed that terrible plagues, such as the bubonic plague, were expressions of divine wrath. People placed more faith in the prayers of priests than help from physicians, whose treatments often degenerated into blends of superstition and magic. Caring for the sick became an act of Christian charity, with little attempt to use medical science to find cures. Eventually, medical science was revived through the establishment of medical schools based on Arab practices and the rediscovery of Greek teachings, which had been preserved in the Arab world.

MYTH, MAGIC, BUT VERY LITTLE MEDICINE

Treatments remained much as they had been in Galen's day, with a reliance on blood-letting to balance the humors. Uroscopy, the examination of urine samples to look for disease symptoms, was an important form of diagnosis, and many treatments used herbal medicine. Physicians seeking guidance for the use of herbs looked for divine signs by following the Doctrine of Signatures – plants that resembled bodily parts were believed to have been shaped by God to draw attention to their beneficial uses. Purveyors of folk remedies also flourished, offering such unlikely cures as crabs' eyes for sight defects. Major surgery was rare, but minor operations, such as cauterizing wounds with hot irons, were carried out by barbers as a lucrative sideline to shaving and cutting hair.

CARING FOR THE SICK

The Christian Church played an important part in caring for the sick during the Middle Ages. Throughout Europe, hospitals were established and the sick were fed, sheltered, and prayed for, but there were few medical advances that could offer any hope of improved cures. Monks often acted as physicians and followed those parts of Galen's teaching that fitted comfortably with their religious beliefs.

CHRISTIAN CHARITY
Hospitals offered their patients care and comfort but, beyond the use of prayer, there was no method of treating disease.

Rat flea

***Yersinia pestis*
bacteria**

CAUSES OF PLAGUE
The Black Death was caused by the bacterium
Yersinia pestis, named after the French bacteriologist
Alexandre Yersin, who identified it in the late
19th century. The bacterium was transmitted
by biting fleas that lived in the fur of rats.

Black rat

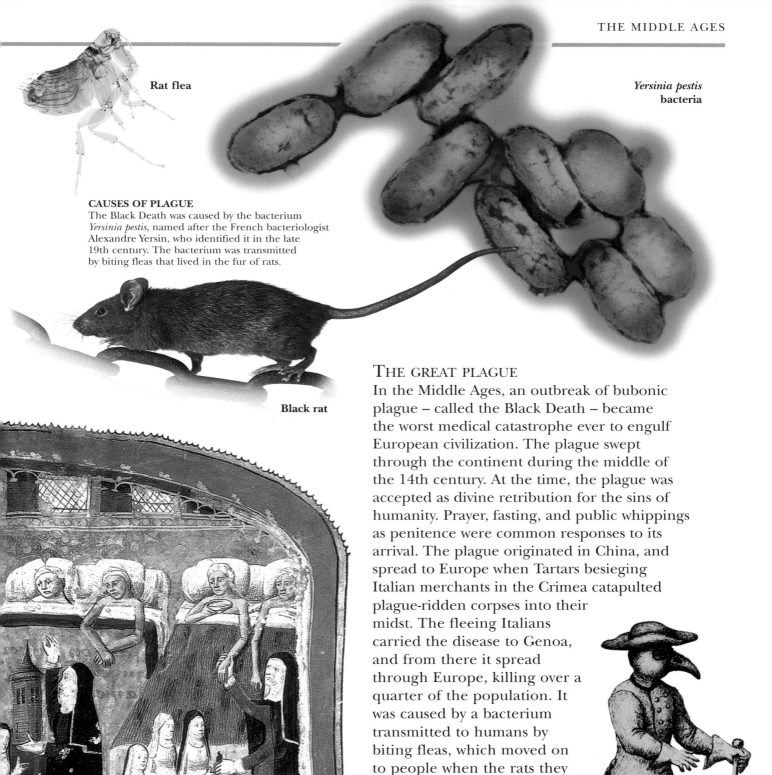

THE GREAT PLAGUE
In the Middle Ages, an outbreak of bubonic
plague – called the Black Death – became
the worst medical catastrophe ever to engulf
European civilization. The plague swept
through the continent during the middle of
the 14th century. At the time, the plague was
accepted as divine retribution for the sins of
humanity. Prayer, fasting, and public whippings
as penitence were common responses to its
arrival. The plague originated in China, and
spread to Europe when Tartars besieging
Italian merchants in the Crimea catapulted
plague-ridden corpses into their
midst. The fleeing Italians
carried the disease to Genoa,
and from there it spread
through Europe, killing over a
quarter of the population. It
was caused by a bacterium
transmitted to humans by
biting fleas, which moved on
to people when the rats they
lived on began to die.

SWEET SMELLS
People tried desperate remedies to
keep the plague at bay. Physicians
wore beaked masks (right) filled
with aromatic herbs that offered
no real protection, but
might have hidden the
stench of decaying bodies.

Renaissance discoveries

BY THE END OF THE MIDDLE AGES, public confidence in physicians and surgeons had reached a low ebb. Then, during the 14th and 15th centuries, the rebirth of interest in arts and sciences in Western Europe, known as the Renaissance, brought important advances in medicine. Physicians and surgeons who read the rediscovered Greek and Roman medical texts questioned their ancient teachings. The anatomical discoveries made during this period finally corrected errors made by Galen over 1,300 years earlier, and new, more accurate knowledge became widely available. Drastic medieval treatments gave way to a philosophy that physicians should try to do as little harm as possible and should encourage natural healing processes.

ACCURATE DRAWINGS
During Galen's lifetime, human dissection was forbidden. His mistaken ideas on anatomy, based on dissections of animals, remained unchallenged until Andreas Vesalius (1514–64) dissected human corpses. His book *De Humani Corporis Fabrica*, published in 1543, provided accurate drawings of human anatomy, such as this woodcut of the circulatory system (left).

ARTIST AND SCIENTIST
Leonardo da Vinci (1452–1519) combined brilliant dissecting and drawing skills with great attention to detail, allowing him to produce scientifically accurate anatomical drawings that were not influenced by Galen's mistakes. Unfortunately, Leonardo's drawings of his dissections, conducted in secret, remained undiscovered for 300 years after his death.

Leonardo's drawing of a fetus in the womb

TREATING THE PATIENT
During the Renaissance, Philipp von Hohenheim, a Swiss physician, questioned the teachings of Galen. He traveled widely and consulted everyone he met about medical treatments. He came to the conclusion that the diet, surroundings, and treatment of the patient all contributed to the recovery process, and that the body and its illnesses needed to be understood before treatments were prescribed. He also rejected complicated herbal potions in favor of simple drugs administered one at a time until a beneficial effect was identified. Paracelsus's ideas shocked many doctors of the time who clung to their belief in the ancient teachings of Galen. But Paracelsus set the tone for a new approach to treatment.

RENAISSANCE REBEL
Philipp von Hohenheim (1493–1541) renamed himself Paracelsus, meaning "above Celsus," because his ideas went beyond those of the Roman physician Celsus.

FAMOSO DOCTOR   PARESELSVS.

TEACHING ANATOMY

During the 15th century, some of the restrictions on human dissection were lifted. This led to a better understanding of human anatomy and helped produce accurate anatomical models such as these, used as teaching aids in medical schools.

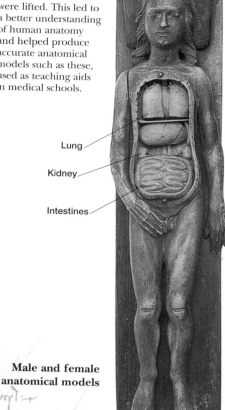

Lung

Kidney

Intestines

Male and female anatomical models

links the ear to the throat. Thanks to the invention of the printing press, their knowledge could be made widely available, aiding the teaching of anatomy and surgery.

BATTLEFIELD DEVELOPMENTS

During the 16th century, new treatments developed amid the carnage of the battlefield. The introduction of gunpowder had produced horrific gunshot wounds that quickly became infected. The injured often died of pain and shock when these wounds were treated by scorching them with hot oil or sealing them with hot irons. It was only by chance that a French barber-surgeon, Ambroise Paré, developed a wound dressing made from egg yolk, rose oil, and turpentine that was more effective and less painful. Paré also realized that after an amputation, tying a ligature around the blood vessels would help to stem the flow of blood. He continued to help wounded soldiers by designing artificial limbs. Paré had no formal medical training, so his ideas were not always adopted by other surgeons.

THE ANATOMIST'S KNIFE

Religious disapproval of dissection of human bodies finally gave way under pressure from Renaissance anatomists, who wanted to test the accuracy of Galen's observations. Andreas Vesalius was typical of the new breed of scientific inquirer. While professor of anatomy at Padua University, Italy, he publicly dissected corpses of executed criminals and proved that the human liver was not identical to that of a pig, as Galen had claimed. Vesalius also trained assistants, including Gabriel Fallopius (1523–62) and Bartolommeo Eustachio (1520–74). Fallopius investigated the female reproductive system and discovered the tubes leading from the uterus to the ovaries, now called fallopian tubes. Eustachio dissected the head and found the tube that bears his name, the eustachian tube, which

TREATING WOUNDS

Ambroise Paré (1510–90) had firsthand experience of battlefield wounds. He replaced boiling oil with gentle dressings as a treatment for gunshot wounds. He also rejected hot irons for cauterizing amputated stumps, in favor of tying off cut blood vessels with ligatures.

The scientific age

THE PERIOD CALLED THE ENLIGHTENMENT, between the 17th and 18th centuries, brought new understanding of the workings of the human body. Galen's teachings were swept aside by the scientific methods of William Harvey and other anatomists who revealed the true functions of the body's organs. French philosopher René Descartes (1596–1650) described the body as a machine, and illness as a breakdown of its functions. Technical advances laid the foundations for the study of the body's tissues, cells, and infections. At last, science was directing medical progress, but understanding how the body worked did not guarantee that illnesses could be treated.

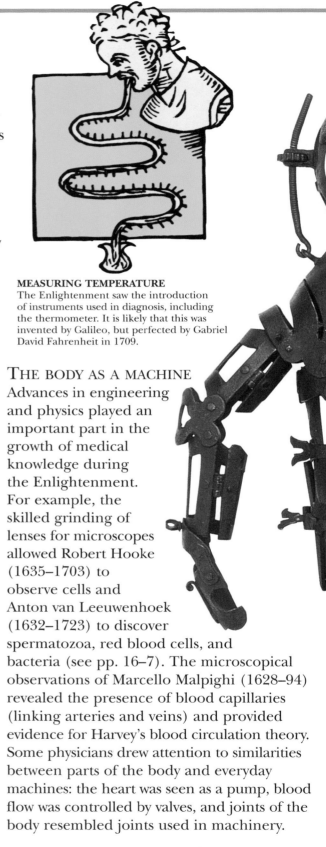

MEASURING TEMPERATURE
The Enlightenment saw the introduction of instruments used in diagnosis, including the thermometer. It is likely that this was invented by Galileo, but perfected by Gabriel David Fahrenheit in 1709.

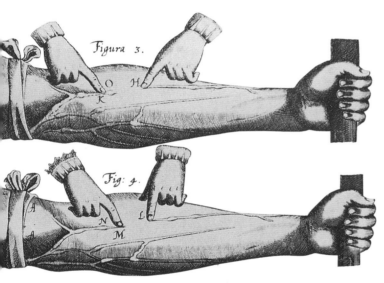

BLOOD CIRCULATION
William Harvey first recorded his belief that blood circulates around the body in 1603, but fierce opposition deterred him from publicizing his ideas until he had experimental proof. By applying and releasing pressure to veins (above), he showed that they emptied, then refilled with blood, demonstrating that valves allow blood to flow in one direction only.

THE ECLIPSE OF GALEN

The old idea that balancing the body's "humors" would maintain health gradually fell out of favor, as anatomists' dissections revealed that diseased organs often caused illness and death. Then, in 1628, William Harvey (1578–1657) published his *De Motu Cordis*, proving through a series of careful experiments that blood circulated through arteries and veins, pumped by the heart. The ancient belief that the body manufactures and consumes blood each day was swept aside.

THE BODY AS A MACHINE

Advances in engineering and physics played an important part in the growth of medical knowledge during the Enlightenment. For example, the skilled grinding of lenses for microscopes allowed Robert Hooke (1635–1703) to observe cells and Anton van Leeuwenhoek (1632–1723) to discover spermatozoa, red blood cells, and bacteria (see pp. 16–7). The microscopical observations of Marcello Malpighi (1628–94) revealed the presence of blood capillaries (linking arteries and veins) and provided evidence for Harvey's blood circulation theory. Some physicians drew attention to similarities between parts of the body and everyday machines: the heart was seen as a pump, blood flow was controlled by valves, and joints of the body resembled joints used in machinery.

BODY MECHANICS
This model, designed to teach students the principles of bone setting and the workings of joints and limbs, may have been invented by Hieronymous Fabricius (1537–1619).

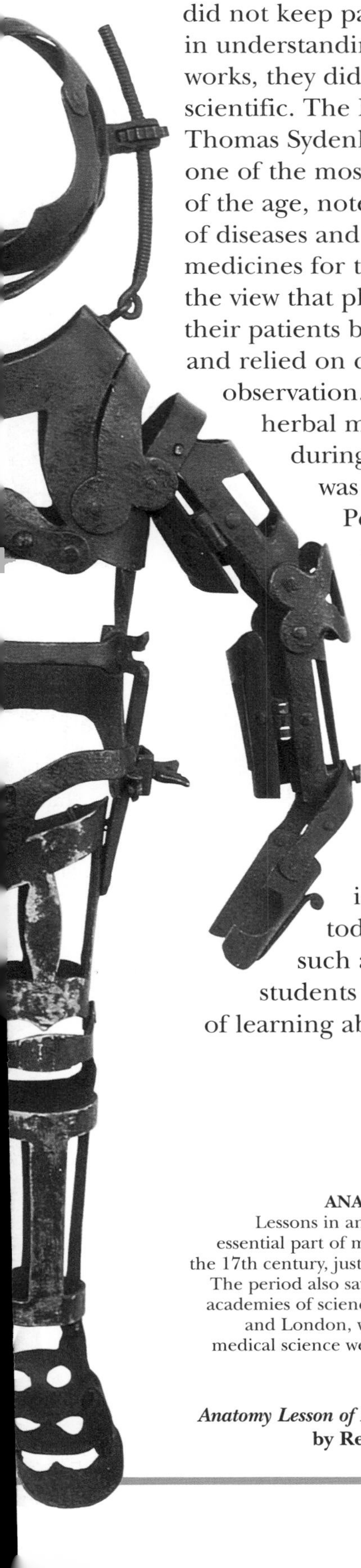

TREATING PATIENTS

Although treatments for illnesses did not keep pace with advances in understanding how the body works, they did become more scientific. The English physician Thomas Sydenham (1624–89) was one of the most respected physicians of the age, noted for his descriptions of diseases and prescription of specific medicines for treating them. He held the view that physicians should put their patients before testing theories, and relied on common sense and observation. Understanding of herbal medicines improved during this period. Sydenham was the first to prescribe Peruvian bark (the source of quinine) to treat malaria. Dutch physician Herman Boerhaave (1668–1738), who greatly admired Sydenham's ideas, established a reputation for encouraging careful scientific diagnosis and recording detailed case histories. Some of his ideas are still used in today's teaching methods, such as the involvement of students in postmortems as a way of learning about the cause of death.

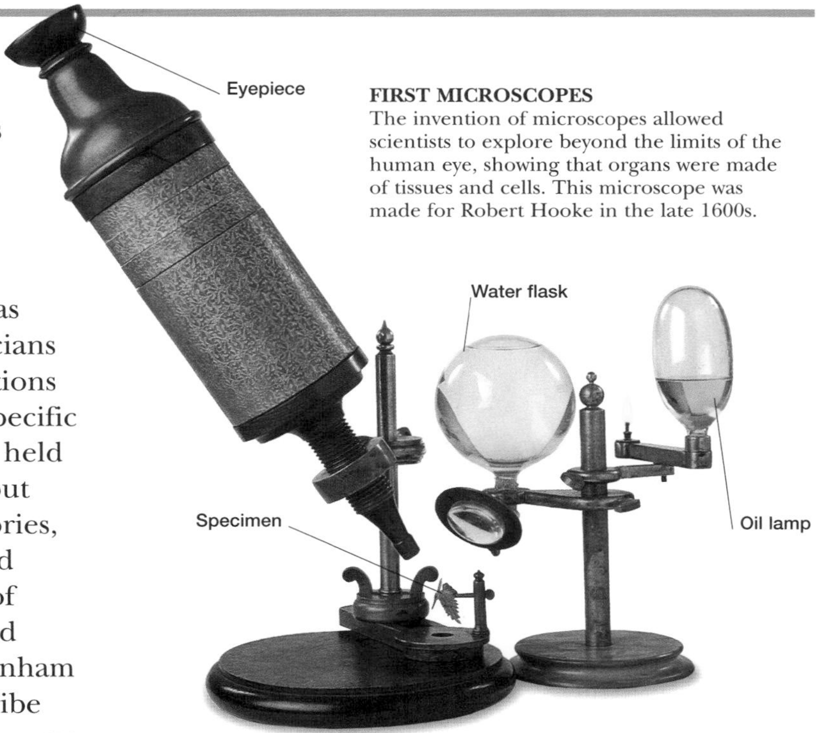

FIRST MICROSCOPES
The invention of microscopes allowed scientists to explore beyond the limits of the human eye, showing that organs were made of tissues and cells. This microscope was made for Robert Hooke in the late 1600s.

Eyepiece

Water flask

Specimen

Oil lamp

MEDICINE AS A PROFESSION

The status of surgeons rose as knowledge of the workings and defects of the internal organs increased, but surgery remained a frightening and risky ordeal. Lack of anesthetics meant that conscious patients screamed in agony when surgeons operated, and abdominal surgery was rare because many patients died of postoperative infections. But by the end of the 17th century, the scientific approach to anatomy, surgery, and the treatment of illness was firmly established. Medicine in all its forms was becoming a respected profession.

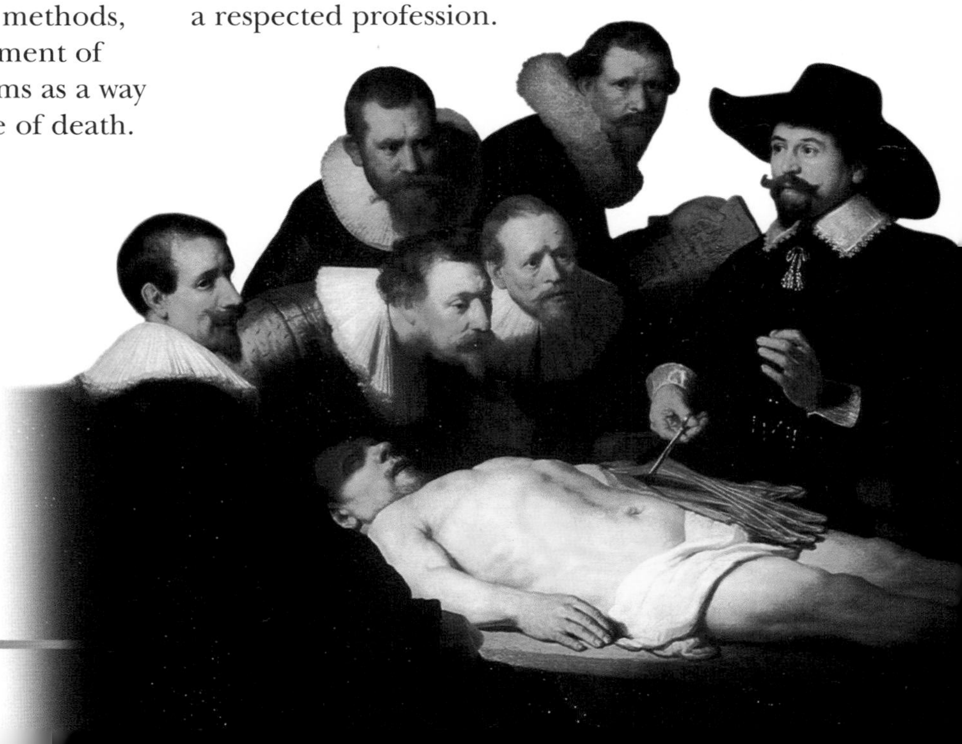

ANATOMY LESSONS
Lessons in anatomy became an essential part of medical training in the 17th century, just as they are today. The period also saw the founding of academies of science in Rome, Paris, and London, where advances in medical science were hotly debated.

Anatomy Lesson of Dr. Nicolaes Tulp
by Rembrandt (1632)

Advances in surgery

JOHN HUNTER
John Hunter turned surgery into a science. He dedicated his career to comparative anatomy and experimental surgery.

Aᴛ ᴛʜᴇ ʙᴇɢɪɴɴɪɴɢ ᴏꜰ ᴛʜᴇ 19ᴛʜ ᴄᴇɴᴛᴜʀʏ, people who discovered that they needed an amputation received the news almost as a death sentence. Enduring the pain, at a time when no effective anesthetics were available, was bad enough. The best they could hope for was a surgeon who worked swiftly. And after the operation, wounds always became infected, so as many as half of all amputees died. By the end of the century, two major advances – the introduction of anesthetics and the use of antiseptics – had drastically reduced the trauma of surgery and the risk of death from infections.

Sᴡɪꜰᴛ, ᴀɢᴏɴɪᴢɪɴɢ ᴏᴘᴇʀᴀᴛɪᴏɴs

During the 18th century, brothers John (1728–93) and William Hunter (1718–83) transformed surgery from a lowly trade into a medical science. But for patients it remained a subject of dread and despair. They remained fully conscious throughout major operations, often screaming in agony. Many surgeons prided themselves in being able to work quickly, cutting off a leg in less than three minutes and so minimizing their patients' suffering.

Pᴀɪɴʟᴇss sᴜʀɢᴇʀʏ

Several dentists experimented in the 1840s with ether as an anesthetic for numbing pain during tooth extractions. In 1846, American dentist William Morton (1819–68) persuaded a surgeon called John Collins Warren (1778–1856) to use ether on a patient during the removal of a neck tumor at Massachusetts General Hospital in Boston. The unconscious patient barely murmured during the 25-minute operation. The era of painless surgery had arrived. The introduction of anesthetics allowed surgeons to operate slowly and carefully, and to attempt complicated operations that were impossible when patients struggled in agony.

SURGICAL INSTRUMENTS
It is no coincidence that these instruments (right), used for amputations, look more like a carpenter's tools. Until the 18th century, surgery was a craft, not a science. Although surgical instruments were made of polished wood and steel to allow easy cleaning, surgeons did not sterilize instruments between operations.

FAST WORK
Before anesthetics became available, patients cried out in pain throughout the operation, and had to be tied down, as shown above. The need to minimize patients' suffering meant that surgeons achieved fame for speed, not precision.

KILLER INFECTIONS

Before the mid-19th century, deaths from infections after surgery were so common that patients had less chance of survival than a soldier at the Battle of Waterloo. Hungarian doctor Ignaz Semmelweiss (1818–65) showed that deaths of new mothers could be reduced if medical staff washed their hands, but surgeons rarely did this or sterilized their instruments (see pp. 232–3). The turning point came in 1865, when Joseph Lister (1827–1912) introduced carbolic acid spray to kill germs. Until Lister's day, surgeons did not realize that bacteria caused infections. Like Galen (see p. 259), they believed that pus in wounds was part of the natural healing process.

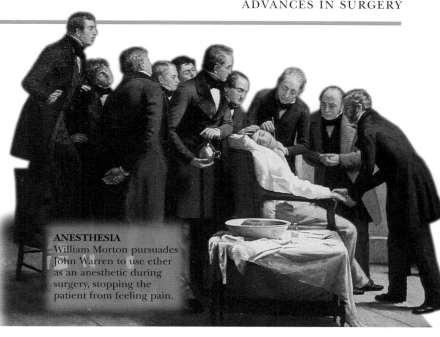

ANESTHESIA
William Morton pursuades John Warren to use ether as an anesthetic during surgery, stopping the patient from feeling pain.

THE OPERATING ROOM

Operating rooms were built as theaters, where students – sometimes coughing and sneezing – sat in tiers of seats, watching surgeons perform. Lister insisted on thorough cleaning of operating rooms, so he used carbolic acid spray to kill germs. His first great success came when he saved the leg of an 11-year-old boy who had been run over by a cart. The compound fracture of the boy's leg was so bad that the leg would normally have been amputated immediately, but Lister set the fracture and sterilized it with carbolic acid. The boy's leg healed, enabling him to walk out of the hospital within six weeks. Lister struggled to overcome doubts from rival surgeons, but when he successfully operated on Queen Victoria using carbolic acid spray, his reputation was made, and antiseptics became a feature of surgical operations.

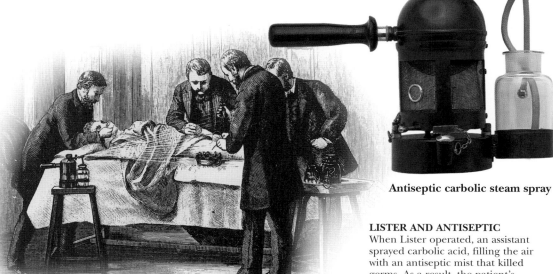

Antiseptic carbolic steam spray

LISTER AND ANTISEPTIC
When Lister operated, an assistant sprayed carbolic acid, filling the air with an antiseptic mist that killed germs. As a result, the patient's chances of surviving surgery dramatically increased.

Microbe hunters

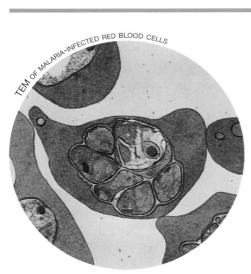

TEM OF MALARIA-INFECTED RED BLOOD CELLS

MALARIAL MICROBE
These red blood cells are infected with *Plasmodium*, the single-celled parasite identified in 1880 by Charles Laveran as the cause of malaria. Infected cells rupture periodically, releasing parasites that invade other red blood cells, and causing the high fever that is typical of the disease.

Tʜʀᴏᴜɢʜᴏᴜᴛ ʀᴇᴄᴏʀᴅᴇᴅ ʜɪsᴛᴏʀʏ, humankind has been plagued by diseases. But at the beginning of the 19th century, doctors and scientists still had no clear idea of what caused diseases, apart from rather vague notions of poor hygiene or bad air. One hundred years later, everything had changed, thanks to two pioneering scientists: French bacteriologist Louis Pasteur (1822–95) and German doctor Robert Koch (1843–1910). Together Pasteur and Koch developed the "germ theory" of disease. This states that it is microbes – microorganisms such as bacteria – that are the cause of many diseases. Once germ theory had been established, microbe hunters rapidly identified the causes of prominent diseases, including cholera, tuberculosis (TB), and malaria. Other researchers investigated how diseases are passed from person to person.

Mɪᴀsᴍᴀs ᴀɴᴅ ᴍɪsᴜɴᴅᴇʀsᴛᴀɴᴅɪɴɢ

Although Dutch microscopist Anton van Leeuwenhoek (see pp. 16–17) first described the microorganisms now called bacteria in 1683, this had little impact on medicine. By the mid-19th century, many doctors still held that diseases were caused by miasma, a mysterious toxic vapor that arose from stagnant water, slums, and feces. Although doctors knew that bacteria occurred in wounds and diseased tissues, it was generally assumed that their presence was incidental and could be explained by "spontaneous generation" – the belief that new life could arise from decaying material, just as maggots seemed to "appear" on rotting meat.

LOUIS PASTEUR
The groundbreaking work of this pioneer microbe hunter simultaneously established the germ theory of disease and demolished the old notion of spontaneous generation. Although he trained to be a chemist, and had been a professor of chemistry, Pasteur was to become the first-ever bacteriologist – a scientist who studies bacteria.

MIASMAS
The theory that these mysterious vapors caused disease was still widely believed in the mid-19th century.

ROBERT KOCH
A brilliant observer, Robert Koch (left) examines bacteria under the microscope, carefully drawing what he sees. Beside him are petri dishes – circular, shallow glass dishes with an overlapping lid – in which he grew bacteria on a solid, nutrient-rich gel.

Robert Koch's drawing of cholera bacteria

GERM THEORY

It was this idea that bacteria were "innocent bystanders" that would be put to the test by Louis Pasteur and Robert Koch. Pasteur's initial interest in microbes arose because of research he undertook into winemaking and milk production. He devised simple experiments to show that micro-organisms caused both wine and milk to go sour. Pasteur went on to explore the role of microbes in causing diseases in silkworms, farm animals, and eventually humans. He also designed experiments to prove that bacteria could not appear from nothing, thereby destroying the idea of spontaneous generation. Pasteur's germ theory of disease was further strengthened by a man 21 years his junior. Robert Koch was a meticulous investigator who was the first to show that each infectious disease – one caught by coming into contact with microbes – is caused by a specific microorganism. He laid down rules to prove the bacterial causes of specific diseases, which included isolating bacteria from an infected person and injecting them into an animal to see if it caught the disease. Two of his great

discoveries were the bacterium that causes TB, in 1882, and the bacterium that causes cholera, in 1884.

IDENTIFYING MICROBES

Pasteur and Koch's discoveries triggered a wave of new research. The microbes that caused a wide range of diseases, including diphtheria, leprosy, and tetanus, were identified. Microbes called viruses, which are much smaller than bacteria, were discovered. French doctor Charles Laveran (1845–1922) identified *Plasmodium* – a single-celled organism known as a protist – as the cause of the tropical disease malaria. How diseases spread was also investigated. Some were found to be communicated by direct contact, air, food, or water, but others remained a mystery. But, in 1897, British scientist Ronald Ross showed that malaria was spread by *Anopheles* mosquitoes as they fed on human blood. Then, in 1900, an American team of doctors in Cuba found another mosquito, called *Aëdes aegypti*, to be the carrier of the virus that caused the deadly disease yellow fever.

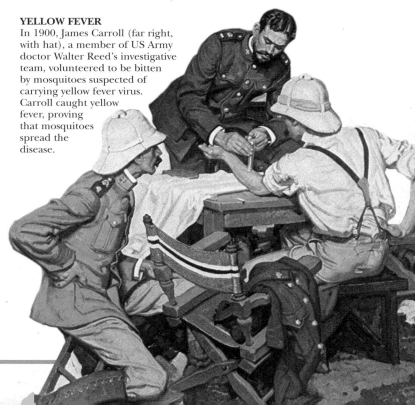

YELLOW FEVER
In 1900, James Carroll (far right, with hat), a member of US Army doctor Walter Reed's investigative team, volunteered to be bitten by mosquitoes suspected of carrying yellow fever virus. Carroll caught yellow fever, proving that mosquitoes spread the disease.

Public health

SCOURGE OF CHOLERA
Cholera caused panic when it reached Europe from India in the early 19th century. This woman is taking extra precautions. The disease strikes victims with devastating suddenness, kills by causing uncontrollable diarrhea and dehydration, and spreads quickly in polluted water supplies. The first cases of cholera in England occurred in 1831.

CITIES GREW QUICKLY during the Industrial Revolution, when millions of people migrated into cities in search of employment. In these rapidly expanding cities, polluted air and water, poor nutrition, and overcrowding in slums with primitive sewer systems were all factors that encouraged epidemics of contagious diseases. Particularly feared were epidemics of cholera that swept through European and American cities at different times throughout the 19th century. Boats arriving in the United States that were suspected of carrying cholera-infected immigrants from Europe were turned away. As the century advanced, measures were taken in European and American cities to improve public health and prosperity by providing clean water and safe sanitation. London was one of the first cities to take such steps.

RECIPE FOR DISASTER

People flooded into London and other European cities during the Industrial Revolution, seeking employment in the new factories that paid regular wages. They often lived in narrow streets of hastily built slum dwellings that sprang up around factories, sometimes with as many as 50 people in a single house. They drew their water from a communal well, poured sewage into drains and rivers, and went about their daily lives in surroundings that were polluted by their local industries. No wonder, then, that when infectious disease struck these communities, the disease spread like wildfire.

THE SPECTER OF CHOLERA

Cholera first arrived in Europe in 1817. It has a short incubation period of as little as one day, causes violent vomiting and diarrhea, and, if not treated, kills half of its victims. When the disease arrived in the crowded slums of industrialized cities, it created terror and panic.

One outbreak, in 1848, killed 7,000 Londoners in a single month. John Snow (1813–58) studied the disease and by 1849 already suspected that it infected the body via food and water, rather than as a miasma in the air.

POOR CONDITIONS
In the 18th and 19th centuries, the development of factories in urban areas lured increasing numbers of people into cities in search of work and a better life. Crowded slums with primitive sanitation sprang up in poor districts, creating perfect conditions for disease to take hold.

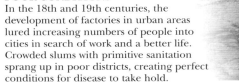

JOHN SNOW AND THE BROAD STREET PUMP
In 1854, English doctor John Snow (1813–58) mapped the homes of 700 cholera victims during an outbreak in London and found that they were clustered around a single pump on Broad Street that they had all used as a water supply. Snow persuaded the authorities to take the pump out of action by removing its handle, and in three days the epidemic was over. Later analysis of the water supply showed that it had been contaminated with sewage.

Broad Street water pump

But few people accepted his theory that it was transmitted through the victims' dried vomit and feces, which contaminated drinking water. Then, in 1854, another epidemic broke out in the part of London called Soho, killing 700 people. Snow found that most local people drew water from a hand pump on Broad Street. His suspicions that this was the source of the epidemic were strengthened when he mapped the location of cases and found that they were all within 500 yd (450 m) of the pump. He persuaded the local authorities to take the pump out of use by removing the handle, and the epidemic stopped. Later investigations showed that cholera-contaminated sewage had leaked into the water supply. Snow's deductions became a classic example of epidemiology – the study of the spread of infectious disease – and drew attention to the urgent need for safe water supplies.

THE POLITICS OF PUBLIC HEALTH
It was social reformer Sir Edwin Chadwick (1800–90) who realized that poor public health and disease

epidemics were more than a matter of human misery. In a report to the British government in 1842, he described the links between living conditions, disease, and poverty, and described how an unhealthy workforce caused economic losses. His Public Health Act of 1848 focused attention on the need for clean water supplies and better sewers in towns and cities. Flush toilets, sewage treatment plants, and piped clean water supplies played a vital role in preventing the spread of infectious diseases. With better hygiene, better food, and the development of public hospitals for treatment of the poor, the health of the urban population improved, and the high infant mortality rates in major cities declined.

SEWAGE CONTROL
In 1842, Edwin Chadwick produced a report for the British government that highlighted the problem of sewage as a cause of disease. This led to the passing of the Public Health Act of 1848. The overpowering stench of the sewage-laden Thames River, flowing past the Houses of Parliament, also helped to persuade politicians that London needed a new sewage system. The construction of sewers (above) in the second half of the 19th century allowed sewage to be removed and treated efficiently.

FLUSH TOILET
Although water washed away waste in Roman times, it was not until the late-19th century that water closets, like this one, were introduced into homes. These water closets helped to flush waste into sewers.

Modernizing medicine

A CENTURY OF SCIENTIFIC DISCOVERIES has produced spectacular improvements in the diagnosis and treatment of illnesses, and in a patient's prospects for recovery. Progress in detecting internal damage to the body has allowed doctors to diagnose internal diseases that once could only have been found with major surgery. The development of drugs targeting specific diseases helped to produce more effective treatments. Cleaner surgical techniques and the discovery of antibiotics have kept bacteria, the surgeon's old enemy, at bay. Scientific research continues to revolutionize medicine, providing ever-improving prospects for recovery from illness and injury.

ANTIBIOTICS
The bacteria-destroying properties of penicillin were discovered by Alexander Fleming (above) in 1928.

MODERN SURGERY
Absolute cleanliness is the first line of defense against bacterial infections during surgery. Thorough sterilization of operating rooms, use of sterilized or disposable instruments, scrubbing of hands, and wearing of surgical gowns, masks, and rubber gloves all minimize the risk of infection.

HIDDEN PROBLEMS REVEALED

In 1895, Wilhelm Roentgen (1845–1923) discovered X-rays and found they could be used to produce an image of bones and hard objects inside the body. Roentgen's discovery led to the development of noninvasive medicine, in which radiation is used to form images of the body's internal condition without the use of surgery. Today, hospital scanning machines can produce detailed images of soft tissues and assess their condition using ultrasound or electrical sensors. The development of tests that aid diagnosis – such as blood and urine tests to check for chemical abnormalities, and tests using a microscope to detect abnormal cells – has allowed doctors to identify early signs of illness, which is essential for improving chances of a complete cure.

MAGIC BULLETS

Paul Ehrlich (1854–1915) developed the idea of the "magic bullet" – a drug that would attack the diseased part of the body without damaging healthy cells and tissues. In 1910, after a long search, Ehrlich identified a compound called salvarsan, which could be used to treat potentially fatal syphilis infections. The modern pharmaceutical industry still searches for magic bullet drugs to treat specific diseases without harmful side effects.

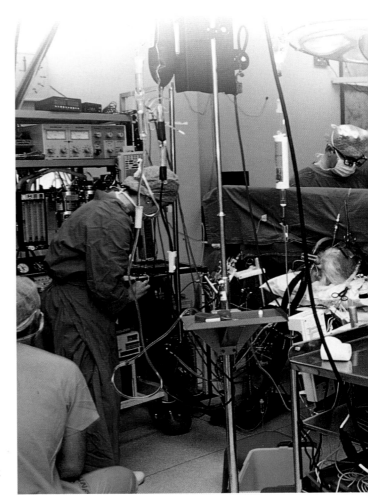

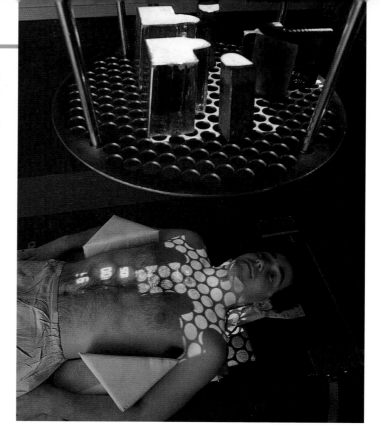

RADIOTHERAPY
High-energy radiation kills cells. If it is carefully targeted, the radiation can be used to destroy abnormal growths, tumors, and cancerous cells without long-term damage to the rest of the body. The rays can be focused on the cancerous cells using a machine (right), or capsules of radiation-emitting chemicals can be implanted next to a tumor.

BEATING BACTERIA

Antibiotics were the most important 20th-century drug discoveries, because they kill a broad range of bacteria. Bacterial infection of burns and wounds was a major cause of death until antibiotics became available. The first, penicillin, was discovered by Alexander Fleming (1885–1955) in 1928, but only went into large-scale production in 1938, just in time to save millions of lives during World War II. Preventing diseases is as important as curing them, especially when they are caused by bacteria that can become resistant to antibiotics. Aseptic techniques in surgery, which demand absolute cleanliness, have become vital in preventing these infections and ensuring that antibiotics remain an effective weapon against bacteria.

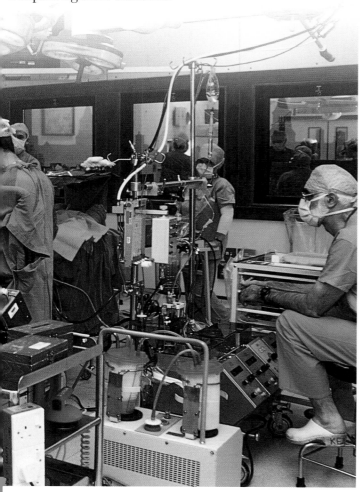

TREATMENTS AND ARTIFICIAL ORGANS

Today many more illnesses can be cured, thanks to accurate diagnosis and treatments that more precisely target the source of diseases. Techniques such as radiotherapy, using high doses of focused radiation to kill diseased cells, can be combined with drug treatments to cure diseases, such as some cancers, that would once have been fatal. Worn and damaged body parts can be replaced with artificial joints, while advances in medical technology, using microelectronics and microprocessors, have produced artificial limbs that mimic arms and hands. And while organ transplant technology can replace damaged hearts, the shortage of donor organs has led to the development of the first mechanical hearts, which can prolong the life of a patient until a donor organ becomes available.

REPLACEMENT PARTS
Microelectronic circuits and compact, long-lasting batteries have allowed medical technologists to develop artificial limbs that can perform the complicated movements of a real hand, arm, or leg.

Alternative therapies

TODAY, IF PEOPLE ARE SICK, we expect modern medical science to provide a cure, which might come in the form of a drug or drastic surgery. Our ancient ancestors had to rely on simpler treatments. These included meditation, herbal remedies, and treatments applied to the body surface in an effort to promote better health. These ancient medical methods have survived and can be used, in combination with modern alternative therapies, such as osteopathy and aromatherapy, to complement modern medicine.

Map of the body's acupuncture points

Chamomile plant **Mother tincture** **Diluted tincture** **Further diluted tincture**

LIKE CURES LIKE
German doctor Samuel Hahnemann devised the therapy called homeopathy, based on the claim that if high doses of a substance produce symptoms resembling an illness, then small doses of the same substance could be used to cure that illness. Homeopathic treatments are based on plants, such as chamomile, or mineral, or animal products, diluted hundreds of thousands of times.

HOLISTIC MEDICINE
Modern science-based medicine has produced great benefits for humanity, eliminating diseases such as smallpox and providing effective treatments for illnesses that were once always fatal, such as diabetes. But many people argue that the achievements of modern medicine should not eclipse the benefits of traditional treatments, which have much to offer in our search for health. There is a growing belief that modern medical science and the older teachings can complement one another. Modern scientific medicine often uses technologically advanced treatments that target specific parts of the body, while holistic medicine treats the health of the whole – body and mind together. Many supporters of holistic medicine believe that we would not need drastic modern treatments so often if we recognized the benefits of traditional Chinese and Indian medicine, combined with more recently developed alternative techniques, such as osteopathy and reflexology.

ACUPUNCTURE
In the ancient Chinese practice of acupuncture, the balance of yin and yang in the body is corrected by inserting fine needles in specific places, stimulating the body's energy channels. Different acupuncture systems have mapped as many as 600 points on the body (right) where insertion of needles may have a beneficial effect.

ANCIENT PHILOSOPHIES
The ancient medical methods of Indian Ayurvedic and Chinese medicine are still practiced in their countries of origin, and many people in the Western world also choose to have their ailments treated in this way. Chinese acupuncture clinics use the insertion of needles in places that influence one or more of the 12 major energy pathways in the body.

According to Chinese medical philosophy there are two opposing forces in the body, yin and yang, which are balanced in the healthy body and disturbed during illness. Acupuncture, aided by herbal treatments, rebalances yin and yang.

Herbal treatments also play a major role in Indian Ayurvedic medicine, and there is scientific proof that some of these are effective. For example, snake root, used in Ayurvedic medicine, contains a compound called reserpine, which acts as a sedative and reduces blood pressure. Ayurvedic medicine also emphasizes the importance of meditation and whole-body relaxation in the maintenance of health, while the postures and breathing exercises used in yoga are designed to promote mental and physical well-being.

AYURVEDIC MEDICINE
Ayurveda is the traditional Indian holistic system of medicine, which evolved between 600 and 100 BC. Ayurveda makes extensive use of herbs to treat imbalances, but it is also a philosophy for physical health, based on moderation in lifestyle, meditation, and a harmonious relationship with the environment.

developed the concept of reflexology, in which foot massage is used to treat health problems in other parts of the body. Aromatherapy uses essential oils, or aromatic essences, such as lavender oil. These oils are diluted with vegetable oil and massaged into the skin. At the same time, the patient breathes in the aromatic essences as they evaporate. Each oil is believed to have its own medicinal effect.

RECENT DEVELOPMENTS

More recent developments in holistic medicine have been added to those that were handed down from ancient physicians. Samuel Hahnemann (1755–1843) developed the therapy of homeopathy. He described herbal potions that cause symptoms of common illnesses when they are given at high doses, and claimed that the same potions cured these illnesses when they were administered in extremely diluted doses. American doctor Andrew Taylor Still (1828–1917) promoted the practice of osteopathy, in which the maintenance and manipulation of the spine is considered to be a key to health. In 1930, Eunice Ingham

OSTEOPATHY
Osteopathy emphasizes the importance of good walking, sitting, standing, and lifting postures, and uses manipulation and massage of the spine to correct defects.

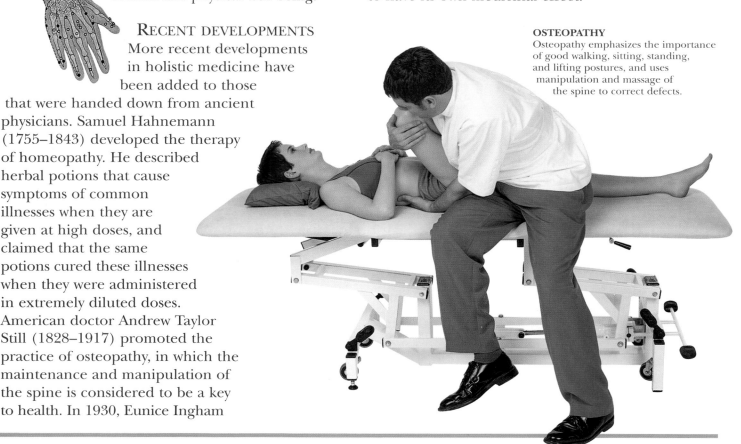

The body today

FOOD GATHERERS
Humans evolved as energetic hunter-gatherers, spending part of every day collecting food. The body has changed very little over the last 10,000 years, since agriculture and settled civilization developed.

MOST HUMAN SOCIETIES have left their Stone Age hunter-gatherer origins far behind. Our reasoning ability and technological skills have provided large sections of the population in the developed world with work that needs little physical effort. Our diet delivers surplus energy from fatty food, and we have a choice of tempting leisure activities that exercise our minds but not our bodies. Lifestyles in the developed world have changed a great deal, but our bodies, which evolved to cope with the daily physical stresses of gathering food, have not. Obesity and stress-related illness now rival infectious diseases as major threats to human health. Medical science can provide us with a better understanding of the way our body works, and with better treatments for its illnesses, but regular exercise and a balanced and varied diet are as important for our survival today as they were for our ancestors.

STONE AGE VERSUS MODERN AGE

Imagine for a moment that you are a hunter-gatherer. As dawn breaks, your first thought is to collect and catch food for the day. You will need to travel many miles on foot to find it, always alert to dangers posed by predatory animals and ready to run for your life. Physical fitness is vital for your survival. Now imagine daily life as an urban office worker. Your first thought in the morning is to grab a quick breakfast. Then you worry about the traffic jams that will make you late for work. All day you sit at a computer, dealing with stressful problems, with just a short break for a burger at lunch. When you arrive home, you are so tired that all you can do is microwave a frozen dinner and sit in front of the television until bedtime.

HEALTHY EXERCISE
Enjoying the full benefits of modern society depends on recognizing the nutritional and physical needs of the body. We no longer chase and trap our next meal, but by taking full advantage of sports and exercise facilities, we can maintain our health.

MODERN DIET
Preprepared foods that can be cooked quickly may be very convenient for busy modern lifestyles, but a diet based on these alone, combined with lack of physical exercise, is a recipe for obesity and heart disease. Fresh foods, particularly fruits and vegetables, are essential for a healthy diet.

YOUR BODY

Physical fitness is still vital for your survival today, because your 21st-century body works in exactly the same way as the body of a Stone Age hunter. Our lifestyles may have changed, but our bodies have not evolved to cope with a life that involves sitting down all day, eating a diet with a high fat intake and fewer vegetables and fruits, and living with constant levels of background stress. If we ignore the physical and nutritional requirements of the body, we can expect to suffer from obesity, heart problems, diseases like diabetes, and a shortened lifespan. The key to maximizing our chances for a long and healthy life in our modern society is to take the time and trouble to maintain fitness through a balanced diet and regular exercise.

STRESS
The stresses of modern life often arise from daily frustrations at work or during travel. These stresses operate continuously over long periods of time, undermining mental and physical health.

LESS ACTIVITY
Technological advances have removed much of the physical effort from daily life. Travel, work, and leisure activities involve more sitting down. Modern society has invented sophisticated ways to communicate and to stimulate mental activity, but often at the expense of physical health.

LEVELING INEQUALITIES

While health problems in the developed world are often rooted in too much food and too little activity, millions of people in the developing world live shortened lives because their basic human needs are not met. In many major cities in the developing world, sanitation and clean water, housing, simple health care, and adequate food are still in short supply. Providing these basic essentials for the world's poor is the major challenge.

THE CHALLENGE

Medical science has come a long way since Mesopotamian priests called on the gods to cure the sick. With the development of modern biomedical technology, we can hope to cure diseases that only a decade ago were considered untreatable. But maintaining health requires more than just scientific skill. For millions of the world's poorest people, it depends on providing the basic necessities for healthy living. For people in affluent nations, it depends on realizing that we need to take responsibility for maintaining the fitness of our own bodies.

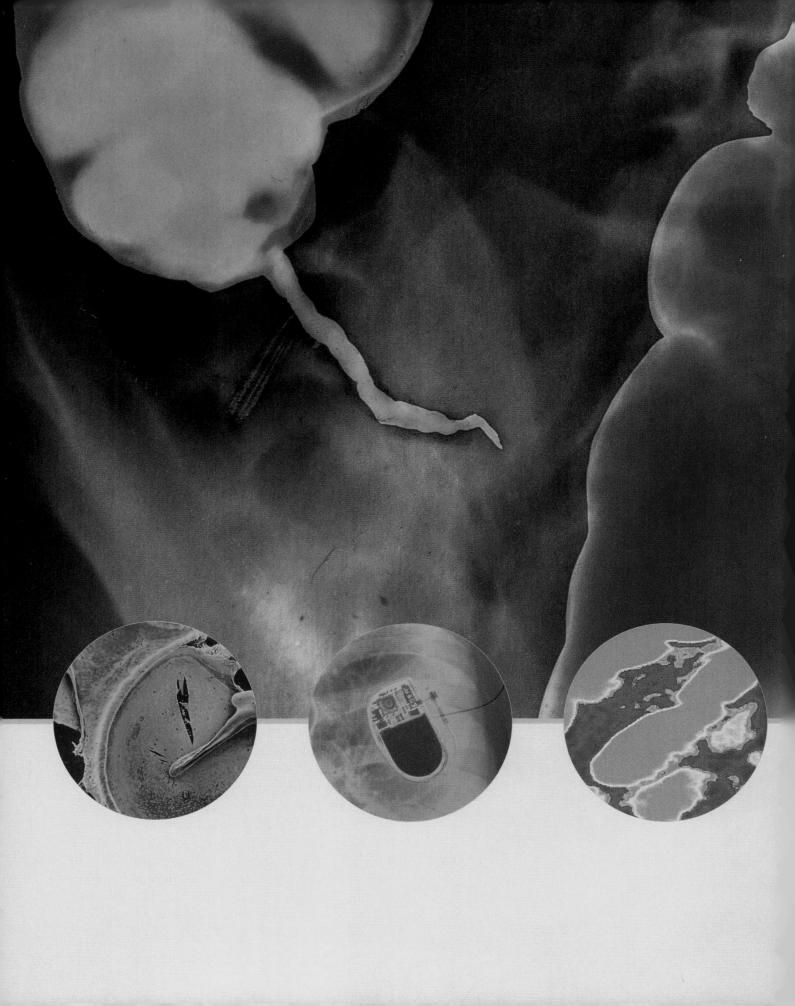

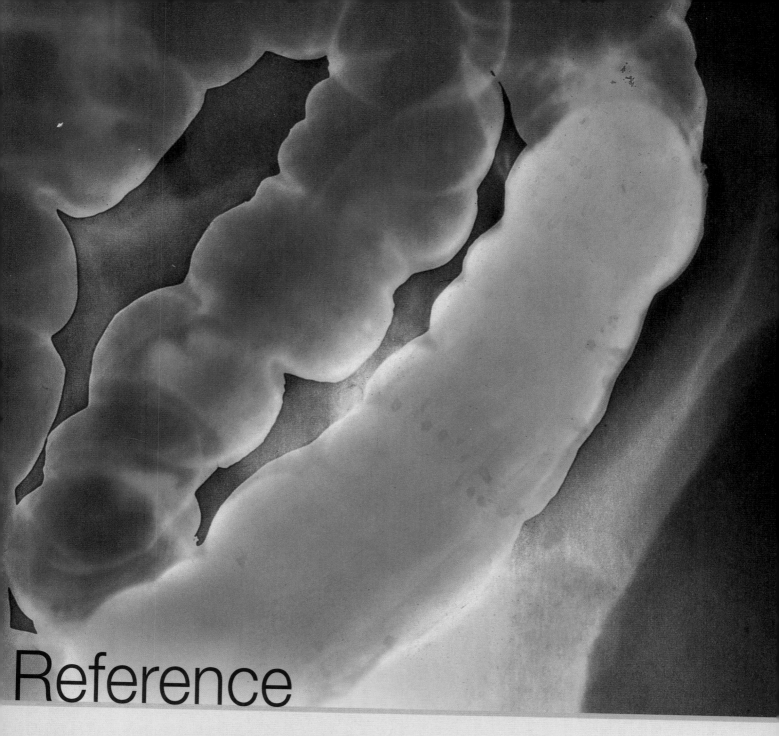

Reference

THIS FINAL SECTION PROVIDES invaluable reference resources in the form of a timeline and glossary. Spanning the millennia from 100,000 BC to the present day, the timeline lists significant milestones in both the study of the human body and the development of medicine. Any confusion over words used in the book can be solved by looking them up in the glossary, which gives easy-to-understand explanations of nearly 300 scientific terms, from "Abdomen" to "Zygote."

TIMELINE

c. 100,000 BC
Modern humans (*Homo sapiens*) first appear in Africa.

c. 70,000 BC
Humans spread from Africa to other continents.

c. 30,000 BC
Humans produce cave paintings and sculptures of themselves and other animals.

c. 10,000 BC
Transition from hunter-gatherer lifestyle to agricultural, settled communities.

c. 2650 BC
Earliest known physician, the Egyptian Imhotep, later given full status as a god.

c. 2600 BC
Chinese Emperor Huang Ti believed to have laid down the basic principles of the *Nei Ching*, a standard manual of Chinese medicine.

c. 1750 BC
King Hammurabi of Babylonia establishes a set of laws, called the Code of Hammurabi. The laws help to regulate the work of physicians.

c. 1500 BC
Date of origin of the Ebers papyrus (discovered in Egypt in 1873), which remains the oldest known medical text.

c. 500 BC
Greek physician and philosopher Alcmaeon of Croton proposes that the brain, and not the heart, is the organ of thinking and feeling.

c. 420 BC
Greek physician Hippocrates teaches the importance of observation and diagnosis over magic and myth in medicine.

c. 350 BC
Greek philosopher Aristotle states that the heart is the organ of feeling and intelligence, a belief held centuries before by the ancient Egyptians.

c. 280 BC
Herophilus of Alexandria reinstates the brain as the organ of thinking. He also describes the cerebrum and cerebellum, and discovers that nerves are channels of communication.

AD 40
Roman philosopher Cornelius Celsus publishes *On Medicine*, a medical handbook based on earlier Greek sources.

c. AD 200
Influential Greek-born Roman doctor Claudius Galen describes, often incorrectly, the workings of the body. With his ideas remaining unchallenged until the 1500s, few advances are made in the understanding of the human body.

AD 890–932
Persian physician Abu Bakr ar-Razi (Rhazes) produces many influential medical texts, and accurately describes measles and smallpox.

1000

c.1000
Publication of medical texts by Arab doctor Ibn Sina (Avicenna) that influence European and Middle Eastern medicine for the next 500 years.

c.1000
Arab surgeon Abulcasis publishes surgery textbooks that describe complicated operations.

1200

1268
Roger Bacon, an English scientist, records the use of glasses to correct eye defects.

c. 1280
Arab physician Ibn an-Nafis shows that blood flows through the lungs.

1300

1347–1350
Black Death (a bubonic plague pandemic) spreads through Europe, killing more than a quarter of its population.

1500

c. 1500
From his own dissections, Italian artist and scientist Leonardo da Vinci produces accurate anatomical drawings of the human body.

1543
Andreas Vesalius, a Flemish doctor, publishes *The Structure of the Human Body*, the first accurate description of human anatomy.

1545
Ambroise Paré, a French surgeon, publishes *Method of Treating Wounds*, in which he describes his less painful, more successful techniques for treating wounds.

1561
Italian anatomist Gabriello Fallopio (Fallopius) publishes *Anatomical Observations*, in which he describes the duct linking the ovary to the uterus.

1562
Italian anatomist Bartolommeo Eustachio is the first to describe the ear in detail in his book *The Examination of the Organ of Hearing*.

1565
Swiss physician Paracelsus (Philipp von Hohenheim) publishes *Opus Chyrurgicum*, in which he attacks the works of Galen and Avicenna.

1590
Dutch instrument maker Zacharias Janssen invents the microscope.

1600

1603
Italian anatomist Hieronymus Fabricius publishes *On the Valves of Veins*, the first detailed description of vein structure.

1614
Italian physician Santorio Santorio (Sanctorius) publishes *The Art of Statistical Medicine*, the results of a 30-year study of his own bodily functions.

1628
William Harvey, an English doctor, publishes *On the Movement of the Heart*

and *Blood*, describing how blood circulates around the body, pumped by the heart.

1662
René Descartes' book *De homine*, published 12 years after his death, puts forward ideas about the brain and mind, and describes reflexes.

1663
Marcello Malpighi, an Italian physiologist and microscopist, discovers blood capillaries, helping to confirm that blood circulates around the body.

1664
Thomas Willis, an English doctor, describes the blood supply to the brain.

1665
English physicist Robert Hooke publishes *Micrographia*, in which he coins the term "cell."

1667
English physician Richard Lower carries out first blood transfusion to a human, using blood from a sheep.

1672
Dutch doctor Regnier de Graaf describes the structure and workings of the female reproductive system.

1674–1677
Dutch draper and pioneer microscopist Anton van Leeuwenhoek observes and describes red blood cells, sperm, and skeletal muscle cells using an early microscope.

1691
English doctor Clopton Havers makes the first description of the microscopic structure of bones.

1700

1717
Lady Mary Wortley Montagu, a British writer, brings the Turkish practice of smallpox inoculation to England.

1747
British naval doctor James Lind discovers that citrus fruits prevent the deficiency disease scurvy during long sea voyages.

1763–1793
British doctor John Hunter makes significant advances in knowledge about human anatomy, and elevates surgery from a craft to a science.

1775
French chemist Antoine Lavoisier discovers oxygen, and later shows that cell respiration is, like burning, a chemical process that consumes oxygen.

1780
Italian doctor Luigi Galvani experiments with nerves, muscles, and electricity.

1785
British doctor William Withering shows that the extracts of the foxglove plant could be used to treat heart failure.

1792
Austrian doctor Franz Gall begins his investigations into the link between behavior and bumps on the skull. The investigations help to form the basis of his "science of phrenology."

1796
First vaccination against smallpox is carried out by British doctor Edward Jenner, when he takes pus from a cowbox blister and introduces it into the arm of an eight-year-old boy.

1800

1800
French doctor Marie François Bichat publishes *Traité des Membranes*, in which he shows that organs are made of different groups of cells called "tissues."

1801
Philippe Pinel, a French doctor, suggests that mentally ill people should be treated more humanely.

1811
Scottish anatomist Charles Bell describes spinal nerve roots and shows that nerves are bundles of nerve cells.

1816
The stethoscope is invented by French doctor René Laënnec.

1817
English doctor James Parkinson first describes a brain disorder that affects movement in some older people, later to be called Parkinson's disease.

1818
British doctor James Blundell performs the first successful transfusion of human blood to a human patient.

1833
American surgeon William Beaumont publishes *Experiments and Observations on the Gastric Juice and the Physiology of Digestion*. The book records the results of his research into the mechanism of digestion made on Alexis St. Martin, a man seriously wounded in a shooting accident.

1837
Czech biologist Johannes Purkinje first observes neurons (nerve cells) in the cerebellum of the brain, later called Purkinje cells.

1838
German scientists Theodor Schwann and Jakob Schleiden put forward their "cell theory," which states that all living things are made from cells.

1840
German anatomist Jakob Henle states in his book *On Miasmas and Contagions* that infectious diseases are caused by microorganisms.

1840
French doctor Charles Laveran identifies the protist *Plasmodium* as the cause of the disease malaria.

1842
British surgeon William Bowman first describes the microscopic structure and function of the kidney.

1844
German doctor Carl Ludwig shows that nephrons in the kidneys act as filters for the production of urine.

1846
American dentist William Morton uses ether as an anesthetic to make a patient unconscious during an operation at Massachusetts General Hospital in Boston.

1848
American railroad worker Phineas Gage survives an accident that drives an iron rod through the front of his brain, but suffers a behavior change. This indicates to scientists that the frontal lobe of the cerebrum controls personality.

1848
Claude Bernard, a French scientist, demonstrates the function of the liver, and later shows that body cells need stable surroundings, thereby establishing the principles of what will later be called homeostasis.

1848
Hungarian doctor Ignaz Semmelweis demonstrates that hand-washing by medical staff dramatically reduces deaths of women from puerperal (childbirth) fever.

1849
English-born American Elizabeth Blackwell becomes the first woman to qualify as a doctor in the United States.

1851
Hermann von Helmholtz, a German physicist, invents the ophthalmoscope (an instrument for looking inside the eye).

1854
British doctor John Snow halts an outbreak of cholera in London by removing the handle of a public water pump, suggesting that the disease is spread by contaminated water.

1858
In his book *Cellular Pathology*, German biologist Rudolf Virchow states that all cells are made from existing ones, and that diseases occur when cells stop working normally. This establishes the basis for the branch of medicine called pathology.

1859
British scientist Charles Darwin puts forward the theory of evolution in his groundbreaking book *The Origin of Species*.

1860s
Louis Pasteur, a French scientist, explains how microorganisms cause infectious diseases.

1861
French doctor Pierre Paul Broca identifies the area of the brain (Broca's area) that controls speech.

1865
British doctor Joseph Lister first uses carbolic acid as an antiseptic during surgery and dramatically reduces deaths from infection.

1870
Elizabeth Garrett Anderson begins practicing as the first woman doctor in Britain.

1872
Italian doctor Camillo Golgi devises a stain that, for the first time, shows the brain's nerve cells clearly under the microscope.

1874
Carl Wernicke, an Austrian doctor, identifies the area on the left side of the brain (now called Wernicke's area) that controls the understanding of spoken and written words.

1882
German doctor Robert Koch identifies the bacterium (*Mycobacterium tuberculosis*) that causes TB (tuberculosis).

1888
French microbiologists Emile Roux and Alexandre Yersin show that bacteria release toxins (poisons), which cause the symptoms of many diseases.

1889
Spanish physiologist Ramón Santiago y Cajal states that the nervous system is made up of a network of distinct nerve cells (later called neurons) that do not touch.

1895
X-rays are discovered by German physicist Wilhelm Roentgen.

1897
Ronald Ross, a British doctor, shows that the microorganism (a protist) causing malaria is spread from person to person by *Anopheles* mosquitoes.

1900

1900
Christiaan Eijkmann, a Dutch doctor, shows that the deficiency disease beriberi can be treated by a change of diet. This helps to establish the concept of "essential food factors," later called vitamins.

1900
Austrian doctor Sigmund Freud publishes *The Interpretation of Dreams*, which contains the basic ideas of psychoanalysis.

1900–1901
American army surgeon Walter Reed and his team demonstrate that yellow fever is transmitted by *Aëdes* mosquitoes and is caused by a virus.

1901
Austrian American doctor Karl Landsteiner demonstrates the existence of blood groups (later classified as A, B, AB, and O), paving the way for safe blood transfusions. He was awarded the Nobel Prize for Medicine in 1930.

1901
Japanese biochemist Jokichi Takamine is the first scientist to isolate crystals of a pure hormone, adrenaline.

1902
British physiologists Ernest Starling and William Bayliss isolate secretin, the first substance to be called a hormone (a term that was devised by Starling in 1905).

1903
An early version of the ECG (electrocardiograph), a device for monitoring heart activity, is invented by Dutch physiologist Willem Einthoven.

1905
British physiologist Ernest Starling devises the term "hormone" to describe the newly discovered "chemical messengers" that coordinate body processes.

1906
Charles Sherrington, a British physiologist, publishes *The Integrative Action of the Nervous System*, a landmark work describing how the nervous system works.

1906–1912
Frederick Gowland Hopkins, a British biochemist, demonstrates the importance of "accessory food factors" (vitamins) in food.

1907
German neurologist Alois Alzheimer first describes the brain disorder (later to be called Alzheimer's disease) that causes a progressive decline in mental abilities.

1910
German scientist Paul Ehrlich discovers salvarsan, the first drug used to treat a specific disease.

1912
Polish-American biochemist Casimir Funk coins the term "vitamin" to describe essential nutrients needed in small amounts for normal body functioning.

1912
American Harvey Cushing publishes *The Pituitary Gland and its Disorders*, in which he describes the functioning of the gland.

1914
American doctor Joseph Goldberger shows that pellagra is not an infectious disease but is caused by poor diet (later shown to be lack of the vitamin niacin).

1916
American birth control pioneer Margaret Sanger opens her first clinic in Brooklyn, New York.

1918
Edward Mellanby, a British scientist, discovers vitamin D, which is essential for normal bone growth.

1921
British birth control pioneer Marie Stopes opens her first clinic in London.

1921
Canadian physiologists Frederick Banting and Charles Best isolate the hormone insulin, allowing the disease diabetes to be controlled.

1921
German-born American scientist Otto Loewi detects chemicals called neurotransmitters involved in carrying signals between neurons.

1926
William Castle, an American doctor, demonstrates the intrinsic factor secreted by the stomach that aids the body's intake of vitamin B_{12}.

1928
Scottish bacteriologist Alexander Fleming discovers penicillin, the first antibiotic, when he notices mold growing on a plate of bacteria.

1928
Hungarian American biochemist Albert von Szent-Györgyi isolates vitamin C.

1929
English physiologists Henry Dale and H.W. Dudley demonstrate the chemical transmission of nerve impulses between neurons, and identify acetylcholine as the first neurotransmitter.

1930
American physiologist Walter Cannon devises the term "homeostasis" – from the Greek for "standing still" – to describe the mechanisms whereby the body maintains a stable internal state.

1933
German electrical engineer Ernst Ruska invents the electron microscope.

1937
German-British biochemist Hans Krebs discovers the sequence of reactions called the Krebs cycle (or the citric acid cycle), which breaks down glucose during aerobic respiration to release energy.

1943
Dutch doctor Willem Kolff invents the kidney dialysis machine to treat people with kidney failure.

1948
World Health Organization (WHO) formed within the United Nations.

1952
British scientists Alan Hodgkin and Andrew Huxley describe nerve impulses.

1953
Using research by British physicist Rosalind Franklin, US biologist James Watson and British physicist Francis Crick discover the structure of DNA.

1953
American surgeon John Gibbon develops the heart-lung machine to pump blood during heart surgery.

1954
First use of polio vaccine developed by American doctor Jonas Salk.

1954
First successful kidney transplant carried out in Boston, Massachusetts.

1958
Ultrasound first used to check health of fetus in its mother's uterus by British professor Ian Donald.

1965
American biochemist Marshall Nirenberg finishes deciphering the genetic code through which DNA controls production of proteins inside a cell.

1967
South African surgeon Christiaan Barnard carries out first successful heart transplant.

1967
Introduction of mammography, an X-ray technique for detecting breast cancer.

1969
British biochemist Dorothy Hodgkin determines the structure of insulin using X-ray crystallography, having previously described that of penicillin in 1946 and vitamin B_{12} in 1956.

1970s
Discovery of natural painkillers, called endorphins and enkephalins, produced by the body.

1972
CT (computerized tomography) scanning first used to produce images of body organs.

1977
Last recorded case of smallpox; the disease is declared eradicated in 1979.

1978
Successful IVF (in vitro fertilization) by British doctors Patrick Steptoe and Robert Edwards results in first "test tube" baby, Louise Brown.

1980
Introduction of "keyhole" surgery, using an endoscope to look inside the body through small incisions.

1980s
PET scans first used to produce images of brain activity.

1981
AIDS (acquired immune deficiency syndrome) identified as a new disease.

1982
First artificial heart, invented by US scientist Robert Jarvik, implanted into a patient.

1984
French scientist Luc Montagnier discovers the virus called HIV (human immunodeficiency virus), which causes AIDS.

1990
Human Genome Project is launched to identify the genes in human chromosomes.

1999
Chromosome 22 becomes the first human chromosome to have its DNA sequenced.

2000

2000
First "draft" of Human Genome Project completed.

2002
Gene therapy used to cure boys suffering from an inherited immunodeficiency disease which would otherwise leave the body defenseless against infection.

GLOSSARY

Abdomen
Lower part of the trunk (central part of the body) between the thorax (chest) and the hips.

Absorption
Process by which the products of digestion pass through the wall of the small intestine into the bloodstream.

Accommodation
Adjustment made by changing the shape of the lens of the eye so it can focus on near or distant objects.

Acne
Skin disorder causing pimples that results from inflamed sebaceous glands and hair follicles.

Adolescence
Transition period between childhood and adulthood that occurs during the teenage years.

Aerobic respiration
Release of energy from glucose that takes place inside cells and requires oxygen.

Alimentary canal
Hollow tube which extends from the mouth to the anus, and includes the pharynx, esophagus, stomach, and small and large intestines.

Allergy
Illness caused by over-reaction of the body's immune system to a normally harmless substance.

Alveoli (sing. alveolus)
Microscopic air bags inside the lungs through which oxygen enters, and carbon dioxide leaves, the bloodstream.

Amino acid
One of a group of 20 chemical compounds that are the basic building blocks from which proteins are made.

Amputation
Surgical removal of all or part of an arm or leg.

Anaerobic respiration
Release of energy from glucose that takes place inside cells and does not use oxygen.

Anatomy
Study of the structure of the body, and how its parts relate to one another.

Anesthetic
Drug used to temporarily block feelings of pain in a patient during surgery or while giving birth.

Angiogram
Special type of X-ray that reveals the outline of blood vessels after a dye that absorbs X-rays has been injected into them.

Antibody
Substance released by lymphocytes of the immune system that disables a pathogen and marks it for destruction.

Antigen
Foreign substance, usually found on the surface of pathogens such as bacteria, that triggers the immune system to respond.

Antiseptic
Chemical applied to the skin to destroy bacteria and other microorganisms before they can cause infection.

Apgar score
System of scoring used to assess the condition of a newborn baby.

Appendicular skeleton
Part of the skeleton made up of the bones of the pectoral and pelvic girdles, and those of the upper and lower limbs.

Arteriole
Very small artery that delivers blood to a capillary.

Artery
Blood vessel that carries blood from the heart towards the tissues.

Association neuron
Neuron (nerve cell) that relays nerve impulses from one neuron to another, and processes information.

Atom
Smallest particle of an element, such as carbon or hydrogen, that can exist, and one of the building blocks from which all matter is made.

ATP (adenosine triphosphate)
Substance that stores, carries, and releases energy.

Atrium (pl. atria)
Left or right upper chamber of the heart.

Autonomic nervous system (ANS)
Part of the nervous system that controls the involuntary activities of internal organs, such as heart rate and blood pressure.

Axial skeleton
Central part of the skeleton consisting of the skull, backbone, ribs, and sternum.

Axon
Also called a nerve fiber, this is the long "tail" of a neuron that carries nerve impulses away from its cell body.

Bacteria (sing. bacterium)
Group of single-celled microorganisms, commonly known as germs, some of which cause diseases such as typhoid and TB.

Base
One of four nitrogen-containing substances – adenine, cytosine, guanine, and thymine – that spell out the instructions written in genetic code in molecules of DNA.

Biopsy
Removal of a small piece of tissue from the body for examination under the microscope to look for signs of disease.

Blind spot
Also called the optic disk, this is the part of the retina of the eye where the optic nerve leaves the eye, and where light cannot be detected.

Blood vessel
Tube, such as an artery or vein, that carries blood through the body.

Body language
Form of nonverbal communication that uses body position, gestures, and facial expressions.

Brain stem
Lowest part of the brain. It is connected to the spinal cord and controls vital functions such as breathing.

Cancer
One of a number of different diseases caused by body cells dividing out of control and producing growths called tumors.

Capillary
Microscopic blood vessel that carries blood from arterioles to venules and supplies individual cells.

Carbohydrate
One of a group of organic compounds, made up of carbon, hydrogen, and oxygen, that includes glucose and glycogen, and provides the body's main energy supply.

Carbon dioxide
Gas that is a waste product of cell respiration, which is released into the air from the lungs during exhalation (breathing out).

Cardiac muscle
Type of muscle found only in the heart.

Cartilage
Tough, flexible connective tissue that helps support the body and covers the ends of bones where they meet at joints.

Catalyst
Substance that speeds up the rate of a chemical reaction but does not change itself.

Cell body
Part of a neuron (nerve cell) that contains its nucleus.

Cell division
Process by which cells multiply by dividing into two.

Cell membrane
Also called a plasma membrane, this is the thin membrane that surrounds a cell and separates it from its environment.

Cell (internal) respiration
The release of energy from glucose and other fuels that takes place inside cells.

Central nervous system (CNS)
The part of the nervous system that consists of the brain and spinal cord.

Cerebellum
Part of the brain that controls balance and ensures that movements are smooth and coordinated.

Cerebral cortex
Thin surface layer of the cerebrum that processes information relating to thought, memory, the senses, and movement.

Cerebrospinal fluid
Watery fluid that circulates within and around the central nervous system, and helps protect and nurture the brain and spinal cord.

Cerebrum
The largest part of the brain, involved in conscious thought, feelings, and movement.

Chemical digestion
The breakdown of food into simple molecules using enzymes.

Chemoreceptor
Receptor, such as those in the nose and tongue, that responds to chemicals dissolved in water.

Chromosome
One of 46 threadlike packages of DNA, found inside most body cells, that contain genes, the instructions needed to construct and run a body.

Chyme
Creamy, souplike liquid containing semidigested food that passes from the stomach into the small intestine during digestion.

Cilia (sing. cilium)
Microscopic, hairlike projections from certain cells that beat in a rhythmic, wavelike manner to move things, such as mucus, across their surface.

Cochlea
Coiled structure inside each ear that detects sounds.

Collagen
Tough, fibrous protein that helps to strengthen cartilage, tendons, and other types of connective tissue.

Compact bone
Also called cortical bone, this is the very hard material that forms a bone's outer layer.

Computed tomography (CT)
Scanning technique that uses X-rays and computers to produce visual "slices" through living tissues.

Conception
The period between fertilization and the implantation of an embryo in the lining of the uterus.

Cone
One of two types of light receptors in the retina of the eye, cones provide color vision and work in bright light.

Connective tissue
Tissue, such as bone or cartilage, that supports the body and holds together its various structures.

Consciousness
Awareness of self and surroundings produced by the cerebrum, which enables a person to make decisions and to know what they are doing.

Contagious disease
Infectious disease, such as the common cold or measles, that is easily passed from person to person.

Contraception
Use of various methods to prevent pregnancy.

Convex lens
Lens, such as the one found in the eye, that curves outward on both surfaces and makes light rays converge (come together).

Cornea
Clear area at the front of the eye that allows light in and refracts (bends) light rays.

Cranial nerve
One of the 12 pairs of nerves that arise from the brain.

Cranium
Upper part of the skull, made from eight interlocking bones, that surrounds the brain.

Cytoplasm
Jellylike fluid that fills a cell between the cell membrane and nucleus.

Deficiency disease
Disease caused by a lack of a particular nutrient in the diet, especially a vitamin or a mineral.

Dendrite
Short filament that carries nerve impulses to the cell body of a neuron.

Dentine
Hard, bonelike tissue that surrounds the pulp of a tooth and gives the tooth its basic shape.

Dermis
Deeper, thicker layer of the skin that contains blood vessels, sweat glands, and sensory receptors.

Diaphragm
Dome-shaped sheet of muscle that separates the thorax (chest) from the abdomen and plays a key role in breathing.

Diastole
Part of the heartbeat cycle when either the atria or the ventricles are relaxed.

Diffusion
Random movement of molecules in a gas or liquid from an area of high concentration to one of low concentration until they are evenly distributed.

Digestion
Breakdown of complex molecules in food into simpler substances that can be absorbed into the bloodstream.

Diploid cell
One, like most body cells, that contains two sets of 23 chromosomes.

Dissaccharide
Sugar, such as maltose, sucrose, or lactose, that is made up of two monosaccharide units.

DNA (deoxy-ribonucleic acid)
One of a number of large molecules, each consisting of two intertwined nucleic acid strands that are found inside cells and carry the genetic instructions needed to build and operate those cells.

Double helix
Name given to the twin strands of nucleic acids that spiral around each other like a twisted ladder in each DNA molecule.

Duct
A tube that leads from a gland and carries its products, such as the tear duct that carries tears from the tear glands.

Eardrum
Thin membrane at the end of the ear canal that vibrates when sounds hit it.

Egestion
Elimination from the body, in the form of feces, of the undigested waste remaining after digestion.

Elastin
Protein whose fibers can stretch and recoil like a rubber band and give elasticity to connective tissues, such as those in the dermis of the skin.

Electrocardiogram (ECG)
Recording of the electrical changes that occur as the heart beats, made by an electrocardiograph.

Electroencephalogram (EEG)
Recording of brain waves produced by electrical activity in the brain, made by an electroencephalograph.

Electron microscope
Powerful microscope that uses an electron beam instead of light to produce highly magnified views of body cells and tissues.

Embryo
Name given to an unborn child during the first eight weeks of development after fertilization.

Enamel
The hardest material found inside the body; it covers the crown of a tooth.

Endocrine gland
Gland, such as the pituitary gland, that secretes hormones into the bloodstream.

Enzyme
Protein that acts as a biological catalyst to speed up the rate of chemical reactions both inside and outside cells.

Epidemic
Outbreak of an infectious disease that affects many people in the same location at the same time.

Epidermis
Upper, thinner, protective layer of the skin, from which the topmost layer of dead cells is constantly worn away and replaced from below.

Epithelium
Also called epithelial tissue, a sheet of cells, one or more cells thick that covers the body, lines its internal cavities, and forms glands.

Excretion
Elimination from the body of waste products produced by cell metabolism or of substances that have entered the bloodstream and are surplus to requirements.

Exhalation
The movement of air out of the lungs; also called expiration or breathing out.

Exocrine gland
Gland, such as a salivary or sweat gland, that secretes chemicals along a duct onto the body surface or into a body cavity.

Fat
Type of lipid that is solid at room temperature, and is found in many foods.

Fatty acid
Building block, with glycerol, of fats and oils.

Feces
Solid waste consisting of undigested food, dead cells, and bacteria that remains after digestion and is eliminated from the body through the anus.

Feedback system
Control mechanism that maintains a stable state in the body by correcting unwanted changes and regulates, for example, body temperature.

Fertility
Ability of a man and a woman to produce children without undue difficulties.

Fertilization
Joining together of an ovum and a sperm to make a new individual.

Fetus
Name given to the unborn child from the ninth week after fertilization until birth.

Fiber (dietary)
Also called roughage, this is indigestible plant material that gives bulk to food and improves the efficiency of intestinal muscles.

Fiber (muscle)
Name given to a muscle cell.

Follicle
Cluster of cells found inside the ovary that contains an ovum (see also Hair follicle).

Fracture
Break in a bone, often caused by a fall.

Fungi (sing. fungus)
Group of living organisms, including yeasts and mushrooms, some of which are parasitic on humans, causing diseases such as athlete's foot.

Gas exchange
Movement of oxygen from the lungs into the bloodstream, and of carbon dioxide in the opposite direction.

Gene
Carries the instructions to make a specific protein, and is one of the 30,000–50,000

genes stored in the DNA that makes up chromosomes inside a body cell.

Genetic code
Code used to convert the "message" carried by the sequence of bases in DNA into a sequence of amino acids to make a protein.

Genetic engineering
Artificial alteration made to the genetic makeup of an organism.

Genetics
Study of inheritance and transmission of genes from one generation to the next.

Girdle
Ring of bones that attaches the limbs to the rest of the skeleton.

Gland
Group of cells that produce chemical substances and release them into or onto the body.

Glial cells
Also called neuroglia, these cells protect and nurture neurons (nerve cells).

Glucose
Main sugar found circulating in the bloodstream, and the body's primary energy source.

Glycogen
Polysaccharide made of glucose subunits that forms a carbohydrate energy store in liver cells and muscle fibers.

Gray matter
Surface layer of the cerebrum and inner part of the spinal cord; consists mainly of neuron cell bodies.

Hair follicle
Deep, hollow space in the skin from which a hair grows.

Haploid cell
A cell, such as a sperm or ovum, that is formed by meiosis and contains only a single set of 23 chromosomes.

Haversian system
Also called an osteon, this is a cylindrical collection of concentric bony tubes that is the basic units of compact bone.

Hemoglobin
Oxygen-carrying, iron-containing protein found inside red blood cells.

Hepatic
Related to the liver, such as the hepatic artery that supplies blood to the liver.

Heredity
The passing on of characteristics controlled by genes from one generation to the next.

Homeostasis
Maintenance of stable conditions, including body temperature and blood glucose levels, regardless of external conditions.

Hormone
Chemical messenger that is produced and released by an endocrine gland and carried to its "target" by the blood.

Hunter-gatherer
Person who lives by hunting animals and gathering plants rather than through agriculture. Typical of early human societies but rarer today.

Hypothalamus
Small but important part of the brain that regulates many body activities, including thirst and body temperature, via the pituitary gland and the autonomic nervous system.

Immune system
Collection of cells within the circulatory and lymphatic systems that protect the body from disease-causing microorganisms.

Immunity
Ability of the immune system to "remember" and provide resistance to specific disease-causing microorganisms.

Immunization
Provision of immunity against a disease by injecting a vaccine containing a weakened form of the microorganism that causes that disease.

Infant mortality rate
Number of infants who die during the first year of life per 1,000 live births.

Infection
Establishment of disease-causing microorganisms, such as bacteria, in the body.

Infectious disease
Disease, such as chickenpox, that is caused by a specific microorganism.

Infertility
Inability of either a man or a woman, or both partners, to produce a child.

Ingestion
Taking food or drink into the body through the mouth.

Inhalation
The movement of air into the lungs; also called inspiration or breathing in.

Insertion
Point of attachment of a muscle, by its tendon, to a bone that moves.

Insoluble
A substance that does not dissolve in water.

Integumentary system
External protective covering of the body provided by the skin, hair, and nails.

IVF (in vitro fertilization)
Technique used to help infertile couples conceive by fertilizing an ovum outside the body, then returning it to the uterus to develop.

Karyotype
Complete set of chromosomes inside a cell, photographed and arranged in pairs in descending size order.

Keratin
Tough, waterproof protein found inside cells making up hair, nails, and the upper epidermis of the skin.

Labor
Contractions of the muscular wall of the uterus before and during birth.

Ligament
Tough strips of fibrous connective tissue that hold bones together where they meet at joints.

Light microscope
Instrument that uses light rays focused by glass lenses to produce a magnified image of an object.

Limbic system
Part of the brain at the base of the cerebrum that controls emotions.

Lipid
One of a group of organic compounds, made up of carbon, hydrogen, and oxygen, that includes fats and oils (made of fatty acids and glycerol), phospholipids, and steroids, such as cholesterol.

Lymph
Fluid that flows through the lymphatic system from the tissues to the blood.

Lymphocyte
Type of white blood cell that plays a key role in the immune system.

Macronutrient
Nutrient – such as carbohydrate, fat, or protein – needed in large amounts by the body.

Macrophage
White blood cell present in a number of tissues that engulfs bacteria and foreign debris and plays a part in the immune system.

Magnetic resonance imaging (MRI)
Scanning technique that uses magnetism, radio waves, and a computer to produce images of the inside of the body.

Magnetoencephalo-graphy (MEG)
Scanning technique that produces real-time images of brain activity.

Mammal
Living organism that belongs to a group of animals that are "warm-blooded," have a covering of fur, and feed their young with milk.

Marrow
Soft fatty tissue, either red or yellow, found in the spaces within bones.

Mechanical digestion
Breakdown of food into smaller particles through chewing or the churning action of stomach muscles.

Mechanoreceptor
Receptor that can detect pressure produced by touch, sound waves, or the stretching of muscles.

Medieval
Relating to the Middle Ages (between the 5th and 15th centuries).

Meiosis
Type of cell division that occurs in the ovaries and testes to produce sex cells – ova and sperm – that contain a single set of chromosomes.

Melanin
Brown-black pigment found in the skin, hair, and the iris of the eye that gives them their coloring.

Membrane
Thin layer made up of epithelial tissue supported by connective tissue that covers or lines an external or internal body surface (see also Cell membrane).

Meninges (sing. meninx)
Protective membranes that cover the brain and spinal cord.

Menopause
Point in a woman's life, usually between the ages of 45 and 55, when ovulation and menstrual periods cease.

Menstrual cycle
Sequence of changes, repeated about every 28 days, that prepares the lining of a woman's uterus to receive an ovum should it be fertilized.

Mesopotamia
Ancient region of south-western Asia between the Rivers Tigris and Euphrates, known today as Iraq.

Metabolism
Sum of all the chemical processes that take place within the body, particularly within its cells.

Metabolic rate
Rate at which energy is released by metabolism.

Microbe
General name for a micro-organism that causes disease.

Micrograph
Photograph taken with the aid of a microscope.

Micronutrient
Nutrient – such as a vitamin or mineral – needed in small amounts by the body.

Microorganism
Tiny organism, such as a bacterium, that can only be seen with a microscope.

Middle Ages
Period of Western European history between the 5th and 15th centuries.

Mineral
One of about 20 chemical elements, including calcium and iron, that must be present in the diet to maintain good health.

Mitochondria (sing. mitochondrion)
Organelles inside cells that carry out aerobic respiration to release energy.

Mitosis
Type of cell division used for growth and repair that produces two identical cells from each "parent" cell.

Molecule
Chemical unit that is made up of two or more linked atoms, such as the two hydrogen atoms and one oxygen atom in a water molecule.

Monosaccharide
Sugar, such as glucose, fructose, or galactose, that is the simplest type of carbohydrate.

Motor neuron
Neuron (nerve cell) that carries nerve impulses from the central nervous system to muscles and glands.

Mucous membrane
Layer that lines body cavities that open to the exterior – for example, the respiratory system – and secretes mucus.

Mucus
Thick, slimy fluid, secreted by mucous membranes, that moistens, protects, and lubricates.

Muscle tone
Partial contraction of a muscle that maintains the body's posture.

Mutation
Change to the DNA in one of a cell's chromosomes that may have harmful effects, and can be passed on to the next generation.

Myelin sheath
Insulating sheath wrapped around most axons (nerve fibers) that increases the speed of conduction of nerve impulses.

Myofibril
One of thousands of tiny rodlike strands inside a muscle fiber (cell).

Nephron
One of about a million filtration units inside each kidney that produce urine.

Nerve
Cablelike bundle of neurons (nerve cells) that relays nerve impulses between the body and central nervous system.

Nerve fiber
Also called an axon, this is the long "tail" of a neuron that carries nerve impulses away from its cell body.

Nerve impulse
Tiny electrical signal that passes along a neuron (nerve cell) at high speed.

Neuron
One of the billions of interconnected nerve cells that carry electrical signals at high speed and make up the nervous system (the brain, spinal cord, and nerves).

Neurotransmitter
Chemical released when a nerve impulse reaches the end of a neuron, and triggers a nerve impulse in a neighboring neuron.

Nitrogen
Gas, like oxygen, that is found in the air but normally plays no part in body functions.

Nobel Prize
Prestigious award given annually for outstanding achievement in one of five fields, including physiology or medicine.

Noninfectious disease
Disease, such as cancer or heart disease, that is not caused by a disease-causing microorganism.

Nucleic acid
Organic compound, such as DNA or RNA, which contains carbon, hydrogen, oxygen, nitrogen, and phosphorus, and is made up of units called nucleotides.

Nucleotide
Basic building block of nucleic acids such as DNA consisting of a phosphate group, a deoxyribose sugar, and a nitrogenous base (adenine, cytosine, guanine, or thymine).

Nucleus
Control center of a cell; contains chromosomes.

Nutrient
Substance – such as carbohydrate, protein, fat, vitamin, or mineral – needed in the diet to maintain good health and normal body functioning.

Obstetrician
Doctor who specializes in pregnancy and childbirth.

Ophthalmoscope
Instrument used to view the inside of the eye.

Orbit
Socket in the skull that surrounds, supports, and protects the eyeball.

Organ
Body part, such as the kidney or brain, that has a specific role or roles and is made up of two or more different types of tissues.

Organic compound
Substance, such as carbohydrate, protein, lipid, or nucleic acid, that has a carbon "skeleton," and is made only by living systems.

Organelle
Microscopic structure inside a cell, such as a mitochondrion, that has a specific function.

Origin
Attachment point of a muscle, by its tendon, to a bone that is stationary.

Osmoregulation
Maintenance of the correct levels of water and salts in blood and tissue fluids, carried out by the kidneys.

Ossicle
One of the three small, sound-transmitting bones found inside the middle ear.

Ossification
Process of bone formation.

Ovarian cycle
Sequence of changes, repeated about every 28 days, that causes an ovum to be released from a woman's ovary.

Ovulation
Release of an ovum from a woman's ovary.

Ovum (pl. ova)
Also called an egg, this is the female sex cell, which is produced by, and released from, a woman's ovary.

Oxygen
Gas found in the air that is taken into the bloodstream through the lungs and used by body cells in aerobic respiration to release energy from glucose.

Paleontologist
Scientist who studies fossils.

Papillae (sing. papilla)
Small bumps projecting from the tongue's surface, some of which house taste receptors called taste buds.

Paraplegic
Weakness or paralysis of both legs and sometimes part of the trunk caused by damage to the spinal cord.

Pathogen
Disease-causing microorganism such as a bacterium, virus, protist, or fungus.

Pectoral girdle
Girdle formed by the two collar bones and two shoulder blades, which attaches the arms to the skeleton.

Pelvic girdle
Girdle formed by the two hip bones that anchors the legs to the skeleton and, with the sacrum, forms the basin-like pelvis.

Periosteum
Membrane that covers the surface of bones and contains blood vessels.

Peripheral nervous system (PNS)
The part of the nervous system that consists of the nerves that relay nerve impulses between the body and the central nervous system.

Peristalsis
Wave of muscular contraction through a hollow organ that, for example, pushes food down the esophagus or urine down a ureter.

Phagocyte
General name for white blood cells – including neutrophils and macrophages – that engulf and digest disease-causing microorganisms.

Phagocytosis
Process by which phagocytes engulf and digest disease-causing microorganisms.

Phantom pain
Sensation of pain felt in a limb that is no longer present because it has been amputated.

Phospholipid
Type of phosphate-containing lipid that makes up the cell membranes around cells, and the membranes around organelles.

Physiology
Study of how the body works and functions.

Pitch
Quality of a sound – whether high- or low-pitched – that depends on the frequency of sound waves, that is, how quickly one wave is followed by the next.

Placenta
Organ that develops in the uterus during pregnancy; forms an interface between the blood supplies of the mother and fetus through which the fetus receives food and oxygen.

Plasma
Liquid part of the blood that is mainly water.

Polysaccharide
Complex carbohydrate, such as glycogen, that does not have a sweet taste and is made up of long chains of monosaccharides, such as glucose.

Portal system
Veins that carry blood from one organ to another rather than toward the heart.

Positron emission tomography (PET)
Scanning technique that uses radioactive substances injected into the body to show parts of the body at work, especially the brain.

Pregnancy
The period from conception to birth; dated from the start of a woman's last menstrual cycle and so lasts about 40 weeks.

Primates
Group of mammals that includes monkeys, apes, and humans.

Protein
One of a group of organic compounds, made up of carbon, hydrogen, oxygen, nitrogen, and sulfur, that perform many roles inside the body, including making enzymes.

Protists
Group of single-celled organisms, some of which cause diseases in humans, such as malaria.

Puberty
Period during adolescence when the body grows and develops an adult appearance, and the reproductive system starts working.

Pulmonary circulation
Part of the circulatory system that carries blood from the heart to the lungs and back to the heart.

Pupil
Opening in the center of the iris through which light enters the eye.

Radionuclide scanning
Scanning technique that uses radioactive substances to reveal the functioning of organs such as bones.

Receptor
Special cells or neurons that detect stimuli, such as light, and trigger sensory neurons.

Reflex
Automatic, unconscious, split-second response to a stimulus that often protects the body from danger.

Reflex arc
Nervous pathway, often through the spinal cord but not the brain, involved in a reflex.

Renaissance
Term meaning "rebirth" that describes the period between the 14th and early 17th centuries in Europe when there was a creative revolution in the arts, sciences, and medicine.

Renal
Related to the kidney, as in the renal artery that supplies blood to the kidney.

Retina
Inner lining of the eyeball that is packed with light receptors.

Rod
One of two types of light receptors in the retina of the eye, rods provide black and white vision, and work best in dim light.

Saliva
Fluid released into the mouth, especially during chewing, by the salivary glands.

Scanning electron micrograph (SEM)
Photograph produced using a scanning electron microscope.

Sebaceous gland
Gland connected to a hair follicle that produces an oily liquid called sebum.

Sebum
Oily liquid that keeps hair and skin soft, flexible, and waterproof.

Secretion
Chemical substance made and released by a gland.

Semen
Fluid produced by male reproductive glands that activates and nurtures sperm, and in which they swim.

Semicircular canal
Part of the inner ear that is involved in balance.

Sensory neuron
Neuron (nerve cell) that carries nerve impulses from sensory receptors to the central nervous system.

Septum
Dividing wall within body part, such as in the nose.

Skeletal muscle
Type of muscle that is attached to the skeleton and moves the body.

Smooth muscle
Type of muscle found inside the walls of organs that, for example, pushes food along the small intestine.

Soluble
Describes a substance that dissolves in water.

Solution
Mixture of one substance (called a solute) dissolved in another (the solvent); glucose and carbon dioxide are both solutes that dissolve in the water (solvent) in blood.

Species
A group of living things in the natural world that can breed with each other.

Sperm
Also called spermatozoa, these are the male sex cells, which are made in and released from a man's testes.

Spermatogenesis
Process of sperm production inside the testes.

Sphincter
Ring of muscle around a passage or opening that opens or closes to control the flow of, for example, food or urine along it.

Spinal cord
Column of nervous tissue that runs down the back and relays nerve signals between the brain and body.

Spinal nerve
One of the 31 pairs of nerves that arise from the spinal cord.

Spongy bone
Also called cancellous bone, this is the tough but lightweight honeycomb of struts and cavities that forms the inner part of a bone.

Stain
Dye used to color cells and tissues so they can be seen under a light microscope.

Sterilization
Surgical procedure that takes away a person's ability to reproduce. Also the process used to destroy any microorganisms on surgical instruments and other materials used in hospitals, to minimize the risk of infection to patients.

Steroid
One of a group of lipids that includes cholesterol and some hormones and vitamins.

Stethoscope
Instrument used to listen to heart sounds and breathing.

Stimulus (pl. stimuli)
Any change in external conditions that causes a change in body activities, such as the smell of food causing the release of saliva.

Sugar
A simple, sweet-tasting carbohydrate such as glucose or sucrose.

Surgery
Treatment of disease or injury by direct intervention, often using instruments to open the body.

Sweat
Watery liquid produced by sweat glands that cools the body when it evaporates from the skin's surface.

Symptom
Indication of a disease or disorder that is noticed by a patient.

Synapse
Junction between two neurons in which they do not touch but come very close to each other.

Synovial joint
Most common type of joint in the body, a movable joint with a fluid-filled space between the bones.

System
Group of linked organs that work together to perform a particular task or tasks.

Systemic circulation
Part of the circulatory system that carries blood from the heart around the body and back to the heart.

Systole
Part of the heartbeat cycle when either the atria or the ventricles are contracted.

Taste bud
Taste receptor found in the surface of the tongue.

Tendon
Cord or sheet of strong connective tissue that connects muscle to bone.

Terminal hair
Thick hair that grows on the scalp and forms the eyebrows and eyelashes.

Thermogram
Color-coded image produced by a special camera that shows the amount of heat released by different parts of the body.

Thorax
Also called the chest, the upper part of the trunk (central part of the body) between the neck and abdomen.

Tissue
Group of one type of cell, or similar types of cells, that work together to perform a particular function, such as epithelial cells forming a protective lining in the mouth.

Toxin
Poisonous substance released into the body by a disease-causing bacterium.

Transmission electron micrograph (TEM)
Photograph produced using a transmission electron microscope.

Transplant
Replacement of a diseased organ or tissue with a healthy living organ or tissue provided by a donor, who has usually just died.

Trepanning
Ancient practice of cutting or drilling holes into the skull, probably to release "evil spirits."

Trunk
Also called the torso, the central part of the body, consisting of the thorax and abdomen, to which the head and limbs are attached.

Tumor
Abnormal growth of tissue produced when tissue cells multiply at an increased rate.

Ultrasound scanning
Scanning technique that uses high-frequency sound waves to produce images of the inside of the body, including those of the developing fetus.

Ultraviolet (UV) radiation
Radiation that occurs naturally in sunlight, but can be harmful if the skin is overexposed to it.

Umbilical cord
Ropelike structure that connects the fetus to the placenta.

Urination
Release of urine from the bladder to the outside of the body.

Urine
Liquid produced by the kidneys that contains wastes, and surplus water and salts removed from the blood.

Vaccination
Also called immunization, this is the process whereby a vaccine is injected into the bloodstream to stimulate the body to produce antibodies against a disease.

Vaccine
Medication containing a weakened form of a disease-causing microorganism.

Vein
Blood vessel that carries blood from the tissues towards the heart.

Vellus hair
One of the millions of fine, soft hairs that grow all over the body.

Ventricle
One of the two (left and right) lower chambers of the heart.

Venule
Very small vein that collects blood from a capillary.

Villi (sing. villus)
Tiny, fingerlike projections from the lining of the small intestine that greatly increase its surface area for absorption.

Viruses (sing. virus)
Infectious nonliving agents, much smaller than bacteria, that invade cells and cause diseases such as the common cold and measles.

Vitamin
One of over 13 organic compounds, including vitamin A and niacin, that are needed in small amounts in the diet for normal body functioning.

White matter
The inner part of the brain and the outer part of the spinal cord, made up mainly of axons (nerve fibers).

X-ray
Form of radiation that reveals bones when projected through the body onto a photographic film.

Zygote
Cell produced when a sperm fertilizes an ovum.

INDEX

Page numbers in bold indicate the principal reference to a subject. Page numbers with the suffix g indicate a glossary entry.

ACKNOWLEDGMENTS

The team at Dorling Kindersley would like to thank:
Carole Oliver, Clair Watson, and Willie Wood for design help; Caryn Jenner and Brad Round for editorial help; Sophie Young for DTP help; Alyson Lacewing for proofreading; and Marie Lorimer for the index.

The publisher would like to thank the following for their kind permission to reproduce their photographs:
Key: a=above; b=below; c=center; l=left; r=right; t=top; bi=background image; mi=main image

10 Telegraph Colour Library/Getty Images: Alistair Berg bl; **10–11** Science Photo Library: mi, l; Simon Fraser c; r Professors P. M. Motta, S. Makabe & T. Naguro r; **12–13** Harry Cutting mi; **14–15** Liam Bailey bl; source unknown cl; **16–17** Science Photo Library: Professor P. Motta, mi (circular), bl, tr (circular), Astrid & Hanns-Frieder Michler (cutout), Pascal Goetgheluck cb; Science Museum ct (cutout); Ann Ronan Picture Library: ct (circular); **18–19** Science Photo Library: mi, c (circular), br, Eric Grave tl, Quest bl, Professor P. Motta cl (circular); Mary Evans: tr; **20–21** Denis Models mi; Science Photo Library: Alfred Paskia l; Professors P. M. Motta, S. Makabe & T. Naguro tr, CNRI cr (circular), Dr. Kari Lounatmaa br; **22–23** Science Photo Library: bi, Dr Arther Tucker cl, Professor K. Seddon & Dr T. Evans cr, Ken Eward br; **20–21** Denis Models mi; Science Photo Library: Alfred Paskia l, Professors P. M. Motta, S. Makabe & T. Naguro tr, CNRI cr (circular); Dr Kari Lounatmaa br; **22–23** Science Photo Library: bi, Dr. Arther Tucker cl, Professor K. Seddon & Dr. T. Evans cr, Ken Eward br; **24–25** Science Photo Library: bl; A. Barrington Brown ct, Dr. Gopal Murti tr; **26–27** Science Photo Library: Quest mi and ct, David M. Martin cl (circular), BSIP Laurent/H. Amercain cb (box), Professor P. Motta rt, Manfred Kage rc, cr; **28–29** Science Photo Library: Simon Fraser mi; **30–31** Science Photo Library: Volker Steger mi, SNRI tl, GJLP c, Dr. John Mazziotta et al/Neurology rt, Alfred Paskia tr (cutout), cl, Simon Fraser/Royal Victoria Infirmary, Newcastle-upon-Tyne br; **32–33** Science Photo Library: Professor P. Motta mi, all other images Science Photo Library; **34–35** Geoff Brightling l and tr (cutout); Corbis Images c; Science Photo Library: Martin Dohrn c (box), Andrew Syred tr (circular); Andy Crawford cb (cutout and circular); Dave King br (cutout) and (circular); **36–37** Science Photo Library: Dr. Jeremy Burgess mi, Christina Pedrazzini c, Dr. P. Marazzi cr, D. Phillips tr; Richard Wehr/Custom Medical Stock Photo/SPL cl; **38–39** Science Photo Library: bl, Dr. P. Marazzi ct, Quest c, Geoff Brightling cb; Corbis Images: tr; Anthony Duke, digital artwork br; **40–41** Science Photo Library: D. Phillips mi; Andrew Syred bl and cr, Eye of Science r and br; Andy Crawford ct photograph (digitally amended by Peter Bull); **42–43** Science Photo Library: b (box), Professor P. Motta bi,

Biophoto Associates tr, CNRI bl, GJLP/CNRI bl; Mary Evans c (box); Andy Crawford mi; **44–45** Philip Dowell tl; Science Photo Library: Alfred Paskieka c (oval), Dave Roberts tr, Dave King br; **46–47** Science Photo Library: r, Allsport c, GJLP/CNRI tr (circular); **48–49** Science Photo Library: Department of Clinical Radiology, Salibury District Hospital bi, CNRI tl; Mehau Kulyk cb, tr; Ann Ronan Picture Library c (box); Philip Dowell r; **50–51** Science Photo Library: Hugh Turvey tl and ct, Mehau Kulyk bl; Andy Crawford c (x2); **52–53** Science Photo Library: bi; sources unknown bl and tr; Corbis Images: br; **54–55** Science Photo Library: Andrew Syred l, c and r, Professor P. Motta ct, Robert Becker/Custom Medical Stock Photo br; **56–57** Science Photo Library: Department of Clinical Radiology, Salibury District Hospital bi, bl, and tr, Quest cl, Scott Camazine ct; Mary Evans: bc (box); **58–59** Ray Moller cb; Dave King tr (cutout); Science Photo Library: Dr P. Marazzi and Department of Clinical Radiology, Salibury District Hospital (digitally amended by Anthony Duke) tr, Mike Devlin br (circular), Brad Nelson/Medical Stock Photo br; **60–61** Andy Crawford: mi photography, tc (digital artwork Peter Bull), and r; 6 artworks surrounding skeleton by Colin Salmon; **62–63** Science Photo Library: cl and c, Dr R. Clark & M. Goff br; M.I. Walker ct and br (box); **64–65** Andy Crawford c circular images (x2); Raymond Evans/Unit of Art in Medicine, University of Manchester, London r; **66–67** Science Photo Library: bl and rc; Andy Crawford tr; **68–69** The Royal Collection Picture Library bl (and bi); Wellcome Library, London: tl and cb; Science Photo Library: c; **70–71** Corbis c ; Getty Images cb; **72–73** Getty Images: mi; Corbis Images: bl; Quest c (circular); Andy Crawford and Steve Gordon tr; Science Photo Library: Will McIntyre br; **74–75** Science Photo Library: GJLP/CNRI r; all other images Science Photo Library; **76–77** Getty Images: mi; Science Photo Library: BSIP VEM tl, bl (box) and c (circular); Andy Crawford br photography (head and hand); brain artwork, eye and heart DK; **78–79** Science Photo Library: Quest bl, Nancy Kedersha ct, BSIP, Sercomi cb (box); Corbis Images tr; **80–81** Peter Bull bl; Science Photo Library: Eye of Science ct (circular), tr and br; Frank Greenaway cr; **82–83** Science Photo Library: Quest bl, Sue Ford tr; **84–85** Andy Crawford mi photography; Getty Imags br; **86–87** Andy Crawford l photography (superimposed image DK); Corbis: cr; Andy Crawford cb; Science Photo Library: CC Studio tr; Mary Evans: br; **88–89** Science Photo Library: bl, clt, and crt (box); Andy Crawford r photography (superimposed image DK); **90–91** Imperial War Museum: crb (and bi); Department of Neuorology and Image Analysis Facility, University of Iowa cl; Andy Crawford ct; Science Photo Library: Hank Morgan bl, BSIP Astier br; **92–93** Science Photo Library: GJLP/CNRI bi, ct, Getty Images: tr; **94–95** Steve Gorton bl; Corbis Images: c; Science Photo Library: tr; Dave

King br (x3); **96–97** Andy Crawford bl photography (superimposed image DK); Science Photo Library: Hank Morgan ct, BSIP Buntschucr cr; **98–99** Andy Crawford mi photography (superimposed artwork DK); Science Photo Library: Jean-Loup Charmet cr; **100–101** Geoff Dann and Andy Crawford l; Andy Crawford ct, c, and cb; Science Photo Library: Montreal Neuro Institute, McGill University/CNRI cr; **102–103** Science Photo Library: Mehau Kulyk, bi, US National Library of Medicine cl, Simon Fraser (RNC Newcastle-upon-Tyne) cr; Mary Evans: cb; Science Museum: tr; **104–105** Andy Crawford mi photography (digitally amended by Anthony Duke); Corbis: bl; The Bridgeman Art Library: tr (box); Corbis Images: cr; Science Photo Library: BSIP Leca br; **106–107** Andy Crawford bi and l photography (superimposed artwork DK); Getty Images: tr; Science Photo Library: cb and br; **108–109** Andy Crawford tl photography (superimposed artwork DK); Science Photo Library: Quest cl, James King-Holmes cr (circular) and tr; Corbis: br; **110–111** Getty Images: mi; Andy Crawford tl photography (superimposed artwork DK); Science Photo Library: Mark Clarke br; **112–113** Andy Crawford mi photography (superimposed artwork Peter Bull) and br; Science Photo Library: cl and cr; **114–115** Mary Evans bl; Science Photo Library: PIR-CNRI tl, Bill Longcore l, cbr Mark Burnett cbr; Custom Medical Stock Photo br; **116–117** Science Photo Library: Mehau Kulyk br (plus superimposed artwork DK); Ronald James cl; **118–119** Getty Images: mi; Science Photo Library: bl and tr; **120–21** Andy Crawford cl (superimposed artwork DK); Getty Images: tr; Science Photo Library: br Pascal Goetgheluk; **122–23** Andy Crawford mi photography (superimposed artwork Anthony Duke); Science Photo Library: bl; **124–25** Science Photo Library: Astrid & Hanns-Frieder Michler bi, tl, Saturn Stills c, J.C. Revy cr, Volker Steger bl; Banting House National Historic Site tr; **126–27** Science Photo Library: Quest mi, Professor P. Motta l, c, CNRI r; **128–29** Science Photo Library: National Cancer Institute bi; Simon Fraser tr, Quest bl; **130–31** Science Photo Library: Quest bl, tl, St Bartholomew's Hospital ct, Robert Becker, Custom Medical Photo Stock br; Andy Crawford cbr; **132–33** Science Photo Library: bi, CNRI br (circular), Francis Leroy, Bicosmos tr, Eye of Sciencebr; **134–35** Science Photo Library: Jurgen Berger mi, Max Planc Institute, Nigel Dennis bl; CNRI tr (circular) and br, Dr Gopal Murti tr; Quest cr, NIBSC br (circular), Secchi-Lecaque bcr; **136–37** Science Photo Library: bl and tl, NIBSC bcl, tl Volker Steger; Mary Evans: bl; **138–39** Corbis: br; Mary Evans: ct and cb; Science Photo Library: David Scharf bi; Jerry Mason br; **140–41** Science Photo Library: bl and tr, BSIP, Carvallini James ct, Quest cb, Phillipe Plailly br; **142–43** Science Photo Library: Phillipe Plailly ctr, bc; Getty Images: br; **144–45** Science Photo Library: CNRI bi and bl, Will & Denis

Mcintyre tr, D. Ouellette c, Ouellete & Theroux bl; Corbis: ctl ; **146–47** Science Photo Library: CNRI bi; **148–49** Science Photo Library: cl, ct, and tr (digitally manipulated by Anthony Duke); Mary Evans: br; **150–51** Science Photo Library: Saturn Stills tr; Corbis: cbr and br.; **152–53** Science Photo Library: tl John Griem; **154–55** Science Photo Library: Secchi Lecaque bi, Alferd Pasieka ctl, tl, Dr. P. Marazzi cr; **156–57** Science Photo Library: Dr. Linda Stannard tl; Eye of Science bl and ctr, Dr. P. Marazzi bcl, Dr. Gary Gaugler c, Quest tr; Mary Evans br; **158–59** Andy Crawford cl phography (superimposed image DK); Science Photo Library: circular images, clockwise from top: Manfred Kage, Professor P. Motta, Science Photo Library, Biophoto Associates, Professors P.M. Motta, K.R. Porter, and P.M. Andrews, Science Photo Library, Philip A. Harington tr, Juergen Bergercr and bi, Oscar Burriel r; **160–61** Science Photo Library: cl, Dr Andrejs Liepins tr, Jerrican br; **162–63** Science Photo Library: tl, br, c, cb, and bi; **164–65** Science Photo Library: Eye of Science br, James King-Holmes tl, cbr, ctr, and br, J. F. Wilson cr; Corbis: tr; **166–67** Science Photo Library: BSP Vem tl; bl, cl, and cr; **168–69** Science Photo Library: Clinique Ste Catherine, CNRI tl, tr, Alain Dex ctr ; Matt Meadows br, H. Schleichkorn br; **170–71** Science Photo Library: CNRI bi; SPL tr; Getty Images: br; **172–73** Andy Crawford bl photography (superimposed images); Science Photo Library: br; **174–75** Mary Evans: tl; Ann RonanPicture Library: bl; Science Photo Library: National Library of Medicine ct, Bill Longcore br; Corbis: bi; Mary Evans; **176–77** Science Photo Library: Mehau Kulyk l, Professor C. Ferland bcl and bcr; Labat tr; Andy Crawford c (x2) photography (superimposed images (x2) Peter Bull); cr (x2) Andy Crawford; Getty Images: br; **178–79** Andy Crawford c photography (superimposed images DK); Science Photo Library: Eye of Science br; **180–81** Andy Crawford mi; Science Photo Library: BSIP Vem tcr, CNRI cr, Dr Tony Brain br; **182–83** Science Photo Library: Biophoto Associates tr; Andy Crawford: bi, l photography (superimposed imges DK); Dr Klaus Schiller cl; **184–85** Science Photo Library: bl and bcr, Eye of Science bcl, Dr. K. R. Schiller tr; Corbis: br; **186–87** Science Photo Library: Manfred Cage cl, bl and br, Professor P. Motta tcr; Andy Crawford mi photography (superimposed images DK); **188–89** Science Photo Library: Eye of Science cl, David M. Martin cl, Professor P. Motta tr; Andy Crawford mi and ctr photography (superimposed images DK); **190–91** Science Photo Library: cr, Professors P. Motta & F.M. Magliocca br; **192–93** Andy Crawford bi; Science Photo Library: Adam Hart-Davis far bl, Dr Jeremy Burgess bl, c; Corbis: tcl and tr; Getty Images: br; **194–95** All images DK; **196–97** Science Photo Library: Alfred Pasieka tl, (superimposed image DK), Dr Jeremy Burgess ctr **198–99** Andy Crawford tl photography (superimposed image DK); bl, c, tr and br DK; Professor P. Motta cr, bl; **200–01** Corbis: mi; Andy Crawford bl photography (superimposed image DK); **202–03** Science Photo Library: Brian Yarvin cr, br; **204–5** Science Photo Library: Quest mi, Brad Nelson bl, Biophoto Associates tl, Professors P. Motta and M.

Castellucci br (circular); Corbis: bl **206–07** Janos Marffy l; Science Photo Library: BSIP Vem cl, Mauro Fermariello tr, Andrew Syred br (circular); r DK; Andy Crawford bl photography, (superimposed image DK); br Corbis; **208–09** Science Photo Library: Quest bl, Ed Reschke, Peter Arnold Inc tl, tr, CNRI b; James Stevenson br; **210** Science Photo Library: BSIP VEM br; Professor P. Motta, G Macchiarelli, SA Nottola bl; Petit Format– Nestle bl; **210–211** Science Photo Library: TEK Image –211; **212** The Image Bank–Getty Images: Larry Dale Gordon br; **213** Science Photo Library: D. Phillips tr; Science Pictures Ltd br; **215** Corbis: Bohemian Nomad Picturemakers tr; Science Photo Library: Ed Reschke, Peter Arnold Inc. tl; National Library of Medicine br; The Wellcome Institute Library, London: Dr. Joyce Harper bc; **216** Science Photo Library: CNRI bc; Astrid & Hanns-Frieder Michler ac; **216-217** Science Photo Library: Science Source tl; **217** Corbis: tr; Science Photo Library: Peter Cull tc; Custom Medical Stock Photo br; **218** Science Photo Library: br; Professor P. Motta, G. Macchiarelli, S. A. Nottola cl; **219** Science Photo Library: CNRI br;Custom Medical Stock Photo tr; Dr. Yorgos Nikas tl; **221** Science Photo Library: Professor P. M. Motta & E. Vizza tr; Professors P. M. Motta & J. Van Blerkom tl; **223** Science Photo Library: Dr Yorgos Nikas tl, cla, clb; The Wellcome Institute Library, London: Yorgas Nikas br; **224** Corbis: Bettmann bl; **224–225** Science Photo Library: Pascal Goetgheluck c; **225** Corbis: Bettmann tr; Science Photo Library: Pascal Goetgheluck br; **226** Science Photo Library: Petit Format– Nestle crb; **227** Science Photo Library: Custom Medical Stock Photo br; **228** Science Photo Library: Dept. of Clinical Radiology, Salisbury District Hospital crb; **229** Science Photo Library: Petit Format– Prof E. Symonds br; **231** The Wellcome Institute Library, London: l; **232** Corbis: Dick Clintsman cla; Science Photo Library: tr; Jean–Loup Charmet b; **233** Science Photo Library: Lawrence Migdale cr; Alfred Pasieka tr; **234** Corbis: Reed Kaestner br; Barnabas Kindersley: tr; Guy Ryecart: cr; **235** Barnabas Kindersley: c, cr, bc; Guy Ryecart: c; **236** Science Photo Library: Christopher Briscoe tr; Ron Sutherland cl; **237** Telegraph Colour Library–Getty Images: Stephanie Rausser br; **238** Telegraph Colour Library–Getty Images: Jim Cummins b; **239** Corbis: O'Brien Productions tl; Science Photo Library: BSIP VEM clb; Mehau Kulyk br; **240** Science Photo Library: Scott Camazine tl; Quest cl; **241** The Image Bank–Getty Images: Ghislain & Marie David de Lossy tr; Science Photo Library: Dr. P. Marazzi c; Telegraph Colour Library–Getty Images: tl; **242** Science Photo Library: Dr. P. Marazzi r; Telegraph Colour Library–Getty Images: Larry Bray cl; **243** Science Photo Library: Custom Medical Stock Photo r; Dr. P. Marazzi tl; Alfred Pasieka cl; **244** Science Photo Library: CNRI cl, crb, bc; Mike Bluestone tr; **245** Pa Photos: bl; **246** Science Photo Library: Peter Menzel tl; **246–247** Science Photo Library: Biophoto Associates; **247** Science Photo Library: tr; **249** Science Photo Library: CNRI bc; Lauren Shear br; **250** Science Photo Library: Andrew Syred bl; **250–251** Science Photo Library: TEK Image; **251** Science Photo Library: BSIP, PIKO

tl; BSIP VEM cr; Klaus Guldbrandsen bl; **252** Bridgeman Art Library, London – New York: Bibliotheque des Arts Decoratifs, Paris, France; Science Museum: bc; Science Photo Library: National Library of Medicine bl; **254–255** American Museum Of Natural History: Denis Finnin & Craig Chesek b; **255** Corbis: Kevin Schafer br; Science Museum: tr; Werner Forman Archive: Tanzania National Museum, Dar es Salaam cr; **256** AKG London: Erich Lessing tr; © Michael Holford: cla; Science Photo Library: Christian Jegou, Publiphoto Diffusion br; **257** Science Museum: br; Charles Walker Collection: tl; **258** AKG London: tr; Erich Lessing bc; Charles Walker Collection: c; **258–259** Scala Group S.p.A.: **259** Mary Evans Picture Library: tr; World Health Organisation: cra; **260** Mary Evans Picture Library: tl; Science Museum: tr; Science Photo Library: National Library of Medicine bl; **260–261** AKG London: b; **261** Museum of the Royal Pharmaceutical Society: cla; Hulton Getty Archive: cr; **262** Science Photo Library: Jean-Loup Charmet tl; **262–263** AKG London: b; **263** Corbis: © Bettmann br; Science Photo Library: John Burbidge tl; CAMR–A B Dowsett tr; **264** AKG London: tl; Erich Lessing bc; Bridgeman Art Library, London – New York: Bibliotheque des Arts Decoratifs, Paris, France cr; **265** Science Museum: tl; Mary Evans Picture Library: br **266** Corbis: Bettmann tr; Science Photo Library: cl; **266–267** Science Museum: **267** AKG London: Erich Lessing br; Science Museum: tr; **268** Hulton Getty Archive: bc; Science Photo Library: Sheila Terry tl; **268–269** Science Museum: **269** AKG London: tr; Science Museum: crb; Hulton Getty Archive: bc; **270** AKG London: Musee d'Orsay br; The Image Bank–Getty Images: Roine Magnusson bl; Science Photo Library: Dr Gopal Murti tl; **271** AKG London: br; Mary Evans Picture Library: tl, ac; **272** AKG London: tl; Hulton Getty Archive: br; **273** Science Museum: br; Hulton Getty Archive: c; Sean Hunter: tc; Science Photo Library: tl; **274** Mary Evans Picture Library: tl; **274–275** Science Photo Library: Antonia Reeve b; **275** Science Photo Library: Martin Dohrn tr; James King-Holmes br; **276** The Image Bank–Getty Images: Wayne H. Chasan c; **277** Corbis: Lindsay Hebberd tc; **278** Science Photo Library: Simon Fraser tl; **278–279** Telegraph Colour Library–Getty Images: VCL–Paul Viant b; **279** Science Photo Library: CC Studio tc; Telegraph Colour Library–Getty Images: Bill Losh tr; **280** Science Photo Library: Custom Medical Stock Photo br; **282–83** Science Photo Library: CNRI mi, Quest l, cl; J. Croyle/Custom Medical Stockc; **288–289** Science Photo Library: Nancy Kedershami; **294–95** Science Photo Library: Professor P. Motta mi; **290–291** Science Photo Library: Astrid & Hanns-Frieder Michler; **292–293** Science Photo Library: Dr. Gopal Murti;
Endpapers Science Photo Library: Juergen Berger, Max-Planck Institute.

Jacket: Science Photo Library: back tl, back tcl; CNRI front tl; Mehau Kulyk front tr, back tr; Dr. Yorgos Nikas front tll; Alfred Pasieka front c, front tc; D. Phillips back tcr.

All other images © Dorling Kindersley. For further information see: www.dkimages.com